CARLA I. KOEN

Comparative International Management

The **McGraw·Hill** Companies

London · Boston · Burr Ridge, IL · Dubuque, IA · Madison, WI · New York · San Francisco
St Louis · Bangkok · Bogotá · Caracas · Kuala Lumpur · Lisbon · Madrid · Mexico City · Milan
Montreal · New Delhi · Santiago · Seoul · Singapore · Sydney · Taipei · Toronto

Comparative International Management
Carla I. Koen
ISBN-10: 0-07-7103912
ISBN-13: 978-0-07-7103910

 **Education**

Published by McGraw-Hill Education
Shoppenhangers Road
Maidenhead
Berkshire
SL6 2QL
Telephone: 44 (0) 1628 502 500
Fax: 44 (0) 1628 770 224
Website: www.mcgraw-hill.co.uk

British Library Cataloguing in Publication Data
A catalogue record for this book is available from the British Library

Library of Congress Cataloguing in Publication Data
The Library of Congress data for this book has been applied for from the Library of Congress

Acquisitions Editor: Kate Mason
Development Editor: Catriona Watson
Marketing Manager: Marca Wosoba
Senior Production Editor: Eleanor Hayes

Text Design by Fakenham Photosetting
Cover design by Fielding Design
Printed and bound in the UK by The Bath Press

ISBN-10: 0-07-7103912
ISBN-13: 978-0-07-7103910

The **McGraw·Hill** Companies

Brief Table of Contents

Foreword   ix

Preface   x

Acknowledgements   xi

Guided Tour   xii

Technology to Enhance Learning and Teaching   xiv

General Introduction   xvii

Introduction   to the Approaches to Comparative International Management   2

Chapter 1   The Societal Environment and Economic Development   26

Chapter 2   National Cultures and Management   52

Chapter 3   Organizational Culture Research   94

Chapter 4   National Diversity and Management   152

Chapter 5   Managing Resources: Human Resource Management   198

Chapter 6   Comparative Corporate Governance   254

Chapter 7   Managing Resources: Production Management   308

Chapter 8   Managing Resources: National Innovation Systems   358

Chapter 9   Multinational Corporations: Structural Issues   406

Chapter 10   Multinational Corporations: Comparative Corporate Strategy   444

Chapter 11   Networks and Clusters of Economic Activity   490

Chapter 12   Globalization, Convergence and Societal Specificity   522

Index   552

Detailed Table of Contents

Foreword   ix

Preface   x

Acknowledgements   xi

Guided Tour   xii

Technology to Enhance Learning and Teaching   xiv

General Introduction   xvii

Introduction   **to the Approaches to Comparative International Management**   2
Introduction to the Theoretical Debate   4
Universalistic Theories   5
Particularistic Theories   8
Globalization   15
Study Questions   19
Further Reading   19
References   20

Chapter 1   **The Societal Environment and Economic Development**   26
1.1   Introduction   28
1.2   The Economist's Point of View   29
1.3   How the Economy Influences Culture: the Sociologist's Stance   43
1.4   Conclusions   49
Study Questions   49
Further Reading   50
References   50

Chapter 2   **National Cultures and Management**   52
2.1   Introduction   54
2.2   Methodological Dilemmas   55
2.3   The Etic Approach   62
2.4   Cultural Clusters   74
2.5   The Emic Approach   78
2.6   National Cultures and Cross-cultural Negotiations   82
Study Questions   86
Further Reading   87
References   91

Chapter 3   **Organizational Culture Research**   94
3.1   Organizational Culture: What and Why?   96
3.2   Research Streams: the Etic and Emic Approaches   97
3.3   Multi-level Shaping of Culture   104

3.4   Culture Issues in Mergers and Acquisitions   111
3.5   Organizational and Industry Culture   119
3.6   Organizational Culture and Strategy   121
3.7   Organizational Culture and Economic Performance   123
3.8   Creation and Consolidation of Organizational Culture   127
3.9   Organizational Culture Change   131
Study Questions   135
Further Reading   136
References   145

Chapter 4   **National Diversity and Management**   152
4.1   Institutional Analysis: What and Why?   154
4.2   The Business Systems Approach   155
4.3   Business Systems Research Applied to Taiwan and South Korea   167
4.4   The Societal Effect (SE) Approach   179
4.5   Institutional Change   185
Study Questions   189
Further Reading   190
References   195

Chapter 5   **Managing Resources: Human Resource Management**   198
5.1   Introduction   200
5.2   Work Relationships   202
5.3   Employment Relationships   217
5.4   Reward Structure   227
5.5   Conclusions   238
Study Questions   243
Further Reading   243
References   249

Chapter 6   **Comparative Corporate Governance**   254
6.1   Introduction   256
6.2   Corporate Governance: a Societal Explanation of Major
        Capitalist Models   259
6.3   Conclusions   294
Study Questions   297
Further Reading   298
References   304

Chapter 7   **Managing Resources: Production Management**   308
7.1   Introduction   310
7.2   Characteristics and Types of Production System   311
7.3   Production Systems and the Societal Environment   332
7.4   Conclusions   345
Study Questions   348
Further Reading   348
References   354

Chapter 8   **Managing Resources: National Innovation Systems**   358
8.1   Introduction   360
8.2   Technological Advancement: a Taxonomy   361
8.3   Innovation: Overview of the Major Institutions Involved   363
8.4   The American Innovation System   367
8.5   The Japanese Innovation System   371
8.6   The German Innovation System   377
8.7   The French Innovation System   381
8.8   Conclusions   387
Study Questions   388
Further Reading   389
References   401

Chapter 9   **Multinational Corporations: Structural Issues**   406
9.1   Introduction   408
9.2   The Internationalization Processes of MNCs   409
9.3   Coordination and Control within MNCs   420
9.4   Knowledge Management in the MNC   427
9.5   The MNC and Cultural and Institutional Differences   430
Study Questions   435
Further Reading   436
References   440

Chapter 10   **Multinational Corporations: Comparative Corporate Strategy**   444
10.1   Introduction   446
10.2   Corporate Strategy   447
10.3   Theoretical Approaches to Corporate Strategy   448
10.4   Comparative Empirical Studies   457
10.5   Model   464
10.6   Conclusions   472
Study Questions   473
Further Reading   473
References   485

Chapter 11   **Networks and Clusters of Economic Activity**   490
11.1   Introduction   492
11.2   Balancing Competition and Cooperation   493
11.3   Networks from a Theoretical Perspective   494
11.4   From Networks to Clusters   503
11.5   Innovative Milieux   508
11.6   Conclusions   511
Study Questions   513
Further Reading   513
References   518

Chapter 12   **Globalization, Convergence and Societal Specificity**   522
12.1   Introduction   524
12.2   Corporate Governance   525
12.3   The Personnel and Industrial Relations Systems   535
12.4   Conclusions   540
Study Questions   545
Further Reading   545
References   547

Index   552

Foreword

In April 2004, the Royal Netherlands Academy of Sciences published a report and held a discussion on the future of sociology. As the main priority for research it identified the subject of internationalization and cross-cultural understanding. Clearly, under present conditions of globalization, emerging economies, immigration, political upheaval, and violent confrontations between ideologies and religions, an understanding of different cultures is of crucial importance in dealing with problems of conflict and rivalry. This book satisfies that priority, in the area of management and organization. Thus, it is very timely. While it has suffered from neglect, in comparison with the more domestic areas of research, the subject of internationalization and cross-cultural comparison in management and organization is not new. Authors writing on 'business systems', 'varieties of capitalism' and 'societal effects' have conducted extensive cross-cultural studies in this area for some time. However, this work has, understandably for an emerging field, been fairly descriptive and taxonomic, and causal explanations have been scarce. The present volume aims to provide a more causally explanatory account, not only identifying cross-cultural differences, but also trying to explain them. In particular, it offers a fruitful combination of cultural and institutional approaches, with elements of economic theory and insights derived from the field of business strategy.

This book is intended as a text for advanced students and scholars. It will be of interest to a wide range of students and scholars, in management and organization, business, economics and sociology. It yields a comprehensive account of relevant topics, on different levels, across a wide range of countries, including some countries in transition, and some underdeveloped countries. In the environment of the firm it discusses the wider economic, institutional and cultural environment and, somewhat closer to the firm, innovation systems and networks, and regional clusters. Within the firm, it deals with corporate governance, personnel management, production management, organizational structure, strategy and internationalization processes. Particularly useful, from a conceptual, theoretical point of view, is its attempt to combine and integrate cultural and institutional approaches, from both an economic and a sociological perspective. This book looks not only at institutional differences, but also at institutional change. An important theme, of course, is convergence between economic systems: will cross-national differences disappear or will they persist, and, if so, how? This theme runs through the book and is reviewed at the end. In short, the book is well designed, with a good range of relevant subjects and issues, on different levels of analysis. The book is also well informed, being based on sound and thorough research. Above all, it is to be commended for taking a critical approach, and avoiding hype, stereotype and cliché.

Professor Bart Nooteboom
Erasmus University
The Netherlands

Preface

Two years ago, I embarked on this project not really knowing what I was getting myself into. I was driven by the sheer lack of teaching material in the field of comparative international management. It was hard, if not impossible, to find material that was accessible for my undergraduate and graduate students, and that would provide them with a broad and critical view on international business or international management.

Now, two years on, and looking back on the process of writing and redrafting, I must admit that the challenge of writing a truly comparative international textbook, covering as many topics as we have in this book, was often a daunting task and could not have been completed without the unfailing support of my colleagues and co-authors. I would like to take this opportunity to express my deep gratitude to them.

I am also most grateful to Ad van Iterson from Maastricht University, Glenn Morgan from Warwick Business School, Can-Seng Ooi from Copenhagen Business School, Jan Ulijn from Eindhoven University of Technology, and other anonymous reviewers of the book for their constructive comments and useful suggestions. Each of them had a major input in improving the book and taking it to its current level.

I should also like to take this opportunity to express my appreciation to the team at McGraw-Hill who have worked on this book. Special thanks go to Kate Mason (acquisitions editor), for her deep belief in, and enthusiasm and support for, the project. Most sincere thanks also go to Emily Jefferson, Catriona Watson, Rachel Crookes (development editors) and to Eleanor Hayes (senior production editor) for their professional assistance and wonderful support throughout the project.

I am also grateful to our secretarial staff, Nienke Boelhouwer, Nancy Kanter and Heidi van den Borne, for their secretarial assistance and endless encouragement.

Last but not least, I would like to express special thanks to colleagues other than my current co-authors in the Department of Organization and Management at Tilburg University for their wonderful support and interest in the project.

Carla I. Koen
Erasmus University
The Netherlands

Acknowledgements

Thanks go to the following reviewers for their comments at various stages in the text's development.

Joost Bucker – University of Nijmegen
Robert Carty – London Metropolitan University
Abby Cathcart – University of Sunderland
David Chesley – Doncaster College
Peter Miskell – University of Reading
Patricia Nelson – University of Edinburgh
Can-Seng Ooi – Copenhagen Business School
Frances Tomlinson – University of North London
Jan Ulijn – Eindhoven University of Technology
Ad Van Iterson – Maastricht University
Nimal Wijayaratna – Loughborough University

Thanks to the companies and organizations who granted us permission to reproduce material in the text. Every effort has been made to trace and acknowledge ownership of copyright. The publishers would be pleased to make suitable arrangements to clear permission with any copyright holders whom it has not been possible to contact.

Guided Tour

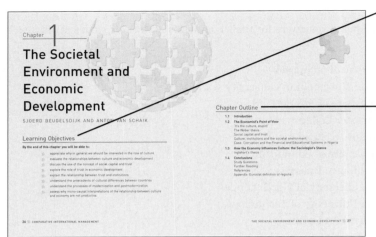

Learning Objectives
Each chapter opens with a set of learning objectives, which introduce the ideas to be discussed within the chapter.

Chapter Outline
Each chapter contains a brief outline at its opening that highlights the key topics to be covered in the chapter.

Figures and Tables
Each chapter provides a number of figures and tables to help you to visualize the various models, provide extra data, and to illustrate and summarize important concepts.

Boxed Examples
Brief boxed examples in the text demonstrate a variety of different management scenarios from across the world, illustrating the main text's discussion with examples from contemporary business practice.

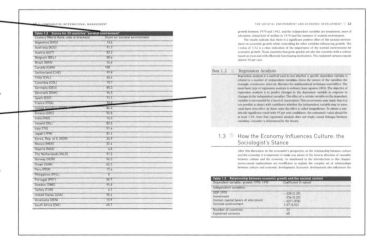

Study Questions

These encourage you to review and apply the knowledge you have acquired from each chapter and can be used to test your understanding.

Further Reading

Each chapter ends with a section of guided further reading, providing details of importance sources and useful articles and texts for further research and study.

Cases

Chapters end with relevant and up-to-date case studies featuring real organizations, offering examples of management from a variety of different cultures. Case study questions encourage students to analyse each case and the management issues it raises.

References

Each chapter ends with a full listing of the books and other sources referred to in the chapter, providing the student with an opportunity to undertake further study.

Technology to Enhance Learning and Teaching

Visit www.mcgraw-hill.co.uk/textbooks/koen today

Online Learning Centre (OLC)

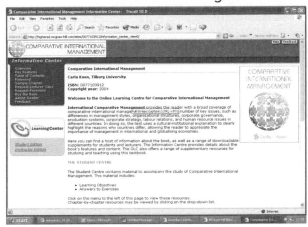

After completing each chapter, log on to the supporting Online Learning Centre website. Take advantage of the study tools offered to reinforce the material you have read in the text, and to develop your knowledge in a fun and effective way.

Resources for students include:

- Learning objectives
- Answers to exercises

Also available for lecturers:

- PowerPoint slides
- PowerPoints for print handouts
- Lecture outline
- Case study solutions
- Mini-case solutions

For lecturers: Primis Content Centre

If you need to supplement your course with additional cases or content, create a personalized e-book for your students. Visit www.primiscontentcenter.com or e-mail primis_euro@mcgraw-hill.com for more information.

Study Skills

Open University Press publishes guides to study, research and exam skills to help under-graduate and postgraduate students through their university studies.

Visit www.openup.co.uk/ss/ to see the full selection.

Computing Skills

If you'd like to brush up on your computing skills, we have a range of titles covering MS Office applications such as Word, Excel, PowerPoint, Access and more.

Get a £2 discount off these titles by entering the promotional code **app** when ordering online at www.mcgraw-hill.co.uk/app.

General Introduction

Comparative international management is the field of inquiry that focuses on differences in management and organization between countries. By now, there is sufficient awareness of the usefulness of studying management and organization in an international context. Also, the use of comparison to aid explanation and to enhance understanding of social phenomena has always been recognized as a valuable tool of social scientific research and hence as an end in itself. Despite this wisdom, however, in general, the field of comparative international management is undervalued and few efforts have been made to apply the insights of the field in textbooks. This book is the first of its kind to take this type of comparison seriously and to show the reader the usefulness of broadening its horizons beyond the familiar and the known to understand better, and hence function more efficiently within international and globalizing economies.

In doing so, we aim to answer calls from prominent scholars (e.g. Vernon, 1994; Shenkar, 2004) to emphasize the enormous value of comparative work for international business (IB). In 1994 Vernon was already concerned that, 'while comparative national business systems was one of the three core IB areas (the others being international trade and the multinational enterprise), it was the one most at risk of being overrun by US ethnocentrism as well as by high opportunity cost' (cited in Shenkar, 2004: 164). He argued that 'the omission of comparative business and its related components, such as cross-cultural research and comparative management, from the IB agenda is a fundamental error' (2004: 164). 'It amounts to no less than negating the value of local knowledge and assuming no scholarly 'liability of foreignness' (Zaheer, 1995, cited in Shenkar, 2004: 164). In a similar vein, Shenkar (2004: 164) argues that 'the disappearance of the comparative perspective has robbed IB of one of its most important theoretical and methodological bases, and has stripped it of one of its most unique and valuable assets'.

In this book, we try to do justice to the field by studying comparative international management in its broadest sense. Among other things, we will discuss management styles, decision processes, delegation, spans of control, specialization, organizational structure, organizational culture, typical career patterns, corporate governance, production systems, corporate strategy and labour relations. Moreover, all chapters of this book use examples from different countries and from different sectors within those countries to illustrate its approach. However, the purpose of these examples is not just to serve as an illustration; the acquisition of knowledge of management and organization in different countries and sectors is also one of the objectives of this book. It covers most EU countries, the USA, Japan and other Asian countries, some African countries, and Russia.

All chapters depart from the question of whether differences in management and organization between countries do indeed exist. Do managers in France have a more autocratic management style than managers in Germany? Do organizations in Japan have more hierarchical layers than organizations in the USA? These questions are difficult to answer because, if one is interested in *cross-national* differences in management and organization, one has to rule out differences caused not by nationally determined variables, but, for instance, by industry characteristics. In other words, one has to isolate differences that have to do with nationality from all other kinds of differences between organizations and management practices. When trying to explain cross-national differences, it is not, for example, particularly useful to compare companies in the automobile industry in Korea with professional service firms in the UK. Nor is it useful to compare the management style of elderly supervisors in Belgium with the actions of young executives in the Netherlands.

Once cross-national differences have been identified, two additional questions are asked: how can they be explained, and are they likely to disappear or will they persist? These questions form the core of each chapter and are answered in a theoretically informed way, based on cultural and institutional analysis. The book takes a critical approach not only by evaluating critically the different theoretical strands but also by assessing the usefulness of the approaches for explaining issues in non-western, non-capitalist, less-developed countries and countries in transition. This may mean that, in some instances, the book appears intensive and highly focused. This approach is in accordance with the philosophy of the book, which is to offer thorough and well-founded knowledge rather than provide an easy descriptive tour through the material, and this approach requires a strong foundation in order to be meaningful.

Plan of the Book

The book consists of 12 chapters, each of which deals with major aspects of comparative international management and organization, in a comparative way. Each chapter starts with a learning objectives section and an outline of the chapter, and ends with study questions followed by an annotated recommended further reading list, one or more closing case studies, and a full list of references. Each chapter also includes some real-life examples and brief cases related to the topics discussed. These brief studies usually involve the application of the topics discussed in countries in transition such as China and Russia or in less-developed African countries such as Nigeria.

The first chapter sets the scene by introducing the main approaches to comparative international management as well as the globalization debate. The cultural and institutional theories, which are introduced in this chapter, are treated in a more in-depth way in Chapters 2 to 4. These two theoretical strands form the cornerstone of the explanations of the international management and organization issues that are covered in the subsequent chapters of the book. The globalization debate is introduced early on in the book in order to facilitate the understanding of the convergence–divergence question, which is the thread that connects all chapters. As will be clear from the text, the convergence–divergence question is quite controversial and, until now, there has been no definite answer to it. Hence, while I offer my own perspective in Chapter 12, this should be seen more as an encouragement to further reflection than a definite answer.

Before digging into the theory, however, Chapter 1 deals with the broader question of the role of national culture and national institutions in socio-economic development. The word 'societal' is used in the title of this chapter to express the dialectical relationship between culture and institutions. Chapter 1 deliberately takes a macro perspective, taking the economy at large instead of the organization as the unit of analysis. Since organizations are not only economic but also social phenomena that are part of, as well as operate within, the economy of a country, it is important to acquire some knowledge of the social functioning of this broader context.

Chapter 2 discusses several theoretical approaches to national culture in a critical and balanced way. It shows how national culture shapes organization and management differently in different countries. In order to further stress the influence of national culture on the micro level of the organization, the chapter also includes a section on the popular topic of cross-cultural negotiation.

Following this chapter on national culture, the influence of organizational culture on management and organization is explored in Chapter 3. This chapter emphasizes the relationship between national and organizational culture, and explains why organizational cultural differences are important in an international management context.

Chapter 4 discusses important aspects of institutional theory, concentrating on two major European approaches: the business systems approach and the societal effects approach. It explains the influence of the national institutional context on the development process of two Asian business systems: the Korean *Chaebol* and the Taiwanese business system. In order to be able to answer the convergence–divergence question theoretically, it tackles the issue of institutional change.

Chapters 5 and 6 concentrate on micro topics, discussing international human resource management issues and corporate governance aspects respectively. These two chapters serve dual purposes. First, they provide the background knowledge that is essential to an understanding of Chapters 7 and 8, which deal with production and innovation management respectively. Next, they help the reader to understand how the cultural and national institutional approaches that are explained in the previous chapters affect two important areas at the micro level of the organization. In particular, Chapters 5 and 6 explain how nationally specific institutions and national culture shape human resource management and corporate governance in organizations in different countries. As such, they are important in their own right.

As mentioned above, Chapter 7 explores how the societal environment shapes production systems and management in different countries. It concentrates on the major production systems – that is, on mass and flexible production systems, and the forms they take in different countries. Chapter 8 discusses the relationships between the societal environment and national systems of innovation. By means of examples of US, Japanese, German and French innovation systems, it clarifies these relationships.

Chapter 9 concentrates first on explaining the internationalization process of multinational corporations (MNCs). It discusses issues of coordination and control, and of learning. It also deals with the MNCs' responses to cultural and institutional differences. Chapter 10 analyses the influence of the societal environment on corporate strategy. Since this is a rather new and so far under-researched topic, there is scant literature available. The chapter concentrates on the major existing studies in the field. To a greater or lesser extent, all chapters of this book can be applied to and are useful for both MNCs and small and medium-sized organizations – since they also operate in an increasingly international and multicultural context. In view of the special position of MNCs in an international context, Chapters 9 and 10 are devoted to them. More than any other organization, these corporations have to decide how to deal with cross-national diversity in management and organization. They can adapt to local circumstances, but this means that the diversity is internalized. Alternatively, they can choose one particular approach in all countries, but that gives rise to the question of how effective local operations will be. Moreover, individuals who move from one country to another as expatriates will have to be aware of differences in rules and values.

Most chapters of this book take the organization as the core unit of analysis or examine how the macro influences the micro. Over the past ten years, however, networks and clusters have been a growing focus of attention in international business. From this literature it is clear that different types of network and cluster develop in different national contexts. To date, however, these topics have hardly been addressed in international management textbooks. In view of the growing importance of this research and management field, we felt it essential to dedicate a chapter – Chapter 11 – to these topics, in order to offer some background knowledge.

Chapter 12 concludes the book by trying to answer the question of whether differences in cross-national management and organization practices are likely to disappear or to persist in the future. In order to be able to answer this question, the chapter concentrates on developments in human resource management, labour relations and corporate governance in the two major capitalist models: the Anglo-Saxon and the Rhineland models. We concentrate on these two since, to a greater or lesser extent, the models of most countries – including countries in transition – tend to be variants of these two main models.

References

Shenkar, O. (2004) One more time: international business in a global economy. *Journal of International Business Studies* 35, 161–71.

Vernon, R. (1994) Contributing to an international business curriculum: an approach from the flank. *Journal of International Business Studies* 25, 215–27.

Zaheer, S. (1995) Overcoming the liability of foreignness. *Academy of Management Journal* 38(2), 341–63.

Introduction to the Approaches to Comparative International Management

Learning Objectives

By the end of this chapter you will be able to:

- understand the differences between universalistic and particularistic theories
- evaluate the use and usefulness of contingency theory
- assess the explanatory role of culture
- distinguish between emic and etic approaches to cultural analysis
- reflect critically upon the link between institutions and organization and management issues
- appreciate the differences between the two main institutional clusters
- appreciate the complexity of globalization research
- reflect upon the possible consequences of globalization.

Chapter Outline

Introduction to the Theoretical Debate
Universalistic Theories
  The Contingency Perspective
Particularistic Theories
  The cultural approach
  The institutional approach
Globalization
Study Questions
Further Reading
References

Introduction to the theoretical debate

In the introduction to this book it was suggested that comparative international management is concerned with the study of management and organization in different societal settings. Consequently, comparisons focus on the interplay between societal settings on the one hand, and various management and organizational forms and processes on the other. In the process of comparing these phenomena we find both similarities and differences. Depending on the goals and interests of the analyst, research designs will favour either the search for similarities or the search for differences.

This book focuses on differences in management and organization that are caused by nationally determined variables and that exist despite similarities in technology, environment, strategies, and so on. We ask ourselves how these differences can be explained and whether they are likely to disappear or to persist. To be able to answer these questions, we need to acquire a theoretical framework that guides comparative analysis and explanation of business organization and management.

Theories that try to answer the first question fall into two categories. 'Universalistic' theories claim that the phenomena of management and organization are subject to the same universal 'laws' everywhere in the world. An example is the positive relationship between the size of an organization and its degree of internal differentiation, which has been found in many studies. Universalistic theories posit that this relationship is valid everywhere in the world, because it is based on fundamental characteristics of human behaviour. 'Particularistic' theories, conversely, posit that organization and management in different countries can differ fundamentally, and that different explanations are necessary for different countries.

Universalistic theories tend to predict that cross-national differences in management and organization, in so far as they exist, will disappear in the future. A driving force for this homogenization process is globalization. As more and more markets become subjected to worldwide competitive pressure, less efficient ways of management and organization will give way to 'best practices', regardless of the nationality of company, management or employees. Existing cross-national differences may be seen as temporary disequilibria, which will disappear when obstacles to the free market are removed. The concept of globalization and its consequences are discussed more extensively in the section of this chapter that deals with globalization.

Particularistic theories, on the other hand, predict that cross-national differences in management and organization will persist. The reason is that management and organization reflect expectations and preferences that differ between countries. Furthermore, particularistic interpretations of organization and management imply that history matters, as national systems of management and organization are path-dependent. For instance, the question may be asked whether Japanese management and organization can be truly understood without taking into account Japan's late industrialization halfway through the nineteenth century, leading to dramatic changes in a society that still bore the characteristics of the feudal era.

An influential universalistic approach (discussed in the section of this chapter that focuses on universalistic theories) is contingency theory. Two important particularistic approaches that guide contemporary comparative analysis and explanation of organization and management and, hence, the chapters of this book, are the cultural and institutional approaches. These are introduced in the section on particularistic theories, and are discussed more extensively in later chapters.

The two alternative theoretical orientations – that is, the universalistic and the particularistic theories – have particular strengths and weaknesses, some of which will be discussed below. They should not be seen as mutually exclusive, however; rather they can usefully complement each other. Most studies from a cultural or institutional perspective tacitly utilize the insights of contingency theory. Hickson *et al.* (1974: 29) underline the contribution contingency theory can make when they point out that 'we can only start to attribute features to culture when we have made sure that relations between variables, e.g. between size and degree of specialization, are stable between cultures'. Contingency theory thus permits the researcher to highlight cultural or societal differences by controlling for the stable relationships identified. This means that the researcher selects his or her cross-national sample in such a way that the units of analysis are carefully matched according to certain factors. Size, degree of dependency, and production technology or product are the variables usually matched in the comparison of business organizations in different societies.

The cultural and institutional approaches could also usefully be seen as complementary and could best be integrated into one single framework. Adherents of the cultural approach, however, have made little effort in this direction. Cross-cultural studies explain organizational variance between nations solely by cultural aspects and do not complement their research by inquiry into the influence of the institutional environment. If the cultural perspective is to examine the historical emergence and perpetuation of cultural values, however, it is bound to recognize the important role played by institutions.

Institutional scholars, while incorporating culture into their theoretical ideas, seem to lack the analytical tools to address the concept of culture in a satisfactory way. While institutions are conceived as concrete manifestations of societal values and norms, little effort has been made within institutional research to analyse and specify what values and norms are seen to be congruent with given institutional structures. Such an analysis would be helpful in explaining the differences between institutions in different countries, a question that has not yet been answered sufficiently clearly. Similarly, the openness of societies to institutional change – an as yet unresolved research topic – might fruitfully be examined within a truly integrated cultural–institutional framework.

The approach adopted in this book is to use a framework that integrates institutional and cultural perspectives. In so doing, it aims to provide both cultural and institutional explanations for cross-national differences in organization and management. It tries to avoid favouritism and emphasizes that, until now, there has been no one best approach.

Universalistic Theories

The contingency perspective

The contingency approach was developed by the so-called Aston School from the 1960s onwards, and is associated primarily with the names of Hickson and Pugh (see Hickson *et al.*, 1969, 1979). Much of contingency theory research has studied organizational structure, and this tradition is referred to as structural contingency theory. This theory posits that, given similar circumstances, the structure of an organization – that is, the basic patterns of control, coordination and communication – can be expected to be very much the same wherever it is located (Hickson *et al.*, 1974). The theory further posits that, if they are to be successful, organizations must structure in response to a series of demands or contingencies posed by the scale of operations, usually expressed as size, the technology employed and the environment within which operations take place. Table 1 shows the relationship between these contingencies and organizational structure.

The contingency theory states that the mechanistic structure (hierarchical, centralized, formalized) fits a stable environment because a hierarchical approach is efficient for routine operations. Given the routine nature of operations, the management at upper levels of the hierarchy possesses sufficient knowledge and information to make decisions, and this centralized control fosters efficiency (Table 2). In contrast, the organic structure (participatory, decentralized, unformalized) fits an unstable environment and situations of high task uncertainty. A major source of task uncertainty is innovation, much of which comes ultimately from the environment of the organization, such as technological and market change. The mechanistic organizational structure is shown to fit an environment of a low rate of market and technological change. Conversely, the organic organizational structure is shown to fit an environment of a high rate of market and technological change.

Moreover, each of the contingencies – that is, the environment, technology and size – is argued to affect a particular aspect of structure. This means that change in any of these contingencies tends to produce change in the corresponding structure. In this way the organization moves its structure into alignment with each of these contingencies, so that structure and contingency tend to be associated.

Cultural and societal specifics are perceived as negligible. While these influences are not entirely denied, contingency constraints are argued to override them. The contingency perspective claims that variance in organizational structure is due primarily to the contingencies faced and not to societal or cultural location. Any deviation from this

Table 1 Efficient fit between organizational forms, and some contingency factors

Factors/forms	Mechanistic	Organic
Environment	Stable	Turbulent
Technology	Mass production	Single product and process production
Size	Large	Small(er)

Table 2 Organic and mechanistic organizational forms

Dimension/form	Mechanistic	Organic
Tasks	Narrow, specialized	Broad, enriched
Work description	Precise, procedures	Indicative, results
Decision-making	Centralized, detailed	Decentralized
Hierarchy	Steep, many layers	Flat, few layers

pattern is explained by the fact that some organizations (in some cultures) have yet to catch up, in structural terms, with contingencies. Because the fit of organizational features to contingencies leads to higher performance, organizations seek to attain fit.

Relationships between contingencies and aspects of organization structure are seen as constant in direction but not necessarily in magnitude. For example, in all societies, increases in the size of organization bring increases in formalization, but not necessarily the same degree of increase. Contingency theorists posit merely a stable relationship between contingencies and structure across different societies. They do not maintain that organizations in different countries are alike because the contingencies still vary across countries; for example, the UK has more large-scale corporations than France (Lane, 1989).

The strengths of contingency theory are that the theory is straightforward and the methodology, though complex, is highly standardized. The various dependent and independent variables are operationalized so that they can be quantified and measured in a precise way (i.e. size equals number of employees). Multivariate analysis of these empirically measurable dimensions, each constructed from scalable variables (64 scales were devised for this purpose), was used to develop a taxonomy (or multidimensional classification) of organizational structures.[1] These strengths gained the contingency approach considerable influence, and for a long time it displaced the approach from culture, which had remained both theoretically and methodologically unsophisticated.

The contingency approach, however, also has numerous weak points and blind spots. It has been pointed out that although this theory is able to show the consistency and strength of correlation between the two sets of variables – that is, between contingency variables such as size, or technology and the structural features of an organization – it has never provided an adequate explanation for this. Furthermore, the theoretical status of contingencies has remained uncertain (Child and Tayeb, 1981). Are they imperatives or do they merely have the force of implications if a certain threshold is crossed?

In addition, the contingency approach only elucidates properties of *formal* structure and neglects informal structures (Lane, 1989). For example, German business organizations usually come out as highly centralized. However, when the relationships between superiors and subordinates are analysed in detail it turns out that autonomy in staff working practices is actually greater in Germany than in the UK and France (for details, see Chapter 5). This shortcoming is due to the fact that the theory focuses only on structure – moreover, only on limited aspects of the latter – and completely leaves out of the picture the actors involved and the informal interaction between them. It thus operates at a high level of abstraction and generality. It is in fact argued that contingency theory, which is a culture-free theoretical framework, can only be maintained because the actor is left out of the picture (Horvath *et al.*, 1981). However, while formal structure may be remarkably alike across societies, different national actors perceive, interpret or live with them in very different ways, due to deep-rooted cultural forces.

Moreover, contingency theory also seems to suffer from the fact that it evolved from western traditions of rational design of organizations and from research on organizational populations in mostly Anglo-American institutional settings. A comparative study

---

[1] As this complex methodology cannot be explained here, the reader could usefully refer to the articles by Pugh *et al.* (1963, 1968 and 1969) cited in the References section.

of 55 manufacturing plants in the USA and 51 plants in the same manufacturing industries in Japan confirms the bias that is inherent in this sample (see Lincoln *et al.*, 1986). The results of this research are consistent with the thrust of much writing on Japanese industrial organization and relations (see e.g. Meyer and Rowan, 1977; Carroll and Huo, 1986). These writings show that the 'institutional environment' – the society's distinctive set of highly established and culturally bound action patterns and expectations – has a particularly strong influence on organizational forms in Japan.

Japanese organizational structures were found to differ in certain particulars from US designs. Compared with those in the USA, Japanese manufacturing organizations have taller hierarchies, less functional specialization and less formal delegation of authority, but more de facto participation in decisions at lower levels in the management hierarchy. These structures are consistent with the internal labour market processes (lifetime employment, seniority-based promotion) that characterize Japanese companies and the general emphasis on groups over individuals as the fundamental units of organization. These findings seem to indicate that organizational theories are 'culture bound', limited to particular countries or regions in their capacity to explain organizational structure.

The popularity of the culture-free approach has declined significantly in the past decade. Nowadays, most cross-national thinking and research focuses on difference rather than similarity. Instead of trying to find universally applicable practices, research warns against the ill-considered adoption of foreign ideas.

Particularistic Theories

The cultural approach

Comparative cultural research has expanded greatly in the past decade and a half. In part, this is a response to the biases of culture-free researchers, who have tended to focus on macro-level variables and structure context relationships, rather than the behaviour of people within the organization (Child, 1981). The move away from contingency theory and towards the cultural approach was also spurred by the globalization of markets and business. Greater integration and more dynamic commercial environments meant that structures could not remain static and individual cross-cultural interactions became more frequent. There was a need to understand the entirety of the organization and not just the structural features.

Culture-bound research is carried out at different levels of analysis. *Cross-cultural* research takes place at two distinct levels of analysis: individual and cultural. In comparative management studies, the focus is on the cultural rather than the individual level. Culture is considered to be a background factor, almost synonymous with country. Similar to contingency theory, this research has a macro focus, examining the relationship between culture and organization structure. However, in comparative management research, the concept of culture has also been expanded to include the organizational or corporate level. In this case, culture is considered to be an explanatory variable. This research has a micro focus, investigating the similarities and differences in attitudes of managers of different cultures.

Irrespective of the level of analysis, in social science there are two long-standing approaches to understanding the role of culture: (1) the *inside* perspective of ethnographers, who strive to describe a particular culture in its own terms, and (2) the *outside* perspective of comparativist researchers, who attempt to describe differences across cultures in terms of a general, external standard. These two approaches were designated the *emic* and *etic* perspectives, respectively, by analogy to two approaches to language: phonemic analysis of the units of meaning, which reveals the unique structure of a particular language, and phonetic analysis of sound, which affords comparisons among languages (Pike, 1967).

The emic and etic perspectives have equally long pedigrees in social science. The emic, or inside, perspective follows in the tradition of psychological studies of folk beliefs (Wundt, 1888) and in cultural anthropologists striving to understand culture from 'the native's point of view' (Malinowski, 1922). The etic, or outside, perspective follows in the tradition of behaviourist psychology (Skinner, 1938) and anthropological approaches that link cultural practices to external, antecedent factors, such as economic or ecological conditions (Harris, 1979).

The two perspectives are often seen as being at odds – as incommensurable paradigms. An important reason for this perception lies in the differences in constructs, assumptions and research methods that are used by the two approaches (see Table 3). Emic accounts describe thoughts and actions primarily in terms of the actors' self-understanding – terms that are often culturally and historically bound. In contrast, etic models describe phenomena in constructs that apply across cultures. Along with differing constructs, emic and etic researchers tend to have differing assumptions about culture. Emic researchers tend to assume that a culture is best understood as an interconnected whole or system, whereas etic researchers are more likely to isolate particular components of culture, and to state hypotheses about their distinct antecedents and consequences.

As indicated, in general, both approaches use differing research methods.[2] Methods in emic research are more likely to involve sustained, wide-ranging observation of a single cultural group. In classical fieldwork, for example, an ethnographer immerses him or herself in a setting, developing relationships with informants and taking social roles (e.g. Geertz, 1983; Kondo, 1990). Emic description can also be pursued in more structured programmes of interview and observation.

Methods in etic research are more likely to involve brief, structured observations of several cultural groups. A key feature of etic methods is that observations are made in a parallel manner across differing settings. For instance, matched samples of employees in many different countries may be surveyed to uncover dimensions of cross-national variation in values and attitudes (e.g. Hofstede, 1980), or they may be assigned to experimental conditions in order to test the moderating influence of the cultural setting on the relationship among other variables (e.g. Earley, 1989).

The divide between the emic and the etic approaches persists in contemporary scholarship on culture: in anthropology, between interpretivists (Geertz, 1976, 1983) and comparativists (Munroe and Munroe, 1991), and in psychology between cultural psychologists (Shweder, 1991) and cross-cultural psychologists (Smith and Bond, 1998). In the literature on international differences in organizations, the divide is manifest in the

---

[2] The association between perspectives and methods is not absolute, however. Sometimes, in emic investigations of indigenous constructs, data are collected with survey methods and analysed with quantitative techniques. Likewise, ethnographic observation and qualitative data are sometimes used to support arguments from an etic perspective.

Table 3 Assumptions of emic and etic perspectives and associated methods

Features	Emic, or inside, view	Etic, or outside, view
Assumptions and goals	Behaviour described as seen from the perspective of cultural insiders, in constructs drawn from their self-understandings Describes the cultural system as a working whole	Behaviour described from a vantage point external to the culture, in constructs that apply equally well to other cultures Describes the ways in which cultural variables fit into general causal models of a particular behaviour
Typical features of methods associated with this view	Observations recorded in a rich qualitative form that avoids imposition of the researchers' constructs Long-standing, wide-ranging observation of one or a few settings	Focus on external, measurable features that can be assessed by parallel procedures at different cultural sites Brief, narrow observation of more than one setting, often a large number of settings
Examples of typical study types	Ethnographic fieldwork; participant observation along with interviews	Comparative experiment treating culture as a quasi-experimental manipulation to assess whether the impact of particular factors varies across cultures

Source: Morris *et al.* (1999: 783).

contrast between classic studies based on fieldwork in a single culture (Rohlen, 1974), as opposed to surveys across many (Hofstede, 1980). Likewise, in the large body of literature on organizational culture, there is a divide between researchers employing ethnographic methods (Gregory, 1983; Van Maanen, 1988) and those who favour comparative survey research (Schneider, 1990).

Given the differences between the two approaches to culture, it is hardly surprising that researchers taking each perspective have generally questioned or ignored the utility of integrating insights from the other tradition. A common tendency is to dismiss insights from the other perspective based on conceptual or methodological weaknesses (see Chapter 2 for an extended explanation). Some scholars, however, recognize that the two are in fact best seen as complementary, and have suggested that researchers should choose between approaches depending on the stage of the research programme. For example, it has been argued that an emic approach serves best in exploratory research, whereas an etic approach serves best in testing hypotheses.

Some scholars (i.e. Berry, 1990) propose a three-stage sequence. In the first stage, initial exploratory research relies on 'imposed-etic' constructs – theoretical concepts and measurement methods that are simply exported from the researcher's home culture. In the second stage, emic insights about the other culture are used to interpret initial findings, with an eye to possible limitations of the original constructs, such as details that are unfamiliar or meaningless outside of the home culture. On this basis, then, the constructs in the model are *filtered* to eliminate details that cannot be measured with equivalence across cultural settings. The factors that survive this filter – 'derived-etic' constructs – are culture-general dimensions of persons, such as value orientations, or of their environments, such as economic or ecological factors. In the third and final stage, the researcher tests an explanation constructed solely of derived-etic constructs (Morris *et al.*, 1999).

Sequential selection models, such as the one from Berry (1990), have been influential in guiding psychological and organizational researchers in their approaches to culture. Yet these analyses only begin to explore the synergies between perspectives. Although they address the role of emic insights in refining etic explanations, they say little about how etic insights stimulate emic investigation. In fact, they do not lead to the full integration of both research streams. Thus far, there have been only limited attempts in that direction (i.e. Morris *et al.*, 1999).

The plea for full integration is based on the fact that the different strengths of the two approaches create complementarities. Findings from the two perspectives could challenge each other and stimulate each other's new questions. Moreover, the two kinds of explanation could complement each other in contributing to rich accounts of culture. The emic and etic perspectives each provide only half of the explanation of culture. Because emic studies tap into the explanations held by cultural insiders, the emic perspective leads inherently to an emphasis on the causes of phenomena that are internal and local to the cultures and organizations being studied. Because etic perspectives attune one to relationships between external structural variables and behaviours, a functionalist story is more likely to result.

The lack of general awareness (outside the small group of scholars) of the complexity of the concept of culture and of the different analytical possibilities to carry out research on culture spurs this book on to cover extensively major studies within the national and organizational culture field of research, as well as to treat the special methodological problems that are often overlooked. It is felt that, in order to get a clear understanding of cultural research, it is essential to understand the ways in which research is, or ought to be, carried out. In Chapters 2 and 3, national and organization culture research, respectively, are discussed in depth. In these chapters the methodological issues and dilemmas of the cultural approach are explained in a more detailed way.

The institutional approach

Since the mid-1970s, comparative organizational analysis based on the institutional perspective have proliferated. In a similar way to cultural research, institutional analysis formed a challenge for the universal theory of the contingency perspective. Institutionalists in particular criticized the fact that contingency theorists implicitly generalize the results of empirical studies based on a population of organizations limited to a single society or family of societies, thus, promoting them to the status of universal, theoretical propositions. Institutionalists argue that such a research approach cannot but lead to finding evidence of convergence.

In contrast to contingency theorists, comparative institutional research focuses on comparisons that highlight differences that cannot be attributed to different goals, contexts, environments or strategies of enterprises. Their interest is focused on differences between organizations that cannot be attributed to common explanatory variables in organization theory, such as technology, firm size, products made, innovation rates, variability in products made, ownership, and so on. 'Intriguing differences are those, which arise despite similarities in the factors just mentioned' (Sorge, 2003). As a consequence, institutional analysis has moved 'towards an increasingly explicit insistence upon the maintained diversity and qualitative specificity of social forms in the advanced societies' (Rose, 1985: 66).

Institutionalists differ from culturalists in that they focus on 'wider norms and standards supported or enforced by institutional machineries or less daunting interested networks', as opposed to 'the culturalists' focus on the mind of the individual as the place where differences reside' (Sorge, 2003). When comparing definitions of institutions and culture, however, distinguishing clearly between the two is not always a straightforward matter. A broad and encompassing definition is given by Douglass North, who sees institutions as

> the humanly devised constraints that structure political, economic and social interaction. They consist of both informal constraints (sanctions, taboos, customs, traditions, and codes of conduct), and formal rules (constitutions, laws, property rights). (1991: 97)

Similarly, Scott (1995) points to three types of institutional support:

> The regulative (formal rules and incentives constructed by the state and other empowered agents of the collective good), normative (informal rules associated with values and explicit moral commitments), and cognitive (abstract rules associated with the structure of cognitive distinctions and taken-for-granted understandings).

These definitions suggest that *informal* and *normative* institutions and culture are alike – that is, they express customs, traditions, values, and so on. In fact, cultural beliefs are seen as central ingredients of institutions (North, 1995: 49). It is very difficult, therefore, to disentangle the impact of *informal* and *normative* institutions from that of culture. In this book, we concentrate on formal institutions as these are less complicated to identify and easier for outsiders to understand; they also lend themselves better to comparative analysis.

Similar to cultural analysis, there is little consensus on the definition of key concepts, measures or methods within the institutional tradition. Institutional theory has developed no central set of standard variables, nor is it associated with a standard research methodology or even a set of methods. Studies have relied on a variety of techniques, including case analysis, historical analysis, cross-sectional regression, longitudinal models of various types, and so on (Tolbert and Zucker, 1996).

Most European organizational institutional analysis uses qualitative research methods and concentrates on case studies and, to some extent, on (descriptive) statistical analysis. The methodological approach is that of comparing carefully matched pairs in different societies, controlling for such well-known constants as size and product. This method gives a relatively small, non-randomly chosen sample and hence dictates a more qualitative and 'in-depth' study, with attention to detail and thick description.

Similar to cultural research, too, varieties of institutional theory differ in terms of the level at which they are applied (Scott, 2001: 83–8). Levels identified differ greatly in terms of whether the investigator is focusing on more micro or more macro phenomena. For institutions, level may be usefully operationalized as the range of influence of the institutional form. For our purposes, it makes sense to distinguish between the level of society (i.e. to examine the institutional foundations of the differences in state regulation), organizational field or industrial sector (i.e. the differences in governance mechanisms at work in different industries), organization (i.e. to explain varying types of organizational forms to govern and reduce transaction costs), and organizational subsystem (i.e. the institutional foundations of the power of the engineering department).

What we are most interested in, in this book, is the question of how organizations and industrial sectors are influenced by institutionalized rules and institutional environments. Chapter 4 discusses two European institutional approaches that help us to answer this question – the 'business systems approach' and the 'societal effect' approach. Most of the empirical literature using these approaches treats institutions as independent variables. These studies examine the effects of institutions on some organizational entity or process, the units ranging from trans-societal systems to organizational subsystems. This focus is understandable because organizational research is primarily interested in assessing whether and to what extent institutional systems affect individual organizations or collections of organizations. Clearly, if such influences cannot be demonstrated, there would be little incentive to pursue institutional analysis.

With this in mind, the relevant versions of institutional analysis today agree on the fact that different sets of institution result in divergent organization and management practices, and different advantages and disadvantages for engaging in specific types of activity. In other words, firms can perform some types of activity that allow them to produce some kinds of goods more efficiently than others because of the institutional support they receive for those activities; the institutions relevant to these activities are not distributed evenly across nations (Streeck, 1992; Whitley, 1999; Maurice and Sorge, 2000; Hall and Soskice, 2001).

Different versions of institutional analysis have developed different typologies on the basis of linkages between social institutions (i.e. Soskice, 1996, 1999; Streeck, 1996; Whitley, 1999; Amable, 2000). Two major ideal types that are identified in all typologies are the liberal market, or Anglo-Saxon, and the coordinated market economies (see Table 4). Since both ideal types are currently commonly used in the popular press and both recur frequently throughout this book, it was decided to introduce them early on and to explain them in this introductory chapter.

The first ideal type is said to be dominant in the Anglo-Saxon cluster of countries, including the USA, the UK, Ireland, Australia, New Zealand and Canada.[3] The model is characterized by:

- a financial system that imposes relatively short-term horizons on companies, but at the same time allows high risk-taking
- an industrial relations system in a deregulated labour market that discourages effective employee representation within companies – hence, weak unions – but that facilitates unilateral control by top management

---

[3] The following section is based on Soskice (1999: 106–12).

- an education and training system that emphasizes general education and discourages long-term initial vocational training, but encourages subsequent bit-by-bit skill acquisition, especially for those with sufficient general education

- an inter-company system that imposes strong competition requirements and, hence, limits possible cooperation between companies.

Coordinated market economies include most northern European economies (the Netherlands, Scandinavian economies, Germany, Switzerland, Austria) and Japan. The model is characterized by:

- a financial system that allows the long-term financing of companies

- an industrial relations system in which unions play an important part and that allows cooperative industrial relations within the company and coordinated wage bargaining across companies

- an education and training system that encourages serious initial vocational training of young people, and in which organized business and/or individual companies are closely involved

- an inter-company system that enables substantial technology and standard-setting cooperation to take place between companies.

The coordinated market economy family has two quite distinct sub-branches. These sub-branches are defined by the way in which business is organized: whether the primary unit of business coordination is the industry (or part of an industry); or whether the primary unit of business coordination is across industry grouping of companies.

Table 4 Institutional typology			
National institutions	**Liberal cluster**	**Coordinated cluster**	
	Anglo-Saxon	Northern Europe + Germany	Japan
Business organization and coordination	Weak	Strong and well-organized at the industry level	at the group level
Relations between institutions and actors	Arm's length; short-term; low trust	Long-term; high trust	
Financial institutions	Market	Banks and market	banks
Education and training system for lower-level workers	Ineffective	Effective	
Unions	Weak	Important role	
Career patterns of managers	Between firms	Within firms	
Labour market	Flexible; deregulated	Regulated	

Industry-coordinated (or northern European) market economies: in these economies, which include Germany, the primary locus for coordination of activities between companies with respect to technology transfer, initial training, industrial relations, and so on, is at the industry level. Coordination across industries usually takes place via industry bodies, rather than individual firms.

Group-coordinated market economies: in Japan, the primary locus of inter-company coordination takes place within across-industry groupings of large companies, to which the great majority of very large companies belong. These groupings include companies from each major industry, with relatively little product-market overlap between the companies in any one group. Many smaller supplier companies have close and exclusive relations with a larger company, and, hence, fall within the sphere of influence of the relevant group.

As suggested, the different social institutional features of different constellations help us to explain differences in international competitiveness. The Anglo-Saxon model is argued to foster product market strategies that emphasize competition over prices, accompanied by more radical forms of innovation. The coordinated market economies' model pushes manufacturers towards a product-market strategy that emphasizes high-quality products and incremental innovation (Soskice, 1996).

Liberal market economies and coordinated market economies are not the only type of *advanced* economy, however. France is an example of a different type of economy: in France, the state still plays a much more important role in the coordination of large companies than it does in other countries. Some advanced economies do not fall easily into any type: Spain, for example, is in transition towards the liberal market model (Soskice, 1996). Moreover, to make the typology more generally applicable, developing countries and/or countries in transition should be taken into account. Similar to cultural analysis, until now, institutional analysis has largely concentrated on advanced (and usually western) economies. Needless to say, both approaches would benefit from expanding their empirical basis to include other parts of the world.

From the 1990s onwards, as recession in Germany and Japan set in, some scholars predicted the erosion and convergence of the Rhine model towards Anglo-Saxon capitalism. The first question to answer in this respect is whether institutional change of this type, as well as in general, can be explained theoretically. This question is answered in Chapter 4. The concluding chapter of this book, Chapter 12, provides an empirical examination of this question.

Globalization

The concept of globalization has become extremely popular over the past decade. Both the concept and the impact of globalization forces have been discussed widely within different disciplinary contexts. The widespread interest of different disciplines in the concept seems to lead to different opinions on the contents of the concept and on its consequences. In economics, for example, globalization refers to economic internationalization and the spread of capitalist market relations. In Cox's words: 'The global economy is the system generated by globalizing production and global finance' (1992: 30). Research in this direction usually predicts the increasing influence of integrated and global capital markets upon the domestic context and in most cases points to Americanization as the end result. Globalization has been defined in business schools as the production and distribution of products and services of a homogenous type and quality on a worldwide basis. Simply put: providing the same output to countries everywhere (Levitt, 1983; Rugman and Hodgetts, 2001). Or in Levitt's words: 'The global corporation operates with resolute constancy – at relatively low cost – as if the entire world (or major regions of it) were a single entity; it sells the same things in the same time everywhere' (1983).

Levitt emphasizes that globalization leads to benefits from economies of scale and standardization. Contingent upon this definition of economic globalization is the need for products to be uniform across countries. For Levitt the global is more present than the local. In this sense, he argues that 'only global companies will achieve long-term success by concentrating on what everyone wants rather than worrying about the details of what everyone thinks they might like' (Levitt, 1983: 1). The most commonly articulated consequences of globalization in this type of literature focus essentially on transnational corporations.

A much broader definition of globalization is formulated by writers such as Albrow, for whom globalization refers to 'all those processes by which the peoples of the world are incorporated into a single world society, a global society' (Albrow, 1990: 9). Similarly, Anthony Giddens defines globalization as 'The worldwide interconnection at the cultural, political and economic level resulting from the elimination of communication and trade barriers' (Giddens, 1999).

Giddens further states that 'globalization is a process of convergence of cultural, political and economic aspects of life' (1999). Convergence of cultures, tastes, regulations, and the like, is of course an extreme version of homogeneity of products and services.

In a large part of the literature, globalization is interpreted as a multidimensional force that has an impact on different levels of analysis (see e.g. Berger and Dore, 1996; Lane, 2000; Meyer, 2000; Nye and Donahue, 2000). The focus of this literature is on the dynamics of change and on the relationships between global and local. It is recognized that change does not occur everywhere in the same way and at the same rate, and that the particular character of individual societies interacts with the larger-scale general processes of change to produce specific outcomes (Dicken, 1998).

This literature is based on the ideas of many contemporary globalization theorists on the nature of transnational processes (i.e. Hannerz, 1987; Robertson, 1992, 1995, 2001; Garcia Canclini, 1995; Pieterse, 1995; Appadurai, 1996; Tomlinson, 1999). These theorists coin the term *glocalization* to indicate the interpenetration of the global and the local. They emphasize global heterogeneity and reject the idea that forces emanating from the West in general and the USA in particular are leading to economic, political, institutional and cultural homogeneity. Similar to the more simplistic writings on globalization, however, this research has been unable to provide a concrete answer to the consequences of the dynamics of change and integration.

In general, according to Lane (2000), the divergent opinions on the consequences of globalization in this literature – irrespective of the meaning that is given to the concept – can be summarized in four possible scenarios: (1) convergence towards the Anglo-American neoliberal market system (i.e Dore, 1996; Streeten, 1996; Streeck, 1997); (2) greater specialization of national models in accordance with domestic institutional and cultural characteristics (Vitols, 2001; Sorge, 2003); (3) incremental adaptation of the domestic institutional context in a largely path-dependent manner (i.e. Casper, 2000; Whitley, 1994a, 1994b); and (4) hybridization with change in a path-deviant manner (i.e. Whitley, 1999; Lane, 2000).

The ideas about the first scenario, convergence of national models, were first systematically articulated in postwar writings about industrial societies.[4] However, while in those days globalization was often interpreted as a process of homogenization or convergence, the postwar writings, while postulating convergence, did not make mention of the concept of globalization. Rather, as suggested at the beginning of this chapter, the social sciences of the 1950s and 1960s located the engine of convergence in technology. The core notion was that as countries sought to increase levels of well-being for their citizens and to maintain the military requirements for survival in an anarchic world, they progressed along a common trajectory of technological possibilities. The path of innovation along which they moved was the same for all. They would advance, more or less rapidly, passing through common stages and adopting over time more and more of the same social, political and economic structures.

Starting in the 1970s and 1980s, new research played an important role in undermining the grip of technological explanations within the social sciences. The new research stimulated new lines of speculation on the societal, cultural, political and organizational factors that might explain the differential performance of firms using the same technologies in different national settings. This new research agenda appeared at the end of the 1980s at a time of an apparent weakening of the American economy and triumph of quite different economic institutions and practices in Japan and Germany. These two countries' remarkable postwar growth and prosperity seemed striking demonstrations that economies work in ways quite different from those described by neoclassical economics and US practice. The notion of different forms of capitalism – each type characterized by different institutions, practices, values and politics – began to appear in both scholarly and popular writing (Berger, 1996: 2–9).

The globalization concept became popular at the time of the resurgence of the US economy in the 1990s, and the demise of the German and Japanese models. It is hardly coincidental, then, that some of the most common interpretations of globalization today are that the world is becoming more uniform and standardized, through a technological, commercial and cultural synchronization emanating from the West – and, in particular, from the Anglo-Saxon countries (Nederveen Pieterse, 1994). While it is clear that the increasing openness of national economies, the swelling volume of funds flowing across national frontiers, and the growing ease of transferring capital and production from one country to another create severe pressures to match others' macro-economic results, it is also clear that Anglo-Saxon capitalism seems to revive in this context. It is less clear that these pressures do actually work to align diversities generated by different national traditions into an ever more common set of institutions and practices. And, if they do so, that this common set of institutions and practices will necessarily be dominated by the Anglo-Saxon type of capitalism (Berger, 1996: 2–9).

Rather, it could be argued that the varied dimensions of globalization all point to the inherent fluidity, indeterminacy and open-endedness of the concept. And that, when we depart from this point of view, it becomes less obvious to think of globalization in terms of

---

[4] For postwar writings on the case for convergence see Aron (1962), Kerr *et al.* (1960) and Bell (1973).

standardization and less likely that globalization can be in terms of uni-directional processes, either structurally or culturally. Moreover, if we accept that culture is embedded in institutions and culture, and that institutions are deeply rooted in societies and, hence, difficult to change, then it would be difficult indeed to conceive of globalization in terms of homogenization.

The second scenario – increased specialization and sharper accentuation of the domestic system – implies that, under pressure of globalization and integration, 'the domestic' will adapt by specializing more vigorously in what it does best. It is important to distinguish here between two views: 'greater specialization in national industrial profiles' (Vitols, 2001: 360) and development of greater societal specificity (Sorge, 1996). Greater industrial specialization demands that domestic industries will focus more closely than before on the activities in which they have an international competitive advantage. It does not necessarily also imply greater specialization (and, thus, increasing divergence) at the level of the domestic institutions, but rather assumes incremental improvements in existing institutions as a result of integration. The development of societal specificity, on the other hand, implies both, increasing differences between societies and, as a result, increasing differences in national industrial specialization. In this research, internationalization and universal technical change is argued to trigger development of societal specificity, rather than bringing about convergence between societies (Sorge, 1996: 84). Greater specialization in industrial profiles is seen as inevitable since industries are influenced by the context in which they are embedded.

The third scenario – incremental path-dependent adaptation – focuses essentially on the institutional level and rules out convergence of one societal system towards the other. The argument is based on the fact that institutions are socially constructed in the sense that they embody shared cultural understandings ('shared cognitions', 'interpretive frames') of the way the world works (Zucker, 1983: 5; Meyer and Rowan, 1991; Scott, 1995: 33). In accordance with the actor–structure logic, emergent and changing institutional forms are argued to be 'isomorphic' with (i.e. compatible, resembling and similar in logic to) existing ones because actors extract causal designations from the world around them and these cause-and-effect understandings inform how they approach new problems (DiMaggio and Powell, 1991: 11; Dobbin, 1994). This means that even when actors would set out to redesign institutions, they are constrained in their actions by these embedded cultural constraints.

Finally, hybridization, the fourth scenario, also tends to be a gradual process. In contrast to path-dependent adaptation, however, hybridization implies some change in a path-deviant manner. Hybridization is argued to result from the process of integration into the global system of individual companies. Subsidiaries, which enjoy a high level of resources and a relatively high degree of autonomy, are argued to become embedded in their host countries. This will lead to learning processes and to the adoption of new organizational structures, practices and competences. Organizational learning from host country experience by affiliates will, in integrated transnational corporations (TNCs), initiate organizational learning and hybridization at company level. Such hybrid companies, it is argued, if they belong to the core companies of a country, may eventually affect the domestic business system (Lane, 2000).

The different opinions on the consequences of global forces serve as a background dilemma in this book. The debates on the existence, non-existence or degree of globalization are not dealt with. It is far more interesting to concentrate on the less systematically explored effects of the processes of integration – whether these are global, regional or local. These effects are not only interesting in their own right, but should help us to answer the question of whether globalization is actually taking place. If globalization would, indeed, be an ongoing process, then obviously we should be able to identify its consequences. These consequences are addressed throughout the book by tracing the impact of processes of international integration and change upon major interrelated societal complexes. This is important, as changes in the societal context translate themselves at the corporate firm and industrial level, and have implications for management and organization. Chapter 12 winds up this entire discussion and aims to provide a substantiated and theoretically supported perspective on the question of which of the aforementioned scenarios the corporate world should be prepared for in the future.

Study Questions

1. Explain the difference between universalistic and particularistic theories.

2. What are the main arguments of the contingency approach, and how can this approach be reconciled with the cultural and institutional approaches?

3. Explain the differences between the 'emic' and 'etic' approaches to cultural research.

4. Assess under what conditions you would choose one or another type of research.

5. Comment on the compatibility of, and the possibility of integrating the two approaches.

6. Explain the importance of national institutions for management and organization.

7. Explain the broad differences between the liberal and the coordinated institutional cluster.

8. Explain and legitimize how, according to you, the concept of globalization could best be defined.

Further Reading

Hall, E.T. and Hall, M.R. (1990) *Understanding Cultural Differences.* Yarmouth, USA: Intercultural Press.

The authors offer yet another framework within the emic approach to national culture, elaborating on the concepts of low and high context, and their implications for understanding and communicating with people from different cultural backgrounds.

Hall, P.A. and Soskice, D. (2001) *Varieties of Capitalism.* Oxford: Oxford University Press.

This book offers another framework for carrying out institutional analysis.

Hofstede, G. (2001) *Culture's Consequences* (2nd edn). London: Sage.

This book offers a complete picture of culture research.

Maurice, M. and Sorge, A. (2000) *Embedding Organizations.* Amsterdam: John Benjamins.

This book offers the latest position and empirical examples in societal effect research.

Punnett, B.J. and Shenkar, O. (1998) *Handbook for International Management Research.* New Delhi: Beacon Books.

This book deals in an accessible way with research design and methodology for international management research.

Quack, S., Morgan, G. and Whitley, R. (1999) *National Capitalisms, Global Competition, and Economic Performance.* Amsterdam: John Benjamins.

This book offers the latest position as well as empirical examples in business systems research.

References

Albrow, M. (1990) Introduction, in Albrow, M. and King, E. (eds) *Globalization, Knowledge and Society.* London: Sage.

Amable, B. (2000) Institutional complementarity and diversity of social systems of innovation and production. *Review of Political Economy* 7(4), 645–87.

Appadurai, A. (1996) *Modernity at Large: Cultural Dimensions of Globalization.* Minneapolis, MN: University of Minnesota Press.

Aron, R. (1962) *Dix-huit leçons sur la Société industrielle.* Paris: Gallimard.

Bell, D. (1973) *The Coming of Post-industrial Society.* New York: Basic Books.

Berger, S. (1996) Introduction, in Berger, S. and Dore, R. (eds) *National Diversity and Global Capitalism.* London: Cornell University Press.

Berger, S. and Dore, R. (eds) (1996) *National Diversity and Global Capitalism.* London: Cornell University Press.

Berry, J.W. (1990) Imposed etics, emics, derived etics: their conceptual and operational status in cross-cultural psychology, in Headland, T.N., Pike, K.L. and Harris, M. (eds) *Emic and Etics: the Insider/Outsider Debate*. Newbury Park, CA: Sage, 28–47.

Carroll, G.L. and Huo, Paul Yangchung (1986) Organizational task and institutional environment in ecological perspective: findings from the local newspaper industry. *American Journal of Sociology* 91, 838–73.

Casper, S. (2000) Institutional adaptiveness, technology policy, and the diffusion of new business models: the case of German biotechnology. *Organization Studies* 21(5), 887–914.

Child, J. (1981) Culture, contingency, and capitalism in the cross-national study of organizations. *Research in Organizational Behavior* 3, 303–56.

Child, J. and Tayeb, M. (1981) Theoretical perspectives in cross-national organizational research. *International Studies of Management and Organization* 10(1), 23–70.

Cox, R.W. (1992) Global perestroika, in Miliband, R. and Panitch, I. (eds), *New World Order? Socialist Register 1992*. London: Merlin.

Dicken, P. (1998) *Global Shift: Transforming the World Economy* (3rd edn). London: Sage.

DiMaggio, P. and Powell, W. (1991) Introduction, in Powell, W. and DiMaggio, P. (eds) *The New Institutionalism in Organizational Analysis*. Chicago: University of Chicago Press, 1–40.

Dobbin, F. (1994) *Forging Industrial Policy: the United States, Britain and France in the Railway Age*. New York: Cambridge University Press.

Dore, R. (1996) Convergence in whose interest?, in Berger, S. and Dore, R. (eds) *National Diversity and Global Capitalism*. London: Cornell University Press.

Earley, P.C. (1989) Social loafing and collectivism: a comparison of United States and People's Republic of China. *Administrative Science Quarterly* 34, 565–81.

Garcia Canclini, N. (1995) *Hybrid Cultures: Strategies for Entering and Leaving Modernity*. Minneapolis, MN: University of Minnesota Press.

Geertz, C. (1976) From the native's point of view: on the nature of anthropological understanding, in Basso, K. and Selby, H. (eds) *Meaning in Anthropology*. Albuquerque: University of New Mexico Press, 221–37.

Geertz, C. (1983) *Local Knowledge: Further Essays in Interpretive Anthropology*. New York: Basic Books.

Giddens, A. (1999) *Runaway World: How Globalization is Reshaping our Lives*. London: Profile Books.

Gregory, K. (1983) Native-view paradigms: multiple cultures and culture conflicts in organizations. *Administrative Science Quarterly* 28, 359–76.

Hall, P. and Soskice, D. (2001) *Varieties of Capitalism: the Institutional Foundations of Comparative Advantage*. New York: Oxford University Press.

Hannerz, U. (1987) The world in Creolization. *Africa* 57, 546–59.

Harris, M. (1979) *Cultural Materialism: the Struggle for a Science of Culture*. New York: Vintage.

Hickson, D.J., Pugh, D.S. and Pheysey, D. (1969) Operations technology and organization structure: an empirical reappraisal. *Administrative Science Quarterly* 14, 378–97.

Hickson, D.J., Hinings, C.R., McMillan, C.J. and Schwitter, J.P. (1974) The culture-free context of organization structure: a trinational comparison. *Sociology* 8, 59–80.

Hickson, D.J., McMillan, C.J., Azumi, K. and Horvath, D. (1979) Grounds for comparative organization theory: quicksands or hard core?, in Lammers, C.J. and Hickson, D.J. (eds) *Organizations Alike and Unlike*. London: Routledge & Kegan Paul.

Hofstede, G. (1980) *Culture's Consequences*. London: Sage.

Horvath, D., Azumi, K., Hickson, D.J. and McMillan, C.J. (1981) Bureaucratic structures in cross-national perspective: a study of British, Japanese, and Swedish firms, in Dlugos, G., Weiermair, K. and Dorow, W. (eds) *Management Under Differing Value Systems*. Berlin: Walter de Gruyter.

Kerr, C., Dunlop, J.T., Harbison, F. and Myers, C.A. (1960) *Industrialism and Industrial Man.* Cambridge: Harvard University Press.

Kondo, D.K. (1990) *Crafting Selves: Power, Gender, and Discourses of Identity in the Japanese Workplace.* Chicago: University of Chicago Press.

Lane, C. (1989) *Management and Labour in Europe.* Aldershot: Edward Elgar.

Lane, C. (2000) Globalization and the German model of capitalism – erosion or survival? *British Journal of Sociology* 51(2), 207–34.

Levitt, T. (1983) The globalization of markets. *Harvard Business Review* 61 (May–June), 92–102.

Lincoln, J.R., Hanada, M. and McBride, K. (1986) Organizational structures in Japanese and US manufacturing. *Administrative Science Quarterly* 31, 338–64.

Malinowski, B. (1922) *Argonauts of the Western Pacific.* London: Routledge.

Maurice, M. and Sorge, A. (2000) *Embedding Organizations.* Amsterdam: John Benjamins Publishing.

Meyer, J.W. (2000) Globalization: Sources and effects on national states and societies. *International Sociology* 15(2), 233–48.

Meyer, J.W. and Rowan, B. (1977) Institutionalized organizations: formal structure as myth and ceremony. *American Journal of Sociology* 83, 340–63.

Meyer, J.W. and Rowan, B. (1991) Institutionalized organizations: formal structure as myth and ceremony, in Powell, W. and DiMaggio, P. (eds) *The New Institutionalism in Organizational Analysis.* Chicago: University of Chicago Press, 41–62.

Morris, M.W., Kwok Leung, Ames, D. and Lickel, B. (1999) Views from inside and outside: integrating emic and etic insights about culture and justice judgement. *Academy of Management Review* 24(4), 781–96.

Munroe, R.L. and Munroe, R.H. (1991) Comparative field studies: methodological issues and future. *HRAF Journal of Comparative Management* 25(1–4), 155.

Nederveen Pieterse, J. (1994) Globalization as hybridization. *International Sociology* 9(2), 161–84.

North, D. (1991) Institutions. *Journal of Economic Perspectives* 5(1), 97–112.

North, D. (1995) *Institutions Matter* (mimeo). Washington University.

Nye, J.S. and Donahue, J.D. (2000) *Governance in a Globalizing World.* Washington: Brookings Institution Press.

Pieterse, J.N. (1995) Globalization as hybridization, in Featherstone, M., Lash, S. and Robertson. R. (eds) *Global Modernities.* London: Sage, 45–68.

Pike, K.L. (1967) *Language in Relation to a Unified Theory of the Structure of Human Behavior.* The Hague: Mouton.

Pugh, D.S., Hickson, D.J., Hinings, C.R., MacDonald, K.M., Turner, C. and Lupton, T. (1963) A conceptual scheme for organizational analysis. *Administrative Science Quarterly* 8(3), 289–315.

Pugh, D.S., Hickson, D.J., Hinings, C.R. and Turner, C. (1968) Dimensions of organization structure. *Administrative Science Quarterly* 13(1), 65–105.

Pugh, D.S., Hickson, D.J., Hinings, C.R. and Turner, C. (1969) The context of organization structure. *Administrative Science Quarterly* 14(1), 91–114.

Robertson, R. (1992) *Globalization: Social Theory and Global Cultures.* London: Sage.

Robertson, R. (1995) Globalization: time–space and homogeneity–heterogeneity, in Featherstone, M., Lash, S. and Robertson. R. (eds) *Global Modernities*. London: Sage, 24–44.

Robertson, R. (2001) Globalization theory 2000+: major problematics, in Ritzer, G. and Smart, B. (eds) *Handbook of Social Theory*. London: Sage, 458–71.

Rohlen, T. (1974) *For Harmony and Strength: Japanese White-collar Organization in Anthropological Perspective*. Berkeley: University of California Press.

Rose, M. (1985) Universalism, culturalism and the Aix group: promise and problems of a societal approach to economic institutions. *European Sociological Review* 1(1), 65–83.

Rugman, A. and Hodgetts, R. (2001) The end of global strategy. *European Management Journal* 19(4), 333–43.

Schneider, B. (1990) *Organizational Climate and Culture*. San Francisco: Jossey-Bass.

Scott, W.R. (1995) *Institutions and Organizations*. Thousand Oaks, California: Sage.

Scott, W.R. (2001) *Institutions and Organizations*. London: Sage.

Shweder, R.A. (1991) *Thinking Through Culture: Expeditions in Cultural Psychology*. Cambridge, MA: Harvard University Press.

Skinner, B.F. (1938) *The Behavior of Organisms: an Experimental Analysis*. Englewood Cliffs, NJ: Prentice Hall.

Smith, P.B. and Bond, M.H. (1998) *Social Psychology: Across Cultures* (2nd edn). Boston: Allyn & Bacon.

Soskice, D. (1996) *German Technology Policy, Innovation, and National Institutional Frameworks*. Wissenschaftszentrum Berlin, Discussion Paper FS I, 96–319.

Soskice, D. (1999) Divergent production regimes: coordinated and uncoordinated market economies in the 1980s and 1990s, in Kitschelt, H., Large, P., Marks, G. and Stephens, J.D. (eds) *Continuity and Change in Contemporary Capitalism*. Cambridge: Cambridge University Press.

Sorge, A. (1996) Societal effects in cross-national organization studies, in Whitley, R. and Kristensen, P.H. (eds) *The Changing European Firm*. London: Routledge.

Sorge, A. (2003) Cross-national differences in human resources and organization, in Harzing, A.-W. and Van Ruisseveldt, J. (eds) *Human Resource Management* (2nd edn). London: Sage.

Streeck, W. (1992) *Societal Institutions and Economic Performance: Studies of Industrial Relations in Advanced Capitalist Economies*. London: Sage.

Streeck, W. (1996) Lean production in the German automobile industry? A test for convergence theory, in Berger, S. and Dore, R. (eds) *National Diversity and Global Capitalism*. New York: Cornell University Press.

Streeck, W. (1997) German capitalism: does it exist? Can it survive?, in Crouch, C. and Streeck, W. (eds) *Political Economy of Modern Capitalism*. London: Sage.

Streeten, P. (1996) Free and managed trade, in Berger, S. and Dore, R. (eds) *National Diversity and Global Capitalism*. London: Cornell University Press, 353–65.

Tolbert, P.S. and Zucker, L.G. (1996) The institutionalization of institutional theory, in Clegg, S.R., Hardy, C. and Nord, W.R. (eds) *Handbook of Organization Studies*. London: Sage Publications, 175–90.

Tomlinson, J. (1999) *Globalization and Culture*. Chicago, IL: University of Chicago Press.

Van Maanen, J. (1988) *Tales of the Field: on Writing Ethnography.* Chicago: University of Chicago Press.

Vitols, S. (2001) Varieties of corporate governance: comparing Germany and the UK, in Hall, P.A. and Soskice, D. (eds) *Varieties of Capitalism.* Oxford: Oxford University Press.

Whitley, R. (1994a) The internationalization of firms and markets: its significance and institutional structures. *Organization Studies* 1(1), 101–24.

Whitley, R. (1994b) Dominant forms of economic organization in Market economies. *Organization Studies* 15(2), 153–82.

Whitley, R. (1999) *Divergent Capitalisms: the Social Structuring and Change of Business Systems.* Oxford: Oxford University Press.

Wundt, W. (1888) Über Ziele und Wege der Volkerpsychologie. *Philosophische Studien* 4.

Zucker, Lynne G. (1983) Where do institutional patterns come from? Organizations as actors in social systems, in Zucker, L.G. (ed.) *Institutional Patterns and Organizations: Culture and Environment.* Cambridge, MA: Ballinger.

1

The Societal Environment and Economic Development

SJOERD BEUGELSDIJK AND ANTON VAN SCHAIK

Learning Objectives

By the end of this chapter you will be able to:

- appreciate why in general we should be interested in the role of culture
- evaluate the relationships between culture and economic development
- discuss the use of the concept of social capital and trust
- explore the role of trust in economic development
- explain the relationship between trust and institutions
- understand the antecedents of cultural differences between countries
- understand the processes of modernization and postmodernization
- assess why mono-causal interpretations of the relationship between culture and economy are not productive.

Chapter Outline

1.1 Introduction

1.2 The Economist's Point of View
'It's the culture, stupid!'
The Weber thesis
Social capital and trust
Culture, institutions and the societal environment
Case: Corruption and the Financial and Educational Systems in Nigeria

1.3 How the Economy Influences Culture: the Sociologist's Stance
Inglehart's thesis

1.4 Conclusions
Study Questions
Further Reading
References

1.1 ✦ Introduction

Where do cultural differences come from? This is a useful question with which to begin a study of comparative international management. An awareness of the antecedents of cultural features can help us to improve our understanding of the differences between cultures. A better understanding of cultural differences, in turn, can help us to enhance our approach to them in an international management context.

As is explained more extensively in Chapter 2, the term *culture* has a multiplicity of meanings. Narrowly understood it refers to the arts and entertainment, whether upmarket or popular. More generally, it can be understood as the perceptual frames, values and norms used in social life: as the way society looks at itself and filters what it sees.

The two are connected, in that arts and entertainment provide symbols of identity and representations of social norms, holding up a more or less distorting mirror to society. Numerous broader definitions of the word culture exist, and most include elements like meanings, values, and religion or ideology. One of the most accepted and extensive definitions is that proposed by Clifford Geertz, who defines culture as 'an historically transmitted pattern of meanings embodied in symbols, a system of inherited conceptions expressed in symbolic forms by means of which men communicate, perpetuate, and develop their own knowledge about and attitudes toward life' (1973: 89).

Hofstede's more succinct definition of culture as the 'collective programming of the mind' comes close to the one by Geertz (cited in Hofstede, 2001: 1). Hofstede adds that culture does not only manifest itself in values but also in more superficial ways, in symbols, heroes and rituals (2001: 1). A central element in most definitions of culture is the concept of values. Similar to culture, numerous definitions of values exist. Building on a large body of literature, Hofstede (2001: 5) defines a *value* as a 'broad tendency to prefer certain states of affairs over others'.

This chapter examines the relationship between economy and culture. Specifically, it deals with the relationship between economic development and cultural differences, and aims to provide a broader perspective on the complex relationship between culture and economy. The chapter consists of two parts, which correspond to the two views on the relationship. These are the economist's and the sociologist's perspectives, respectively.

1. Economists argue that cultural differences may cause differences in economic growth.
2. The core question for sociologists is where cultural differences come from. It is argued that one of the most important factors driving cultural differences is the level of economic development.

The chapter thus discusses both directions of causality between culture and economic development. Since mono-causal explanations are unable to explain sufficiently the relationship between culture and economic development, it is essential to have an understanding of both paradigms.

The first part of this chapter is devoted to the economist's stance and examines the question of whether cultural traits have economic consequences. It provides a general background to the role of culture in the economic sciences. Next, the chapter discusses the Weber thesis, since this was one of the first studies to suggest a link between culture and economic growth. The first part of the chapter also deals with the concept of social capital, and the important role of trust and institutions for economic development. This discussion on the economist's perspective is followed by the sociologist's discussion on the causes of cultural differences. We have chosen to discuss here Inglehart's thesis, as he is one of the most celebrated authors on this topic.

1.2 ❧ The Economist's Point of View

'It's the culture, stupid!'

Why are some countries rich while others are poor? This is perhaps one of the most crucial research questions, if not *the* core question in economics. For many decades this question has triggered many economists to study growth differences between countries. One of the groundbreaking contributions has been Solow's neoclassical growth model, in which the core factors determining growth are investment in physical capital (K) and labour (L). The neoclassical growth model was formulated as national income (Y) and is a function of K and L.

However, economists studying growth differences between countries also found that these two factors alone are not sufficient to explain the differences in economic growth. From then onwards, the standard neoclassical model has been extended with factors that are thought to contribute to some countries growing faster than others. Subsequently, economists have concentrated on the level of education or human capital; the way in which society is formally organized in terms of, for example, laws (institutional differences); and, finally, they have turned to the role of culture as a potentially explanatory factor for cross-country diversity in levels of growth and welfare.

In the second half of the 1980s and at the beginning of the 1990s, it was popular among economists to study a range of variables that might cause growth differences. Authors like Baumol (1986), Barro (1991), and Mankiw, Romer and Weil (1992) have made important contributions to the question of why some countries are poor and others rich. During the 1990s, more and more economists felt that existing models of economic growth could be further improved by including culture. Aside from the improvement of existing growth models, however, the interest in the role of culture in explaining growth and welfare differences has been emphasized for other reasons.

One important reason has been the formidable growth performance of Japan in the 1970s and 1980s. The major stimulus that has made economists more attentive to macro-level forces (e.g. culture) other than the aforementioned orthodox ones (investment in physical capital and labour) has been the rise of the global economy and the recognition that the USA and western Europe had lost their hegemonic position within it (Zukin and DiMaggio, 1990). Although the Japanese economy has been in crisis since the beginning of the 1990s, the Japanese economic miracle of the 1970s and 1980s has led to a recognition that a variety of successful economic models exists. The Japanese success has led economists to rethink the idea that there is only a single model that brings economic success. In other words, the recognition of the heterogeneity of successful economic models has accorded a new prominence to institutional and cultural factors.

The importance of the broader societal environment to economic development has been strengthened further by the policy experiences of the World Bank. The main task of the World Bank is to fight poverty across the world. One of the ways that the World Bank tries to do this has been to introduce market-based policies in poor and less-developed countries (LDCs). Typically, some of the instruments used to reduce poverty are cutting budget deficits, and reducing the number of import barriers and other market-disturbing policies. In other words, the focus has been very much on the introduction of a free-market system by taking away all kinds of obstacle, mostly created by the governments of LDCs. Together with the International Monetary Fund (IMF) the World Bank has followed a neoliberal market-based approach.

However, this approach – sometimes referred to as the Washington Consensus – has increasingly been criticized for not always yielding beneficial results or for yielding different results across different countries. The latter has led to the acknowledgement of the crucial influence of the broader societal environment in which these adjustment policies have taken place. The hidden social basis of neoliberal success and failure has led economists and policy-makers to think of development in a broader way than just the neoliberal market-orientated one (Portes, 1997). The interest in culture and the possibility of culture facilitating economic development and growth has been further emphasized by the impressive economic development of South-east Asia and the assumed role of culture, in particular religion.

A related reason why a critique of the neoliberal market view emerged has been the development of new methods of research in economics. Experimental economics, or game theory, has led many economists to recognize that some core assumptions in economics are not realistic, the most important being the assumption of rationality. The use of experiments has shown that individuals do not always take decisions that are rational. Instead, many decisions are taken because 'we always do it like this' or 'because we are expected to do so'. Based on insights from psychology and sociology, a richer picture of human behaviour has been introduced in economics. At a more abstract level, the development of new methods like game theory has led to a broader acceptance of socio-cultural factors in economic analysis.

Besides the above-mentioned factors, it has been suggested that the interest in culture should be linked to the process of increased internationalization or globalization. Globalization implies a reduction in the effectiveness of traditional economic policy instruments because there are leakage effects in a globalized world economy. However, it is not only policy-makers that have to take the effect of globalization forces into account. Multinational firms are affected, too. Rapid flows of trade, capital and information have significantly reduced the advantages that a firm gets from inputs sourced from elsewhere. Buying products in a foreign country is not unique, and these strategies have therefore been neutralized as a competitive advantage in today's global economy. The remaining sources of competitive advantage are increasingly local, including special buyer–supplier relationships, specialized access to local knowledge and knowledge of local human resource traditions. To paraphrase Michael Porter (2000: 17), since many of the external sources of advantage for a nation's firms have been nullified by globalization, potential internal resources of advantage must be cultivated if a country wishes to upgrade its economy and create prosperity for its citizens.

There are, then, a number of reasons why the role of culture has increasingly been emphasized as a potentially relevant variable in explaining differences in economic growth between countries. However, the literature is far from clear on how, exactly, culture influences the process of economic development. The remainder of this section discusses the economic function of culture.

The Weber thesis

One of the first studies describing the economic function of culture has been Max Weber's study on the Protestant ethic and the rise of capitalism (2001). According to Weber (2001), Protestantism, especially its Calvinist branches, promoted the rise of modern industrial capitalism. Protestantism did so not so much by easing or abolishing those aspects of the Roman faith that might hinder free economic activity or by encouraging the pursuit of wealth, but by defining an ethic that contributed to economic success.

An important element in Weber's thesis was the doctrine of predestination in Calvinist Protestantism. In contrast with the Roman faith, predestination meant that one could not gain salvation by faith or deeds (e.g. by buying a letter of indulgence), but that this question had been decided upon for everyone from the beginning of time. Nothing could alter one's fate. Although the idea of predestination could easily have been dismissed as a fatalistic attitude, it was not. Instead it was converted into a secular code of behaviour, based on hard work, honesty, seriousness and the thrifty use of money.

Although heavily criticized, the Weber thesis has generally been accepted as plausible. Criticisms mainly point to the fact that it was not so much the influence of Protestantism on the development of industrial capitalism, but at most a matter of coincidence that these two developments took place in a similar period of time. Nevertheless, there are at least three historical facts that are related to the Protestant faith and that, it can be argued, have economic consequences.

1. First, there was the emphasis placed by Protestantism on instruction and literacy for boys and girls. Good Protestants were expected to read the Bible themselves, whereas Catholics were catechized but did not have to read, and in some cases were even discouraged from reading the Bible. The result was increased literacy among Protestants.

2. The second element was the importance Protestants accorded to time. The making and buying of clocks and watches was much more common in the UK and the northern part of the Netherlands than in Catholic countries and regions.

3. Third, the Protestant faith resulted in a significant reduction of holy days on which people were not expected to work, thus increasing productivity.

On the whole, the Protestant reformation helped to loosen the hold of the medieval Christian worldview; but it would be an overemphasis of the role of religion to argue that it was only the Protestant reformation that contributed to this. The emergence of scientific inquiry had already started to undermine the existing worldview and initiated the modernizing change from a traditional religion-orientated society to a secular-rational one. Nevertheless, during the three centuries after the Reformation, capitalism mainly emerged in Protestant countries. Generally speaking, Weber's concept of the Protestant ethic is outdated if it is taken as something that can only exist in Protestant countries, but the general idea that culture influences economic growth offers an important insight.

Social capital and trust

Contemporary research on culture and economic development, however, has departed from the historical analysis of Weber and instead focuses on the concept of social capital. As the term suggests, the social and the capital stand for the non-economic and the economic respectively. Although the definition of the concept of social capital is ambiguous, most of us have some idea of what it means. Broadly speaking, it has to do with the norms and values present in a society. As a result of the general interest in the role of culture described earlier, the concept of social capital has been developed. Numerous definitions of social capital exist, but one of the most encompassing is that proposed by Robert Putnam (2000): '*Social capital* refers to those features of social organization, such as norms, trust, and networks that can improve the efficiency of society by facilitating coordinated actions.' The World Bank uses a similar definition, in which social capital refers to the institutions, relationships and norms that shape the quality and quantity of a society's social interactions.

In his groundbreaking analysis of 20 Italian regions, Putnam studied the role and function of social capital in the efficient functioning of government and the economy. From this work it follows that the critical factor in explaining the effectiveness of the regional governments in Italy is to be found in differences in social capital. It was found that rich regions in the northern part of Italy have more social capital than the poorer southern regions. In the northern regions, relationships between people are based on mutual trust and shared values. In the southern regions, the contrary state can be observed, and relationships are based more on power and control. Whereas in the northern regions trust between people is of a general nature, in the southern regions this is more likely to be restricted to the closed social circle (i.e. family and friends).

One of the cultural characteristics in which this is reflected is the degree to which people are embedded and active in all types of clubs and associations, like choirs, soccer clubs, bowling clubs, reading groups, church and political parties. Regional and national differences in membership of these kinds of association are hard to relate to differences in welfare, nevertheless, a dense network of associational activity in a country or region is an indication of the level of 'civicness' of society, and provides some indication of whether a society is geared towards opportunistic behaviour or horizontal relations based on mutual trust.

Generally, it has been recognized that trust is one of the most important dimensions of social capital. Besides the economic function of trust, there are also sociological arguments for trust. According to sociologists, trust is a social mechanism that reduces complexity and enables individuals to deal with the complexities and contingencies of modern life (Luhmann, 1979). Trust is also seen as central to the construction of social order (Parsons, 1969). In this view, a common value system based on widely shared norms and values stabilizes interactions in a social system. Trust is grounded in pre-existing consensus and is the product of an effective integration of norms and values. Trust fulfils an integrative function in the establishment of social order. Consequently, generalized trust also fulfils an economic function (e.g. Fukuyama, 1995).

It is argued that increased trust within a society reduces the need to set up institutional and organizational mechanisms to overcome principle–agent problems.[1] Trust in this case serves as a substitute for contracts. In more developed countries, trust enables the organization of complex transactions that cannot be 'arranged' in contracts (incomplete contracts). The lack of a proper institutional system makes even relatively straightforward transactions complex and unsafe, and trust is needed to solve the problem of uncertainty associated with the transaction. In other words, the more trust there is, the lower the transaction costs (such as the costs of organizing and transacting exchanges).

Trust is mostly seen as the perception and interpretation of the other's expected dependability. Trust refers to the confidence that a partner will not exploit the vulnerabilities of the other (Barney and Hansen, 1995). The concept of trust may be framed as an expectation of a partner's reliability with regard to his or her obligations, predictability of behaviour, and fairness in actions and negotiations while faced with the possibility of behaving opportunistically (Zaheer et al., 1998). Trust has to do with signalling that the actor will not play one-shot games and behave opportunistically. Since the literature on trust is extensive, it is impossible (nor is it the aim here) to do justice to its richness. In the following we will focus on only the main insights that are relevant to a discussion of the relationship between culture and economic development.

Two levels of trust

There are two important levels of trust (Luhmann, 1979).

1. The micro level, based on the emotional bond between individuals, is more characteristic of primary and small-group relationships. Micro-level trust is more personalized and therefore yields 'thick' trust.

2. The macro level involves more abstract relationships where trust is related to the functioning of bureaucratic systems (e.g. legal, political and economic). Macro sources of trust apply apart from any specific exchange relationship, arising from the institutional environment of laws, norms and standards.

This distinction has also been phrased in terms of honesty (Putnam, 2000). There is an important difference between honesty based on personal experience and honesty based on a general community norm. Trust embedded in personal relationships that are strong, frequent and nested in wider networks is sometimes called thick trust (as in point 1, above). On the other hand, a thinner trust in 'the generalized other' also rests implicitly on some background of shared social networks and expectations of reciprocity (Putnam, 2000: 136). Thin or generalized trust may be even more useful than thick or personal trust, however, because it extends the radius of trust beyond the roster of people whom we can know personally (Putnam, 2000: 136).

---

[1] Principal–agent problems are problems that stem from the fact that the principal – or the person who delegates responsibility to another, known as the agent – wants to induce the agent to take some action but is not always able to directly observe the action of the agent. The principal's problem is then to design an incentive payment from the principal to the agent that induces the agent to take the best action from the viewpoint of the principal. The simplest example of a principal–agent problem is that of a manager and a worker. The manager wants the worker to exert as much effort as possible, in order to produce as much output as possible. The worker, of course, wants to make a choice that maximizes his or her own benefit given the effort and the incentive payment.

At the micro level, numerous typologies of trust have been developed. The most commonly accepted typologies of trust besides the distinction macro (generalized)/micro (personal) are calculus-based trust, knowledge-based trust and identification-based trust (Janowicz and Noorderhaven, 2002; Nooteboom, 2002). Calculus-based trust has to do with the fear of the consequences of not doing what one promised to do. In this case the shadow of the future is dark enough to create pressure to do what has been promised and not behave opportunistically. Knowledge-based trust is grounded in the predictability of the other's behaviour. This may be experience-based or established through reputation. Identification-based trust is based on the perceived similarity between partners yielding empathy and trust. In this case the bond of friendship is an important vehicle for the creation of trust.

More generally, it has been argued that trust is based on rational reasons and psychological causes (Nooteboom, 2002). Reasons arise from a rational evaluation of the trustee's trustworthiness. This can be based on knowledge of the trustee inferred from reputation, records, norms and standards, or one's own experience. A psychological cause is empathy. This is the ability to share another person's feelings and emotions as if they were one's own, thereby understanding the motives behind the action of the other. Empathy affects both one's own trustworthiness, in the willingness to make sacrifices for others, and one's trust, in the tolerance of behaviour that deviates from expectations. One will more easily help someone when one can identify with his or her needs:

> One can more easily forgive someone's breach of trust when one can identify with the lack of competence or the motive that caused it. Since one can identify with the other, one may sympathize with his or her action, seeing perhaps that this action was in fact a just response to one's own previous actions. (Nooteboom, 2002: 81)

Trust is also related to networks. Through the role of reputation, social networks can serve as a basis for deterrence-based trust. Burt and Knez (1995) show that what they call 'third-party gossip' amplifies both the positive and the negative in relationships, because it makes actors more certain of their trust (or distrust) in one another. Trust is associated with the strength of a relationship. Trusting relationships may develop inside a (closed) network; actors build up a reputation for trustworthiness that may become important information for other actors in the network. Networks may then fulfil the function of implicit contracts (see the information on network theory in Chapter 11).

At the individual level, trust is regarded as a property of individuals or characteristic of interpersonal relationships. Through ongoing interactions, firms develop trust around norms of equity or knowledge-based trust (Gulati, 1998). Numerous studies have shown the importance of trust in economic transactions. These studies can also be seen as a critique or extension of Williamson's (1975, 1985) transaction cost theory (see Chapters 10 and 11). In this respect, it has been shown that informal, personal connections between and across organizations play an important role in determining the governance structures used to organize transactions (Ring and Van de Ven, 1992). It has also been pointed out that both transaction cost elements, as well as social factors, are relevant and important in studying inter-firm relationships and cooperation (Gulati, 1995). Repeated ties between firms engender trust that is manifested in the form of the contracts used to organize subsequent alliances. Trust and contractual safeguards are to some degree substitutes. Hence, besides a transaction cost perspective, trust is an important component of the control mechanisms that are used within alliances.

Another question is how those trust relationships that are not embedded in structures of personal relationships come into being. The principal–agent framework has been used to discuss the role of several mechanisms that control trust relationships that are *not* embedded in structures of personal relations (Shapiro, 1987). It seems that all kinds of mechanism come to life in an atomistic market when transactions are not embedded in a social network where trust and personal relationships are present. In the Weber thesis discussed earlier, God fulfilled such a function. The possibility of being punished was and, in some countries still is, an important incentive to behave according to some generally accepted rules of behaviour and not play opportunistic games. In these cases, this is referred to as the economic function of God. However, an authority figure does not have to be present in all cases in order to enforce non-opportunistic behaviour. In such cases, the role of a moral sense of duty has been highlighted as a potential source of cooperation.

Functions of trust

Trust fulfils several economic functions. Through third parties, trust provides options for control in social networks. Trust is also linked with the facilitation of highly uncertain transactions. It reduces the uncertainty involved in these kinds of transaction, especially the relational risk involved. In this respect, it has been shown that 'trust facilitates the exchange of resources and information that are crucial for high performance but are difficult to value and transfer via market ties' (Uzzi, 1996: 678). Moreover, trust is argued to be related to its information function. 'Through the economic and social relationship in the network, diverse information becomes inexpensive to obtain' (Malecki, 2000: 195). Moreover, trust not only enables greater exchange of information, but also promotes ease of interaction and a flexible orientation on the part of partners in an alliance (Gulati, 1998: 308). It operates as a mechanism that facilitates communication and cooperation between firms. Trust relationships can result in a supplier exceeding contractual requirements, whether by early delivery, higher quality or some other means of assuring goodwill (Sako, 1992). Trust yields more flexibility and economizes on the costs of governance. Another benefit of trust as a vehicle in forming alliances is the reduction of search costs for alliance partners. Firms in social networks of trusting relationships can ally with someone they already know (Gulati, 1995: 107). In sum, from an economic point of view, trust has a number of pecuniary and non-pecuniary advantages. Trust is argued to reduce the costs of an economic transaction. At the aggregate level this implies that it can be expected that high-trust countries are richer than low-trust countries (see Figure 1.1).

Figure 1.1 illustrates the relationship between the degree of generalized trust and the level of economic development (GDP) in a number of European countries in 1999. Information on GDP per capita (1998) is taken from Maddison (2001). Although the way trust is operationalized can be criticized for being a too-crude measure, the upward slope of the line in this graph suggests that there is a positive relationship between trust and level of economic development. Countries in which people are more inclined to trust one another are richer than countries with lower scores on generalized trust. However, a closer look at the figure reveals that there are three 'clouds' of observations: there is one group of Scandinavian countries, including the Netherlands, one including the other relatively advanced European economies in the middle of the figure, and one including the relatively less advanced eastern European countries in the lower-left corner of the graph. It is well known that these former Soviet satellites have great difficulty in creating efficiently functioning institutions. If these countries were left out, no relationship between trust and GDP per capita would be found. For similar levels of GDP per capita (approximately US$20,000) the graph shows trust scores ranging between 20 per cent (France) and just below 70 per cent (Denmark). This suggests that institutions are closely related to trust.

Figure 1.1 Trust and GDP per capita in European countries

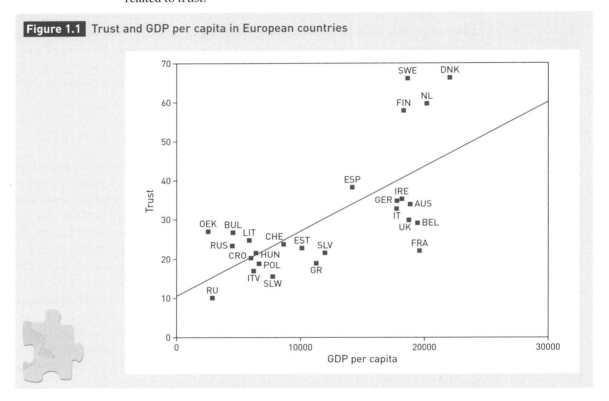

Culture, institutions and the societal environment

Trust is not a cultural trait that is independent of institutional factors. In fact there are close relations between the degree of generalized trust and the degree to which institutions function well in society. Institutions can be defined here as the informal and formal rules of the game (North, 1991). Institutions are the humanly devised constraints that guide and structure political, social and economic interaction.

Institutions are important for the incentive structure of an economy. It is generally assumed that efficiently functioning institutions are important to the effective functioning of the market economy and process of economic development.

After Putnam (2000) had studied the culture and institutions in Italian regions extensively, he concluded that citizens in a community based on trust and characterized by relatively strong civic virtues deal fairly with one another and expect fair dealing in return. They expect the government to follow high standards and they willingly obey the rules that this government imposes on them. In a less trust-based society, laws are made to be broken, and everyone expects the other to violate the rules. In other words, if the majority of the people are inclined to follow the rules, there is a social pressure on individuals to do so as well. If, however, the majority of the people are used to cheating and opportunistic behaviour, this will 'force' individuals to behave in a similar way. This mechanism theoretically yields two types of society:

1. societies in which opportunistic behaviour is the default, and
2. societies where people are inclined to invest in relationships that are based on reciprocity.

In a study of trust in Germany and the UK, it has been shown that differences in institutions result in differences in the process of trust building and types of trust present in society (Bachmann, 2001). The British socio-economic system is characterized by extensive deregulation compared to the German system. In several chapters of this text, the differences between the Rhineland model (Germany) and the Anglo-Saxon (UK and USA) model will be further elaborated upon. For now it is enough to know that the German business environment is characterized by strong and extensive institutional order and by tight regulation. The type of trust present in British society is likely to be personal trust based on individual experiences: 'I trust you because I know you, or because someone told me you can be trusted.' In Germany, trust is likely to be based on system trust, because it is the strict institutional system of laws which guarantees that a person can be trusted. Evidently these differences between types of trust are greater once less-developed countries come into the equation. In most less-developed countries (LDCs) the institutional system does not function properly or is not even present. There are no laws, or laws are broken.

In this respect, the close relationship between the degree of generalized trust and the degree of corruption in a country is an illustrative example. A correlation between these two measures for 39 countries yields a value of -0.73, which can be considered rather strong. This correlation is illustrated in Figure 1.2, where the horizontal axis shows information on the level of trust and the vertical axis reflects the degree of perceived corruption. Information on the degree to which people claim that others can be trusted is gathered by the Values Survey (EVS/WVS). Information on the perceived level of corruption is gathered by an organization called Transparency International (TI). For a limited number of countries, World Bank codes are used as labels. It is clear that the negative relationship between trust and corruption is rather strong. Countries that score high on trust and low on corruption are, for example, the Scandinavian countries, Sweden (SWE), Denmark (DNK) and Norway (NOR); at the other end of the spectrum are countries like Colombia (COL), Mexico (MEX) and Ghana (GHA), which score low on trust and high on corruption.

Case: Corruption and the Financial and Educational Systems in Nigeria

Case written by Carla Koen on the basis of information from the Federal Government of Nigeria (1980) and Olopoenia (1998).

The legacy of corruption and malpractice in the Nigerian banking sector can be traced back to the liberation days. After gaining independence from the UK in the 1960s, the Nigerian government's rapid drive towards industrialization and modernization led to large-scale borrowing in order to finance the prestigious projects undertaken. Large industrial loans required political support, some of which was thought to have had a price attached to it. These loans were dispensed liberally to favoured persons. Moreover, the government's policy of mandated credit for exploitation of, say, the oil sector was disbursed through local-level officials, cooperating with the military government. There were reports of borrowers bribing bank officials in order to get loans. In addition, interference by senior government officials in lending decisions, directing the bankers to lend to dubious projects owned by political or business allies of the ruling party, resulted in an increased level of corruption. It was common to use bribes to mobilize scarce deposit funds from owners or controllers of government and military funds. This behaviour was facilitated by the fact that the majority of the banks were nationalized and under the direct control of the bureaucrats. Moreover, the different governments in power did not have the commitment necessary to combat this disease, nor did they consider it politically advantageous to take action against defaulters who had strong business or political links with the ruling dictators. In many cases, the influential ruling party members or the lawmakers themselves have been direct or indirect beneficiaries of bank corruption. Inadequate and ineffective internal controls within banks, and weak supervision and monitoring by the Central Bank of Nigeria (CBN) further encouraged the maintenance and growth of corruption. It is perhaps noteworthy that the CBN is not an independent institution, but acts as the government demands.

Various forms of corruption to which teachers resort in much of Africa (including Nigeria) have been listed. An important form is absenteeism. Many teachers collect their government salaries and do not show up to teach. Children are usually much more eager to learn than teachers are to teach. The Nigerian educational system seems to reflect the fact that the main objective of many civil services in Nigeria is to provide employment for school leavers and/or political support. The areas most vulnerable to corruption are procurement and recruitment. Teachers demand money from students for letting them pass exams or for after-school tutoring programmes. The catch is that the most popular tutors are professors who also sit on the committees that decide who is admitted to college and who is refused. The examinations are oral. Grading criteria are wholly subjective. This clearly creates an environment that will encourage corruption and bribing. The lack of funds for higher education also creates the climate for corruption. Government spending on higher education was only 0.5 per cent of the federal budget in 2001. Undergraduate students eligible for scholarships received $160, which the government believes is the cost of a year's education. A Nigerian lecturer who refuses bribes earns $23 per month. With overtime and extra work, this rounds out to about $64. To live honestly on such a salary is almost impossible. Such lecturers can hardly pay for decent housing, food, transportation and other basic amenities. As a result they seek other ways to increase their income, in the form of corrupt practices. Corruption in the educational sector is also strengthened by the fact that the country's minister of education is heavily engaged in textbook sales. Textbooks in Nigeria sell for more than twice the price at which they are sold in the UK and the USA. Ministry of Education staff force themselves upon authors as co-authors in order to reap royalties on sales, and issue directives forcing schools and parents to buy new textbooks every year, ensuring profits are kept high.

Questions

1. Could you, on the basis of the information in this case, provide evidence of the close relationships between the degree of generalized trust and the degree of corruption?

2. What is the role of trust in economic development in Nigeria? Use evidence from the case to substantiate your argument.

3. What is the relationship between trust and the financial and educational institutions in Nigeria?

4. Trust is said to reduce contact, contract and control costs. Can you find evidence in the case of the opposite – that is, that the absence of trust would involve an increase in contact, contract and control costs if a society or organization is to function effectively?

To test whether measures of institutions and the trust measure of social capital are related, several statistical techniques exist. One technique that can be used is factor analysis (see Box 1.1).

Box 1.1:   Factor Analysis[2]

Factor analysis is a method used to reduce the number of variables or to achieve better measurement of a certain theoretical construct. It is a statistical approach that can be used to analyse the relationship between a large number of variables and to explain these variables in terms of their common underlying factors. Factor analysis is also referred to as 'principal components analysis'. Although the mathematical approach used differs slightly between these two techniques, many researchers use

[2] See Hair *et al.* (1998) for an introduction to this methodology.

them interchangeably. By using factor analysis on, for example, nine variables, the goal is to test to what extent these nine items can be reorganized in a more limited number of factors. Say the statistical results show that three factors each containing three items exist. This means that the differences *within* the three groups (or factors) are minimal and at the same time the differences *between* these groups are maximal. In other words, there is (almost) no correlation between the factors, but the items within a factor are very strongly correlated.

A number of methods of factor analyses exist. The two basic methods are the so-called oblique and orthogonal rotations. These methods are similar, except that oblique rotations allow correlated factors instead of maintaining independence between rotated factors. There are no specific rules on which to base the selection of a particular orthogonal or oblique principal component analysis. Generally, the choice of research method depends on the research problem. If the goal of the research is simply to reduce the number of variables, regardless of how meaningful the factors may be, the most appropriate solution would be the orthogonal one, in which there is no correlation between the factors. More relevant perhaps is that if the researcher wishes to reduce the number of variables to a smaller set for subsequent use in regression, orthogonal is again best because of the required independence in regression techniques (see Box 1.2). But if the goal of the research is to obtain meaningful factors that can be expected to be correlated on theoretical grounds, an oblique rotation might be more appropriate.

Figure 1.2 Trust and corruption

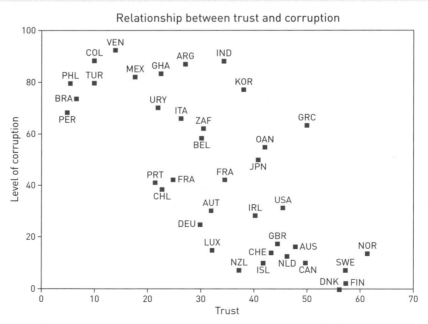

Data: trust data from EVS/WVS; corruption data from Transparency International

Factor analysis has been performed on a number of existing measures of institutions and on the trust measure (see Table 1.1). Factor analysis indicates that there is one factor in which all these variables fit. The numbers in Table 1.1 reflect the weights of the different variables in this factor. The advantage of creating this new variable is that one single variable reflects the general societal environment in a country, including both institutions and trust as a component of culture. The resulting factor, including trust as well as these measures of institutional strength, confirms our earlier theoretical reasoning: trust is related to the presence and effective functioning of institutions.

Table 1.2 depicts, for 33 countries, the score on the variable 'societal environment', the components of which were outlined in Table 1.1. Scores range from 0 (Philippines) to 100 (Canada). This variable is a general measure of the effective functioning of institutions and degree of social capital in a society. A low score for a particular country means that its institutions do not function well and that the country did not develop much social capital; vice versa, a high score means that the institutional environment in the country functions well and the country has built substantial social capital. The advantage of this measure is that instead of individual items measuring culture or institutions independently, this single measure explicitly recognizes that culture and institutions are related. Evidently it is a crude measure, but at least it provides some empirical intuition.

In order to show the importance of the societal environment for economic development it is important to relate the country scores on 'societal environment' to measures of economic success. A technique that can be used to test the relevance of the societal environment for economic success is regression analysis (see Box 1.2). Table 1.3 summarizes the main results of the regression analysis. The goal is to explain differences in economic growth between the 33 countries for which the variable 'societal environment' has been calculated.

The dependent variable is economic growth between 1970 and 1992. Following neoclassical growth theory, economic investment in physical capital, investment in human capital and the initial level of welfare can explain growth. The latter variable controls for convergence effects, meaning that poorer countries grow faster than richer countries (*ceteris paribus*). In sum, in the analysis performed, the dependent variable is economic

Table 1.1 Components of 'societal environment'	
Items	**Weights**
1. Trust (EVS/WVS)	.800
2. Contract enforceability (Zak and Knack, 2001)	.917
3. TI corruption index (Transparency International)	.925
4. Black market premium (Sala-i-Martin)	−.659
5. Revolutions/coups per year, average over the period 1960–84 (Sala-i-Martin)	−.659
6. Rule of law (Sala-i-Martin)	.910
7. Degree of capitalism (Sala-i-Martin)	.646
8. Index of social infrastructure (Hall and Jones, 1999)	.936

Table 1.2 Scores for 33 countries' 'societal environment'	
Country (World Bank code in brackets)	Score on 'societal environment'
Argentina (ARG)	13.6
Australia (AUS)	91.7
Austria (AUT)	82.2
Belgium (BEL)	80.6
Brazil (BRA)	24.6
Canada (CAN)	100
Switzerland (CHE)	99.8
Chile (CHL)	44.4
Colombia (COL)	15.7
Germany (DEU)	85.3
Denmark (DNK)	96.5
Spain (ESP)	71.1
France (FRA)	70.8
United Kingdom (GBR)	84.6
Greece (GRC)	55.8
India (IND)	16.0
Ireland (IRL)	82.5
Italy (ITA)	51.6
Japan (JPN)	82.4
Korea, Rep. of S. (KOR)	24.9
Mexico (MEX)	32.4
Nigeria (NGA)	4.8
The Netherlands (NLD)	91.2
Norway (NOR)	96.0
Oman (OAN)	62.2
Peru (PER)	17.4
Philippines (PHL)	0
Portugal (PRT)	55.7
Sweden (SWE)	95.6
Turkey (TUR)	4.1
United States (USA)	95.6
Venezuela (VEN)	13.9
South Africa (ZAF)	45.7

growth between 1970 and 1992, and the independent variables are investment, years of education, initial level of welfare in 1970 and the measure of societal environment.

The results indicate that there is a significant positive effect of the societal environment on economic growth while controlling for other variables influencing growth. The t-value of 3.52 is a clear indication of the importance of the societal environment for economic growth. Those countries that grow quickly are also the countries with a culture based on trust and with efficiently functioning institutions. The explained variance equals almost 50 per cent.

Box 1.2: Regression Analysis

Regression analysis is a method used to test whether a specific dependent variable is related to a number of independent variables. Given the nature of the variables (e.g. continuous, interval, discrete) the mathematical technique used differs. The most basic type of regression analysis is ordinary least squares (OLS). The objective of regression analysis is to predict changes in the dependent variable in response to changes in the independent variables. The effect of a certain variable on the dependent variable is surrounded by a band of uncertainty. This uncertainty may imply that it is not possible to detect with confidence whether the independent variable may in some cases have zero effect. In these cases the effect is called insignificant. To obtain a statistically significant result with 95 per cent confidence, the estimated t-value should be at least 1.96. Note that regression analysis does not imply causal linkages between variables. Causality is determined by the theory.

1.3 How the Economy Influences Culture: the Sociologist's Stance

After this discussion on the economist's perspective on the relationship between culture and the economy, it is important to make you aware of the inverse direction of causality between culture and the economy. As mentioned in the introduction to this chapter, mono-causal explanations are insufficient to explain the complex set of relationships between culture and economic development. Economic development also influences the

Table 1.3 Relationship between economic growth and the societal context	
Dependent variable: growth 1970–92	**Coefficient (t-value)**
Independent variables:	
GDP 1970	−.328 (2.39)
Investment	.036 (2.23)
Human capital (years of education)	−.027 (.876)
Societal environment	1.57 (3.52)
Number of countries	33
Explained variance	.48

generally shared norms and values in a society. In the remainder of this chapter this debate, or the sociologist's perspective, is discussed.

Inglehart's thesis

In numerous publications, Inglehart has described and empirically analysed the relationship between cultural values and economic development (including Inglehart, 1997, and Inglehart and Baker, 2000). He writes that 'in marked contrast to the growing materialism linked with the industrial revolution, the unprecedented existential security of advanced industrial society gave rise to an intergenerational shift towards post-materialist and postmodernist values' (Inglehart and Baker, 2000: 21). Industrialization is linked with an emphasis on economic growth at almost any price, whereas in affluent societies elements like quality of life, environmental protection and self-expression are emphasized. Industrialization brought less dependence on nature, and the world became mechanical, bureaucratic and rationalized (Bell, 1973). The rise of the service economy coincides with the reduced emphasis on material objects and a growing emphasis on self-expression (Inglehart, 1997). To sum up, the shift from industrial to service economies goes together with a shift in value priorities from an emphasis on economic and physical security towards an increasing emphasis on subjective well-being and quality of life.

Inglehart's central thesis is that economic development has systematic and, to some extent, predictable cultural and political consequences. These consequences are not iron laws of history, but probabilistic trends. In other words, the probability is high that certain changes will occur as societies develop economically, but it also depends on the specific cultural and historical context of the society in question.

Inglehart's thesis differs from those of traditional modernization theorists, who argue that the decline of 'traditional' values and their replacement with 'modern' values occurs as a result of economic and political forces. Modernization theory borrowed heavily from Marxism as it, essentially, takes an economic view of the underlying forces of historical change. The dialectical process of historical evolution should be reasonably similar for different human societies and cultures. As Marx stated in the preface to the English edition of *Das Kapital*, 'the country that is more developed industrially only shows, to the less developed, the image of its own future'. In other words, this modernization school predicts the convergence of values in the long run.

Modernization theory is somehow not really satisfactory, however (Fukuyama, 1992). It is a theory that works to the extent that man is an economic creature, to the extent that he is driven by the imperatives of economic growth and industrial rationality. The undeniable power of this theory derives from the fact that human beings, particularly in the aggregate, do in fact act out of such motives for much of their lives. However, there are other aspects of human motivation that have nothing to do with economics, and it is here that discontinuities in history find their origin (Fukuyama, 1992: 133–4).

Nevertheless, modernization theory looks much more persuasive after 1990 than it did in the 1960s or 1970s when it came under heavy attack in academic circles (Fukuyama, 1992). In particular, since the collapse of the Soviet Union, modernization theorists would argue that almost all countries that have succeeded in achieving a high level of economic development have come to look increasingly similar to each other. Modernization theory eventually fell victim to the accusation that it was ethnocentric –

that it elevated the western European and North American development experience to the level of universal truth, without recognizing its 'culture-boundedness'. The critique focused on the idea in modernization theory that the western model was supposedly the only valid one.

Inglehart's thesis also differs from the competing school, which emphasizes the persistence of values despite economic and political changes. More precisely, this second school 'predicts that convergence around some set of "modern" values is unlikely and that "traditional" values will continue to exert an independent influence on the cultural changes caused by economic development' (Inglehart and Baker, 2000: 20). Though this second school of thought has been criticized for its cultural determinism, it has become quite popular to take cultural differences as independent and stable entities in explaining the process and speed of (economic) development. The former discussion on social capital and trust clearly shows the current popularity of this type of thinking in social sciences, especially economics (Putnam, 1993; Fukuyama, 1995; Knack and Keefer, 1997; Zak and Knack, 2001).

Inglehart and Baker (2000) show that it is in fact the combination of these two schools that does most justice to the complex reality of value changes around different societies. Modernization theorists are therefore partly right. The rise of industrial society is linked with coherent cultural shifts away from traditional value systems, and the rise of a postindustrial society is linked with a shift away from absolute norms and values towards a syndrome of increasingly rational, tolerant, trusting postindustrial societies.

Values are path-dependent, however, which fits the second school. Inglehart and Baker (2000) show that a history of Protestant or Orthodox or Islamic traditions gives rise to cultural zones that persist after controlling for the effects of economic development. Hence, 'economic development tends to push societies in a common direction, but rather than converging, they seem to move on parallel trajectories shaped by their cultural heritages' (Inglehart and Baker, 2000: 49). Culture should not be seen in an essentialist or reductionist manner, as something that is inherent to a society or that condemns it to path dependency, but as something that is continuously created and recreated (Keating, 1998). Therefore, economic development brings cultural changes, but the fact that a society was shaped, for example, by Protestantism leaves a permanent imprint and has enduring effects on subsequent value development.

Given the cultural heritage of a country, Inglehart's thesis is that countries pass through several societal stages, from a traditional via a modern to a postmodern society in which the societal goals and individual values change. Table 1.4 summarizes this idea of cultural change.

The culture in a *traditional society* is to maintain social cohesion and stability in a mainly agrarian economy. Evidently, traditional societies differ greatly, but the majority of them emphasize individual conformity to societal norms, usually codified and legitimated in a religious framework. Norms of sharing in families or kinship-based groups are crucial to survival. In poor countries like Nigeria and Congo, even today people feel a strong obligation to help take care of the family.

In *industrial societies* this sense of obligation has eroded to some extent. The main goal in the period of modernization is economic growth through industrialization. At the individual level the rise of achievement motivation is embedded in a broad shift towards instrumental rationality weakening traditional norms. During the period of modernization,

Table 1.4 Cultural change according to Inglehart			
	Traditional	*Modern*	*Postmodern*
Core societal project	Survival in a (mainly agrarian) economy	Maximize economic growth	Maximize subjective well-being
Individual value	Traditional religious and communal norms	Achievement motivation	Postmaterialist and postmodern values
Authority system	Traditional authority	Rational–legal authority	De-emphasis of both legal and religious authority

economic growth and scientific discovery form the core of the progress and are almost good by definition.

The *postmodern shift* implies a change from the aforementioned priorities with an emphasis on economic growth to individual-level priorities like self-expression and a meaningful job. Instead of economic imperatives like the provision of food, shelter and clothing, individuals in a postmodern society stress subjective measures of well-being like the quality of life: 'Economic growth continues, but output consists less and less of tangible things that contribute directly to survival, and more and more of intangibles whose values is subjective' (Inglehart, 1997: 76).

The shift from traditional society to industrial society coincided with a shift from traditional authority to rational bureaucratic authority. This basically meant a shift from religious to political authority in most western countries. But in postmodern societies, concepts like authority and centralization are de-emphasized. In postmodern societies this may lead to declining confidence in hierarchical institutions.

In the shifts from traditional to modern and modern to postmodern societies, two major processes occur in both stages.

1. The first is *secularization*, being the decline of traditional religious beliefs in an institutionalized setting. The publics in most advanced postmodern societies show declining confidence in churches and there are declining rates of church attendance. Less emphasis is placed on organized religion. This does not, however, imply that there is no role for spiritual thinking in general. In line with the process of individuation (see below), it is typical for postmodern societies that people spend more time thinking about the meaning and purpose of life. The crucial difference is that people do so on an individual basis and not in a predetermined institutionalized setting like the Catholic Church.

2. The second is *individuation*. Both in the process of modernization and the process of postmodernization individual rights have taken priority over other obligations. In the process of modernization, it is the erosion of traditional religious beliefs and controls that increased individual autonomy. This increased personal freedom, however, was largely taken up by obligations to the state. In postmodern societies the shift away from religious and state authority has given an even greater push to individuation.

In their groundbreaking analysis Inglehart and Baker use two basic dimensions to measure the aforementioned cultural differences around the globe. Evidently there are several ways to measure the character of societies (e.g. Hofstede, 2001). But having studied dozens of items and variables, Inglehart argues that two dimensions tap the basic cultural orientations of societies when comparing the worldviews of the peoples of rich societies with those of low-income societies across a wide range of political, social and religious norms and beliefs. Inglehart labels these dimensions the *traditional/rational dimension* and the *survival/self-expression dimension*.

1. The *traditional/rational dimension* reflects a value system in which people at the traditional pole of this dimension reject divorce, emphasize the importance of God, support deference to authority, seldom discuss politics and have high levels of national pride (Inglehart and Baker, 2000). At the rational pole of this dimension, opposite values are emphasized.

2. The *survival/self-expression dimension* taps values that emerge in a postindustrial society with high levels of security. A central component of this dimension involves the difference between materialist and postmaterialist values. This component measures the relative priority that is given to economic and physical security over self-expression and quality of life.

Based on extensive data research, Inglehart has measured culture by these two dimensions. Using factor analysis (see Box 1.1) he has reduced the number of potentially relevant variables to two factors each containing five items (see Table 1.5).

Figure 1.3 shows the location of 43 societies on the two cultural dimensions. The vertical axis corresponds with the traditional/rational dimension and a position on the left

---

Table 1.5   The two cultural dimensions of Inglehart

Traditional/rational dimension

Traditional values emphasize the following:
- God is very important in respondent's life
- respondent has a strong sense of national pride
- respondent favours more respect for authority
- abortion is never justifiable
- it is more important for a child to learn obedience and religious faith than independence and communication

(Rational values emphasize the opposite)

Survival/self-expression dimension

Survival values emphasize the following:
- respondent gives priority to economic and physical security over self-expression and quality of life
- respondent describes him or herself as not very happy
- respondent has not signed and will not sign a petition
- homosexuality is never justifiable
- respondent feels one has to be very careful in trusting people

(Self-expression values emphasize the opposite)

Source: Inglehart (1997).

Figure 1.3 Country location according to Inglehart's two cultural dimensions

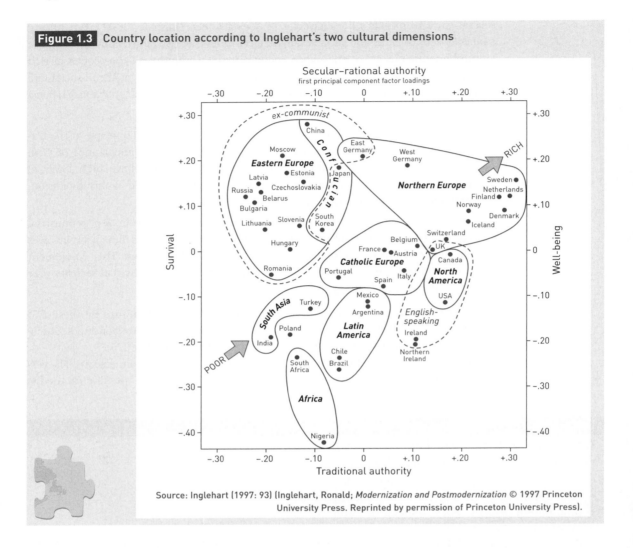

Source: Inglehart (1997: 93) (Inglehart, Ronald; *Modernization and Postmodernization* © 1997 Princeton University Press. Reprinted by permission of Princeton University Press).

side of the horizontal axis implies a low score on the survival/self-expression dimension. Inglehart has aimed to plot the societies with similar cultural orientations in intuitively plausible clusters (in the next chapter we discuss cultural clusters based on different types of dimensions).

The first observation is that the value systems of rich countries differ from those of poorer countries. The figure suggests a direction from the lower-left corner to the upper-right corner where poor countries are on the lower-left side and rich countries are in the upper-right. It is interesting to note that the USA seems to be a deviant case. It seems to have much more traditional values than its level of economic development would predict.

For the rest, however, the figure suggests clusters of countries that correspond to the theory. The Latin American countries for which data has been gathered fall into one cluster, as do the two African countries, the Confucian-influenced societies of East Asia and the historically Catholic societies of western Europe. It is interesting to observe that although church attendance has fallen due to the process of secularization, the historically

Protestant and Catholic countries of Europe fall in different clusters. The USA and Canada form a North American cluster to which the UK could easily be added. The figure suggests that Poland is an outlier, having more traditional values than the other ex-communist countries of eastern Europe.

Although the definition of these clusters could be discussed, the figure suggests that value systems are not random. Culture is shaped by a variety of factors of which levels of welfare and history (Catholic, Protestant, ex-communist) seem important elements. This corresponds to Inglehart's thesis that value differences can be explained both by differences in welfare levels and by cultural heritage.

1.4　Conclusions

In this chapter the relation between the societal environment and economic development has been discussed. It has been argued that culture, in particular the degree of social capital and trust in a society, differs between countries and regions, and that this difference may have economic consequences.

On the other hand, it has been shown that economic development influences the present norms and values in a society. In addition to cultural heritage, differences in level of economic development are an important explanation of differences in culture. Processes of modernization and postmodernization are, to a large extent, driven by rising welfare levels.

From this chapter it follows that mono-causal discussions of the relationship between culture and economic development are not productive. Whereas the remaining chapters concentrate on the role of societal differences, the aim of this chapter has been to sketch out the broader picture of the complex relationship between the societal environment and economic development.

Study Questions

1. Explain why economists have become increasingly interested in the role of culture.

2. Evaluate the contention that cultural traits have economic effects.

3. Explain and provide some examples of how economic developments influence cultural values.

4. Assess the usefulness of mono-causal interpretations of the relationship between culture and economic development.

5. Explain the effects of modernization and postmodernization on culture.

6. Assess the economic functions of trust.

7. Discuss the relationship between generalized trust and institutions.

8. From the text it is clear that trust reduces contact, contract and control costs. Illustrate these three Cs by providing examples.

Further Reading

Batjargal, B. (2003) Social capital and entrepreneurial performance in Russia: a longitudinal study. *Organization Studies* 24(4), 535–56.

This article is one of the few studies on the topic of social capital in Russia. It provides strong evidence on the effect of relational embeddedness on company performance in Russia.

Nooteboom, B. (2002) *Trust: Forms, Foundations, Functions, Failures and Figures.* Cheltenham: Edward Elgar.

Provides an interesting and extensive overview of the roles, limits, origins, and so on, of trust in an organizational context.

References

Bachmann, R. (2001) Trust, power and control in trans-organizational relations. *Organization Studies* 22(2), 337–65.

Barney, J.B. and Hansen, M.H. (1995) Trustworthiness as a source of competitive advantage. *Strategic Management Journal* 15,175–90.

Barro, R.J. (1991) Economic growth in a cross section of countries. *Quarterly Journal of Economics* 106(2), 407–43.

Baumol, W. (1986) Productivity growth, convergence, and welfare: what the long run data show. *American Economic Review* 76(5), 1072–85.

Bell, D. (1973) *The Coming of Post-industrial Society.* New York: Basic Books.

Burt, R. and Knez, M. (1995) Kinds of third-party effects on trust. *Rationality and Society* 7, 255–92.

Federal Government of Nigeria (1980) *Crime and the Quality of Life.*

Fukuyama, F. (1992) *The End of History and the Last Man.* London: Penguin.

Fukuyama, F. (1995) *Trust: the Social Virtues and the Creation of Prosperity.* New York: Free Press.

Geertz, C. (1973) *The Interpretation of Cultures.* New York: Basic Books.

Gulati, R. (1995) Does familiarity breed trust? The implications of repeated ties for contractual choice in alliances. *Academy of Management Journal* 38, 85–112.

Gulati, R. (1998) Alliances and networks. *Strategic Management Journal* 19, 293–317.

Hair, J.F., Anderson, R.E., Tatham, R.L. and Black, W.C. (1998) *Multivariate Data Analysis.* New Jersey: Prentice Hall.

Hall, R.E. and Jones, C. (1999) Why do some countries produce so much more output per worker than others? *Quarterly Journal of Economics* 114(1), 83–116.

Hofstede, G. (2001) *Culture's Consequences: Comparing Values, Behaviors, Institutions and Organizations Across Nations* (2nd edn). Beverly Hills: Sage.

Inglehart, R. (1997) *Modernization and Postmodernization: Cultural, Economic and Political Change in 43 Societies.* Princeton: Princeton University Press.

Inglehart, R. and Baker, W. (2000) Modernization, cultural change and the persistence of traditional values. *American Sociological Review* 65, 19–51.

Janowicz, M. and Noorderhaven, N.G. (2002) The role of trust in inter-organizational learning in joint ventures. *CentER Discussion paper* 119. The Netherlands: Tilburg University.

Keating, M. (1998) *The New Regionalism in Western Europe.* Cheltenham: Edward Elgar.

Knack, S. and Keefer, P. (1997) Does social capital have an economic pay-off? A cross country investigation. *Quarterly Journal of Economics* 112, 1251–88.

Luhmann, N. (1979) *Trust and Power.* Chichester: John Wiley & Sons.

Maddison, A. (2001) *The World Economy: a Millennial Perspective.* Paris: OECD.

Malecki, E.J. (2000) Network models for technology-based growth, in Acs, Z. (ed.) *Regional Innovation, Knowledge and Global Change.* London: Pinter, 187–204.

Mankiw, N.G., Romer, D. and Weil, D. (1992) A contribution to the empirics of economic growth. *Quarterly Journal of Economics* 107, 407–31.

Nooteboom, B. (2002) *Trust: Forms, Foundations, Functions, Failures and Figures.* Cheltenham: Edward Elgar.

North, D. (1991) Institutions. *Journal of Economic Perspectives* 5, 97–112.

Olopoenia, R.A. (1998) *A Political Economy of Corruption and Underdevelopment.* Faculty Lecture Series No. 10, Faculty of Social Sciences, University of Ibadan (October).

Parsons, T. (1969) *Sociological Theory and Modern Society.* New York: Free Press.

Porter, M. (2000) Attitudes, values, beliefs and the micro economics of prosperity, in Harrison, L. and Huntington, S. (eds) *Culture Matters.* New York: Basic Books, pp. 14–28.

Portes, A. (1997) Neoliberalism and the sociology of development: emerging trends and unanticipated facts. *Population and Development Review* 23(2), 229–59.

Putnam, R. (2000) *Bowling Alone: the Collapse and Revival of the American Community.* New York: Simon & Schuster.

Putnam, R. (with Leonardi, R. and Nanetti, R.Y.) (1993) *Making Democracy Work.* Princeton: Princeton University Press.

Ring, P.S. and Van de Ven, A.H. (1992) Structuring cooperative relationships between organizations. *Strategic Management Journal* 13, 483–98.

Sako, M. (1992) *Prices, Quality and Trust: Interfirm Relations in Britain and Japan.* Cambridge: Cambridge University Press.

Shapiro, S.P. (1987) The social control of impersonal trust. *American Journal of Sociology* 93, 623–58.

Uzzi, B. (1996) The sources and consequences of embeddedness for the economic performance of organizations: the network effect. *American Sociological Review* 61, 674–98.

Weber, M. (2001 [1930]) *The Protestant Ethic and the Spirit of Capitalism.* London: Routledge.

Williamson, O.E. (1975) *Markets and Hierarchies, Analysis and Antitrust Implications.* New York: Free Press.

Williamson, O.E. (1985) *The Economic Institutions of Capitalism.* New York: Free Press.

Zaheer, A., McEvily, B. and Perrone, V. (1998) Does trust matter? Exploring the effects of interorganisational and interpersonal trust on performance. *Organisation Science* 9, 141–59.

Zak, P. and Knack, S. (2001) Trust and growth. *The Economic Journal* 111, 295–321.

Zukin, S. and DiMaggio, P. (eds) (1990) *Structures of Capital, the Social Organization of the Economy.* Cambridge: Cambridge University Press.

National Cultures and Management

NIELS NOORDERHAVEN AND CARLA I. KOEN

Learning Objectives

By the end of this chapter you will be able to:

- understand the 'levels of analysis problem' in cultural research
- evaluate the usefulness of the emic and etic approaches to cultural analysis
- assess when and how to use the culture dimensions identified by Hofstede, Schwartz and Trompenaars
- appreciate the strengths and weaknesses of the aforementioned approaches
- comprehend the 'logics of cultures' as identified by d'Iribarne
- recognize the implications of cultural differences at the national level for international negotiations.

Chapter Outline

2.1   **Introduction**

2.2   **Methodological Dilemmas**
Etic versus emic
Research methods
Boundaries of cultures
Levels of analysis
Dimensions and typologies

2.3   **The Etic Approach**
Geert Hofstede: five dimensions of work-related values
Shalom Schwartz: three bipolar dimensions of motivational values
Fons Trompenaars: cultural dilemmas

2.4   **Cultural Clusters**

2.5   **The Emic Approach**
Philippe d'Iribarne: the logics of culture

2.6   **National Cultures and Cross-cultural Negotiations**
Study Questions
Further Reading
Case: Unisource
Case: Management of Phosphate Mining in Senegal
References

2.1 ❋ Introduction

The introductory chapter briefly introduced the cultural approach to comparative international management. In this chapter we will discuss this approach in more depth. In doing so, we aim to provide the reader with a balanced view. Too many contributions to cultural management theory are one-sided, arguing for the importance of one particular source of cultural differences (e.g. nationality), and reasoning from one particular theoretical point of view (e.g. 'etic' versus 'emic'). The importance of national differences in culture is undeniable, and we will discuss these differences extensively. There are also other cultural distinctions, however, that may remain unobserved if we continue to look at the nation-state as the main (or sole) source of cultural identity. The reality is that countries have always harboured cultural diversity and are increasingly doing so. The complex influences of cultural differences on management can probably never be understood from only one methodological perspective, hence our discussion of multiple approaches and our emphasis on their complementarity. In particular, we will discuss various approaches that fall under the 'etic' perspective, as well as the main outlines of the 'emic' perspective.

However, before going into a description of the contents of these approaches we will discuss some key methodological issues. The reason for this is that an insight into the methods used in cross-cultural research is of vital importance in understanding the strengths *and* weaknesses of the various approaches. The distinction between the various approaches to culture is also largely a matter of research methods, and the same can be said of the distinction between cultural and institutional approaches.

Following the section on methodological issues, we will first discuss three main representatives of the etic approach: Geert Hofstede, Shalom Schwartz and Fons Trompenaars. After that, we will show how on the basis of these and other studies the national cultures of the world can be grouped into a number of more or less homogenous clusters. This is of obvious importance to managers, as cultural differences may be assumed to be more pronounced, and their implications more serious, if the boundaries between cultural clusters are crossed.

Next, we will turn to the emic approach. It is more difficult here to distinguish the most important representatives, in particular regarding the application to comparative international management. We will discuss the approach in more general terms, referring to some major contributors, and subsequently discuss in more depth the work of one author who explicitly addresses management issues, and who has also explicitly reflected on the difference between his approach and the etic perspective as exemplified by, for example, Hofstede. This author is Philippe d'Iribarne.

In the final part of the chapter we focus on one particular, but very important, aspect of the influences of culture on management, namely international negotiations. International negotiations are of crucial importance to an increasing number of firms, whether in the context of buying or selling across national boundaries, in the context of the formation of an international alliance or joint venture, or in the course of the internal management of a multinational corporation (the subject of Chapter 9).

2.2 Methodological Dilemmas

As mentioned in the introductory chapter, two main traditions can be distinguished in cross-cultural research: the etic and the emic. We will start with a characterization of both approaches, and then go on to discuss the related subjects of levels of analysis, dimensions and typologies of cultures, boundaries of cultures, and research methods.

Etic versus emic

The comparison of cultures presupposes that there is something to be compared – that each culture is not so unique that any parallel with another culture is meaningless. Throughout the history of the study of culture there has been a dispute between those stressing the unique aspects (the emic approach) and those stressing the comparable aspects (the etic approach). The emic approach emphasizes the need to understand social systems from the inside and through the definitions of their members. It attempts to analyse the internal coherence of single examples and condemns any attempt at classification across cultures as denying the uniqueness of each culture. Because of this emphasis on the unique features of each culture, the approach can also be characterized as 'idiographic'. Pure idiographic research is usually based on qualitative data analysis such as participant observation and interviews. Etic research, in contrast, attempts to establish general laws governing large numbers of examples. It looks at the variances and covariances of variables *between* cultures (between-society correlations). Because of the emphasis on general laws, this approach can be characterized as 'nomothetic'.

The words 'etic' and 'emic' come from linguistics; they are taken from the terms 'phonetic' and 'phonemic', the distinction between which can be seen as paradigmatic for the major debate within cultural studies. Phonetics is the study of sound and sound changes in human speech. Historically, this branch of science was conceived as a natural science, which tried to uncover the general laws determining human speech sounds. Phonemics, in contrast, is the study of sound units in language that enable speakers to distinguish between meanings. Phonemes differ between languages, and can only be studied within the context of a given language. North Sea Ferries once coined the slogan 'North Sea Ferries, Ferry Good'; however, the pun was lost on most members of the Dutch public, for whom the difference between the 'f' and 'v' sounds is not phonemic.

The difference between etic and emic approaches is partly parallel to that between psychological and sociological approaches to culture on the one hand, and anthropological approaches on the other. However, there have also been anthropologists with nomothetic-etic ambitions. This was particularly true of the early generations of anthropologists, like Edward Tyler (1832–1917), who developed a general evolutionary theory of cultural development. All cultures were assumed to progress through a series of stages, from 'primitive' to 'civilized'. It is true that later generations of anthropologists, following in the footsteps of Franz Boas (1858–1942), emphasized that cultures are integrated wholes that need to be studied in detail before any generalization can be made (if it ever can), but more recently, Claude Lévi-Strauss's structural anthropology again sought to identify general regularities. Lévi-Strauss (1908–90), through painstakingly detailed analysis, tried to demonstrate that, at a deeper level, the bewildering variety of cultural phenomena, like kinship systems and myths, can in fact be grouped into a very limited number of basic forms or structures. These structures were seen to reflect the structures of the human unconscious processes that shaped the forms of cultural life (Moore, 1997: 219). Hence, important anthropologists have nourished the ideals of building an objective 'science of society' normally associated with etic approaches. However, since the 1970s, anthropology has 'moved quite rapidly from being a (would-be) science of society to being (once again) one of the humanities, concerned with interpretation and meaning' (Chapman, 1996–97: 4). The consequence is that contemporary anthropological research is predominantly of the emic kind, and hence is fundamentally different from the etic sociological and psychological work. Another consequence, which we will try to avoid here, is that representatives of both perspectives act as if they have nothing to say to each other. We think, in contrast, that it is important for students of comparative international management to familiarize themselves with both approaches in order to be able to construct a balanced view of what we know and do not know about cultures and their impact on management.

Research methods

Although the differences between the etic and the emic approach cannot be reduced to issues of method alone, it is clear that the different foci of the two perspectives do call for divergent research methods, and that these different methods in turn further sharpen the differences between the two perspectives. Etic culture research aims to generalize across the boundaries of individual countries. If a researcher wants to identify dimensions in which cultures differ, he or she has to study a sufficient number of different societies in order to be able to verify the general nature of the proposed dimensions. Hofstede's research, described briefly in the introductory chapter and discussed in more depth later in this chapter, illustrates this. Hofstede used factor analysis to identify two of his dimensions. In such an analysis, the unit of analysis is the culture. This means that in order to have a sufficient number of observations, many cultures need to be studied.

In large-scale studies, covering many cultures, it is important that observations from the different cultures studied are comparable. For this reason the nomothetic-etic approach has a partiality for standardized instruments, in particular standardized questionnaires. In constructing these instruments one of the main concerns is that the data collected in different societies are indeed comparable. This is the quest for 'equivalence' in etic research. If a particular question is asked of respondents in country A, the same question has to be asked of respondents in country B in order for the answers to be comparable.

Translation into local languages is one aspect of the quest for equivalence. It is standard practice in cross-cultural research to translate a questionnaire into a local language, and then have it 'back-translated' into the original language by a different translator. In this way, inconsistencies between the translated and the original instrument can be identified. However, equivalence issues go beyond translation into different languages. Even if the translation is faithful, the question may have quite different connotations from one country to another. An example is one of the questions used by Hofstede (1980): 'How long do you think you will continue working for this company?' (part of the scale measuring uncertainty avoidance). We may expect that it makes a big difference whether this question is asked of respondents in a country like the USA, with bountiful alternative employment options, or in a country like, say, Peru, with at the time of the research far fewer comparable employment possibilities. Hence, differences between answers to the question may partly be due to differences in other context factors than the national culture that is targeted.

With the preference for standardized, equivalent research instruments and large samples, a preference for quantified data becomes inevitable. Quantified data also make it possible to address issues of equivalence post hoc – that is, after the data collection. If we have included in the instrument a number of items that are supposed to measure a particular construct, we can test whether the answers to these items are correlated in the different societies studied. If this is not the case, this is a sign that the items do not measure the construct in question reliably. Items that do not in all countries studied correlate significantly with the other items measuring the construct can then be dropped from the further analysis, and in this way the scale is purified. This procedure would be impossible with qualitative data, of course.

Anthropologist Malcolm Chapman (1996–97: 12) notes that the search for equivalence in etic research seems strange from an emic perspective:

> Faced with 'differences in connotation' or 'different divisions and structures of categories', the instinct of a psychologist has been to remove these in order to ask culturally neutral and 'objective' questions. To the anthropologist, by contrast, any 'lack of equivalence' is precisely where research should focus and precisely where objective knowledge must be sought.

In other words, from an emic perspective in the quest for equivalence the etic researchers risk throwing out the baby (the 'real' cultural differences) with the bath water ('measurement errors'). Because it focuses on meaning, contemporary anthropologic research by necessity espouses different research methods. It would be futile to try to gauge differences in meaning in and using large-scale questionnaires. Instead, emic researchers study cultures from within, which involves living within the society being researched for a prolonged period of time, learning the language, engaging in interactions with local people, and so on. The aim is to develop an understanding of the meaning of culturally specific behaviours, symbols and artefacts to the members of the society or group in question. In the words of Clifford Geertz, 'the trick is to figure out what the devil they think they are up to' (Geertz, 1983: 58). The data collected with this 'ethnographic' method are of a rich, qualitative nature, but difficult to compare with those from other studies, because they are also more subjective than the data collected in etic research. If another emic researcher studied the same culture, there is no guarantee that he or she would come up with the same interpretation of meaning. To put it very simply, one could say that data collected in etic research are shallow but reliable, and data collected in emic research rich but less reliable. However, an emic researcher would say, 'What's the use of "reliable" data when they miss the essential point of a culture – that is, its meaning to local people?'

Boundaries of cultures

Another noteworthy problem with cross-cultural research is that the boundaries of the level of analysis cannot always be defined clearly. Within the cross-cultural literature (in particular, in etic studies) the dominant approach has been to equate nations with cultures, and thus to study culture by comparing samples from different countries. However, national boundaries often do not encompass homogenous societies with a shared culture. Examples are Canada, which has an English- and a French-speaking population with different cultural features; Belgium, with a Flemish- and French-speaking population with different cultural traits; Germany, with cultural differences between the different states (Bundesländer), and so on. Moreover, the nation-state is essentially a western invention; elsewhere (e.g. in Africa) the nation-state is relatively young and hardly corresponds to any sense of cultural homogeneity or identity. It is argued, however, that in nations that have existed for some time there are strong forces towards integration (Hofstede, 1991: 12). There is usually a single dominant language, educational system, army, political system, shared mass media, markets, services and national symbols (e.g. flag, sports teams). These can produce substantial sharing of basic values among residents of a nation. This is less the case, of course, in nations with sharp divisions between ethnic groups. Most etic research, however, concentrates on the more homogenous societies, avoiding this problem but posing limits on the generalizability of the framework. Emic research, in contrast, has always had a tendency to focus on cultural groups that are not defined by national boundaries, like the indigenous peoples of North America, or the Nuer people of the southern Sudan.

To be able to make valid comparisons, research should be based either on representative samples or on more narrow, but carefully 'matched', samples. In order to be representative, a sample should cover (in the right proportions) all the relevant subgroups or categories of people in a society, also taking into account age, gender and occupation. As a result this strategy calls for large samples. The national samples used in the 1999/2000 European Values Survey, for instance, vary between 967 and 2500 respondents. As for the strategy of matched samples, depending on the nature of the characteristics scholars want to compare, they can compose matched samples of individuals, situations, institutions (such as families) or organizations. An example of the last of these is a study about hierarchy conducted by Tannenbaum *et al.* (1974) that covered ten industrial companies, matched for size and product, in each of five countries. When comparing cultural aspect of nations, one should try to match for categories such as educational level, socio-economic status, occupation, gender and age group. In addition, there may also be linguistic, regional, tribal, ethnic, religious or caste divisions within nations. We can compare Spanish nurses with Swedish nurses, or Spanish policemen with Swedish policemen; in the case of such narrow samples, however, we have to be careful in interpreting the differences and similarities found. For instance, if differences are found in the values espoused by military personnel in different countries (Soeters and Recht, 1998) this can reflect value differences between these countries in general, but before drawing any conclusion we will have to ascertain whether these institutions are functionally equivalent in the nations concerned. If one of the countries has a conscription system and another country a regular (professional) army, there may be a self-selection bias in the second sample that makes it incomparable with the first. A more solid research strategy, if we have to use narrow samples, is to take several samples from different parts of society. With a fourfold sample of Spanish and Swedish nurses and Spanish and Swedish policemen, we can test not only the nationality effect but also the occupation effect (nurses versus policemen) and the possible interaction between the two, which can give clues as to functional equivalence. The quality of the matching of narrow samples can often only be proven ex post facto: if the differences we find between cultures in one sample set are confirmed by those found by others in other matched samples, our matching was adequate (Hofstede, 2001: 23–4).

Levels of analysis

The nomethetic-etic approach presupposes data on a greater number of cultures and tends to proceed from a study of 'ecological' correlations. The latter are calculated either from *mean values* of variables for each society or (in the case of categorical variables) from percentages (Hofstede, 2001). *Comparative research* with an idiographic-emic concern (if statistically inclined) will express itself in a focus on relations between variables *within* cultures (within-society correlations), followed by a comparison of the patterns found from culture to culture. The within-society indexes are calculated from variables correlated at the *individual* level.

Two common areas of confusion in nomothetic-etic studies concerning the levels-of-analysis problem are the *ecological fallacy* and the *reverse ecological fallacy*. The ecological fallacy is committed when conclusions concerning individuals are drawn from higher-level data. The classic example is discussed in Hofstede (2001: 16). In 1930 data, there was a strong $r=.95$ correlation between skin colour and illiteracy across US states: states with a higher percentage of blacks also had higher percentages of illiterates. However, if the same data were analysed at the individual level, across 97 million individuals, the correlation dropped to $r=.20$. The ecological fallacy is particularly tempting when data at higher levels of aggregation are available, but individual-level data are not.

The *reverse* ecological fallacy implies that conclusions regarding cultures are drawn from individual-level data. It is committed in the construction of *ecological indexes* from variables correlated at the *individual* level. Indexes are, for example, constructed through addition of the scores on two or more questionnaire items. In constructing indexes for the individual level, we ought to make sure that the items correlate across individuals; in constructing indexes for the national level, we ought to make sure that the country mean scores correlate across countries. The reverse ecological fallacy in cross-cultural studies occurs when research compares cultures on indexes created for the individual level (Hofstede, 2001: 16). In other words, within-society correlations are used instead of between-society correlations. One reason the reverse ecological fallacy occurs easily is that studies with data from more than a few societies (more than two or three) are rare, and ecological dimensions can be detected clearly only with data from ten or more societies.

Hofstede (2001: 17) maintains that the reverse ecological fallacy is more than just inadequate data treatment, and that it betrays 'an inadequate research paradigm in which cultures are treated and categorized as if they were individuals'. However, when individual-level questionnaire data are aggregated and analysed at the ecological level, as is the case in nomothetic-etic research, it is unfortunate if the data cannot be interpreted in terms of the individuals who provided the answers in the first place. Culture exists in the minds of people. Hence, one would expect the logic of the culture also to be reflected in the logic of the individual bearers of the culture. For this reason dimensions based on items or questions that do not correlate at the individual level within the cultures studied (as is the case for some of Hofstede's dimensions) are not entirely satisfactory. It would be preferable to construct culture-level scales, which also have good statistical characteristics at the individual level (Maznevski *et al.*, 2002).

While less relevant in *comparative* management research, for the sake of completeness and to emphasize further the levels-of-analysis problem, we discuss here briefly the *pan-cultural* and *individual* levels of analysis. Imagine we have a sample that consists of *N* individuals who belong to *n* different societies. Pan-cultural analysis pools the data from all *N* individuals together regardless of the culture they belong to. The pan-cultural analysis, thus, deals with the combined variance from both the ecological and the individual analysis. This makes sense when we try to identify general, not culture-specific, characteristics of individuals. An individual analysis is performed on the pooled data for the *N* individuals after elimination of the culture-level effects. This can be done by deducting from each individual score the unit's mean score on the question, so that the new unit mean becomes 0 and the ecological variance is eliminated. It can also be done by full standardization of the individual scores, which results in standard scores with a mean (for each question, across the individuals within each country) of 0 and a standard deviation of 1. In both cases, the individual analysis considers precisely that part of the variance in the data that has been eliminated in the ecological analysis. It is a way of pooling the within-culture analyses across all *n* cultures or units (Leung and Bond, 1989).

It should be obvious by now that the choice of the appropriate level of analysis for the problem at hand is of extreme importance. Briefly, the levels-of-analysis problem in social and behavioural research occurs when conclusions applying to one level have to be drawn from data only available at another level. If the fact that the two levels do not correspond is not recognized and accommodated by the researcher, a cross-level fallacy occurs (Rousseau, 1985). This fallacy can logically go two ways: interpreting data from the social-system level as if they were data about individuals – called the *ecological fallacy* – and the reverse, as we have just seen, called the *reverse ecological fallacy.*

To complicate things further, the different levels of analysis interact in a complex way. Most cross-cultural studies, however, tend to concentrate on one level of analysis, neglecting the interplay between different levels. This means, among other things, that the influence of national culture on organizational- and industry-level culture is not often explicitly examined (see Chapter 3).

Dimensions and typologies

Contemporary *comparative* cross-cultural research is mainly carried out by scholars who lean towards the nomothetic-etic approach, focusing on the *ecological* level. An essential step in such research is to define the concept of culture. Without definition, culture cannot be operationalized and, without operationalization, it cannot be measured. Measurements are exactly what etic research is all about. For years, research on culture has been hampered by the lack of a widely accepted definition of the concept and until now there has been little agreement on how cultural features are best conceptualized and operationalized in empirical studies. The lack of conceptual and operational consistency in cross-cultural research is expressed most clearly in the fact that different studies have developed different dimensions of national culture.

Dimensions are developed to yield greater cultural understanding and to allow for cross-cultural comparisons. Cross-cultural research focuses on 'values' in order to characterize culture. There are, however, hundreds, perhaps thousands, of values on which societies and other cultural groups could be compared. Some values are relevant in all societies, others are known only in particular societies. Hence, to be able to compare societies effectively, the profusion of cultural values must be organized into a limited number of dimensions. Theorists who address this issue make the assumption that cultural dimensions of values reflect the basic issues or problems that societies must confront in order to regulate human activity (Smith and Schwartz, 1997).

It is clear, however, that while useful tools in explaining cultural behaviour, dimensions have limitations that we ought to acknowledge. It is obvious that any description of culture in a few dimensions cannot do justice to the complexity of the concept and is limiting in the way it constrains individuals' perceptions of behaviour in another culture. Moreover, by simplifying the reality of culture into dimensions, we neglect within-country differences, sacrificing completeness. Not surprisingly, dimensions are found to be more beneficial in making comparisons between cultures than in understanding the wide variations of behaviour within a single culture. The existence of so-called cultural paradoxes reveals the limitations in our thinking. For example,

> based on Hofstede's value dimension uncertainty avoidance, the Japanese have a low tolerance for uncertainty avoidance while Americans have a high tolerance. Why then do the Japanese intentionally incorporate ambiguous clauses in their business contracts, which are unusually short, while Americans dot every i, cross every t, and painstakingly spell out every possible contingency? (Osland and Bird, 2000: 65)

Hofstede himself warned against expecting too much of these dimensions and of using them incorrectly. For example, he defended the individualism–collectivism dimension as a useful construct, but went on to say:

> This does not mean, of course, that a country's individualism index score tells all there is to be known about the background and structure of relationship patterns in that country. It is an abstraction that should not be extended beyond its limited area of usefulness. (Hofstede, 1994: xi)

The use of dimensions and/or the simplification of the construct of culture should also be seen against the background of the emic–etic debate. As indicated, an emic perspective looks at a culture from *within* its boundaries, whereas an etic perspective stands *outside* and compares two or more cultures. Most cultural approaches in management adopt a between-culture or etic approach. To make between-culture differences more prominent, the etic approach downplays inconsistencies within a culture or, in other words, neglects within-culture differences. Consequently, it could be argued that the dimension approach does not replace in-depth studies of country cultures but, on the contrary, invites them. The most complete, certain and precise understanding of societies would arguably be obtained through a combination of both research approaches. Culture needs to be both observed and measured if we are to take the concept seriously. The combined use of the two research methods would offer the possibility of achieving greater conceptual consistency (i.e. consistency in the features of culture being compared cross-nationally) and equivalence in operational measurement.

Instead of using dimensions, some researchers construct *typologies* to illustrate differences between countries. A typology describes a number of ideal types, each of which is easy to imagine. The division of countries into the first, second and third worlds is such a typology. The identification of culture areas as ideal types represents a compromise solution between the purely emic position and the extreme etic of the index values. Rather than considering each country as an entirely different whole, we recognize that some cultures are more alike than others (d'Iribarne, 1996–97). However, whereas typologies are easier to understand than dimensions, they are problematic in empirical research. Real cases seldom correspond fully to one single ideal type. Most cases are hybrids, and arbitrary rules have to be made for classifying them as belonging to one of the types. With a dimensions model, such as those from Hofstede, Trompenaars and Schwartz (all are discussed below), cases can always be scored unambiguously. In practice, typologies and dimensional models can be reconciled. On the basis of their dimension scores, cases (countries) can be sorted empirically afterwards into clusters with similar scores. These clusters then form an empirical typology. Hofstede, for example, sorted into 12 clusters more than 50 countries in a study of IBM (see the section on Hofstede, below), on the basis of four dimension scores. In fact, Hofstede uses a kind of typology approach for explaining each of the five dimensions. For every dimension, he describes the two opposite extremes, which can be seen as ideal types. Some of the dimensions are subsequently taken two by two, which creates four ideal types. However, the country scores on the dimensions locate most real cases somewhere in between the extremes (Hofstede, 2001: 28).

Despite all methodological difficulties cross-cultural research has allowed us to make important steps towards understanding cultural differences and their consequences for management and organization. In the remainder of this chapter we will discuss in some detail a number of empirical studies, starting with the main representatives of the etic approach, and then shifting to the emic approach. After that, we will discuss the impact of cultural differences on international negotiations, deferring a discussion of the empirical consequences for management and organization of cultural influences to subsequent applied chapters.

2.3 The Etic Approach

To be able to explain cross-cultural differences, nomothetic-etic research has concentrated on identifying dimensions of cultural variation. To identify such dimensions, it is desirable for studies to include as many and as wide a range of cultures as possible. Most extant cross-cultural work has been confined to a small number of cultures, although there are notable exceptions. Two such exceptions are pioneering research projects, which have aimed directly at identifying cultural dimensions of values, namely the projects of Hofstede (1980, 1991, 2001) and Schwartz (Schwartz and Bilsky, 1987, 1990; Schwartz 1992). Related work by Bond and colleagues, and by Trompenaars, will also be discussed. Trompenaars' work is based on different theoretical frameworks from those used in Hofstede's model. Nevertheless, Trompenaars' dimensions, though different from those of Hofstede, have been shown to be conceptually related principally to 'individualism' and 'power distance', and as such have been interpreted as supportive of Hofstede's model in that they emphasize some of the consequences of 'individualism' and 'power distance' for organizational behaviour, attitudes and beliefs (Gatley *et al.*, 1996: 109).

Geert Hofstede: five dimensions of work-related values
Overview

Comparative cross-cultural research at the societal or national level gathered significant impetus through the well-known work of the Dutch scholar Geert Hofstede (1980, 1991, 2001).

Hofstede, citing Inkeles and Levinson (1997), suggests that three basic societal problems underlie cultural value dimensions:

1. relationship to authority
2. conception of self, including the individual's concept of masculinity and femininity
3. primary dilemmas or conflicts, and ways of dealing with them, including the control of aggression and the expression versus inhibition of affect.

One of the most imposing features of Hofstede's original study (1980) is its sheer size. Data was generated from 116,000 questionnaires collected from IBM employees in over 40 countries. Both the size of the sample and the geographic coverage were unprecedented. Since the respondents were all sales and service employees of a single company, a number of factors could be controlled for. All respondents were doing the same general task (selling and servicing IBM products) within the same overall company framework. Thus, the technology, job content and many formal procedures were the same. Only the nationalities of the subjects differed. Any variation in attitudes and values would, Hofstede claimed, be related to cultural differences rather than organizational ones (for a critical view of this claim, see McSweeney, 2002).

'Eclectic analysis' (starting with two single focal items seen as measuring issues of hierarchy and work stress respectively, and then looking for correlated items) yielded the dimensions of 'power distance' and 'uncertainty avoidance'. Factor analysis of responses to 32 questions about the importance of work goals revealed two additional dimensions of culture: 'individualism–collectivism' and 'masculinity–femininity'. Hofstede defined these dimensions such that they reflect the way members of a society typically cope with each of the 'basic societal problems': power distance to (1), uncertainty avoidance to (3), and both individualism–collectivism and masculinity–femininity to (2) (Hofstede, 2001: 31).

Hofstede's study also allowed for a 'modest' quantitative assessment of cultural change and stability (Hofstede, 2001: 34–6). He did this on the basis of the IBM survey cycles of 1967–69 and 1971–73, through a comparison of answers from respondents in different age brackets. He found that differences in values among respondents of the same national culture but of different ages and/or at different points in time may be due to three different causes: age (maturation), generation and Zeitgeist. Age effects simply mean that respondents' values shift as they grow older. Shifts over time are due only to the ageing of the respondents. Generation effects occur for values that were absorbed by the young people of a certain period and accompanied their age cohort over its lifetime. If conditions of life have changed (i.e. due to fast technological change), subsequent generations may carry forward different values that they have absorbed in their youth. Zeitgeist effects occur when drastic system-wide changes in conditions cause *everyone's* values to shift, regardless of age. The changes found within the IBM data are small, which can be taken as an indication that cultural values do not change easily or quickly. This finding could perhaps be an indication of the fact that globalization effects will not lead to cultural convergence in the short or medium term (there is more on this below).

Moreover, Hofstede interprets the consequences of differences in the four original dimensions for work and organization (see Tables 2.1–2.4). He addresses the structural concerns of the contingency theorists by relating two of his dimensions – power distance and uncertainty avoidance – to the structure of organizations. Power distance is similar to concentration of authority (centralization), and uncertainty avoidance to structuring of activities. Hofstede has little empirical evidence to support his interpretation, however (Tayeb, 1994). In later chapters, we will see that scholars working within the institutional framework find results that support Hofstede's interpretations, thus to some extent providing the empirical evidence required.

Hofstede's dimensions are described below.

Power distance (PDI) describes the extent to which 'the less powerful members of institutions and organizations within a country expect and accept that power is distributed unequally' (Hofstede, 1991: 262). Power distance is relevant for organizational structure, the dimension 'is clearly related to the Aston dimension of "concentration of authority"' (Hofstede, 2001). Organizations in high power distance countries will tend to prefer greater centralized organizational structures than those in low power distance countries. Other consequences for organizations and work proposed by Hofstede are summarized in Table 2.1.

Table 2.1 Some consequences of national PDI score differences for work and organization	
Low PDI countries	**High PDI countries**
Decentralization	Centralization
Low concentration of authority	High concentration of authority
Flat organizational pyramids	Tall organizational pyramids
Hierarchy means inequality of roles, established for convenience	Hierarchy reflects existential inequality between higher-ups and lower-downs
Small proportion of supervisors in workforce	High proportion of supervisors in workforce
Narrow salary range between top and bottom; lower differential in status and qualifications	Wide salary range between top and bottom; higher differential in qualifications and status
Consultative relationship between superior and subordinate leads to satisfaction, performance and productivity	Authoritative leadership and close supervision lead to satisfaction, performance and productivity
Ideal boss is resourceful and democratic	Ideal boss is benevolent and paternal
Privileges and status symbols for managers are frowned upon	Privileges and status symbols for managers are expected and popular
Openness with information, also to non-superiors	Information constrained by hierarchy

Source: based on Hofstede (2001: 107–8).

Uncertainty avoidance (UAI) describes the extent to which 'the members of a culture feel threatened by uncertain or unknown situations' (Hofstede, 1991: 263). A summary of Hofstede's proposed consequences for work and organizations of different UAI scores is shown in Table 2.2.

Individualism versus collectivism (IDV) describes whether 'the ties between individuals are loose, with everyone being expected to look after himself or herself and his or her immediate family only' (individualism) or whether 'people from birth onwards are integrated into strong, cohesive ingroups, which throughout people's lifetime continue to protect them in exchange for unquestioning loyalty' (collectivism) (Hofstede, 1991: 260–1). Principal consequences proposed by Hofstede for national differences in the IDV index on organizations and work are summarized in Table 2.3.

Masculinity versus femininity (MAS) describes whether 'social gender roles are clearly distinct: men are supposed to be assertive, tough, and focused on material success; women are supposed to be more modest, tender, and concerned with the quality of life' (femininity), or whether 'social gender roles overlap; both men and women are supposed to be modest, tender, and concerned with the quality of life' (Hofstede, 1991: 261–2). The fundamental consequence for the workplace is in attitudes to work centrality, in that the work ethos in masculine cultures tends towards 'live in order to work' rather than in feminine cultures where the ethos is more inclined towards 'work in order to live' (Hofstede, 1991). Principal consequences proposed by Hofstede for work and organizations of differences in national scores on the MAS index are summarized in Table 2.4.

Hofstede later added a fifth dimension to his framework, in response to the work of Bond and colleagues (Chinese Culture Connection, 1987). The IBM studies, which yielded the data from which Hofstede distilled his dimensions, used a questionnaire composed by western minds. The team that first designed it consisted of British, Dutch, French, Norwegian and US members. This exclusively western input into the research instrument introduced a bias in the sense that the values of non-western respondents would possibly not be fully expressed by the questionnaire results. In other words, the content validity of the instrument used by Hofstede was doubtful. Recognizing this bias, Bond decided to introduce a deliberate eastern bias by having Chinese colleagues from Hong Kong and

Table 2.2 Consequences of UAI score differences for work and organization	
Low UAI countries	**High UAI countries**
Tolerance for ambiguity in structures and procedures	Highly formalized conception of management
Power of superiors depends on position and relationships	Power of superiors depends on control of uncertainties
Managers more involved in strategy	Managers more involved in details
Relationship orientation	Task orientation
Weak loyalty to employer; short average duration of employment	Strong loyalty to employer, long average duration of employment

Source: based on Hofstede (2001: 169–70).

Taiwan prepare an alternative questionnaire. This instrument was subsequently used in a study among university students in 23 countries (20 of which overlapped with those covered by Hofstede's IBM studies). The analysis of the data from this survey revealed four dimensions, three of which showed a certain resemblance to Hofstede's power distance, individualism–collectivism and masculinity–femininity. However, none of the dimensions identified by Bond and colleagues correlated with Hofstede's uncertainty avoidance. Instead another, bipolar, dimension was identified 'Confucian dynamism', with values at one of the poles reflecting more future-orientated and dynamic values related to the teachings of Confucius, and those at the other pole more past and present-orientated and static (Hofstede, 1991: 166). Hence, the dimension can be seen as distinguishing between more and less dynamic and between future-orientated and past-orientated readings of the work of the Chinese philosopher Confucius (Kong Fu Ze).

Later, Hofstede adopted Confucian dynamism as the fifth dimension in his framework, under the name 'long-term versus short-term orientation'. However, it is important to note that the empirical basis of this fifth dimension is much less robust than that of the other four (Fang, 2003). Both numbers of countries included as the sample sizes per country were much smaller in the study in which the fifth dimension was identified than in the IBM studies. Furthermore the respondents in the Chinese culture survey were university students, whereas Hofstede had more samples of IBM employees, which were arguably more representative for the working populations of their countries. Nevertheless, we will, following Hofstede, treat long-term versus short-term orientation as an integral part of Hofstede's system of work-related values.

> *Long-term versus short-term orientation* is related to the 'fostering of virtues oriented towards future rewards, in particular perseverance and thrift' (long-term orientation) versus 'the fostering of virtues related to the past and the present, in particular respect for tradition, preservation of "face", and fulfilling social obligations' (short-term orientation) (Hofstede, 1991: 261–3). Partly because of the smaller number of countries for which index values have been computed, less is known about the consequences of this dimension for work and organization. Table 2.5 summarizes the main implications.

An overview of country scores on Hofstede's original four dimensions and on long-term versus short-term orientation can be found in Table 2.6.

Criticism

As with all studies, Hofstede's has provoked praise as well as criticism. Some criticism has to do with the empirical basis of his study, other criticism concerns methodological issues. A brief summary of much of this criticism has been offered by Hunt:

> There has been much formal and informal debate on the suitability of IBM employees as the target for his study, on the breakdown of the massive sample (116,000) into country samples, on the dominance of male responses (especially in countries where females are not found in executive positions), on the built-in bias of the sort of people (are they a minority?) who are attracted to and selected by IBM as employees, on the use of a survey to collect data and on items from the survey used to establish the indices of difference. (Hunt, 1981: 55)

Table 2.3 Consequences of IDV score differences for work and organization

Collectivist countries	Individualist countries
Employer–employee relationship is basically moral, like a family link	Employer–employee relationship is a business deal in a 'labour market'
Employees perform best in in-groups	Employees perform best as individuals
Treating friends better than others is normal and ethical: particularism	Treating friends better than others is nepotism and unethical: universalism
Belief in collective decisions	Belief in individual decisions
Direct appraisal of performance is a threat to harmony	Direct appraisal of performance improves productivity
Employee has to be seen in family and social context	Employee can be seen as individual

Source: Hofstede (2001: 244–5).

The issue of the adequacy of the sample should be seen in the light of our discussion of sampling strategies, above. Hofstede argues that it does not matter that samples are atypical 'as long as they are atypical in the same way from one country to another'. He also recognizes that 'multinational corporations have organizational cultures of their own', but argues that 'to the extent that these reduce the variability in the data from one country to another, the remaining variability will be a conservative estimate of the true variability among countries' (Hofstede, 2001: 24). Whether this is true depends on the functional equivalence of the national subsamples. It is not impossible that IBM employees diverged more from the general population in some than in other countries in the sample. This selection bias could be particularly important in comparing industrialized nations with third world countries (McSweeney, 2002).

The second criticism indicated in the extract from Hunt (1981), above, concerns the inherent limitations of the use of the survey method in identifying characteristics of cultures.

Table 2.4 Consequences of MAS score differences for work and organization

Masculine countries	Feminine countries
Managers hold ambitious career aspirations	Managers hold modest career aspirations
Managers expected to be decisive, firm, assertive, aggressive, competitive, just	Managers expected to use intuition, deal with feelings, and seek consensus
Fewer women in management; larger wage gap between genders	More women in management; smaller wage gap between genders
Job applicants oversell themselves	Job applicants undersell themselves
Resolution of conflicts through denying them or fighting until the best 'man' wins	Resolution of conflicts through problem solving, compromise and negotiation
Higher job stress: more burnout symptoms among healthy employees	Lower job stress: fewer burnout symptoms among healthy employees
Preference for higher pay	Preference for fewer hours worked

Source: Hofstede (2001: 318).

Table 2.5 Consequences of LTO score differences for work and organization	
Short-term orientated countries	**Long-term orientated countries**
In business, short-term results: the bottom line	In business: building of relationships and market position
Family and business sphere separated	Vertical coordination, horizontal coordination, control and adaptiveness
Meritocracy: economic and social life to be ordered by abilities	People should live more equally

Source: Hofstede (2001: 366).

The possibility of bias because of low content validity of the survey instrument (there is no guarantee that all relevant aspects of the cultures investigated are covered by the research instrument) has been admitted by Hofstede, and partially addressed by including the 'fifth dimension' identified later. More generally the use of the survey instrument in culture research is one of the bones of contention between representatives of the etic and emic approaches. We do not pretend to be able to solve this dispute here, but the spirit in which this book is written is that both approaches, with their own research methods and instruments, can yield complementary insights of importance to issues of comparative international management.

Third, Hunt raised questions about the suitability of the items used to establish the dimensions of culture. Indeed, many of the items Hofstede used to operationalize his dimensions lack face validity (we will return to this issue in our discussion of the work of d'Iribarne). This is due to the fact that Hofstede's work is an example of 'survey archeology': the IBM studies were never designed to measure national cultures, the interest of the company was more in the area of employee morale. The identification of dimensions of culture was the result of the coincidence of the inclusion of a number of questions concerning personal goals and beliefs, which happened to tap cultural differences, and Hofstede's serendipity and persistence in analysing the data. The problem is that many of the items used by Hofstede at first sight have little connection to the construct measured. For instance, why would a preference for a job that provides training opportunities to improve one's skills or learn new skills be negatively related to individualism? Hofstede's reply could be that the robustness of the findings from the IBM studies depends not so much on the face validity of the items in the instrument used, as in the fact that the dimensions found could be statistically linked to other data sources in an interpretable way (for an extensive overview, see Appendix 6 in Hofstede, 2001). This effectively belies the statement sometimes made that Hofstede's dimensions are statistical artefacts (see, e.g., McSweeney, 2002). All the same, the low face validity of Hofstede's items may be one of the reasons for the slow and hesitant acceptance of Hofstede's work in some parts of the scientific community (see Chapman, 1996–97).

An even more general issue, not mentioned by Hunt, is the question of whether national culture may indeed be expected to exist – that is, whether the country is an appropriate level of analysis for cultures. This is of course a fundamental question, which is relevant to this chapter as a whole, but as the criticism of using the country as the unit of analysis has been most forcefully voiced in the criticism of Hofstede's work we will discuss it here. The nation-state is a relatively recent development; during most of the history of mankind no 'countries' or 'nations' existed. However, once in existence the nation-state can exert a strong influence on the culture of its inhabitants, in particular through the institutionalization of the educational system. As education is one of the two main mechanisms for the transfer and change of culture (the other being the child-rearing practices of parents), it is plausible that as a country has been in existence for long enough, it will have had sufficient influence on the population to enable us to speak of a 'national culture'. The extent to which this is true will of course depend on many factors, like the initial linguistic, ethnic or cultural homogeneity of the population, the pervasiveness and adequacy of national institutions, and so on. But, as Hofstede himself concedes (1991: 12), the nation-state is not always the appropriate level of analysis, as nations may harbour culturally diverse populations, or as members of one particular culture may be spread out over many countries (as, say, in Africa). Moreover, nations sometimes lack stability (McSweeney, 2002). Some fragment into smaller countries, as in the case of the former Yugoslavia. Or nations may merge into new units, as in the case of Hong Kong and mainland China.

One final question, also not mentioned by Hunt but gaining in significance in the years that have passed since his data were collected, is to do with the applicability of Hofstede's findings to the present situation. There are good reasons to assume that cultures change only very slowly, and some research suggests that the relevance of the cultural differences between countries originally found by Hofstede remains undiminished (Barkema and Vermeulen, 1997). In addition, a 1984 study in 19 European countries replicated Hofstede's dimensions reasonably well (Hoppe, 1990); but the likelihood that all countries in Hofstede's sample will continue to change in the same direction and at the same pace, and that this will be the case in all four (or five) dimensions, seems to be very small. Therefore it seems to be increasingly necessary to obtain new and reliable estimates of the relative positions of countries on Hofstede's dimensions, if the paradigm is to continue to help researchers to make sense of culture (Triandis, 1994).

Shalom Schwartz: three bipolar dimensions of motivational values

Schwartz (1992) provides the most recent research of note and the most substantive challenge to Hofstede's model in that, if validated further, it is likely to become regarded as both more refined and more complete than Hofstede's work. In recognition of the seminal status of Hofstede's work, Schwartz included in his analysis values suitable for uncovering Hofstede's dimensions, and this serves as a 'check on the replicability of the Hofstede dimensions with a different method of measurement' (Schwartz, 1994). The claim is that a more exhaustive examination of values based upon his 1992 study and a more adequate sample of nations will enable the determination of a more universally inclusive model of cultural dimensions which, by implication, will provide a more refined model than Hofstede's (Gatley et al., 1996: 105).

Schwartz's study was originally carried out in 20 countries, but has been expanded continuously (Smith and Schwartz, 1997). Schwartz composed a survey instrument of 56 values from the literature. He used two types of matched sample to enable a check on the robustness of the value dimensions generated. The respondents included schoolteachers and university students, and data was collected between 1988 and 1992 from 86 samples drawn from 41 cultural groups in 38 nations. Schwartz's analysis used the mean scores of his teacher values and, separately, of his student values per country. Schwartz suggested that the content of cultural value dimensions reflects the alternative solutions that emerge as groups cope with basic societal problems. He began with three basic societal problems.

1. Relationships between individual and group: to what extent are persons autonomous versus embedded in groups?

2. Assuring responsible social behaviour: how to motivate people to consider others' welfare and coordinate with them?

3. The role of humankind in the natural and social world: is it more to submit, to fit in or to exploit?

The cultural adaptations that evolve to resolve each of these issues are arrayed along bipolar cultural dimensions. In various phases of his research, Schwartz proposed different model specifications and has used different labels for the value dimensions he distinguishes. We will discuss the most recent version, in which Schwartz specified three bipolar dimensions of national culture, which, to some extent, overlap with some of Hofstede's dimensions (Schwartz and Ros, 1995; Smith and Schwartz, 1997; Sagiv and Schwartz, 2000). In a similar way to Hofstede, Schwartz explains the consequences of differences in national culture for organizations. Schwartz's dimensions are described below.

Embeddedness versus autonomy

In *embedded* cultures, people are viewed as entities embedded in the collectivity who find meaning in life largely through social relationships. Values such as social order, respect for tradition, security and wisdom are especially important. Embedded cultures emphasize maintaining the status quo and restraining actions or inclinations that might disrupt the solidarity of the group or the traditional order. Organizations in such cultures function as extended families. They are likely to take responsibility for their members in all domains of life, and to expect members to identify with and work dutifully towards shared goals.

In *autonomy* cultures, people are viewed as autonomous, bounded entities who find meaning in their own uniqueness and who are encouraged to express their preferences, feelings and motives. Schwartz and colleagues distinguish two types of autonomy: *intellectual autonomy* and *affective autonomy*. Intellectual autonomy encourages individuals to pursue their own ideas and intellectual directions independently (important values are curiosity, broadmindedness and creativity); affective autonomy encourages individuals to pursue actively positive experiences for themselves (values include pleasure, and an exciting and varied life). Organizations in such cultures may be relatively open to change and diversity. They are likely to treat their members as independent actors with their own interests, preferences, abilities and allegiances.

This dimension from Schwartz's model is argued to overlap conceptually to some degree with Hofstede's individualism/collectivism dimensions. Both concern the relationship between the individual and the collective, and both contrast an autonomous view of people with an interdependent view. However, while Schwartz's dimension of autonomy/embeddedness strongly contrasts openness to change with maintaining the status quo, individualism/collectivism does not explicitly do so. Rather, Hofstede sees openness to change (modernism) and maintaining the status quo (traditionalism) as *consequences* of individualism and collectivism, respectively (see Table 2.3).

Hierarchy versus egalitarianism

In *hierarchical* cultures, the unequal distribution of power, roles and resources is seen as legitimate (values include social power, authority, humility and wealth). People are socialized and sanctioned to comply with the obligations and rules attached to their roles. In hierarchical cultures, organizations are likely to emphasize the chain of authority, to assign well-defined roles in a hierarchical structure, and to demand compliance in the service of goals set from the top.

Cultural *egalitarianism* seeks to induce people to recognize one another as moral equals who share basic interests as human beings. It emphasizes transcendence of selfish interests in favour of voluntary behaviour that promotes the welfare of others (values include equality, social justice, responsibility and honesty). People are socialized to internalize a commitment to voluntary cooperation with others and to feel concern for everyone's welfare. Organizations are likely to express egalitarianism by acknowledging the legitimacy of cooperative negotiation among members who flexibly enact their roles and try to affect organizational goals. These goals may include the welfare of group members and of the larger society, not only profitability. Leaders are likely to motivate others by enabling them to share in goal setting and by appealing to the joint welfare of all.

The hierarchy–egalitarianism dimension is said to overlap with Hofstede's power distance. Both are to do with legitimizing social inequality. Power distance refers to the acceptance of inequality by less powerful people. It also expresses their fear of authority. Hofstede sees it as a response to the inevitability of social inequality. Schwartz's hierarchy–egalitarian dimension addresses a different issue: assurance of responsible behaviour that preserves the social fabric. Their capacity to assure responsible behaviour gives hierarchical systems of ascribed roles their legitimacy. Hierarchy does not necessarily entail a preference for distance from authority. Egalitarianism emphasizes the moral equality of individuals, their capacity to internalize commitments to the welfare of others and to cooperate voluntarily with them. These key elements of egalitarianism are absent from low power distance (Sagiv and Schwartz, 2000: 421).

Mastery versus harmony

Mastery-orientated cultures encourage active self-assertion in order to master, change and exploit the natural and social environment to attain personal or group goals (values include ambition, success, daring and competence). Organizations in such cultures are likely to be dynamic, competitive and strongly orientated towards achievement and success.

Harmony-orientated cultures accept the world as it is, trying to comprehend and fit in rather than to change or exploit (values include unity with nature, protecting the environment and world peace). In this view, applying technology to manipulate the environment is problematic and may even be seen as illegitimate. Where harmony is important, organizations are likely to be viewed holistically as systems to be integrated with the larger society, which should minimize competition. Leaders are likely to try to understand the social and environmental implications of organizational actions and to seek non-exploitative ways to work towards organizational goals.

The mastery dimension corresponds to some extent to Hofstede's masculinity dimension. Both emphasize assertiveness and ambition, and both have similar consequences for organizations. However, Hofstede contrasts masculinity with femininity – tenderness, care and concern for others. This implies that masculinity neglects or rejects the interests of others. Schwartz contrasts mastery to harmony – being in tune with others and the environment. Mastery calls for an active, even disruptive, stance, but it does not imply selfishness. Harmony might seem to overlap conceptually with uncertainty avoidance, because both idealize a harmonious order. However, harmony stresses that people and nature can exist together comfortably without the assertion of control. In contrast, uncertainty avoidance emphasizes controlling ambiguity and unpredictability through institutions and beliefs that provide certainty (Sagiv and Schwartz, 2000: 421). The consequences for organizations of harmonious cultures do seem to reflect some of the consequences of feminine cultures, however. Whereas harmony is argued to reduce competition, femininity encourages achievement in terms of service, human contacts, and so on (Table 1.4). Whereas leaders in a harmonious culture are likely to seek non-exploitative ways to work towards organizational goals, feminine cultures are likely to stress equality and solidarity, thus hampering exploitation.

Schwartz's work has some advantages over that of Hofstede, the most important of which are the higher face validity of the items used to operationalize the dimensions, and the measurement characteristics of the scales. On the other hand, the items used by Schwartz are broader than those of Hofstede, which focus on work-related values. This may limit the applicability of Schwartz's framework in the field of comparative international management. Although it has strong theoretical foundations, the usefulness of Schwartz's framework has not yet been established to the same extent as that of Hofstede (Steenkamp, 2001).

Fons Trompenaars: cultural dilemmas

Independently from the above approaches, Trompenaars drew on sociological literature to theoretically derive dimensions of culture that may affect behaviour in business organizations. He developed a questionnaire intended to measure preferred ways of handling five basic elements of social relationships specified by Parsons and Shils (1951), as well as preferred ways of managing in organizations. The questionnaire was meant to tap the values of organizational employees. Questions have been raised, however, regarding the format of many of the items used to measure values (Smith and Schwartz, 1997). During the past decades, about 46,000 managers from over 40 countries have completed the questionnaire. In contrast to Hofstede and Schwartz, Trompenaars did not match the demographic profiles of his samples. Respondents were mostly managers and other employees who attended his training programmes. As indicated, Trompenaars' cultural model consists of six (in earlier work, seven) bipolar dimensions or 'dilemmas'. We will look at each in turn (on the basis of Hampden-Turner and Trompenaars, 2000) and, as far as possible, relate them to Hofstede's dimensions.

Universalism versus particularism

This dimension concerns 'rules' in contrast to 'relationships' as the principal determinants of interpersonal behaviour. In a strongly universalist culture, personal relationships should not interfere with business decisions. Nepotism is frowned on and contractual agreements are the referees of conduct. Logical, rational analytical thinking and impartial professionalism are ideal characteristics to cultivate and standards to maintain. In particularist cultures, institutionalized obligations to friendship and kinship are considered 'moral' requirements, which are maintained through personalism, paternalism and other social network mechanisms. Particularism is statistically associated with Hofstede's individualism–collectivism dimension as particularist cultures are normally also collectivist and, therefore, also high on the power distance dimension (Hofstede, 1980: 229).

Individualism versus communitarianism

Trompenaars' second dimension is almost identical to Hofstede's dimension of individualism–collectivism.

Specificity versus diffuseness

This dimension highlights the difference between cultures that analyse phenomena into *specifics* (i.e. parts, facts, targets, tasks, numbers, units, points), and cultures that integrate and configure such details into diffuse patterns, relationships and wider contexts.

Achieved status versus ascribed status

In some societies, status is accorded on the basis of achievement, whereas others ascribe status on the basis of durable characteristics such as age. This dimension seems conceptually related to both power distance and individualism–collectivism. Achievement in ascriptive cultures is less an individual and more of a collective concern, and organizations in these societies justify a high power distance and the resulting hierarchy as requisite 'power-to-get-things-done'. Power in such cultures does not require legitimizing in the same way as in achievement-orientated cultures and abuse of power is checked by the moral responsibilities inherent in patron–client-type relationships.

Inner-directed orientation versus outer-directed orientation

This dimension distinguishes between cultures in which action is guided by inner-directed judgements, decisions and commitments, and cultures in which action is guided by signals, demands and trends in the outside world. At stake is whether virtue and right direction is located *within* us or *outside* us.

Sequential versus synchronous time

Different attitudes towards time (past, present and future) are reflected by the contrast between notions of time as linear and 'sequential', and notions of time as circular and 'synchronic'. Such differences affect how we coordinate, plan and organize. A 'sequential' culture, where the focus is rational efficiency, is focused on getting things done in the shortest possible sequence of passing time. In contrast, a synchronic culture allows parallel activities and is less orientated towards punctuality. The focus in synchronic cultures is more likely to be on effectiveness than on efficiency.

There is a connection between this dimension and Hofstede and Bond's dimension of long-term versus short-term orientation as 'Individualist cultures with a sequential view of time are usually short-term in their business strategies. Collectivist cultures with a synchronous view of time are typically long-term strategically' (Trompenaars, cited in Gatley *et al.*, 1996: 111).

In Trompenaars' early work a seventh dimension was also distinguished: affective versus neutral. This dimension concerned the extent to which emotions or feelings may be expressed in interpersonal communication. In a later study (Hampden-Turner and Trompenaars, 1994), this dimension was replaced with another one, which was called 'equality versus hierarchy', which appears to resemble closely Hofstede's power distance.

Trompenaars' work is seen as less academically rigorous than Hofstede and Schwartz's work (for a criticism of Trompenaars' work, see Hofstede 1996). For instance, it is not clear to what extent the dilemmas do indeed form independent dimensions. The attractiveness of his work, however, lies in the fact that, more than the other two studies, it offers some practical and intuitively appealing answers for managers involved in cross-cultural ventures.

The message of Trompenaars and Hampden-Turner is to submit that as cultures face dilemmas in relationships with people, with time and with the environment differently, it is necessary to recognize and reconcile differences and attempt to synthesize the advantages inherent in all cultures. It is a reiteration of the view that there is no 'one best way' of managing and no objective truth in how best to generate wealth.

Each of these major studies of culture-level dimensions has yielded mappings of national culture relative to one another. To explore further the relationship between Hofstede, Schwartz and Trompenaars' work we will now compare these mappings.

2.4 Cultural Clusters

Two key questions may be asked here.

1. Do the world's national cultures form meaningful clusters? That is, do the clusters of countries that emerge in an empirical analysis of their value profiles have common or similar histories and/or socio-demographic characteristics that might account for why they have evolved similar cultures?

2. What value profiles characterize these clusters?

The practical implications of cultural clusters can be illustrated through the following example (Ronen and Shenkar, 1985: 447).

An MNC is establishing a venture in Switzerland. The corporation's directors must determine if management skills will be imported from its subsidiaries in France, Germany or Italy. All three languages are spoken in Switzerland, albeit in different areas. The country clustering [see Table 2.6] suggests that managers be brought from Germany because Switzerland and Germany belong to the same cluster of work values. German managers, therefore, can be expected to be closer to and more familiar with workers' attitudes in Switzerland.

Hofstede (2001) reported a hierarchical cluster analysis of 53 countries based on their scores on the four IBM indexes (PDI, UAI, IDV and MAS). This analysis yielded 12 cultural clusters. Hofstede provided value profiles for each culture area. For reasons of brevity, not all of Hofstede's cultural clusters are mentioned here (see Table 2.6).

Schwartz (1994) and Schwartz and Ros (1995) conducted multidimensional scaling analyses using nation scores on the seven culture-level value types Hofstede identified. They replicated these analyses with data both from teachers (44 nations) and students (40 nations). The same six culture areas were clearly distinguishable in both analyses: West European, Anglo, East European, Islamic, East Asian and Latin American. Again, Japan was distinctive. The similarity between the Hofstede and Schwartz culture areas is remarkable. Some of the differences doubtless reflect the different sampling of nations – for example, there are hardly any East European nations in Hofstede.

The value profiles that Schwartz reported for culture areas may also be noted. Similar to Hofstede's findings, he found that western European nations are characterized by a high importance of egalitarianism (or low PDI) and intellectual autonomy (or high IDV), and a low importance of hierarchy (or low PDI) and embeddedness (or collectivism) (Sagiv and Schwartz, 2000).

A second region, encompassing the samples from eastern Europe (Slovenia, Estonia, Slovakia, the Czech Republic, Poland and Hungary) reveals a shared culture that empha-sizes harmony (or high UAI) and embeddedness (low IDV or collectivism), rather than mastery (or low MAS) and both types of autonomy (or low IDV). The indexes from Yugoslavia and Slovenia, the only eastern European countries Hofstede analysed, confirm Schwartz's picture.

Samples or countries from the English-speaking nations share a culture that tends to emphasize mastery (or high MAS) rather than harmony (or low UAI) and affective autonomy (or high IDV) rather than embeddedness (or collectivism).

Schwartz's sample of sub-Saharan African countries (Ghana, Uganda, Namibia, Nigeria and Zimbabwe) reflects strong cultural emphasis on embeddedness (low IDV or collectivist) and hierarchy (or high PDI), little importance placed on affective autonomy (or low IDV) and harmony (low UAI), and very little importance placed on intellectual autonomy (low IDV) and egalitarianism (or high PDI). Hofstede's sample of East and West African countries, to a large extent, shows similar features, the only difference being that Hofstede's sample shows high UAI while the sample from Schwartz tends to reflect that relatively little importance is placed on harmony, which, expressed in Hofstede's dimen-sions, would be low UAI.

Schwartz's samples from East Asia (Singapore, Thailand, Malaysia, Indonesia, the Philippines and Taiwan) also give little emphasis to egalitarianism (or high PDI) and intel-lectual autonomy (low IDV). However, they vary substantially in their emphases on

Table 2.6 Hofstede's country clusters

Clusters	PDI	UAI	IDV	MAS	LTO
Australia	36	51	90	61	31
USA	40	46	91	62	29
Canada	39	48	80	52	23
UK	35	35	89	66	25
Ireland	28	35	70	68	43
New Zealand	22	49	79	58	30
	low	**medium**	**high**	**high**	**low**
Germany	35	65	67	66	31
Switzerland	34	58	68	70	40
South Africa	49	49	65	63	
Italy	50	75	76	70	34
	medium	**high**	**high**	**high**	**medium**
Denmark	18	23	74	16	46
Sweden	31	29	71	5	33
Netherlands	38	53	80	14	44
Norway	31	50	69	8	44
Finland	33	59	63	26	41
	low	**low to medium**	**high**	**low**	**low to medium**
Belgium	65	94	75	54	38
France	68	86	71	43	39
	high	**high**	**high**	**medium**	**low**
Japan	54	92	46	95	80
	medium	**high**	**medium**	**high**	**high**
Austria	11	70	55	79	31
Israel	13	81	54	47	
	low	**high**	**medium**	**high**	
Yugoslavia	76	88	27	21	
Slovenia	71	88	27	19	
Turkey	66	85	37	45	
Arab countries	80	68	38	53	
Greece	60	112	35	57	
Argentina	49	86	46	56	
Spain	57	86	51	42	19
Brazil	69	76	38	49	65

	high	high	low	medium	
Venezuela	81	76	12	73	
Colombia	67	80	13	64	
Mexico	81	82	30	69	
	high	high	low	high	
Indonesia	78	48	14	46	
Thailand	64	64	20	34	56
Taiwan	58	69	17	45	87
East Africa	64	52	27	41	25
West Africa	77	54	20	46	16
	high	high	low	medium	
Malaysia	104	36	26	50	
Philippines	94	44	32	64	19
India	77	40	48	56	61
Singapore	74	8	20	48	48

Source: adapted from Hofstede (2001).

mastery and harmony. China and, to a lesser extent, India attribute high importance to mastery (or high MAS) and low importance to harmony (or low UAI); other countries from East Asia are more moderate on these values. This is largely confirmed by Hofstede's findings (see Table 2.6). In comparison with adjacent countries, Japan places more emphasis on intellectual autonomy (or higher IDV in Hofstede's model), and on mastery (Japan scores higher on MAS than India in Hofstede's model). Japan places higher emphasis on harmony, which is expressed in a higher score for UAI in the Hofstede model.

Smith *et al.* (1996) present a plot of 43 nations on their two meaningful dimensions. Two clear culture areas emerge, one for eastern Europe and the other for northern Europe. Somewhat less clear Far Eastern, Latin and Anglo areas are also discernible. The overlap of these results with those reported by Hofstede and Schwartz is substantial. The northern European cluster was high on egalitarian commitment and on utilitarian involvement. According to the items that formed these dimensions, this profile signifies a cultural emphasis on achievement of status through personal merit, equality of individual rights and rejection of paternalism, together with an emphasis on utilitarian rather than loyalty considerations in interpersonal relations. This profile is virtually the same one as found by Schwartz for western Europe (Smith and Schwartz, 1997: 105).

The eastern European cluster, like the northern European one, was high on utilitarian involvement, but it was also high on conservatism. Thus it differed in emphasizing acceptance of a hierarchical, paternalistic system of ascribed roles rather than an emphasis on individual rights and responsibilities. This profile is very similar to the one Schwartz found for the eastern European culture area, one that emphasized conservatism and hierarchy at the expense of autonomy, egalitarianism and mastery values (Smith and Schwartz, 1997: 106).

The convergence regarding two culture-level dimensions in all the studies that have covered numerous countries could be taken as an indication that the major dimensions of culture-level variation in values have been identified. Moreover, because these studies used data obtained in different ways and from different types of sample, it is apparent that they are relatively robust. There is also evidence that they are relatively stable over time. They emerged both from Hofstede's data, collected nearly 30 years ago, and from much more recent studies. Moreover, the Schwartz (1994) analysis yielded similar structures of values among samples of rich and of poor nations. This would not be expected if the massive changes that accompany socio-economic development also cause change in the structure of values.

A warning is apposite, however. The dimensions that emerge from these studies are affected by the locations that are sampled. No study has sampled many more than 50 of the nearly 200 current national entities. Europe, North America and the Pacific Rim are well represented, but African and Arab countries are badly under-represented in all studies. Moreover, the dimensions that emerge are affected by the values included in the survey questionnaires. It is clearly too early to foreclose on the possibility that further theorizing and consideration of values found in indigenous studies will yet point to additional major dimensions (Smith and Schwartz, 1997).

2.5 The Emic Approach

There seems to be an imbalance in the use of etic and emic approaches to culture in comparative international management. Clearly the etic approaches are better known among management scholars. These approaches also come up with quantitative yardsticks for comparing different national cultures, which can be used to operationalize the cultural factor in comparative international research. This is one of the main reasons for the very extensive use of Hofstede's work in management studies, in particular international management. However, there is a danger to this rather one-sided concentration on the etic approach. This is that scholars and practitioners less familiar with the background of the studies will apply the dimensions scores uncritically, as if these represented *the* culture of the countries in question. This is also at least partly due to the fact that emic scholars have so far shown far less interest in cross-cultural management issues. However, the overemphasis on etic approaches, and in particular the quantitative findings, isolated from more qualitative interpretations, leads to *reification* of the dimensions: what was developed as a tool for interpreting complex datasets comes to be seen as an inherent aspect of reality. The conceptual lenses developed by Hofstede and other etic scholars can thus become blinkers: because we expect to find differences in, for example, power distance, we see them everywhere, and we are likely to miss the many other differences that may also exist. Therefore we think that it is essential that students of comparative international management are familiar with both the etic and the emic approach, as this will provide them with a more balanced and critical view. Below we will briefly present the work of one emic researcher who focuses explicitly on management and organization from a cross-cultural perspective: Philippe d'Iribarne.

Philippe d'Iribarne: the logics of culture

The French researcher Philippe d'Iribarne explicitly confronts in his work the findings of etic research using findings from his own emic studies. From this perspective, the limitations of etic research are serious. We will discuss d'Iribarne's criticism of the application of Hofstede's power distance scale in France as an example. After that, we will discuss d'Iribarne's concept of culture, which is representative for today's emic researchers, and then present a summary of the findings of d'Iribarne's main work, *La Logique de l'Honneur* (d'Iribarne, 1989).

Limitations of the etic approach

On the basis of his own ethnographic research into French work organizations, d'Iribarne takes issue with Hofstede's finding that French culture would be characterized by a rather large power distance (68, compared with 40 and 38 for both other countries studied in detail by d'Iribarne, the USA and the Netherlands, respectively). This large power distance raises questions for d'Iribarne, for it is higher than that of, for instance, Iran, South Korea, Chile, Turkey or Colombia. It puts France (and Belgium, which in Hofstede's study is closely associated with France) out on a limb as the only non-autocratic nation between the large power distance countries (d'Iribarne, 1996–97). The core of the problem, according to d'Iribarne, is that in Hofstede's power distance dimension the notions of power and hierarchy are conflated. From his own research, as well as from other ethnographic studies of French work organizations, d'Iribarne concludes that 'in the case of France, the notions of hierarchy and power are by no means the same' (d'Iribarne, 1996–97: 36):

> In fact, the existence of a large *symbolic distance* among the various levels of the hierarchy does not in any way mean that the *balance of power* in France particularly favors the upper levels of the hierarchy. One could even say that, to some degree, the existence of a large hierarchical distance tends not to strengthen but rather to limit the power of the bosses. (d'Iribarne, 1996–97: 37; original emphasis).

Looking at how the high score for France was obtained in Hofstede's study, d'Iribarne demonstrates clearly the limitations of questionnaire approaches in general, and Hofstede's instrument in particular. Hofstede's power distance scale is made up of the following three questions:

1. How frequently are employees afraid to express disagreements with their managers?
2. Under which manager would the respondent prefer to work (choosing between descriptions of what can be described as 'autocratic', 'persuasive/paternalistic', 'consultative' and 'democratic' (Hofstede 2001: 85)?
3. To which of the above-mentioned four types of manager does the respondent's own manager correspond most closely?

Unsurprisingly, the less often employees are afraid to express disagreement with their managers, the lower the power distance score. But the interpretation of the 'preferred manager' and 'perceived manager' questions is less straightforward. In the 'preferred manager' question, a preference for a consultative manager is associated with a lower score on power distance. But in the 'perceived manager' question, lower scores on power distance are associated with *not* preferring an autocratic manager or a persuasive/paternalistic manager. Note that a preference for a democratic manager is *not* associated with a lower score on power distance. Hofstede sees this choice as unrealistic, as it is unlikely to be effective in work organizations. He interprets this choice as a 'counterdependent reaction' to a situation of large power distance (Hofstede, 2001: 86). But d'Iribarne notes that the Netherlands scores less hierarchically than the USA with regard to the *preferred* manager, but more hierarchically than the USA with regard to the *perceived* manager. In d'Iribarne's own research, the Americans emerged as much more hierarchical than the Dutch, who, among other things, 'vigorously resisted American methods of command, which they judged too authoritarian' (d'Iribarne, 1996–97: 40).

According to d'Iribarne the hierarchical distance in France may be large, but this is mainly symbolic. Hierarchical position does not yield much power to managers, because it actually separates them from their subordinates.

> Thus, forepersons can be observed stressing the lowly nature of their practical skills, compared with the more theoretical knowledge possessed by engineers, while at the same time they exploit this divergence to keep engineers out of the sphere under their own control. (d'Iribarne, 1996–97: 37)

On the basis of these and other observations, d'Iribarne questions the adequacy of Hofstede's interpretation of the French situation. He calls for a more idiographic approach, using ethnographic methodology. Although d'Iribarne gives little detail of his preferred methodology, some elements are clear from his work. In the preface to his book *La Logique de l'Honneur* (1989) he states that he could not be satisfied with the superficial view that would arise from surveys and some interviews with top managers. Instead he chose to concentrate on a very restricted research object: one single plant of an internationally operating company in each of three different countries (France, the USA and the Netherlands). In these plants, direct observations were combined with documents reflecting daily life and with open interviews (d'Iribarne, 1994: 82). These plant-level data were coupled with multiple data sources concerning the countries in which these plants were located. Putting such data next to each other, the observations at plant level started to resonate with country-level sources about the ways in which individuals relate to collectivities, in which good can be distinguished from bad, legitimate from illegitimate, what is respectable from what is not respectable or what is indifferent (d'Iribarne, 1989: 11–12). In this way the logic governing the phenomena, both at the micro level and at the level of the society, was uncovered. In essence, d'Iribarne's study was a quest for *meaning*:

> I have made an effort, in each of the localities, to understand the behaviours that could be observed, sometimes odd to the stranger's eye, starting from what gave them meaning to those who adopted those behaviours. (d'Iribarne, 1989: 14; our translation)

This method of trying to comprehend the meaning attributed to behaviour by local actors, in d'Iribarne's view, leads to 'a more certain and precise understanding of the societies under investigation [even if] it does not give the same impression of objectivity' (d'Iribarne, 1996–97: 46). We will now examine d'Iribarne's findings concerning the cultural logics of France, the USA and the Netherlands.

The logics of honour, contract and consensus

In his principal book, Philippe d'Iribarne (d'Iribarne, 1989; summarized briefly in d'Iribarne, 1996–97) reports on a study of three aluminium production units of the French company Péchiney, in France, the USA and the Netherlands. The plants were selected to employ the same technology, so that they would be comparable with regard to the main contingency factors. Nevertheless, marked differences between the 'collective lives' within the three plants are noticeable.

In France, d'Iribarne observes that the various professional groups are attached to the privileges determined by the particular traditions of each group. These traditions define what individual members of an occupational group should do, and also what they cannot stoop to. The interesting thing is that this definition of what one should and should not do is completely independent from instructions or orders from superiors. Professional pride does not allow an employee to bow to pressure from above, if this would go against the honour of his or her professional group. This emphasis on pride and honour is connected by d'Iribarne to Montesquieu's analysis of French society in the eighteenth century. The influence sphere of each professional group in the organization, from top to bottom, should be respected if managers want to avoid revolt or deceit.

> It would be degrading to be 'in the service of' (*au service de*) anybody, in particular, of one's superiors. By contrast, it is honorable to devote oneself to a cause, or to 'give service' (*rendre service*) with magnanimity, at least if one is asked to do so with due ceremony. Under these circumstances, the realization of hierarchical relationships requires a great deal of tact and judgment. (d'Iribarne, 1996–97: 32)

In the USA a different logic prevails: the logic of the contract, freely entered into by equals. According to d'Iribarne in the US culture, an organization is seen as 'an interlocking set of contractual relationships', and 'great importance is attached to the decentralization of decision making, to the definition of objectives, and to the rigor of evaluation' (d'Iribarne, 1996–97: 31). The link between the individual employee and the organization, as well as that between the subordinate, and the superior, is an agreement specifying what the parties may expect of each other. The employee may expect to be evaluated against explicit criteria that are well known in advance; there should be no room for subjective opinions or feelings from the side of the superior. Hence, on one hand the American manager has more degrees of freedom than his or her French counterpart, as he or she is considered free to set the goals for the employee (who in turn is free to accept or reject these goals, and face the consequences of either option). However, once the superior and subordinate agree on a set of goals, the evaluation criteria the manager can employ are also defined. The resulting style of management and organization is linked by d'Iribarne by Tocqueville's description of the 'democratic' relationships between masters and servants in nineteenth-century America.

In the plant in the Netherlands, d'Iribarne identified yet another cultural logic. Here there were no sharp divisions between occupational groups, each with their own traditions and pride, nor was there strict adherence to agreements. Instead, what struck d'Iribarne was the process of discussion and argument necessary to settle disputes, which were reopened as soon as the conditions of the environment changed. The use of discussion and argumentation, on the basis of factual information, was used both between equals and between superiors and subordinates. To be a manager in Holland means to be a master of argument and persuasion, as the use of severe sanctions is not acceptable. Overt, or even covert, pressure is to be avoided. D'Iribarne's view of Dutch work organizations corresponds very well to what is found in a number of Dutch sources (summarized in Noorderhaven, 2002).

The Dutch style of consensus management is linked by d'Iribarne to the political history of the Netherlands. The origin of Dutch institutions lies in the association of provinces in the Union of Utrecht (1579). In the delicate balance between the provinces, lengthy processes of persuasion and mutual accommodation were necessary to reach decisions. Also in more recent times, the cohabitation of the different religious groups (mainly the Protestants and the Catholics) was regulated through the same mechanisms (d'Iribarne, 1996–97: 33).

2.6 National Cultures and Cross-cultural Negotiations

In this final section of the chapter we will discuss from a cross-cultural perspective a very important aspect of doing business across borders, namely international negotiations. Negotiations play an important role in business, as the essential characteristic of economic transactions in a market system is that the parties enter into an agreement of their own free will. In an efficiently functioning market, both parties can also consider alternatives (i.e. there are multiple potential sellers and buyers). In the negotiation process with a particular potential business partner what is at stake is closing a deal that is better than that which could be effected with the most attractive alternative partner. The negotiation process takes place under the shadow of the 'best alternative to negotiated agreement', or BATNA (Lewicki *et al.*, 1994). Each party's BATNA will strongly influence what their minimally acceptable outcome in the negotiation process is. If the other party is not willing to make sufficient concessions, it is better to break off the negotiations and go to the most attractive alternative business partner.

Looking at negotiation processes in a schematic way, two possibilities exist. Either there is an overlap between the parties' 'zones of acceptance' (the set of possible deals they are willing to accept, with the lower limit defined by their BATNAs), or there is no overlap. In the latter case an effective communication process should make this clear to the parties, and the negotiation process will come to an end. The problem is that communication processes are not always very straightforward, and this is particularly the case in international negotiations. In the first case (when there is overlap between the parties' zones of acceptance), the ultimate outcome of the negotiation remains indeterminate. The parties may end up with any deal that is acceptable to both, depending on their negotiation skills, the quality and quantity of available information, and the circumstances in which the negotiation takes place. But they may also end up without a deal, simply because the communication process makes them believe that there is *no* overlap between their zones of acceptance. The reason for this is that information is often deliberately misrepresented in negotiations, as negotiators try to get the best deal possible.

Negotiation processes may be ubiquitous in business in general; they are an even more salient characteristic of international business, and levels of complexity and uncertainty in the international arena are also greater. Multinational corporations (MNCs) may negotiate with national governments over the conditions under which they are allowed to invest and to do business in a country. For instance, before Intel Corporation decided to invest in a US$300 million chip plant in Costa Rica it went through a lengthy and complex negotiation process with local political authorities and representatives of institutions (Spar, 1998). Companies may also, however, negotiate with other companies in countries that they seek to enter through exports or licensing, or with a strategic alliance or joint venture. Once active in another country, managers of a company may find themselves engaged in negotiations with local institutions like trade unions or employers' associations. Furthermore, processes *within* MNCs often have characteristics of negotiation, even if the parties involved are not independent, but parts of the same company. For instance, an MNC's headquarters may find itself negotiating certain policies with a local subsidiary (rather than commanding it to act in a certain way) because it believes local subsidiary managers' views and interests have to be taken into account if good results are to be achieved. Finally, managers of one subsidiary of an MNC may negotiate deals with other subsidiaries without much interference from company headquarters, as is increasingly common in complex 'networked' MNCs (see Chapter 9). In many of these cases, the negotiators and their constituencies (the companies or parts of companies they represent in the negotiation process) are from different cultures. We will now take a quick look at the ways in which cultural differences may influence negotiation processes.

Figure 2.1 shows the elements of an intercultural negotiation process in a schematic form. Each negotiation process takes place within a particular social situation.[1] This means, for instance, that the negotiators fulfil certain roles (e.g. that of buyer or seller), stand in particular relationships with their constituencies (e.g. as senior manager or as country representative), and may face certain deadlines or other restrictions. These situational factors influence the negotiators, their perception of the situation, their judgement, and their motives and goals. All these factors in turn influence their behaviour in the negotiation process (e.g. more cooperative or more competitive behaviour, the amount of information disclosed, etc.). What makes negotiation processes so complex is the feedback loop from the other party's behaviour to the negotiator's interpretation of the negotiation process. There is a dynamic interplay between one's behaviours, the interpretation of these behaviours by the counterpart, his or her response, and one's own interpretation of the negotiation process (Bazerman and Carroll, 1987). For this reason, negotiation processes always have an element of unpredictability.

Possible cultural influences on international negotiation processes are also indicated in Figure 2.1. Previous research on intercultural negotiation processes has often yielded unclear, or even inconsistent, results. For instance, some researchers find that the extent to which negotiators reciprocate cooperative problem solving behaviour by their counterparts does not differ significantly between cultures. However, in other studies such differences *are* identified, for example the Japanese were more likely to reciprocate than

---

[1] The discussion in this section is based on Gelfand and Dyer (2000).

both Americans and Brazilians (Allerheiligen *et al.*, 1985). This suggests that the influences of culture on negotiations are not very straightforward. This is reflected in Figure 2.1. Cultural influences work out on (1) the social situation in which the negotiations take place; (2) the way in which this social situation influences the perceptions, judgements, motives, goals, and so on, of the negotiators; (3) directly on these perceptions, and so on; and (4) on the way in which these perceptions and so on influence the behaviour of the negotiators. We will give some examples of each of these.

Figure 2.1 Influences of culture on negotiations

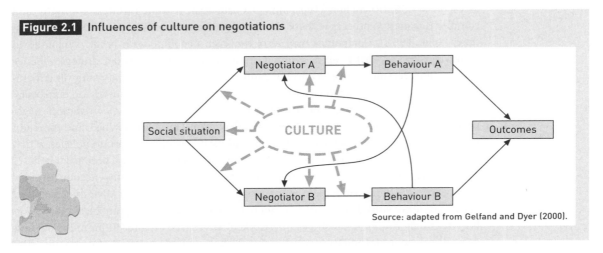

Source: adapted from Gelfand and Dyer (2000).

Gelfand and Dyer (2000) state that the prevalence of types of social situation is likely to differ between cultures. For instance, in more collectivist cultures the negotiator is more likely to be a member of a group, even at the negotiating table, than in more individualistic cultures. Japanese companies are well known for sending large delegations to negotiations with other companies, to the representatives of which the roles of the various Japanese delegates often remain unclear. These authors also expect that in cultures high on Schwartz's mastery dimension negotiators, because they strive for achievement and success, will feel more time pressure during the negotiation than negotiators from cultures orientated towards harmony. The organizational context is also likely to vary with the cultural environment. Organizations from large power distance societies will have more centralized control, with the effect that key negotiations have to be concluded by the top authority (Hofstede and Usunier, 1997).

Culture may also mediate the influence of the social situation on the negotiator. Laboratory experiments show that if negotiators are required to justify their actions to their constituencies after the negotiations, this leads to more cooperative behaviour in terms of ego and cooperative interpretations of the behaviour of the other for collectivists, but to more competitive behaviour and interpretations of the other's behaviour among individualists (Gelfand and Realo, 1999). In large power distance cultures, roles have a stronger influence on negotiation processes and outcomes than in cultures with a smaller power distance (Graham *et al.*, 1994).

Culture also influences directly the perceptions, judgements, motivations, goals, and so on, of negotiators. The negotiation context is not given objectively, but is a cognitive construct of the negotiators, based on the information they receive, but also on their culturally coloured expectations. Individuals use various kinds of 'cognitive heuristics' (subconscious 'rules of thumb') to make sense of ambiguous situations. One way to make sense of a situation is to use metaphors linking the unfamiliar with the familiar. Americans may be more likely to use (competitive) sports metaphors in interpreting negotiation situations, whereas the Japanese would rather be expected to use (more cooperative) family household metaphors (Gelfand and Dyer, 2000). Culture may influence the goals negotiators pursue particularly strongly. Whereas each party will try to get the best outcome of the negotiation process for him or her and his or her constituency, there are also subsidiary goals like the preservation of a good relationship, which may carry more or less weight, depending on the culture. In more collectivist cultures maintaining a good relationship and saving both the 'face' of the negotiation partner and the respect he or she has for ego may be expected to carry relatively more weight. In more masculine (Hofstede) or mastery-orientated (Schwartz) cultures, there will be a strong emphasis on competitive goals ('winning' the negotiation), if necessary at the expense of the relationship (Hofstede and Usunier, 1997; Gelfand and Dyer, 2000).

Case: Who has Formal Decision Rights?[2]

"When Honda invested heavily in an extensive relationship with British car manufacturer Rover, workers and managers at the two companies developed very positive working relationships for more than a decade. The partnership intensified after the government sold Rover to British Aerospace (BAe), but as Rover continued to lose money, BAe decided to discard the relationship, abruptly selling Rover to BMW through a secretive deal that caught Honda completely unaware. The Japanese auto maker had considered its connection with Rover a long-term one, much like a marriage, and it had shared advanced product and process technology with Rover well beyond its effective contractual ability to protect these assets. Honda's leaders were dumbfounded and outraged that BAe could sell – and to a competitor no less. Yet, while Honda's prized relationship was at the level of the *operating* company (Rover), the Japanese company had not taken seriously enough the fact that the decision rights over a Rover sale are vested at the *parent* (BAe) level. From a financial standpoint, the move made sense for BAe, and it was perfectly legal. Yet Honda's cultural blinkers made the sale seem inconceivable, and its disproportionate investment in Rover in effect created a major economic opportunity for BAe. The bottom line: understanding both formal decision rights and cultural assumptions in less familiar settings can be vital."

Finally, culture may mediate the relationship between a negotiator's psychic state and his or her behaviour in the negotiation. In other words, the same interpretations, goals, and so on, may lead to different behaviours in different cultures. For instance, the norms concerning the display of emotions differ between cultures. Hence, negotiators

[2] An excerpt from Sebenius, J.K. (2002) The hidden challenge of cross-border negotiations. Harvard Business Review 80(3) p. 6.

from different cultures may be equally infuriated by certain kinds of behaviour, but show their anger to a different extent. This, in turn, may lead to inaccurate interpretations by their counterparts of the effects of the negotiation tactics employed. In negotiating with the Japanese a westerner may get the impression that rational arguments carry little weight: they do not seem to be able to change the opinion of the Japanese negotiators. But, as observed by Sebenius (2002: 84), 'in Japan, the negotiating table is not a place for changing minds. Persuasive appeals are not appropriate or effectual'. The reason for this is that the position taken by the Japanese negotiators is very often based on consensus within the constituency. Changing that position is only possible if a new consensus is first reached, which tends to be a highly time-consuming process.

As the discussion above illustrates, the influences of culture on negotiation processes are too complex to allow for simple recommendations for managers. But it is clear that managers negotiating across cultures should be aware of the various possible influences depicted in Figure 2.1. This figure may also serve as a warning. Negotiators may be inclined to see the individuals they are dealing with too much as representatives of their culture; but the characteristics of an individual can never be reduced to a cultural stereo-type. Rather, negotiators should try to understand the behaviour of their counterparts by also taking into account the wider situation in which the negotiation process is embedded (and which itself may be culturally influenced, as discussed above). Hence, the negotiator should 'along with assessing the person across the table, [figure out] the intricacies of the larger organization behind her' (Sebenius, 2002: 85). Finally, one should never forget that language deficiencies may play an important role in international negotiations. A sense of humour, for instance, can be very difficult to express in a foreign language, especially when one's command of that language is far from perfect. The use of interpreters may help in some respects, but at the same time may introduce yet other difficulties. For instance, if one directly addresses the interpreter rather than one's counterpart, the latter may take this as a sign of disrespect (Mead, 1998: 246). Interpreters may also make mistakes, particularly in translating slang or jokes.

Study Questions

1. Explain the concept of culture and how can it be measured at different levels of analysis.

2. Explain the differences between 'etic' and 'emic' approaches to the study of cultures.

3. What is meant by the 'ecological fallacy' and the 'reverse ecological fallacy'?

4. What is meant by 'dimensions' and 'typologies' of cultures?

5. Describe and evaluate the most important research methods employed by 'etic' and 'emic' researchers.

6. What are the dimensions of culture identified by Hofstede, and what are their implications for management and organization?

7. Explain and comment on the most important criticisms of Hofstede's work?

8. What are the dimensions of culture identified by Schwartz, and how do they relate to those of Hofstede?

9. What are the dimensions of culture identified by Trompenaars?

10. What are the main limitations of 'etic' approaches, from an 'emic' perspective?

11. Describe the 'cultural logics' of management in France, the USA and the Netherlands according to d'Iribarne.

12. In what ways can culture influence international negotiations?

Further Reading

Bakhtari, H. (1995) Cultural effects on management style. *International Studies of Management and Organization* 25(3), 97–118.

The study examines the effect of culture on the management style of immigrant Middle Eastern managers in the USA.

Hall, E.T. and Hall, M.R. (1990) *Understanding Cultural Differences*. Yarmouth, USA: Intercultural Press.

The authors offer yet another framework within the emic approach to national culture, elaborating on the concepts of low and high context, and their implications for understanding and communicating with people from different cultural backgrounds.

Hofstede, G. (2001) *Culture's Consequences* (2nd edn). London: Sage.

This book offers a quite complete picture of culture research.

Punnett, B.J. and Shenkar, O. (1998) *Handbook for International Management Research*. New Delhi: Beacon Books.

This book deals in an accessible way with research design and methodology for international management research.

Segalla, M., Fischer, L. and Sandner, K. (2000) Making cross-cultural research relevant to European integration: old problem – new approach. *European Management Journal* 18(1), 38–51.

This paper reports the results of a study of European managerial values. The authors conducted a six-country study of over 900 managers working in 70 companies in the European financial sector.

Case: Unisource

Source: Van Marrewijk (1997, 1999).

The opening of European national telecoms markets to (international) competition, which started in the 1980s, constituted both an opportunity and a threat for national providers like the Netherlands' PTT Telecom. The threat was, of course, the possibility that new providers would take away business in the domestic market. The option to expand internationally was the opportunity, and PTT Telecom embarked enthusiastically on this course to compensate for the potential setback of loss of domestic market share. The first large-scale international experience of Dutch PTT Telecom was the cooperation in Unisource. This strategic alliance was meant to help the companies involved to expand their international activities, initially focusing on data communication. (Unisource was established in 1992 as a strategic alliance between Dutch PTT and Telia from Sweden.) In the period 1992–94 Swiss Telecom, Spanish Telefonica and AT&T joined the alliance. However, the cooperation did not last very long: Unisource fell apart in 1998 after various partners had joined rival alliances.

From a cultural point of view, it is interesting to note that perceptions of cultural differences between the members of the alliance shifted over time. Early in the alliance's development, Dutch PTT Telecom managers cherished the following stereotypes (according to Van Marrewijk, 1997: 373).

- 'Swiss colleagues are trustworthy, thoughtful, very formal and love to write official letters. They have no international experience and are afraid of losing control; that's why they have so many rules.'

- 'Spanish colleagues are informal, proud of their advanced technical knowledge and wide international experience. They do not speak English, eat at impossible times and exclude foreigners from their informal networks.'

- 'Swedish colleagues are very much like us, not formal, people orientated and enjoy discussions. But they also differ on many points: they have endless discussions, do not take any decisions, have less planning and control, and their work attitude varies with the climate: in the winter it is too dark to work, in the summer it is too sunny to work.'

However, these early expectations were subsequently put to the test in the evolving process of cooperation. Taking a schematic and static approach, one would expect cultural differences between the Dutch and the Spanish to be much more pronounced than those between the Dutch and the Swedes in terms of the four dimensions of Hofstede (see Figure 2.2).

In practice, the extent to which cultural differences were felt to lead to real difficulties depended very much on how the alliance evolved over time. Whereas the cultural difference between the Dutch and the Swedes was the smallest between the various alliance partners, the negative emotions from the Dutch towards the Swedes became stronger and stronger, as parent company Telia gradually shifted its attention to an alliance with other Nordic providers, and lost interest in Unisource. The cultural gap between the Dutch and the Spanish, in contrast, seemed to disappear as the Spanish came to be seen as the more reliable alliance partners.

Question

1. Use the emic perspective to reflect on the phenomenon of shifting perceptions of cultural differences over time as a function of the evolution of the alliance.

Figure 2.2 Cultural differences between the Netherlands, Sweden and Spain (cumulative over four Hofstede dimensions)

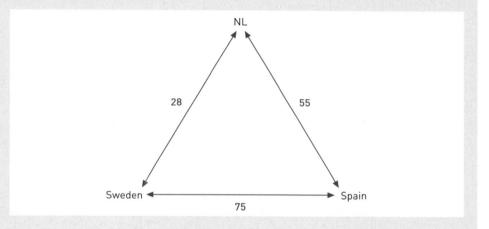

Case: Management of Phosphate Mining in Senegal

Source: Grisar (1997) and general information on Senegalese phosphate mining and processing.

The Senegalese mining industry is dominated by phosphate mining, and phosphate-related exports are a major currency earner for the country. In 1994 a merger between the Compagnie Senegalaise des Phosphates de Taiba (CSPT) and the Industries Chimiques du Senegal (ICS) made CSPT/ICS the dominant player in the regional phosphate mining and processing industry. The CSPT, on which this case focuses, was founded in 1957 with French capital and imported technology. It started production and export in 1960, the year of Senegal's independence. In 1975 the Senegalese state took a 50 per cent interest in the company's shareholdings. In 1980 the process of 'Senegalization' of the management of the company took a new turn when the first Senegalese exploitation manager took over, and for the first time in history the company had more Senegalese than

French managers (27 versus 16). During the 1980s, labour relations and relationships with the unions gradually deteriorated. Concurrently, the company suffered from declining productivity until its absorption by ICS. A superficial reading of the history of the firm might conclude from the simultaneity of Senegalization and decline that the Senegalese managers were less capable than their French predecessors. However, such an attribution would be too easy. Closer inspection shows that the Senegalese managers were trained by the French, and practised the same management style as the French. But, paradoxically, what was effective when practised by the French did not work for their Senegalese successors. Senegalese employees, looking back at the period when the French managed the company, expressed positive sentiments (quoted in Grisar, 1997: 235):

- 'We used to be like a big family in former times.'

- 'Before we were all equal.'

- 'You were respected for good work and efforts no matter what position in the hierarchy you had.'

The perception of equality voiced in these quotes is surprising, as during French rule there was a very clear-cut hierarchy, the French being the bosses and the Senegalese the subordinates. When interviewing Senegalese workers about the conduct of the former French and the present Senegalese managers Grisar (1997: 238) made the striking observation that 'Senegalese managers lost respect among workers for the same behaviour for which the French had been respected.' Apparently what was acceptable, or even laudable when coming from the French, was interpreted very differently when coming from fellow countrymen. According to Grisar the key to understanding this paradox is the isolation of the French expatriates in Senegalese society, and their ignorance of caste and class differences and affiliations, which normally determine an individual's status in Senegalese society. Because the French were in a special position, outside the fabric of the networks of society, Senegalese subordinates tended to accept their decisions as impartial. The same decisions taken by Senegalese managers, in contrast, were often explained on the basis of the social relationships (or lack of such) between superior and subordinate. Hence the acceptability of managerial decisions depended on the motives ascribed to the manager taking the decisions, with systematically different (social) motives being ascribed to fellow Senegalese than to the French.

Questions:

1. To what extent can the relative failure of Senegalese management at CSPT be explained by the positions of France and Senegal in Hofstede's five dimensions of culture (see Table 2.6)?

2. What would you recommend the management of CSPT/ICS do in order to improve the effectiveness of its management?

References

Allerheiligen, R., Graham, J.L. and Lin, C.-Y. (1985) Honesty in interorganizational negotiations in the United States, Japan, and the Republic of China. *Journal of Macromarketing* 5, 4–16.

Barkema, H.G. and Vermeulen, F. (1997) What differences in the cultural backgrounds of partners are detrimental for international joint ventures? *Journal of International Business Studies* 28, 845–64.

Bazerman, M.H. and Carroll, J.S. (1987) Negotiator cognition. *Research in Organizational Behavior* 9, 247–88.

Chapman, M. (1996–97) Social anthropology, business studies, and cultural issues. *International Studies of Management & Organization* 26(4), 3–29.

Chinese Culture Connection (1987) Chinese values and the search for culture-free dimensions of culture. *Journal of Cross-Cultural Psychology* 18, 143–74.

d'Iribarne, Ph. (1989) *La Logique de l'Honneur: Gestion des Entreprises et Traditions Nationales*. Paris: Editions du Seuil.

d'Iribarne, Ph. (1994) The honour principle in the 'Bureaucratic Phenomenon'. *Organization Studies* 15, 81–97.

d'Iribarne, Ph. (1996–97) The usefulness of an ethnographic approach to the international comparison of organizations. *International Studies of Management and Organization* 26(4), 30–47.

Fang, T. (2003) A critique of Hofstede's fifth national culture dimension. *International Journal of Cross Cultural Management* 3, 347–68.

Gatley, S., Leesem, R. and Altmna, Y. (eds) (1996) *Comparative Management: a Transcultural Odyssey*. London: McGraw-Hill.

Geertz, C. (1983) *Local Knowledge: Further Essays in Interpretive Anthropology*. New York: Basic Books.

Gelfand, M.J. and Dyer, N. (2000) A cultural perspective on negotiation: progress, pitfalls, and prospects. *Applied Psychology: an International Review* 49, 62–99.

Gelfand, M.J. and Realo, A. (1999) Collectivism and accountability in intergroup negotiations. *Journal of Applied Psychology* 84, 721–36.

Graham, J.L., Mintu, A.T. and Rodgers, W. (1994) Explorations of negotiation behaviors in ten foreign cultures using a model developed in the United States. *Management Science* 40, 70–95.

Grisar, K. (1997) Globalization of work culture: African and European industrial cooperation in Senegal. *Research in the Sociology of Work* 6, 223–46.

Hampden-Turner, C.M. and Trompenaars, F. (1994) *The Seven Cultures of Capitalism*. London: Piatkus.

Hampden-Turner, C.M. and Trompenaars, F. (2000) *Building Cross-cultural Competence*. Chichester: John Wiley & Sons.

Hofstede, G. (1980) *Culture's Consequences*. London: Sage.

Hofstede, G. (1991) *Cultures and Organizations: Software of the Mind*. London: McGraw-Hill.

Hofstede, G. (1994) Foreword, in Kim, U., Triandis, H.C., Kagitcibasi, C., Choi, S.-C. and Yoon, G. (eds), *Individualism and Collectivism: Theory, Method, and Applications*. Thousand Oaks, CA: Sage, ix–xiii.

Hofstede, G. (1996) Riding the waves of commerce: a test of Trompenaars' 'Model' of national culture differences. *International Journal of Intercultural Relations* 20(2), 189–98.

Hofstede, G. (2001) *Culture's Consequences* (2nd edn). London: Sage.

Hofstede, G. and Usunier, J.-C. (1997) Hofstede's dimensions of culture and their influence on international business negotiations, in Ghauri, P.N. and Usunier, J.-C. (eds) *International Business Negotiations*. Amsterdam: Elsevier-Pergamon, 119–29.

Hoppe, M.H. (1990) *A Comparative Study of Country Elites*. Unpublished doctoral dissertation, University of North Carolina at Chapel Hill.

Hunt, J.W. (1981) Applying American behavioral science: some cross-cultural problems. *Organizational Dynamics* (Summer 1981), 55–61.

Inkeles, A. and Levinson, D.J. (1997) National character: the study of modal personality and sociocultural systems, in Lindzey, G. and Aronson, E. (eds) *Handbook of Social Psychology*, Vol. 4, 418–506. New York: McGraw-Hill (original work published 1954).

Leung, K. and Bond, M. (1989) On the empirical identification of dimensions for cross-cultural comparisons. *Journal of Cross-Cultural Psychology* 20, 133–51.

Lewicki, R.J., Litterer, J.A., Minton, J.W. and Saunders, D.M. (1994) *Negotiation*. McGraw-Hill: New York.

McSweeney, B. (2002) Hofstede's model of national cultural differences and their consequences: a triumph of faith – a failure of analysis. *Human Relations* 55, 89–118.

Maznevski, M.L., DiStefano, J.J., Gomez, C.B., Noorderhaven, N.G. and Wu, P.-C. (2002) Cultural dimensions at the individual level of analysis: the cultural orientations framework. *International Journal of Cross Cultural Management* 2, 275–95.

Mead, R. (1998) *International Management: Cross-cultural Dimensions*. Oxford: Blackwell.

Moore, J.D. (1997) *Visions of Culture*. Walnut Creek: Altamira Press.

Noorderhaven, N.G. (2002) De grenzen van de Nederlandse bedrijfscultuur, in Batenburg, R., van der Lippe, T. and van den Heuvel, N. (eds) *Met het Oog op de Toekomst van de Arbeid*. Den Haag: Elsevier Bedrijfsinformatie, 77–89.

Osland, J.S. and Bird, A. (2000) Beyond sophisticated stereotyping: cultural sensemaking in context. *Academy of Management Executive* 14(1), 65–77.

Parsons, T. and Shils, E.A. (1951) *Toward a General Theory of Action*. Cambridge, MA: Harvard University Press.

Ronen, S. and Shenkar, O. (1985) Clustering countries on attitudinal dimensions: a review and synthesis. *Academy of Management Review* 10(3), 435–54.

Rousseau, D.M. (1985) Issues of level in organizational research: multi-level and cross-level perspectives, in Cummings, L.L. and Staw, B.M. (eds) *Research in Organizational Behaviour: an Annual Series of Analytical Essays and Critical Reviews*, Vol. 7, 1–37.

Sagiv, L. and Schwartz, S.H. (2000) A new look at national culture, in Ashkanasy, N., Wilderom, C.P.M. and Peterson, M.F. (eds) *Handbook of Organizational Culture and Climate*. London: Sage, 417–35.

Schwartz, S.H. (1992) Universals in the content and structure of values: theoretical advances and empirical tests in 20 countries, in Zanna, M. (ed.) *Advances in Experimental Social Psychology*, Vol. 25. New York: Academic Press, 1–66.

Schwartz, S.H. (1994) Beyond individualism and collectivism: new cultural dimensions of values, in Kim, U., Triandis, H.C., Kagitcibasi, C., Choi, S.C. and Yoon, G. (eds) *Individualism and Collectivism: Theory, Method, and Applications*. Newbury Park, CA: Sage, 85–199.

Schwartz, S.H. and Bilsky, W. (1987) Towards a universal psychological structure of human values. *Journal of Personality and Social Psychology* 53, 550–62.

Schwartz, S.H. and Bilsky, W. (1990) Towards a theory of the universal content and structure of values: extensions and cross-cultural replications. *Journal of Personality and Social Psychology* 58, 878–91.

Schwartz, S.H. and Ros, M. (1995) Values in the West: a theoretical and empirical challenge to the individualism–collectivism cultural dimensions. *World Psychology* 1, 91–122.

Sebenius, J.K. (2002) The hidden challenge of cross-border negotiations. *Harvard Business Review* 80(3), 76–85.

Smith, P.B. and Schwartz, S.H. (1997) Values, in Berry, J.W., Segall, M.H. and Kagitcibasi, C. (eds) *Handbook of Cross-cultural Psychology*, Vol. 3, *Social Behavior and Applications*. Boston, MA: Allyn & Bacon, 77–118.

Smith, P.B., Dugan, S. and Trompenaars, F. (1996) National culture and the values of organizational employees: a dimensional analysis across 43 nations. *Journal of Cross-cultural Psychology* 27, 231–64.

Soeters, J. and Recht, R. (1998) Culture and discipline in military academies: an international comparison. *Journal of Political and Military Sociology* 26, 169–89.

Spar, D. (1998) *Attracting High Technology Investment: Intel's Costa Rican Plant*. Foreign Investment Advisory Service Occasional Paper 11. Washington, DC: World Bank.

Steenkamp, J.-B.E.M. (2001) The role of national culture in international marketing research. *International Marketing Review* 18, 30–44.

Tannenbaum, A.S., Kavcic, B., Rosner, M., Vianello, M. and Wieser, G. (1974) *Hierarchy in Organizations*. San Francisco: Jossey-Bass.

Tayeb, M. (1994) Organizations and national culture: methodology considered. *Organization Studies* 15(3), 429–46.

Triandis, H.C. (1994) Cross-cultural industrial and organizational psychology, in Triandis, H.C., Dunnette, M.D. and Hough, L.M. (eds) *Handbook of Industrial and Organizational Psychology* (2nd edn), Vol. 4. Palo Alto, CA: Consulting Psychologists Press.

Van Marrewijk, A.H. (1997) The internationalization of the Dutch PTT Telecom from a cultural perspective. *Telematics and Informatics* 14, 365–81.

Van Marrewijk, A.H. (1999) *Internationalisation, Cooperation and Ethnicity in the Telecom Sector: an Ethnographic Study of the Cross-cultural Cooperation of PTT Telecom in Unisource, the Netherlands Antilles and Indonesia*. Delft: Eburon.

Chapter 3

Organizational Culture Research

Learning Objectives

By the end of this chapter you will be able to:

- understand the different approaches to organizational culture
- appreciate the complexity of organization culture research
- reflect upon the context-versus-actor problem in organization culture analysis
- appreciate the intricate role of organizational culture in domestic and international mergers and acquisitions
- evaluate the link between industry characteristics and organization culture
- analyse the link between organizational culture and strategy
- reflect critically upon the link between organizational culture and performance
- understand the development of organization culture
- assess the plausibility of a cultural dynamics process.

Chapter Outline

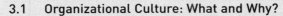

3.1   **Organizational Culture: What and Why?**

3.2   **Research Streams: the Etic and Emic Approaches**
The emic approach
The etic approach
Conclusion to the emic–etic methodological debate

3.3   **Multi-level Shaping of Culture**
The micro perspective
The macro perspective
Societal culture versus organizational context

3.4   **Culture Issues in Mergers and Acquisitions**
Strategic fit?
Cultural fit
Symbols and boundaries
Acculturation
Management styles
Case: Culture Clash at DaimlerChrysler

3.5   **Organizational and Industry Culture**

3.6   **Organizational Culture and Strategy**

3.7   **Organizational Culture and Economic Performance**
Culture as a building block
Culture as a tool and constraint
Culture as a diagnostic instrument

3.8   **Creation and Consolidation of Organizational Culture**
Creation
Consolidation
Case: Glass Ceiling or Sticky Floor? Organizational Culture as a Source of Stickiness at RaboBank

3.9   **Organizational Culture Change**
Three types of organizational culture change
Cultural change versus structural and material change
Study Questions
Further Reading
Case: Atos Origin and KPN
References

3.1 Organizational Culture: What and Why?

The previous chapter explained how organizations are linked to culture at the societal (national) level. A second major way in which organizations and culture are linked is that organizations are themselves culture-producing phenomena. Organizational culture is seen as a metaphor for understanding how organizations differ, how their members cohere, and how organizations and members interact (Adler and Jelinek, 1986).

While most organizational culture research still tends to perceive organizational culture as entirely distinct from the societal or national culture, it is widely recognized that the societal level influences the organizational level. In other words, the members of an organization are influenced by both the national and organizational culture contexts. As a consequence, managing international business means handling both national and organizational culture diversity.

This chapter has been conceived with this observation in mind. It discusses organizational culture issues that are especially important for operating successfully in a multicultural context. In this respect, Section 3.3 of this chapter discusses approaches that focus on intra-organizational culture diversity as well as approaches that specifically incorporate the societal environment in their analysis of organizational culture. It addresses the issue of fit between the societal and organizational cultural level. The section also introduces a taxonomy (classification) of work-related values to analyse the societal effect on organizations.

Section 3.4 continues in this direction by introducing the concept of 'cultural fit' in the context of mergers and acquisitions, both international and domestic. It is argued that, depending on the degree of integration, the cultures of the merging corporations need to 'fit' in order to arrive at successful post-merger coordination and integration. This section also addresses the concept of acculturation, which suggests different ways through which the culture and systems of two companies can be combined. There is a brief discussion of the DaimlerChrysler case at the end of the section, showing how cultural clashes can impede the efficient functioning of a merged company.

Aside from the impact of the societal level, organizational culture is also influenced by the industry in which the organization operates. In fact, industry characteristics impose another type of 'fit' upon organizational culture. In order for a company to survive, both the culture and the form it develops must be appropriate to industry demands. Section 3.5 examines the link between industry characteristics and organizational culture, and addresses some effects of this link for organizational strategy.

The central role of strategy in corporate life explains why we have dedicated a section of this chapter – Section 3.6 – to the link between organizational culture and strategy. The section discusses the main approaches to this issue. The concept of 'fit' is used in this context by research that argues for the alignment of strategy and organizational culture in order for companies to be successful.

In one way or another, Sections 3.3–3.6 of this chapter suggest a link between organizational culture and corporate performance. Section 3.7 broadens this picture by looking at three perspectives, which discuss the scope for management intervention within organizational culture in order to enhance performance. It warns the reader against simplistic solutions to organizational problems. A topic, which is related to this discussion, is the question of organizational culture change in general. This is discussed in Section 3.9.

In some cases, continuity rather than change of organizational culture is desirable. Organizational culture creation and consolidation is discussed in Section 3.8. The issue of undesirable continuation is demonstrated through a case study on Rabobank. At the same time, this case introduces gender issues in relation to organizational culture.

Before tackling these issues, following a structure similar to that of the previous chapter on national culture, Section 3.2 offers a balanced view of contemporary organizational culture research. It discusses the two main perspectives on the topic: the emic and etic approaches – stressing complementarity instead of one-sidedness. We argue that, rather like national culture, organizational culture is a complex research area, which cannot be understood from a single perspective.

3.2 Research Streams: the Etic and Emic Approaches

The body of literature that focuses on organizational culture is large and diverse, crossing disciplinary and methodological barriers. Similar to cross-cultural research, the present state of the art in the field of organizational culture research shows little convergence towards a commonly accepted conceptualization and operationalization of the construct (an *operationalization* is the way a given concept is measured in a particular study).

Conceptualizations of organization culture range from viewing it as a root metaphor for understanding how organizations are (the emic view) to viewing it as an independent variable that managers can manipulate for desired ends – that is, something an organization has (the etic perspective) (Smircich, 1983). The difference in conceptualization of organizational culture results in the use of different definitions, levels of analysis and, hence, different research methods. These differences are discussed below.

The emic approach
Definition and levels of analysis

The first stream of research is rooted in anthropology and ethnography, with Edgar Schein, Marta Calàs, Joanne Martin, Majken Schultz, Mary Jo Hatch and Linda Smircich as important representatives. The conceptualization and definitions of organizational culture in this strand of research all focus on the so-called 'deep levels' of meanings, beliefs and values, which can only be understood and studied from the 'inside' (Figure 3.1). They express the approach's concern with 'understanding', tending to view corporate culture as a way of understanding corporate life and as developed by the members of the organization.

Schein's conceptualization and formal definition of organizational culture are among the clearest expressions of the emic approach. For Schein, organizational culture or the culture of a group can be defined as follows:

> A pattern of *shared* basic assumptions that the group learned as it solved its problems of external adaptation and internal integration, that has worked well enough to be considered valid and, therefore, to be taught to new members as the correct way to perceive, think, and feel in relation to those problems. (Schein, 1992: 17)

Schein's definition expresses his view that the essence of a culture lies in the pattern of basic underlying 'assumptions' that members of an organization come to share as a result of common experiences in their working life. These assumptions, in turn, are reflected in and give meaning to expressed 'values' and observable artefacts and patterns of behaviour. Schein thus differentiates between different levels, addressing questions of depth of organizational culture (see Table 3.1).

In his view, the level of artefacts is at the surface and includes all the phenomena that one sees, hears and feels when one encounters a new group. Artefacts would include the visible products of the group such as the architecture of its physical environment, its language, its technology and product, its style as embodied in clothing, manners of address, observable rituals and ceremonies, and so on. Artefacts are easy to observe but very difficult to decipher. The observer can describe what she sees and feels but cannot reconstruct from that alone what those things mean in the given group, or whether they even reflect important underlying assumptions. Only if the observer lives in the group long enough do the meanings of the artefacts gradually become clear.

If one wants to achieve this level of understanding more quickly, Schein argues that one can attempt to analyse the espoused values, norms and rules that provide the day-to-day operating principles by which the members of the group guide their behaviour. However, Schein also argues that values are often inconsistent with observed behaviour, and may only reflect rationalizations or aspirations for the future. Moreover, large areas of behaviour will be left unexplained.

Schein thus argues that in order to achieve a deeper level of understanding of a group's culture, one must attempt to get at its shared basic assumptions and one must understand the learning process by which such basic assumptions come to be. Schein argues that while any group's culture can be studied at these three levels – the level of its artefacts, the level of its values and the level of its basic assumptions – if one does not decipher the pattern of basic assumptions that may be operating, one will not know how to interpret the artefacts correctly or how much credence to give to the articulated values (Schein, 1992).

Many other 'emic' and 'etic' organization culture researchers prefer the concept of basic 'values' for describing the deepest levels. Schein prefers basic 'assumptions' because these tend to be taken for granted and are treated as non-negotiable. Values can be and are discussed, and people can agree to disagree about them. Basic assumptions are so taken for granted that someone who does not hold them is viewed as crazy and automatically dismissed (Schein, 1992). The question of whether values or assumptions lie at the

Table 3.1 Schein's levels of organizational culture	
Artefacts	Visible organizational structure and processes (hard to decipher)
Espoused values	Strategies, goals, philosophies (espoused justification)
Basic underlying assumptions	Unconscious, taken-for-granted beliefs, perceptions, thoughts and feelings (ultimate source of values and action)

Source: Schein (1992: 17).

core of organizational culture is debatable, however. The fact that values are acquired in early childhood, and afterwards show considerable resistance to change, would seem to be an argument to place them at the deepest level of culture (Noorderhaven, 1995: 151). Moreover, we should not forget that the layers model of organizational culture is no more than a metaphor expressing that some elements of organizational culture are easier to observe and to change than others. The 'deep' elements are not in any real sense embedded more deeply in the organization or in the organization members' minds.

Moreover, the exclusive focus on cognitive components such as assumptions and beliefs has its shortcomings (Martin and Meyerson, 1988: 96). Given that organizations are purposive, the manifestations of ideas in practices are important. Comparing expressed ideas and actual practices as perceived by others can provide valuable information about the worldview of organizational members and its degree of overlap with reality as perceived or experienced by others. Observations of manifestations such as artefacts and behaviours can therefore be used as sources of data to 'triangulate' with information obtained about cognitive components (Sackmann, 1992).

Methodology

The preferred research methodologies of emic cultural research are open interviews and participant observations. Emic researchers have taken several positions supporting qualitative research and countering the use of quantitative culture measures. The rationale for the use of qualitative methods in organizational culture research is largely predicated on the presumed inaccessibility, depth or unconscious quality of culture. Schein (1992), for example, argues that only a complex interactive process of inquiry between insiders and outsiders can uncover fundamental assumptions. Such assumptions, he argues, tend to drop out of awareness and become implicit, because unlike the situation with corporate ideology or slogans, there is no need to remind members of assumptions that are an integral part of their worldview.

While assumptions are, indeed, difficult to assess without interactive probing, characteristic patterns of behaviour (norms) regarding how members should or should not act and members' perceptions of organizational processes – which are seen as reflections of organizational culture – are far more accessible. In this respect one could argue that the method appropriate to assessing culture depends on those elements we choose to examine. In the layered model of culture shown in Table 3.1, observations by outsiders and responses to structured instruments become more appropriate as we move from the bottom to the top. As the elements of culture we are interested in become more conscious (values and perceptions) or observable (artefacts), these are accessible by both standardized and non-standardized assessments.

Another argument that is used in favour of qualitative research is the possible uniqueness of an organization's values and beliefs such that an outsider cannot form a priori questions or measures. Louis (1985) and Smircich (1983) have argued that culture reflects a social construction of reality unique to members of a social unit, and that this uniqueness makes it impossible for standardized measures to tap cultural processes. Stereotypical or over-general categories, reducing the wide variety of possible organizational forms and cultures to an idealized few, might be construed as a weakness of an a priori structured (or etic) approach to tapping culture. Moreover, some argue that the specific types assessed might reflect ethnocentrism among organizational development practitioners or organizational behaviour researchers, something Schein (1985) labels 'American optimism' that anything can be changed or bettered. The very fact, however, that many researchers question the uniqueness of organizational culture (see Section 3.3) is an indication of the ambivalence surrounding the entire methodological and definitional debate. This is especially so since similar elements of culture have been found in different contexts. In other words, there are no sufficiently convincing arguments in favour of an exclusive reliance on qualitative methods for the purpose of organizational culture research.

Moreover, qualitative research has some disadvantages, which can be remedied by using quantitative methods. First, there are the costs of doing this type of labour-intensive research, and the difficulty for the researcher not to impose his or her own views. In most cases it is impossible to involve every organization member, so sampling is needed but is not always easily organized. The analysis of data is also more difficult than with questionnaire-based research. Finally, comparison between organizations, which after all is the goal of comparative international management research, is difficult to realize.

The advantages of qualitative methods to assess organizational culture are the richness of data they provide and the possibility that a close insight will be achieved through empathic listening. The latter idea comes from the research focus on socially constructed knowledge (how people interpret what happens to them).

The etic approach
Definition and levels of analysis

The second stream of literature – neopositivist cultural research – is rooted in organizational psychology and sociology, with Charles O'Reilly, Jennifer Chatman, David Caldwell, Geert Hofstede, Robert Cooke and Janet Szumal its main adherents. In contrast to the emic approach, this approach focuses on the shallow levels of practices or patterns of behaviour, which can be understood from an outsider (etic) point of view (Figure 3.1). It is concerned mainly with change, and predominates among management teachers and consultants. The goal of this approach is to develop generalizable theory (Martin, 2002: 6).

We will elaborate here on Geert Hofstede's (2001 and 1980) view of organizational culture as he is one of the few researchers, if not the only one, who studied culture both at national (see Chapter 2) and organizational levels. Hofstede's organizational culture definition resembles his national culture definition in that it uses the metaphor of the mental programming of the mind. It differs, however, in its focal group. For Hofstede (2001: 373): 'Organizational culture is the differences in collective mental programming of the mind found among people from different organizations, or parts thereof, within the same national context.'

Rather like Schein, Hofstede recognizes that culture manifests itself at different levels. The major difference with Schein's perception of organizational culture is that, instead of assumptions (or values), Hofstede finds that 'shared perceptions of daily practices should be considered the core of an organization's culture' (Hofstede, 2001: 394). Values are at a deeper level and, as explained in Chapter 2, they are the core of national culture.

Hofstede *et al.* (1990) came to this conclusion on the basis of a Danish–Dutch study of 20 organizational units. This study surveyed values as well as organizational practices and found the latter to differ significantly between organizational units, while values were more influenced by nationality. Organizational practices reflect the reality within an organization, 'what is' rather than 'what should be' reflected in values.

Hofstede *et al.* (1990) distinguished between three categories of organizational practice: symbols, heroes and rituals, which Hofstede (1991: 64) collectively labels 'practices' in an 'onion diagram' (Figure 3.1). These practices are visible to outsiders and their meaning is interpretable by both insiders and outsiders. The cultural meaning of these phenomena lies in the way they are perceived by organizational members.

Symbols have been put into the outer layer of Figure 3.1 since they represent the most superficial layer. Symbols are words, gestures, pictures or objects that carry a particular meaning, which is only recognized by those who share the culture. The words in a language or jargon belong to this category, as do dress, hairstyles, Coca-Cola and status symbols. Symbols are not unique as they can be copied by others; they are easily developed and old ones disappear (Hofstede, 1991).

Heroes are persons, alive or dead, real or imaginary, who possess characteristics that are highly prized in a culture, and who thus serve as models for behaviour. Even fictional or cartoon figures, like Batman in the USA and Asterix in France, can serve as cultural heroes.

Rituals are collective activities, technically superfluous in reaching desired ends, but which, within a culture, are considered socially essential; they are therefore carried out for their own sake. Ways of greeting and paying respect to others are examples.

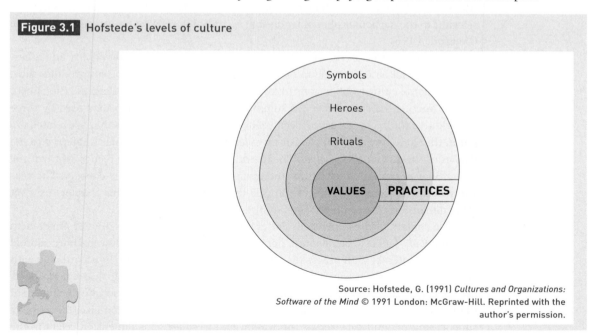

Figure 3.1   Hofstede's levels of culture

Symbols

Heroes

Rituals

VALUES   **PRACTICES**

Source: Hofstede, G. (1991) *Cultures and Organizations: Software of the Mind* © 1991 London: McGraw-Hill. Reprinted with the author's permission.

Not all etic research on organizational culture focuses on practices, however (see below). O'Reilly *et al.* (1991) and Chatman and Jehn (1994), for example, measure organizational values. Cooke and Rousseau (1988) address the behaviours it takes to fit in and get ahead – that is, evidence of behavioural norms attached to a social unit.

Methodology

The etic type of organizational cultural research uses the so-called scientific method to develop and test theory, working from deductively derived hypotheses that can be tested empirically and potentially proven false. Preferred research methods are written surveys and other highly structured data-collection procedures, often complemented by open interviews.

Similar to the etic approach to national culture, the etic stream of organizational culture research 'measures' far more than observes culture, and conducts analysis at the *ecological* (population, group) level. Thus, mean scores are calculated and used rather than individual scores. Organizational culture is seen as a property of the organizational units and not of the individuals within them. Individuals can be replaced over time, but the culture remains. Moreover, the culture of a particular organization can only be studied by comparing it with that of other organizations.

Obtaining information about culture quantitatively involves a priori identification of a feasible set of dimensions, categories or elements likely to be uncovered. Dimensions to be assessed require a basis in theory and previous research, supporting the assumption that certain dimensions are generalizable or generic across situations or organizational settings. When priorities are set among possible dimensions for study, certain variables are assessed and others omitted. Though all research omits some variables while addressing others, admittedly omissions are often quite obvious when measures are specified a priori. Hence, it is important to acknowledge that all quantitative (and in fact any other) assessment captures only part of reality; the exclusion of variables is inevitable (Rousseau, 1990: 168–71). It makes sense, then, to try to identify the dimensions that are relevant to the particular phenomenon that is studied in relation to organization culture (Denison, 1996).

Given the model of culture as layers of elements varying in observability and accessibility, it would be reasonable to expect quantitative assessments of culture and, thus, organizational culture dimensions to focus on the more observable elements (Rousseau, 1990). Such is the case. Table 3.2 summarizes the different dimensions used by three quantitative studies to 'measure' organizational culture. Dimensions that are related are put in the same row of the table. For an extended overview, the reader is referred to the studies of the authors themselves. The intention here is to make the reader aware of the diversity of organizational culture studies and the complexity of the concept. The case study on the IT company Atos Origin (see the case at the end of this chapter) uses yet other dimensions, based on previous studies.

The content of the dimensions varies from values regarding priorities or preferences (O'Reilly *et al.*, 1991) to behavioural norms, expectations regarding how members should behave and interact with others (Kilmann and Saxton, 1983), and, in accordance with Hofstede, practices (Christensen and Gordon, 1999). The task–people distinction underlies the conceptual model used by Kilmann and Saxton (1983). The second dimension in the model is characterized as short term versus long term, operationalized in terms of support and relationships versus innovation and freedom. This dimension refers to the degree to which individuals are encouraged to avoid conflict and protect themselves, or to innovate and take risks. Thus, to some extent, these instruments contrast a risk-averse, behaviour-inhibiting set of norms with behaviour-enhancing growth-orientated expectations (Rousseau, 1990: 173–8).

Table 3.2 Organizational culture dimensions (selected authors)			
	O'Reilly et al.	**Christensen and Gordon**	**Kilmann and Saxton**
	Aspect	Values	Practices
Behavioural Norms	1	Outcome orientation	Results orientation
Results orientation	2		People orientated
Human/technical	3		Confrontation
	4	Innovation	Innovation
Innovation	5	Stability	
Support	6	Respect for people	
	7	Attention to detail	
	8	Team orientation	Team orientation
Social relations 9	Aggressiveness	Aggressiveness/action-planning orientation	
10			
11		Communication	
12			Personal freedom

Source: Noorderhaven *et al.* (2002), and Rousseau (1990).

While values are assessed in the Organizational Culture Profile (O'Reilly *et al.*, 1991) and organizational practices in Christensen and Gordon (1999), the contents of their dimensions show some overlap. For example, outcome or results orientation, innovation, team orientation and aggressiveness feature in both inventories. However, there is as much diversity as overlap. The diversity of these studies could be seen as an indication of the fact that there is still no one best way to measure organizational culture.

The advantages of using the so-called scientific method in the etic approach to organizational culture are the quantification that allows for statistical treatment of the data. The opinions on organizational culture of all members of an organization can be included in the sample, avoiding in this way the problem of identifying the representative sample. In comparison to qualitative methods it is cheaper and much faster, though the development costs of a good questionnaire can be high. A lot of standardized instruments for the analysis of the data are available. Moreover, quantitative approaches provide instruments to examine large samples and to make comparisons, which, after all, is the ultimate goal of comparative management research.

A serious disadvantage of quantitative methodology is that little information on the context is provided. Questionnaires are perceived as impersonal and therefore not suitable for sensitive questions. In order to obtain depth and context information, however, quantitative analysis could be easily complemented by qualitative research. In fact, while the constructs used in the quantitative approach to measure organizational culture are etic, their manifestations in various cultures can be quite different, thus requiring emic or qualitative analysis. For instance, while an organization can be results-orientated, this orientation may be focused upon financial results, innovative or qualitative results, and so on.

Qualitative methods such as in-depth interviews can help us to find out the more specific or detailed perception of the construct.

Conclusion to the emic–etic methodological debate

Nowadays, most scholars seem to agree that, as with national-level culture research, 'what is needed is a combination of a qualitative approach for depth and empathy with a quantitative approach for confirmation' or to look to 'triangulation' – that is, pick the best from both paradigms while recognizing the strengths and limits of each (Hofstede, 2001 and 1980). Combinations of both methods of data collection and analysis create opportunities to synthesize the strengths of both. Traditional qualitative methods combine detailed data collection with interpretative analysis. Classic quantitative methods couple standardized assessments with statistical analysis. Qualitative assessment coupled with quantitative analysis can open up new areas of study where structured instruments are unavailable or possibly inappropriate. Similarly, standardized data collection, combined with interpretative analysis, offers researchers experience with a particular type of instrumentation that can be used to identify a variety of interpretations, implications and parallels (Martin, 2002).

Despite this agreement, however, few apply it. For example, cultural researchers often have strong preferences for either qualitative or quantitative research. Thus, whole bodies of cultural research are dismissed as unworthy: for example: 'That's an ethnography – just anecdotes about a single organization'; 'A journalist could have written it.' Another example: 'there is no proof' or, equally dismissive, 'No one can capture the complexity and richness of a culture in a sequence of numbers.' This kind of dogmatism in the cultural arena severely limits the range of studies that are viewed as able to contribute to understanding (Martin, 2002: 12).

3.3 ❖ Multi-level Shaping of Culture

Most management-orientated approaches to organizational culture commonly assume the existence of a micro culture covering the entire organization that is *unique, coherent* and *independent*, and that can be *shaped by managerial intentions*. One reason why these approaches include the assertion of uniqueness is that cultural members often believe, and take pride in, the idea that their organization's culture is unique (Martin, 1992: 109–10; Martin *et al.*, 1983).

Both the claims of uniqueness and of coherence are also often upheld for managerial reasons. If an organizational culture is not unique, but is influenced by meanings and values originating and anchored in regions, occupations, and the like, there will be considerable pressure from groups outside the specific organization, which may counteract and weaken the influence of management. Managers would then compete with other groups in defining what is correct and good (e.g. work long hours and during the weekends as opposed to family life) (Martin, 1992).

Moreover, in order to be managerially led, employees of a given organization should preferably share similar characteristics, because if not, all managerial interventions become more complicated. When different groups have different cultural orientations, they may respond differently to the same types of intervention. In addition, a considerable amount of time and effort must be spent negotiating various opinions, and dealing with any confusion and conflict emerging from cultural differences.

The micro perspective

Since the 1990s, the 'uniqueness and coherence' view of organizational culture has been disputed and two alternative but complementary forms of critique have emerged (e.g. Martin and Siehl, 1982; Sackmann, 1991, 1992; Phillips *et al.*, 1992). One view, taking a micro perspective of organizational culture, starts from the question of whether the entire organization or a part of it corresponds to (what can be treated as) a culture.

A micro perspective typically views the organization as the macro context and cultures within it as the more important phenomena (Alvesson, 2002: 156). This view is closely associated with an emphasis on work context (i.e. marketing department, engineering department, etc.) and social interaction (i.e. Van Maanen and Barley, 1984, 1985). It is argued that the specific tasks of work groups rather than the overall business of the company is decisive for the meanings and ideas of various groups. Work group situation and group interaction lead to local or subcultures within organizations, which are differentiated from, sometimes even antagonistic against overall and abstract ideas associated with management rhetoric and other initiatives.[1]

In this view,

Unitary organizational cultures are argued to evolve only when all members of an organization face roughly the same problems, when everyone communicates with almost everyone else, and when each member adopts a common set of understandings for enacting proper and consensually approved behavior. (Van Maanen and Barley, 1985: 37, cited in Alvesson, 2002: 156)

These conditions are, of course, rare. Hence, such research emphasizes subcultures created through organizational segmentation (division of labor hierarchically and vertically), importation (through mergers, acquisitions, and the hiring of specific occupational groups), technological innovation (which creates new group formations), ideological differentiation (e.g. when some people adopt a new ideology of work), counter-cultural (oppositional) movements, and career filters (the tendency for people moving to the top to have or develop certain common cultural attributes). (pp. 39–47, ibid.)[2]

The actual existence of organizational culture and different subcultures, however, are both a theoretical and an empirical question. The researcher may choose to decide a priori what represents a culturally meaningful organizational unit. Theoretically it is obvious that in order to be a meaningful subject for the study of organizational culture, a unit should be reasonably homogeneous with regard to the cultural characteristics

---

[1] Reproduced with permission from Alvesson, M., *Understanding Organizational Change* © Mats Alvesson 2002, by permission of Sage Publications Ltd.

[2] Reproduced with permission from Alvesson, M., *Understanding Organizational Change* © Mats Alvesson 2002, by permission of Sage Publications Ltd.

studied. This means that there can be different desirable study levels for different characteristics: some characteristics of a culture can apply corporation-wide, others will be specific to smaller units (Hofstede, 1998: 1). Empirical experience with large organizations, however, shows that at a certain size, the variations among the subgroups are substantial, suggesting that it is not appropriate to talk of 'the culture' of an IBM or a General Motors or a Shell Oil (Schein, 1992: 15). Sometimes, the research method used allows for a post hoc check on subunit variance. In other words, the researcher can, when analysing the data, search for subcultures, and then compare these with structural units in the organization (see Hofstede, 1998).

The micro perspective is not without its weaknesses. This perspective has been guilty of neglecting contextual factors that can significantly constrain the effects of individual differences that lead to collective responses, which ultimately constitute macro phenomena.

> We may, for example, be able to show that an individual's stress resistance helps to improve individual performance under stressful circumstances. However, we cannot then assert that selection systems that produce higher stress resistance will necessarily yield improved organizational performance. Perhaps they will, but that inference is not directly supported by individual-level analyses. Such 'atomistic fallacies', in which organizational psychologists suggest team- or organization-level interventions based on individual-level data, are common in the literature.[3]

The neglect of contextual factors could be argued to stem from the fact that the micro perspective is rooted in social psychology. It thus assumes that there are variations in the ways individuals interact with others, and that a focus on organization-level aggregates will mask important differences between small groups of individuals that are meaningful in their own right. Its focus is thus on variations among individual characteristics that affect interaction patterns and thus the small group.

The macro perspective

In contrast to the micro perspective, the second view of organizational culture and critique of a unitary and unique management-shaped organizational culture takes a macro orientation, and asks whether organizational culture is a reflection of society. The macro approach suggests that societies – nations or groups of nations with similar characteristics – put strong imprints on organizational culture. Cultural manifestations at the micro level are 'not generated in a socioeconomic vacuum, but are both produced by and reproduce the material conditions generated by the political and economic structure of a social system' (Mumby, 1988: 108, cited in Alvesson, 2002: 148). For example, different national cultures have different preferred ways of structuring organizations and different patterns of employee motivation (see Table 3.3 and Tables 2.1–2.4 in Chapter 2).

By drawing attention to the wider cultural context of the firm, the macro approach encourages a broader view of it. It suggests that while (depending on the research question) organizational culture analysis across organizations within the same society could

---

[3] Reproduced with permission from Alvesson, M., *Understanding Organizational Change* © Mats Alvesson 2002, by permission of Sage Publications Ltd.

legitimize focusing on the organizational level only, cross-cultural analysis of organizations cannot neglect the societal level. Macro perspectives argue that the national values of employees have a significant effect on their organizational performance.

Moreover, research within this perspective has found that cultural differences are more pronounced among foreign employees working within the same multinational organization than among personnel working for firms in their native lands. In Adler's words: 'When they work for a multinational corporation, it appears that Germans become more German, Americans become more American, Swedes become more Swedish, and so on' (Adler, 1996: 75–6). Similarly, Schneider (1988: 243) suggests that it is 'a paradox that national culture may play a stronger role in the face of a strong corporate culture. The pressures to conform may create the need to reassert autonomy and identity, creating a national mosaic rather than a melting pot.'

Despite these observations, to date there is no unanimity on whether organizational culture moderates or erases the impact of national cultural values, or whether it maintains and enhances them. There is agreement, however, on the fact that there is an effect of national upon organizational cultures and that this effect should not be ignored in international management. In this respect, the cross-cultural literature points to the need for fit between the two for the effectiveness of 'imported' practices and, as a result, for the performance – human and financial – of the foreign subsidiaries.

> Managers get a clear message from this literature. They are encouraged to adapt their management practices away from the home country standard towards the host country culture. It is argued that corporate initiatives that are created at headquarters and promoted worldwide run the risk of conflicting with defensive societal cultures.

Societal or national culture is argued to be a central organizing principle of employees' understanding of work, their approach to it, and the way in which they expect to be treated. Societal culture implies that one way of acting or one set of outcomes is preferable to another. When management practices are inconsistent with these deeply held societal values, employees are likely to feel dissatisfied, distracted, uncomfortable and uncommitted. As a result, they may perform less well (Newman and Nollen, 1996). Management practices that reinforce societal values are more likely to yield predictable behaviour (Wright and Mischel, 1987), self-efficacy and high performance (Earley, 1994) because congruent management practices are consistent with behavioural expectations and routines that transcend the workplace. In general, alignment between key characteristics of the external environment (societal culture) and internal strategy, structure, systems and practices is argued to result in competitive advantage (Burns and Stalker, 1961; Powell, 1992; Chatman and Jehn, 1994).

Obviously, the more different the host country culture is from the company's home country culture, the more the company will need to adapt. By implication, while there is much to be learned from exemplary management practices in other cultures, the differences between societal cultures limit the transferability of management practices from one to another. The lesson that management practices should not be universal – despite the ongoing drive to globalization and standardization – is illustrated by examples with which most managers are familiar. Pay-for-performance schemes are popular and work well in the USA and the UK, but are less used or adapted and are not so successful outside the Anglo countries (see Chapter 5, on human resource management). Similarly, quality circles are widely used and effective in Japan but have not delivered the same performance results in the USA despite significant efforts (see Chapter 7, on production management). In the last subsection, below, we discuss some further examples of the effect of societal culture for organizations.

Rather like the micro perspective to organizational culture, the macro perspective is not without its weaknesses. As a result of its sociological roots, the macro perspective neglects the means by which individual behaviour, perceptions, affect and interactions give rise to higher-level phenomena. It assumes that there are substantial regularities in social behaviour that transcend the apparent differences among social actors. Given a particular set of situational constraints and demographics, people will behave similarly. Therefore, it is possible to focus on aggregate or collective responses, and to ignore individual variation.

There is a danger of superficiality and triviality inherent in anthropomorphization. Organizations do not behave – people do. Macro researchers cannot generalize to these lower levels without committing errors of misspecification, as they use global measures or data aggregates. This renders problematic the drawing of meaningful policy or application implications from the findings.

> For example, assume that we can demonstrate a significant relationship between organizational investments in training and organizational performance. The intuitive generalization – that one could use the magnitude of the aggregate relationship to predict how individual performance would increase as a function of increased organizational investments in training [– is not supportable because of the problem of ecological inference].[4]

In other words, one cannot and should not infer conclusions for the individual level from ecological (in this case, organization or group level) correlations. Relationships among aggregate data tend to be stronger than corresponding relationships among individual data elements.

Societal culture versus organizational context

The cross-cultural literature generally uses a taxonomy (classification) of work-related national culture values (e.g. the taxonomy of Hofstede, 2001, 1991; Hellriegel *et al.*, 1992; Schwartz, 1994; Trompenaars, 1994; Adler, 1996; Hodgetts and Luthans, 1997) to analyse the effect of societal-level cultures on organization-level phenomena.[5] Three types of value, often studied, are used here for illustration: values governing power relations, orientations to work, and values pertaining to uncertainty. Table 3.3 summarizes several 'hypotheses' illustrating some implications of these values for the structure and processes of organizations, as well as for the behavioural styles of their members. These hypotheses can be theorized and confirmed in the literature. This will not be done here. The main purpose of discussing these values and their implications is to illustrate

---

[4] Reproduced with permission from Alvesson, M., *Understanding Organizational Change* © Mats Alvesson 2002, by permission of Sage Publications Ltd.

[5] Some of these taxonomies are discussed extensively in Chapter 2, which deals with national cultures.

Table 3.3 The effects of cultural values on organizational choices			
Cultural values	**Structure**	**Processes**	**Behavioural style**
Power High/low power	Hierarchy: differentiation high/low	Decision-making: participative/ non-participative	Leadership: authoritarian/ democratic
	Centralization: high/low	Communication vertical/horizontal	Subordinates' compliance strategies high/low authoritarian or coercive/permissive
		Control: tight/loose	
		Coordination vertical/horizontal	
Work orientation Work/ non-work centrality	Span of control: wide/short	Rewards and incentives: intrinsic/extrinsic	Climate: expressive/ instrumental
			Commitment: internal/external
Uncertainty High/low avoidance	Formalization: high/low	Locus of decisions: hierarchical/diffuse	Climate: reserved/open
	Centralization: high/low		

Source: Lachman *et al.* (1994: 48).

the profound effect of societal culture on organizations; and, once again, to emphasize the need to take account of this effect in order to be able to maximize corporate performance.

Power values are cultural values that specify appropriate forms of power relationships and authority in social organizations. They define the appropriate hierarchical arrangements and the power-compliance strategies that should be employed within organizations. Thus, it can be argued that a cultural emphasis on high power distance will be associated with the choice of compatible patterns of structural configurations such as high hierarchical differentiation or high centralization. Similarly, it can be associated with the choice of corresponding organizational processes of non-participative decision-making, and hierarchical rather than collegial or 'clan' control and coordination. Through the effects of cultural values on individual behaviour, it can be argued that preference for high power distance will be associated with preference for an authoritarian leadership style (Lachman *et al.*, 1994).

The literature further argues that congruence between the choice of a highly centralized organizational power structure and non-participative decision processes, on the one hand, and the preference for a style of high distance in interpersonal relations on the other, will enhance organizational effectiveness. A study by Hinings and Badran (1981) illustrates this point. Their study describes how the high degree of participation required by the prescribed structure of public organizations in Egypt was difficult to implement, because the indigenous cultural values emphasized social and hierarchic distance in interpersonal relations. The outcomes of this incongruency were poor internal processes and low levels of participation in the realized organizations, not the high levels required by the prescribed structure.

In this context, Lachman *et al.* (1994) further differentiate between 'core' values, affecting the satisfaction of workers, and 'non-core' values that have less impact. Using this distinction, they explain that Chinese workers in Hong Kong – where the cultural emphasis is on high power distance – are satisfied working in a centralized rather than decentralized structure. Similar assumptions regarding satisfaction with organizational differentiation and formalization were not supported. Lachman *et al.* (1994) explain the latter by arguing that the value governing hierarchical power relations is core to the Chinese culture in Hong Kong, whereas those governing formalization and differentiation are not. Consequently, when a core value is concerned, value incongruency can explain employees' dissatisfaction (i.e. lower effectiveness). However, when variations in practices (differentiation or formalization) among the multinational organizations are incongruent with values that are not core, the work satisfaction of local employees is not affected.

The implication of the distinction between core–periphery values is that not every incongruency in organizational adaptation with local values is dysfunctional and should be avoided. It suggests differential effects of incongruencies with core or periphery values. Lachman *et al.* (1994) thus advocate a contingency approach of 'cultural congruence' describing different incongruencies, which may have different consequences for cross-cultural organizations and may require different managerial approaches or coping strategies. The problem with this approach, however, is the difficulty and often arbitrariness in determining what are core and non-core values, and the consequent adaptation problems. While proposing a more fine-grained approach to cross-cultural management, Lachman *et al.* (1994), at the same time, exacerbate complexity.

The value placed on work itself governs the view of work as a distinct form of social activity, and the centrality of work in life. It specifies the importance of organized work activity to individuals and the preferred methods used to motivate and direct the investment of human energy in this activity. In this respect, cultural preferences may range from a strong emphasis on work as a means of achieving non-work goals and social status (instrumental orientation), to a strong emphasis on work as a highly valued activity in itself (expressive orientation).

Values pertaining to uncertainty govern the culturally preferred reaction to it, which may range from high avoidance of uncertainty to its acceptance. Obviously, the framework presented in Table 3.3 is by no means limited to these values or to an examination of the possible effects of a single value at a time. It is intended as an illustration and can be extended to incorporate other values; the distinction between core and periphery values and congruence can be used to generate testable hypotheses about their effects on organizations. The basic approach underlying the framework is that of 'cultural congruence' with societal (core) values (Lachman *et al.*, 1994).

3.4 🧩 Culture Issues in Mergers and Acquisitions

One of the most obvious situations in which corporations experience the influence of societal culture on organizational context and culture is when two or more cultures are brought together via cross-border or domestic mergers and/or acquisitions. Foreign acquisitions and international mergers are two intensive modes of intercultural encounter. In foreign acquisition, a local company is purchased wholesale by a foreign corporation. The local company's organizational culture and, of course, elements of its national culture are parachuted into the corporation. Foreign acquisitions offer a speedy means of expanding, but their cultural risks are considerable. When integration is imperative, cultural clashes are often resolved through brute power: key people are replaced by the corporation's own agents.

The international merger resembles the foreign acquisition, except that the partners are of roughly equal size or importance. The cultural risk is even greater than in the case of foreign acquisition because cultural problems cannot be eliminated through a one-sided show of power. International mergers, therefore, have a very low success rate. Leyland-Innocenti, Chrysler UK, Imperial Typewriters, Vereinigte Flugzeugwerke-Fokker, Hoogovens-Hoesch, Citroën-Fiat, and Renault-Volvo are some of the more notorious failures (Hofstede, 2001: 445). The DaimlerChrysler case on pages 117–18 is another example of a problematic international merger.

While mergers and acquisitions have been a dominant mode of internationalization, they have also been an important feature of national organizational life during the last two decades. The continuing popularity of international and national mergers and acquisitions is probably a reflection of the widespread belief among managers that acquisitions provide a quicker and seemingly easier route to achieving growth and diversification objectives (Datta, 1991). Paradoxically, however, and as indicated, mergers and acquisitions – whether national or international – have a high failure rate; nearly half of all mergers and acquisitions are rated as being unsatisfactory by managers of the acquiring firms (see Young, 1981; Porter, 1987). On average, the profitability of target firms actually declines after an acquisition (Ravenscraft and Scherer, 1989; Cartwright and Cooper, 1993).

Strategic fit?

Research into strategic management suggests that 'strategic fit' may help explain why some mergers or acquisitions succeed while others are dismal failures. Strategic fit, or relatedness, is the degree to which the acquired or merged firms augment or complement the acquiring firm's strategy, and the degree to which value is created (Jemison and Sitkin, 1986). Relatedness or 'strategic fit' is needed in order to obtain greater synergistic benefits arising out of economies of scale and scope (Salter and Weinhold, 1979; Lubatkin, 1983). Merging firms can reduce unit costs in production, inventory holding, marketing, advertising and distribution, integrating similar departments and functions (Howell, 1970; Rappaport, 1987). In addition, the possibility of transferring core skills across the firms involved is associated with related acquisitions.

The findings of empirical studies, however, have not always been consistent with these expectations. In fact, the considerable diversity in the findings of these studies supports the contention that strategic fit, while important, is not a sufficient condition for superior acquisition performance (Jemison and Sitkin, 1986). In other words, while relatedness indicates that potential synergistic benefits may be present, it will result in superior acquisition performance only if synergies can eventually be realized through effective post-merger or post-acquisition integration. Effective integration in mergers can be defined as the combination of firms into a single entity or group, generating joint efforts to fulfil the goals of the new organization.

Evidence suggests that this goal is not easily accomplished (i.e. Sales and Mirvis, 1984; Buono *et al.*, 1985). While, in theory, integration should result in benefits, in reality the picture can be very different. Impediments associated with the integration of operations can result in the acquiring firm being unable to manage the integration of the target firm effectively. This is especially true when organizational incompatibilities exist in areas such as *organizational culture* and *management style*, both of which are discussed below.

Cultural fit

Many researchers believe that the degree of compatibility between the cultures of the partner organizations in a merger, or 'cultural fit', is a major cause for implementation difficulties (i.e. Davis, 1968; Cartwright and Cooper, 1993; Newman and Nollen, 1996; Weber *et al.*, 1996). When organizations that have developed their own corporate cultures acquire each other, attempt to merge or engage in various kinds of partnership, the culture issue is at its most obvious (Schein, 1999: 8). Fundamental differences, made manifest in differences in the thought, behaviour and actions of employees, are believed to increase conflict potential and may hinder agreement over management issues (Olie, 1994: 384).

This is especially the case when the fusion or integration of some or all of the human resources of the organizations involved is required and thus success becomes heavily dependent on human synergy. The choice of the degree of relatedness between the firms involved in a merger depends on the motives behind the merger. As indicated, these motives can include achieving operating synergies in production, in marketing, and so on. Many companies also merge in order to achieve financial synergies such as risk reduction through diversification and access to more favourable financial terms (Nahavandi and Malekzadeh, 1988). To obtain these synergies, a firm must select a merger target that is, to a degree, related to its business. Depending on the type of merger and the motive, the acquiring company must decide on an implementation strategy. That strategy will determine the extent to which the various systems of the two firms will be combined, and the degree to which the employees of the company will interface.

In contrast to the great conglomerate boom of the 1960s, the wave of mergers and acquisitions in the 1980s and 1990s was dominated by the combination of companies in similar rather than unrelated business activities. In related mergers, the acquirer is more likely to impose its own culture and practices on the acquired company (Walter, 1985), thereby initiating extensive interaction among the employees of the two firms. The integration of two previously separate and often very different workforces and organizational cultures presents a major managerial challenge to those involved. Mismanagement is likely to result in poor morale, employee stress, increased sickness absence, high labour turnover and lowered productivity. The costs of 'culture collisions' resulting from poor integration may typically be as high as 25 to 30 per cent of the performance of the acquired organization. Hence, it could be argued that 'culture fit' is of equal, if not greater, importance than 'strategic fit' (Cartwright and Cooper, 1993: 59).

> The Japanese experience is argued to provide a good lesson. The Japanese consider acquisition a strategy of last resort – that is, when all other alternatives are considered inappropriate. When they decide to take over an organization, in most cases they will have previous experience working with that company on a joint venture or collaborative project (i.e. the Sony–CBS partnership). In other words, they have already learned their partner's culture, and are aware of the suitability of the 'culture fit'. Moreover, in comparison with British and American negotiating teams, which are heavily dependent on legal advisers and financial consultants, Japanese decision-makers are more inclined to seek the opinions of their operational and human resource managers (Cartwright and Cooper, 1993: 68).

While achieving coordination within an international merger is often obstructed by cross-cultural as well as organizational culture differences, as indicated, achieving coordination within a national merger is also a challenging task. According to Hofstede (2001 and 1980), when faced with cultural diversity among home cultures a viable new organization can only be created through the development of a strong organizational subculture or common identity. Merging in this sense implies the reconstruction of a new social identity or a new, enlarged in-group. Obviously, this will take time. Identification with a new organization is often a product of common experiences. Nevertheless, in this respect, it has been argued that it is probably easier to adopt new practices than to change old ones. In fact, the simultaneous adoption of new practices at both of the previously separate organizations is likely to create less internal comparison and fewer negative attitudes than situations where one has to conform unilaterally to the beliefs and practices of the other side (Vaaraa, 1999: 72).

Symbols and boundaries

By removing symbols of previous identities and replacing them with new identification symbols, management can help to define a new category in which both groups are psychologically merged (Olie, 1994: 386). One obvious symbol of identification is the appointment of leaders that can symbolize the new identity. Management is a powerful symbolic means to build organizational commitment, to convey a philosophy of management, to motivate personnel and to facilitate socialization (Smircich, 1983; Schein, 1985). Recent research in the field of leadership suggests that, particularly in organizational transformation processes, charismatic leadership is needed (Bryman, 1992).

Other symbols may also help with the reconstruction of a new identity, such as corporate names, the appointment of key managers, the location of head offices and board membership. Moreover, while cultural differences may decrease the perception of a common identity, the awareness of a common set of goals and objectives, or a subordinate goal, may reinforce integration. Intergroup cooperation for a common goal induces the members of both groups to perceive themselves primarily as one large group rather than separate entities, thereby transforming their categorized representations from *us* and *them* into the more inclusive *we* (Gaertner *et al.*, 1989). However, the effectiveness of this strategy will depend in part on the outcomes of achieving this goal. Failure will reinstitute the group boundaries as members search for scapegoats to justify or to explain the negative outcome.

Another tactic that aims to reduce the salience of boundaries between two or more merging organizational groups is the creation of overlapping memberships, other than the organizational ones. People may belong to different groups, such as pre-merger organizations, yet share common identities in other respects – for example, through the creation of a combined task force. In this way individuals owe loyalty to more than one group. If alternative categorizations can be brought into play in mergers and acquisitions by multiple group memberships, these may help to reduce the conflict surrounding the original division (Olie, 1994: 387).

Acculturation

When two cultures come together, anthropologists use the term *acculturation* to describe the 'changes induced in (two cultural) systems as a result of the diffusion of cultural elements in both directions' (Berry, 1980: 215). The process occurs at the group and individual levels in the three stages of contact, conflict and adaptation.[6] Although acculturation is considered to be a balanced two-way flow, members of one culture often attempt to dominate members of the other. In an organizational context, this implies that people at the acquired unit often face considerable pressure to conform to the values and management practices of the buyer.

Though the concept of acculturation was developed to explain events involving societal groups, it can be applied to the merger situation (Figure 3.2) to accommodate different cultural dynamics and outcomes. Societal and industrial groups share many defining characteristics. Both exist and adapt within a specified environment and have well-defined (though permeable) boundaries that encompass a number of individuals who interact and are interdependent to varying degrees (Sales and Mirvis, 1984). They have a functional and adaptive quality, and provide their members with a system of shared symbols and cognition to deal with each other and with the outside world.

Acculturation is argued to occur through four different modes, depending on the extent to which organizational members are satisfied with and value their existing culture, and their evaluation of the attractiveness of the other culture.

Assimilation

Assimilation is a unilateral process in which the members of the acquired firm willingly relinquish their culture, and adopt and become absorbed into the culture of the acquirer or dominant merger partner: they *assimilate*. In effect, the acquirers conduct a 'culture-stripping' exercise. If members of the acquired organization resist and are unwilling to abandon their culture, separation occurs. Resistance results in lower levels of commitment and cooperation among acquired employees (Sales and Mirvis, 1984, Buono *et al.*,

---

[6] The following discussion is based on Berry (1983); Nahavandi and Malekzadeh (1988); and Cartwright and Cooper (1993).

Figure 3.2 Modes of organizational and individual acculturation in mergers and acquisitions, and their potential outcomes

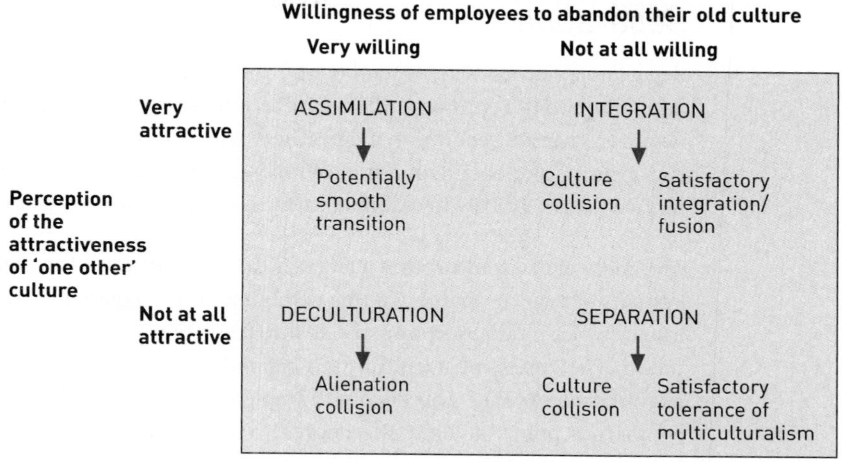

Source: Cartwright and Cooper (1993: 65).

1985), greater turnover among acquired managers (Hambrick and Cannella, 1993; Lubatkin *et al.*, 1999), a decline in shareholder value at the buying firm (Chatterjee *et al.*, 1992) and a deterioration in operating performance at the acquired firm (Weber, 1996; Very *et al.*, 1997). Often, acquirers seek to escalate assimilation and avoid the problems of resistance and separation by displacing resistors.

Deculturation

When members of the acquired organization are dissatisfied with their existing culture, but unconvinced as to the attractiveness of the other culture, deculturation occurs. Deculturation thus involves losing cultural and psychological contact both with one's group and with the other group, and it implies remaining an outcast from both. As a consequence, employees experience a great deal of confusion, as well as feelings of alienation, loss of identity, and what has been termed 'acculturative stress'.

Integration

Integration occurs when the interaction and adaptation between the two cultures spontaneously result in the evolvement of a new culture. However, this requires change and ultimate balance between the two cultural groups, which, as merger is rarely a marriage between equals, seems to occur infrequently in practice. This situation represents considerable potential for culture collisions and fragmentation.

There is some evidence that collisions and fragmentation can be avoided when the buying firms rely on 'social controls'. It is argued that, by participating in such activities as introduction programmes, training, cross-visits, retreats, celebrations and similar socialization rituals, employees will create, of their own volition, a joint organizational culture, regardless of expectations of synergies, the relative organization size, and differences in nationalities and cultures (Larsson and Lubatkin, 2001).

Separation

Separation occurs when members of the acquired organization resist any attempt at adaptation to the culture of the acquirer, and they try to remain totally separate from the acquirer. Overall, separation means there will be minimal cultural exchange between the two groups, and each will function independently. The consequent maintenance of separate cultures is likely to result in culture collision and a lack of cohesiveness.

The concept of acculturation addresses the different ways through which the culture and systems of two companies can be combined. It is suggested that when two groups come into contact, total absorption of one into the other is by no means the only mode of adaptation. The course of acculturation depends on the way in which the acquirer and the acquired companies approach the implementation of the merger. From the acquired company's point of view, the degree to which members want to preserve their own culture and the degree to which they are willing to adopt the acquirer's culture will determine their preferred mode of acculturation.

In the case of the acquirer, the culture – that is, the degree to which an organization values cultural diversity and is willing to tolerate and encourage it – and the diversification strategy regarding the type of merger (i.e. the degree of relatedness) will, to a large extent, determine the preferred mode of acculturation. As indicated, if the merger is with a firm in a related business, the acquirer is more likely to impose some of its culture in an attempt to achieve operating synergies. On the other hand, an acquirer is less likely to interfere with the culture of an unrelated acquisition. This mode corresponds to the original goal of an unrelated merger, which is to achieve financial rather than operating or managerial synergy.

Given that the members of the two organizations may not have the same preferences regarding a mode of acculturation, the degree of agreement regarding each one's preference for a mode of acculturation will be a central factor in the successful implementation of the merger. Indeed, when two organizations agree on the preferred mode of acculturation for the implementation of the merger, less acculturation stress and organizational resistance will result, making acculturation a smoother process (Nahavandi and Malekzadeh, 1988: 84).

Because of the time, energy and sunk costs involved in merger and acquisition negotiation, there is strong reluctance on the part of management to abandon a deal because of potential cultural incompatibility. In practice, financial and strategic considerations are always likely to outweigh any selection criteria based on cultural compatibility. It is important, however, that managers make some cultural assessment of the target company or potential merger – international as well as national – in advance of any legal combination. A culture audit is a valuable source of information, with implications not only for partner selection but also for long-term management.

The Atos Origin case study at the end of this chapter is an example of such an audit. The case shows that organizational culture can differ significantly between companies that are located in the same country and that operate in the same sector. The case points to potential problem areas, offers directions for avoiding potential problems but also stresses the opportunities for learning from cultural differences.

Indeed, while cultural differences are often causes of organizational problems in post-merger change processes, we would like to comment here that they can also be sources of value and learning. Different ways of doing things can provide an opportunity to develop 'best practices' that can be the core of the emerging new culture of the developing large organization. Too little research has focused on these positive aspects, however.

Management styles

As already indicated, a noteworthy element of 'cultural fit' in mergers and acquisitions is the extent of compatibility in the styles of management of the acquiring and the acquired firms (Datta, 1991: 283–4). Management style has been described as an element of the managerial or the subjective culture of an organization (Bhagat and McQuaid, 1982; Sathe, 1985). It has been conceptualized in the organization's literature as comprising a number of factors, including the management group's attitude towards risk, its decision-making approach, and the preferred control and communication patterns.

Management styles are unique to organizations and may differ considerably across firms – for example, management groups may have very different risk-taking propensities. It is, therefore, not unusual to find that policies and procedures, which seem to be reckless and extremely 'risky' to one management group appear to another to be justifiable approaches. Similarly, one management group's tolerance for change may be much greater than another's. Top management groups may also differ in their approach to decision-making.

As pointed out by Mintzberg (1973), while some management teams rely almost exclusively on common sense, gut feeling and 'rules of thumb', others emphasize formal-ized strategic planning systems, market research and various management science techniques. Consequently, rather like what has been argued for 'cultural fit' in general, compatible management styles facilitate post-acquisition assimilation, while major differences in management styles and philosophies can prove to be serious impediments to the achievement of acquisition success.

Moreover, like cultural fit, in general, the extent to which management styles impact acquisition performance is likely to vary depending on the level of interaction required among the two management groups in the post-acquisition management of the combined entity. The potential for conflict due to differences in management style is likely to be greatest in acquisitions followed by considerable operational integration, given that such acquisitions invariably involve much higher levels of managerial interaction. Since integration of operations makes the coexistence of two different styles virtually infeasible, it inevitably raises the issue of whose style will dominate (as indicated, generally it is the style of the acquiring firm that prevails).

Case: Culture Clash at DaimlerChrysler[7]

In January 1998, Jürgen Schrempp, chairman of the DaimlerBenz management board, and Robert Eaton, chairman and CEO of Chrysler Corporation, met to discuss a possible merger. Within four months, there was a signed merger agreement. The merger was announced on 7 May 1998 and, within ten months, the first DaimlerChrysler stock was trading on stock exchanges worldwide. The merger was announced to be a joining of equals. The driving force behind the merger was the need to create ever larger globally based enterprises, which could compete in all the major markets of the world. The goal was to create synergies based on complementary product and geographic markets. Before the merger, Chrysler and DaimlerBenz were essentially regional producers – Chrysler with the third-largest market share in North America, Daimler-Benz with the majority of its sales revenues made in Europe. Immediate growth opportunities would be created through using each other's facilities. The united corporation would also develop a low-cost car to conquer the Asian market.

However, after four years, it turned out that the merger did not pay off as was expected and propagated by the management boards in 1998. Sales did not increase, synergy effects were minimal and stock prices declined dramatically in the years following the merger. The *New York Times* called the Daimler–Chrysler marriage 'one of the most disastrous mergers in history'. The US partner was in serious trouble. Chrysler's profits fell from US$4.9 billion to US$1.2 billion, and its shares from US$109 to US$48 over the second half of 2000. Daimler's operating loss for 2001 may be as large as 1.7bn euros.

The question to answer of course is what went wrong with this merger. The potential for synergies and growth looked promising. Of course, during the merger there were several hurdles that had to be negotiated, but it seemed that the companies were prepared for that. The biggest hurdle, it turned out, was related to cultural differences and the inequality between the two parties. Despite the announcement that it was a marriage between equals, it was clear that DaimlerBenz has been the 'more equal' partner and that it was imposing its own corporate imprint on the merged company. In fact, Chrysler's shareholders could do nothing else than approve the merger since the company was at that time already in serious problems. Hence, Daimler has been the dominant partner from day one. The fact that German employees took over many key positions in the organization and that Chrysler top manager Robert Eaton resigned in 2000 made it evident that DaimlerBenz in fact *acquired* Chrysler.

The main problems arose during the integration phase. Top management did not experience cultural clashes in 1998. Only after that did middle and lower management clash severely. Chrysler managers resisted the dominant role of DaimlerBenz and defended their own interests and culture. The corporate clash came down to a confrontation between the engineering culture of Daimler, with its systems, precision, safety- and quality-orientated approach, as opposed to the

---

[7] This case study draws on Blasko *et al.* (2000).

pay-for-performance culture of Chrysler, with its sales, marketing and risk-orientated approach. Discussions of a new corporate culture had been avoided deliberately at the start of the merger. Later in the integration process, employees were unexpectedly confronted with this issue and resisted any form of adaptation.

Questions

1. Explain how national culture affects organizational culture at DaimlerBenz and Chrysler.

2. During the integration phase the cultural clash became evident. Explain whether and how this could have been foreseen and avoided.

3. In what mode of the acculturation process do you situate the merger? Explain whether and why any other mode of acculturation would have been more appropriate in this case.

3.5 ⚫ Organizational and Industry Culture

Until now we have discussed how organizational phenomena are influenced by societal-level culture. However, aside from the influence of the societal level, organizational culture is also strongly affected by the characteristics of the industry in which the company operates. Industries are argued to exert influence that cause organizational cultures to develop within defined parameters. By implication, within industries, certain cultural characteristics will be widespread among organizations, and these will most likely be quite different from the characteristics found in other industries (Gordon, 1991: 396). Theoretical support for the existence of industry-based mind-sets is found in diverse strands of the literature (i.e. in institutional theory, industrial economics, marketing, organization behaviour and strategy).

Strategy theorists, who traditionally focus on the industry level, propose that commonly held mind-sets exist across firms within industries and drive decision-making by individuals within those firms (Phillips, 1994: 386). In particular, industry-driven assumptions[8] are argued to lead to the development at the organizational level of value systems that are consistent with these assumptions. These value systems, in turn, prevent the company from developing strategies, structures or processes (hereafter referred to as 'forms') that would conflict with these assumptions and be 'antagonistic' to the culture (Gagliardi, 1986). Such conflicts are argued to arise only in the relatively rare situations where very significant changes in the environment mean that the assumptions are no longer valid. Under such circumstances, cultural change involving changes in assumptions is required (see Section 3.9).

Moreover, in order for a new company to survive, both the culture and the forms that

---

[8] As a reminder, the concept of 'assumptions' has been introduced by Schein to indicate the deepest cultural level. Most authors, however, prefer *values* to indicate the deepest cultural level.

it develops must be appropriate to the industry imperatives. Under these conditions the company's survival and prosperity are limited only by that of the industry. It must be noted, however, that within the context of the industry assumptions, various compatible strategies, structures or processes are available. Thus, culture is not argued to be deterministic of specific forms, but to exert an influence upon the *nature* of the forms that will be developed (Gordon, 1991: 398).

There are two main approaches to studying the effect of industry characteristics on organizational or corporate culture. The first approach focuses narrowly on top managers' mental models for strategic decision-making (see Huff, 1982; Porac *et al.*, 1989; Spender, 1989; Caroll and Thomas, 1994). It argues that top managers of organizations active in the same industry reveal the same patterns of thinking. They have similar opinions about their environment and think in the same way about how their organizations should function. Managers active in a certain industry think the same because they have experienced the same developments (Huff, 1982; Spender, 1989). In particular, in industries that have enjoyed long periods of stability, the thought patterns of management become a copy of institutionalized interaction patterns (Caroll and Thomas, 1994). In contrast, within dynamic industries uniformity cannot be found, which suggests the existence of differences in the thought patterns of management.

The second approach considers broad-based assumption sets, comprising the cultural knowledge shared widely among organizational participants within industries. Rather than concentrating only on those members of the industry who are responsible for positioning their individual organizations in relation to their competitors, a focus on the broader spectrum of industry participants is advised (Phillips, 1994). An industry is perceived in this literature as a community with its own structure and culture (i.e. Räsänen and Whipp, 1992; Whitley, 1992). The way in which different parties and stakeholders within a certain industry deal with each other is regarded as a consequence of a process of institutionalization. Institutionalization implies the development of regularities in both patterns of thinking and behaviour. The institutionalized patterns of thinking are regarded as industry culture.

Industry-shared values and beliefs have both negative and positive consequences. They might facilitate negotiation among top managers, increase trust, and generally reduce transaction costs. Moreover, in more homogenous industry cultures, top managers tend to pay attention to the same strategic issues, recognize the same challenges to their industry, more readily see their common interest, and, therefore, may have greater capacity to engage in the collective strategies necessary to counter threatening events and trends (Abrahamson and Fombrun, 1994).

Authors pointing to the potential negative consequences of industry-based assumptions and beliefs argue that industry-shared assumptions may cause future collective inertia and technological traditionalism. Industry-shared assumptions and beliefs are said to encourage managers of member firms to interpret environments in similar ways, to identify similar issues as strategic, and so to adopt similar competitive positions (Abrahamson and Fombrun, 1994). An illustrative example is the US car industry during and after the oil crisis of 1973–74. At that time, the US car industry collectively denied the fact that increased sales of small cars was a structural rather than a temporary phenomenon. As a consequence, in the 1980s, European and Japanese competitors captured 25 per cent of the total market. Moreover, despite the fact that the US car industry has been producing small cars since 1974, imported cars are still more economical than their US equivalents (Huff, 1982). By benchmarking against each other rather than against global rivals, US manufacturers converged in making similarly misguided resource commitments over the years and in disregarding looming threats from seemingly peripheral producers (Halberstam, 1986; Keller, 1989).

Finally, because not all organizational assumptions and values are driven by industry imperatives, one should not be surprised to find significant variations in culture within industries. Companies in the same industry can encompass very different elements in their corporate cultures, as long as those elements are not driven by basic industry assumptions. Variations may stem from founders' convictions, successful coincidences (see Schein, 1985) or changes in management.

Variations may also stem from changes in the industry environment and the fact that companies react in different ways. When, for example, some of the successful past behaviours that have evolved from industry-shared cultural elements are no longer effective, companies will feel pressure to search for new actions that will be more effective. However, because the competing firms will have had little, if any, experience with such actions (i.e. the previous industry context did not call for them) it is likely that a variety of alternative actions will be attempted by the various companies. Some of these actions will be successful and will lead to new values (as suggested by Schein, 1985) that are compatible with the new environmental influences, thereby creating cultural diversity within the industry. Thus, to some extent, cultural diversity within an industry may be a function of the dynamism of that industry (Gordon, 1991).

3.6 Organizational Culture and Strategy

Section 3.3 suggested that the link between national culture and organizational culture is important for employees and thus for corporate performance. Section 3.4 discussed the link between 'cultural fit', or the fit between the cultures of merging corporations, and corporate performance. Another way in which organizational culture is linked to economic performance is by means of its relationship to strategy (see Figure 3.3). It has been suggested that in order to be successful, a company's strategy should be aligned with, or 'fit', its organizational culture. This relationship is far from straightforward, however. Hence, while there are several approaches to the relationship between organizational culture and strategy, only one suggests the link with success. Below we briefly discuss the different approaches and clarify why one should be wary of the link with success.

One less popular approach to the link between strategy and organizational culture suggests that the two are essentially synonymous because they are both 'deeply ingrained patterns of management behavior', and they both '[emerge] out of the cumulative effect of many informed actions and decisions taken daily and over years by many employees' (Greiner, 1983, cited in Weick, 1985: 384).

Another approach sees organizational culture as the driving force behind all movements in the organization (an approach that is advocated by, among others, Mintzberg, 1979, and Saffold, 1988). This approach argues that the chosen strategy depends to, a large extent, on the existing culture. As an illustration of this relationship between culture and strategy, Gordon (1991: 399) considers an electric utility where a basic assumption is that customers need continuous, uninterrupted service. Within that assumption and the values it produces there might be variations. For example, a utility might focus on either industrial or residential businesses because either strategy would not conflict with the basic assumption of continuous service. In contrast, a strategy of selling power at higher prices outside the service area, which might result in periodic service interruptions within the service area, would conflict with the basic beliefs regarding continuous service and, therefore, would not be considered an acceptable direction for the company to pursue. Moreover, in the case of the regulated utility industry, such a strategy would not be tolerated by the regulating authority and, thus, would be directly affected by societal expectations as well.

The contrasting perspective on this view argues that culture is best seen as directed by the strategy of a company. It is thereby asserted that one starts with a competitive strategy, and then defines and implements – parallel to other parts of the strategy – the required culture (i.e. Davis, 1984; Morgan, 1993). This approach is very technocratic, and is preferred by those consultants who tout the 'cultural turnaround'. Major drawbacks of the approach are the assumption that organizational culture is *consciously* constructed and is not at all affected by environmental influences.

Finally, some scholars (i.e. Scholz, 1987a, 1987b) claim that both aspects are heavily interrelated, which makes the fit between culture and strategy the relevant variable. The problem with this approach is the assumed connection between fit and success. In this respect, it is argued that a necessary condition for success is the degree of alignment between culture and strategy. For instance, an empowerment culture is more likely to underpin a strategy where staff creativity is a critical success factor resulting in a high level of innovation (Ghobadian and O'Regan, 2002: 30).

However, even though fit is considered to be the main reason for success, it is often defined as that particular combination of variables that is successful. Critics (i.e. Schreyögg, 1989), therefore, rightly claim that this approach is tautological and, therefore, theoretically unsound. Moreover, the difficulties with understanding and defining existing strategy and culture might lead us to argue that the creation of a culture–strategy fit is a modern 'mission impossible'. If we cannot operationalize two (or more) elements adequately, how can we make them fit?

Related to the fit argument, Ghobadian and O'Regan (2002) point broadly to a circular interrelationship between organizational culture, strategy and performance (Figure 3.3). Culture influences strategy and, in turn, is influenced by strategy. They both affect performance and, in turn, are affected by the firm's performance. Most research in this direction, however, examines the bilateral relationship between strategy and performance, culture and performance or strategy, but not the three variables within the same

Figure 3.3 The culture–strategy–performance relationship

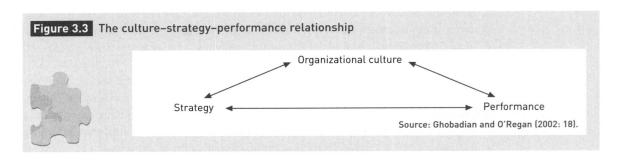

Source: Ghobadian and O'Regan (2002: 18).

domain as a single integrated study. We would, therefore, urge caution when strong statements are made about the relationship between the three variables. It is clear that more research is needed in this area before definite conclusions can be drawn.

3.7 Organizational Culture and Economic Performance

In a managerial context, organizational culture gains importance when it can be linked to economic performance. We have already discussed how organizational culture can be linked to employee and corporate performance by using the concept of 'cultural fit'. This section broadens the picture by discussing some ideas from the management literature regarding whether and the extent to which organizational culture can be used as a management instrument to improve corporate performance. There are several viewpoints on this topic.[9] Broadly speaking, these can be classified into the three approaches described below.

Culture as a building block

The most popular approach is the view that culture is a 'building block'. This view is the most instrumentally orientated of all views, giving rise to the idea that a particular input leads to a predictable effect. Culture is assumed to be designed by management and to have a strong impact on results. Accordingly, this type of research on corporate culture and organizational symbolism has been dominated by a preoccupation with a limited set of meanings, symbols, values and ideas presumed to be manageable and directly related to effectiveness and economic performance (i.e. Deal and Kennedy, 1982; Peters and Waterman, 1982; Kilmann *et al.*, 1985). The values and ideas to which this type of organizational culture research pays attention are primarily connected with the means and operations employed to achieve predefined and unquestioned goals. Associated with this is a bias towards the trivialization of culture, over-stressing the role of management and the employment of causal thinking.

Within this approach, corporate cultures are evaluated in terms of whether they are more or less 'good', 'strong', 'valuable', 'dysfunctional', and so on. Often, good or valuable is equated with strong. Strong is defined in various ways: as coherence (Deal and Kennedy, 1982; Weick, 1985); as stability and intensity (Schein, 1985); as homogeneity (Ouchi and Price, 1978); as congruence (Schall, 1983); as 'thickness' (Sathe, 1983); as penetration (Louis, 1985); as internalized control (DiTomaso, 1978). A strong culture is argued to facilitate goal alignment and, to increase motivation, and is often directly related to the level of profits in a company (i.e. Denison, 1984). One problem, however, is that the literature is ambiguous about the content of the beliefs or values thought to produce a strong organizational culture. Moreover, few empirical studies have actually related cultural characteristics to some measure of corporate financial performance (Gordon, 1992).

---

[9] See Alvesson (2002, chapter 3) for a more complete discussion of this topic. Unless indicated otherwise, the following discussion draws on this chapter.

Another problem is that some research argues for the reverse relationship between culture and performance, suggesting that high performance leads to the creation of a 'strong' corporate culture (or cultural homogeneity). While it seems plausible that success brings about a common set of orientations, beliefs and values, this culture may be more than just a by-product of high performance. Furthermore, it may also be a source of conservatism and a liability in situations calling for radical change.

Yet another view within this train of thought draws upon contingency thinking to suggest that, under certain conditions, a particular type of culture is appropriate, even necessary, and contributes to efficiency. Still another version argues that 'adaptive' cultures are the key to good performance (i.e. cultures that are able to respond to changes in the environment). Such cultures are characterized by people willing to take risks, trust each other, be proactive, work together to identify problems and opportunities, and so on. It may be tempting to say that 'adaptive cultures' are self-evidently superior. However, an element of tautology easily comes into play here: 'adaptive' implies successful adaptation, and this is, by definition, good for business (Alvesson, 2002: 54).

> There are organizations that are relatively stable and fit with a relatively stable environment, and risk-taking and innovation are not necessarily successful. Indeed, too much change can lead to instability, low cost-efficiency, risky projects and a loss of sense of direction. (Brown, 1995 as in Alvesson, 2002: 54)[10]

Culture as a tool and constraint

A second approach linking organizational culture with performance emphasizes the reality-defining powers of management action. It is assumed that the leaders of an organization exercise more or less far-reaching influence on the way in which employees perceive and understand their tasks and on the workplace by creating and maintaining metaphors and myths. One result of this type of influence, from management's point of view, might be the sharing of a 'favourable' definition of organizational reality and work by the whole organization or a part of it. (i.e. Berg, 1986; Pfeffer, 1981; Smircich and Morgan, 1982 as in Alvesson, 2002: 49–50)[11]

Other possible consequences include mobilization/motivation, satisfaction of demands, implementation of change, and attitudes and feelings of satisfaction.

> The most important behaviour patterns, however, are basically determined by external constraints. The cultural dimension is more a stabilizing force: 'Shared understandings are likely to emerge to rationalize the patterns of behavior that develop, and in the absence of such rationalization and meaning creation, the structured patterns of behavior are likely to be less stable and persistent.' (Alvesson, 2002: 50)[12]

[10] Reproduced with permission from Alvesson, M., *Understanding Organizational Change* © Mats Alvesson 2002, by permission of Sage Publications Ltd.

[11] Reproduced with permission from Alvesson, M., *Understanding Organizational Change* © Mats Alvesson 2002, by permission of Sage Publications Ltd.

[12] Reproduced with permission from Alvesson, M., *Understanding Organizational Change* © Mats Alvesson 2002, by permission of Sage Publications Ltd.

The approach sees culture as mediated in actions, language use and arrangements primarily affecting beliefs and understandings, having merely consequences for attitudes and orientations, and less directly so for substantive outcomes (such as profits). Clever symbolic action, however, may serve to appease groups that are dissatisfied with the organization, thereby ensuring their continued support of the organization and the reduction of opposition and conflict.

> Pfeffer is more careful, then, than most writers on 'corporate culture' about postulating causal relations between cultures and corporate performance, instead stressing the avoidance of problems which might negatively affect organizational performance such as conflict, resistance, wide-spread frustration, high turnover, and absenteeism. (Alvesson, 2002: 50)[13]

Culture as a diagnostic instrument

The third approach in using the idea of organizational culture in relation to corporate performance is to treat culture as a diagnostic instrument,

> A third position using the idea of organizational culture in relation to corporate performance is to treat culture as a diagnostic instrument, as an aid in making decisions and avoiding traps. It stresses the deep values and basic assumptions of organizations – unconscious or half-conscious beliefs and ideals about objectives, relationships to the external world, and the internal relations that underlie behavioural norms and other 'artefacts'. Culture is viewed as relatively resistant to attempts to control and change and only occasionally manageable. This approach is not much concerned about giving advice on how culture can be controlled, but it does attempt to be of practical relevance by informing managers of what may be difficult or impossible to accomplish and providing ideas for constructive action in the light of culture. . . . The focus here is not on the effects of managerial action but rather on the consequences of organizational cultures on how the initiatives and change efforts are reacted upon. (Alvesson, 2002: 51)[14]

The three perspectives discussed above reflect different assumptions of senior management opportunities to shape organizational members' ideas, meanings, values and norms according to their business goals. The first approach posits the influential position of management; in the second, management and culture are intertwined and carry similar weight; in the third, culture is a resistant force to which management must adapt.

> Management's possibilities to shape culture vary with circumstances – in a young company in a fast-growing market the chances are much better than in a situation of managing a highly experienced workforce on a mature market. (Alvesson, 2002: 53)[15]

---

[13] Reproduced with permission from Alvesson, M., *Understanding Organizational Change* © Mats Alvesson 2002, by permission of Sage Publications Ltd.

[14] Reproduced with permission from Alvesson, M., *Understanding Organizational Change* © Mats Alvesson 2002, by permission of Sage Publications Ltd.

[15] Reproduced with permission from Alvesson, M., *Understanding Organizational Change* © Mats Alvesson 2002, by permission of Sage Publications Ltd.

Generally, some wariness about assuming too much in terms of the ability of management to control and intentionally change culture is recommended (Alvesson, 2002).

Furthermore, it is very difficult to link simply and unambiguously corporate culture to corporate results. Not only is corporate culture difficult to capture, but so is performance. It is of course plausible to argue that what we call 'corporate culture' will have an effect on many aspects of corporate life, and also on corporate financial performance. Any such influence, however, can hardly be disentangled from all the factors and interaction patterns that have something to do with these results. Moreover, to interpret a phenomenon as complex as culture in terms of 'good' and 'bad' is not easy to do. For instance, while Peters and Waterman (1982) outlined eight characteristics of 'excellent' (i.e. effectively performing) organizations, within two years after the publication of their book, a third of the companies identified as excellent experienced poor performance.

In this respect,

> Instead of giving up the idea of finding clear-cut empirical answers to the questions of 'corporate culture's' effect on performance, some researchers have argued that a more refined approach which takes into account the complexity of culture should guide empirical research. (Alvesson, 2002: 55)[16]

Saffold (1998: 546), for example, argues that it is reasonable to expect that 'a phenomenon as pervasive as organizational culture affects organizational performance', but that existing models oversimplify the relationship.[17]

He points to five important shortcomings of empirical studies:

(1) 'strong culture' studies tend to emphasize a single, unitary organizational culture even though multiple subcultures rather than unitary cultures seem to be the rule;

(2) measures of the 'strength' of culture are ambiguous partly because in the study of culture 'meanings are central, not frequencies' (Van Maanen and Barley, 1984: 307);

(3) there is a preference for broad-brush cultural profiles, focusing on very general values and norms, which fail to do justice to the complexity of culture;

(4) there is insufficient attention to the variety of possible culture-performance links. A particular cultural feature may affect different performance-related organizational processes in different directions. Development of shared meanings may, for example, have a positive effect on organizational control but at the same time create conformism and reduce the organization's capacity to learn and change;

(5) there are many methodological problems in existing studies, ranging from over-reliance on top management views to the absence of control groups.

Saffold suggests an enriched framework, which involves the 'use of appropriate measures of culture's impact', the use of contextual rather than modal analysis

---

[16] Reproduced with permission from Alvesson, M., *Understanding Organizational Change* © Mats Alvesson 2002, by permission of Sage Publications Ltd.

[17] The following discussion is based essentially on Alvesson (2002: 55–6).

(i.e. avoidance of static and abstract categorizations), and attention to multiple interaction effects. This framework involves:

(1) measures of cultural dispersion, the degree to which cultural characteristics are dispersed throughout an organization (sociologically, psychologically, historically and artefactually);

(2) measures of cultural potency (the power of the culture itself to influence behaviour);

(3) studies of 'how specific culturally conditioned processes contribute to outcomes'; and

(4) the recognition of multiple, mutually causal interactions. (Alvesson, 2002: 55–56)[18]

Saffold admits the complexity of the suggested approach but, at the same time, argues that this is unavoidable since only such a framework 'reflects the true richness of culture–performance relationships'.

3.8 ❖ Creation and Consolidation of Organizational Culture

An intriguing aspect of organizational culture is how it originates. How do two companies with similar external environments (e.g. in the same country, industry) and founders of similar origins come to have entirely different ways of operating over the years? Moreover, an organizational culture is not created from one day to the next, but evolves over time. The question, then, is: 'Does evolvement mean change or continuity?' These matters are addressed in this section. At the end of this section (pages 128–9) there is a case study that addresses the issue of the evolution of particular features of organizational culture. The lesson to take away from this case is that, while continuity can be desirable, it can also involve undesirable rigidities, which are hard to tackle.

Creation

Schein identifies three mechanisms through which culture is created: leadership identification, the social trauma or critical incident model, and the success model (Schein, 1990, 1992). When groups or organizations first form, there are usually dominant figures or 'founders' whose beliefs, values and assumptions provide a visible and articulated model for how the group should be structured and how it should function. Founders not only choose the basic mission and the environmental context in which the new group will operate, they also choose the group members and bias the original responses that the group makes in its efforts to succeed in its environment and to integrate well. As the founder's beliefs are put into practice, some work out and some do not. The group then learns from its own experience what parts of the 'founder's' belief system work out for the group as a whole. The joint learning is argued to gradually create shared assumptions.

[18] Reproduced with permission from Alvesson, M., *Understanding Organisational Change*, © Mats Alvesson 2002, by permission of Sage Publications Ltd.

Even in mature companies one can trace many of the assumptions to the beliefs and values of the founders and early leaders. The special role that these leaders play is to propose the initial answers to the questions that the young group has about how to operate internally and externally. The group cannot test potential solutions if nothing is proposed. However, while founders have an influence on organizational culture, the cultural literature neglects the impact of industry characteristics upon initial culture formation. As explained in Section 3.5, in order to survive, a company's culture should be congruent with the industrial environment in which it operates.

The social trauma model sets in when an organization is confronted with uncertainty: uncertainty regarding the chance of survival, productivity and cooperation. When the measures provided (mostly by the management) help to remove this uncertainty and create a more predictable future, next time, in similar situations, the same measures will be used to avoid the unpleasant feeling of uncertainty. Crisis and uncertainty are especially significant in culture creation and transmission because the heightened emotional involvement during such periods increases the intensity of learning. Crises heighten anxiety, and anxiety reduction is a powerful motivator of new learning. The big threat in this learning mechanism is that it leads to the avoidance of problems. When the members of organizations have once been exposed to an unpleasant situation and they have learned to solve it, they will continue to use the solution but will not deal with the root of the problem.

The success model has a different basis. This model implies that when a certain behaviour from the past leads to success, members will repeat this behaviour up to the point where there is common agreement that the behaviour is correct. The main difference with the social trauma mechanism is that learned behaviour is tested continuously by its environment; when this behaviour is no longer successful, it will be recognized and adapted. Members of an organization repeat things that do work and point out things that do not work.

Consolidation

While the aforementioned mechanisms help to explain how culture is created, practices such as (self-)selection and socialization help to explain its perpetuation and reproduction (Schein, 1990; Noorderhaven, 1995). During a selection process an organization selects and recruits individuals who not only have the knowledge and capability to be part of the organization, but also have the 'right' set of assumptions (Schein, 1990: 115). In contrast, individuals who do not identify themselves with the organization and its culture will in most cases not seek to become a member of the organization (see the case on pages 128–9). The process of (self-)selection thus keeps an existing culture in place.

However, even when the selection process is performed well, there will always be differences between the practices and values of a new member and those of the existing members of the organization. The process of socialization then stimulates new employees to adapt to the organization. The socialization process can be guided and strengthened by introduction programmes. Several instruments can be used to do so (e.g. articles in the company's internal magazine, intranet, speeches by managers, group discussions, internal and external training, and 'brainstorming' session). However, socialization is not always achieved deliberately. Socialization normally takes place during interactions with colleagues, inducing the spontaneous adaptation of opinions. Furthermore, adaptation to an organizational culture by the members of the organization mostly happens without awareness of it. After being exposed for a longer period to the organization, organizational practices become familiar.

A problem one has to be wary of with approaches to organizational culture creation, and more so with approaches to organizational culture perpetuation, is that they seem implicitly to presume cultural homogeneity throughout the organization. The idea that whole organizations can have distinct cultures and that top managers are the central architects behind these was an idea widely embraced in the 1980s. This view – sometimes referred to as an integration perspective – still seems to dominate in popular (and in a few academic) writings. It is often linked closely to an idealistic notion of culture in the sense that a set of overall meanings, ideas and values communicated by senior management will lead to a strong sense of direction and priorities shared broadly within the organization. As suggested in Section 3.3, the existence of subcultures, professional cultures, external influences, and so on, renders the idea of 'one corporate culture' problematic. We are not saying here that it is impossible to foster a common organizational pattern of behaviours, practices and ideas, but we do wish to emphasize that a common pattern does not necessarily imply that *all* practices, behaviours and ideas will be common.

Case: Glass Ceiling or Sticky Floor? Organizational Culture as a Source of Stickiness at RaboBank

Few women gain access to the highest positions as executive heads of organizations. Depite some improvements, the progress of advancement of women is slow, given the large number of qualified women in the labour market today. While women have captured an ever increasing share of the labour market, improvements in the quality of women's jobs have not kept pace. Surveys reveal that even in the largest and most powerful companies worldwide, women's presence at the very top of the organization is limited to a mere 2 to 3 per cent. This phenomenon is called the 'glass ceiling'. This is because there seems to be an invisible ceiling that stops women from rising higher than a certain level.

An examination of several banks in the Netherlands shows that, in particular, the well-known Dutch multinational, RaboBank, is facing problems of under-representation of women at managerial levels. While women represent 60 per cent of the total workforce, men still occupy 80 per cent of the executive positions. In 1990, RaboBank introduced an Emancipation Policy both at RaboBank Netherlands and in the local banks. Among other things, the policy implied that RaboBank management had to increase the number of women in managerial postions and experiment with part-time work in higher and management functions. The policy was updated in 1998 and 1999, but the backlog compared to competitors in the banking sector remained large. Rather like its competitors, RaboBank provides its employees with comfortable secondary work conditions that should help improve the position of women at higher levels. But, unlike its competitors, RaboBank does not succeed in attracting women to managerial positions.

The under-representation of women in managerial positions has several explanations. In recent years, however, organizational culture has been pointed to as a major explanatory variable. Specifically, 'male-orientated' organizational cultures, characterized by hierarchical authority, independence, autocratic leadership styles and top-down communication, are argued to be barriers to women's progress. Moreover, organizations become more homogenous as one moves up the organizational hierarchy. At the lower levels, there are many employees performing different kinds of task. At the top of the organization, tasks are less varied and are essentially managerial. The homogeneity is also reflected in the type of people performing such jobs. Very often they have the same demographic features, come from a certain socio-economic background and are mostly men. It has been argued that only those who fit the organizational culture at the top have a chance of ending up there.

A closer look at RaboBank's emancipation initiatives shows that the initiatives come from RaboBank Netherlands, which functions as an advisory body for the local banks. It assists the local banks with formulating strategy and policies. The local banks are entirely independent, however, and make their own decisions. Moreover, the local banks received the information on the Emancipation Policy by e-mail and had not been involved in the original discussions. The policy was communicated at board of directors and management team levels, but not at the lower levels at which most female employees are working. Furthermore, no attention was paid to the implementation part of the policy, which makes it difficult for the local banks to put the advice into practice. In addition, there are no women on the board of RaboBank Netherlands. The local banks used this as an excuse not to take the Emancipation Policy too seriously.

In general, RaboBank is a very traditional bank with traditional customers. In rural areas, such as Gelderland, Groningen, Friesland and Limburg, in particular, it seems that the traditional societal culture has an effect upon corporate culture. Indeed, in these areas, many of the customers are farmers, and local bank managers argue that their male clients prefer a male adviser. Also, RaboBank still perceives jobs in terms of typically 'male' and 'female'. For example, jobs that are more commercially orientated and require responsibility are argued to be typically 'male', while other tasks, such as desk and secretarial functions, are said to be typically 'female'. Such viewpoints are also expressed in selection and recruitment procedures. Moreover, it is argued that women who are ambitious and career-orientated will not apply for a RaboBank job but will go for a job at ABN AMRO or ING banks instead. In addition, those female employees with ambition often leave RaboBank after a few years because they feel they are stuck at one level. It could, in fact, be argued that female employees at local RaboBanks have not yet been confronted with the glass ceiling because they are still struggling with the sticky floor!

Questions

1. How can organizational culture block women from top positions?

2. Explain the relationship between organizational and regional subcultures.

3. Explain that, despite the fact that according to Hofstede's dimensions the Netherlands is a 'female' country, RaboBank seems to have a 'male' culture.

4. What would you advise RaboBank Netherlands to do to solve the problem of the under-representation of women in managerial positions?

5. Explain, on the basis of this case, the mechanisms through which RaboBank's male culture survives despite emancipatory initiatives.

3.9 Organizational Culture Change

The final topic we wish to discuss in this chapter deals with the possibility of changing organizational cultures. In the above case, we suggest that organizational cultures tend to have features that are strongly embedded in an organization and, hence, are difficult to change. In general, it is recognized that although cultures are always somewhat in motion, intentional and systematic organizational cultural change is a difficult task. This section discusses whether and the extent to which organizational culture change is feasible.

In the popular management literature, there is much optimism, but most reflective writers treating this topic downplay the chances of intentional cultural change, at least of the grand technocratic type (Lundberg, 1985; Fitzgerald, 1988; Brown, 1995; Grey, 1999). While the following discussion implies that cultures can be changed, or 'managed', the question of how much change in culture can be planned for and implemented by existing or new management remains unanswered. Although many authors have described processes for managing culture (i.e. Davis, 1984; Allen, 1985; Kilmann *et al.*, 1985; Schein, 1985), there is still little empirical evidence on just how effective such processes are (Gordon, 1991: 412).

The task of organizational culture change is highly constrained by the variety of cultural manifestations, and the multitude of group identifications and commitments. There are also cultural constraints, related not only to a large proportion of the employees, but also to many top executives themselves, especially those promoted from within. In addition, the middle-management layers are also disinclined to implement change, as they often have little to gain and much to lose. Moreover, the relationship between organizational and industry culture limits the potential to change a company's culture to actions that are neutral to, or directionally consistent with, industry demands (Gordon, 1991).

In contrast, when a company's industry environment changes in terms of the competitive environment, customer requirements or social expectations, behaviours based on past assumptions (values) might be ineffective; thus the company is likely to experience negative results. Such a condition is argued to create pressures for change; but the culture, based upon successful lessons from the past, will resist change. Cultural change at the levels of assumption (the deepest level) may not be possible unless many of the people or their positions change (Dyer, 1985). At the same time, it is argued that environmental changes that require cultural changes at the deepest level rarely occur, because these would involve the total restructuring of an industry.

Environmental changes that require cultural changes at less deep levels, such as the levels of values (for Schein), rituals, heroes, symbols and artefacts, are less encompassing and are likely to occur more often (Gordon, 1991). The cultural changes required in these situations are argued to occur through experimentation and learning. Such changes require readjustment with the direction of environmental pressures, but this does not involve any change in basic assumptions (values).

Experimentation and change will normally be initiated by those who are not a product of the dominant culture (i.e. those who are not committed to the existing value system). Such facilitators of cultural change can include new management (Dyer, 1985; Lorsch, 1985), members of counter-cultures (Martin and Siehl, 1982) and consultants (Gagliardi, 1986). Organizational learning leading to a change in the less deep cultural levels (i.e. values, beliefs, artefacts) takes place because actions that are in conflict with established values, rituals, and so on (but consonant with the current environment), are successful and are considered successful by others in the organization (Gordon, 1991).

Three types of organizational culture change

The extent to which industry and organizational culture constraints play a role is related to the cultural level at which change is to take place but also to the type of change or the scale at which change is required or demanded. In this sense the literature distinguishes between three types of organization culture change: the grand project, organic movement and everyday reframing.[19]

The most popular type of organization culture change is the *grand technocratic project*, which is related to the instrumental approach to organization culture.

> Most descriptive and even more normative models of large-scale cultural change are of this type. It portrays or promises the possibility of an intentional large-scale transformation from a particular cultural situation to another, more superior and profitable one.[20]

This view posits that organization culture change is a top-down project. Top management is assumed to develop superior insights about the required change and is also the chief architect behind the plan for change.

> Aside from planning and allocation of resources to change projects and making decisions in line with the wanted change, the acts of senior executives – public speeches, highly visible acts drawing attention to ideals – also symbolize re-framing

---

[19] For an extended explanation of these three types, see Alvesson (2002: 177–81). I am indebted to Alvesson for this typology of change.

[20] Reproduced with permission from Alvesson, M., *Understanding Organizational Change* © Mats Alvesson 2002, by permission of Sage Publications Ltd.

of how people should think, feel, and act in accordance with new ideals and values.[21]

Usually, consultants are used to back up senior managers in this kind of change project.
The second type of organization culture change is the *organic social movement*.

Change is then mainly something emergent. There is no strong, uniform will acting as the center in the change, neither is there that much of intentionality and a clear plan. Groups within the organization revise their thinking, valuing and giving meaning to phenomena 'spontaneously'. These new ideas may originate within the organization as many people feel discontent with dominant ideas and practices and want to consider another set of ideas, but they may also originate outside the organization and then gradually take root there. It may be a matter of people in the organizations noticing changes in customers when interacting with them, calling for new responses and potentially involving reconsideration of some important ideas and beliefs. It may also be broadly shared new ideas in society, e.g. on gender, a common European currency or sustainable development, that affect people who then 'carry' and insert and express these ideas in the organization.

Cultural change as an organic movement means that groups within an organization follow the flow of the new ideas gradually leading to organization cultural change. . . . For organic movement changes to have a strong impact on organizations, senior managers need to share and support the new ideas and orientations. (Alvesson, 2002: 179)[22]

Sometimes broad societal or industry-level changes are so strong that individual organizations must respond to these. There is then an institutional pressure to adapt to new ideas – inability or unwillingness to do so leading to legitimacy problems (DiMaggio and Powell, 1983; Scott, 1995 as in Alvesson, 2002: 179).[23]

The third view on cultural change – *everyday reframing* – is the more relevant mode of cultural change for the large majority of managers, not being at the top of large organizations.

Everyday re-framing is mainly an informal culture-shaping agenda, involving pedagogical leadership in which an actor exercises a subtle influence through the re-negotiation of meaning. . . . Everyday re-framing is, on the other hand, strongly anchored in interactions and 'natural' communication. It is also better adapted to the material work situations of people and has thus stronger action-implications. (Alvesson, 2002: 180)[24]

It is, typically, mainly incremental and is a matter of local cultural change.

---

[21] Reproduced with permission from Alvesson, M., *Understanding Organizational Change* © Mats Alvesson 2002, by permission of Sage Publications Ltd.

[22] Reproduced with permission from Alvesson, M., *Understanding Organizational Change* © Mats Alvesson 2002, by permission of Sage Publications Ltd.

[23] Reproduced with permission from Alvesson, M., *Understanding Organizational Change* © Mats Alvesson 2002, by permission of Sage Publications Ltd.

[24] Reproduced with permission from Alvesson, M., *Understanding Organizational Change* © Mats Alvesson 2002, by permission of Sage Publications Ltd.

The three types of change are not contradictory but may also go hand in hand. New ideas and values in society may 'soften up' an organization for change; top management may experience a combination of legitimacy problems and convictions that there are good 'internal' reasons for change and therefore take initiatives to changes. Specific managers, without getting specific instructions to do something special but encouraged by societal changes and new signals from top management, may take initiatives to re-frame local thinking on the issue concerned. Within a specific domain, a division, department or a work group, the re-shaping of ideas, values and meaning then may be more drastic than in other parts of the organization, without necessarily deviating from these in the direction of the change. (Alvesson, 2002: 181)[25]

Cultural change versus structural and material change

Aside from the *type* of cultural change, there is also the question of whether cultural change also involves matters such as structural and material arrangements, directly implying behavioural changes. Broadly speaking, there are two schools of thought on this issue. Most authors on organizational culture emphasize the level of assumptions (values), ideas and beliefs in order to make any 'real' change possible. Occasionally, writers stress the more material side of organizations. This approach suggests that

> Another would be that making people behave differently is what matters; cultural changes will follow from this. Re-allocation of resources and rewarding different behaviour would then be sufficient. (Alvesson, 2002: 181)[26]

One could plausibly argue, however, that the relevant level and/or aspects of change are matters of the problems or questions concerned.

> If it is a matter of core business with direct perceived links to production, performances and performance measures, then a 'pure' cultural change appears unrealistic. (Alvesson, 2002: 182)[27]

If we talk about something less material, like greater openness or new ways of interacting with customers, then cultural elements become involved. Often, however, the interplay between the level of meaning and the level of behaviour, material and structural arrangements must be considered in organizational change. There are sufficient examples of these dilemmas in the literature.

> There are various estimations whether a change towards knowledge sharing calls for structural measures, such as performance evaluations and incentives (as argued by e.g. Davenport and Prusak, 1998), or whether 'true' knowledge sharing

---

[25] Reproduced with permission from Alvesson, M., *Understanding Organizational Change* © Mats Alvesson 2002, by permission of Sage Publications Ltd.

[26] Reproduced with permission from Alvesson, M., *Understanding Organizational Change* © Mats Alvesson 2002, by permission of Sage Publications Ltd.

[27] Reproduced with permission from Alvesson, M., *Understanding Organizational Change* © Mats Alvesson 2002, by permission of Sage Publications Ltd.

presupposes value commitments (O'Dell and Grayson, 1998), that may be counter-acted by formal control extrinsic rewards. (Alvesson, 2002: 182)[28]

Regarding gender issues, of which the above case study on RaboBank is an example, there is debate as to whether increased gender equality in organizations can be accomplished through cultural change measures or if this calls for structural elements such as changes in the ratio of men/women in particular senior positions.

Greater representation by women would then lead to cultural changes, it is assumed (Kanter, 1977; Ely, 1995). Another position assumes that the use of structural measures – setting targets and controlling that these are attained – to recruit or promote greater numbers of females in order to fill the quota does not imply a qualitative change and may backfire as those recruited/promoted will be negatively evaluated as the merits will be seen as less significant for their promotion and stereotypes to be reinforced. (Alvesson, 2002: 182)[29]

Study Questions

1. What are the main differences between the emic and etic approach to organizational culture? Under what circumstances would you use either approach?

2. How would you go about analysing the effects of the societal environment on organizational culture?

3. Explain whether it always makes sense to distinguish between the different levels (societal, industrial, individual) at which organizational culture can be analysed?

4. Explain the relationship between industry characteristics and organizational culture.

5. Discuss the relationship between organizational culture and strategy.

6. Discuss whether, how and when organizational culture affects organizational performance?

7. Explain whether organizational culture can *always* be changed readily. Discuss whether there are aspects of organizational culture that are more easily changed than others and, if so, whether this change can be called *real* change.

8. How can industry features limit organizational culture change, and how can a change in the industrial environment enforce organizational culture change?

9. What are the mechanisms that help organizations to perpetuate and reproduce some of the widely shared assumptions within the organization?

10. Explain whether cultural fit is always essential for successful mergers and acquisitions.

[28] Reproduced with permission from Alvesson, M., *Understanding Organizational Change* © Mats Alvesson 2002, by permission of Sage Publications Ltd.
[29] Reproduced with permission from Alvesson, M., *Understanding Organizational Change* © Mats Alvesson 2002, by permission of Sage Publications Ltd.

Further Reading

Alvesson, M. (2002) *Understanding Organizational Culture.* London: Sage Publications Ltd.

Critical book on organizational culture research. Deals with a wide range of topics that have been touched upon in this chapter.

Cartwright, S. and Cooper, C.L. (1993) The role of culture compatibility in successful organizational marriage. *Academy of Management Executive* 2, 57–70.

Interesting article examining the role of culture compatibility in determining venture outcomes.

Datta, D.K. (1991) Organizational fit and acquisition performance: effects of post-acquisition integration. *Strategic Management Journal* 12, 281–97.

Excellent article that deals explicitly with the link between differences in top management styles, and acquisition integration and performance.

Hempel, P.S. and Ching-yen Daphne Chang (2002) Reconciling traditional Chinese management with high-tech Taiwan. *Human Resource Management Journal* 12(1), 77–95.

This article offers initial evidence on the adaptation of management 'culture' in Taiwan in order to enable industrial development in new sectors.

Klein, K.J. and Kozlowski, S.W.J. (2000) *Multilevel Theory, Research and Methods in Organizations.* San Francisco: Jossey-Bass.

This book offers a thorough treatment of multilevel theorizing and analysis in the organizational context.

Martin, J. (2002) *Organizational Culture: Mapping the Terrain.* London: Sage.

Highly accessible and instructive book on organizational culture. It provides a balanced and critical overview of the chaotic field of organizational culture research.

Case: Atos Origin and KPN: an Organizational Culture Analysis in the Complex World of ICT Mergers[30]

 Atos Origin is a relatively young organization, which resulted from the merger in 2000 between the Dutch company Origin and the French company Atos. The entire staff and management of Atos Origin is Dutch and management of the company is independent of the French Atos.

[30] This case study is based on fieldwork carried out by one of my students, Dion Plouvier, between March 2002 and November 2002, at Atos Origin DTS in Eindhoven and KPN WD in Amsterdam, both in the Netherlands. I owe him many thanks.

In May 2002, Atos Origin acquired KPN WerkplekDiensten (WD) (workplace services), which is a subdivision of the services division of the Dutch KPN, and which administered 27,000 internal workplaces (desktop computers, portable computers, etc.) for KPN. The acquisition meant that around 700 employees of KPN WD became Atos Origin employees. More specifically, KPN WD was merged with the business unit Desktop Services (DTS) at Atos Origin. The latter employed almost 800 people. From summer 2002 onwards, a new management team has headed the new business unit – called Atos Origin End User Services. The head of the new unit is the former head of KPN WD, Geert Wapstra.

In general, before and during the merger process most, if not all, attention is paid to questions with respect to product market relationships, continuity and finance. Issues such as cultural differences receive less attention because they cannot be expressed in financial or strategic terms. However, research shows that more than half of mergers and acquisitions fail, and that culture is a major explanatory variable. It is surprising, then, that the merging world continues to focus on strategic analysis and planning issues essentially. Atos Origin DTS and KPN WD are exceptions to this rule. Aware of the problems that can occur as a result of cultural differences, during the merging process the two companies had their organizational cultures examined and prepared measures to ensure the successful integration of the two subdivisions. In the following text, some background information on the two companies – Atos Origin and KPN – is offered (see also Figure 3.4). Next, the results of the organizational culture analysis at the Dutch Atos Origin DTS and the Dutch KPN WD are discussed, together with potential problem areas.

Background
The formation of Atos

In January 1997, the French companies Axime and Sligos merged. The merged company was named Atos. In 1995, Axime was admitted for quotation on the stock market. At that time Paribas held 88 per cent of its shares. This was reduced to 26 per cent in 1996. The Sligos Group was established in 1970 as a result of the merger between Cegos Informatique – a consulting company, which also developed management systems – and Sliga – a division of Crédit Lyonnais, involved in data processing.

After the merger, Atos implemented a new organization structure based on four service lines: Services, Multimedia, Outsourcing and Systems Integration. All service lines delivered international services.

In January 2000, Atos established a joint venture with Euronext, called Atos Euronext. From that time on, the company has been the European leader in financial and IT services. At the time of the merger with Origin in 2000, the Atos Group had approximately 11,000 employees working in 11 European countries. In 1999, the Group reported a turnover of 1.1bn euros, 67 per cent of which was realized in France.

The formation of Origin

In 1996, Origin came into existence as a result of the merger between the Dutch BSO/Origin and Philips Communication and Processing Services (C&P).

Philips C&P was a division of the large Dutch Philips concern and encompassed Philips' IT services. The origin of Philips C&P can be traced back to 1968, when Philips established the division called Information Systems and Automation (ISA). This division focused on the development of software, the administration and maintenance of the computer centre and networks, and internal customer support. In 1989, this division was reorganized and split into two separate divisions: Philips C&P, and Philips Application and Software Services (PASS).

In 1976, BSO was set up as an independent IT services company. The company was commercially orientated and had a flat structure, consisting of independent units called 'cells'. The intention was to stimulate flexibility and entrepreneurship. The cell structure seemed to stimulate growth and geographic spread.

In 1990, BSO set up a joint venture with Philips PASS. Philips Electronics was the majority shareholder of the joint venture. The new company was called BSO/Origin. Philips PASS was different from BSO in that it delivered services to other Philips divisions. The customer was, in fact, perceived as a colleague. In addition, PASS had a more bureaucratic style of management. A major change for BSO was that the expansion was accompanied by an increased emphasis on professionalism, centralization and rules. Cells were cut in half and 'full service' cells were developed, which offered the entire package of services. The differences in organizational culture and the change in organization structure resulted in problems that were not to be forgotten easily by the management team. Despite the fact that all employees were Dutch, during the initial phase of the joint venture (BSO/Origin) employees seemed unable to cooperate, communication was difficult and, despite major efforts on the part of management, former BSO and former PASS employees continued to form subgroups within the organization. This split within the organization hampered effectiveness and slowed down productivity.

The formation of Atos/Origin and DTS

In August 2000, Atos and Philips Electronics, the majority shareholder of Origin, signed an agreement for the merger of Atos and Origin. The merger resulted in the formation of the company Atos Origin, which is a worldwide operating ICT services company.

Atos Origin offers an entire ICT service package from the consulting phase to the development and operationalization of large ICT projects. To this end, Atos Origin established three service lines: Consulting and Systems Integration (C&SI), Managed Services (MS) and On-Line Services. A service line consists of a service package targeted at a specific market. The first service line, C&SI, offers advice, and develops and operationalizes innovations in ICT applications. The second service line, MS, manages ICT systems on a world scale. This entails the integrated management of servers, networks and desktop systems. The services are delivered on the basis of long-term contracts and entail daily support of the business operations of customers. On-Line Services manages transactions – for example, by Internet hosting, e-brokerage, e-publishing, payment processing and call-centre management.

The annual turnover of Atos Origin amounts to over 3 bn euros. Atos Origin operates in over 30 countries and has over 27,000 employees, of which over 7500 are in the Netherlands. Customers include ABN AMRO, Akzo Nobel, BNP Paribas, Crédit Lyonnais, Euronext, Fiat, KPN, Lucent, Philip Morris, Philips, Shell and Unilever.

From November 2001, Atos Origin MS consisted of five business units and a number of supporting units. Desktop Services (DTS), which acquired KPN WD in May 2002, is one of the five business units. DTS had a turnover of 120 mn euros in 2001 and has approximately 800 employees, who manage around 40,000 workplaces. The mission of AO DTS is to design, implement, migrate and manage ICT workplace infrastructure to increase the productivity of its customer end-user community and to optimize the utilization of ICT investments to exceed the business objectives of the customer. Some of the services of DTS are: demand management, transformation consulting, infrastructure consulting and design, implementation and migration projects, call management, automatic remote back-up services, process management, functional helpdesk and field service.

KPN – KPN WD – Atos Origin End User Services (EUS)

KPN, a former state-owned company, is one of the Netherlands' largest organizations with a worldwide annual turnover of 12.4 bn euros. Whereas the emphasis used to be on telephony, in recent years, there has been a shift towards information and telecommunications services. This shift in technology, combined with market deregulation, induced different organizations to enter the telecoms market in the Netherlands from the 1997 onwards. KPN thus lost its monopoly position and had to reorganize in order to adapt to the new market environment. The company established divisions that focused on specific market segments. In 2000, increased competition forced KPN to implement more and faster changes. Costs were growing faster than ever, which led to the deterioration of KPN's competitive position. This induced KPN management to combine new and old change programmes into one major project called Vision. Vision has three purposes: to increase customer satisfaction, to lower costs, and to optimize management and control systems.

By the end of 2001, the executive board had decided on further adjustments of the organization to the changed environment. Among other things, it decided to concentrate on the core activities in the main market segments. As a result of this process, KPN WD was sold to Atos Origin. KPN WD did not perform core activities, and the services it delivered could be outsourced more cheaply to the merged organization. As indicated, in May 2002, KPN WD was sold to Atos Origin's business unit DTS, and the integrated unit was called Atos Origin End User Services (EUS).

For several reasons, it was beneficial for Atos Origin to acquire KPN WD:

1. KNP would become a large customer

2. WD is a professional, process-orientated organization

3. Atos Origin would get national coverage through the Service Delivery organization of WD

4. WD has specific skills to develop and maintain standardized and reliable desktop systems

5. Atos Origin would acquire experienced IT employees, at a time when there was a shortage in the market

6. by combining existing businesses, the new organization would become one of the largest 'desktop solutions' organizations in the Netherlands.

The downside of the acquisition was that KPN was the only customer of KPN WD. This meant that, before the acquisition, KPN WD was not exposed to market competition. Hence, KNP WD would need to shift mentality from an internal service delivery unit to a commercial organization. Moreover, the market in which KPN WD was operating had become extremely competitive and many well-established companies were offering high-quality services at remarkably low prices. KPN WD was said to be expensive and, in order to be able to compete, it had to cut costs.

Figure 3.4 Atos Origin – KPN WD: background of the companies

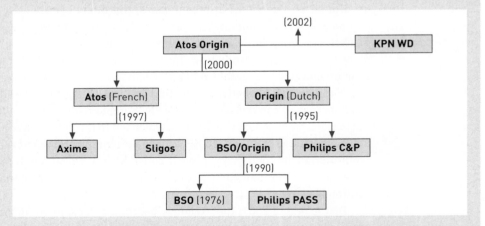

Organizational culture analysis

Because of their seemingly different mentalities, Atos Origin DTS and KPN WD decided to have their organizational cultures analysed. Atos Origin DTS was especially alert to the problems that could result from organization culture clashes as some of the members of the management team had experienced such problems before, as a result of the establishment of the joint venture by BSO and Philips PASS. This time, the management team wanted to prevent similar problems from occurring and decided to take measures alongside the integration process between the two subdivisions.

First, though, it needed to have a clear view of the differences between both groups of people. Only then could it implement appropriate measures. A change in organizational culture, management knew from experience, was impossible in the short run. However, employees could be made aware of the differences and this awareness, in turn, could improve mutual understanding and communication.

The survey was sent out to approximately 10 per cent of the employees of the two organizations. The response rate was high enough to ensure a representative sample. Employees from all layers and subdivisions of the organizations were included in the sample to have as complete as possible a picture of the organizational cultures of the two groups of employees. The survey used items and dimensions from Hofstede et al. (1990), Verbeke (2000), O'Reilly et al. (1991), and Christensen and Gordon (1999). A combination of the validated items enabled us to obtain a clear picture of the organizational cultures of both subdivisions. The survey results are shown in Table 3.4.

From the table it is clear that the main differences in organizational culture dimensions between the two groups of employees are reflected in large differences in team orientation, employee orientation and stability. Less important differences were found with respect to results orientation, communication and ethical norms. Both groups have similar perceptions of organizational innovativeness.

The question to answer now is as follows. What do these differences tell us

Table 3.4 Organizational culture dimensions: mean scores Atos Origin DTS (AO DTS) and KPN WD

Dimension	AO DTS	KPN WD	Difference	α
Results orientation	3.60	3.79	0.19	0.043
Employee orientation	**2.82**	**3.37**	0.55	0.000
Communication	3.02	3.38	0.36	0.001
Ethical norms	3.21	3.52	0.31	0.002
Innovation	3.58	3.57	0.01	0.863
Stability	**2.78**	**3.21**	0.43	0.000
Team orientation	**2.72**	**3.30**	0.58	0.000

Note: scores run from 1 = disagree to 5 = agree; differences between the mean scores noted in the table are significant when α < 0.05.

and what consequences can they have? We will start by trying to explain the differences, substantiating them using information obtained through observation and semi-structured interviews.

The first dimension, *process-orientated versus results-orientated*, opposes a concern with means (process-orientated) against a concern with goals (results-orientated). The results show that both AO DTS employees and KPN WD employees perceive their organization as results-orientated. Interviews, however, indicate major differences in the perceptions of the concept of results-orientatedness. Both organizations are said to be results-orientated with respect to the high quality they demand of the services they deliver. The major difference, however, lies in the fact that AO DTS is also very much focused on financial results. After the merger between Atos, which is quoted on the stock market, and Origin, Dutch AO DTS was forced to focus more on financial results. Some interviewees refer to the 'good old BSO and Philips days', during which there was less emphasis on financial results and profit-orientatedness. Moreover, AO has deliberately assigned responsibility for financial results to the lowest layers of the organization, at the level of the individual division of a business unit. The dominant emphasis on profit-making has resulted in a management style that is focused on figures. Until recently, this style was absent at KPN and foreign to KPN WD employees. KPN WD has always been an internally orientated subdivision of KPN, with no profit concerns. Whereas AO DTS is focused on turnover and profits, KPN WD continues to pay more attention to the management of organization processes.

The second dimension, *employee-orientated versus job-orientated*, opposes a concern for people against a concern for getting the job done. Employee-orientation reflects an organization's commitment to personal development and education, attention to personal events and accomplishments, as well as taking care of work pressure (Verbeke, 2000). Perhaps as a corollary to AO's focus on financial results, AO DTS scores lower on this dimension than KPN WD. Interviews confirm this result. At AO DTS, employees are dissatisfied with the focus on financial results as opposed to a concern for the employees. Employees complain about the lack of personal development opportunities, absence of additional training possibilities and attention to the individual, absence of promotion chances, the abolition of social events and many other cost-cutting measures, which are said to have a demotivating impact. KPN WD employees are more positive about the employee orientation of their division. There seems to be a lot of attention paid to the concerns of employees, for instance in terms of personal problems and personal development possibilities; incoming employees are helped structurally, promotion opportunities are good, and so on. KPN WD employees do, however, mention that the reforms have left their mark upon the organization in the sense that cost-cutting is also taking place, although this is gradual and not as abrupt as at AO DTS.

The third dimension, the *open versus closed system*, describes the *communication* climate. More specifically, it refers to the way in which employees and management deal with (self-)criticism (Verbeke, 2000). Also with respect to this dimension, results show that AO DTS employees are less satisfied than KPN WD employees. The interviews confirm this picture. AO DTS employees complain about the communication from management to the lower layers of the organization. Communication is top-down only and last-minute so that employee reactions cannot be taken into account. Communication also often happens informally, through different channels, which often leads to misinterpretation. Moreover, communication most often deals with positive issues, hiding the more critical points. Finally, criticisms are discussed among colleagues not usually with management. KPN WD has different formal channels to communicate information from management to the floor and vice versa. Among other departments, KPN WD has its own communication division. Criticisms are debated openly with management and, when found to be legitimate, are taken into account. Decisions are taken in teams and can be overruled by individuals. This is a feature of the widely known 'Poldermodel', which predicates consensus decision-making to obtain commitment.

Dimension four, *normative versus pragmatic*, is tied by Verbeke (2000) to the mission of the organization: socially responsible (= normative) organizations have an *ethical* mission and urge employees to behave according to that mission; other organizations are driven by self-interest (= pragmatic). Both AO DTS and KPN WD employees respond positively to this dimension, though KPN WD scores somewhat higher. Qualitative research shows that while KPN WD tends to be a normative organization, AO DTS is more pragmatic. AO DTS employees explain that social responsibility at Atos is not stimulated by the organization itself but by some of the employees. Some employees organize specific projects such as food expeditions to countries in need. The organization itself is more concerned with aspects of its reputation that influence the shareholders' public in view of its stock market results. In fact, employees argue that the company's interests are given absolute priority. Employees point in particular to the poor fulfilment of promises and agreements. KPN WD employees, in contrast, point to the donation of computers and other projects, organized by KPN to support its argument that KPN is a normative, or socially responsible, organization. Moreover, it has not been demonstrated that company interests dominate, and the company sticks to the promises and agreements it makes.

Dimension five concerns *innovation*. An organization scoring high on this dimension is seen by its members as being innovative, quick to take advantage of opportunities, risk-taking, and displaying a willingness to experiment. It is uncharacteristic for these organizations to be careful and rule-orientated. In the survey, both AO DTS and KPN WD employees described the company as innovative. Interviews, together with the market position of both companies, point to the need to substantiate this result. With respect to AO DTS, interviewees explain that, although knowledge is available, innovation is not stimulated, except for when the customer asks explicitly for the latest technology. In general, however, the company tends to concentrate on proven technology and a customer basis that demands a solid solution to problems that occur, but not the most innovative one – the so-called 'comfort zone'. Employees refrain from taking risks, do not have the opportunity to express innovative ideas and have to ask permission to continue when risk is involved in projects. Hence, Atos is not a truly innovative company, as is suggested by the survey responses. Similarly, qualitative research at KPN WD shows that it is not really innovative despite the survey result. Even KPN WD does not have this ambition, and instead emphasizes stability and solidity. Like AO DTS, KPN WD uses proven technology, and employees have to ask permission when risk is involved. Unlike AO DTS, however, KPN WD employees are encouraged to come up with new ideas and, in particular, ideas that help to cut costs. KPN WD has established Telecom Idea Management (TIM), which screens new ideas, provides feedback and rewards good ideas. Moreover, KPN WD also has an engineering division, which used to concentrate on innovative activities but, as a result of cost-cutting measures, is now unable to continue to do so. It is clear, however, that rather like the results of the survey at AO DTS, survey results at KPN WD paint a different picture from the results that stem from qualitative research sources. Presumably this contradiction is due to the fact that surveys can induce people to answer in an 'appropriate' way and/or that the items of each dimension, though validated, are not always interpreted correctly.

The sixth dimension is *stability*. Characteristic of organizations scoring high on this dimension is being rule-orientated, emphasizing stability, predictability, and security of employment; employees are constrained by many rules. From the survey results it is clear that AO DTS employees do not see stability as a feature of the organization. In contrast, KPN WD employees responded positively and hence see KPN WD as an organization that emphasizes stability and predictability. In this case, interviews support the survey results.

The last dimension, *team orientation*, refers to the extent to which people are encouraged to cooperate and coordinate within and across units. The survey results show that AO DTS employees do not see team-orientatedness as a feature of the organization. Two out of three employees responded negatively. In fact, qualitative research shows that employees experience the lack of cooperation within AO DTS as a major weakness. KPN WD employees, on the other hand, responded positively and emphasized that team orientation is definitely a feature of the organization.

Main organizational culture differences

Quantitative research, combined with qualitative results, shows the following organizational culture differences between Atos DTS and KPN WD.

1. Both, AO DTS and KPN WD are results-orientated with respect to the quality achieved but only AO DTS is results-orientated in financial terms.

2. AO DTS is less employee-orientated than KPN WD.

3. AO DTS is less open (to criticism) than KPN WD.

4. AO DTS is less ethical than KPN WD.

5. Neither organization is truly innovative, but KPN WD is characterized by structures that could help to improve 'innovativeness' if wanted.

6. AO DTS is less rule-orientated, and emphazises less stability and predictability than KPN WD.

7. AO DTS is less team-orientated than KPN WD.

Questions

1. Explain the concept of organizational culture.

2. Discuss how organizational culture can be measured, and how this has been approached in the case study. What would be the best way to measure culture, given that there are shortcomings to the etic and emic approaches?

3. Explain whether the examination of culture in the case study should also include national culture analysis to provide the companies with valid results?

4. Discuss the factors that can aid understanding of the differences in organizational culture between AO DTS and KPN WD.

5. Explain whether the organizational culture differences between AO DTS and KPN WD are such that they should be taken into account during the integration process of the two subdivisions?

6. Explain the types of measure you think the management of the merged subdivisions should take in order to ensure the successful integration of the two organizations?

7. Explain to what extent institutions (e.g. the stock market) have an influence on organizational culture. Can you give any other examples of this type?

References

Abrahamson, E. and Fombrun, C.J. (1994) Macrocultures: determinants and consequences. *Academy of Management Review* 19(4), 728–55.

Adler, N. (1996) *International Dimensions of Organizational Behavior.* Cincinnati, OH: South-Western College Publishing.

Adler, N. and Jelinek, M. (1986) Is 'organization culture' culture bound? *Human Resource Management* 25, 73–90.

Allen, R.F. (1985) Four phases for bringing about cultural change, in Kilmann, R.H., Saxton, M.J., Serpa, R. *et al.* (eds) *Gaining Control of the Corporate Culture.* San Francisco: Jossey-Bass, 137–47.

Alvesson, M. (2002) *Understanding Organizational Culture*. London: Sage Publications Ltd.

Berg, P.O. (1986) Symbolic management of human resources. *Human Resource Management* 25, 557–79.

Berry, J.W. (1980) Social and cultural change, in Triandis, H.C. and Brislin, R.W. (eds) *Handbook of Cross-cultural Psychology*. Boston: Allyn & Bacon, 211–79.

Berry, J.W. (1983) Acculturation: a comparative analysis of alternative forms, in Samuda, R.J. and Woods, S.L. (eds) *Perspectives in Immigrant and Minority Education*. Lanham, MD: University Press of America, 66–77.

Bhagat, R.S. and McQuaid, S.J. (1982) Role of subjective culture in organizations: a review and directions for future research. *Journal of Applied Psychology* 67(5), 653–85.

Blasko, M., Netter, J. and Sinkey, J. (2000) The DaimlerChrysler merger: short-term gains, long-run wealth destruction? *Issues in International Corporate Control and Governance*.

Brown, A. (1995) *Organizational Culture*. London: Pitman.

Bryman, A. (1992) *Charisma and Leadership in Organizations*. London: Sage.

Buono, A.F., Bowditch, J.L. and Lewis, J.W. (1985) When cultures collide: the anatomy of the merger. *Human Relations* 38(5), 477–500.

Burns, T. and Stalker, G.M. (1961) *The Management of Innovation*. London: Tavistock.

Caroll, C. and Thomas, H. (1994) Linking economic, organizational, and psychological perspectives: an examination of collectivities of firms within industries. Working paper, College of Commerce and Business Administration, University of Illinois, Urbana-Champaign.

Cartwright, S. and Cooper, C.L. (1993) The role of culture compatibility in successful organizational marriage. *Academy of Management Executive* 2, 57–70.

Chatman, J.A. and Jehn, K.A. (1994) Assessing the relationship between industry characteristics and organizational culture: how different can you be? *Academy of Management Journal* 37, 522–53.

Chatterjee, S., Lubatkin, M., Schweiger, D. and Weber, Y. (1992) Cultural differences and shareholder value in related mergers: linking equity and human capital. *Strategic Management Journal* 13, 319–34.

Christensen, E.W. and Gordon, G.G. (1999) An exploration of industry, culture and revenue growth, *Organization Studies* 20, 397–422.

Cooke, R.A. and Rousseau, D.M. (1988) Behavioral norms and expectations: a quantitative approach to the assessment of organizational culture. *Group & Organization Studies* 13, 245–73.

Datta, D.K. (1991) Organizational fit and acquisition performance: effects of post-acquisition integration. *Strategic Management Journal* 12, 281–97.

Davenport, T. and Prusak, L. (1998) *Working Knowledge*. Cambridge, MA: Harvard Business Press.

Davis, R.L. (1968) Compatibility in organizational marriages. *Harvard Business Review* 46(4), 86–93.

Davis, S.M. (1984) *Managing Corporate Culture*. Cambridge, MA: Ballinger.

Deal, T.E. and Kennedy, A.A. (1982) *Corporate Culture*. Reading: Addison-Wesley.

Denison, D.R. (1996) What is the difference between organizational culture and organizational climate?: a native's point-of-view on a decade of paradigm wars. *Academy of Management Review* 21, 619–54.

Denison, D.R. (1984) Bringing corporate culture to the bottom line. *Organizational Dynamics* 13(2), 5–22.

DiMaggio, P. and Powell, W. (1983) The iron cage revisited: institutional isomorphism and collective rationality in organizational fields. *American Sociological Review* 48, 147–60.

DiTomaso, N. (1978) Symbolic media and social solidarity: the foundations of corporate culture. *Research in the Sociology of Organizations* 5, 105–34.

Dyer, W.G. Jr (1985) The cycle of cultural evolution in organizations, in Kilmann, R.H., Saxton, M.J., Serpa, R. *et al.* (eds) *Gaining Control of the Corporate Culture*. San Francisco: Jossey-Bass, 44–65.

Earley, P.C. (1994) Self or group? Cultural effects of training on self-efficacy and performance. *Administrative Science Quarterly* 39, 89–117.

Ely, R. (1995) The power in demography: women's social construction of gender identity at work. *Academy of Management Journal* 38(3), 589–634.

Fitzgerald, T. (1988) Can change in organizational culture be really managed? *Organizational Dynamics* 17(2), 4–15.

Gaertner, S.L., Mann, J., Murrell, A. and Dovidio, J.F. (1989) Reducing intergroup bias: the benefits of recategorization. *Journal of Personality and Social Psychology* 57, 239–49.

Gagliardi, P. (1986) The creation and change of organizational cultures: a conceptual framework. *Organization Studies* 7, 117–34.

Ghobadian, A. and O'Regan, N. (2002) The link between culture, strategy and performance in manufacturing SMEs. *Journal of General Management* 28(1), 16–35.

Gordon, G.G. (1991) Industry determinants of organizational culture. *Academy of Management Review* 16(2), 396–415.

Gordon, G.G. (1992) Predicting corporate performance from organizational culture. *Journal of Management Studies* 29, 783–98.

Greiner, L.E. (1983) Senior executives as strategic actors. *New Management* 12, 11–15, in Weick, K., The significance of corporate culture, in Frost, P., Moore, L., Louis, M., Lundberg, C. and Martin, J. (eds) *Organizational Culture*. Beverly Hills, CA: Sage (1985), 381–9.

Grey, C. (1999) *Change in Organizations?* Judge Institute of Management, Cambridge University, working paper.

Halberstam, D. (1986) *The Reckoning*. New York: William Morrow.

Hambrick, D. and Cannella, B. (1993) Relative standing: a framework for understanding departures of acquired executives. *Academy of Management Journal* 36(4), 733–62.

Hellriegel, D., Slocum, L. and Woodman, R. (1992) *Organizational Behavior*. St Paul, MN: West Publishing.

Hinings, C.R. and Badran, M. (1981) Strategies of administrative control and contextual constraints in a less developed country. *Organization Studies* 2, 3–22.

Hodgetts, R. and Luthans, F. (1997) *International Management*. New York: McGraw-Hill.

Hofstede, G. (1991) *Cultures and Organizations: Software of the Mind*. London: McGraw-Hill.

Hofstede, G. (1998) Identifying organizational subcultures: an empirical approach. *Journal of Management Studies* 35(1), 1–12.

Hofstede, G. (2001 and 1980) *Culture's Consequences*. London: Sage.

Hofstede, G., Neuijen, B., Ohayv, D.D. and Sanders, G. (1990) Measuring organizational cultures: a qualitative and quantitative study across twenty cases. *Administrative Science Quarterly* 35, 286–316.

Howell, R.A. (1970) Plan to integrate your acquisitions. *Harvard Business Review* 48(6), 66–76.

Huff, A. (1982) Industry influences on strategy reformulation. *Strategic Management Journal* 3, 119–31.

Jemison, D.B. and Sitkin, S.B. (1986) Corporate acquisitions: a process perspective. *Academy of Management Review* 11(1), 145–63.

Kanter, R.M. (1977) *Men and Women of the Corporation*. New York: Basic Books.

Keller, M. (1989) *Rude Awakening*. New York: Morrow.

Kilmann, R.H. and Saxton, M. (1983) *The Kilmann–Saxton Culture-Gap Survey*. Pittsburgh, PA: Organizational Design Consultants.

Kilmann, R.H., Saxton, M. and Serpa, R. (1985) *Gaining Control of Corporate Culture*. San Francisco: Jossey-Bass.

Lachman, R., Nedd, A. and Hinings, B. (1994) Analyzing cross-national management and organizations: a theoretical framework. *Management Science* 40(1), 40–55.

Larsson, R. and Lubatkin, M. (2001) Achieving acculturation in mergers and acquisitions: an international case survey. *Human Relations* 54(12), 1573–1607.

Lorsch, J.W. (1985) Strategic myopia: culture as invisible barrier to change, in Kilmann, R.H., Saxton, M.J., Serpa, R. *et al.* (eds) *Gaining Control of the Corporate Culture*. San Francisco: Jossey-Bass, 44–65.

Louis, M.R. (1985) An investigator's guide to workplace culture, in Frost, P., Moore, L., Louis, M., Lundberg, C. and Martin, J. (eds) *Organizational Culture*. Beverly Hills: Sage, 381–9.

Lubatkin, M. (1983) Merger and the performance of the acquiring firm. *Academy of Management Review* 8(2), 218–25.

Lubatkin, M., Schweiger, D. and Weber, Y. (1999) Top management turnover in related M&As: an additional test of the theory of relative standing. *Journal of Management* 25(1), 55–73.

Lundberg, C.C. (1985) On the feasibility of cultural intervention in organizations, in Frost, P.J. *et al.* (eds) *Organizational Culture*. Beverly Hills: Sage.

Martin, J. (1992) *Cultures in Organizations*. New York: Oxford University Press.

Martin, J. (2002) *Organizational Culture: Mapping the Terrain*. London: Sage.

Martin, J. and Meyerson, D. (1988) Organizational culture and the denial, channeling and acknowledgment of ambiguity, in Pondy, L., Boland Jr, R. and Thomas, H. (eds) *Managing Ambiguity and Change*. New York: John Wiley, 93–125.

Martin, J. and Siehl, C. (1982) Organizational culture and counterculture: an uneasy symbiosis. *Organizational Dynamics* 12(2), 52–64.

Martin, J., Feldman, M., Hatch, M. and Sitkin, S. (1983) The uniqueness paradox in organizational stories. *Administrative Science Quarterly* 28, 438–53.

Mintzberg, H. (1973) Strategy making in three modes. *California Management Review* 16(3), 44–58.

Mintzberg, H. (1979) *The Structuring of Organizations*. Englewood Cliffs, NJ: Prentice-Hall.

Morgan, M.J. (1993) How corporate culture drives strategy. *Long Range Planning* 26(2), 110–18.

Mumby, D. (1988) *Communication and Power in Organizations: Discourse, Ideology and Domination.* Norwood, NJ: Ablex.

Nahavandi, A. and Malekzadeh, A.R. (1988) Acculturation in mergers and acquisitions. *Academy of Management Review* 13(1), 79–90.

Newman, K.L. and Nollen, S.D. (1996), Culture congruence: the fit between management practices and national culture. *Journal of International Business Studies* 27(4), 753–79.

Noorderhaven, N.G. (1995) *Strategic Decision Making.* Reading: Addison-Wesley.

Noorderhaven, N.G., Koen, C.I. and Beugelsdijk, S. (2002) Organisational culture and network embeddedness. CentER Discussion paper 91, Tilburg University.

O'Dell, C. and J. Grayson (1998) If only we knew what we know: identification and transfer of best practices. *California Management Review* 40(3), 154–73.

Olie, R. (1994) Shades of culture and institutions in international mergers. *Organization Studies* 15(3), 381–405.

O'Reilly, Ch.A., Chatman, J. and Caldwell, D.F. (1991) People and organizational culture: a profile comparison approach to assessing person–organization fit. *Academy of Management Journal* 34, 487–516.

Ouchi, W. and Price, R. (1978) Hierarchies, clans, and theory Z: a new perspective on organizational development. *Organizational Dynamics* 7, 25–44.

Peters, T.J. and Waterman, R.H. (1982) *In Search of Excellence.* New York: Harper & Row.

Pfeffer, J. (1981) Management as symbolic action: the creation and maintenance of organizational paradigms, in Cummings, L.L. and Staw, B.M. (eds) *Research in Organizational Behavior*, Vol. 3. Greenwich, CT: JAI Press.

Phillips, M.E. (1994) Industry mindsets: exploring the cultures of two macro-organizational settings. *Organization Science* 5(3), 384–402.

Phillips, M.E., Goodman, R.A. and Sackmann, S.A. (1992) Exploring the complex cultural milieu of project teams. *PmNETwork-Professional Magazine of the Project Management Institute* VI(8), 20–6.

Porac, J.F., Thomas, H. and Baden-Fuller, C. (1989) Competitive groups as cognitive communities: the case of Scottish knitwear manufacturers. *Journal of Management Studies* 26(4), 397–416.

Porter, M.E. (1987) From competitive advantage to competitive strategy. *Harvard Business Review* 65(3), 43–59.

Powell, T.C. (1992) Organizational alignment as competitive advantage. *Strategic Management Journal* 13, 119–34.

Rappaport, A. (1987) Converting merger benefits to shareholder value. *Mergers and Acquisitions* 21(3), 49–55.

Räsänen, K. and Whipp, R. (1992) National business recipes: a sector perspective, in Whitley, R. (ed.) *European Business Systems: Firms, Markets and their National Context.* Newbury Park: Sage, 46–60.

Ravenscraft, D.J. and Scherer, F.M. (1989) The profitability of mergers. *International Journal of Industrial Organization* 7, 101–16.

Rousseau, D.M. (1990) Assessing organizational culture: the case for multiple methods, in Schneider, B. (ed.) *Organizational Climate and Culture.* San Francisco: Jossey-Bass.

Sackmann, S.A. (1991) *Cultural Knowledge in Organizations: Exploring the Collective Mind.* Newbury Park, CA: Sage.

Sackmann, S.A. (1992) Cultures and subcultures: an analysis of organizational knowledge. *Administrative Science Quarterly* 37(1), 140–61.

Saffold, G.S. (1988) Culture traits, strength, and organizational performance: moving beyond 'strong' culture. *Academy of Management Review* 13(4), 546–58.

Sales, A.L. and Mirvis, P.A. (1984) When cultures collide: issues of acquisition, in Kimberly, J.R. and Quinn, R. (eds) *Managing Organizational Transitions.* Homewood, IL: Irwin, 107–33.

Salter, M.S. and Weinhold, W.A. (1979) *Diversification through Acquisitions: Strategies for Creating Economic Value.* New York: Free Press.

Sathe, V. (1983) Implications of corporate culture: a manager's guide to action. *Organizational Dynamics* 12, 5–23.

Sathe, V. (1985) *Culture and Related Corporate Realities.* Homewood, IL: Irwin.

Schall, M. (1983) A communications-rules approach to organizational culture. *Administrative Science Quarterly* 28, 557–81.

Schein, E.H. (1985) *Organizational Culture and Leadership.* San Francisco: Jossey-Bass.

Schein, E.H. (1990) Organizational culture. *American Psychologist* 45(2), 109–19.

Schein, E. (1992) *Organizational Culture and Leadership.* London: Jossey-Bass.

Schein, E.H. (1999) *The Corporate Culture Survival Guide: Sense and Nonsense about Cultural Change.* San Francisco: Jossey-Bass.

Schneider, S.C. (1988) National versus corporate culture: implications for human resource management. *Human Resource Management* 27, 231–46.

Scholz, C. (1987a) *Strategisches Management: ein integrativer Ansatz.* Berlin: Walter de Gruyter.

Scholz, C. (1987b) Corporate culture and strategy: the problem of strategic fit. *Long Range Planning* 20(4), 78–87.

Schreyögg, G. (1989) Zu den problematischen Konsequenzen starker Unternehmenskulturen. *Zeitschrift für Betriebswirtschaftliche Forschung* 41, 94–113.

Schwartz, S.H. (1994) Beyond individualism and collectivism: new cultural dimensions of values, in Kim, U., Triandis, H.C., Kagitcibasi, C., Choi, S.C and Yoon, G. (eds) *Individualism and Collectivism: Theory, Method, and Applications.* Newbury Park, CA: Sage, 85–199.

Scott, R. (1995) *Institutions and Organizations.* Thousand Oaks: Sage.

Smircich, L. (1983) Concepts of culture and organizational analysis. *Administrative Science Quarterly* 28, 339–58.

Smircich, L. and Morgan, G. (1982) Leadership: the management of meaning. *Journal of Applied Behavioral Science* 18, 257–73.

Spender, J.-C. (1989) *Industry Recipes.* Oxford: Basil Blackwell.

Trompenaars, F. (1994) *Riding the Waves of Culture.* New York: Irwin.

Vaaraa, E. (1999) Cultural differences and post-merger problems: misconceptions and cognitive simplifications. *Nordiska Organisasjonsstudien* 1(2), 59–88.

Van Maanen, J. and Barley, S.R. (1984) Occupational communities: culture and control in organizations, in Staw, B.M. and Cummings, L.L. (eds) *Research in Organizational Behavior.* Vol. 7. Greenwich: JAI Press.

Van Maanen, J. and Barley, S.R. (1985) Cultural organization: fragments of a theory, in Frost, P.J. *et al.* (eds) *Organizational Culture*. Beverly Hills: Sage.

Verbeke, A. (2000) A revision of Hofstede *et al.* (1990) organisational practices scale. *Journal of Organisational Behaviour* 21, 587–602.

Very, P., Lubatkin, M., Calori, R. and Veiga, J. (1997) Relative standing and the performance of recently acquired European firms. *Strategic Management Journal* 18(8), 593–614.

Walter, G.A. (1985) Culture collisions in mergers and acquisitions, in Frost, P.J., Moore, L.F., Louis, M.R., Lundberg, C.C. and Martin, J. (eds) *Organizational Culture*. Beverly Hills: Sage.

Weber, Y. (1996) Corporate cultural fit and performance in mergers and acquisitions. *Human Relations* 49, 1181–202.

Weber, Y., Shenkar, O. and Raveh, A. (1996) National and corporate cultural fit in mergers/acquisitions: an exploratory study. *Management Science* 42(8), 1215–27.

Weick, K. (1985) The significance of corporate culture, in Frost, P.J. *et al.* (eds) *Organizational Culture*. Beverly Hills: Sage, 381–9.

Whitley, R. (1992) Societies, firms and markets: the social structuring of business systems, in Whitley, R. (ed.) *European Business Systems: Firms, Markets and their National Context*. Newbury Park: Sage, 5–45.

Wright, J.C. and Mischel, W. (1987) A conditional approach to dispositional constructs: the local predictability of social behavior. *Journal of Personality and Social Psychology* 53, 1159–77.

Young, J.B. (1981) A conclusive investigation into the causative elements of failure in acquisitions, in Lee, S.J. and Colman, R.D. (eds) *Handbook of Mergers, Acquisitions, and Buyouts*. Englewood Cliffs: Prentice Hall, 605–28.

Chapter 4

National Diversity and Management

Learning Objectives

By the end of this chapter you will be able to:

- understand what comparative institutional research is about

- explain the major differences between the two main European institutional models – that is, between the business systems approach and the societal effect approach

- evaluate the relationship between culture and the national institutional environment

- reflect critically upon the explanatory power of societal and institutional analysis

- assess the value of institutional typologies

- appraise whether the business systems and the societal effect approach, aside from explaining national diversity in organization, also help to explain sector-level diversity

- evaluate whether these two approaches are able to help us understand globalization pressures

- explore the main features of the Korean business system or the *Chaebol*, and of the Taiwanese business system.

Chapter Outline

4.1 Institutional Analysis: What and Why?

4.2 The Business Systems Approach
Main features of business systems
Institutional typology
Background versus proximate institutions
Major societal institutions
Connections between dominant institutions and business system features

4.3 Business Systems Research Applied to Taiwan and South Korea
The Korean business system
Institutional influences on the Korean business system
The Taiwanese business system
Institutional influences on the Taiwanese business system

4.4 The Societal Effect (SE) Approach
Actor–structure relationship
Institution as a process and a structure
Institutional interdependence

4.5 Institutional Change
Causes of institutional change
Theorizing institutional change
Study Questions
Further Reading
Case: The Japanese *Keiretsu*
References

4.1 ✦ Institutional Analysis: What and Why?

The importance of institutions for management and organization is widely recognized nowadays. Much of the important work by institutional theorists over the past two decades has been in documenting the influence of social forces on organizational structure and behaviour. Empirical institutional research on organizations has shown that corporations do not operate in a vacuum, but are influenced by contextual variables. Contextual variables not only provide corporations with constraints (i.e. certain levels of (technical) training; capital constraints, etc.) but also with opportunities (i.e. the provision of sufficient high-risk capital, tax-free loans, etc.).

Rather like cultural analysis, from the 1970s, within the institutional camp, several approaches developed to analyse how societal institutions influence organizational forms (usually) in capitalist economies. Sections 4.2 and 4.4 of this chapter discuss the theoretical features of the two main European institutional approaches: the 'business systems' and the 'societal effect' approaches, respectively. Both approaches have made major contributions to the study of management and organization in market economies. They compare institutional systems across two or more societies, and examine their effects on organizations and industrial structure. They emphasize the importance of history, attending to when and how developments occurred.

The 'business systems' approach, which is discussed in Section 4.2, was developed by Whitley (1990, 1992a) and is a manifestation of the idea that organization is significantly conditioned by national belonging. Whitley's principal use of the national business system concept is to explain why different countries have evolved different sets of institutions to coordinate apparently similar types of economic activity (Casson and Lundan, 1999).

In most approaches in sociology, economics, and organization and management studies, which accept the idea that organization (in a broad sense) – including corporate governance, the market-hierarchy choice and firms' internal organization – is strongly influenced by the national context, economic organization only enters the picture as a secondary concern. The main point of interest in most of these studies is to understand how a firm's international competitiveness, or the type and amount of innovation, is nationally conditioned (e.g. see Kogut, 1991, 1993; Lundvall, 1992). In the business systems approach, in contrast, economic organization occupies centre stage.

The complexity of business systems research may be illustrated by the brief explanation of Whitley's empirical research on the South Korean and Taiwanese business systems in Section 4.3. It is widely acknowledged that Asian firms behave very differently from those in western countries, especially the USA and UK, and that these differences are connected to distinctive features of dominant societal institutions (Whitley, 1999). Besides the success of these specific business systems, there is also the fact that we are living in an international, often referred to as 'global', business world, which makes it useful to be knowledgeable about them. To retain the clarity of Richard Whitley's explanations, I have directly quoted from his work in the chapter (with permission).

The 'societal effect' approach, which is discussed in Section 4.4, has been developed by Maurice and Brossard (1976); Maurice *et al.* (1976/1986); Maurice *et al.* (1980); and Sorge and Warner (1986). The theorizing and empirical methods of these scholars represent a determined refutation of the universal hypothesis of the contingency approach that, given similar circumstances, the structure of an organization is very much the same wherever it is located. These scholars proclaimed the societal level as the key explanatory level. The societal effect approach posits that the structures of organizations reflect the institutional arrangements of their societal environments. While the original studies refrained from addressing the 'efficiency' question of the contingency theorists, later studies within the societal effect framework added a contingency element to the theory by highlighting the central importance of firms making a strategic choice, which fits the society's dominant pattern of organization (Sorge, 1991).

While classified as institutional, the 'societal effect' approach goes beyond the institutional to integrate both cultural and institutional viewpoints in one conceptual framework.[1] The approach argues that the explanation of organizational differences between societies never lies in culture *or* institutions. The approach is theoretically more sophisticated than the business systems approach but, perhaps due to its complexity and open-endedness, somewhat less widely used and less well understood. The societal effect approach is applied in the case at the end of Chapter 7, which discusses national production systems.

Rather like cultural analysis, which assumes culture to be relatively stable over time, institutional research (i.e. the business systems approach) is largely static, viewing institutions as a source of stability and order. If the nature of actors (organizations) and their modes of acting are constituted and constrained by institutions, how can these actors change the very institutions in which they are embedded? Much of the scholarly attention to change tends to look at the formation of new institutional forms and associated changes in industries and individual organizations, as these entities respond to pressures to adopt new structures or practices. This focus assumes that institutions are put in place and then exert their effects but are not themselves subject to further change.

Only in the last decade have theorists and researchers begun to examine arguments and situations involving institutional change that witness the 'de-institutionalization' of existing forms and their replacement by new arrangements that, in time, undergo institutionalization (Scott, 2001). A discussion of this topic is especially relevant in this book to an understanding of the consequences of globalization pressures (see Chapter 1). In general, globalization is argued to involve institutional change. If we are to understand institutional change, we should first theorize it. This is done in Section 4.5.

4.2 ✸ The Business Systems Approach

The 'business systems' approach has been developed by Richard Whitley on the basis of his research into East Asian organizations and their institutional contexts (Whitley, 1990, 1991). The approach is useful in a comparative international management context in that it helps us to understand how different institutional arrangements shape different forms of economic organization or different forms of business systems (i.e. the Japanese *Keiretsu*, Korean *Chaebol*, etc.).

---

[1] Throughout this chapter and the remaining chapters of the book, the term 'societal' is used whenever use is made of the integrated viewpoint of the approach.

The concept of a business system is conceived by Whitley (1992b: 125) as 'particular ways of organizing, controlling, and directing business enterprises that become established as the dominant forms of business organization in different societies'.

The main features of business systems that the approach seeks to explain are:

- the nature of firms as economic actors, including the extent to which firms dominate the economy and how they share risk
- the nature of authoritative coordination and control systems within firms, including the types of authority exercised, and the extent of differentiation and decentralization, and
- the nature of market organization, including the extent of interdependence among firms and the role of competitive versus cooperative ties. (Whitley, 1992b: 129–30)

Unique business systems are argued to arise 'wherever key associated institutions are both mutually reinforcing and distinctive from other ones' (Whitley, 1999: 44). In this sense, nation-states often develop distinctive business systems because 'state actions determine the effectiveness and role of formal institutions in governing many important aspects of economic coordination' (Whitley, 1999: 44).

The core argument of the approach is that:

differences in societal institutions encourage particular kinds of economic organization and discourage other ones through structuring the ways that collective actors are constituted, cooperate, and compete for resources and legitimacy, including the standards used to evaluate their performance and behavior. (Whitley, 1999: 27)

However, while similar to cross-cultural analysis, the business systems approach is most often used to understand cross-national differences; the national level is not the only level at which business systems can be analysed. It is true that in general, the institutions that help us explain business systems (i.e. the financial system, the educational and training system) are situated at the level of the nation. This does not necessarily need to be the case, though. It could well be that, for example, regional institutions (such as EU-level institutions), and broad cultural norms and values are distinct from national ones and able to exert considerable discretion in the economic sphere. In such cases, Whitley expects distinctive kinds of economic organization to become established at the regional level. This is especially so if national agencies and institutions are less effective in coordinating activities and implementing policies.

Business system features are argued to be general and long term in nature, implying that they do not change very rapidly or in response to the behaviour of individual firms. Moreover, the approach assumes that business systems interact with the institutional environment but that the pattern of interaction is seen as a co-evolutionary process that is strongly path-dependent. Path-dependency equals, at best, incremental change.

At the same time, change is argued to be dependent on the cohesiveness and integration of institutional frameworks and business systems. It is assumed that where major institutions are strongly interdependent, and business systems are highly integrated and cohesive, change is unlikely to occur unless there are significant changes in the institutional framework. In contrast, where institutions are more differentiated and their interdependence weaker, business system characteristics and particular institutions may undergo change without leading to a radical departure from established patterns. Thus, the strongly interdependent nature of institutions in postwar Japan is argued to have resulted in the Japanese business system being much more integrated than its Anglo-American counterparts, and as a result, more difficult to change.

There are several problems with Whitley's explanation of change. First, Whitley does not explain the mechanisms behind major institutional change and for this reason is unable to explain this type of change. Next, on the one hand, Whitley argues that strongly interdependent institutions result in highly integrated business systems while, on the other hand, business system change is assumed to be dependent on both the extent of institutional interdependence and business system cohesiveness. This argument is tautological. When institutions are strongly interdependent, they result in cohesive business systems. Because business systems are cohesive and institutions strongly interdependent they are difficult to change. The business systems approach is clearly unable to explain change and needs further development in that direction.

Main features of business systems

The first step in business systems research is to describe the basic features of business systems and their interconnections. Whitley (1999: 33) suggests that differences in the nature of relationships between five broad kinds of economic actors are particularly important in contrasting business systems:

1. the providers and users of capital
2. customers and suppliers
3. competitors
4. firms in different sectors, and finally
5. employers and different kinds of employee.

As Richard Whitley says in his book, Divergent Capitalisms,* 'these vary in both the extent of organizational integration and whether this is achieved primarily through ownership-based hierarchies, formal arrangements, personal obligations, informal commitments, etc.' (Whitley, 1999: 33). The relationships between these categories of actors that make up a business system are also reflected in the primary features that Whitley (1999) accords to business systems (see Table 4.1).

The first feature – *ownership coordination* – concerns the relationship between owners and managers, and the extent of owners' direct involvement in managing business. Whitley distinguishes between:

- direct control of firms by managers
- alliance control, in which owners delegate considerable decision-making to managers but remain committed to particular firms, and
- market, or arm's length, portfolio control.

---

* All material by Richard Whitley in this chapter is taken from *Divergent Capitalisms* (1999), Whitley, R., by permission of Oxford University Press.

Table 4.1   Key characteristics of business systems
Ownership coordination   Primary means of ownership control (direct, alliance, market contracting)   Extent of ownership integration of production chains   Extent of ownership integration of sectors
Non-ownership coordination   Extent of alliance coordination of production chains   Extent of collaboration between competitors   Extent of alliance coordination of sectors
Employment relations and work management   Employer–employee interdependence   Delegation to, and trust of, employees (Taylorism, task performance discretion, task organization discretion)

Source: Whitley (1999: 34).

The two further characteristics of ownership coordination concern the scope of ownership integration of economic activities – that is, the extent to which the activities of firms are vertically and horizontally diversified.[2]

Whitley states 'these three characteristics of ownership relations are often interrelated, in that alliance forms of owner control tend to inhibit unrelated diversification while market ones encourage it as a way of spreading risks that cannot easily be shared with business partners' (Whitley, 36). He goes on to say that 'where owners become locked into the fates of particular firms, they tend to develop expertise and knowledge about their technologies and markets in order to manage their greater exposure to risk and uncertainty. Diversification into unknown fields increases owners' risks and so is unlikely to be encouraged by them. Portfolio holders in capital markets, on the other hand, can usually sell their assets on liquid secondary markets if diversification fails and so are unlikely to oppose it strongly' (Whitley, 1999: 36–7).

With respect to the second broad area, *non-ownership coordination*, Whitley identifies three sets of inter-firm relationship:

1. those between members of a production chain
2. those between competitors, and
3. those between firms in different industries.

These different types of relationship can range from zero-sum, adversarial contracting and competition to more cooperative, long-term and mutually committed relationships between partners and competitors.

As Whitley states, 'Production chains, for example, may be quite fragmented in ownership terms, but exhibit strong networks of obligational contracting between relatively stable suppliers and customers – sometimes with limited exchanges of shares, as in Japan. Similarly, competitors may compete fiercely for customers and yet collaborate over the introduction of new technologies, employment policies, and state lobbying through various formal associations and alliances, as numerous studies have shown' (Whitley,

---

[2] These three broad types of ownership vary in terms of six characteristics. While it is beyond the scope of this chapter to offer a discussion of this issue, the interested reader is referred to Whitley (1999: 35–7).

1999: 37). Finally, firms may develop different types of alliance across sectors in order to enter new markets, acquire new technologies (i.e. joint ventures) or reduce the risk of specialization. In comparing the role of alliance relationships or inter-firm networks across sectors in different market economies one should pay attention to the extent to which economic activities are consciously and repeatedly coordinated across sectors.

Of the last category, *employment relations and work organization*, the former is characterized in terms of the degree of employer–employee interdependence – that is, the extent to which societies encourage reliance on external labour markets in managing the bulk of the labour force, and those encouraging more commitment and mutual investment in organizational capabilities. Organization-based employment systems, such as those institutionalized in many large Japanese firms represent perhaps the greatest extent of mutual dependence between employer and the bulk of the workforce (see Chapter 5 for an extended explanation of this issue). The Anglo-Saxon pattern of 'flexible' external labour markets and high rates of employment change represents the other extreme of this dimension (see also Chapter 5).

The second item in this category of business system characteristics – that is, patterns of work organization – can be distinguished in terms of the discretion and trust employers grant to the bulk of the workforce. 'The pure case of 'scientific management' removes all discretion from manual workers and fragments tasks to simplify them for unskilled and easily replaced employees. 'Responsible-autonomy' strategies, on the other hand, trust manual workers to carry out tasks with more discretion and independence from managers.

This autonomy, though, need not extend to questions of work organization and task definition. Few Japanese companies, for example, and even fewer Korean or Taiwanese ones, delegate the allocation and organization of jobs to manual workers, while being keen to involve them in problem-solving activities and grant many considerable discretion over task performance' (Whitley, 1999: 39).

'Employment strategies and work systems are interrelated in that it is difficult to envisage a firm pursuing a radically Taylorist system of work organization and control at the same time as seeking long-term commitments from the manual workers and investing in their skill development. Taylorism and market-based employment systems would then seem to be highly consonant. However, it clearly is possible to combine considerable fluidity in external labour markets with reliance on highly skilled workers who exercise high levels of discretion over work performance, as Kristensen's account of Danish work systems and many Anglo-Saxon professional service firms illustrate' (Whitley, 1999: 39). 'The connections between high mutual commitment employment systems and work-control practices are more clear-cut. As Lazonick, Best, and others have emphasized, integrating the bulk of the workforce into large, dominant enterprises as loyal and committed partners encourages firm-specific skill development, functional flexibility strategies, and the delegation of considerable autonomy over task performance' (Whitley, 1999: 39).

Institutional typology

As Whitley goes on to explain, 'These interconnections suggest that a limited number of combinations of business-system characteristics are likely to remain established over historical periods, because contradictions between them can be expected to generate conflicts between social groupings and prevalent institutional arrangements. . . . Similarly, business systems based on market types of ownership relations are unlikely to be supportive of long-term risk-sharing between suppliers and customers or employers and employees, because portfolio owners usually prefer liquidity to lock-in' (Whitley, 1999: 41).

On the basis of these connections, Whitley (1999: 41–4) identifies *six major ideal types of business systems* (Table 4.2). He distinguishes four types of market economies in terms of:

- their degree of ownership-based coordination of economic activities, and
- the extent of non-ownership or alliance form of organizational integration.

'First, there are those where both forms are low, so that the overall level of coordination is quite limited. These can be termed *fragmented* business systems' (Whitley, 1999: 41). '*Fragmented* business systems are dominated by small owner-controlled firms that engage in adversarial competition with each other and short-term market contracting with suppliers and customers. Typically, employment relations are also short-term and dominated by 'efficient' external labour markets' (Whitley, 1999: 43). Short-term results orientation abounds and, along with this, a pronounced flexibility to convert the firm from one product or service to another. The most useful example of such a low-commitment economy is Hong Kong.

'Second, *coordinated industrial district* business systems combine relatively low levels of ownership integration – and so are dominated by small firms – with more extensive inter-firm integration and co-operation' (Whitley, 1999: 41), and stronger links across sectors. Economic coordination is more geared to long-term perspectives, and cooperation, commitment and flexibility are emphasized in the sphere of work relations and management. 'As the title suggests, these kinds of economies are exemplified by the postwar Italian industrial districts and similar European regional business systems' (Whitley, 1999: 43). See Chapter 11 for more examples.

'Third, *compartmentalized* business systems are dominated by large firms but exhibit low levels of co-operation between firms and business partners' (Whitley, 1999: 41). Moreover, in both commodity and labour markets more adversarial competition or confrontation abounds. 'Usually, owner control is exercised at arm's length, through financial markets. Firms here are islands of authoritative control and order amidst market disorder, as in the stereotypical Anglo-Saxon economy' (Whitley, 1999: 43).

Finally, Whitley distinguishes between three types of business system that combine relatively large units of ownership coordination with extensive alliances and collaboration between them. The three types are further differentiated by owner-control type, size of firm, and extent of alliance integration between firms and within them.

State-organized business systems are dominated by large firms that are dependent on state coordination and support to integrate production chains and activities in different sectors. 'However, they differ in their ownership patterns. Families and partners in these economies are typically able to retain direct control over large firms because the state supports their growth through subsidized credit' (Whitley, 1999: 43), and thus dominates economic development and guides firms' behaviour. Prominent examples are France in Europe and Korea in Asia.

'*Collaborative* business systems, on the other hand, manifest more collective organization and cooperation within sectors, but less ownership integration of activities in technologically and market-unrelated sectors. Owner control of these large forms is typically alliance in nature and they tend to focus on particular industries rather than diversify across different ones. They develop a greater degree of employer–employee interdependence and trust of skilled workers than employers in compartmentalized and state-organised business systems' (Whitley, 1999: 43–4). Prominent examples are to be found in western continental Europe, in German-speaking countries, and also in Scandinavia.

Highly coordinated business systems are also dominated by alliance forms of owner control and, in addition, have extensive alliances between larger companies, which are usually conglomerates, and a differentiated chain of suppliers. Employer–employee interdependence is high, and a large part of the workforce is integrated into the enterprise in a more stable way. Japan is the most prominent example of this type of system.

Whitley's typology is not the only one that has been developed within the institutional literature, but in organization studies in Europe it is the most frequently used and most differentiated one.[3] Typologies are, of course, very crude tools that help us to sketch broadly the differences between, say, Korea and Japan, but that are unable to capture the more specific differences thus failing on more demanding analysis. In general, and also in Whitley's case, typologies fail to explain why a particular country develops a specific type of business system at a particular time. In other words, there is a lack of theory building. Typologies are useful, though, in forcing us to identify linkages between different institutional domains (Sorge, 2003).

Background versus proximate institutions

In considering the key social institutions that influence the sorts of business system that become established in different market economies, and the ways in which they vary, Whitley (1992a: 19) distinguishes between more basic, or 'background' institutions and 'proximate' institutions.

Background institutions are social institutions (norms and legal rules such as property rights) that structure general patterns of trust, cooperation, identity and subordination in a society (i.e. commitment of employees, corporate culture) (see Table 4.3).

They are reproduced through the family, religious organizations and the education system, and often exhibit considerable continuity. They are crucial because they structure exchange relationships between business partners, and between employers and employees. They also affect the development of collective identities and prevalent modes of eliciting compliance and commitment within authority systems. Variations in these institutions result in significant differences in the governance structures of firms, the ways in which they deal with each other and other organizations, and prevalent patterns of work organization, control and employment. For example, how trust is granted and guaranteed in an economy especially affects the level of inter-firm cooperation and tendency to delegate control over resources. Another example is the impact of a society's level of individualism or collectivism. Individualistic societies such as the USA and the UK tend to have 'regulatory' states, a preference for formal, contractual regulation of social relationships, and market-based employment and skill development systems.

Proximate institutions are more directly involved in the economic system and constitute the more immediate business environment. They are often a product of the industrialization process and frequently develop with the formation of the modern state (see Table 4.3).

---

[3] Soskice (1991, 1994) develops a similar but less diversified typology.

Table 4.2 Six types of business system

Business system features	Business system type					
	Fragmented	Coordinated industrial district	Compartmentalized	State organized	Collaborative	Highly coordinated
Ownership coordination						
Owner control	direct	direct	market	direct	alliance	alliance
Ownership integration of production chains	low	low	high	high	high	some
Ownership integration of sectors	low	low	high	some to high	limited	limited
Non-ownership coordination						
Alliance coordination of production chains	low	limited	low	low	limited	high
Collaboration between competitors	low	some	low	low	high	high
Alliance coordination of sectors	low	low	low	low	low	some
Employment relations						
Employer–employee interdependence	low	some	low	low	some	high
Delegation to employees	low	some	low	low	high	considerable
	Hong Kong	Italian districts	Anglo-Saxon countries	France Korea	Germany Scandinavian countries	Japan

Source: Whitley (1999: 34).

Proximate social institutions affect forms of business organization and, in turn, become influenced by long-established and successful business systems. While there is no doubt about the existence of these causal relationships, the overemphasis of the business systems approach on 'thick' description is not matched by equally meticulous efforts at spelling out and theorizing the causal relationships between the relevant variables (Foss, 1999). This is perhaps due to the fact that the approach is 'aggregative and is not rooted in any spelled-out theory of individual behavior' (Foss, 1999: 4). Aside from being a theoretical flaw, the neglect of the actor within the framework is also a lost opportunity to explain (institutional) change and institutionalization. As is explained in more detail below, the societal effect approach surpasses this problem by using structuration theory (Giddens, 1986) or the 'actor–structure' argument.

Major societal institutions

Unlike societal effect analysis, the business systems approach is not open-ended but concentrates on a fixed number of *dominant* societal institutions that help to explain the variations between the business systems in different countries. The framework of a priori defined institutions and business system features, which have to be researched within the approach, helps the researcher to focus during his/her analysis, and probably contributes to the widespread use of the framework.

According to Whitley, the crucial institutional arrangements, which guide and constrain the nature of ownership relations, inter-firm connections and employment relations – or, in other words, that help us to explain business systems – are argued to be those governing access to critical resources, especially labour and capital. In particular, these institutions are the state, the financial system, and the skill development and control systems (Table 4.3).

Particularly important aspects of the *state* are its dominance of the economy, its encouragement of intermediary economic associations and its formal regulation of markets. The crucial aspect with regard to the *financial system* concerns the processes by which capital is made available and priced (see Chapter 6 for an extended explanation of this topic). A central distinction is made between capital-market-based and credit- or bank-based financial systems. In the former, resources are allocated through competition in capital markets, whereas in the latter they are allocated by the state or by financial institutions. In terms of the *skill development* and *control systems*, important factors are, first, the types of skill produced by education and training systems, and the extent to which employers, trades unions, and the state are involved in developing and managing such systems. This area also concerns the organization and control of labour markets, in particular the strength and organization of independent trade unions and the coordination of bargaining (see Chapter 5 for a discussion of this topic).

Connections between dominant institutions and business system features

In the same way as the characteristics of business systems are seen as interconnected, interrelations between the institutions are also stressed. The political, financial and labour

Table 4.3 Key institutional features structuring business systems

Proximate institutions

The state
Dominance of the state and its willingness to share risks with private owners
State antagonism to collective intermediaries
Extent of formal regulation of markets

Financial system
Capital market or credit-based

Skill development and control system
Strength of public training system and of state–employer–union collaboration
Strength of independent trade unions
Strength of labour organizations based on certified expertise
Centralization of bargaining

Background institutions

Trust and authority relations
Reliability of formal institutions governing trust relations
Predominance of paternalist authority relations
Importance of communal norms governing authority relations

Source: adapted from Whitley (1999: 48).

institutions, together with cultural features, are argued to work interdependently to structure business systems. Hence the explanation of differences between individual business systems, and of changes in their characteristics, depends on an analysis of all the major institutions and how they interdependently structure the specific form of economic organization that has developed.

The connections between dominant institutions (Table 4.3) and business system features (Table 4.1) enable us to identify the different institutional contexts that are associated with each of the six types of business system outlined in Table 4.2.[4] In general, the overall level of organizational integration of economic activities in an economy is argued to be connected to the existence and nature of general coordinating institutions in the wider society. Specifically, low levels of state risk-sharing, weak intermediaries and low market regulation, coupled with weak unions, a poor public training system and low trust in formal institutions limit the degree of organizational integration in an economy. More organizationally integrated business systems develop in societies where institutional mechanisms for managing uncertainty and trust are more established, and the political and social order encourages collaboration between social actors.

Fragmented business systems

As Whitley explains, 'fragmented business systems, then, develop in particularistic business environments with low trust cultures where formal institutions are unreliable, risks are difficult to share, and the state is at best neutral, and at worst predatory' (Whitley, 1999: 59).[5]

---

[4] For an explanation of the link between dominant institutions and business system features see Whitley (1999: 54–9).

[5] The following explanation of the institutional context of different business system types draws on Whitley (1999: 59–64).

Coordinated industrial districts

Coordinated industrial districts develop and continue to be reproduced in an institutional context in which both formal and informal institutions limit opportunism and provide an infrastructure for collaboration to occur. 'Local governments, banks, and training organizations typically work with quite strong forms of local labour representation in these situations to restrict adversarial, price-based competition in favour of high-quality, innovative strategies based on highly skilled and flexible labour. Firm size is limited in these localities by strong preferences for direct owner control by 'artisanal' entrepreneurs and consequent high levels of skilled labour mobility, often coupled with preferential tax and credit arrangements for small firms' (Whitley, 1999: 61).

Compartmentalized business systems

Compartmentalized business systems develop in arm's length institutional contexts with large and highly liquid markets in financial assets and unregulated labour markets with a highly mobile workforce. 'States are here regulatory rather than developmental, and often quite internally differentiated. ... Unions may be influential at times but are usually organized around craft skills rather than industries, and bargaining is decentralized. Practical manual worker skills are not highly valued and training in them is typically governed by *ad hoc* arrangements with little or no central coordination. ... Such a relatively impoverished institutional infrastructure restricts organizational integration between ownership units and leads to a strong reliance on ownership-based authority relations for coordinating economic activities' (Whitley, 1999: 61).

State-organized business systems

'State-organized business systems develop in less pluralist, *dirigiste* environments where the state dominates economic decision-making and tightly controls intermediary associations. ... Firms and their owners are highly dependent on state agencies and officials. As a result, they delegate little to employees and find it difficult to develop long-term commitment with business partners or competitors' (Whitley, 1999: 61–2).

Collaborative and highly coordinated business systems

'In contrast, both collaborative and highly coordinated business systems are established and reproduced in more collaborative institutional contexts that encourage and support cooperation between collective actors. The state here performs a greater coordinating role than in the previous case, and encourages the development of intermediary associations for mobilizing support and implementing collective policy decisions' (Whitley, 1999: 62). Markets are typically quite regulated in these societies, limiting the mobility of skilled workers and the price-based allocation of capital through impersonal market competition. 'Similarly, these kinds of business systems are much more likely to develop in economies with credit-based financial systems in which the providers of capital are strongly interconnected with its users and cannot easily exit when conditions alter' (Whitley, 1999: 62). 'Corporatist-type bargaining arrangements based on strong unions often lead to considerable employer–employee collaboration here. . . . Often organized around strong public training systems in which strong sectoral or enterprise unions cooperate with employers, labour systems in these economies encourage investment in high levels of skills which are cumulative and linked to organizational positions' (Whitley, 1999: 62). Whitley also adds that 'Additionally, societies where trust in the efficacy of formal institutions governing exchange relations and agreements is considerable are more likely to encourage joint commitments between the bulk of the workforce and management to enterprise development than those where trust is overwhelmingly dependent on personal obligations' (Whitley, 1999: 62).

Whitley concludes by stating that 'Essentially, I suggest that these result from variations in the extent of institutional pluralism across societies, especially with regard to those governing the organization and control of labour power, and the concomitant dominance of the state's coordinating role. Highly coordinated business systems are more likely to develop and continue in societies where the state dominates the coordination of economic development and the regulation of markets, as distinct from those where banks, industry associations, and similar organizations perform coordinating functions independently of state guidance' (Whitley, 1999: 62–3).

'Perhaps, even more important in separating the two types of business system, though, are the autonomy and influence of unions and other forms of labour representation in policy-making processes' (Whitley, 1999: 63). Collaborative business systems develop when unions are strong at the national and sector level. Strong unions at the national level limit the capacity of state–business coalitions to coordinate and integrate economic development and restructuring on a significant scale. In particular, strong sector-based unions, involved in national policy networks, limit state coordination of economic changes across sectors. Additionally, powerful national unions, coupled with strong public training systems, limit worker dependence on particular employees, which, in turn, restricts the extent of organizational integration of manual workers within firms. Whitley adds that 'centralized bargaining, collaboration in the management of training systems, and other factors do, of course, encourage greater integration of the bulk of the workforce in many firms in continental Europe than in the Anglo-Saxon economies' (Whitley, 1999: 63).

Societies, such as Japan, that develop highly coordinated business systems have less strong unions at the national and sector level. Japan has company-based unions, which do not form a strong counterweight against state dominance of economic coordination. Japan has limited public training systems. Training is organized at the company level, resulting in high employer–employee interdependence.

Conclusions

To sum up, differences in economic organization or business systems arise from contrasting processes of industrialization and are reproduced by different kinds of institutional context.

Variations in political arrangements and policies, as well as in the institutions governing the allocation and use of capital, have major effects on the extent and direction (vertical/horizontal) of organizational integration.

Equally, the ways that skills are developed, certified and controlled exert significant influence on prevalent employment relations and work systems, as do the dominant norms governing trust and authority relationships.

All these institutional arrangements, in addition, affect the management of production and market risks, and structure the ways that dominant firms are organized and controlled in market economies, as well as the sorts of competitive strategy they pursue.

4.3 Business Systems Research Applied to Taiwan and South Korea[6]

As indicated, the business systems approach argues that different societal contexts or dominant institutions encourage and constrain the development of distinctive and effective ways of organizing economic activities, or business systems, which constitute the dominant hierarchy-market configurations. Of course there are deviant patterns from the dominant one, but these can easily be identified. For instance, while there are some large capital-intensive firms in Taiwan, these are either state owned, or controlled and supported (such as Formosa Plastics), and do not reflect the dominant pattern of specialized, family businesses interconnected through elaborate personal networks. The focus here is on forms of business organization in South Korea (henceforth referred to as Korea) and Taiwan that compete effectively in the world markets or, in other words, on the ways of organizing competitive economic activities. The analysis of the business systems features deals with the situation in the 1980s and 1990s. The dominant institutions that together help to explain these features, and how they do so, are also discussed briefly. The intention is to help you understand how to apply the business systems approach, as well as to provide you with a brief account of two less well-known business systems.

The major distinguishing features of the postwar business systems in Korea and Taiwan are summarized in Table 4.4. These features were established between 1960 and 1990, and remained largely unchanged in the 1990s. Some features are quite similar in both business systems, particularly those concerned with employment relations and ownership control. There are also, however, significant differences between the two; these are to do with firm size, ownership integration and horizontal linkages in particular.

The Korean business system
Ownership relations

The Korean economy is dominated by very large family-owned and controlled conglomerate enterprises called *Chaebol* (well-known examples are Hyundai, Daewoo and Samsung). 'These quite diversified and vertically integrated firms have been the main agents of industrialization in Korea since the war under the strongly directive and coordinating influence of the authoritarian state' (Whitley, 1999: 141). They dominate many manufacturing industries (i.e. the heavy and chemical industries), as well as significant parts of the service sector – in particular, the construction industry, transport services, insurance and related financial services. 'Finally, seven large general trading companies which are members of the largest ten *Chaebol* have come to dominate Korea's export trade' (Whitley, 1999: 142).

---

[6] The explanation on these two business systems is based on Whitley's research (1999: Chapters 6 and 7). For a more detailed elaboration see the original text, as well as Whitley (1992a).

Table 4.4 The postwar business systems of Korea and Taiwan

Business system features	Korea	Taiwan
Ownership coordination		
Owner control	direct	direct
Ownership vertical integration	high	low except in intermediate sector
Ownership horizontal integration	high	high in business groups, low elsewhere
Non-ownership coordination		
Alliance-based vertical integration	low	low
Alliance-based horizontal integration	low	limited
Competitor collaboration	low	low
Employment relations and work management		
Employer–employee interdependence	low except for some managers	low except for personal connections
Worker discretion	low	low

Source: Whitley (1999: 140).

'The *Chaebol* remain largely family owned and controlled, despite their rapid growth and state pressure to sell shares on the stock market' (Whitley, 1999: 142). In the large *Chaebol* most of family holdings are indirect in the sense that owner control is exercised through a number of core companies rather than direct family ownership in all firms. The smaller *Chaebol* are more directly dominated by family owners. As Whitley states, 'This continuance of high levels of family ownership despite the rapid expansion and very large size of these conglomerates was facilitated by most of their expansion being funded by state-subsidized debt which did not dilute family shareholdings. Family ownership continues to mean largely family control and direction, with most of the leading posts held by family members and/or trusted colleagues from the same region or high school as the founding entrepreneur' (Whitley, 1999: 142). Family ownership also continues to imply strong central control over decision-making. 'This high level of direct owner control is implemented by substantial central staff offices that intervene extensively in subsidiary affairs. These offices typically deal with financial, personnel, and planning matters, including internal auditing and investment advice, and some have as many as 250 staff. . . . The high level of centralized decision-making encouraged considerable integration of economic activities, as capital, technology, and personnel could be centrally allocated and moved between subsidiaries' (Whitley, 1999: 143). The *Chaebol* are in fact managed as cohesive economic entities with a unified group culture focused on the owner.

Whitley goes on, saying that 'These strong owner-controlled large groups of firms are highly diversified, both vertically and horizontally. According to Hamilton and Feenstra, most are vertically integrated, with many individual *Chaebol* business units themselves being quite integrated and the network of firms increasing this even more so' (Whitley, 1999: 143). Horizontal diversification is considerable, with the average *Chaebol* operating in five different manufacturing industries. For example, Samsung's 55 firms were active in textiles, electronics, fibre optics, detergents, petrochemicals, shipbuilding, property development, construction, insurance, mass media, healthcare and higher education in the early 1990s.

The *Chaebol* have grown extremely fast since the 1950s, with high growth at the expense of profitability. Detailed analysis of the *Chaebol* suggests that the objective of the firms of the large *Chaebol* is not to maximize profits but to maximize sales. Ownership rights are held for control purposes more than for income, and, as indicated, growth has been financed by state-provided and subsidized credit, rather than from retained profits.

Non-ownership coordination

Whitley explains that 'the large size and self-sufficiency of the Korean *Chaebol* mean that they exhibit low interdependence with suppliers and customers and are able to dominate small and medium-sized firms. Typically, their relations with subcontractors are predatory. As Fields comments: "Core firms are able to increase their working capital by squeezing the subcontractors associated with the *Chaebol* . . . the *Chaebol* are able to keep the small and medium-sized contractors under their thumbs, pass recessionary shocks on to them, or even merge with them if it suits their plans." . . . Relations between the *Chaebol*, and between ownership units in general in Korea, tend to be adversarial, with considerable reluctance to cooperate over joint projects, such as complementary R & D programmes. . . . New industries especially are often the site of intense competition for dominance, and the major driving force behind many new investments often appears to be corporate rivalry for the leading position in them' (Whitely, 1999: 144–5). In general, markets are not organized around the long-term mutual obligations that characterize the postwar Japanese economy, but rather are characterized by predominantly short-term, single-transaction relationships. 'These sometimes develop from personal contacts, as when subcontracting firms are set up by ex-employees. Where cooperation does occur between firms, direct personal ties between chief executives are usually crucial to reaching agreements. Alliance-based modes of integration, then, are weak in the postwar Korean business system' (Whitley, 1999: 145).

Whitley states that 'the high degree of competition between the leading *Chaebol*, which has been fuelled by the state's policy of selecting entrants to new industries and opportunities on the basis of competitive success, has severely limited the development of independent sector-based organizations in Korea. . . . In the 1980s and 1990s, however, the umbrella organization, the Federation of Korean Industries, together with a few other associations, attempted to diverge from and publicly influence state policies' (Whitley, 1999: 145).

Employment policies and labour management

Whitley's explanation of employment policies states that 'In most *Chaebol* the level of employer–employee commitment is limited for manual workers. Although seniority does appear to be important in affecting wage rates, and employers do provide accommodation and other fringe benefits in the newer capital intensive industries, most notably perhaps at the Pohang Iron and Steel Company, Korean firms are reluctant to make the sorts of long-term commitments to their workforce that many large Japanese ones do. Mobility between firms, both enforced and voluntary, has been considerably greater for manual workers – and some non-manual – than is common in the large firm sector in Japan. Annual labour turnover rates of between 52 per cent and 72 per cent were quite usual in the 1970s in Korea and were especially high in manufacturing industries. Additionally, leading firms in Korea sometimes poach skilled workers from competitors rather than invest in training programs. . . . White-collar employees are more favoured and tend more to remain with large employers, not least because their pay and conditions are usually substantially better than they could obtain by moving' (Whitley, 1999: 145–46).

The centralized and personal nature of authority relations in the *Chaebol* is accompanied by a largely authoritarian, not to say militaristic, management style. As Whitley discovered, 'According to the Japanese managers involved in joint ventures with Korean firms interviewed by Liebenberg, the Korean management style is characterized by top-down decision-making, enforcement of vertical hierarchical relationships, low levels of consultation with subordinates, and low levels of trust, both horizontally and vertically. Superiors tend to be seen as remote and uninterested in subordinates' concerns or their ability to contribute more than obedience. . . . This authoritarian management style encourages close supervision of task performance' (Whitley, 1999: 146). In order to facilitate supervision, the physical layout of offices is arranged in a specific way and tasks are usually described carefully. Because of the importance of personal authority in the Korean *Chaebol*, jobs and responsibilities are determined more by supervisors' wishes than by formal rules. 'Such strong supervision of task performance was allied to considerable specialization of roles for manual workers. . . . Unskilled workers continue to carry out relatively narrow tasks without much movement between jobs and skill categories. However, non-manual workers do appear to be moved between tasks and sections, and sometimes develop more varied skills, in the larger and more diversified *Chaebol* ' (Whitley, 1999: 146). Managers in particular are often transferred across subsidiaries and have more fluid roles and responsibilities.

Institutional influences on the Korean business system

The dominant institutions structuring the postwar Korean business system stem from both pre-industrial Korean society and the period of Japanese colonial rule, as well as the Korean war and the post-1961 period of military-supported rule (Table 4.5). The dominant and risk-sharing nature of the Korean state can be traced back to the period between 1392 and 1910, when Korea was ruled by the *Yi*, or *Chosun* dynasty. This dynasty entrenched Confucianism as the official ideology. This ideology is based on the idea that the stability of society is based on unequal relationships between people. The Confucian heritage in Korea helps to explain the population's respect for hierarchy. During the *Yi* period, 'political power was highly centralized by the pseudo-bureaucratic elite, who claimed moral superiority over the population on the basis of examination successes' (Whitley, 1999: 152). The elite were awarded official posts by the king, and access to examinations for the leading posts was restricted to those of aristocratic status. In addition, because the possibility of obtaining a state office was always present for the Korean aristocracy, they were discouraged from developing non-official corporate interest groups at the local level. As Whitley states, 'Military institutions had little prestige in the Confucian-dominated political culture; equally Korea lacked a strong commercial class'. The merchant class was subjected to strict surveillance. 'In both preindustrial China and

Table 4.5   Dominant institutional influences on the postwar Korean business system
The state
Dominant and risk sharing
Antagonistic to independent collective intermediaries
Strong formal and informal state regulation of markets
Financial system
State-dominated, credit-based financial system
Skill development and control system
Weak public training system; no collaboration with unions
State-controlled official unions
Weak occupational associations
Little institutionalized bargaining
Trust and authority
Low trust in informal institutions and procedures
Patriarchal authority relations

Source: Whitley (1999: 159).

Korea, successful merchants were considered to be potential threats to the official élite as manifesting an alternative basis of prestige and power to the official examinations and constituting an independent source of power. Private accumulation of wealth was officially regarded as an indicator of corruption . . .' (Whitley, 1999: 154). Hence, traders were considered to be exploiters and pedlars were organized into a state-controlled guild to be used for political control of any threats to the established order.

As Whitley's book explains, the 35 years of Japanese rule (1910 until approximately 1945) and the subsequent US occupation of Korea intensified some of the features of the pre-industrial political system, such as its high level of centralization. Among other things, the Japanese developed a formal administrative apparatus that enabled the state to control rural communities directly, without needing the local elites, and thus enhanced the centre's power over society as a whole. 'However, as Jacobs suggests much of this "modernization" of Korean society by the Japanese retained crucial elements of the earlier patrimonial system and, in particular, the capricious and unpredictable behaviour of the executive' (Whitley, 1999: 155). During the colonial period, indigenous enterprises experienced as much insecurity and instability as during the *Yi* period, encouraging further the dependence on close family ties among top managers and the intensive cultivation of personal connections with the governing elite. Whitley goes on to say that 'As well as inhibiting the development of new indigenous political institutions, the Japanese occupation also prevented the growth of an independent Korean entrepreneurial élite and technical strata. Koreans were systematically excluded from middle- and senior-ranked posts in both the state bureaucracy and privately owned businesses that were dominated by the Japanese. The few indigenous firms that did develop and survive were mostly in textiles and food-processing industries and were heavily dependent upon the toleration of the colonial administration. The bulk of the productive land, manufacturing, and industrial enterprises was owned and managed by Japanese and the forced industrialization of Korea in the 1930s and 1940s was directed almost entirely towards supporting Japanese military expansion in mainland Asia' (Whitley, 1999: 155–6). The Japanese did, however, provide a model of how industrial enterprises and banks could be organized, and they did develop the physical and social infrastructure necessary for an industrial economy, albeit one designed to support the colonial power.

When Korea recovered its independence in 1948, many of the traditional patterns recurred, especially the dependence on the centre. This dependence grew even more in the 1950s after land reform weakened the landlord class and rural elites. 'Particularly important also was the virtual giving-away of the formerly Japanese-owned businesses between 1947 and 1957 to favoured businessmen. These firms formed the basis of many of the leading *Chaebol*.

'The high levels of business dependence on the state, and especially upon personal relations with the chief political executive and/or bureaucratic elite, during the period of early industrialization became even more intensified after the 1961 military *coup* led by Park Chong-hui. Initially, Park rounded up the richest men together in an anti-corruption campaign and charged them with illicit profiteering. After realizing that this would merely prevent the economy from developing and that it was not particularly popular, the military regime released the major business leaders and much of their property in exchange for paying fines in the form of establishing new enterprises and cooperating with the state in its ambitious industrialization plans.

'The one exception to this return of expropriated property was the banking system, which was systematically used to direct investment, reward exports and other achievements desired by the state, and punish inefficiency and/or political opposition. Thus, the state controlled the flow of cheap credit, and especially access to foreign loans and technology, to the fast-growing *Chaebol* in favour of its developmental priorities, first in light manufacturing exports and later, in the 1970s, in heavy and chemical industries. . . . The direct financial risks for the *Chaebol*-owning families were, therefore, limited since they did not need to find the capital themselves to dilute their control by selling shares on the stock market. However, political risks were obviously very high, either for failing to meet state targets or for not supporting the regime' (Whitley, 1999: 156–7). Big business in Korea was, and remains, highly dependent on the state and especially the president and his close advisers for access to subsidized credit and the means to expand. In return for these resources, the *Chaebol* diversified into heavy industry in the 1970s to fulfil state priorities, and funded the political campaign of the ruling party. This high level of dependence, together with the traditional devaluation of formal legal institutions, engendered a low degree of trust in formal institutions and procedures. Trust, cooperation and loyalty in Korea remain largely based on groups constituted by predominantly ascriptive criteria and/or shared collective experiences.

The difficulty of establishing long-term trust relations outside kinship or similar groupings, inhibits the delegation of control to non-family managers in the *Chaebol*, and this is reinforced by the importance of personal superior–subordinate relationships in authority structures. 'Given the pervasive insecurity of the entrepreneur in Korean society, and the lack of institutional mechanisms for generating trust and loyalty beyond the lineage, or similar personally based groupings, long-term obligations and alliances between firms are also difficult to develop and maintain so that growth has been managed internally by *Chaebol* owners rather than through extensive networks and business groups as in Japan. The overweening power of the central state likewise prevented the establishment of powerful intermediary institutions to coordinate economic activities within and between sectors' (Whitley, 1999: 162).

Aside from providing cheap credit, a further way in which the state reduced the risks for the *Chaebol* was by controlling and restricting trade unions, and by limiting real wage increases. For political as well as economic reasons, the military regime maintained considerable control over the organized labour movement in Korea and often intervened in strikes and other industrial disputes. The weakness of the trade unions has meant that *Chaebol* owners have not had to gain their cooperation or make long-term commitments to workers. The plentiful availability of relatively cheap labour until the mid-1980s, due to population growth and emigration from the land to the major cities, also limited real wage growth and the need to gain workers' commitment to enterprise goals.

As Whitley says, 'The general prestige of educational qualifications and their perceived necessity for high-status white-collar jobs have led to high levels of investment in general education, both public and private' (Whitley, 1999: 158). However, whereas the general academic qualifications enjoy great prestige in Korea, technical education is of relatively low status and limited in provision. Hence, managers were one of the least scarce resources, whereas skilled and experienced workers were most scarce. Moreover, the difficulty of establishing reliable long-term trust relationships and collective commitments beyond kinship and similar groupings prevented the generation of 'Japanese-style' employment policies in the *Chaebol*. Hence, as suggested, turnover among manual workers is great, as is the reliance on external labour markets for scarce skills.

The Taiwanese business system
Ownership relations

Taiwan developed a large state-owned enterprise sector that dominates the capital-intensive, upstream industries together with a large number of small and medium-sized family-owned and controlled firms dominating the export trade in consumer goods. Whitley explains that 'the production of intermediate goods tends to be more dominated by larger enterprises, often exercising quasi-monopoly control and also forming more diversified business groups. These groups are usually under common ownership, although this may be shared between a number of business partners who have established highly personal trust relations with each other' (Whitley, 1999: 148).

Whitley states 'As Wade points out: "From the early 1950s onward Taiwan has had one of the biggest public enterprise sectors outside the communist bloc and Sub-Saharan Africa", and public enterprises contributed about twice as much GDP at factor cost as their equivalents in Korea in the 1970s. Indeed the only Asian countries with a comparable public-sector contribution to capital investment were India and Burma.

'In 1980 the Taiwanese Ministry of Economic Affairs owned firms in the power, petroleum, mining, aluminium, phosphates, alkali, sugar, chemicals, fertilizers, petrochemicals, steel, ship building, engineering, and machinery industries, while the Ministry of Finance owned four banks and eight insurance companies. These public enterprises were very large by comparison with privately owned ones and often dominated, if not monopolized, their sectors. Thus the state has retained ownership and control of the "commanding heights" of the economy in Taiwan, especially the upstream capital-intensive sectors' (Whitley, 1999: 147).

Privately owned Taiwanese businesses follow the traditional pattern of the Chinese family firms that dominate many Asian economies. Most are limited in size, relatively specialized in particular industries, concentrated in light manufacturing industry and commerce, and embedded in highly flexible networks of suppliers, subcontractors and customers. When successful, they often engage in opportunistic, unrelated diversification. Most networks between family firms are not particularly stable or long-lived, except where they are based on strong personal ties of mutual obligation and support.

'Private firms in Taiwan are nearly all owned and controlled by families, as indeed are most Chinese businesses throughout South-east Asia. Owners are highly involved in the running of their firms, and there are strong connections between ownership and the direction of economic activities' (Whitley, 1999: 148). Like many family firms in other economies, authority in Taiwanese companies is highly centralized and personal, with little emphasis on formal rules and procedures. In diversified firms, subsidiaries are coordinated through personal relationships and family domination of multiple top-management positions, rather than by systematic planning or joint activities. This emphasis on family ownership and control means that dominant goals are focused on the acquisition and growth of family wealth rather than on the growth of the firm as a separate entity. The pursuit of large size, irrespective of profitability, is not usually the dominant objective in these firms, especially if it could lead to the loss of personal control or to being considered a threat by the ruling party's interests' (Whitley, 1999: 148).

'Vertical integration is weak in most of these firms and they are rarely self-sufficient in terms of combining the management of key processes and activities in one organization. Instead, they are usually highly interdependent with other enterprises for inputs and for distributing their outputs, and form fluid subcontracting networks. However, this interdependence is not usually accompanied by a willingness to share long-term risks with suppliers and buyers. Rather, more restricted and limited connections are preferred. Some Taiwanese business groups do exhibit a greater degree of backward integration in the production of intermediary goods, but this is much less than in Korea or many western firms' (Whitley, 1999: 148–9).

Whitley explains that 'Diversification of a horizontal nature ... is however, more widespread in private Taiwanese firms, especially those forming business groups of associated companies. While by no means all successful firms develop into highly diversified business groups, including some of the largest, those that do diversify tend to move into a variety of sectors in a seemingly *ad hoc* and idiosyncratic way, often as the result of personal requests or obligations. According to Hamilton, a common pattern of expansion of leading Taiwanese business groups is to establish a dominant presence – quasi-monopolistic in many cases in a particular sector supplying export-oriented firms, and then to set up a number of quite separate and unrelated businesses to be run by the patriarch's sons and other male relatives. Ownership-based horizontal diversification is, then, quite considerable in the intermediate sector, but less so in the capital-intensive state sector or the very small-firm-dominated export sector' (Whitley, 1999: 149).

Non-ownership coordination

Whitley also analyses non-ownership coordination: 'The specialization and interdependence of Taiwanese family businesses mean that they have to rely on each other to obtain inputs for their products and services, and to distribute and market them. Thus multiple market connections between firms are crucial to their operation. These are not necessarily long term or based on mutual obligations. Rather, inter-firm links are often managed in such a way as to reduce risks, and so commitments to other economic actors are restricted. Exchange partners may, then, be numerous and selected on the basis of their personal reputations for competence and reliability, but do not usually form networks of long-term trust and reciprocal loyalty. Market relations can change rapidly and are quite fluid, and flexibility is emphasized over long-term risk sharing'. Indeed, when the Taiwanese state tried to encourage the formation of Japanese-style subcontracting arrangements, it failed. Equally, attempts to establish trading companies as long-term coordinating agencies in Taiwan have been less successful than in Korea.

Whitley explains that: 'Business partnerships, on the other hand, often do involve long-term reciprocal commitments, and can lead to the development of elaborate networks of personal obligations that structure strategic decisions and new ventures. Where significant resources are involved and firms need to undertake activities jointly, connections are highly personal and dependent on trust between the owners. Without high levels of personal trust, such partnerships cannot be formed successfully in Taiwan and, as a result, many medium-sized firms do not grow into large enterprises because they are unable to find partners they can rely on' (Whitley, 1999: 150). In general, the extent of systematic, stable, vertical and horizontal integration of economic activities through alliances and long-term partnerships is limited in Taiwan. Whitley concludes that partnerships based on personal connections and trust, on the other hand, seem easier to develop and to be more sustained than in Korea.

Sectoral cooperation is also 'limited by this concern with personal control, as well as being restricted by the state's intolerance of independent intermediary organizations' (Whitley, 1999: 150). Whitley paraphrases Numazaki in saying that the survival strategies of Taiwanese small and medium-sized enterprises are to seize the opportunities, take full advantage of them and then leave the industry; the result is frequent entry and exit of Taiwanese enterprises, making stable associations of industry-specific associations difficult to maintain. Collective organization and joint action by competitors are therefore lacking in Taiwan.

Employment policies and labour management

'Long-term employment commitments and seniority-based promotion practices tend to be reserved for those workers with whom the owning family has personal obligation ties, while previously unknown staff hired though impersonal channels neither expect nor receive such commitments. In particular, young, female, semi-skilled, non-family workers in the light manufacturing export sector are expected to stay only for a short time and are rarely trained for more demanding posts' (Whitley, 1999: 151).

Whitley also outlines that 'the intensely familial nature of these businesses restricts senior managerial posts to family members or those who have family-like connections to the owner. Thus, many skilled workers and managers prefer to leave and start up their own businesses once they have acquired business skills and some capital especially, in the labour-intensive export sector, where subcontracting is widespread. Both the general cultural preference for personal business ownership over employment, and the unwillingness to trust non-family subordinates on the part of the employers, limit the scope and length of employer-employee commitments in the Chinese family business, where obligations are restricted to close personal connections' (Whitley, 1999: 151).

Whitley also explains that 'the importance of personal relationships and authority in Chinese family businesses additionally means that formal specification of roles and positions is less important than in most Western societies. Equally, jobs and skills are not rigidly defined and separated by formal procedures, but rather are fairly broad and flexible. Similarly, many managers in Taiwanese business groups hold a considerable number of posts and are rarely restricted to a single specialized role' (Whitley, 1999: 151). Their responsibilities are liable to be changed suddenly at the behest of the owner.

Whitley goes on to say that 'the strong commitment to patriarchal relationships in the workplace, and in society as a whole, means that superior-subordinate relations are quite remote and distant, particularly those between the owner-manager and employees. Similarly, as in Korea, paternalism implies a lack of confidence in the abilities and commitment of staff, so that close supervision of work performance is a feature of Taiwanese firms, as is considerable personal discretion in how authority is exercised, especially at the top of the enterprise' (Whitley, 1999: 152).

Institutional influences on the Taiwanese business system

Some of the institutional features of Korean society can be found in Taiwan, but there are also significant differences, which have resulted in a different kind of business system being developed there. The dominant institutions in Taiwan during its industrialization combine some features from pre-industrial society – such as the strong identification with, and loyalty to, the family – with a number of quite distinctive features resulting from Japanese colonialism and the imposition of the *Koumintang* (KMT) rule after the war (Table 4.6). Whitley believes that perhaps the most important feature of Taiwan's industrialization since the end of Japanese colonialism in 1945 has been the large-scale movement of the Chinese nationalist government and its followers to Taiwan in 1949 following its defeat in the civil war by the communists. 'This take-over of Taiwan by Chiang Kai-shek and the KMT not only effectively created a new state but also established a major division in its population between the 6 million or so Taiwanese and the 1 to 2 million "mainlanders", which had major consequences for the organization and control of economic activities' (Whitley, 1999: 164).

Whitley explains this by saying that 'In particular, it resulted in the exclusion of most Taiwanese from the state bureaucracy and political leadership as well as from the management of the large publicly owned industrial sector. . . . This domination of Taiwan society by outsiders continued the pattern established by the Japanese occupation in which the indigenous population learnt to obey and fear their rulers, and to develop economic activities within the context and framework established by an external power' (Whitley, 1999: 164).

He goes on to say that 'the lack of trust between the KMT and its mainlander followers and the Taiwanese, together with the military objective of retaking control of the mainland, which justified the continuance of martial law and the authoritarian state – at least in the eyes of the leadership – resulted in the state maintaining ownership of the larger, upstream, and capital-intensive sector of the economy. . . . Additionally, many state officials and leading KMT politicians continued to regard the establishment of large privately owned concentrations of economic resources with considerable suspicion and a potential threat to their power, and so were reluctant either to privatize state enterprises or to encourage large Taiwanese firms to develop independently of the state' (Whitley, 1999: 168).

Whitley explains the Taiwanese business system, saying that 'This ownership extended to the banks and the bulk of the formal financial sector, and enabled the regime to provide jobs for its followers as well as influencing the development of the small-firm, Taiwanese-dominated export sector . . . The KMT domination of the economy was different from that of the military-backed regime in Korea, in that it concentrated more on state ownership and control of tariffs, import licenses, etc., than on direct control over the flow of credit to privately owned firms. Although the formal banking system in Taiwan has been owned and controlled by the state since the war, the regime has not used this control to direct the flow of capital to favoured private firms pursuing state priorities. Rather, it has been more concerned to prevent the growth of large Taiwanese enterprises that had close links to major banks and so has enacted legislation that prohibits banks from owning shares in borrowers' companies or forming holding companies that combine industrial and financial businesses. In general, the banks prefer to lend to the state enterprises and the largest privately owned firms that have good mainlander connections, since the risks are lower and function more as arms of the bureaucracy than as risk-sharing supporters of industry . . . As a result, the bulk of the firms in the export-oriented sector rely more on the informal "curb" market and capital from family and friends for growth funds than on the formal banking system. This is especially true for the smaller and newer enterprises that have little or no collateral to support their applications for bank loans. . . . Consequently, informal, personal networks of trust and support are crucial to firms' survival and growth in Taiwan, and the development of large-scale capital-intensive industries is difficult without strong state support' (Whitley, 1999: 168–70).

Whitley explains that 'the regime's antagonism to large privately owned enterprises that are independent of the state – buttressed by references to Sun Yat-sen and sharpened by the ethnic divide – of the state – has prevented long-term collaboration between the state and large-scale private interests, except in a few cases, such as Formosa Plastics. Instead, the private, Taiwanese-dominated part of the economy has been largely treated with official disdain, and relations between state officials and Taiwanese businessmen are often described as 'cool' and 'distant' in contrast to those between officials and the leaders of publicly owned enterprises. As a result, the degree of direct dependence on the state of most Taiwanese businesses is limited, and the state has found it difficult to gain the cooperation of firms in a particular sector when it did want to achieve a specific objective through collaboration. This is exacerbated, of course, by the large number of small firms in most sectors and the traditional distrust of the regime and its agents' (Whitley, 1999: 170).

Continuing his argument, Whitley states that 'the traditional Chinese leaders' concern with limiting the power of private wealth holders, exacerbated by the ethnic divide between the Taiwanese and the mainlanders, was expressed most strongly in the conflict over the liberalization of the economy and movement to a more export-oriented policy at the end of the 1950s. . . . However, more for political reasons than for economic ones, coupled with strong US pressure, Chiang Kai-shek supported the reform group in 1958, and Taiwan adopted a more liberal, though still state-dominated approach, to economic management.

'This boosted the largely Taiwanese-owned export-oriented sector and confirmed the distinctive division of the political and economic system between mainlanders and

Table 4.6   Dominant institutional influences on the postwar Taiwanese business system

The state
Dominating state controlled by mainlanders; commitment to state-led development with little risk sharing with Taiwanese firms
Antagonistic to independent collective intermediaries
Strong state control of upstream capital-intensive sectors, agriculture and new industries; low control of small firms in export sector

Financial system
State-directed, credit-based financial system; limited state control of informal curb market in SME sector

Skill development and control system
Stronger state technical training system for technicians and engineers than elsewhere in East Asia
State-controlled and repressed labour organizations
Weak occupational associations
Little institutionalized bargaining

Trust and authority
Low trust in formal institutions and procedures
Patriarchal authority relations

Source: Whitley (1999: 171).

Taiwanese. The former dominated the military, the political system, the bureaucracy, and the state enterprises, while the latter concentrated on building up family businesses in export-focused light manufacturing and commerce. Although this division became attenuated in the 1980s as the proportion of mainlanders declined and economic growth increased the regime's security, it remains a distinctive feature of Taiwan's society and has had major consequences for the business system that has become established' (Whitley, 1999: 169).

'As in Korea, the Confucian emphasis on education has resulted in high rates of private and public investment in education. However, the exclusion of the Taiwanese from leading positions in the bureaucracy has meant that the private sector has been more attractive to college graduates than might be expected. The public education system in Taiwan has produced large numbers of engineers over the past thirty years, and the appeal of technical subjects such as electrical and electronic engineering seems to have been greater than in Korea. This has not been accompanied, however, by the development of strong craft-based skills credentialled by public institutions. Employers' use of the technical skills then has not been constrained by specialized, publicly certified and standardized practical competences but remains largely determined by individual firm's organization of tasks and on-the-job training. Consequently, the education and training system develops certified technical skills without standardizing jobs around them or institutionalizing highly specialized roles within firms. Although university education remains highly prized and competition to enter universities is highly competitive, traditional literary qualifications and official positions are not as highly regarded as in traditional Chinese society' (Whitley, 1999: 170).

Whitley goes on to say that 'state control over the labour movement has been strongly enforced, as in Korea. As in Korea, too, unions and occupational associations have had little impact on skill development and standardization, and they have not affected the way work is organized and controlled in firms. The KMT maintained firm control over unions for political as well as economic reasons, and the right to strike was prohibited under martial law.' Whitley concludes by saying that 'state control over, and repression of, trade unions meant that business owners have not had to formalize employment procedures nor to elicit long-term commitment from employees, especially those to whom personal obligations are not due' (Whitley, 1999: 173). In addition, the combination of the strong preference for family entrepreneurship, close rural–urban linkages, and the relatively decentralized nature of industrial development throughout much of Taiwan has restricted the development of large concentrations of urban workers wholly dependent on employment. This, in turn, has limited the formulation of a self-conscious working-class movement that could exert pressure on employers and the state (Whitley, 1999: 170–1). Furthermore, the predominance of small to medium-sized family-controlled businesses, in which traditional conceptions of paternalistic management remained important, has inhibited the growth of unions. The significance of personal relationships, and foundations of trust in Taiwanese society, limit the establishment of formal collective organizations representing workers' interests in favour of personal obligations and commitments. Skill-based occupational identities and organizations are, similarly, unimportant in Taiwan' (Whitley, 1999: 171).

Conclusions

Internationalization, growth and institutional developments have not, then, constituted such strong and discontinuous changes as to lead to major shifts in dominant forms of economic organization in Korea and Taiwan.

    While the democratization of the Korean and Taiwanese states has limited the extent of authoritarian direction of economic development and firms' policies in recent years, the state remains the dominant collective agent of economic decision-making in these economies.

    Moreover, the lack of strong intermediary organizations in both countries remains, as does the limited extent of collaboration between competitors over such issues as training, bargaining and technological development.

    Risk sharing continues to be largely absent beyond personal ties in Korea and Taiwan.

    Finally, democratization in both countries does not yet seem to have developed such radical discontinuities with the recent past as to generate major changes in business-system features.

4.4 The Societal Effect (SE) Approach

The second main European institutional approach is the societal effect approach. Societal effect analysis is not a theory in the conventional sense but an 'approach' that is open to further development. For example, as suggested, unlike the business systems (BS) approach, which focuses on an a priori fixed set of institutions, for the SE approach this is an empirical question. Unlike the BS approach, the SE approach offers a balance between structure, action and actor-centric elements. As is explained more extensively below, the attention for the actor or agency means that the approach is better able to explain change than the BS approach.

Note that *the notion of actor* as used in SE analysis is not confined to the 'individual subject'. It can equally well be applied to categories and groups of actors (i.e. occupational categories) and to the collective actors making up a particular organizational entity, such as a firm's R&D department or the firm itself.

Unlike etic approaches to organization and management (see Chapter 2), SE analysis seeks to *contextualize* phenomena and, by doing so, is able to show that they are the expression of the different logics operating in different societies. Indeed, a major characteristic of societal analysis is that it aims to relate organizations to the institutional and cultural systems of the surrounding society, and thus attempts to overcome the split between institutionalism and culturalism.

Societal analysis, then, addresses a weakness of etic cultural analysis, which tends towards methodological individualism, using value surveys that target individuals to explain systemic characteristics. It also addresses a weakness of institutional analysis, which neglects the individual in favour of system characteristics. Faced, for example, with organizational outcomes in Japan, compared with other societies, institutional analysis (such as the business systems approach) would play down the role of Japanese culture to the extent that this refers to individual mental programmes and general socialization processes. Institutionalists would argue that the specificity of Japanese practices resides in a different construction of professional careers, labour markets (life-long employment), payment systems and industrial relations, or, in other words, in system characteristics. They would argue that, if Europeans and Americans were to be transplanted into a Japanese-type context, they would reproduce or generate the same organizational patterns (Sorge, 2003). They do of course hereby ignore the question of why Japanese institutions developed in Japan in the first place and not in Europe or the USA. Cultural analysis would argue the opposite – that is, it would stress the importance of mental programmes as opposed to system features in explaining organizational outcomes. The aim of societal analysis is to capture the interrelationship between all these influences and their effect on organization.

Actor–structure relationship

The aim of contextualizing phenomena, and thus overcoming this gap between cultural and institutional analysis, is reflected in one of the major theoretical features of the SE approach, which insists on the reciprocal, interactive constitution of 'actors' and 'spaces', or the dialectical relationship between the micro (the cultural) and the macro (the institutional). The approach draws on structuration theory (Giddens, 1986: Chapter 4), which has made the point that individual behaviour and social structure are reciprocally constituted: it is impossible to imagine a normative regularity, instituted to be more or less binding, as not being kept in place by acting individuals. Likewise, individuals do not make behavioural choices without regard for norms (Sorge, 2003).

It is precisely by recognizing that actors (individuals and organizations) are able to influence institutions (i.e. laws, rules, systems) and processes that societal analysis is able to overcome the stasis and inertia that is inherent in business systems analysis. The SE approach argues that actor–space (the notion of space is explained in detail below) interaction patterns do not necessarily reproduce something that remains unchanged. Actors have the ability to innovate practices, which reduces the inertia usually implied by institutions.

The approach argues, however, that since actors are embedded in the social structures, they replicate some more abstract qualities of practices even as they innovate them. Structural properties and rules of the game – that is, the 'systems' properties – it is argued, tend to load the individual 'choices' that actors make in a specific way. Actors tend to see particular 'choices' as generally favourable, and develop a specific 'programming of the mind'. The dynamics in this way link both elements of stability and change within 'non-identical reproduction'. In other words, since individuals or organizations live by, use, accept or are familiar with existing rules, laws, regulations, and so on, they will, almost unconsciously and automatically, base themselves on the existing and the 'known' to innovate or introduce change. As a consequence, change will usually be incremental (non-identical reproduction) rather than revolutionary.

The interactive relationship between actor and spaces may be marked by both correspondence and opposition: faced, for example, with hierarchical organization patterns, the actors may learn to internalize corresponding assumptions and find them legitimate. They may also develop a dislike for them, and attempt to evade them while trying at the same time to comply with them. This means that expressed value preferences and manifest behaviour may both converge and diverge (Sorge, 2003).

The approach further argues that conflicts and contradictions, between values and between institutional arrangements, exemplify the need for a dialectical perspective. This dialectical perspective stresses that the openness of social systems goes with conflict. Openness and conflict, together, account for the ever present tendency to change and modify in ways that go beyond the relatively stable patterns put forward in Whitley's business systems framework.

The SE approach distinguishes two levels of change, one more abstract and the other more concrete. Concrete practices, arrangements and actor predispositions change over time. However, since new practices are linked to existing logics of action, they will take on a specific form that is in accordance with the existing societal identity. In other words, new practices will be moulded by the existing societal institutions while existing societal institutions remain visible in the specific form that changes take on. The SE approach argues that this would happen even after full-scale revolutions.

Like the notion of space, the notion of 'actor' is seen as a 'social construct'. This means that it is not definable a priori, but that it is understood in its relation to, and at the same time as part of, a space or social structure that helps to shape its identity, while the space itself is structured by the action of the actor (dialectic relationship between actor and space). Thus, we are dealing with an actor located in a space that he helps to structure, while that same space helps to determine the conditions under which the actor himself exists.

Moreover, within the societal effect approach, actors have a historical dimension. More concrete, the 'construction of actors' has temporal and historical dimensions that help to shape the actors' identity and their form of existence in society. Recognition of the historical nature of the construction of actors and spaces, and of the historicity of the processes involved, is another way in which the approach is able to take account of the dynamics of change. However, it is not the purpose of the SE approach to go back in time.

Historical analysis is used not to provide a historical interpretation of the phenomena analysed but rather in order to identify better those dimensions of the analysis most relevant to an understanding of the particular processes at work today in the construction of the actors. Societal analysis thus involves another kind of dialectic – that between the synchronic and the diachronic, with the synchronic given a certain degree of methodological priority.

Important points

- There is an interactive relationship between actor, structure and process.
- This relationship can be characterized by correspondence and opposition, and can produce institutional change.
- Relevant actors and spaces should be empirically determined and not theoretically fixed.

Institution as a process and a structure

The notion of 'space', or the 'macro' concept, was originally an 'empirical' concept used to denote the structures and processes of skill acquisition and development in the workforce of German companies – or, in other words, the educational and vocational institutions and processes. As such, it was used instead of the concept of institution or structure in order to develop an analysis in terms of 'processes' and the 'quality' of the relationships between the actors, and of the forms of socialization to which they are subject. The notion of space is thus extensive in both its meaning and its analytical capacity, since it describes both the modes of existence of employees within the firm (the structure) and the way in which the firm manages their mobility, resources and social relations (the process).

Later, the notion was expanded to other spheres of application (or other social structures and processes): organizational space and industrial space. As already suggested, unlike the business systems approach, the SE approach has deliberately refrained from suggesting an exhaustive list of spaces (structures and processes). The classification of spaces and dimensions that the approach offers has been developed in a piecemeal and pragmatic way, and is open to further development as research within the approach progresses.

The classic statement of the societal effect approach (Maurice *et al.*, 1982), which was based on a Franco-German comparison, focused on four spaces of the wider social, economic and political spheres of society:

1. organization of work and of the enterprise
2. human resources, education, training and socialization
3. industrial and sectoral structures, and relationships between such industries and sectors
4. labour markets, as the sum total of events and arrangements that constitute the exchange of labour power for an equivalent, such as intrinsic satisfaction, social affiliation or money (Sorge, 2003).

This approach decrees that each of these four *spaces* can be subdivided into a *structure* and a *process* aspect. The structural aspect refers to the 'stocks' and properties that characterize the composition of an aggregate of people or of a system. The process refers to the changes that occur with regard to a space, over a certain period of time. Interestingly, structures and processes are not set apart. A process – for instance, labour market mobility between enterprises – has a clear structure, being de-composed into relative shares of types of labour differentiated by age, experience, specialism, education and training, and other salient variables. Inversely, a structure is characterized by processes since a structure is never entirely stable. The identity of the structure over time cannot be limited to those elements that remain stable over a period of time; it also includes a relatively stable pattern of changes.

The *organizational space* has structures, such as formal and informal organization structures, of both hierarchical and functional kinds. The process side is characterized by primary and secondary transformation processes, which transform inputs into outputs.

The *human resource space* has, on the structure side, professional structures, the apparatus (schools, instructors, teaching methods, etc.) dedicated to training, and the educational system of a society, both inside and outside enterprises. On the process side, there are personnel flows across stages of education, training and socialization more generally. The latter includes job changes, since even a succession of jobs without a manifest training purpose has a socialization effect.

The *industrial–sectoral space* includes, on the structure side, the subdivision of an economy into sectors and industries, and the subdivision of industries into enterprises of different types (differentiated according to size, age, dependence, etc.). On the process side, there are transactions of commodities and goods between industries and sectors, including ideas and information, rather in the manner of an input–output table. There are also processes that involve the leaving and entering of enterprises in industries.

The *labour market space* has structures such as organizations, contractual, informal and statutory rules, which govern processes in the transaction of labour power. Professional structures are also a structural aspect, since they affect the supply of and demand for labour. Such professional structures also form part of the human resource space, which is, in a way, close to the labour market space.

More recently, a *technical space* has been added; this comprises the structural features of physical artefacts, of their mode of development, design and employment, plus processes of information, knowledge and experience, which constitute and change technology. Innovation comes under the process aspect of the technical space, being concerned with changes to structures of technical experience and knowledge.

As indicated, the societal effect approach does not aim to define a rigid de-composition of the society and the economy into subsystems; the capital market could, for instance, be added. Proponents of this approach do not think that classifications, such as those offered by the business systems approach, are very helpful. Instead, they stress the relationships between events, arrangements, structures and processes, across any classification scheme. This means that it is essential to explore the *societal* aspect of any social, economic and political phenomenon with which we are concerned. The definition of society, then, does not separate society from the economy or the polity. Societal analysis is concerned with lateral, reciprocal relationships between any subdivided components of reality. Briefly, this means that what happens in a specific space – be it technology, social stratification, labour markets, enterprise organization or whatever – has to be explained with reference to a set of cross-relationships with as many other spaces as possible.

Institutional interdependence

In addition to the principle of reciprocal constitution of actors and spaces, there is the principle of the interactive constitution of spaces with regard to each other. For example, capital market and labour market arrangements are complementary. The short-term view, which capital finance implies, goes hand in hand with short-term labour contracts. The reciprocal constitution of spaces does not happen in a mechanical or impersonal way: it rests on the operation of the actor–space interaction, which is explained above.

Action spaces (or social institutions and processes within different functional areas) are interlinked in such a way that they condition each other reciprocally, thus safeguarding the 'coherence' between the spaces. This means that specific patterns of work organization and enterprise structures are linked with specific patterns of human resource generation, of industrial and sectoral structures, and of industrial relations. What happens in one space has implications for what happens in the others.

Societal effects are argued to originate from this reciprocal constitution of spaces; and the distinctiveness of a particular society (or the so-called societal identity) lies in the features that a specific type of reciprocal constitution has brought about. This is the more static aspect of the approach, which tries to summarize features that are relatively stable over time.

Important point

Spaces (institutions and processes) are complementary and reinforce each other.
The implication of this is that change in one space will affect the other spaces.

The theoretical features of the SE approach show to what extent societal analysis is open to further development, through rearrangement of spaces and reconsideration of societal specificity over time. The openness of the approach has never been recognized as such in the literature but has often been perceived as theoretical weakness.

It is clear, however, that the openness of the approach will also allow us to use it to examine whether the notions of globalization (which is discussed in Chapter 1) and convergence (discussed in the concluding chapter) are useful and relevant perceptions of reality. The rhetoric of globalization is usually based on analysis of financial flows and commercial exchanges, without any consideration being given to the organizations or actors involved in them. The SE approach could widen the debate by including an analysis of the *context* in which globalization forces are active, highlighting the diversity of reactions from actors at national level.

This would mean that a certain priority would be given to the 'local', which serves as a basis for revealing the 'global'. The notion of 'societal' will then need to be reformulated, making it no longer necessarily associated solely with national spaces (that is, spaces enclosed by the boundaries of the nation-state). The analytical dialectic that characterizes the approach allows for forging links between the forms of sectoral, regional, national, supranational and international regulation to which the various actors active in the different spaces contribute. While this extension of the approach will undoubtedly add to its complexity since these spaces usually overlie or cut across each other, it can be concluded that it would in any case be a feasible option.[7]

Important point

The fact that relevant spaces and actors have to be empirically identified and are not a priori fixed, combined with the analytical dialectic of the SE approach, implies that it can be used to examine globalization effects on management and organization.

4.5 Institutional Change

One last topic that we wish to approach in a theoretical way in this chapter concerns institutional change. Most versions of institutional analysis (e.g. the business systems approach) are static and unable to explain change. This is a result of the fact that most institutional analysis rests on the basic assumption that institutions are stable over time and difficult to change. In reality, however, we observe that institutions do change, both incrementally and in a revolutionary way. The literature points to many causes of institutional change. Three general types of pressure towards institutional change, which are relevant in the context of this book, are functional, political and social (Oliver, 1992).

Causes of institutional change
Functional pressures

Functional pressures are those that arise from perceived problems in performance levels associated with institutionalized practices. For example, the Japanese *keiretsu* have been questioned in recent years as a consequence of the, in general, deteriorating performance of *keiretsu* members. Worsening performance leads to a loss of legitimacy. Reduced legitimacy, in turn, allows increased consideration of reform or change.

Political pressures

Political pressures result from shifts in interests or underlying power distributions that provided support for existing institutional arrangements. Scott *et al.* (2000), for example, show how the long-term reduction in membership of the American Medical Association, associated with the rise of speciality associations, resulted in the weakening and fragmentation of physician power and, as a consequence, a reduction in professional control over the healthcare field.

---

[7] Unless indicated otherwise, most of the explanation of the SE approach is based on Maurice and Sorge (2000: Chapters 1 to 3).

Social pressures

Social pressures are associated with differentiation of groups, and the existence of heterogeneous divergent or discordant beliefs and practices. When particular social pressures gain strength this can stimulate institutional change. Consider, for example, how pressures from an initially small group of environmentalists has gained widespread interest and put increased pressure on governments to enforce cleaner technology by law.

Theorizing institutional change

As indicated in the introductory chapter, one of the questions we wish to examine in this book is whether globalization pressures lead to institutional and organizational change. We also explained that, in general, the literature debates four possible change scenarios as a result of globalization:

1. convergence towards the Anglo-American neoliberal market system
2. greater specialization of national models in accordance with domestic institutional and cultural characteristics
3. incremental adaptation of the domestic institutional context in a largely path-dependent manner
4. hybridization with change in a path-deviant manner.

These four scenarios were explained in the introductory chapter. In this section we will examine which of these four scenarios have theoretical support. As you will notice, we will draw quite heavily on the societal effect approach discussed in the previous section. This approach incorporates dynamic elements, which we consider useful for our purposes.

In our explanation of the societal effect approach, we have suggested that if we want to be able to explain institutional change, we must examine institutions not only as a *property* or state of an existing social order, but also as a *process*. By looking at 'spaces', which are interpreted as structures and processes, instead of just structures, the societal effect approach introduces a dynamic element to its theory. As suggested, the structural aspect of the space refers to the properties of a system, while the process refers to the changes that occur with regard to a system.

Moreover, we have also discussed the fact that the SE approach posits the existence of dialectical relationships between the actor and the structure, and argues that systemic variables are reproduced in a non-identical way as a result of this dialectic relationship. The pattern of actor–structure interactions and the ability of the actor to innovate practices, means that the inertia, which is usually connected with institutions, is reduced. However, since new practices are linked to existing logics of action they will take on a specific form, which is in accordance with the existing societal identity. The latter implies that convergence of one institutional setting to another, as proposed in scenario 1, above, is excluded since convergence would imply a complete shift away from the existing logics and identity.

The actor–structure logic also implies that institutional design and change are not necessarily driven primarily or exclusively by economic rationality, as implied by the majority of convergence proponents. Economic performance is one feedback loop into institutional dynamics that are by nature *social* and, hence, involve political struggles, the role of both ideas and interests in these struggles, the power differentials between groups, and the legitimization of institutionalized solutions to these struggles (Knight, 1992). Institutions require both economic and social/political viability over time. Hence, while one could plausibly explain theoretically how similar economic pressures lead to international convergence, we argue that one can only do so by using an inadequate view of the nature of institutions and institutional change (see Boyer, 1996, cited in Jackson, 1997, for a similar line of reasoning).

Moreover, even if at the national level, international (or global) pressures would stimulate developments in the direction of convergence (e.g. convergence of regulations and laws), this does not necessarily mean that convergence would take place at the micro level (the firm level). While external conditions (market and institutional) shape the opportunities and constraints faced by firms, the logic of goal formation and decision-making within organizations requires one to look inside at the internal constitution of the firm (Cyert and March, 1963, cited in Jackson, 1997: 5). The diverging interests and bargaining processes between potential stakeholders within the firm impose constraints on the goals and the capacities of the business firm to adapt to changes in its environment.[8] We can thus explain the deviations in the behaviour of German and Japanese firms from the profit-maximization model (e.g. the inclination to pursue high growth, the stickiness of corporate employment, and the high level of firm-specific investments) in terms of different internal coalitions among the stakeholders of those German and Japanese firms that strive to preserve acquired rights.

As was also explained in the previous section, in addition to the principle of reciprocal constitution of actors and social structures, there is the principle of the interactive constitution of social structures with regard to each other. Social structures are interlinked in such a way that they condition each other reciprocally, thus safeguarding the 'coherence' between them (Maurice, 2000). This principle of coherence is related to the notion of complementary institutions (Amable, 2000) and what North (1994) calls the 'institutional matrix', a framework of interconnected institutions that, together, make up the rules of the economy. The basic hypothesis is that several institutions – in the broad sense – taken together, reinforce each other so that they form a coherent and stable, but not everlasting, structure. The concept of complementary institutions is based on multilateral reinforcement mechanisms between institutional arrangements: each one, by its existence, permits or facilitates the existence of the others. Complementary institutions make one another more or less efficient according to their respective characteristics. Specifically, the influence of one institution is reinforced when the other complementary institution is present. For instance, the set of incentives to the firm defined by the German and Japanese bank-based system makes long-term employment possible and efficient, which in return reinforces the efficiency of the bank-based system.

The complementary character is fundamental for defining the coherence as well as

---

[8] This view is consistent with Aoki's definition of the firm (1988: 33, cited in Jackson, 1997: 5), which is characterized 'as a field of bargaining among the firm-specific resource-holders including the body of employees, rather than simply as a bundle of individual exchange relationships supplemented by the existence of marketable residual claims (equity). There does not seem to exist a single objective of the firm such as the maximization of residual (profits); rather, the firm internalized a bargaining process in which the conflicting objectives of firm-specific resource-holders are brought in equilibrium with a framework of the co-operative relations.'

the pattern of evolution of a societal system. The 'coherence' of a given societal system is the expression of the complementarity between specific institutional arrangements and the outcome in terms of economic performance (i.e. a certain pattern of industrial specialization, a certain type of innovation, certain specific characteristics of the labour force in terms of skills or adaptability, a structure of wage differentials, etc.). Institutional complementarity also involves that change in one element of the system may have consequences well beyond the area concerned and threaten a certain pattern of complementarity. The effects of financial liberalization, for example, may not only be a decrease in the intermediation margin and a cheaper cost of capital as, one assumes, is intended. The introduction of more competition in the financial system is also argued to threaten the stability of long-term relationships (Allen and Gale, 1997; Amable, 2000).

The argument is that the decrease in intermediation margins may reduce the investment projects-monitoring capacity of intermediaries, which will lead them to reorientate their lending policy towards projects where monitoring matters less or is less intensive – for instance, short-term projects. Moreover, the increase in competition in financial intermediation in general is argued to promote arm's-length finance and undermine relationship banking (Amable, 2000). The consequence of these arguments would be that globalization pressures (i.e. financial liberalization and integration of capital markets) would lead to hybridization or change in a path-deviant manner in systems where institutional complementarities with relationship banking are important (i.e. Japan and Germany). Rather like the scenario of incremental path-dependent adaptation, hybridization implies gradual change. In contrast to path-dependent adaptation, however, hybridization implies change in a path-deviant manner.

The notion of complementarity also implies, however, that change in one element of the system would lead to instability of the system. For instance, a decentralized financial system and arm's-length relationships with centralized labour market institutions would generate contradictory incentives and constraints, making the system unstable and less efficient. The actor–system dynamic, though, could be assumed to prevent the development of such contradictions. However, even if there were to be a temporary disequilibrium, one could assume that the actor–structure dialectic would, in any case, be able to push the system to the next equilibrium defined by, but non-identical to, the previous one. In view of the actor–structure dialectic, and thus the tendency for existing system properties to load actors' preferences, the next equilibrium could not be characterized by change in a path-deviant manner. Instead, the combination of the notion of complementarity with the actor–structure dialectic could be assumed to provide theoretical support for the scenarios of greater specialization in accordance with existing social features and incremental path-dependent change.

Finally, the notion of complementarity also helps to explain that the same institution (i.e. regulation or law) may affect outcomes differently depending on the other institutions. For example, in the 1980s, Germany and Spain enacted laws that encouraged temporary contracts. In Spain the proportion of workers covered by these contracts increased massively, until about one-third of employees worked under such contracts. In Germany there was virtually no growth of temporary contracts. German apprenticeships and works councils preserved permanent jobs (Freeman, 2000).

Conclusions

As regards institutional dynamics, then:

- institutions are a state of an existing order as well as a process
- there is a dialectical relationship between actors and institutions and processes
- institutional design and dynamics are not only characterized by economical imperatives but also by social forces
- the complementary character of institutions has implications for the pattern of evolution of institutional change
- organizations experience external opportunities and constraints and form their reactions based on internal logics.

In Chapter 12, we examine whether these theoretical arguments can help us explain contemporary developments in the Rhineland model.

Study Questions

1. Provide a brief outline of the main differences and/or similarities between the 'societal effect' and the 'business systems' approaches.

2. What is methodological individualism?

3. A major aim of the societal effect approach is to contextualize phenomena.

   (a) Explain what this means and how the approach goes about theorizing this aim.

   (b) Explain how contextualization can help the approach to overcome the gap between culturalism and institutionalism.

4. Explain how the notion of 'space', as it is used within the societal effect approach, is more extensive than the concept of an institution.

5. Explain the differences between the concept of background institutions, as it is used in the business systems approach, and national culture.

6. Assess whether and how both approaches that have been studied in this chapter can help you to understand differences between organizations in different countries, in different regions and in different sectors.

7. Explain why it is important to use 'matched' samples in comparative analysis.

8. Assess whether typologies, such as the one developed within the business systems approach, are useful analytical tools.

9. Explain how the societal effect approach is able to account for change as well as the type of change it accounts for.

10. Explain why the business systems framework is a static as opposed to a dynamic

approach.

11. Explain how, despite the dynamic nature of the societal effect approach, there is a static aspect to the approach.

12. Explain whether and how both the business system and the societal effect approaches recognize and are able to incorporate globalization pressures within their framework.

13. Explain whether and how institutional interconnectedness can hamper convergence despite globalization pressures.

Further Reading

Foss, J.N. (1999) The challenge of business systems and the challenge to business systems. *International Studies of Management and Organization* 29(2), 9–24.

Critical article reflecting on the weaknesses of business systems research and how economics can help to overcome them (and vice versa), pointing to ways in which business systems research offers opportunities to enhance economics research.

Hall, P.A. and Soskice, D. (2001) *Varieties of Capitalism*. Oxford: Oxford University Press.

This book offers another framework for carrying out institutional analysis.

Maurice, M. and Sorge, A. (2000) *Embedding Organizations*. Amsterdam: John Benjamins.

This book offers the latest position in and empirical examples from societal effect research.

Müller, F. (1994) Societal effect, organizational effect and globalization. *Organization Studies* 15(3), 407–28.

Critical article reflecting on the influence of societal effects as opposed to globalization and organizational effects.

Quack, S., Morgan, G. and Whitley, R. (1999) *National Capitalisms, Global Competition, and Economic Performance*. Amsterdam: John Benjamins.

This book offers the latest position in as well as empirical examples from business systems research.

Case: The Japanese *Keiretsu*[9]

The existence and functioning of interorganizational groups or corporate groups has long been a focus of economic research on Japan. This is unsurprising since the basic structure of Japanese business consists of business groups, the so-called *keiretsu*. There are two main kinds of corporate grouping in Japan. The best known of these are the horizontal or financial *keiretsu*, or groups of firms organized around a large bank. While member firms may buy and sell to each other, the glue that holds the group together is argued to be mutual stockholding and bank loans to members, supplemented by personnel exchanges and meetings between the presidents or leaders of the organizations belonging to the groups. In short, these organizations are linked primarily by finances rather than products.

The bank at the core of a financial *keiretsu*, called the 'main bank', does much more than simply make loans available. It is also the central clearing house for information about group companies and coordinator of group activities. It monitors the performance of its group, holds equity in most of the major companies, and provides management assistance when it deems this necessary. In the worst case, if one of the group's firms is in serious trouble, the main bank is expected to step in both with financial assistance and with a whole new management team selected from among the bank's executives.

Three of the six financial *keiretsu* (Mitsui, Mitsubishi and Sumitomo) are direct descendants of the famous pre-Second World War *zaibatsu* (financial cliques), while the remaining three (Fuyo, Sanwa and Dai-Ichi Kangyo) have less direct links to earlier organizations. The connections in all three, however, are definitely both historical and financial. In contrast to the *zaibatsu*, however – which were controlled by a single family, usually through a central holding company – the contemporary *keiretsu* are horizontally structured groupings. Stockholding and influence move in both directions between pairs of firms, although loans and personnel are likely to come mainly from the commercial banks and the insurance companies within the group and to go to the others.

The driving force behind the re-establishment of the major prewar *zaibatsu* and the formation of the new groups was a combination of weak stock markets in Japan after the war, the stagnant share prices of major Japanese companies and the resulting vulnerability to take-over threats. In this situation, cross-shareholdings and dependence on group financial institutions formed a protection mechanism. (See Chapter 6 for an in-depth explanation of the financial aspects.)

In addition, between the 1950s and 1970s, the government made it difficult for business to raise the funds it needed from any source other than the banking system, and at the same time encouraged the city banks to lend to important industries. It rewrote the law to make it legal for the banks to own stocks in their clients (contrary to the Antimonopoly Law that was put in place by the US occupation right after the Second World War). Moreover, because the government

---

[9] This case study is based on the following sources: Teranishi (1994), Ostrom (1990), Miyashita and Russell, (1994) and Miwa (1996).

wanted to control the limited flows of capital in the economy, the Ministry of Finance (MoF) also devised strict regulations to make sure that the stock market would not mature and rival the banks. Thus the government helped to build and shape the new bank-led *keiretsu* and the banks became the source of funds for postwar industry. This primacy remained essentially unchallenged until the late 1980s.

Until the late 1970s, the structural paradigm for the *zaibatsu* descendants as well as for the new groups was based on the concept of 'one firm in each major industrial sector'. Hence, aside from a large bank, the nucleus of the *keiretsu* would also include a trading company and a major manufacturer. There would also be a trust bank, a life insurance firm and a non-life firm, so that, together with the bank and the trading company (which provides trade credit), most of the group's financial needs could be met internally. Then there would ideally be one key company in each important industrial sector, including chemicals, construction, steel, electricals, cement, paper, glass, oil, autos, shipping, warehousing and non-ferrous metals. When a sector became prominent, all *keiretsu* would jump into it, whether there was room for six major firms or not. The result was intense competition, much more than in the prewar days when the *zaibatsu* could privately carve up markets among a few strong players and close everyone else out. After the Second World War, the government – more specifically, the Ministry of International Trade and Industry (MITI) – decided on the industries to be developed. As a result, the growth of certain sectors would be assured and all the *keiretsu* wanted to be part of it.

However, while the big six financial *keiretsu* did not simply drift together, they were not assembled according to some master plan formulated by the government. The MITI prepared the ground that allowed the 'big six' to emerge, then nurtured their core companies, steered them, and protected them from outside competition until the 1970s. The actual formation of the *keiretsu* and much of their activities were left up to the groups and the individual companies.

By the 1970s, the big six had achieved the government's goals of building up Japan's heavy industries to internationally competitive levels. By the 1980s, as calls were going up around the world for Japan to open up to free competition, the *keiretsu* no longer needed protection, although the vestiges of it remained for years in many sectors, and some are still intact today.

A second major type of inter-firm collaboration is the vertically structured group, or vertical *keiretsu*. There are two types of vertical *keiretsu*: production *keiretsu*, in which a myriad of parts suppliers and assemblers put together products for a single end-product manufacturer, such as in the auto (i.e. Toyota) or electronics industries; and distribution *keiretsu*, in which a single firm, usually a manufacturer, moves products out to market through a network of wholesalers and retailers that depend on the parent firm for goods. Most manufacturers have both types of *keiretsu*.

Production and distribution *keiretsu* exist in almost every industry in Japan, from oil to cosmetics to advertising to broadcasting. Hence, Japan has dozens of these large independent groups or vertical *keiretsu*. Stockholding in these groups is more pyramidal than in financial *keiretsu*, strengthening control in the core firm. Hence, the structure consists of vertical relationships rather than horizontal, which is characteristic of the financial *keiretsu*. The goods and services produced by the group are often complementary, but they need not be. Moreover, the core company has the best-known name, and may or may not lend this to other members of the group. It owns the largest shareholdings in other group companies and is also the most likely source of personnel or technical assistance to other group members, particularly those just beneath it in the group pyramid.

Otherwise, enterprise groups differ considerably. In some groups, such as the Hitachi Group, member firms have moved into a broad range of businesses, such as construction, consumer electronics and financial services. Other groups consist of related companies that produce the same kinds of product as the core firms. For example, Victor Co. of Japan, Ltd, the developer of the VHS format for videocassette recorders, and today mainly a manufacturer of that type of product as well as audio equipment, is 50.8 per cent owned by Matsushita Electric Industrial Co., Ltd, which is best known to consumers for its Panasonic and Quasar lines of consumer electronics products.

While not centred around a bank, some large enterprise groups have significant holdings in financial services firms. For example, Toyota is the largest individual stockholder, at 40.6 per cent, in Chiyoda Fire & Marine Insurance Co., Ltd, Japan's tenth largest non-life insurance firm. In addition to being the largest lender to Nissan Fire & Marine Insurance Co., Ltd, Japan's 12th largest firm, Nissan Motor Co., Ltd, has a 7.3 per cent stake in the company, making it the second largest shareholder.

In general, as noted above, the flow of financial and other resources is mostly one-way in all the enterprise groups. The list of 20 largest stockholders in Matsushita Electric Industrial does not include JVC or much other representation from the Matsushita Group. Only one firm, Matsushita Electric Works Co., Ltd, ranks 19th, holding 1.1 per cent of the stock. However, until his death in 1989, Konosuke Matsushita, the group's founder, ranked eighth, holding 2.1 per cent of the shares. This illustrates another characteristic of such groups and one that distinguishes them from financial *keiretsu*: one family or individual may hold substantial power. The fact that firms belonging to groups organized around independent firms are usually much younger than companies associated with *zaibatsu* or their descendants explains why company founders still play leading roles in some relatively independent companies such as Sony.

Some of the core firms of the leading independent groups, however, are themselves members of the financial *keiretsu*, at least in name. Toyota is an example of such a firm, officially a member of the Mitsui *keiretsu*, but operating at the periphery of group affairs. Nissan belongs to the Fuyo Group. The companies to which they are linked may or may not belong to the same financial *keiretsu*. For example, despite Toyota's position as the largest stockholder in Chiyoda Fire & Marine Insurance, the insurer belongs to the inner circle of the Fuyo Group. Nissan Fire & Marine Insurance is part of the Dai-Ichi Group, not of the Fuyo Group with Nissan. Moreover, some companies, while strongly associated with financial *keiretsu*, have their own enterprise groups. For example, Mitsubishi Heavy Industries, Ltd, which plays a major role in the Mitsubishi financial *keiretsu*, has dozens of firms under it. And, to make things even more complex, there are a few very large companies that claim allegiance to more than one group. Hitachi is the best-known example of a firm that considers itself above the *keiretsu* and boldly flies the flag of three different groups.

In short, financial *keiretsu* and enterprise groups may be related in several ways. In some situations, the leading members of financial *keiretsu* themselves are at the core of other, distinct large groups of firms, a sort of circle within a circle. In others, industrial firms are more independent, with some group members linked to a financial *keiretsu* (intersecting circles) or two or more financial *keiretsu* (one circle intersecting with two other circles) or with no strong ties at all. Even where the circles intersect, members of enterprise groups often have a high degree of independence from other members of the financial *keiretsu*.

Consequently, while, as suggested in the above, there is competition between the member firms of the different *keiretsu*, there is also cooperation. In general, one of the most striking characteristics of Japan's industrial organization is the predominance of stable, long-term inter-firm relationships, which are non-exclusive. For example, Matsushita, the largest consumer electronics products and robotics manufacturer in Japan, sells its component-inserting machine to its rivals, contributing to their high productivity. Another example is Nikon, a firm that dominates the lithography market. Although Nikon is a core member of the Mitsubishi Group, it maintains long-term relationships with firms outside it. Similarly, Toyota has advised its suppliers, even firms of which Toyota is the largest shareholder, to do business with other manufacturers, even if they are Toyota's rivals. As a result, many members of the Toyota suppliers' association also belong to another car manufacturer's association, such as Nissan, Mazda or Mitsubishi. The long-term relationships are based on trust and reciprocity. Even when a long-term relationship ends at some point, there is sufficient confidence, trust and loyalty between partners to avoid the leaking of trade secrets.

Finally, the *keiretsu* structure expresses the dislike of major Japanese firms for dealing with 'independent' subcontractors. In fact, in the subcontracting pyramid, Japanese manufacturers effectively control their subcontractors. It is quite common, for example, for Japanese manufacturers to instruct the subcontractor to invest in new equipment. Over time, this brings the parent firm all the advantages of state-of-the-art production equipment with little or none of the cost. In addition to arranging for equipment investment by their affiliated suppliers, the parent companies can push their subcontractors to work extra hours, deliver parts at the parent's convenience (part of the famous just-in-time (JIT) system, which is explained further in Chapter 7), and accept payment when the parent's cash flow permits. Most important, the parent firm tells the supplier how much it will pay for the parts. In addition, the parent firm adjusts these prices – always downwards – at least twice a year and usually by at least 5 to 10 per cent each time. In fact, subcontractors are treated as 'shock absorbers' by the manufacturing firms. In crisis situations, price cuts are passed on to the smallest bottom-level subcontractors. Often these do not survive the hard times since they do not have much of a profit margin to work with in the first place.

Questions

1. According to Whitley's framework, ownership coordination is one of the features of a business system. The concept of ownership coordination consists of owner control, ownership vertical integration and ownership horizontal integration. Use the information in this case to describe these features for the dominant business system in Japan – that is, for the *keiretsu*.

2. The second major feature of a business system is the degree of non-ownership coordination. Non-ownership coordination consists of alliance-based vertical integration, alliance-based horizontal integration and competitor collaboration. Use the information in this case to describe these features for the Japanese *keiretsu*.

3. Discuss the institutions that help explain the development of the characteristics of the Japanese business system that you were asked to describe in Questions 1 and 2.

4. Explain the main differences and similarities of the patterns of ownership and non-ownership coordination between the Japanese *keiretsu* and the Korean *Chaebol*.

References

Allen, F. and Gale, D. (1997) Financial markets, intermediaries and intertemporal smoothing. *Journal of Political Economy* 105, 523–46.

Amable, B. (2000) Institutional complementarity and diversity of social systems of innovation and production. *Review of International Political Economy* 7(4), 645–87.

Aoki, M. (1988) *Information, Incentives, and Bargaining in the Japanese Economy.* Cambridge: Cambridge University Press.

Boyer, R. (1996) Elements for an institutional approach to economics. Mimeo, Paris: CEPREMAP.

Casson, M. and Lundan, S.M. (1999) Explaining international differences in economic institutions. *International Studies of Management and Organization* 29(2), 25–42.

Cyert, M. and March, J.G. (1963) *A Behavioral Theory of the Firm.* Englewood Cliffs, NJ: Prentice-Hall.

Foss, N.J. (1999) Preface: perspectives on business systems. *International Studies of Management and Organization* 29(2), 3–8.

Freeman, R. (2000) Single peaked vs diversified capitalism: the relation between economic institutions and outcomes. *NBER Working Paper* No. 7556.

Giddens, A. (1986) *The Constitution of Society.* Berkeley, CA: UCP.

Jackson, G. (1997) Corporate governance in Germany and Japan: development within national and international contexts. Mimeo, Max-Planck-Institut für Gesellschaftsforschung, Cologne.

Knight, J. (1992) *Institutions and Social Conflict.* Cambridge: Cambridge University Press.

Kogut, B. (1991) Country capabilities and permeability of borders. *Strategic Management Journal* 12, 33–47.

Kogut, B. (ed.) (1993) *Country Competitiveness: Technology and the Organizing of Work.* Oxford: Oxford University Press.

Lundvall, B.-A. (1992) *National Systems of Innovation.* London: Pinter, 1992.

Maurice, M. (2000) The paradoxes of societal analysis: a review of the past and prospects for the future, in Maurice, M. and Sorge, A. (eds) *Embedding Organizations.* Amsterdam: John Benjamins Publishing.

Maurice, M. and Brossard, M. (1976) Is there a universal model of organization structure? *International Journal of Management and Organization* 6, 11–45.

Maurice, M., Sellier, F. and Silvestre, J.-J. (1982) *Politique d'education et organisation industrielle en France et en Allemagne.* Paris: Presses Universitaires de France.

Maurice, M., Sellier, F. and Silvestre, J.-J. (1976/1986) *The Social Foundation of Industrial Power: a comparison of France and Germany.* Cambridge, MA: MIT Press.

Maurice, M. and Sorge, A. (2000) *Embedding Organizations.* Amsterdam: John Benjamins Publishing.

Maurice, M., Sorge, A. and Warner, M. (1980) Societal differences in organizing manufacturing units: a comparison of France, West Germany and Great Britain. *Organization Studies* 1, 59–86.

Miwa, Yoshiro (1996) *Firms and Industrial Organization in Japan.* New York: New York University Press.

Miyashita, K. and Russell, D. (1994) Keiretsu: *Inside the Hidden Japanese Conglomerates.* New York: McGraw-Hill.

North, D. (1994) Institutions matter. Mimeo, Washington University.

Oliver, C. (1992) The antecedents of deinstitutionalization. *Organization Studies* 13(4), 563–88.

Ostrom, D. (1990) *Keiretsu* and other large corporate groups in Japan. *Japan Economic Institute Report* No. 2A.

Scott, W.R. (2001) *Institutions and Organizations.* London: Sage.

Scott, W.R., Ruef, M., Mendel, P.J. and Caronna, C.A. (2000) *Institutional Change and Healthcare Organizations: from Professional Dominance to Managed Care.* Chicago: University of Chicago Press.

Sorge, A. (1991) Strategic fit and the societal effect: interpreting cross-national comparisons of technology, organization and human resources. *Organization Studies* 12(2), 161–90.

Sorge, A. (2003) Cross-national differences in human resources and organization. Draft manuscript.

Sorge, A. and Warner, M. (1986) *Comparative Factory Organization: an Anglo-German Comparison of Management and Manpower in Manufacturing.* Aldershot: Gower.

Soskice, D. (1991) The institutional infrastructure for international competitiveness:

a comparative analysis of the UK and Germany, in Atkinson, A.B. and Brunetta, R. (eds) *Economics for the New Europe*. London: Macmillan.

Soskice, D. (1994) Innovation strategies of companies: a comparative institutional approach of some cross-country differences, in Zapf, W. and Dierkens, M. (eds) *Institutionenvergleich und institutionendynamik*. Berlin: Sigma.

Teranishi, J. (1994) Loan syndication in war-time Japan and the origins of the main bank system, in Aoki, M. and Patrick, H. (eds) *The Japanese Main Bank System*. Oxford: Clarendon Press.

Whitley, R. (1990) Eastern Asian enterprise structures and comparative analysis of forms of business organization. *Organization Studies* 11(1), 47–74.

Whitley, R. (1991) The social construction of business systems in East Asia. *Organization Studies* 12(1), 1–28.

Whitley, R. (1992a) *European Business Systems: Firms and Markets in their National Context*. London: Sage.

Whitley, R. (1992b) The social construction of organizations and markets: the comparative analysis of business recipes, in Reed, M. and Hughes, M. (eds) *Rethinking Organizations: New Directions in Organization Theory and Analysis*. Newbury Park, CA: Sage, 120–43.

Whitley, R. (1999) *Divergent Capitalisms: the Social Structuring and Change of Business Systems*. Oxford: Oxford University Press.

Chapter 5

Managing Resources: Human Resource Management

Learning Objectives

By the end of this chapter you will be able to:

- understand differences in human resource management practices between countries

- provide a societal explanation for the diversity in human resource practices between countries

- reflect on the differences in human resource systems between advanced and newly developed nations

- analyse the impact of elements of human resource and industrial relations systems upon firm structure

- appreciate the effects of increased competition and globalization on human resource management systems.

Chapter Outline

5.1   **Introduction**

5.2   **Work Relationships**
Work classification, design and coordination
Functional specialization
Organizational hierarchy and spans of control

5.3   **Employment Relationships**
Recruitment and selection methods
External recruitment versus promotion
Dismissal procedures

5.4   **Reward Structure**
Wage systems
Performance-related pay
Case: Human Resource Management in China

5.5   **Conclusions**
Study Questions
Further Reading
Case: Human Resource Management in Korea, among Dutch Affiliates in the
    Consumer Industry
References

5.1 🧩 Introduction

In the 1980s, a modest but growing literature started to deal with the international dimension of human resource management. At that time in particular, the field of human resource management had a strong managerialist orientation, assuming that employees and managers have a great deal of freedom in determining the design and implementation of human resource practices and policies. The literature was essentially prescriptive and had an implicit tendency to assume that one model, at that time generally the Japanese or the German one, was superior. This model was then elevated as universally applicable, and was seen as one to which all organizations and nations should aspire. The result was that research designed in one country was transplanted to another, as if this was an easy thing to do. This research ignored the fact that knowledge of societies, of their language(s), their concepts, values and culture is fundamental to understanding the behaviour of people within employing organizations (Hofstede, 1980; Laurent, 1983).

Alongside this research another stream developed (i.e. Adler, 1984; Smith, 1992; Rosenzweig and Nohria, 1994), which warned of the problems in assuming the generalizability of models, as this would assume the stability of factors across contexts – a demand not usually met in the international arena. Cross-national diversity in societal frameworks is likely to create management practices that vary from country to country. In the human resource management field in particular, the societal environment is likely to impose constraints on the freedom that employers have to determine their own human resource management systems. This is due to the fact that human resource management practices are subject to nationally idiosyncratic institutional pressures, such as the scrutiny of labour unions, whose strength and attitudes towards management vary.

Different types of human resource management practices may be determined to a considerable degree by the imperative of maintaining external credibility through adherence to institutional structures, rules and norms at the national level, and may vary as a result of dissimilar national contexts (Gooderham *et al.*, 1999). Moreover, it has been argued that the constraints imposed upon human resource practices by societal factors are needed for employers to make choices that are conducive to the long-run competitiveness of the firm and the nation (Dore, 1989; Streeck, 1989; Purcell, 1993).

Inevitably, such a perspective has implications for the labour market and employment policies of government, for firms and for human resource management theory. For the role of public policy, this perspective argues that the government's use of policy levers may be designed to impose constraints, which may be beneficial for the community at large as well as for individual firms (i.e. the protection of long-term employment in Germany, Japan and the Netherlands). For the theory of human resource management, and for firms, this perspective treats management not as 'free agents' (Purcell, 1993: 520), but as actors whose choices are constrained – for better or worse – by the circumstances in which they find themselves.

The existence of societal constraints on human resource management combined with the fact that effective firm performance and competitive advantage also result from fitting the human resource management systems consistently with the requirements of the external environment make it essential for management practitioners and business students to develop a better understanding of the impact of different national settings on the management of human resources.

By drawing on the differences between human resource practices in the USA, the UK, Sweden, Japan, Germany, the Netherlands and China, this chapter aims to fulfil this need. These countries have not been chosen at random. Aside from the last two, they represent the major types of industrial relations and human resource systems worldwide (Begin, 1997). The Netherlands is added as an example of a European country where companies use a hybrid human resource system, with features of both the Anglo-Saxon and the German type. China is added in the form of a case study to extend the analysis to the evolution of human resource systems in nations in transition.

Moreover, a comparative international view of human resource management systems also helps to distinguish between what is general and universal in the management of human resources, and what is particular or specific to one nation or culture. While stressing the particular, the chapter does not deny the ability of actors to change, innovate or borrow designs from other human resource practices, thus reducing the inertia usually connected with institutions. However, since actors are embedded in the societal context, they replicate some more abstract qualities of practices even as they change them, and they adapt borrowed practices to fit the existing societal logic.

The examples of change in the different national human resource systems discussed in this chapter show that an explanation of change must incorporate constraints by external institutions; especially in the form of previous human resource policies, which exercise inertial forces, management values as shaped by norms accepted in the society, legal constraints and unions' bargaining agendas. In this light, an extended discussion is offered on the changes that have taken place in the Japanese human resource system, due to pressure from increased competition and recession.

Given that the precise nature of human resource management is contested, two pillars of Gospel's (1992) broad typology are adopted here. Human resource management is thus taken to cover the two areas of (1) work relations (i.e. the way work is organized or structured), and (2) employment relations (i.e. the arrangements governing such aspects of employment as recruitment, promotion, job tenure and the reward of employees). An understanding of these two pillars is also essential to grasping the details of the concept of institutional advantage, which, in the context of this chapter, is the link between human resource systems and industrial competitiveness (this link is explained extensively in Chapter 7).

Gospel's third pillar – that is, industrial relations (i.e. the representational aspirations of employees and the voice systems that may exist, such as joint consultation, employee involvement practices, works councils and collective bargaining) is seen here as a societal factor, influencing human resource management systems. Similarly, institutional arrangements such as the national education and training systems, and labour market policy, are also shown to be prominent societal influences. These various societal elements are shaped by the historical as well as by the immediate settings in which they are embedded and are intrinsically interconnected, such that they form a whole. This societal logic also holds the human resource management components together, makes them recognizably interconnected and guides their functioning. For example, in Germany, high employment stability is imposed on firms through collective agreements, codetermination and legislation. Firms are thus forced to adjust through the internal labour market by redeployment. As a consequence, employment protection encourages employer invest-ment in training and long-term human resource development. Moreover, shaped and reproduced in a non-identical way by the societal setting, human resource systems, in turn, influence organizational shapes (as explained in the following section) and, as indi-cated, firm performance.

The organization of the chapter is as follows: as indicated, the next section discusses various aspects of work relationships. Sections 5.3 and 5.4 deal with the second pillar of Gospel's typology; specifically, Section 5.3 explains the differences in the hiring, dismissal and promotion procedures in the aforementioned countries, while Section 5.4 focuses on differences in reward systems, explaining the variations in wage systems between the selected countries, and the introduction and use of performance-related wages. Section 5.5 provides a summary of the chapter, emphasizing the link between societal and human resource practices.

5.2 Work Relationships

As indicated above, this section discusses various aspects of work structuring. It discusses job classification, design and coordination, and functional specialization in the aforemen-tioned countries in a comparative way. These human resource management aspects are shown to be influenced essentially by the national education and vocational training system, and by the national system of industrial relationships. For example, the relative emphasis on general versus specialist education impacts on the scope of the job, the cen-tralization as well as stratification of the workforce, and the relative reliance on bureaucratic procedures. Equally important is the relative amount of practical and tech-nical training that is perceived to be part of the formation process, especially at staff levels. This dimension has a countervailing impact on the division of labour. Technical and scientific education is likely to be more specialized, leading to shorter hierarchies, more consensual decision-making and less bureaucracy (Hage, 2000). At the end of the first and second subsections, we provide a summary in the form of tables (Tables 5.1 and 5.2). The Netherlands is not included since its model lies somewhere on the continuum between the German and the Anglo-Saxon ones.

Work classification, design and coordination

The traditional job design practices of large **US** firms differentiate jobs into hundreds of dis-crete titles, carry out systematic job evaluations to ascertain the scope and depth of job responsibilities, record these in great detail in formal job descriptions, and make them the basis of compensation decisions. One powerful historical force behind the preoccupation of US firms with formal job design and classification has been the scientific management move-ment, which, in Taylor's teachings, saw the minute analysis and delineation of job duties, and the elimination of worker discretion as critical elements in the rationalization of pro-duction and the transfer of control to management. Another force in the same direction was the emergence of 'job control' unionism in the USA. Unions took up formal job classification and description as devices for curtailing management discretion in the task-assignment process and giving workers rights to tightly circumscribed areas of job responsibility

(Lincoln, 1993). Moreover, in the USA, vocational education in schools has been accorded a low status and offered only narrow training to workers. Hence workers were not flexible in taking on a broader range of tasks in times of change, nor were they capable of participating in more complex business decisions. Taken together, job classifications define a sort of plant hierarchy in which gradations are based on income and working conditions.

In US factories, work is controlled through the direct supervision of foremen, who in the typical factory do not perform manufacturing operations. Foremen and industrial engineers are relied upon to find and resolve problems, not the employees. The low degree of worker autonomy in the USA is partly explained by the virtual absence of vocational education, apprenticeship, training in craft skills relevant to manufacture, job-related training for foremen and technicians, and so on, in the European tradition (Lawrence, 1996). The 'Cook's tour' traineeship, or rapid succession of assignments, is very common in US organizations. This can be related to the deregulated nature of most labour law, which creates an extremely active labour market. The active labour market, in turn, makes employers less willing to invest in training and retraining. Furthermore, the financial system creates a host of incentives to develop short-term business strategies, since most US companies view stockholders as their primary stakeholders. Investment in human capital, to say nothing of investments in efforts to transform the labour–management relationship, offers only long-term returns. Moreover, since they are in many regards qualitative these returns are hard to measure (Turner *et al.*, 2001). Since many managers' salaries are tied to financial performance on a quarterly basis they are often unwilling to invest in long-term qualitative improvements.

The numerous job classifications have, however, created strong property ownership of jobs, and thus have 'hinder[ed] . . . flexible and fluid job assignments' (Aoki, 1990: 52). During the 1990s, as many US manufacturing firms adopted innovative work practices (i.e. some of the flexible work system features), the number of job classifications declined, as job designs became less specialized both horizontally and vertically. Moreover, as manufacturing organizations move towards relying more on work teams, they are also beginning to place a higher priority on worker training. However, the investment still lags substantially behind that in Japan and Germany, and the strategies being used do not sufficiently promote flexible employment systems. For example, formal differences between production and maintenance work remain. In general, it has been argued that Taylorism and job control unionism have been difficult to override (Begin, 1997).

Similar to the situation in the USA, **UK** manufacturing work systems are characterized by many vertically and horizontally specialized jobs, and factories are peopled by low-skilled production workers doing repetitive tasks with little authority. Skilled craft workers in UK factories have a low division of labour with a high degree of discretion. The crafts create job territories so there is a high degree of job demarcation among crafts, and between the crafts and the production jobs (Lane, 1989). Occupational segmentation and the limited training of employees restrict the ability of employers to transfer employees within the plant to wherever they are needed. In fact, the reaction of unskilled or semi-skilled operatives to craft segmentation is to practise segmentation among factory jobs by refusing to move to another machine (Lane, 1989: 155). The result is a type of job control unionism, but it is practised in a different way than that used in the USA. The UK's unions' commitment to demarcation is argued to be related to the absence of any type of employment security in the UK. The control over access to jobs through occupational demarcations and the creation of limits on output through manning and work assignment decisions are seen as strategies for providing some security for workers (Kahn-Freund, 1979). Moreover, the practice of negotiating agreements on pay and work practices with shop stewards for a job or groups of jobs, often without any element of control on the part of human resource managers, creates varying practices within plants that impede the ability of firms to move employees to different areas. Recently, internal transfers have been used more frequently to adjust to needs, or to reduce or reallocate the workforce in the private sector (Begin, 1997).

Rather like the USA, the UK has neither the German vocational training system nor the Japanese firm-level training system to prepare individuals for work. In comparison with their counterparts in the USA, however, UK production workers have a higher degree of control over job design, task allocation and manning practices through a strong shop-steward system (Lane, 1989: 154; Lorenz, 1992: 463–4). Taylorism is less diffused in the UK due to the absence of shop-floor control by managers. The anomaly of the UK system is that work is controlled neither by the standardization of skills as in Germany (this form is incompatible with unskilled workers) nor by standardization of process as in the USA (which is compatible with unskilled workers) (Begin, 1997: 119). At best, there is a weak form of standardization of process control, an outcome in part caused by the low level of technical training of supervisors and managers, which reduces their ability to systematically manage the production process (Lane, 1989: 154–5). UK first-line supervisors, unlike those in Germany, stand above the work group as supervisors and are not part of the work group; in many firms they must relate to the work group through shop stewards (Dore, cited in Begin, 1997: 119).

As with the situation in the USA, the highly segmented internal labour market in the UK limits functional flexibility and work reorganization since employee job rights are tied to job definitions. Though in recent times, efforts to broaden out jobs have increased, the occupational demarcation of UK factory workers remains a fact. Most of the attempts to change have aimed to increase functional flexibility by expanding the range of tasks within jobs, rather than through multiskilling (Cross, cited in Begin, 1997: 120). Neither management nor unions have really embraced work redesign: management because of the perceived threat to their autonomy and unions because they had other priorities, namely pay, job security and involvement in management decision-making.

Sweden has been a pioneer in developing autonomous work teams at companies like Volvo and Saab (see Chapter 7 for an extensive discussion of this). The advanced state of Swedish technology in some sectors has permitted the development of more flexible job designs. Job design and task assignments are to a striking degree the prerogatives of the production team. Workers enjoy real autonomy in choosing the operations to be performed and who does what (Lincoln, 1993). The development of this type of work organization in Sweden should be understood against the background of sharpened demands on the product market, labour shortage and consequent improved prospects for union influence (Berggren, 1992). The tight labour market, combined with high and rising rates of short- and long-term absenteeism, was of great concern to the business community, the government and the unions, and furnished the motivation for a growing number of projects in the 1980s aimed at changing work organization. The excellent education system, which delivers a well-trained labour force, enabled the development of flexible job designs and worker autonomy. The Swedish education system does not duplicate the German apprenticeship system (Martin, 1995); most job skills are developed through limited on-the-job training. In addition, the educational system is particularly well integrated with employing organizations. Educational reform in the early 1970s eliminated a separate vocational education system, and two- or four-year vocational programmes were integrated into the school system. By the early 1990s, vocational routes were three years in length (Begin, 1997).

The 'modernized' plants (i.e. in the car industry) contrast sharply with the many traditional plants (i.e. in the metal sector) that are still using the old Taylorist job design principles, or that are only in the early phase of changing job designs. Thus, many workers on assembly lines have jobs that are specialized both horizontally and vertically as on assembly lines in the USA and the UK. In fact, the diffusion of the Swedish 'socio-technical' system (see Chapter 7 for an extensive explanation) has not been high, and production jobs are not being changed enough to draw upon or expand worker knowledge. In many factories, job enlargement is often limited to providing workers with multiple skills to improve functional flexibility, but the work organization is otherwise unchanged (Kjellberg, 1992). However, unlike in the USA, where job analysis and evaluation mechanisms form the core of job control unionism, in Sweden job descriptions are used (if used at all) primarily for determining relative wage differentials among different types of job (Begin, 1997: 204).

Finally, in general, Swedish employers also have a great deal of flexibility in moving workers among different kinds of job, including jobs in different geographical areas, as long as the movement of a worker to a less skilled job does not reduce the worker's income. Rather like Japanese practice, employee transfer is a major device for adjusting workforces. Seniority is not a determinant of transfer, and management determines who is to go based on the firm's needs and the specific requirements of the case. Hence workers have a right to work and to income protection if shifts among jobs are necessary, but not to a specific type of work. Thus Swedish employers have more flexibility in moving workers among different types of job than their counterparts in the USA or the UK, but less flexibility in reducing the level of the workforce, the primary means used by US and UK employers to balance production levels and employment.

Job classifications are kept simple and broad in **Japanese** firms, with most factory production workers, for example, falling within a single classification. Job descriptions, if they exist at all, are typically short and couched in vague terms. Detailed job titles, formal job descriptions, and job-related criteria for pay and advancement have been conspicuously absent from Japanese employment practices, whereas job rotation and extensive cross-training are the rule (Lincoln, 1993). Extensive on-the-job training is used to train workers through 'learning by doing', while off-the-job training is used to supplement this process with systematic and codified knowledge about the firm, industry and functions of which employees are in charge (Morishima, 1995). The employee development systems require employees at all levels to acquire experience over time in different aspects of the business (Nishida and Redding, 1992).

Womack *et al.* (1991) study of the automotive industry found that new production workers in Japanese plants received about 370 to 380 hours of training in their first year; comparable figures for European and US plants were 173 and 46 hours, respectively.

Workers are expected to perform what technical staff do in the USA. Specifically, they are expected to identify and resolve ongoing contingencies without the intervention of management or staff (Aoki, 1989). Moreover, Japanese foremen are working members of the team who can fill in for absentees as well as coordinate the team. However, rather like the case in Sweden, production teams and job rotation are central features of Japanese factory organization; where things differ from the case in Sweden, however, is that Japanese workers experience little freedom in determining how production tasks are to be performed. A refined set of work specifications is usually provided for them by the company's industrial engineers. Workers do have input into job design, but the criteria against which all refinements are made are rigorous industrial engineering standards. The use of job evaluation is quite limited in Japanese factories. It is used primarily in fixing wage levels rather than job duties since the tasks performed by individual workers are neither fixed nor permanent.

The simple and broad job designs in Japan are related to Japanese collective bargaining contracts and other legal instruments used in this society. These are phrased in very flexible and general language. Japanese unions, particularly in the tumultuous formative period of Japanese labour relations (the 1920s and 1930s), have certainly, at times, shown strong resistance to the exercise of arbitrary supervisory authority. In general, however, they have not challenged the prerogative of management to set the criteria for job design and labour allocation, so long as employment security guarantees have been preserved (Lincoln, 1993). Moreover, the extreme flexibility with which Japanese companies rotate, retrain and transfer workers is also very much an adaptation to the constraints imposed by permanent employment and seniority wage systems. In sharp contrast with US and UK norms, these systems set severe limits on a company's flexibility to terminate the contracts of employees whose particular skills and specialities are no longer in demand. Lifetime employment and seniority wage systems are two institutions in which postwar Japanese unions have had a considerable stake and they have fought hard to defend them. Japanese unions have also been active partners in the development and diffusion of joint consultation committees, quality circle programmes and other participatory workplace arrangements. Strong cultural arguments have also been made for the low level of job or occupation consciousness in Japan. It is proposed that there are deep-seated differences in the social-structural attachments of Japanese and western people. Westerners (perhaps Americans in particular) identify heavily with their occupational positions and roles, and only secondarily with the organizations and groups in which those positions and roles are embedded. In contrast, the Japanese are argued to link themselves first to groups and only secondarily to functional positions within them (Lincoln, 1993).

Worker flexibility and permeable boundaries, due to 'all-round' training and a strongly developed internal labour market are also evident in **Germany**. Germany is known for its highly developed system of vocational education and training (VET), sustained by the long history of its craft sector, and diffused throughout industry. It provides nationally standardized courses for both manual and lower manual occupations, from apprenticeship level up to master craftsman and/or engineer. It thus offers career ladders and ensures homogeneity of competence and orientation at various hierarchical levels. Financing is a joint effort by employers and the state, and the coverage of both theoretical (at school) and practical aspects of VET results in broadly based skills and competencies. Unions are involved in course design in a consultative manner (Lane, 1992).

Rather like the situation in Japan, in Germany there is no union control over the allocation of tasks, and job classifications are broad and can be flexibly changed through a variety of informal and formal negotiation processes (Thelen, 1991). The fact that a strong craft tradition, underpinned by an extensive apprenticeship system, still survives and thrives is proof of these conclusions. The extensive training (some would say over-training), of German workers explains their polyvalence. Work has also been less specialized horizontally due to the existence of polyvalent workers capable of carrying out a wide range of tasks.

The control of work is achieved via the standardization of skills through extensive training rather than by the standardization of processes – the method commonly used in the USA and the UK. The fact that first-line supervisors are considered to be 'technical experts' rather than direct controllers of the work process is an indication of a standardization of skills approach to work coordination (Lane, 1989: 150). As a consequence of this type of standardization, workers have a high degree of control in carrying out work tasks and the jobs are not specialized vertically (Begin, 1997). Together with their foreman, workers exercise greater discretion than their European counterparts in terms of how jobs are carried out, referring to 'craft' judgement and making informal arrangements (Lane, 1989).

While German work systems never adopted the highly vertically and horizontally specialized jobs typical of the USA and the UK, neither did they approach the much less vertically and horizontally specialized Japanese work systems. Japanese work systems show a greater degree of task sharing, with workers alternating between assembly line and non-assembly line work, and job enrichment through involvement in so-called 'indirect' activities (i.e. materials preparation, quality control, maintenance, scheduling, etc.). Moreover, while German workers have a great degree of control within their jobs, in carrying out job tasks and through informal negotiations with supervisors, in contrast to Japan, formal authority over changing conditions at the work site has been low. Only in recent years have German workers begun to participate directly in job-level policy through mechanisms such as quality circles and work teams (Begin, 1997).

US and German unions pursue very different goals in terms of work organization, but in both cases plant-level bargaining is key, and the primary channels for negotiation and conflict resolution are legalistic. In this respect, a distinction has been made between the contractually based rights of US unions and the constitutionally anchored rights of their German counterparts. The key difference is that, in Germany, works councils negotiate over work organization on the basis of a set of stable shop-floor rights, whereas in the USA negotiations over work organization are, perforce and by definition, inextricably linked to negotiations over labour's core rights in the plant. The character of labour's shop-floor rights reflects Germany's general pattern of regulation through a broad and flexible framework (*Rahmenbedingungen*) that structures relationships between actors in the market without dictating outcomes directly. This contrasts sharply with the US pattern of shop-floor relationships premised on detailed contracts, which are themselves, in turn, embedded in a broader system of state regulation resting on a 'tangled web of statute and precedent' (Thelen, 1991: 52). Specifically, the US system has a multitude of rules and no overarching framework, while the German system has a broad but clearly articulated framework, which contains a coordinated set of general rules (Thelen, 1991).

In the **Netherlands**, there is a tendency to formalize rules and to specialize work roles. Consequently, job classification and design are more detailed and dedicated than in Germany. Production and services are more rationalized, so that division of labour, segmentation or organizational subunits and specialization of work roles prevail. Although an apprentice system exists and expediting initiatives have been taken in recent years, both play only a minor role. Apprenticeship figures are substantially lower than in Germany, and apprenticeships are predominantly served by those who have not succeeded in gaining entry into 'proper' secondary, and subsequent vocational or university, education (Sorge, 1992). In addition, in contrast with Germany, the practice of mixing normal work experience with further education and training is not widespread. Generally, education is concentrated in the period before sustained work activity.

In the USA and the UK, the more rigid division of labour also means deficient communication and more disputes, and hence more time spent on resolving labour disputes and grievances. In the Netherlands, however, this is not the case. Within Dutch companies there is a strong emphasis on consensus, negotiation and consultation between employees, top management and shareholders. This emphasis is institutionalized by a number of laws. In managing a large corporation, the executive board has to consult and cooperate, on the one hand, with the employees' representatives (the works council) and, on the other hand, with the supervisory board on all major decisions. The shareholders then evaluate the outcomes of this careful balancing act once a year (Heijltjes *et al.*, 1996).

Dutch industrial relations at national and industry levels are interlinked with company- and plant-level relationships in a way that is similar to the German system, except that company collective agreements are frequent in the Netherlands and very rare in Germany (Sorge, 1992). Dutch labour organizations have a tradition of broad unionism. The relationship between companies and unions is mainly indirect. The Enterprise Council mostly handles matters that are related to work and working conditions in companies. The labour unions' main focus is working out collective labour agreements, the so-called *Collectieve Arbeidsovereenkomsten* (CAOs). CAOs are legally established series of agreements, which result from bargaining sessions between labour and management (Iterson and Olie, 1992). In order to determine these CAOs job classifications are needed.

Functional specialization

Institutional arrangements like management education and vocational training have been found to be the most prominent societal influences on the degree of functional specialization. In this sense, generalist management education can be related to functional specialization; while a more specialist management education enhances functional agglomeration. Furthermore, vocational training with more specialization on offer, some of which is specific to a branch of industry or type of work, leads to a more specialist management orientation. At the same time, the degree of functional specialization in a country is strongly related to the career management policies of firms.

Generalist education, combined with formal business school training and the competitive labour market for executive manpower, relates to high functional specialization in **US** companies. The USA has a thriving market for further management development, epitomized by its business schools, which attract students from all over the world to obtain

Table 5.1   Work relationships: workers

	Job design	Societal determinant
USA	highly specialized jobs formal job descriptions systematic job evaluations direct supervision of foremen standardized processes	job control unionism low status/narrow vocational training deregulated labour market market finance
UK	highly specialized jobs except for craft workers shop steward system absence of shop-floor control	a type of job-control unionism low level of vocational training deregulated labour market market finance
Japan	broad job classifications refined job specifications job rotation and cross- training no fixed or permanent tasks limited job evaluation	unions – employment security collective bargaining contracts in flexible/general language lifetime employment seniority wage system
Germany	broad job classifications all-round training standardization of skills no job specifications high degree of discretion for workers	high-quality vocational training nationally standardized courses apprenticeship system unions – employment security
Sweden *In the modernized plants* *In the traditional plants*	 flexible job design autonomous production team Taylorist job design no systematic control employee transfers possible	 tight labour market union influence excellent education system integrated with employing organizations limited on-the-job training

the highly prized MBA (Finegold and Keltner, 2001). The US generalist education, on the other hand, has implications for management behaviour and careers. It goes hand in hand with a conscious professionalism; it facilitates an 'arm's-length' approach, and enhances the standing of forecasting, planning, marketing and control activities. It encourages, or at least legitimizes, mobility between both functions and companies in personal careers, and stresses the importance of the overall view at the top. The US view is that there are general principles of management that have validity across a range of operations and branches of industry.

Similar to the US situation, the **UK** business organization is highly departmentalized, with different functional areas. Also like the USA, the UK is characterized by a national culture of generalist, as opposed to specialist, managers (Lehrer and Darbishire, 1999). And, like the USA, but unlike Germany, employees who have had a specialist education, such as engineers, are employed as technical specialists, 'whose assumed lack of wider knowledge and social skills makes them ineligible for promotion to top management posts' (Lane, 1989). In the UK context, a degree in accounting was held to be an ideal qualification for a top management position. Generally, it was argued that the promotion to top-level posts of 'gifted amateurs' was a uniquely UK phenomenon. As in the USA, too, from the 1960s onwards in the UK, business schools were established, and these provide a general management education at a high level (Lane, 1989).

In general, and rather like the situation in Germany, **Swedish** management is characterized by specialist education with a high level of technical training. The qualifications of Swedish managers are overwhelmingly in three subjects: engineering, economics and law (in that order of frequency). Production managers and managers in technical functions have engineering qualifications. Commercial managers usually have a degree in economics. Personnel managers are a mixed bunch; the traditional qualification is a law degree, as in Germany, but many have an economics qualification. Unlike in Germany but similar to the case in the UK, there is in Sweden a relative absence of managers with a doctorate degree.

From the 1960s onwards, there seems to have been some change in the pattern of qualifications among heads of companies in Sweden. Sweden's traditional strength was in engineering, and most of the big-name companies were engineering firms. In the past, the great majority of these firms had an engineer as managing director. In fact, if one takes an overview of all ranks, not just the top ones, engineers still predominate in Swedish industry. However, at the top, it is generally agreed that there has been change; since the 1960s there has been a tendency to appoint as managing director people with a sales or marketing background, who also tend to have an economics background (Lawrence and Spybey, 1986). From the mid-1980s, there has been a new development, going beyond the move from managing directors qualified in engineering or economics. Indeed, the current fashion seems to be to appoint as managing director someone who is strongly profit-orientated and alert to business opportunities, rather than being simply production- or market-orientated. This development is by no means a widespread one and refers merely to the top manager's state of mind rather than to his qualifications and training.

Finally, unlike the case in the Anglo-Saxon countries, the Swedish universities and related institutions do not engage in continuing education activities for managers, and general management degrees are not widespread. Only two higher educational institutes train senior and middle management in both functional areas of management and general management (Begin, 1997).

The **Japanese** propensity to reject western (and especially Anglo-Saxon) habits of organizing around functional specialities is not confined to job design. Narrow specialization is likewise typical neither of organizational subunits nor of management careers. Japanese companies rarely have the array of specialist staff departments – finance, planning, law, and so on – found in US firms (Lincoln, 1993). The generalist thrust of Japanese education, and the relative absence of formal business school training for Japanese managers, which in the USA produces large numbers of functional specialists committed to a professional career in marketing, finance or accounting, has been a factor in the low specialization of the Japanese company (Lincoln, 1993). In the unitary system of Japan, the state focuses on the provision of academic education, leaving firms to organize their own technical training. The Japanese education system produces highly disciplined and literate school, college and university graduates, who have faced severe competition in achieving entry into the higher-ranking schools and universities. Their selection by leading companies is on the basis of the rank of their school and/or university, their academic achievements and their character. Japanese factories screen for talented generalists fresh out of school and invest heavily in training them for a wide array of responsibilities. High-school graduates are recruited for technical and clerical work, university graduates for technical and administrative work. The technical training and education received by Japanese employees is entirely firm specific. The employee development system requires employees at all levels to acquire, over time, experience in different aspects of the business (Nishida and Redding, 1992).

As in the case of production jobs, another factor in the low specialization of management occupations is the premium the Japanese firm places on a flexible, multiskilled workforce that can be redeployed as circumstances change. The traditional assumption that managers will spend their entire careers within the firm and that higher positions are filled through internal promotion and reassignment plays a major role in this respect. Effective top management is said to demand long experience across a range of specialities and divisions within a single organization. Management-track employees in manufacturing industries typically begin their careers with a stint on the production line, undergoing the same training that production workers receive. The US pattern of terminating surplus employees in a declining speciality and recruiting to a growing one experienced people from outside has simply not been an option for Japanese companies (Lincoln, 1993).

Unlike in Japan, the USA and the UK, in **Germany**, the generalist approach to education and skill formation has received no institutionalized recognition, and additional qualifications that are highly rewarded are either a doctorate in science or engineering or, alternatively, an apprenticeship (Lane, 1992). Germany has traditionally exemplified a specialist approach in management education, with an emphasis on specific knowledge and skills, especially technical ones. Most German managers are trained as engineers, and more than a few have passed through apprenticeship training too. It is worth mentioning that, in Germany, first degrees in subjects such as engineering encompass management education as an integral part of the course, which is part of the more general tendency for technical courses to be broader-based than they are in many competitor countries (Warner and Campbell, 1993).

German managers, as individuals, will often identify themselves in specialist terms as, for instance, an export salesman, a production controller, a design engineer, a research chemist, and so on, rather than using the general label 'manager' (Lawrence, 1991). This specialism also enhances the integrity of particular functions, and careers are formed within functions. Specialism is also apparent in the German organizational format, with companies being agglomerations of functions, coordinated by a 'thin layer' of general management at the top.

The more rigid division between functions is also evident in the **Netherlands**. Management, design, development, planning and other 'indirect' functions will be more separate from direct work, and concentrated into specific departments or at specific levels

(Sorge, 1992). The educational background of Dutch managers shows a strong patterning according to the subjects studied; the three traditional subjects for people entering commercial or industrial management are law, economics and engineering (Lawrence, 1991). In addition, there has been a significant increase in the study of management itself as a university subject, and a vast increase in its popularity. In this respect the Netherlands has much in common with US generalism. However, Dutch higher vocational education (where courses are, as its name suggests, more vocational), with a greater degree of specialism on offer, resembles the German specialism approach. Furthermore, the expectation that new recruits will go into a particular function, learn it through experience and demonstrate their abilities in it has much in common with the situation in Germany. In a certain way, functional specialization does fit the Dutch highly stratified education and training system. Although equality may be a strong value in the Netherlands, the Dutch education system is marked by a high level of differentiation, not only along confessional lines or through state affiliation, but also according to educational level. However, virtually every different level of education guarantees a sound standard of knowledge and skill in employees, whatever the institution the student graduated from.

Organizational hierarchy and spans of control[1]

The contingency theory of organizations (discussed in Chapter 1) explains organization structures – that is, the structuring of activities and centralization – largely with reference to the size, technology and task environment of organizations. This approach has been criticized in particular for the fact that it ignores the effect of societal variables. Research that focuses on the interrelationships between the social fields (i.e. the interaction of people at work, work characteristics of jobs, education, training and industrial relations) is able to explain the more detailed differences in organization shape and structure between countries in carefully matched pair comparisons (Maurice *et al.*, 1980). These differences are played down or ignored by the contingency approach.

In the societies that are examined, 'societal effect' research found organizations divided according to task performance into the same categories of employees, arranged in the same hierarchical manner. It seems that a basic division of labour between 'staff' (that is, those doing management tasks) and 'works' (that is, those in lower-level jobs), between those who engage in conceptual work and those who merely execute these plans, and between those who control and those who submit to control, is an indispensable feature of the capitalist enterprise. Further horizontal division of labour developed with the increasing complexity of the capitalist enterprise (Lane, 1989: 40). These common structural features are illustrated in Figure 5.1.

Most importantly, research into societal effects also found that the size of each category, relative to other categories, differed significantly between the societies. These differences in organization configurations were shown to arise because of the joint emergence of different work structuring and coordination, and qualification and career systems (Maurice *et al.*, 1980). The societal effect took place primarily by way of the latter two systems. Two of the countries that are discussed in this chapter – the UK and Germany –

---

[1] This section draws largely upon Lane (1989: Chapter 2), and Maurice *et al.* (1980).

Table 5.2 Work relationships: management

	Functional specialization	Societal determinant
USA/UK	high	generalist management education i.e. sales/marketing background formal business school training competitive labour market for executive manpower external career paths
Sweden	low	specialist management education i.e. engineering/economics/ law limited formal business school training
Japan	low	generalist management education firm-specific technical training absence of formal business school training internal career paths
Germany	low	specialist management education i.e. engineering/science limited formal business school training internal career paths

Figure 5.1 A basic organizational configuration

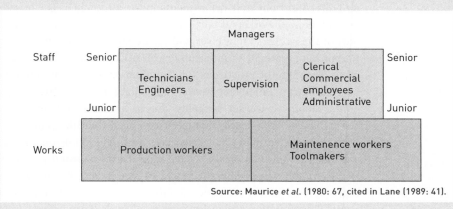

Source: Maurice et al. (1980: 67, cited in Lane (1989: 41).

were also examined in the aforementioned research on societal effects, and are elaborated upon here by way of example.

The differences between German and UK manufacturing units in the division of labour and in the allocation of tasks to positions are expressed in the following detailed features (see Figure 5.2).

1. The relation of 'works' to 'staff' differs significantly between Germany and the UK. Germany has the highest 'works' component, reaching an average of 71.8 per cent of all employees. In the UK organizations take an intermediate position with an average of 63 per cent of 'works'.

2. With respect to the ratio of supervisory staff (foremen) to 'works', German enterprises have the lowest ratio and the UK again occupy a rather intermediate position.

3. If all managerial/supervisory staff (i.e. all staff positions with authority over other employees) are considered in relation to the 'works' component, UK business organizations have the fewest, while German organizations occupy an intermediate position. This result is due to the fact that in German enterprises there is no strong distinction between those in supervisory/managerial positions and those with 'technical staff' status. Consequently, many of those in authority positions are, at the same time, technical experts. In the UK, in contrast, this distinction is strong and technical experts are rarely found in supervisory/managerial positions.

4. The ratio of technical staff to 'works' was found to be lowest in Germany (an average of 12.8 per cent) and medium–high in the UK (21 per cent).

As indicated, the qualification and career systems in particular have a societal effect on the organizational configuration in different countries. Employment relations play a role as well. As indicated, among German manual workers, both skilled and semi-skilled, a high proportion have a relatively high level of skill, have received 'all-round' training and demonstrate a capacity for self-motivation. They do not exercise union control over the allocation of tasks. Consequently they can be utilized highly flexibly, with operators rotating between all the jobs in the plant, thus blurring the distinction between maintenance and production. In addition, German workers carry out many supervisory tasks themselves. Hence, technical staff have a less prominent role on the German shop floor.

In UK enterprises, in contrast, worker autonomy as regards work structuring is less, and direction from staff departments more entrenched. The lesser degree of autonomy among manual workers is partly explained by generally lower levels of skill, both on the part of the workers themselves and the foremen directing them. In the UK, too, the craft unions have retained a significant degree of control over labour recruitment and deployment. Through the practice of job demarcation, they maintain a rigid division of labour both between maintenance workers and operators, and between the various maintenance crafts. Moreover, worker flexibility, due to training methods, is not as developed as in Germany. The high degree of supervision needed in UK manufacturing units, combined with the poor flexibility of UK workers and rigid job demarcation practices by unions, explains why UK organizations have a lower works-to-staff ratio than German ones.

Inevitably, these different modes of structuring the work of manual labour have repercussions for task allocation at other levels of the hierarchy, as well as affecting horizontal differentiation and integration at all levels. They are also reflected in the shapes of

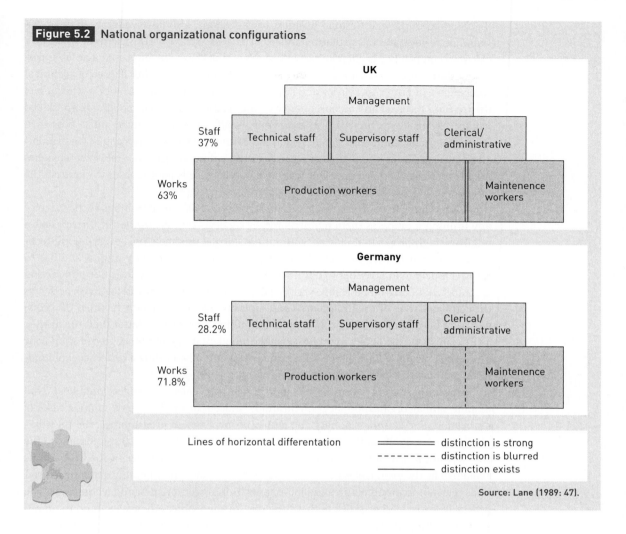

Figure 5.2 National organizational configurations

Source: Lane (1989: 47).

organizational hierarchy and spans of control, or the number of subordinates responsible to a manager.[2] In this respect, the shape of German organizational structures is generally said to be flat, with wide spans of control, particularly at the supervisory level. German business organizations manage with a relatively low overall staffing level because of the way jobs are designed and supervised. Organizational boundaries, and formal and hierarchical coordination mechanisms are softened and complemented by informal and professional modes of coordination (Sorge, 1991).

The UK organizational structure is more hierarchical and, generally, the spans of control are significantly narrower than in German enterprises. However, although the ratio of staff to works and the ratio of supervisory labour to works are greater in the UK than in Germany, the ratio of managerial/supervisory staff taken together is lower. Thus, spans of control must get wider as we ascend the management hierarchy in UK units.

In addition, the different kinds and degrees of competence, and the resulting role of

---

[2] A narrow span exists when this number is small, and a wide span denotes the opposite.

the foreman in UK and German business organizations, also have widespread repercussions for organizational structure. Indeed, the wide scope of the German foreman's (*Meister*) competence is often linked with the fact that there are fewer managerial/supervisory staff in German firms than there are in UK ones. The higher degree of technical competence of both supervisory and line management in Germany is both a reflection of the training received and a consequence of the relatively frequent mobility from 'skilled worker' status to technical and supervisory staff. German foremen must possess a foreman's certificate (*Meisterbrief*), which indicates the successful passing of an examination, awarded after attendance of a two-year (part-time) training course, which teaches mainly technical competence. This technical competence is passed on to workers via the foreman in his role as chief teacher of apprentices.

UK foremen, in contrast, rarely receive such formal technical training. If they receive any training it prepares them mainly for their supervisory role. In the UK, there exists a relatively high proportion of staff without any formal qualifications, even among technical staff. Hence, whereas the UK foreman has mainly supervisory duties, and has to refer technical matters either to higher managerial or technical staff, the German *Meister* is competent to take on both supervisory/administrative and technical tasks. He performs the combined roles of the UK foreman and superintendent (found only in larger UK firms) and is, in his degree of qualification and in his duties closer to the latter than the former. The German *Meister* differs from the UK superintendent in his greater degree of shop-floor experience, which affords him a better understanding of, and thus a better level of communication with, the workers (Sorge and Warner, 1986: 101).

The similarities between the UK and US relevant societal variables could lead us to assume similar organizational configurations. Indeed, in spite of many famous cases of innovation, and countless quality and employee involvement programmes, the **US** workplace remains significantly hierarchical and authoritarian (Wever, 2001). Similar to the case in the UK, the taller organization with narrow spans of control in the USA can be explained by the virtual absence of vocational education, apprenticeship, training in craft skills relevant to manufacture, and job-related training for foremen and technicians. The generally lower level of skills, both on the part of the workers themselves and the managers directing them, results in a reduced degree of worker autonomy. A number of studies have revealed that US firms tend to exercise greater centralized control over labour relations than do the UK or other European firms (Dowling *et al.*, 1999).

Since, to our knowledge, no research has been done on this topic in Swedish companies, it is impossible to provide hard facts. However, in view of the features explained above it would probably not be wrong to assume that Swedish modernized operations would resemble German ones, while Swedish traditional manufacturing units would show configurations similar to the Anglo-Saxon ones. The latter can be confirmed by the fact that, in traditional industries, a clear distinction is made between production and maintenance workers, and between technical staff and workers (Lawrence and Spybey, 1986). As in the Anglo-Saxon model, this clear distinction between functions leads to more staff and an expanded hierarchy.

The professional background and ethos of Dutch management shows, in a way, a middle position between the German-style specialism and 'cult of engineering', and the Anglo-Saxon generalism and 'cult of short-term financial responsibility' (Sorge, 1992). Also, in terms of hierarchical structure, the Dutch organization takes an intermediate position. Production and services are more rationalized, so that division of labour, segmentation or organizational subunits, and specialization of work roles prevail. This breeds a bureaucratic structure of formalization and hierarchical intensity. However, employees are more skilled and greater worker autonomy is typical in Dutch companies. Hence, spans of control are less narrow compared to those in the USA, and bear a closer resemblance to those in the German organization.

A finely layered status and authority pyramid with narrow spans of control is highly characteristic of Japanese organization. The structure of the Japanese firm's authority and status hierarchy is distinctive in a number of important respects. Moreover, along with low degrees of job fragmentation and functional specialism, it is widely regarded as a factor contributing to the cohesion and loyalty for which the Japanese firm is renowned (Lincoln, 1993). For one thing, Japanese organizations decouple status ranking and job responsibility to a striking extent. Whereas shifts in status within US companies typically involve changes in job responsibility as well, Japanese status systems are more closely analogous to civil service, military and even academic ranking systems in the USA – that is to say, an upward move is a reward for merit, experience and seniority, but does not necessarily entail a change in responsibility or an increase in management authority. Although Japanese organizations have a large number of hierarchical layers, a common observation is that they often show advanced decentralization of decision-making, an aspect often referred to as employee participation or involvement. Involvement by blue-collar workers through such means as quality control circles and team production, and greater involvement of middle- to low-level managers in firms' strategic decision-making are often cited as examples of the decentralization of decision-making (Morishima, 1995).

5.3 Employment Relationships

Selecting the best-qualified people to fill job vacancies seems to be a universal goal for both human resource and line managers around the world, as a mismatch between jobs and people could dramatically reduce the effectiveness of other human resource functions (Huo *et al.*, 2002). Recruitment is crucial to an organization in so far as it has important implications for organizational performance. It has therefore to be understood and analysed as a strategic act in all its implications. The strategic impact of recruitment is great, since decisions have long-term consequences.

The methodology of personnel selection has never been uniform around the world. Moreover, whether a specific personnel selection practice should be adopted universally remains an unresolved issue. However, given the crucial role played by this personnel function, especially in managing a multinational workforce, understanding the similarities and dissimilarities of existing practices in different nations ought to be the first step taken by human resource managers and researchers. This section, therefore, considers some of the core characteristics of the recruiting system in the countries under discussion. First, we answer the question of whether significant differences do indeed exist among nations in terms of commonly used recruitment and selection methods. Next, we focus on the alternative of external recruitment versus promotion. At the end of this subsection, we provide a table which offers a summary of these issues (Table 5.3). Lastly, we examine dismissal procedures in the specific countries.

Recruitment and selection methods

Even in the most democratic organizations, personnel selection criteria are rarely set by a consensus generation process; more likely, they are the result of trial and error over the years, bound by legal requirements, and subject to many other institutional constraints (Huo *et al.*, 2002). Recruitment practices are complex and difficult to comprehend through the filter of written studies. The diversity of practices is such that the same concepts might cover different realities. For example, what does 'interview' or 'CV analysis' mean for German, Japanese, Dutch or US organizations? Also, the recruitment methods used to hire a manual worker, a technician, a 'technical manager' and a 'top manager' will differ (Dany and Torchy, 1994). While recruitment and selection covers a wide array of subjects, this section will concentrate on the leading features in the selected countries.

The selection criteria standing out as the most commonly used in the **USA** are: a personal interview, a person's ability to perform the technical requirements of the job, and proven work experience in a similar job (Huo *et al.*, 2002). The US system prizes a close match between the requirements of a specialized position and the capacities of a specialized person. As indicated, the generalist thrust of US education and formal business school training for managers together produce large numbers of functional specialists committed to a professional career in marketing, finance, accounting or organization. Most US companies are not willing to invest in training and the US-style competitive labour market for manpower is grounded in the belief that talented employees can be effective across a range of corporate cultures and business settings. These factors clarify the special emphasis on a person's ability to perform the technical requirements of the job and their proven work experience in a similar job. Moreover, the fact that demonstrated ability counts for more than academic credentials relates to the influence of the decentralized educational system in the USA. The decentralization of the US educational system implies that the quality of some educational programmes is highly variable compared with those of other nations.

Most UK management does not pay recruitment and selection the attention they deserve, and does not make use of many of the techniques and procedures available. In recruitment, they continue to place a great deal of reliance on word of mouth. In selection, they place near-total reliance on the application form to pre-select, and also on the interview, supported by references, to make the final decision. Testing and assessment centres, let alone some of the more recent developments such as the use of biodata, are conspicuous by their absence. Significantly, too, all groups are affected from the bottom to the very top of the organization. Indeed, contrary to what might be expected, testing in particular is even less in evidence in the case of managers than it is in other groups (Watson, cited in Begin, 1997: 128).

Intensively used recruitment methods in **Sweden** (and in all Scandinavian countries) are references, interview panel data and biodata. Psychometric testing, aptitude tests and assessment centres are also used, but to a lesser extent. The determination of recruitment and selection policies is decentralized and is done most of the time at site level and not at national level. Line managers are very much involved in the management of recruitment and selection, the human resource department being supportive of line management (Dany and Torchy, 1994).

The selection criteria standing out as those most commonly used in **Japan** are:

personal interview, a person's ability to get along well with others already working at the firm, and a person's *potential* to do a good job, even if that person is not great at it when they first start. Another interesting finding is that Japan places relatively little emphasis on a person's ability to perform the technical requirements of the job. This is related to the fact that the Japanese state focuses only on the provision of academic education, leaving firms to organize their own technical training. As we saw above, Japanese factories screen for talented generalists fresh out of school, and invest heavily in training them for a wide array of responsibilities. Hence, the important selection criteria used by Japanese firms revolve around 'trainability' or the ability to learn, rather than the ability to execute tasks and duties (Huo *et al.*, 2002).

The heavy emphasis placed by Japanese companies on a person's potential and his/her ability to get along with others may be traced to that country's lifetime employment system (Huo *et al.*, 2002). As noted by some researchers (e.g. Pucik, 1984), large Japanese organizations usually conduct recruitment and selection on an annual basis and tend to hire a cohort of fresh school graduates annually in April rather than conduct recruitment throughout the year as vacancies arise. This phenomenon reflects the importance of harmonious human relationships in Japan, since people from the same schools would find it easier to develop a smooth interpersonal relationship within a team due to their common educational backgrounds (Huo *et al.*, 2002).

Since a large internal labour market operates in Germany and the Netherlands, recruitment mainly takes place at entry-level positions, rendering extensive selection methods less essential (Heijltjes *et al.*, 1996). **German** companies emphasize the application form, interview panel and references as recruitment methods. Recruitment is on the basis of specialist knowledge and experience, especially in technical areas. German companies regard university graduates as good abstract thinkers, but prefer recruiting from among the more practically educated graduates from the senior technical colleges and the MBAs specializing in management because they are considered to be better prepared for jobs as specialists (Scholz, 1996). As mentioned above, since the German system of initial vocational training is standardized, it is less important to test the technical knowledge of those employees who hold such a qualification.

Dutch firms emphasize the three methods that are used by German companies and add to these the aptitude test. This result can be related to the fact that virtually every different level of education guarantees the sound standards of knowledge and skills of employees, whatever institution the student graduated from. If you were to ask Dutch personnel managers engaged in recruitment what they look for, you would be given a mix of generalist and specialist factors (Lawrence, 1991). Certainly the latter do not predominate, even for technical jobs, in the way that they do in accounts given by German personnel managers. In the Dutch case, personal qualities, communication skills and variations on the theme of being flexible all figure. Assessment centres, which are considered to be among the more valid techniques, are not used widely for recruitment purposes, except in the Netherlands (Dany and Torchy, 1994). This might be explained by the Dutch perception that the vocational education system is inadequately matched to the demand side of the labour market. An assessment centre is, then, a very valid technique for testing the skills in which the company is interested.

External recruitment versus promotion

Does the organization want to recruit poorly qualified people and develop them through vocational training? Does it want to recruit highly qualified people, assuming that they are best qualified to improve organizational performance? Decisions between an external recruitment policy, on one hand, and a policy relying on internal promotion, on the other, can potentially have a substantial social impact (Dany and Torchy, 1994). Indeed, the choice that is made affects the nature of the employer–employee relationship, the social climate and the innovative ability of the organization, while the choice itself is affected by the flexibility of the labour market.

The deregulated nature of most labour law in the **USA** creates an extremely active external labour market. Hence, US firms are more likely to hire, at all levels of the organization, from the external labour market. Job hopping by employees, particularly skilled or managerial employees, is generally viewed positively by society as the means for an individual to improve his or her lot more quickly, as long as this is done in moderation. Numerous private employment agencies that facilitate the operation of the external labour market are not restricted or regulated by law, and they, to some extent, make up for relatively low government expenditure on labour market services and training (Begin, 1997). Moreover, the generalist education and predominantly financial orientation among top managers and the more diversified nature of US firms makes movement between firms, and even between industries, relatively easy.

The USA has consistently applied the concept of shareholder value. Company law, stock market regulations and take-over rules are all orientated to the defence of shareholder interests. Inter alia, this implies that managers of publicly owned companies focus more intensively on investors' benefits by striving to reward them with the most attractive rate of return on their capital possible. Short-termism and a risk-prone attitude must also be cited as key features of US management, perhaps best illustrated by executives' recurrent obsession with the next quarter's results rather than the long-term health of the organization (Schlie and Warner, 2000). Hence, since investment in human capital offers only long-term returns, US managers are not usually willing to invest in training and internal promotion.

The external labour market in the **UK** is active at all levels of the organization. There seems, however, to be a tendency to recruit more heavily at the low end of the skill range and to rely to a greater extent on internal promotions and transfers to fill higher skilled and management positions. The recruiting of top managers has been reported to be balanced between an internal and external recruitment pattern, neither recruiting externally as much as the Scandinavian countries and France, nor promoting internally as much as countries like Germany and Japan. Many of the best UK companies promote managers from within, but the external labour market for managers is very active and most managers choose to move up by taking better jobs with different firms rather than by long-term service with one firm. As a result, and in a similar way to US managers, UK managers focus more on short-term results that will improve their external marketability rather than on long-term business goals (Begin, 1997).

External labour market flexibility for UK firms is aided by the high incidence and low degree of state regulation of part-time, female and temporary employment (Lane, 1989: 275). Hence, similar to the situation in the USA, it is easy to hire and fire instantly. The internal labour market is highly segmented, with employees having little opportunity to work themselves up; thus there is a low ceiling for careers in factory-type environments. Unskilled or semi-skilled operators cannot usually move into the craft maintenance occupations because they are given little training, and because recruitment and assignment are controlled by the craft unions. Nor do such workers have much leverage in the external labour market to improve their position, due to their lack of technical skills. The growing subcontracting of skilled work has further limited the internal promotional opportunities of core workers (Lane, 1989).

Promotion through the supervisory route is also limited. In Germany technically trained supervisors are promoted up the organization, thus enhancing the technical knowledge of higher managers. First-line supervisors in the UK rarely move beyond that level, and the technical specialists who are in the techno-structure of UK organizations remain there, for the most part, throughout their careers. Many of these technical specialists were promoted from skilled crafts in the works without further technical training; thus the limited technical backgrounds of the skilled crafts are carried upwards in the techno-structure.

Employers in **Swedish** firms have a major influence over who gets promoted; seniority is not a major determinant. Promotion-from-within policies are not uncommon in Swedish organizations. For managerial personnel, the incidence of such a policy is highly variable across organizations. Most supervisors are promoted internally from the general workforce. However, the promotion of supervisors into higher management positions is most unusual because most middle managers are recruited externally (Faxen and Lundgren, 1988). For management, Sweden is one of the least likely countries in Europe to use succession plans to regularize internal promotions. Moreover, middle managers tend to be functional specialists and are not exposed to other functions by being rotated through promotions to other functional areas (Begin, 1997).

The hierarchy in **Japanese** firms is constructed almost exclusively on the basis of career paths that are internal to the organization. As a result, any links with the external labour market are confined to a certain number of low-status jobs, while access to the higher levels, or to managerial or supervisory positions, cannot be gained through external mobility. This detachment from the external labour market tends to channel actors towards internal strategies (promotion) and to create a 'balkanized' labour market (Nohara, 1999). The internal labour market organization of the Japanese firm includes recruitment of new graduates into entry-level positions after an intensive screening process, subjecting them to intensive on-the-job training in skills and values that are heavily firm-specific (Lincoln, 1993). University graduates constitute a more or less undifferentiated population of recruits from which, after a period of between ten and fifteen years, the new generation of senior managers will be selected. In other words, the entire population of new recruits is treated as a single reservoir of human resources from which specific resources are gradually extracted (Nohara, 1999). Not having any immediately useful skills, all these new recruits undergo the same occupational and organizational apprenticeship. Their skills develop during a long process of socialization: the new recruits begin by exploring technically limited tasks carrying little responsibility, gradually extending their sphere of competence by moving on to related tasks. As noted by a number of researchers, one of the most important implications of long-term employment practices in Japan is their ability to encourage firms to invest in intra-firm training

(Morishima, 1995). It is argued that, since employers are not likely to lose their invest-ment in human capital, they are motivated to provide in-house training to their workers more intensively than otherwise.

In recent years, however, the rapid technological change in some industries has called into question the effectiveness of on-the-job training, which is a linchpin of the entire system. The demands of new technologies, it turns out, are not well met through an experience-based system of skill formation. Increasing competition in product markets requires breakthrough innovations more than incremental adjustments in product devel-opments. The incremental adjustments, which have been regarded as a competitive advantage for Japan's manufacturing industries, are consistent with on-the-job training, while the breakthrough innovations are compatible with more flexible personnel policies based on external labour markets (Thelen and Kume, 1999).

In **Germany** and the **Netherlands**, where mobility between companies is also fairly low, the internal search is likely to be more prominent than recruitment from external sources. This implies that the recruitment function is less important than in countries with prominent external recruitment. In both countries, promotion into supervisory or managerial positions, although dependent on further formally certified training, is ren-dered more likely by loyalty to a given firm and, thus, pursued in internal labour markets.

In the **Netherlands**, frequent changes in career paths are generally regarded as a sign of disloyalty and even ingratitude. Larger Dutch firms are inclined to promote pos-itions internally and fill most positions in this way, including those on the executive board. However, this promotion occurs at a slow rate. Mobility between sectors is even more insignificant. In particular, mobility from public service to business, or vice versa, is more the exception than the rule, although some exchange of managers occurs with respect to the Ministries of Economic Affairs and Finance, as well as government agricultural departments. Mobility between large companies, notably the multinational firms and the smaller Dutch firms, is equally rare. In this respect it looks as if a distinct labour market circuit exists (Iterson and Olie, 1992). This supports employers and employees to invest in company-specific training and skills.

In **Germany**, most companies place special emphasis on the training and selection of apprentices and management trainees. This is in line with the preference for internal labour markets. Moreover, codetermination has an impact on selection and induction, as works councils have the power to influence the design of selection instruments (Lane, 1992). By foreclosing ready access to the external labour market, institutional rigidities force as well as enable firms to invest in long-term human resource development (Streeck, 1991). The German training regime is capable of obliging employers to train more workers and afford them broader skills than required by immediate product or labour market pressures. German firms train large numbers of apprentices and retain most of them on completion of their training. Although such training is not firm-specific, its broad and flexible nature nevertheless makes it a valuable resource that large firms are anxious to retain. Further flexibility is acquired by more informal and firm-specific upgrading of training (*Weiterbildung*), which greatly increased in volume during the 1980s, and by works councils' support for the flexible utilization of core labour (Lane, 1992). Rather like the Japanese human resource system, however, the German system of in-company training and internal promotion does not fit with radical innovation indus-tries. Hence, Germany experiences the same problems with high-tech innovation.

Dismissal procedures

US firms have substantial freedom in adjusting the size of their manufacturing labour forces due to the absence of employment security programmes (except for job control mechanisms) and the absence of restrictions on their ability to reduce workforces using a number of staffing policies. Indeed, US manufacturing firms evolved employment policies that gave them great freedom to move employees in to and out of organizations, thus using the external labour market to regulate the allocation of workers among jobs. At the same time, many manufacturing firms developed staffing policies, often in the collective bargaining process, that limited their ability to flexibly allocate employees within firms in accordance with need (Begin, 1997). Employees higher up in the organization – the

Table 5.3 Employment relationships	Recruitment and selection criteria	External recruitment versus promotion
USA	ability match – technical work experience	external recruitment for all levels limited promotion possibilities
UK	word-of-mouth application form interview	external – for lower end internal/external – for management limited promotion possibilities
Sweden	wide scale of sophisticated techniques	external recruitment for all levels internal/external – for management
Japan	personal interview ability match – personal potential to do a good job	external recruitment for low-status jobs internal labour market includes new graduates internal career paths
Germany	personal interview application form references specialist knowledge and experience	external recruitment for apprentices and management trainees internal career paths
Netherlands	personal interview application form references specialist knowledge and experience aptitude test	external recruitment for apprentices and management trainees internal career paths

managers, professionals and technical employees paid by salary – often enjoy an implicit type of job security, but this security was undermined substantially in the late 1990s under a new social contract.

In recent years, US employers have successfully fended off union efforts at both state and federal levels to restrict their freedom to lay off employees. Currently, there are no substantial limits except for a 60-day federal notice requirement for plant closures or layoffs in firms with 100 or more employees. Moreover, firms do not have to justify layoffs with an economic analysis acceptable to a government agency. Neither do they have to negotiate with unions their decisions to close plants; they only have to negotiate the effects on workers (Begin, 1997: 94).

> ❧ After painful restructuring, US companies in the mid-1990s are counted among the most competitive in the world. Some observers argue, however, that the evidence of mismanaged downsizing and restructuring by US companies suggests that complacency is uncalled for (Mroczkowski and Hanaoka, 1997).

> ❧ 'Downsizing has gone too far and it is time to invest in factories and skilled workers.'[3]

> ❧ In the Japanese *Keidanren Review*, it was argued that the recent resurgence of US industry is due in part to the adoption by US firms of employee-orientated Japanese management practices such as small-group activities and the establishment of a productive dialogue between management and employees.[4]

Similar to the situation for US firms, **UK** companies also have a great deal of freedom from legal or social limits on reducing the size of their labour forces or dismissing individuals. The layoff of employees is a major strategy used by employers to adapt to changes in demand; indeed, it is generally believed that it is easier and less expensive to lay off a worker in the UK than in any other European country (Anderton and Mayhew, 1994: 37). Unskilled workers are highly interchangeable with the external labour market. Unless an employee has been with a firm more than two years, he/she can be laid off without any legal or financial obligation. Employers must give notice of layoffs (redundancies) to the Department of Employment, and must consult with the unions. Usually, firms will reach agreement with the unions on who is to be laid off (Begin, 1997).

In **Sweden**, layoffs are considered a last resort rather than a primary adjustment strategy, due to government policy that substantially restricts layoffs. However, in times of severe economic duress, firms lay off many employees (Begin, 1997). The Security of Employment Act 1974 established strong statutory employment security for Swedish employees, which impacted on the substantial flexibility that Swedish employers previously enjoyed to lay off, deploy and dismiss employees. Now employees are considered to be hired indefinitely unless there are 'reasonable grounds' for dismissal. Previously, employment security was provided by mobility in the external labour market, which was enhanced by government programmes (Martin, cited in Begin, 1997). Under the provisions of the act noted above, the ability of employers to dismiss workers either for poor work performance or because of shortage of work is severely restricted. In addition, older

---

[3] *Financial Times*, America's recipe for industrial extinction (14 May 1996).
[4] *Keidanren Review*, special issue on the Japanese Economy (1994).

workers (over 45) have special 'layoff protection'. It is difficult for an employer to adjust a workforce in relation to market needs unless it can establish by a thorough investigation that transfers to other duties are not appropriate. Both notice and transfer obligations have been expanded by bargaining agreements. Before any workers can be laid off, primary negotiations with the unions affected under the Codetermination Act must take place, a time-consuming process that could involve several levels of negotiation. Employees also have input to potential layoff decisions through their participation on boards of directors. In the final analysis, the employer, after having given the unions an opportunity to affect the outcome, has the right to determine the scope and organization of operations. In a ranking of nations as to whether the obstacles to the termination of employment contracts were 'insignificant, minor, serious, or fundamental', Sweden, together with Japan and the Netherlands, was given a 'serious' ranking; Germany was given a 'fundamental' ranking (Begin, 1997: 213).

As already indicated, an important feature of **Japanese** human resource management is lifetime employment. An important implication of the Japanese lifetime employment system is not to discharge or lay off core employees except in very unusual circumstances. Lifetime employment is not a contract, rather it is a particular way of thinking on the part of both employer and employee. Once a person enters an organization he devotes himself to it and stays until he retires at 60. He will not move from organization to organization. The organization, on the other hand, will take care of him throughout his working life and will not terminate his employment lightly. When profits decline, a company will take many measures to reduce its costs, including the curtailing of dividends and the bonuses of top management, but it will retain its employees for as long as possible. This is in contrast to US corporations, which tend to lay off employees to keep the dividend rate high, and increase the value of stock options for top managers even while laying off employees (Kono and Clegg, 2001). It is important to mention, however, that the Japanese lifetime employment system does not apply and never has applied to all employees (it omits temporary workers, subcontractors, seasonal workers, part-timers and dispatched employees). The system applies only to larger companies, and the definition of lifetime employment refers to core employees' long-term training and employment within the enterprise group or *keiretsu*. It does not state that they *never* leave their particular companies, either for another company within the *keiretsu* or to pursue a career at another company (Ornatowski, 1998).

A misconception about lifetime employment is that the staffing level is never reduced. After the oil crisis and following the recession in the 1990s many companies reduced the size of their workforces, but this was done on a phased basis rather than through sudden redundancies or layoffs (Kono and Clegg, 2001). This is undoubtedly linked to the nature of corporate governance in Japan, which is less subject to short-term financial discipline and tends to put off radical restructuring of industrial activities and to avoid taking drastic measures if at all possible (Nohara, 1999). Moreover, in order to avoid the need to discharge employees because the jobs they do have become redundant, employees' skills are updated to meet the organization's new requirements. These updated skills are also needed by other organizations and, while inter-organizational mobility was restricted in the past, companies are increasingly helping employees to move to other firms. Tokyo Gas, for example (12,000 employees in 1999) offers six 'second life paths' to employees aged 50. The options include taking early retirement or finding a new job, working fewer hours, taking standard retirement at the age of 60, signing a new, obligation-free contract with the company at the age of 60, work sharing after 60, or permanent secondment to an affiliated company. A counselling service is available to help employees decide which path to follow. Hence, while a plethora of articles in the Japanese and US popular business press predict the demise of lifetime employment, these new conditions of employment clearly represent modification of lifetime employment, not a contradiction of it (Kono and Clegg, 2001: 12–13). Indeed, while many companies are implementing changes, it would be inaccurate on this basis to proclaim the end of the current system, since the system has always been evolving rather than remaining stable (Ornatowski, 1998).

There are some very good reasons to continue protecting employment security in Japanese labour markets. First, Japanese employment security is firmly grounded in legal precedents set by the Japanese court, which has made it almost impossible for employers to dismiss or lay off their regular-status employees without the employees' or their unions' consent. Second, both long-term employment and employment security have been explicit policies of the Japanese government. Third, among the bargaining areas of Japanese enterprise unions, wage increases have always been considered in tandem with the protection of employment security for the firm's permanent workforce. Wage issues have always been relegated to second place relative to employment security and, when employment security has been threatened, Japanese enterprise unions engaged in tough and often violent negotiations (Morishima, 1995). Moreover, lifetime employment is, in fact, an important part of Japanese management practices as a whole because it reduces the incredible commitment problems associated with firm-based private-sector training. Lifetime employment provides incentives for workers to stay with the company that trains them which, in turn, makes it safe for the firm to invest heavily in skills without fear of workers leaving, and taking these skills to other firms (Thelen and Kume, 1999). While, as indicated, lifetime employment, combined with internal promotion ladders and continuous in-company training, hampers radical innovation, it is an essential ingredient of the cooperative relationship between producers and suppliers working on a high-quality and just-in-time basis.

Similar to the situation in Sweden and Japan, in general, **German** manufacturing firms do not have a great degree of flexibility in adjusting the size of their workforces through layoffs, subcontracting, or transfers or loans to other firms. In international comparisons, Germany is generally believed to have the most extensive restrictions on layoffs and dismissals (Büchtemann, 1993: 274). Layoffs are costly, complex, restricted by law as to required notice, and essentially must meet a 'just cause' test. Moreover, high employment stability is imposed on firms through collective agreements, codetermination and legislation. While there are no formal laws stipulating long-term employment, German labour has used its power on supervisory boards, as well as its formal consultative rights under codetermination law over training, work organization and hiring, to demand unlimited employment (Casper, 2000). The employment relationship, which has evolved under the influence of legislation on the rights and obligations of workers within the enterprise during the postwar period, has given workers high de facto employment security (Lane, 1989).

For a major employee dislocation like a plant closure, the German regulations contained in the Dismissal Protection Act 1951 (amended in 1969) are among the most comprehensive among advanced nations. Approximately 80 per cent of those workers with permanent employment contracts are protected by its provisions. The works council and the regional government must be notified 12 months prior to the final decision to close a plant. The notice to the works council of a staff reduction must include the reason for the layoffs, the number of workers affected and the planned duration of the layoff. The firm and the works council then discuss options for minimizing layoffs. The law requires employers to make every reasonable effort to prevent layoffs through such mechanisms as retraining, work sharing and reassignment (Büchtemann, 1993: 276).

A significant feature of the relationship between management and unions in the **Netherlands** is the commitment to employee security. Massive layoffs, such as those that occur in the USA and the UK in order to adjust the labour force to the changing demands of industry, are not tolerated. In some ways, this commitment resembles the German and Japanese employment system. Traditionally Dutch people do not like to fire employees for two reasons: first, it involves making judgements about people as individuals and violating corporate security expectations; second, it is expensive – firing managers is legally and procedurally complicated, and it costs a lot in compensation.

Attitudes to mobility have softened, however (Lawrence, 1991). A management philosophy termed *Management en Arbeid Nieuwe Stijl* (MANS) brought a widespread Dutch feeling of 'no-nonsense management' into practice and was a reaction to the human relationship management style of the 1960s. At that time unprofitable companies were subsidized, unions had more power, employees who performed poorly were not dismissed or demoted, and employees were given more time to discuss and participate in corporate policy. MANS emphasized output goals, the needs of the customer, flexible machining techniques, just-in-time inventory, total quality control and doing more with less. In this climate, layoffs became drastic and widespread (Wiersma and van den Berg, 1998).

Furthermore, because of globalization, economic competition has increased dramatically. Companies now need to have greater control over their staffing needs. In recent years, a number of large firms have been forced to downsize and therefore make drastic cuts in to their workforces. As a result employee outplacement has become a prevalent human resource management activity. Where this used to be an activity that was contracted out to specialized agencies, now it takes up a significant amount of the personnel officer's job. This relates to the Dutch emphasis on care for personnel (Heijltjes, 1995). Because it is still difficult to terminate full-time staff in the Netherlands, companies increasingly use temporary personnel, on contracts with the company itself or via recruitment by a manpower agency. Although the interests of employees are increasingly being protected, permanent employment is also being systematically undermined (Wiersma and van den Berg, 1998). Dutch employers have effectively increased the flexibility of labour use through introducing new types of working time, subcontracting production or services, and using temporary labour from employment agencies. This has led to a multiplication of the types of employment relationship and contractual forms (Sorge, 1992).

5.4　Reward Structure

Managing international compensation and benefits successfully requires knowledge of the mechanics of compensation, such as employment and taxation law, customs, environment and the employment practices of foreign countries (Dowling *et al.*, 1999). Yet, with all of this in mind, the three primary objectives of international compensation plans are no different from a domestic-only plan to attract, retain and motivate employees to achieve competitive advantage (Lowe *et al.*, 2002). The loyalty and commitment of employees can be elicited in several ways. This section will cover wage systems as well as performance-related pay in the selected countries (promotion has already been covered). At the end of this section, there is a table (Table 5.4), which offers an overview of the details discussed in this section.

Wage systems

The bargaining system in the **USA** is one of the most decentralized in the world: single employer and single union at local level. Labour contract negotiations are at plant level rather than company level. US companies are autonomous in the matter of the remuneration they offer. Most of them are not unionized and, in any case, the preservation of the managerial prerogative is always a priority. Hence companies take the initiative when it comes to pay. However, in the absence (frequently) of representatives of organized labour telling them what workers want, and before deciding how and where to position them, companies consult salary data (on industry averages or on the local average). In the USA, personnel departments frequently take the initiative in matters of salary data, industry and regional variations, pay relativities and remuneration trends (Lawrence, 1996).

The difference between compensation for a CEO and the average plant worker in the USA is the greatest among advanced nations. The average US CEO is paid 160 times as much as the average plant worker, compared to ten to twenty times in Japan (Tsurumi, 1992: 15). Moreover, many firms offer top executives a number of different 'perks', including executive dining rooms, cars, stock options, fancy offices and travel on corporate jets. At lower levels of the organization, managers and professionals are offered many perks not available to white- and blue-collar employees, such as special parking privileges and dining rooms. Most blue-collar workers are still not paid salaries, but are paid on an hourly basis (Begin, 1997). The majority of US states have minimum-wage laws or wage boards that fix minimum wage rates industry by industry.

In the USA benefits are frequently a competitive weapon. Companies attract and retain employees with the quality of the benefits they offer. Benefits administration has to be good, and companies put much creative energy into the development of benefits. On a rank ordering of OECD states by social funding of pensions, healthcare, unemployment insurance and the like, the USA is second to last. As a consequence, the well-being of workers depends on market earnings and employer-provided benefits more in the USA than in most other countries. Taxes and cash transfers are less redistributed than in other countries. US decentralized wage setting, with rent sharing between prosperous firms and their workers, and limited provision of social wages, puts the country at the top of the developed world in terms of wage inequality (Rogers, 1995). Furthermore, the system of equity finance and frequent profit reporting has led to an attempt to enhance profits by squeezing wages (Lawrence, 1996). Consequently, by the 1990s, labour contract discussions centred on benefits, the new battleground, rather than on wages where any gain would be small.

In the **UK**, during the 1980s, under successive Conservative governments, an emphasis on collective bargaining as the most effective method of determining pay and conditions was abandoned in response to the feeling that unions were responsible for wage 'stickiness' in response to changes in supply and demand, which was undermining the performance of the economy (Sisson, 1989: 25–6). Since the UK labour market was already essentially unregulated, the nation's strategy for achieving greater flexibility was to weaken the power of one of the major players. A unique feature of the UK bargaining system is, in the absence of a legal framework setting the rights and obligations of the parties, the emergence of the workplace as the focus of problem solving under collective bargaining. The shop steward system evolved after the Second World War, and has been described as giving workers direct and substantial authority over decisions relevant to their work group, including pay determination and a broad range of benefits. The written labour agreements are only the tip of the iceberg, since informal custom and practice comprise the bulk of agreements between labour and management at the workplace (Begin, 1997: 140). In many industries, the steward system took over from formal multi-employer bargaining (Edwards et al., cited in Begin, 1997: 140).

The rewards system in the UK has always been closely tied to the operation of the labour market due to the absence of government restrictions on pay determination. Moreover, in the 1980s, whatever restrictions there had been were weakened. As indicated, the role of the unions has been reduced, bargaining has become decentralized and minimum wages have become essentially non-existent. Around 75 per cent of UK workers are paid a fixed wage per hour, shift, week, month or year, with no provision for individual performance. Local work group negotiations between lower management and shop stewards often add supplements to cover such things as seniority, dirtiness of work, complexity of work, safety, and work away from the plant site. The number and size of these additions to pay often vary across work groups within plants, which can make worker transfer across groups with varying payment difficult. Even in the days when multi-employer bargaining was more common, wage settlements were often added at the firm level, and further local shop steward negotiations shaped the final economic package. Except for the work group variations over which they have little control, and which probably account for a relatively small amount of the pay package, top firm managers maintain strong control over wage increases, even with the substantial decentralization of pay determination to divisions of corporations (Brown and Walsh, cited in Begin, 1997: 143).

Salary differences between manual workers and managers in the UK are not as high as in the USA, but are greater than those in Germany (Lane, 1989: 130) and Sweden. Payment systems for non-manual workers in the UK are based on monthly salaries, and merit pay of some type is usually available, while manual workers are paid on an hourly or weekly basis. The number of single-status payment systems introduced for blue- and white-collar workers has been very limited. The existence of separate white-collar unions that want to maintain differentials, as well as a decentralized bargaining structure, are among the factors reinforcing the differentials (Begin, 1997: 146).

As in Germany, worker governance through unions and codetermination has been substantial in **Sweden**.[5] The Swedish codetermination system, however, has not been as extensive and is provided by unions at the firm/plant level and not by works councils as in Germany. The Swedish Codetermination Act, one of the major legislative initiatives of the Swedish union confederations during the 1970s, provided for labour–management negotiations over pay and other terms and conditions of employment, which culminated in a contract requiring the mutual agreement of the parties. The organization of Swedish employers in a strong coalition through the SAF – the sole peak employer association – contributed to the subsequent development of centralized wage negotiations in Sweden.

Up until the early 1990s, negotiations between the SAF and the LO, the Swedish blue-collar trade union federation, traditionally followed a pattern that involved three stages. At the highest level, there were centralized negotiations between the SAF and LO, which established the basic wage agreement. No SAF member could agree to pay less than the agreed settlement. The mid-level of negotiations took place between industry employers' associations and the LO to develop agreements responsive to industry-level conditions. Issues such as the type of wage payment (hourly, salary, piece rates, profit sharing), over-time pay, shift pay, the definition of normal working hours, and compensation when no work is available are discussed at this level. Finally, at the third level, individual companies negotiated with local unions on issues specific to the company. Throughout the nego-tiations, the parties preferred to manage their negotiations without significant government intervention, an outcome that no doubt derived from the substantial political power of the unions.

One similarity with Germany is in the unionization of management, although the unions are different in Sweden. A total of 90 per cent of the supervisors and 70 per cent of the mid-level managers are in unions, so their salaries are determined by collective bar-gaining. Hence, the shift from manufacturing to service employment in Sweden did not result in a decline in union membership, as in the USA. Instead it resulted in some tension among those unions that represent the different occupational groups of employees: the LO, the blue-collar employees; TCO, the white-collar employees; and the SACO/SR, the professional employees. As the structure of the labour market has shifted to more white-collar and professional employees, power has shifted from the manual unions to the highly unionized white-collar and professional groups.

Consequently, whereas, since the Second World War, the centralized wage determi-nation process was controlled by the manufacturing industries through the LO/SAF agreements, from the 1970s service workers and public employee unions were no longer accepting of the blue-collar control of wage settlements. Employers operating the export market also preferred the flexibility provided by decentralized negotiations in adapting to international competition, including the flexibility to compete within Sweden for highly qualified workers in the very tight labour market. As a result, there was growing 'informal' decentralization of bargaining, and a large gap developed between the central-ized LO/SAF wage agreements and what was actually agreed to at many work sites (the Swedes call this difference the 'wage drift'). More recently, wage bargaining has become more firm based, as the SAF refused, from 1991, to participate in peak negotiations with the LO. The metal industry had withdrawn from centralized negotiations in 1983.

For blue-collar workers, collectively determined pay is primarily job based and some-what seniority and skill based, too. For white-collar workers, collective bargaining determines the pot to be distributed, but wage increases are determined individually within the context of a job structure outlined by a job evaluation scheme. The salaries for low- and mid-level managers are negotiated by unions, in much the same way as for white-collar workers, although starting salaries are subject to individual negotiations.

---

[5] I am indebted to Begin (1997: Chapter 6) for the information in this section.

Seniority-based pay and promotion is a familiar feature of the **Japanese** reward structure. The Japanese Ministry of Labour's definition of seniority-based pay and promotion is 'a system or practice which emphasizes number of years of service or age and educational background in determining pay and promotion'. This does not mean that seniority measured by the number of years with the company is the only means to determine pay, but rather it is a primary means. Even in companies that use a seniority-based pay and promotion system, there has always been a fair amount of competition among same-year entrants to the company. Informal evaluation of individual performance begins soon after new employees enter the company, even though they are treated equally in terms of pay and promotion for a number of years (Ornatowski, 1998). In fact, since the 1960s, the Japanese system has been premised not so much on pure seniority wages but on job capability and skill-based wages (Thelen and Kume, 1999). In the Japanese job capability wage system, wage development reflects the accumulation of experience by a worker over the course of his/her career in the firm, as skills are acquired through on-the-job training.

The Japanese skill-grade system, using a set of very detailed criteria, assesses each employee according to what he/she is capable of performing, not what he/she actually performs. In this system, employee capabilities are considered to be formed on the basis of cumulative on-the-job experience and internal training, and, therefore, strongly related to their tenure. Behind the strong positive correlation between tenure and average pay, individual differences exist in the levels of achievement of skill development, and they are exactly what the skill-grade system is intended to measure. On the surface, the skill-grade system is quite close to the system of skill-based pay or pay-for-knowledge that is becoming increasingly popular in western countries. The literature suggests, however, that, assisted by very broadly designed job classifications, there is a much larger number of skills to be learned in a Japanese skill grade relative to those of a skill grade in, for example, a US workplace. The skill-grade pay system encourages learning over the long term during one's career. Since there are, on average, seven to eight skill grades for an employee's occupational category, and advancement to a certain skill grade is required as a precondition for promotion to managerial positions, this system takes on added incentive value. Thus skill-grade pay offers a strong incentive for Japanese employees to learn and improve their skills (Morishima, 1995).

With very few exceptions (e.g. the Seamen's Union), Japanese unions are enterprise unions, each representing the employees of a different firm. The enterprise union organizes both blue- and white-collar employees. The fact that a single union represents employees in diverse occupational groups within a common firm has been a significant force for standardizing working conditions, payment levels and systems across occupational boundaries. The enterprise union is considerably more dependent on the company than the typical craft or industrial union. This connection places limits on how far the union is willing to push the company in a labour–management dispute, and it fosters an impulse on the union's part to identify with company goals (Lincoln, 1993). Observers of Japanese industrial relations, while acknowledging the structural dependence of enterprise unions on Japanese firms, none the less see Japanese unions bargaining hard on wage, benefit and job security issues. Unions can be credited with the rapid postwar rise of aggregate wage levels in the Japanese economy, and with many of the distinctive institutions of the Japanese employment system (permanent employment, seniority wages, etc.) (Lincoln, 1993).

In the early postwar period, unions fought to preserve a guarantee of wages based on workers' minimal living costs: living wages (*Seikatsu-kyu*). The idea was to guarantee wages at a time when high inflation was damaging Japanese workers' ability to keep up with high costs. The system became the basis for seniority-based wages and promotion and, together with the lifetime employment system, was viewed by management as a way to secure labour peace and retain skilled workers. From the unions' viewpoint, on the other hand, lifetime employment and seniority wages were ways to stave off management's tendency to lay workers off in order to adjust labour costs and to beat the threat of an inflated cost of living. At the same time, to achieve flexibility in labour costs and provide lifetime employment to the core workforce, management limited lifetime employment to the core group, created a separate group of temporary workers it could lay off easily, instituted twice-yearly bonuses based on the company's financial results, varied workers' overtime hours and squeezed suppliers in times of recession to adjust overall system labour costs (Ornatowski, 1998).

In the 1980s and 1990s, a number of factors, both internal and external to large firms, have contributed to increasing pressure for change in the seniority system. A major internal factor is the gradual long-term deterioration of returns. This factor, in turn, can be explained by the overwhelming emphasis on market share rather than profitability by the large firms, itself made possible by relatively tolerant, long-term-orientated shareholders. Falling profits can also be explained by a rising percentage of employees in white-collar jobs with much slower productivity growth than blue-collar workers. In addition, with baby boomers reaching middle age, the number of older workers has increased, contributing to steadily rising labour costs under traditional seniority-based wages. An excess of middle-aged and older workers was more easily tolerated when the economy was growing fast and profit margins were higher; now this is no longer the case, the productivity of such excess staff has become a major issue (Ornatowski, 1998: 78–9). The second aspect of seniority is promotion. You generally do not overtake your senior in your own company. The ageing of the population results in what may be called a 'jam effect' (Dirks *et al.*, 2000: 531). It has become difficult for companies to generate the kind of opportunities for advancement within firms that in the past justified seniority-based wage increases. This problem has become even more acute in recent years, which have been marked by corporate retrenchment rather than expansion (Thelen and Kume, 1999: 484). Finally, attitudes among younger employees are much more attuned to the principle of equal opportunity, which is implied by a performance-based pay system. Younger employees are increasingly less tolerant of the principle of equality of results and patiently waiting for the promotion implied by the traditional seniority system (Ornatowski, 1998: 79).

A major external factor is the maturing of the Japanese economy, in terms of both lower growth rates and growth of the service sector, and the end of the catch-up economy. Further economic growth is increasingly dependent on internal technical innovation, a move to higher-value-added products, and major cuts in government regulation. The result is a simultaneous pressure on firms both to develop more high-value-added products through innovation and to shift more of the manufacture of their lower-value-added products out of Japan. Another external factor is the decline in large Japanese companies' international competitive position. Large Japanese firms are in fierce competition with both western firms in high-value-added products on technological grounds and price, and in lower-value-added products with firms in Korea and Taiwan. In the higher-value-added sectors, in which large Japanese manufacturing companies compete, high-quality production of standardized products in mass quantities, or even large varieties of quality products in smaller lots, is no longer sufficient. Rather, large firms increasingly need to develop unique or highly innovative products that cannot easily be copied and continually move up the value-added chain with new innovations. They also need to develop entirely new technologies more often and more quickly. Performance-based wages, rather than seniority wages, help by motivating the more innovative workers and forcing the slackers to either improve their performance or risk lower pay and demotion. Moreover, performance-based wages are also argued to help companies hire the mid-career specialists necessary to develop new technologies or enter new fields. Large companies, therefore, see seniority-based wages as in need of revision (Ornatowski, 1998: 80).

Wage bargaining in **Germany** is characterized by a centralized negotiation structure, which, due to union pressure, emerged after the war and was aimed at pursuing a 'solidaristic wage policy' that averaged out 'market power among the different groups of the working class' (Streeck, 1984: 14). These highly centralized negotiations are usually conducted external to the firm, between unions and employers' associations. The result is that wage negotiations are simply structured and well coordinated nationally since they rarely involve more than one union (Streeck, 1984: 24). Union members are organized regardless of their skill and occupation, and thus are industry unions; craft unions do not exist (unlike the situation in the UK, which is dominated by the special interests of small groups) (Streeck, 1984: 5). The employer associations are also structured by industry, and negotiations are usually conducted on a state level by industry. A decentralization of the bargaining structure has been a recent trend in Germany, with works councils assuming more influence over negotiations so as to better match bargaining outcomes to the economic performance of firms, although centralized negotiations are still prevalent. Pressure on matching bargaining outcomes to firm-level needs has come from the employers' associations (Begin, 1997: 181).

An examination of pay in the German context has to distinguish between tariff and exempt employees (*Aussertarifliche Angestellte*). Whereas tariff employees are fully covered by collective bargaining, exempts are only affected indirectly. Exempts are all those employees that earn significantly more than the highest base salary prescribed by the collective bargaining agreement. Collective bargaining agreements in Germany set a relatively high minimum wage and ensure an adequate basic compensation. In contrast, variable compensation is not generally fulfilled, as effective wages are not much higher than the collectively set ones. Individual bonuses for tariff employees are relatively small. Compared to tariff employees, companies have more freedom with regard to exempt pay. Exempt pay is normally the exclusive province of senior management. However, although exempt pay is little affected by collective bargaining, remuneration decisions for this group of employees are constrained by codetermination. Even if there is no formal system in pay determination, the works council has an influence on exempt remuneration (Müller, 1999a).

Since around 90 per cent of all German employees are covered by a collective bargaining agreement, increases in wages take place every 12 to 15 months. The average wage increases negotiated outside the firm are then tailored to the profitability of individual firms by the works councils, creating a wage drift that varies by industry and region. However, the size of the wage drift has not been the problem that it has been in other countries like Sweden. Although, unlike Sweden, an egalitarian pay system has not been given the priority of German unions, in international comparison the wage differentials across occupations and industries are not high, and the differences between white- and blue-collar workers have been declining. There is a current trend to pay blue-collar workers monthly salaries and to otherwise equalize the employment conditions of blue-collar workers with those of white-collar workers. Some general framework agreements in industries where technological change has blurred the lines between white- and blue-collar workers have provided for a common pay structure (Begin, 1997).

Rather like the situation in Germany, wage negotiations in the **Netherlands** are centralized and take place between the employers' associations and trade unions, with the government playing an active part. However, the persistently high level of national/industry-wide bargaining in the Netherlands has been argued to mask greater scope and flexibility for adjusting these at firm level (Visser, 1992: 351). Company-level agreements are argued to affect approximately one-third of employees. In the case of large firms, in particular, independent agreements are arrived at. The legally prescribed collective-bargaining process between trade unions and employers' associations usually results in (industry- or company-specific) collective labour agreements (CAO, or *Collectieve Arbeidsovereenkomst*). About 700 of these CAOs (at industry level or at company level) are concluded each year. These agreements deal with wages, but also with vocational training and early retirement procedures. They function as minimum standards that apply to entire industries (Heijltjes *et al.*, 1996). The rather centralized system of labour relations traditionally produces salary systems that are more concerned with a reasonable distribution of income than with the creation of performance-related incentives (van Dijk and Punch, 1993).

The Dutch government, employers and employees also consider their societal responsibility for decreasing unemployment and industrial disability. This leads to greater protection, in terms of employment security, for those employees that perform less well. Pay is therefore more often tied to tenure than to performance (Heijltjes *et al.*, 1996). Moreover, many Dutch companies feel that providing employees with additional education, so that they keep abreast of the latest developments, is a significant motivator. This explanation fits well with a cultural emphasis on education and on people's desire to be fully conversant with all aspects of one's chosen occupation. Designing jobs to fit people is another type of intrinsic reward that is valued highly in the Netherlands. This means increasing task variety and flexibility, and having a whole piece of work to complete. In addition, employees are educated to understand how their job fits into the bigger picture (Wiersma and van den Berg, 1998).

Performance-related pay

Human resource management prescriptions tend to favour performance-related over job- or person-based pay systems. The reason for its popularity among managers is that performance-related pay is perceived to increase financial flexibility, to undermine collective bargaining, to strengthen the role of the line manager and to enhance employee commitment to the organization (Müller, 1999b).

With the exception of piece rates and similar incentive systems, historically there has been an insignificant relationship between individual, group and organizational performance, and employee pay in the **USA**. Piece-rate systems in plants were popular earlier in the century, but they have declined subtantially in recent years, primarily because manufacturing systems have changed. Nowaydays, individual merit pay is based on subjective performance evaluations. Rather than objective indicants of performance, like the number of pieces produced, cost savings or profits are used widely. A survey of *Fortune* 1000 firms indicated that 96 per cent used merit pay, 31 per cent using it for all employees. The introduction of performance-related reward systems in the USA was stimulated by the decentralized nature of industrial relations, the short-term orientation of US business and the need to quickly realize a significant return on investment. Profit sharing is used widely, although it is by no means a universal practice. A survey of *Fortune* 500 firms indicated that 60 per cent covered some employees with a profit-sharing plan, with 15 per cent covering all employees (Begin, 1997: 104).

From the 1980s onwards, there has been an increasing interest in pay-for-performance programmes in the UK, although manual workers usually remained untouched by the changes that took place; only a third of manual workers were rewarded with merit pay of some type (Kessler, 1994: 471). Another survey indicated that only a quarter of firms had merit programmes for manual workers, compared to 40 per cent for managers, and one-third for clerical/administrative staff. So the major diffusion of these programmes has been to non-manual staff. These programmes have primarily been based on individual merit pay derived from indicators of financial performance at the individual, subfirm or firm level. Individual and collective bonus payments have declined (Begin, 1997). More common in the UK have been profit-sharing schemes, including employee share ownership based on profits. Aided by government regulations, by 1990, 55 per cent of private-sector firms had some type of share ownership programme (one-third, compared to 23 per cent in 1984 and 13 per cent in 1980) and/or profit-sharing programme (40 per cent of the firms) (Millward *et al.*, 1992: 262–3).

As jobs in **Sweden** have become less specialized in industry, there has been a shift from piece rates towards group incentives, although there appears to be some employer resistance to abandoning piece rates. The use of piece rates in Sweden was very significant compared to their use in other countries, in part because the LO has also been a strong advocate of piece rates in the context of Taylorist job designs. While the use of piece rates is now declining, employers are starting to individualize wage payments to a greater extent through pay-for-performance and profit-sharing or gain-sharing plans, with payments from these sources added to the centrally agreed-upon base increases. The movement towards more flexible pay patterns is illustrated by the degree of diffusion of pay-for-performance systems. In a 1991 survey, 55 per cent of the workers questioned received some type of payment for performance, 27 per cent received fixed pay, while only 17 per cent were compensated by some form of piece rate. Information from SAF membership surveys indicates a somewhat higher degree of flexible compensation, with two-thirds of the employees of SAF members receiving supplements from such compensation programmes as profit sharing or payment by results, although payment by results is much more popular, with over half of Swedish firms using this type of compensation. The use of pay for performance for managerial staff, according to one survey, is the lowest in Europe with only 13 per cent of employer respondents indicating that they use such a system (Begin, 1997: 229–30).

As just indicated, the influence of the recession and the emphasis on the creation of new technological resources in **Japan** has led to attempts to renew incentive mechanisms, particularly the wage system, long considered excessively rigid and ill suited to the new competitive conditions. Up to the late 1980s, almost all white-collar managers and administrative employees were paid on the basis of their skill levels. Consequently, there was little variation in managers' pay from year to year. This began to change in the early 1990s, when firms started to introduce reward arrangements based on individual performance levels (Morishima, 1995). Since then, attempts have been made to put in place a new system – albeit one that takes a wide range of different forms – that combines greater flexibility with increased competition. It must be noted, however, that *the Japanese notion of merit or performance differs from the western focus on work results, and includes communication skills, cooperativeness and sense of responsibility.*

The emerging consensus among larger companies seems to be that, while lifetime employment will be retained, seniority-based pay and promotion will generally be phased out (Ornatowski, 1998). Some firms have already introduced 'nenposei', a lump-sum salary that is renegotiated annually and depends to a large extent on individual performance. Performance-related pay has the advantage of fluctuating, both upwards and downwards, in accordance with individual results, and of individualizing to a large extent the remuneration of each employee. Such strengthening of incentive mechanisms is intended to encourage autonomy and individual creativity, particularly among white-collar workers, whose productivity is considered rather mediocre, even if this development means sacrificing some of the benefits of cooperation (Nohara, 1999).

Moves to reform the wage structure, though typically coded as part of the same managerial offensive that has put long-term employment at risk, are frequently part of a strategy to preserve long-term employment. Patterns of resilience and change are closely interwoven. Technological developments in the past decade have outstripped the skills of experienced workers, and the need to fill the gap has unleashed fierce competition among firms for promising young workers, not so much because of the relatively lower wages that they can be paid but because of their adaptability to new technology. Hence, abolishing seniority wages appears to be less a neoliberal strategy against labour than it is a mechanism for achieving advantage against other firms in competition for the best new recruits. If reforms of the wage system have in part been motivated by the attempt to achieve advantage in competition with other firms over the most desirable young workers, the reforms have also reflected a desire to make it less costly for firms to retain older workers. In other words, such reforms are seen as necessary to maintain the stability of long-term employment. Many specialists argue that the introduction of new performance-based wages will help management to retain younger but highly skilled workers with higher wages (Thelen and Kume, 1999). However, performance-based pay and mid-career hiring are far from being modal practices. That these HR innovations are diffusing slowly in Japan can be attributed to huge sunk costs in the traditional system, which is built on complex interdependencies between micro and macro institutions, and to the historical success of the system's enterprise-orientated incentives (Jacoby, 1995). The current recession is raising concern levels and leading incremental changes that may eventually produce a qualitative transformation. However, Japan is nowhere near that point, yet.

Pay for performance is not common in **Germany** since the centralized collective-bargaining agreements introduce egalitarian pay scales that do not incorporate individual performance. In Germany, managers are least likely among the different staff categories to be subject to performance-related pay. It appears that against the background of a long-standing tradition of profit sharing as part of managerial remuneration, the use of formal performance-related pay schemes has not found much acceptance (Begin, 1997). Moreover, because unilateral decision-making is limited, German firms cannot easily create strong performance incentives for management. As a result, performance rewards tend to be targeted at groups rather than at individuals (Casper, 2000).

The comparatively high uptake for some employee groups is a reflection of particular collective agreements. The collective agreement for the metal industry, for example, includes provisions for appraisal-linked pay increases (Filella and Hegewisch, 1994: 102). In the past, although extrinsic rewards were less popular in Germany, organizations had already used differential rewards and effort bonuses (*leistungszulage*) to reward good performance on the shop floor. These were paid, on the recommendation of foremen, to around 10 per cent of the workforce. The rating system was transparent. Works councils participate in working out the system, and unions have their own REFA (Association for Work Study) expert to help them work with such a system.

From the 1990s onwards, it appears that the ideology of individual performance-related pay has had more impact on German managers. Some firms attempted to link pay more to performance by introducing analytical job evaluation for those exempt, by changing fixed bonuses into variable ones, and by linking merit increases and bonuses to an appraisal scheme. Works councils, however, remain critical of performance-related pay and sometimes prevent its introduction (Müller, 1999b: 135).

Because performance-related pay implies a stimulus of competition between employees to achieve the best performance, which is further enhanced by the knowledge that if the performance criteria are not met the employees can be fired, this reward system is also hard to implement in the **Netherlands**. The underlying assumptions are in conflict with Dutch business culture, where a consensus orientation prevails (Heijltjes *et al.*, 1996). However, changes in industrial relations and human resource management are also occurring gradually in the Netherlands. Whereas, previously, negotiations occurred on a national level and applied to all companies and employees in a particular industry (*Collectieve Arbeidsovereenkomst*), they are now occurring more within individual corporations. The firm has been rehabilitated as the central theatre of labour relations, although the extent and effect of this trend towards greater decentralization differs between economic sectors (Visser, 1992). The sectors that are subject to intense international competition, such as chemicals and consumer electronics, exhibit the most advanced changes in employee relations. These changes afford greater flexibility and more variation across companies in terms of compensation practices. In these companies, the professional personnel managers and the works council play the dominant role in determining working conditions and personnel policy (not the employers' associations or trade unions). In sectors that operate within more stable markets and/or more domestically orientated markets – like building and construction, and retailing – it is unlikely that the traditional labour relations system, characterized by collective bargaining between the employers' associations and trade unions, will change dramatically in the short term. Additionally, little change is likely to occur in the collective and subsidized sectors where union membership is at its highest (Heijltjes *et al.*, 1996).

However, for some, the trend towards pay for performance in the international sector indicates that extrinsic rewards will play a greater role in motivating employees in the Netherlands in the future. Furthermore, Dutch companies changed in that they started competing in terms of differentiation rather than conformity (Wiersma and van den Berg, 1998). This emergent individualism has been accompanied by a franker interest in remuneration. Stock option schemes have become more widespread for senior executives, and fringe benefits more acceptable and more sought after at other levels (Lawrence, 1991).

5.5 Conclusions

International comparative research on the major human resource systems shows that the meaning, importance and composition of human resource techniques are related to the societal settings of each country. Not surprisingly, countries with similar institutions and

Table 5.4   Reward structure

	Wage systems	Performance-related pay
USA	decentralized bargaining system plant-level contracts high wage inequality stress on benefits	profit-sharing plans but not necessarily based on indiv. merit
UK	decentralized bargaining system – craft unions firm-level contracts with local shop steward negot. high wage inequality	profit-sharing plans indiv. merit non-manual workers only
Sweden	centralized wage bargaining firm-based wage bargaining for service workers/high-tech sectors	piece-rate pay group incentives profit-sharing/pay for results for workers
Japan	seniority-based pay and promotion job capability and skill-based wages firm-level bargaining	slow introduction of some types of performance-related pay based on indiv. merit
Germany	centralized wage bargaining industry unions pressures for decentralization works council influence to match firm-level needs	group performance
Netherlands	centralized wage bargaining firm-level agreements stress on reasonable distribution of income	group performance with changes towards pay for performance in the international sectors

| Case: | Human Resource Management in China |

There are great changes taking place in China, not only in the macro-economic sphere, but also at enterprise level. The reforms introduced in the 1980s set the scene, but in the 1990s management–labour relations, employment and human resources moved closer to external models. In September 1997, in particular, approval of the faster reform of state enterprises by the Chinese Communist Party seemed to play a major role in the change process (*The Economist*, 'No job, no house, no welfare', 28 May 1998). Nevertheless, in some ways, institutional and organizational inertia continues to hamper the shift from the older practices, especially in the larger state-owned enterprises (SOEs). What has emerged has been called 'human resource management with Chinese characteristics' (Warner, 1997: 41). Indeed, the imperfect or partial transformation from the old to a newer system of management–labour relations is evidence of specificity rather than universalism.

Until the second half of the 1970s, the Chinese Ministry of Labour exercised tight control over labour allocation. Workers and staff were assigned to particular jobs in a unit for life by the local labour bureau, with an overall quota set by the Ministry of Labour. Neither workers nor enterprises had any say in the allocation process, but had to accept whatever jobs or manpower were given. The recruitment function was practically non-existent in a state enterprise. This system resulted in the mismatching of talents and jobs, and a misallocation of labour resources in SOEs. Moreover, as a result, there was no labour market to speak of in China. From the end of the 1970s, however, the labour control system loosened up somewhat. The reforms in the 1980s and 1990s introduced further change vis-à-vis past hiring practices, and meant a shift from central allocation to marketization of the labour force, with the emergence of a nascent labour market. The legacy of the past cannot easily be dispensed with, however.

The quality of China's labour force is significantly lower than that of other industrialized countries. Recognizing the importance of worker education and industrial training, the reform programmes launched from 1979 onwards emphasized training for technical staff. However, training for management has been carried out with equal vigour. It has been recognized that training a core of managers is the key to successful implementation of the nation's modernization programmes. This view is in great contrast to that of the Cultural Revolution years (1966–76), during which management as a subject of study was abolished by the 35 institutions that offered a programme modelled after the Soviet Union. Nowadays, managers are trained both by the enterprises themselves, as well as by universities and finance/economics colleges. Management courses place a strong emphasis on quantitative methods such as production engineering, operations research and statistics. Qualitative courses such as human resource management, marketing and skill development, on the other hand, are rather weak (Mee-Kau Nyaw, 1995).

A linchpin of the state-owned industrial sector was China's 'iron rice bowl' employment system, which promised job security and cradle-to-grave welfare coverage. Aside from job security, and egalitarian but low wages and limited bonuses, the system provided workers with heavily subsidized services such as low-cost housing, food and transportation, free medical treatment, retirement pensions, childcare, and so on. This practice of a low basic wage with many subsidies is unique to China – a paradox that has yet to be resolved. Indeed, this social support system drains substantial resources from the enterprises, and over the years has become a great burden on them (Mee-Kau Nyaw, 1995).

Since the mid-1980s, Chinese enterprises have slowly begun to abandon the lifetime employment part of the system. After 1986, Chinese enterprises introduced fixed-period labour contracts for new employees. The 1994 labour law extended the phasing-out of the entire system to a wide range of SOEs. However, until the mid-1990s, layoffs of redundant workers were uncommon as there was strong 'unofficial' opposition from the state security unit for fear of social unrest if workers were thrown out of their jobs. From the late 1990s, in those parts of the country where the state economy weighs heaviest, such as Changchun, in China's industrial north-east, being laid off has become a daily threat. Moreover, the city governments in this part of China also announced an end to subsidized housing (*The Economist*, 'No job, no house, no welfare', 28 May 1998). 'China is trying to set up a social-security system to take over the welfare role once played by the enterprises' (*The Economist*, 'Urban discontent', 13 June 2002).

As indicated, the 'iron rice bowl' in state enterprises had co-existed with an egalitarian wage payment system involving a flat reward structure for much of the time. Basic wages were low and fixed according to national scales, and incentive bonuses were developed at plant level but within limits again set by the government. Both wages and bonuses were unrelated to the performance of enterprises. Moreover, lack of proper job evaluation meant that wage levels were more or less arbitrarily determined by state bureaucrats for all Chinese SOEs (Mee-Kay Nyaw, 1995). Recognition of the arbitrariness of the wage system, and of the fact that its overwhelmingly egalitarian nature seriously reduced the initiative and motivation of good workers, resulted in the national abandonment of the old wage grade system. From the mid-1990s onwards, the new 'post plus skills' (*gangji gonzi zhi*) system, with age, position and skill determining the basic wage, has been widely adopted (Warner, 1997). Moreover, the government also lifted the bonus limits to give enterprise management the ability to reward the good and diligent, and to punish the unproductive. This ought to enhance the motivation of workers and technical staff, but in order to have any effect income differences must increase.

For a long time the promotion system in Chinese SOEs has been based on the seniority of workers and staff rather than on performance. In addition, *Guangxi* (or 'connections') is another major factor in determining who should be promoted. Workers and staff with special ties to the superiors in power, either through family connections or via the formation of special cliques, usually get promoted over others lacking these connections. These types of malpractice have denied many capable workers and staff the chance of promotion to higher ranks. Furthermore, a manager can also be said to be 'sitting on an iron chair' while enjoying an 'iron rice bowl' (i.e. he can be promoted to senior ranks but cannot be demoted regardless of capability or performance). This has resulted in a phenomenon where there are too many high-ranking officials with too few rank-and-file staff, and there is overstaffing with too few staff actually performing work. Since the end of the 1970s, governmental reform programmes have tried to rectify such practices. However, there are a number of obstacles that make it difficult to implement change:

1. low wage makes senior management staff unwilling to step down from their positions, as to do so would imply that they would lose many privileges

2. the lack of a rigorous performance appraisal system

3. the lack of regulation that can be implemented and enforced.

From the 1980s onwards, however, there are some indications that promotion is increasingly being based on ability (Mee-kau Nyaw, 1995).

Finally, the role of the Chinese trade unions – in the form of the All China Federation of Trade Unions (ACFTU) – in management–labour relations is also changing. In China, the trade unions play a supportive rather than an adversarial role. The unions have not been bargaining freely or negotiating wage levels, as is normally the case in western countries. The ACFTU was assigned two functions: top-down transmission, mobilization of workers for labour production on behalf of the state and, by bottom-up transmission, protection of workers' rights and interests. Formally at least, trade unions were supposed to implement the details of resolutions passed by enterprise-level Workers' Congresses (the nominally representative workplace mechanism of the ACFTU). In reality, however, the Workers' Congresses themselves had no power to make decisions that were binding on the factory director. Hence managerial authority, together with the power of the party committees, prevailed over others in enterprise management. In the everyday work of the enterprise, union officials were expected to look after the ongoing welfare needs of their members (Warner, 1997). With much greater emphasis now being placed on economic efficiency, the status of the trade union in the enterprise hierarchy is expected to improve, leading to a more active form of worker participation (Mee-Kay Nyaw, 1995). In reality, however, the government is frightened that at some point the ACFTU will, 'break up into independent unions that might actually speak up for the workers' (*The Economist*, 'Getting organized, with western help', 29 November 2001).

Questions

1. Compare the changes in features of the Chinese human resource management system with the Anglo-Saxon and Japanese systems. What are the differences and/or similarities?

2. How would you link the changes that have happened in the Chinese human resource system to Chinese societal and historical features?

3. In what way can the changes help to increase productivity in the SOEs? What would you recommend as further changes that are feasible in view of the societal features?

4. What does the case tell you about the change in the education of works and staff, and how will this affect the organization structure in the SOEs? What would the organizational structure have been before the changes and why?

cultures develop similar human resource systems. With this in mind, the chapter shows that the Anglo-Saxon cluster has developed an entirely different human resource model from that of the Rhineland cluster. This chapter explains how the Anglo-Saxon cluster, with its focus on short-term results, its highly developed external labour markets, generalist management education, low level of vocational training, and arm's-length industrial relations' system, is characterized by a high degree of vertical and horizontal specialization, instant hiring and firing policies, promotion between firms, and poor in-company training. The Rhineland cluster, on the other hand, with its long-term view, its inflexible external labour market, specialist management education, excellent vocational route, and close industrial relations system, focuses on extensive in-company training, long-term employment contracts and internal promotion possibilities, and is characterized by low vertical and horizontal specialization. The Dutch case shows that a hybrid societal environment produces a hybrid human resource model – that is, a model that has features of both the German and the Anglo-Saxon models. The Dutch case also shows that internationally orientated industries exploit the hybrid character and, as a result, increased resilience of national institutions far more than the domestic sectors.

This chapter also emphasizes that the roles that separate human resource elements play in determining the outcomes of the entire human resource system should not be considered in isolation. The interdependent relationships among the elements of human resource systems are institutionalized to constitute a system accepted and legitimated by the parties involved. Consequently, long-term employment in Japan and Germany will not easily be abandoned as it supports the internal promotion ladders and intensive training commitment of companies, which in turn explain worker commitment and functional flexibility. Similarly, unstable and/or competitive employment in US and UK companies help to explain the absence of serious in-company training efforts and the lesser degree of internal promotion opportunities, both of which in turn explain reduced worker commitment and a high degree of functional specialization.

The institutionalization of human resource systems, however, does not imply that they are impossible to change, but rather that change does not happen overnight. The Japanese experience most clearly indicates the interplay between management choices and the constraints upon these choices. The general idea is that some threat to firm survival and prosperity must be perceived by the management in order to initiate the process of change. Management next evaluates the constraints upon change (implied by the societal context) and examines the elements of the human resource system that are most conducive to change. To the extent that firms are constrained in their choices, management will opt for the most efficient solution from a set of possibilities. Consequently, in Japan, a few large employers have made the choice to modify the rules regarding seniority-based pay, but not regarding lifetime employment. The trend away from seniority-based pay, however, appears to be rather slow and cautious overall. Lifetime employment is retained not only because it is a protected right, but also because of the heightened dependence on stable and predictable relationships with labour at the plant level, in the context of tightly coupled production networks and the demands of producing at high quality on a just-in-time basis. In fact, the evolution of human resource features in the countries discussed reveals a mixed picture of cautious and slow change as a result of the resilience and continuity of the relevant societal context.

Study Questions

1. What are the differences between Anglo-Saxon and German work relationships? Explain these differences on the basis of the institutional approach.

2. Explain the differences in employment relationships between the Anglo-Saxon and German models. Use institutional theory in your explanation.

3. Explain the differences between human resource practices in traditional Swedish industry and the 'modernized' sectors.

4. What have been the major changes in the Japanese human resource system? Explain the pressures that have induced these changes.

5. We have studied the human resource management models of the USA, the UK, Sweden, Germany, Japan and the Netherlands. Explain on the basis of institutional theory in which of these countries pay for performance is generally used and in which of them it is not well accepted.

6. Explain whether, under pressure from globalization, human resource systems will converge towards one 'best' model.

7. Explain, in general, which elements of the societal environment and which human resource management practices have an impact on firm structure. Apply your argument to firm structure in Germany and the USA.

Further Reading

Ferner, A. and Quintanilla, J. (1998) Multinationals, national business systems and HRM: the enduring influence of national identity or a process of 'Anglo-Saxonization'. *The International Journal of Human Resource Management* 9(4), 710–31.

Article discussing the 'nationality effect' in the management of human resources by multinational companies (MNCs). The article assesses the elements of the national environments that are most likely to influence MNC behaviour. It explores the tensions arising between the requirements of 'globalized' operations and the characteristics MNCs have adopted from their home environments.

Kogut, B. (1993) *Country Competitiveness: Technology and the Organizing of Work.* Oxford: Oxford University Press.

Though from the beginning of the 1990s, this book remains an excellent example of how the societal has an impact upon the organizing principles of work in different countries. The book adds a further step and analyses the implications for firm performance of diversity and changes in the principles by which work is organized.

Moore, L.F. and Devereaux Jennings, P. (1995) *Human Resource Management on the Pacific Rim: Institutions, Practices, and Attitudes.* Berlin: Walter de Gruyter.

Excellent book on human resource practices in 11 Pacific Rim countries: Australia, Canada, Hong Kong, Japan, New Zealand, China, South Korea, Singapore, Taiwan, Thailand and the USA.

Sorge, A. (1991) Strategic fit and the societal effect: interpreting cross-national comparisons of technology, organization and human resources. *Organization Studies* 12(2), 161–90.

Excellent article on the reciprocal relationship between societal differences in organizing and generating human resources, and business strategies and performance. The argument that is made implies that economies and societies develop Ricardian comparative advantage on the basis of institutionalized organization and human resource patterns.

Case: Human Resource Management among Korean Affiliates in the Dutch Consumer Industry[6]

During the 1990s, many Korean companies established logistics locations in the Netherlands. The Korean multinationals were attracted by the Dutch tax system (which was beneficial to foreign companies), the broad knowledge of the English language and the openness of Dutch society.

Despite these advantages, however, all Korean companies experienced difficulties as a result of societal differences, and some closed their Dutch plants after just a few years. Korean managers suggested that cultural differences, combined with the differences in laws and regulations, and especially the unwritten rules, made it extremely difficult to manage their Dutch sales and distribution plants.

[6] This case study is based on original research in eight Korean subsidiaries in the Netherlands, and on interviews in Korea carried out in the first half of 2003, by Bas A. Daamen. Interviews were obtained from both Korean and Dutch management. I am grateful to Bas for letting me use the original material from his interviews. For reasons of confidentiality, names of companies and persons are not mentioned.

Similarly, Dutch managers pointed to societal differences that made it difficult for them to work in Korean subsidiaries. Dutch managers experienced the relationship with their Korean superiors as tiring in the sense that they had to explain to them time and again 'the Dutch way of working'. 'This requires patience and perseverance,' a Dutch manager comments. In the following we will take a closer look at the difficulties that Korean and Dutch managers experience in working together in Korean subsidiaries in the Netherlands.

A major area in which difficulties were experienced was in human resource management. Korean human resource management policies are quite different from Dutch ones, and Korean managers admit that they often have a hard time understanding and accepting these differences. The problems had already started during the *recruitment* phase. Korean managers asked candidates about their medical history, sexual preferences, and so on. In fact, some candidates were turned down for giving 'undesirable' answers to such questions. These questions are part of standard recruiting practices in Korea; hence it was quite normal for Korean managers to ask them and to turn down candidates when undesirable answers were given. Such questions are, however, illegal in the Netherlands and candidates could take companies to court when discriminated against on the basis of their answers to them.

Further, Korean management mentioned that they could not understand why companies did not have access to employees' medical files in the Netherlands. In fact, Dutch 'sickness' laws in general were not understood. In the Netherlands, an independent doctor needs to be appointed and has to verify the ability of employees to work when illness is reported. Korean management found it upsetting when the doctor, after declaring that an employee was not fit enough to work, refused to explain the employee's physical condition. Moreover, Korean management never really understood why employees could stay home because they had a cold! 'Korean employees will come to work until they are truly unable to do so,' Korean managers argued. Korean views with respect to Dutch illness laws and the like are such that they distrust Dutch employees who call in sick too often.

Initially, some Korean companies had a hard time recruiting and retaining good employees because of their reputation as bad employers. This image was caused partly by Korean human resource practices. For example, some Korean firms dismissed employees without (according to Dutch standards) an acceptable reason. Moreover, some Korean companies maintained a policy of hiring employees on short-term contracts (three weeks) so that they could dismiss them whenever necessary. In Korea, employees can be dismissed when, at the end of a day's work, they have been unable to meet that day's goal or haven't performed as they were expected to. Against this background, a Korean manager said that he couldn't understand the lack of loyalty of Dutch employees. The manager complained about high employee turnover and the fact that employees did not hesitate to switch jobs when they got a better offer.

Korean management was usually experienced as quite authoritarian in their dealings with employees. 'Especially, in the beginning', a Dutch manager states, 'Korean management would call their subordinates by clicking their fingers and pointing at the doors of their offices.' The Dutch manager had a hard time explaining to them that this attitude was considered rude in the Netherlands.

Moreover, employee evaluations were an annual event. Korean management keeps a list of all the comments and criticisms they have and then present them all at once during the yearly evaluation. Dutch employees, who hadn't received any criticism or comments throughout the year, felt completely overwhelmed. During the initial phases of most Korean companies in the Netherlands, in particular, they experienced high turnover rates of local managers and employees as a result of these differences in behaviour and perception. 'The only way to avoid frustration and to be able to work together,' argued a Dutch manager, 'is to be aware of each other's customs and practices.'

Another problematic point proved to be working hours. Dutch employees generally work from 9 am until 5 pm. In Korea, employees will work until the job is done, regardless of the time. Initially, this difference led to serious misunderstandings. Particularly when companies were in the start-up phase, Korean expatriate managers worked long hours and expected the same from their Dutch personnel; 12-hour days and working until around 10 pm was considered normal and was, in fact, expected by Korean management. Dutch employees, in contrast, saw this as extreme overtime. Dutch staff had to constantly explain what were considered 'normal' working hours in the Netherlands, as well as Dutch expectations about work in order for Korean management to understand employee behaviour. In such cases, a question much asked by Korean management was 'But why can't they do this for the company?'

In the Netherlands, there is also a clear distinction between functions; jobs are clearly described in terms of functions, and employees are reluctant to perform any job outside those descriptions. In Korea, people are assigned to a department and can be employed in any job in that department, from cleaning to book-keeping. Hence, Korean management, wanting to reorganize jobs between employees or assign extra tasks outside the regular functional duties of an employee, experienced difficulties.

Furthermore, in Korea 'the boss is the boss'. He can do anything he pleases. He can order people to do certain tasks at any time of day and they will usually work until they are finished. He can hire and fire whenever he feels it essential. Initially, Korean expatriate managers expected the same to hold for managing a workforce in the Netherlands and were quite surprised about the laws and regulations that prevented them from acting in this way. The importance attached to the hierarchical ranking is demonstrated in yet another way: when top management from Korea visits the Dutch subsidiaries, the Korean managers of the subsidiaries seem quite submissive to their superiors from Korea; they would only speak and comment when specifically asked to.

Moreover, Korean management does not accept criticism; it is considered an attack on their honour, or face. Criticism was something Korean managers had to get used to in the Netherlands, as Dutch employees tend to be more critical and direct than Korean staff. Nevertheless, even when they made a mistake and were criticized for it, Korean management would not apologize. Apologizing to subordinates is akin to admitting that you are wrong, and leads to loss of face for Koreans. A Dutch manager once came in to work to find a present on his desk, telling him implicitly that the Korean manager had made a mistake. Honour and face are important in Korean management.

Moreover, Koreans take a long time to build trust. 'It takes years before they trust their Dutch managers and delegate some [more] important tasks to them,' one Dutch manager commented. It also takes time and trust before Korean management will listen to the ideas of Dutch managers and adopt them in the organization. What often happens is that when, initially, Korean management doesn't trust the Dutch managers, they carry out the tasks that are considered important themselves. Here are some examples.

⯄ One of the Korean companies under investigation mainly assembles computers, according to the customer's specifications. A Dutch manager is in charge of acquiring the parts to assemble these computers. In the beginning, however, Korean managers who had more information on new projects ordered the parts without informing the Dutch manager. Parts would be delivered, and the Dutch manager had no idea where they came from or who ordered them.

⯄ A Korean operations manager has a good overview of the production lines from his office. In the beginning, every time he saw something that he believed should be organized differently, he came down from his office and started to interfere with the procedure on the production line. He would tell the workers what to do, and when and how to make changes. The Dutch manager responsible for the production lines and production-line workers was not consulted. The Korean manager didn't feel it was inappropriate to interfere with production directly, without telling or consulting the production manager. The Dutch production manager would sometimes come back to the factory floor and find his line completely reorganized. Indeed, at one point, the Dutch manager commented 'Well, I think I'll leave now, since my job can be done without me anyway.'

Korean managers tend to distribute tasks as problems occur. They focus on one goal that is important at the time and disregard all the other tasks in progress. However, when the task they have asked to be performed first is almost finished, they start enquiring as to why the other projects are falling behind. It is argued that Korean managers have a rather short-term focus and are essentially occupied with ad hoc project management.

Moreover, Dutch employees also experience communication as a considerable barrier to smooth relationships between the Koreans and the Dutch. Korean managers often have a limited working knowledge of English. However, language is not the only obstacle. In addition, the way in which Korean management communicates is different from the Dutch way. While the Dutch are direct and open to all staff, Korean managers tend to consult each other and make decisions without informing the Dutch employees. A Dutch manager recalls a case when potential customers and business partners were informed of certain decisions while he wasn't. This was a most embarrassing experience for him. Korean management, on the other hand, said the Dutch were extremely direct in their communication and did not accept orders. The Dutch complained that Korean management would order something rather than request it.

Moreover, when Korean managers have complaints about performance or when problems occur, Korean management will never confront their Dutch managers in a direct way. The Korean manager assigned to confront the local manager will first walk around a bit, then ask how things are going and talk about various other subjects, while trying to approach the problem. A Dutch manager comments, 'By now, I recognize the "walk" and behaviour of Korean management when they are assigned to talk to you about a problem, and I ask what their problem is and how I can help.'

In the Netherlands, a company with over 50 employees is obliged by law to install a works council (*ondernemingsraad*), in which employees are informed of, evaluate and comment on certain company decisions. Initially, Korean management experienced the concept as a threat to the company and, in some companies, tried to stop employees from introducing this organization. Korean management said they could not understand why their company needed a works council since everything was fine. Korean management failed to understand, even after several attempts from Dutch management to explain, that a works council is meant to involve employees in decision-making and will not, as in Korea, result in violent strikes. Korean management next hired a consulting firm to inform them of the laws and regulations with respect to works councils and to ascertain the necessity for them, as they didn't trust their employees. Finally, when a Dutch manager, who had a trusting relationship with his Korean superior, accepted the role of president of the company's works council, his Korean manager felt betrayed, and asked him time and again how he could do this to the company.

In general, it was admitted by both Korean and local managers that the first five years of operation were difficult, and characterized by underperformance due to the difficulties stemming from differences in practices and customs, lack of trust, and so on. It was argued by both sides that improvement of the situation depends very much on willingness on the part of foreign management to delegate functions to local employees, and to adapt to local customs and practices.

Questions

1. Sketch briefly the main problems experienced by Korean managers in their Dutch subsidiaries.

2. Identify, on the basis of these problems, some Korean societal features.

3. Explain in which EU countries Korean companies would experience similar problems.

4. Explain in which countries of the EU they would avoid most of the problems.

5. Evaluate whether Korean companies would fit into the Japanese societal environment.

6. Assess which of the Korean human resource practices could be applied in the US context.

References

Adler, N.J. (1984) Understanding the ways of understanding: cross-cultural management methodology reviewed, in Farmer, R.N. (ed.) *Advances in International Comparative Management*, vol. 1. Greenwich, CT: JAI Press, 31–67.

Anderton, B. and Mayhew, K. (1994) A comparative analysis of the UK labour market, in Barrell, R. (ed.) *The UK Labour Market: Comparative Aspects and Institutional Developments*. Cambridge: Cambridge University Press, 15–50.

Aoki, M. (1989) The nature of the Japanese firms as a nexus of employment and financial contracts: an overview. *Journal of the Japanese and International Economies* 3, 333–66.

Aoki, M. (1990) Towards an economic model of the Japanese firm. *Journal of Economic Literature* 28, 1–27.

Begin, J.P. (1997) *Dynamic Human Resource Systems: Cross-National Comparisons.* Berlin: Walter de Gruyter.

Berggren, C. (1992) *Alternatives to Lean Production.* Ithaca: ILR Press.

Büchtemann, C. (ed.) (1993) *Employment Security and Labor Market Behavior.* Ithaca, NY: ILR Press, Cornell University.

Casper, S. (2000) Institutional adaptiveness, technology policy, and the diffusion of new business models: the case of German biotechnology. *Organization Studies* 21(5), 887–914.

Dany, F. and Torchy, V. (1994) Recruitment and selection in Europe: policies, practices and methods, in Brewster, C. and Hegewisch, A. (eds) *Policy and Practice in European Human Resource Management*. London: Routledge, 68–88.

Dirks, D., Hemmert, M., Legewie, J., Meyer-Ohle, H. and Waldenberger, F. (2000) The Japanese employment system in transition. *International Business Review* 9, 525–53.

Dore, R. (1989) Where we are now? Musings of an evolutionist. *Work, Employment and Society* 3, 425–46.

Dowling, P.J., Welch, D.E. and Schuler, R.S. (1999) *International Human Resource Management: Managing People in a Multinational Context.* Cincinnati, OH: South-West.

Faxen, K. and Lundgren, H. (1988) Sweden, in Roomkin, M. (ed.) *Managers as Employees: An International Comparison of the Changing Character of Managerial Employment.* New York: Oxford University Press, 150–72.

Filella, J. and Hegewisch, A. (1994) European experiments with pay and benefits policies, in Brewster, C. and Hegewisch, A. (eds) *Policy and Practice in European Human Resource Management*. London: Routledge, 89–106.

Finegold, D. and Keltner, B. (2001) Institutional effects on skill creation and management development in the US and Germany, in Wever, K.S. (ed.) *Labor, Business and Change in Germany and the US*. Michigan: Upjohn Institute for Employment Research, 55–92.

Gooderham, P.N., Nordhaug, O. and Ringdal, K. (1999) Institutional and rational determinants of organizational practices: human resource management in European firms. *Administrative Science Quarterly* 44, 507–31.

Gospel, H.F. (1992) *Markets, Firms, and the Management of Labor*. Cambridge: Cambridge University Press.

Hage, J. (2000) Path dependencies of education systems and the division of labour within organizations: formalizing the societal effects perspective, in Maurice, M. and Sorge, A. (eds) *Embedding Organizations: Societal Analysis of Actors, Organizations and Socio-economic Context*, vol. 4, Amsterdam: John Benjamins.

Heijltjes, M. (1995) *Organizational Fit or Failure: Competitive Environments, Generic and Specific Strategies in Great Britain and the Netherlands*. Maastricht: Universitaire Pers Maastricht.

Heijltjes, M., van Witteloostuijn, A. and van Diepen, S. (1996) The Dutch business system and human resource management, in Clark, T. (ed.) *European Human Resource Management*. London: Blackwell Publishers, 156–84.

Hofstede, G. (1980) *Culture's Consequences*. London: Sage.

Huo, P.Y., Huang, H.J. and Napier, N.K. (2002) Divergence or convergence: a cross-national comparison of personnel selection practices. *Human Resource Management* 41(1), 31–44.

Iterson, A. and Olie, R. (1992) European business systems: the Dutch case, in Whitley, R. (ed.) *European Business Systems*. Newbury Park: Sage, 98–115.

Jacoby, S.M. (1995) Recent organizational developments in Japan. *British Journal of Industrial Relations* 23(4), 645–50.

Kahn-Freund, O. (1979) *Labour Relations: Heritage and Adjustment*. New York: Oxford University Press.

Kessler, I. (1994) Performance pay, in Sisson, K. (ed.) *Personnel Management*. Oxford: Basil Blackwell, 465–94.

Kjellberg, A. (1992) Sweden: can the model survive?, in Ferner, A. and Hyman, R. (eds), *Industrial Relations in the New Europe*. Oxford: Basil Blackwell, 88–142.

Kono, T. and Clegg, S. (2001) *Trends in Japanese Management*. Houndsmills, Basingstoke: Palgrave.

Lane, C. (1989) *Management and Labor in Europe*. Aldershot: Gower.

Lane, C (1992) European business systems: Britain and Germany compared, in Whitley, R. (ed.) *European Business Systems, Firms and Markets in their National Contexts*. Newbury Park: Sage, 64–97.

Laurent, A. (1983) The cultural diversity of western conceptions of management. *International Studies of Management and Organization* 1/2, 75–96.

Lawrence, P. (1991) *Management in the Netherlands*. Oxford: Oxford University Press.

Lawrence, P. (1996) *Management in the USA*. London: Sage.

Lawrence, P. and Spybey, T. (1986) *Management and Society in Sweden.* London: Routledge.

Lehrer, M. and Darbishire, O. (1999) Comparative managerial learning in Germany and Britain, in Quack, S., Morgan, G. and Whitley, R. (eds) *National Capitalisms, Global Competition, and Economic Performance.* Amsterdam: John Benjamins.

Lincoln, J.R. (1993) *Work Organization in Japan and the United States.* Oxford: Oxford University Press, 54–74.

Lorenz, E. (1992) Trust and the flexible firm: international comparisons. *Industrial Relations* 31(3), 455–72.

Lowe, K.B., Milliman, J., De Cieri, H. and Dowling, P.J. (2002) International compensation practices: a ten-country comparative analysis. *Human Resource Management* 41(1), 45–66.

Martin, A. (1995) The Swedish model: demise or reconfiguration, in Locke, R., Kochan, T. and Piore, M. (eds) *Employment Relations in a Changing World Economy.* Cambridge, MA: MIT Press.

Maurice, M., Sorge, A. and Warner, M. (1980) Societal differences in organizing manufacturing units: a comparison of France, West Germany, and Great Britain. *Organization Studies* 1(1), 59–86.

Mee-Kau Nyaw (1995) Human resource management in the People's Republic of China, in Moore, L.F. and Devereaux Jennings, P. (eds) *Human Resource Management on the Pacific Rim.* Berlin: Walter de Gruyter.

Millward, N., Stevens, M., Smart, D. and Hawes, W. (1992) *Workplace Industrial Relations in Transition.* Aldershot: Dartmouth.

Morishima, M. (1995) Embedding HRM in a social context. *British Journal of Industrial Relations* 33(4), 617–37.

Mroczkowski, T. and Hanaoka, M. (1997) Effective rightsizing strategies: is there a convergence of employment practices? *Academy of Management Executive* 11(2), 57–67.

Müller, M. (1999a) Unitarism, pluralism, and human resource management in Germany. *Management International Review*, Special Issue, 3, 125–44.

Müller, M. (1999b) Human resource management under institutional constraints: the case of Germany. *British Academy of Management* 10, 31–44.

Nishida, J.M. and Redding, S.G. (1992) Firm development and diversification strategies as products of economic cultures: the Japanese and Hong Kong textile industries, in Whitley, R. (ed.) *European Business Systems, Firms and Markets in their National Contexts.* Newbury Park: Sage, 241–67.

Nohara, H. (1999) Human resource management in Japanese firms undergoing transition, in Dirks, D., Huchet, J.-F. and Ribault, T. (eds) *Japanese Management in the Low Growth Era.* Berlin: Springer, 243–62.

Ornatowski, G.K. (1998) The end of Japanese-style human resource management? *Sloan Management Review; Cambridge* 39(3), 73–84.

Pucik, V. (1984) White collar human resource management in large Japanese manufacturing firms. *Human Resource Management* 23, 257–76.

Purcell, J. (1993) The challenges of human resource management for industrial relations research and practice. *International Journal of Human Resource Management* 4, 511–27.

Rogers, L. (1995) Labour markets and employment relations in transition: the case of German unification. *Employee Relations* 17(1), 24.

Rosenzweig, P.M. and Nohria, N. (1994) Influences on human resource management practices in multinational corporations. *Journal of International Business Studies* 25, 229–51.

Schlie, E.H. and Warner, M. (2000) The 'Americanization' of German management. *Journal of General Management* (Spring), 33–49.

Scholz, C. (1996) Human resource management in Germany, in Clark, T. (ed.) *European Human Resource Management*. Oxford: Blackwell Publishers, 118–55.

Sisson, K. (ed.) (1989) *Personnel Management in the UK*. Oxford: Basil Blackwell.

Smith, P.B. (1992) Organizational behaviour and national cultures. *British Journal of Management* 3(1), 39–51.

Sorge, A. (1991) Strategic fit and the societal effect: interpreting cross-national comparisons of technology, organization and human resource. *Organization Studies* 12(2), 161–90.

Sorge, A. (1992) Human resource management in the Netherlands. *Employee Relations* 14(4), 71–84.

Sorge, A. and Warner, M. (1986) *Comparative Factory Organization: An Anglo-German Comparison of Management and Manpower in Manufacturing*. Aldershot: Gower.

Streeck, W. (1984) *Industrial Relations in West Germany: A Case Study of the Car Industry*. London: Heinemann.

Streeck, W. (1989) Skills and the limits of neo-liberalism: the enterprise of the future as a place of learning. *Work, Employment and Society* 3(1), 83–104.

Streeck, W. (1991) On the institutional conditions of diversified quality production, in Matzner, E. and Streeck, W. (eds) *Beyond Keynesianism*. Aldershot: Elgar, 21–61.

Thelen, K. (1991) *Union of Parts: Labor Politics in Postwar Germany*. London: Cornell University Press.

Thelen, K. and Kume, I. (1999) The effects of globalization on labor revisited: lessons from Germany and Japan. *Politics and Society* 27(4), 477–505.

Tsurumi, Y. (1992) If Americans were Chinese . . . *Pacific Basin Quarterly* 19 (Fall), 13–19.

Turner, L., Wever, K.S. and Fichter, M. (2001) Perils of the high and low roads, in Wever, K.S. (ed.) *Labor, Business and Change in Germany and the United States*. Kalamazoo: W.E. Upjohn Institute, 123–56.

van Dijk, N. and Punch, M. (1993) Open doors, closed circles: management and organization in the Netherlands, in Hickson, D.J. (ed.) *Management in Western Europe*. Berlin: Walter de Gruyter, 167–190.

Visser, J. (1992) The Netherlands: the end of an era and the end of a system, in Ferner, A. and Hyman, R. (eds) *Industrial Relations in the New Europe*. Oxford: Blackwell.

Warner, M. (1997) Management–labour relations in the new Chinese economy. *Human Resource Management* 7(4), 30–43.

Warner, M. and Campbell, A. (1993) German management, in Hickson, D. (ed.) *Management in Western Europe*. Berlin: Walter de Gruyter, 89–108.

Wever, K. (2001) Mutual learning with trade-offs, in Wever, K. (ed.) *Labor, Business, and Change in Germany and the United States*. Kalamazoo: W.E. Upjohn Institute, 1–16.

Wiersma, U.J. and van den Berg, P.T. (1998) Influences and trends in human resource practices in the Netherlands. *Employee Relations* 21(1), 63–79.

Womack, J., Jones, D. and Roos, D. (1991) *The Machine that Changed the World.* New York: Harper Perennial.

Chapter **6**

Comparative Corporate Governance

Learning Objectives

By the end of this chapter you will be able to:

- understand the concept of corporate governance

- appreciate the differences between the shareholder and stakeholder models of corporate governance

- provide a societal explanation for the differences between these two corporate governance models

- evaluate the position of the Japanese model of corporate governance vis-à-vis the shareholder and stakeholder models

- understand the European difficulties in arriving at one European model of corporate governance

- assess the differences between corporate governance issues in large, small and medium-sized companies

- appreciate the link between the concept of corporate social responsibility and corporate governance

- reflect on the effects of globalization forces on corporate governance systems.

Chapter Outline

6.1 Introduction

6.2 Corporate Governance: a Societal Explanation of Major Capitalist Models
The Anglo-Saxon model
Case: Haier's Purpose
The Rhineland model
Case: Grohe AG
The Japanese model of corporate governance
Case: Corporate Governance in Russia
Corporate governance systems in western Europe
Case: Parmalat
Case: Corporate Governance in China

6.3 Conclusions
Study Questions
Further Reading
Case: Barings
Case: Ahold
References

6.1 Introduction

The literature on corporate governance originates in the USA and the UK, and was initially concerned with a fairly narrow set of issues: how can shareholders monitor and motivate management to act in their interests (the agency problem) – that is, how to improve 'shareholder value' through increasing share price (Vitols, 2001). In this context, *effective corporate governance* rests on two pillars:

1. the ability of owners to monitor and, when required, intervene in the operations of management, and
2. the vigour of the market for corporate control, which should vest the monitoring task in those owners most capable of carrying it out.

From the mid-1990s onwards, corporate governance has become a fiercely debated topic in the comparative management literature. This literature aims to understand the existence of international variations in corporate governance and tries to explain the impact of these differences on the competitive performance of firms. This literature takes a broad view of the relationships involved in governing companies. It distinguishes between two different models of corporate governance for which different terms are used interchangeably in the literature:

1. the **shareholder, outsider** or **market-based model**, also called the **Anglo-Saxon model**, in which the maximization of 'shareholder value' is the primary goal of the firm and only shareholders enjoy strong formalized links with top management, and
2. the **stakeholder, insider** or **bank-based model**, also called the **Rhineland model**, in which a variety of firm constituencies – including employees, suppliers and customers, and the communities companies are located in – enjoy having a say in the firm, and whose interests are to be balanced against each other in management decision-making (Aoki, 1999).

The term *market-based* refers to the fact that, within the system, the financial needs of firms are fulfilled through the capital markets. The term *outsider* refers to the fact that the locus of corporate control and monitoring resides in the disciplines of capital markets. The model presumes that information flows are relatively good and that the regulatory system requires ample disclosure of information, enforces strict trading rules and allows a market in corporate control (via hostile take-over) to flourish. The model is based on liquid stock markets (or stock markets in which there are sufficient numbers of listed shares and share trading) and diversification of portfolios (see Table 6.1).

The contrasting stakeholder, or *insider*, model relies on the representation of specific interests on the board of directors, which is expected to play a strong monitoring and disciplining role with regard to management. Management discipline via securities markets is often weak in this model. There is often concentrated shareholding, with cross-holdings among companies being fairly common. Another feature of the 'insider' or stakeholder, model is that securities regulators often permit asymmetric information policy and are not overly concerned about the rights of minority shareholders. The term *bank-based* refers to the fact that firms generally turn to banks rather than capital markets for finance (see Table 6.1).

In addition, the comparative management literature often treats corporate governance as a facet of the more general debate about the evolution of the different models of capitalism. In this context, scholars have claimed that one or the other corporate governance model is economically superior and that, over time, we should see convergence towards this model of 'best practice'. The shareholder, or outsider, model was heavily criticized in the early 1990s for its tendency to under-invest and focus on short-term results (Porter, 1990). At present, however, the majority view is that the shareholder model will prevail due to the globalization of capital markets and the growing power of institutional investors (Lazonick and O'Sullivan, 2000, cited in Vitols, 2001: 337). (We discuss these issues at length in Chapter 12.)

For a number of reasons, *comparative* corporate governance debates often take place within the contours of the cultural–institutional or societal approach used in this book. First, corporate governance issues can fruitfully be examined within the framework of the approach as it helps to explain the differences between different countries. As governance structures and systems initially developed, differing institutional and cultural factors caused them to vary. Divergent paths resulted in multiple governance forms. The 'institutional clusters' concept of coordinated market economies (CMEs) and liberal market economies (LMEs), which are discussed in Chapter 1, provide a broader institutional context within which stakeholder and shareholder models of governance, respectively, can be discussed.

Moreover, within the cultural–institutional approach, the corporate governance regime itself is perceived as an institution, which helps to explain the comparative institutional advantage of firms. Indeed, some firms appear to view differences in corporate governance as an untapped source of competitive advantage. As part of their efforts to create superior value in this changing global environment, they are adopting structures and mechanisms from different governance systems.

For example, Ford Motor Company has adopted extensive cross-ownership relationships through equity holdings, acquisitions, alliances and research consortia, practices common in the Japanese *keiretsu*. German firms such as DaimlerBenz,

Table 6.1 Differences between the 'shareholder' and 'stakeholder' models

Shareholder model
- financial needs of firms fulfilled through the market
- locus of corporate control and monitoring resides in the disciplines of the market
- assumption of perfect information flows
- effective regulatory system
- model is based on liquid stock markets and diversification of portfolios

Stakeholder model
- financial needs of firms are fulfilled through bank finance
- monitoring and control function resides in the dual-board system
- concentrated shareholding and thus illiquid markets
- regulators often allow for asymmetric information flows
- rights of minority shareholders are not always protected effectively

Deutsche Telecom and Hoechst have altered their financial disclosure practices to gain access to American financial markets (Rubach and Sebora, 1998).

Finally, since the societal approach stresses the embeddedness of national institutions, as well as the possibility of 'complementarities' between different combinations of these institutions, the approach hypothesizes that different responses to internationalizing capital markets, other than convergence, are possible. Companies may respond very differently to similar sorts of pressure, and distinct sets of 'best practice' contingent on the national context may emerge (Vitols, 2001: 338–9). As already suggested, this argument is discussed in Chapter 12.

This chapter applies this broad approach to corporate governance by examining the interaction between corporate governance aspects in large, small and medium-sized firms and national institutions in different countries in the context of internationalizing capital markets. In the absence of a theoretical link between culture and corporate governance aspects, the focus here is on the impact of formal institutions on the corporate governance aspect. Since governance institutions are embedded in the societal, cultural effects can be conceived of as largely reflected in the choice of formal institutions. It could, for instance, be assumed that the lower a country scores on the uncertainty avoidance index of Hofstede, the more it will be market-orientated. Capital market investments entail risks, which risk-averse nations would arguably want to avoid as much as possible.

Against this background, the next section relates the discussion on the two major capitalist corporate governance models – the shareholder (or Anglo-Saxon) versus stakeholder (or Rhineland) models – to the institutional approach through an analysis of the major corporate governance features influencing postwar company decision-making in advanced countries. At the same time, these features together are seen as comprising the *broad definition of corporate governance* used here:

- the structure of ownership of companies
- the relationship between management and the various stakeholders in a company
- the structure of management or top management institutions (i.e. unitary or two-tier boards), and
- the method of bringing about corporate restructuring.

The in-depth explanation of the two main models is followed by an analysis of the Japanese model of corporate governance, which is argued to be similar to the Rhineland model. Next, the Russian model of corporate governance is discussed in the form of a case study. The subsequent section is devoted to continental European models, which are variants of the two main models. The analysis in the two sections shows that differences between the advanced and transitional nations in the aforementioned corporate governance features stem from *differences in key societal institutions* – that is, from differences in

- governmental regulation
- the character of the financial system
- corporate law, and
- cultural values.

The second section concludes with a case study on Chinese corporate governance and financial reforms. The chapter further discusses the major strengths and weaknesses of the two main corporate governance models. At the same time, a summary is provided of the discussion on the direction of change in the two main models. While doing so, an examination is made of the widespread view that, since international capital markets are increasingly dominated by diversified portfolio investors (such as mutual funds[1] and pension funds) seeking higher returns, companies must adopt the shareholder model or be starved of the external capital needed to invest and survive (Vitols, 2001: 338).

Finally, in view of the recent upsurge in interest in corporate social responsibility (CSR), the link with corporate governance issues is discussed, where appropriate, throughout the chapter. Simply put, *corporate social responsibility* can be defined as the duty of organizations to conduct their business in a manner that respects the rights of individuals and promotes human welfare.

One of the main types of CSR process is stakeholder management (Wood, 1991). When implemented, this process helps to keep the firm abreast of, and to address successfully, stakeholder demands. Stakeholder issues are concerns of importance to the groups that can directly or indirectly affect or be affected by the firm's activities (Clarkson, 1995). To an ever greater extent, it seems, corporations are being called upon to respond to the needs of 'stakeholders' other than investors. Yet, this strong interest in CSR comes, ironically, at a time when investors all over the world – many of them large institutions with the capacity and will to topple underperforming CEOs – are escalating their demand that corporations maximize shareholder returns.

The movement for better and more responsive corporate governance seeks to ensure that managers act in the best interests of their shareholders. Compensation of top corporate officers is linked more closely to share prices than ever before (see Chapter 5 for more information on this topic). The steady improvement in corporate profitability over the last few years is due, at least in part, to restructurings that have resulted either in layoffs or in diminished wages and benefits (Reich, 1998). While there are many questions with respect to whether and how companies should be responsible in some way in society, the focal point here is whether there is a new meaning for CSR that is consistent both with the greater need for corporate responsiveness to employees and communities, and with the greater demands from investors for performance. The cases at the end of this chapter, dealing with the Barings and Ahold scandals, should be seen in this light.

6.2 Corporate Governance: a Societal Explanation of Major Capitalist Models

While there is a range of different modes of corporate governance systems in advanced economies, as indicated, two offer clear and distinctly different forms: the shareholder, or outsider, model (also referred to as the 'Anglo-Saxon' form of corporate governance) and

---

[1] Mutual funds are collective investments, run by fund managers. For example, if a small investor has, say, 2000 euros to spend on equities, there are two choices. The money can be spent on just one or two companies' shares or spread widely over ten companies' shares. In the first case, the risk is great if one company performs badly. In the second case, with 200 euros spent on each share, the dealing costs are discouragingly high. The answer may be to put the money into mutual funds.

the stakeholder, or insider, model (referred to as the Rhineland model.) The first is dominant in the Anglo-Saxon cluster of countries, including the USA, the UK, Ireland, Australia and Canada. Rhineland capitalism is attributed to Germany, Japan and continental European countries.

The problem with this distinction between the two main systems is that it does not express the variations that exist between the systems that are classified as 'insider'. Each of the continental European systems has, to a different extent, some elements of the outsider system. For example, the Netherlands, Sweden and Switzerland, three countries considered to have insider systems, have a relatively large number of domestic listed companies and a high stock market capitalization (see below). Comparing Germany and Japan as examples of the insider system is also rather problematic. Both might have some similar mechanisms of corporate control, but their dissimilarities are even greater. The corporate governance systems of continental European countries and Japan could perhaps best be positioned somewhere on a continuum between the Anglo-Saxon model with its strong emphasis on shareholder value and the Rhineland model with its attention to broader societal needs.

By providing an analysis of the Anglo-Saxon, the Rhineland, and the Japanese corporate governance models, this section illustrates how difficult it is to generalize about corporate governance systems. Recent changes in corporate governance aspects are highlighted throughout the section, which concludes with a case on Russia, to illustrate the problems that countries in transition experience in setting up a reliable corporate governance system.

The Anglo-Saxon model
Capital markets and regulation

Broadly speaking, the Anglo-Saxon corporate governance model is based on a system that places emphasis on *equity finance* for business. This means that companies issue shares or bonds rather than relying on bank loans for fulfilling their financial needs. Capital markets tend to be large and regulated in a manner favourable to trading in equities. *Large, diversified and efficiently functioning stock markets* are argued to develop when supported by complementary institutions, such as the legal protection of small shareholders and maximum limits on the shareholdings of financial institutions (Roe, 1994). These are typically institutions that are characteristic of the Anglo-Saxon model.

As in most countries, and akin to the Rhineland model of finance, small firms in the US and the UK rely on bank lending to make investments. The large firm model in Germany and Japan, on the other hand, is converging towards the Anglo-Saxon model. As will become clear later on in this section, the main differences between the two models are found in the medium-sized firm segment.

The structure of ownership

In the Anglo-Saxon model, companies do not generally hold each other's stocks. In other words, unlike in Germany and Japan, one does not find extensive cross-shareholding. Also, unlike the case in Germany and Japan, financial institutions rarely hold stock issued by their customer companies for longer periods, except in certain cases such as venture capital firms. For the USA, the latter can be explained by the fact that US banks were prevented by legislation from holding large stakes in industrial companies. The low incidence of cross-shareholding between companies is reflected in the low figure for shares held by other enterprises compared to Germany (Table 6.2). Instead, ownership of shares is largely in the hands of institutional fund managers, whose focus is on relatively short-term return on capital, rather than longer-term market share issues. The major investors in the UK and the USA – investment funds, pensions funds and (to a certain extent) insurance companies – take a 'portfolio' approach to risk management by taking small stakes in a large number of companies. The types of investor more likely to take large strategic shareholdings – enterprises, the public sector and banks – account for a minority of the shareholdings. In sum, the Anglo-Saxon system is characterized by *dispersed ownership* (that is, shares are not concentrated in the hands of a few shareholders) by *share price-orientated* (investors that are interested in making money by the buying and selling of shares) *financial institutions* (Vitols, 2001).

The relationship between stakeholders and management

The Anglo-Saxon form of corporate governance is characterized by *arm's-length relationships* between all stakeholders and the management of companies. Neither investors nor employees, nor the local communities within which firms invest, have any close links with companies. As banks provide a relatively small share of business finance, the links between banks and companies are not strong either. Consequently, the USA and the other economies where the Anglo-Saxon system of economic governance is widely used depend heavily on active markets for corporate control.

As the ultimate prototype of a 'shareholder' model emphasizing 'shareholder value', the Anglo-Saxon system of corporate governance places importance on investors in more than one way. Company law, stock market regulations and rules all originated in defence of shareholder interests. The conventional proposition of the Anglo-Saxon model is that a company has only one responsibility, both morally and legally: to maximize the value of the shares of those who have invested in it (Friedman, 1962). Corporate board members and executives are 'fiduciaries' under the law – agents solely of those who have invested capital in the corporation. But in fulfilling their responsibility to their investors, according

Table 6.2 Percentage of total shares in circulation held by different sectors in Germany, the USA and the UK (end of 1998)

	US	UK	Germany
Households	49	21	15
Non-financial firms	–	1	42
Banks	6	1	10
Insurance enterprises and pension funds	28	50	12
Investment funds and other financial institutions	13	17	8
Non-residents	5	9	9

Source: OECD (1998).

to this view, boards and executives also indirectly fulfil their core responsibility to the rest of society – to other 'stakeholders' such as their employees, members of their community and fellow citizens – because they help to ensure that society's productive assets are allocated to their most efficient uses.

Optimistic advocates of corporate social responsibility argue that what is good for a company's shareholders over the long term is also good for its other stakeholders over the long term (and, presumably, what is bad for these broader interests is also bad for shareholders, eventually). That is, if one looks far enough into the future, all interests converge: all stakeholders are ultimately the same. All have an interest in a strong economy, well-paid employees, a healthy and clean environment and a peaceful society. However, fuzzy long terms are no match for hard-nosed short terms. Capital markets are notoriously impatient, and are becoming less patient all the time. Most of today's institutional investors have no particular interests in a 'long term' that extends much beyond the next quarter, if that long (Reich, 1998).

While the relationship between investor and company can be seen as a deep-seated 'cultural' feature of the system of corporate governance, it originates from and is supported by regulatory policies that are shaped by interest groups (Woolcock, 1996: 186). So, for example, the combined effect of bankruptcy laws and insider trading legislation contributes to explaining the absence of relationship banking (see pages 263–7 for an explanation) and of closer relations between shareholders and the management of companies in the Anglo-Saxon model.

Bankruptcy regulation militates against relationship banking in that any bank that intervenes in order to assist a customer in difficulties is likely to have its seniority as a debtor reduced. These laws are based on the principle that creditors of any bankrupt company should be treated equally, but the effect of this is to provide a fairly powerful disincentive to active intervention. Insider trading legislation militates against active institutional shareholders, because if they obtain price-sensitive information as a result of involvement in a company they cannot trade without infringing insider trading legislation. As a consequence, corporate restructuring occurs through take-overs as shareholders are tempted to accept bid premia and sell or 'exit' rather than become actively involved in the rescue by 'voicing' concern about the performance of management.

Company law and the structure of top management institutions

Company law is based on a *unitary board system*. The unitary board system is seen as most efficient because it avoids fragmentation of responsibility. Board composition, in both the USA and the UK, tends to reflect a preference for outside directors, or those with no direct affiliations to management. In the UK, listed companies have to comply with a voluntary code that requires the use of non-executive directors on the board. In general, however, executive directors have always been in the majority on UK boards. In the USA, it is rare for there to be more than three executive directors on a board. Consequently, outside (i.e. non-executive directors) are in the majority. Outside directors are often CEOs of other companies, who tend to see things from a management perspective, and other individuals who are felt to add respectability (e.g. prominent academics, persons with political connections, etc.).

Independent directors are seen as a countervailing power against the dominant influence on the board, whether of the management or of the shareholders. Hence, in states where the shareholders have a limited impact on decision-making, independent directors will be seen as a check on the overwhelming influence of the management. This is the case in the USA and the UK, where due to the wide distribution of share ownership, management was able to exercise a dominant influence. The appointment of independent directors is a favourite instrument for the institutional investor to use to bend the company's policies without assuming responsibility for the actual management decision.

The use of outside boards, however, while introducing elements of independent control within the corporate governance system, also introduces information asymmetries to the board: managers who report to the board are intimately connected to the workings of the corporation. Directors, who usually meet up for three to six hours only five to nine times per year, must rely on information solely from management. Moreover, several aspects of the board system may promote the selection of directors sympathetic to incumbent managers, thereby diluting management's accountability to the board.

The existence of the joint chief executive officer (CEO)–chairman of the board blurs the separation between management and oversight functions in many companies. While there are no legal rules related to this issue, in the UK separation is highly recommended by several committees and often practised by large companies. In the USA, in contrast, CEOs often chair the board. And although CEOs can neither hire nor fire directors, they often choose the nominating committee for the directors, or even indirectly nominate the directors themselves (Lightfood, 1992). The US unitary board system could, in fact, be seen as an expression of the CEO-dominated system. The typical leadership role is for the CEO who, after a period of consultation with other managers, makes major decisions unilaterally and takes sole responsibility for these decisions.

Consensus and the institution of employee representation

Another clear distinction between the Anglo-Saxon and continental European forms of corporate governance is on the issue of statutory employee representation. In contrast to most of the rest of continental Europe – especially Germany, which has laws requiring parity co-decision-making in supervisory boards and works councils – in the *Anglo-Saxon model* there are *no legal provisions for employee representatives on company boards*. It is clear, however, that one of the options of a society to have corporate decisions reflect something more than a mere calculation of what is best for shareholders, and when society is uncomfortable giving corporate officials entire discretion over how to arrange the balancing of interests, is to impose, by law, procedures by which stakeholders other than investors can participate directly in corporate decisions. In theory, one can envisage a wide range of means by which all stakeholders could be given voices in corporate decision-making; yet any system of representation tends to prolong and complicate decision-making, something that is not compatible with the short-term demands of the Anglo-Saxon model.

The UK's membership of the European Union has not stopped its government and business from continuing to oppose statutory requirements on employee participation. Underlying the opposition to any form of employee participation in the UK is a legacy of confrontational attitudes to industrial relations, especially during the 1970s, compared to the more consensual approach in Germany (see Chapter 5 for an extended explanation of this topic).

More fundamentally, however, there is a deep-seated difference between the (neo)liberal, free market philosophy of the Anglo-Saxon model and different forms of 'social market economy' in continental Europe. The predominant view in UK industry and government circles is that increased social provision and efforts to seek consensus are costs that undermine competitiveness and thus general economic prosperity. For many continental Europeans, or at least for northern continental Europeans, social provision and consensus are seen as prerequisites of stable (long-term) economic growth. The conviction that cooperative forms of industrial relationship are not possible in the UK continues to shape employers' approaches (Woolcock, 1996).

Corporate restructuring

As indicated, the *take-over mechanism* is at the heart of the Anglo-Saxon open-market model for corporate governance. Any party can bid for the control rights of a listed company by accumulating a large enough ownership stake. *Take-overs* are commonly viewed as playing two related roles.

1. First, the *threat* of take-over may contribute to efficient management by making managers concentrate on maximizing shareholder value, rather than on pursuing their own personal objectives (an example of potential principal–agent problems).

2. Second, in the event of managerial failure, take-overs allow poor management to be replaced with good.

In general, take-overs are not the normal form of corporate control. The USA and the UK are the exception rather than the rule in this regard. The UK accounts for the bulk of mergers and acquisitions within the European Union, (EU). The use of take-overs in corporate restructuring follows, among other things, from the size and regulation of the capital markets.

The legitimacy of the take-over option has militated against enterprise growth from small to medium size (Hughes, 1990, cited in Lane, 1994) and has thus contributed to the creation of a polarized industrial structure in both the UK and the USA. Small family-owned companies choose to remain small because if they grow they will be forced to go to the stock market to obtain funding and will not only lose control of the company but will also face the threat of take-overs. Hence, in comparison with Germany, in the Anglo-Saxon world there is a low incidence of medium-sized companies.

The Rhineland model
Capital markets and regulation

In general, the Rhineland form of corporate governance relies more on *debt finance* by banks. All banks are universal – that is, by law, they can engage in the full range of commercial and investment banking services. Moreover, banks can often adopt a longer-term focus, partly because they know that German firms may credibly offer sustained commitments to

Case: Haier's Purpose

On the face of it, China's leading maker of fridges, washing machines and air-conditioners looks like a global success. Its overseas sales are currently $1 billion. Haier claims 30% of the market for small fridges and half the market for wine coolers in America, and a tenth of Europe's air-conditioner market. Haier is now the world's fourth largest white-goods maker behind Whirlpool, Electrolux and Bosch-Siemens.

But size does not automatically mean quality, just as buying name recognition at any price (that Manhattan HQ) does not equal careful brand-building. Haier's drive into markets abroad mirrors a push into new markets at home. In both, diversification is driven by opportunism and desperation, not good strategy. Predicting that profits in 2004 will be flat at 2 billion yuan for a third successive year, despite an expected 20–30% rise in sales, Mr Zhang admits that plunging returns in his core white goods business are driving him abroad. After China joined the World Trade Organisation, he says, 'every multinational set up in China. Margins are low here. If we don't go outside, we cannot survive.'

Outside China, Haier has so far concentrated on niches – mini-fridges (to which it adds a handy fold-down flap for a laptop) and wine coolers. But to continue to grow globally it will have to compete with the likes of Whirlpool in their main markets. Yet Haier lacks such firm's R & D, their design skills – it employs just ten researchers in America – their distribution or their service networks. Mr Zhang says his biggest headache is hiring decent managers, since he cannot pay as well as rivals. Haier does not have their established brands – or the money to build one.

Nor is Haier being careful to keep costs low. Mr Zhang insists that Haier must produce outside China to be responsive to customers. Yet, at a stroke, that deprives Haier of its greatest advantage: China's vast pool of low-cost labour. Meanwhile, Haier's attempt to reward creativity – allowing every engineer the freedom to design and build his own products – has worked too well, leaving it with a bewildering 96 categories of goods in 15,100 specifications, including a fridge that pickles Korean *kimchee* cabbage and a washing machine that also cleans sweet potatoes. Most of these variants add more to production costs and complexity than they will ever add to sales. Worse, the group has moved beyond white goods into computers, mobile phones (where sales have badly disappointed), and even interior design and pharmaceuticals. All with unlimited potential, insists Mr Zhang.

This attitude is widespread in China. Rather than focusing on a core business or dominating a few markets, as western, Japanese, and South Korean managers have slowly learned to do, their Chinese counterparts quit any market where competition is rising, as so many other profitable opportunities beckon. Lack of accountability – not even Mr Zhang can say who really owns Haier – and cheap loans from state banks encourage this trend.[2]

[2] Extracts from 'Haier's purpose' © *The Economist Newspaper Limited* (20 March 2004).

employees and other stakeholders in the firm, and can often closely monitor the status of their investments through their seats on the supervisory board or by means of direct contacts (Casper, 2000). Despite the recent expansion of capital markets, Germany remains a *bank-centered financial system.*[3] The majority of German firms continue to rely on banks and retained earnings to finance investments.

Small and medium-sized enterprise (SME) owners have been criticized for avoiding listing in order to prevent any dilution of their control and for their unwillingness to reveal profitability (*Herr im Hause Mentalität*). Such SMEs have not made much use of share capital as a means of meeting their growing financing needs, despite reforms aimed at making it easier for them to do so (the 1986 introduction of a 'second market', or *geregelter Markt,* and the 1994 Law on Small Public Companies, or *Gesetz über Kleine Aktiengesellschaften*).

Case: Grohe AG[4]

The disadvantages of being listed from the point of view of small and medium-sized family-owned firms

Friedrich Grohe AG & Co. KG, which was founded in 1911, manufactures sanitation products that range from single taps to electronic water management systems. In 1991, the favourable market situation induced the family to make the company public, both to gain access to funds for growth and to enable the family owners to cash in some of their shares on attractive terms. At the launch, Friedrich Grohe AG floated 1.3 million non-voting shares to the public, with the Grohe family holding all of the remaining 1.7 million ordinary shares. Members of the Grohe family also filled all the seats on the supervisory board. But in the late 1990s, with the stock trading at disappointing levels, the Grohe family decided to delist and go private again. The reasons given were as follows:

1. to avoid ongoing listing costs

2. to prevent a possible hostile takeover by a competitor

3. to achieve greater flexibility from operating as a different legal corporate entity, and

4. the family's unwillingness to raise equity at the low prices commanded by its stock.

As the company's major shareholder, the Grohe family considered that their firm belonged to an industry that investors considered 'boring and unattractive'. As a result, they felt that the company was in the undesirable position of being unable to attract further capital through share offerings, while they were at the same time constrained by the 'inflexible legal duties' of a listed stock corporation.

---

[3] For an extended overview of the measures that have been taken to make the capital markets more attractive in Germany, see Schaede (2000).

[4] This case draws on Nowak (2001).

The SMEs, on the other hand, argue that there remain barriers to listing. For example, continuing credit institutions – in effect, banks – must be involved in the first segment of trading (i.e. issuing shares). As the banks are concerned about their reputation they are thought to be careful about dealing with new entrepreneurs. In contrast to the situation in the USA or the UK, therefore, it is difficult for young entrepreneurs to raise equity capital. This is seen as an impediment to the growth of young dynamic companies in fast-moving technology or services sectors (Vitols and Woolcock, 1997). Another consequence is that capital markets tend to be smaller and to have fewer public companies than in the UK and the USA. Even during the stock market boom of 1999/2000, it was clear that the activity included only a handful of companies in certain industries (Schaede, 2000).

From the late 1990s, this handful of large German companies increasingly turned to the global capital markets for funding. In order to gain access to the liquid US capital markets, German firms had to adopt US accounting standards. The German accounting system adopts a long-term view and is investment rather than trading orientated, profit figures and asset values tend to be *under*stated. Furthermore, it allows for building up 'hidden reserves', also due to the traditional German emphasis on exercising 'commercial caution'. Overall, the adoption of US accounting standards by some large German firms means that they are more in line with international practices and that the transparency of their published accounts has improved significantly (Schlie and Warner, 2000).

The transparency of accounts, or increased information disclosure, in turn, is positively related to corporate social responsibility. Providing increased disclosures is arguably responsive to the needs of several stakeholders. Firms that engage in socially responsive activities are said to provide more informative and/or extensive disclosures than do companies that are less focused on advancing social goals (Gelb and Strawser, 2001). In addition, it has been found that socially responsible firms are more likely to provide this increased disclosure through better investor relations practices. Investor relations, however, have only recently become important in the German model of corporate governance as it is essentially a bank-based model.

The structure of ownership

Owner–company relations in the 'large firm' Rhineland model are most often characterized by *one or more large shareholders* with a strategic (rather than pure share value maximization) motivation for ownership. A total of 90 per cent of listed companies in Germany have a shareholder with at least a 10 per cent stake in the company (Seibert, 1997). The types of investor likely to have strategic interests – enterprises, banks and the public sector – together hold 57 per cent of shares (or 42.1 per cent, 10.3 per cent and 4.3 per cent, respectively). Enterprises generally pursue strategic business interests. The state generally pursues some public goal. The large German banks have tended to view their shareholdings as a mechanism for protecting their loans and strengthening their business relationships with companies rather than as a direct source of income (Vitols, 2001: 342). Until recently, this web of *cross-shareholdings* and *Konzerne* had partly been maintained by a rigid tax of over 40 per cent on the sale of shares by corporations.

From the end of the 1990s onwards, rather like the changes that took place in the large German firms, large banks have reduced the size of most of their equity stakes in non-financial companies in order to reduce risk exposure and the likelihood of having to bail out a client. These changes in the 'large firm' financial model accelerated in the 1990s as a result of financial internationalization and the efforts of the German financial and industrial community to transform Frankfurt into an international financial centre. It could, in fact, be argued that the German financial model is increasingly becoming two distinct (though intertwined) models: a finance and corporate governance model for the small and medium-sized companies (the *Mittelstand*) and a different model for the large firms (Deeg, 1997). The German *Mittelstand* firms are usually family owned, but are sometimes also tied by shareholdings to larger firms.

The ownership types having smaller shareholdings – investment funds, pension funds/insurance companies and households – account for only 35 per cent of total shareholdings of the large German companies (or 7.6 per cent, 12.4 per cent and 14.6 per cent, respectively). The Rhineland system is, then, characterized by concentrated ownership by actors pursuing a mix of financial and strategic goals (Vitols, 2001). Hence, despite the tendency for the German 'large firm' financial model to adopt features of the Anglo-Saxon model of finance, a least one critical distinction remains: the majority of the large German firms continue to have stable, long-term shareholdership, protecting firms from the short-termism of Anglo-Saxon capitalism.

The relationship between stakeholders and management

The relationship between the company and all the stakeholders – investors, employees and local communities dependent on the company for prosperity – tends to be closer than is the case with Anglo-Saxon corporate governance. Consistent with corporate social responsibility views, the German stakeholder model implies that management must pursue actions that are optimal for a broad class of stakeholders rather than those that serve only to maximize shareholder interests. Moreover, the German model emphasizes *long-term relationships built upon trust*. Banks in particular have retained relatively close links with companies through their role as shareholders in their own right, through their role as proxies for smaller shareholders,[5] through participation in supervisory boards or by fulfilling the role of 'lender of last resort' during crises.

The latter implies that when problems arise, the normal practice is for the stakeholders to voice concern and for changes in management to take place, rather than stakeholder 'exit' and a change in ownership. This characteristic enables implicit contractual relationships to develop between management and the stakeholders, and means that take-overs or changes in ownership are not the norm for corporate restructuring. The structure of regulation and practice tends to favour such long-term commitment to companies. For example, insider trading rules were introduced in Germany only in 1998, in part as a result of EU provision. For many years, Germany had subjected its stock exchanges to a 'gentleman's agreement' that supposedly kept bankers and executives from trading on special information.

From the end of the 1990s onwards, however, the relationships between some of the large German firms and the stakeholders have weakened. Against the German traditions

---

[5] German banks have the ability to exercise proxy votes at the shareholders' meetings of the AGs on behalf of shareholders who have deposited their shares with the banks for safe keeping.

of social responsibility, several companies have adopted a cruder form of capitalism by rigorously shifting production away from Germany to lower-cost countries, despite rearguard action by their 'social partners' in the codetermination structures. Moreover, in some large firms, corporate performance is increasingly being measured in terms of share price, thus adopting the Anglo-Saxon shareholder value concept. Having opted for an emphasis on 'shareholder value' over 'stakeholder welfare', the subsequent step large firms made was the introduction of performance-related pay schemes for executives, to ensure that managerial incentives are sufficiently aligned with shareholder interests (Schlie and Warner, 2000).

Company law and the structure of top management institutions

The clearest manifestation of established employee rights in large German companies is the *dual company board system*, with an executive (*Vorstand*) and a supervisory board (*Aufsichtsrat*). The supervisory board is mainly in charge of the selection, appointment or dismissal, and the supervision of the *Vorstand*. Its task is mainly that of supervising the functioning of the company. The supervisory board contains bank representatives and employee representatives. Half of the members of the supervisory board are chosen by shareholders and the other half are elected by workers. Since the supervisory board appoints the management board members, workers can indirectly influence management. The obligatory supervisory board system applies only to stock corporations (*Aktiengesellschaft*, or AG) and companies with limited liability (*Gesellschaft mit beschränkter Haftung*) and more than 500 employees.[6] While there are no supervisory boards in smaller firms, they often have advisory boards (*Beirat*) on which are representatives of one or more banks.

Proponents of the dual-board system argue that the supervisory board provides for more effective independent monitoring of management performance. Specifically, the membership of bankers on their clients' boards is said to provide the financier with better information and better means to control the behaviour of the borrowing firm's management. Strategic decisions, such as major investments, mergers and acquisitions, dividend policy, changes in capital structure, and appointment of top managers, are made by the supervisory board. The day-to-day running of the company, in contrast, is the responsibility of the executive or management board, which generally meets once a week and includes between five and ten of the company's top managers.

The management board is clearly separated from the supervisory board. Hence, one is not allowed to be a member of both the supervisory board and the management board. The management board has a chair, or 'speaker', who is generally considered to be 'first among equals'. Top managers have a great deal of autonomy in their individual areas of responsibility (generally defined by function, such as finance, production, personnel and social policy, etc.). Major decisions or proposals to the supervisory board are reached through consensus. The separate appointment of managers by the supervisory board reduces the dependency of individual members on the chair/speaker (Vitols, 2001: 344).

---

[6] See Baums (1994) for an elaborate explanation of the composition and functioning of the supervisory board.

Consensus and the institutions of employee representation

As indicated, employees in large German companies enjoy strong 'voice' thanks to *corporatist bargaining and codetermination*. Every plant with at least five regular employees is entitled under the Works Constitution Act 1972 (*Betriebsverfassungsgesetz*) to elect a works council. This works council has the right to negotiate key issues with management, including the hiring of new employees, the introduction of new technology, use of overtime and short-working time, and, in the case of mass redundancies, the negotiation of social plans (*Sozialpläne*) covering redeployment severance payments and early retirement.

As indicated, employee representatives are also included on German supervisory boards under the 1976 Codetermination Act (*Mitbestimmungsgesetz*), which applies to almost all companies with 2000 or more employees. This law makes the following key provisions.

- Employee representatives are to comprise half of the supervisory board representatives, and shareholder representatives the other half. Shareholders, however, elect the chairperson, who hold the casting vote in cases of 'deadlock' between shareholder and employee blocs.

- The number of supervisory board seats total 12 in the case of companies with between 2000 and 10,000 employees, 16 in the case of companies with between 10,000 and 20,000 employees, and 20 in the case of companies with more than 20,000 employees.

- In the case of companies with between 2000 and 20,000 employees, two employee representatives can be union functionaries (i.e. non-employees); in the case of companies with more than 20,000 employees, three may be union functionaries.

In practice there is typically a close overlap between codetermination at board level and plant level; the head employee representative on the supervisory board is typically a leading works council member (Vitols, 2001: 343–4).

Consensus has a higher priority than in the Anglo-Saxon system, both within society and within the company. Within the economy as a whole, consensus is supported by the social market economy; within the company it is supported by solidarity in the shape of moderate wage and skill differentials, and institutions such as works councils (Woolcock, 1996).

Corporate restructuring

The German financial system and the greater *protection from hostile take-over* it affords help to explain the survival of many small and medium-sized companies in Germany. The *Mittelstand* model is based on close, long-term relationships between the many regional cooperative and municipal banks and firms to which banks provide not only long-term finance, but also an increasing number of non-financial business services – notably business consulting to their clients. This model is arguably most responsible for the successful adjustment of German industry since the early 1970s (Deeg, 1997). The close relationship of these banks with local industry is demonstrated by the fact that their boards are typically composed of local industrialists (Sabel *et al.*, 1987: 36). This not only provides a close connection between industry and banking, but also forges horizontal links between SMEs in a region. Moreover, the guaranteed financial support enables SMEs to grow into medium-sized firms more easily than is the case for their UK and US counterparts.

As indicated, the use of take-overs in corporate restructuring has been the exception rather than the rule in the Rhineland model. Hostile take-overs were prevented from occurring through legal safeguards and the high degree of concentration of corporate control (in terms of bank ownership and/or voting rights). Groups of banks have acted as 'crisis cartels' to assist in the restructuring of traditional industries or to rescue ailing giants (Lane, 1994). When companies begin to run into difficulties it is the major share-holders, usually the banks, that step in to coordinate a rescue. Rather than sell up to a predatory holding company, which would probably realize the value of assets 'locked up' in its structure, the German approach is to seek to preserve as much as possible.

From the end of the 1990s, however, like their Anglo-Saxon counterparts, large German companies have started to use domestic and foreign take-overs to restructure.

> For example, in 1997, Krupp-Hoesch, a German steel conglomerate, launched a hostile take-over bid for its local rival Thyssen. In April 1999, as part of a shake-up in the German telecommunications industry, Mannesman staged a domestic take-over of rival O.tel.o. and, in May 1999, launched a bid for the UK mobile phone provider Orange.

Other examples can be found in the car industry, and in the chemical and life sciences. The question arises as to whether the Rhineland model is, indeed, adopting elements of the Anglo-Saxon system in response to increasing and new forms of competition. On the surface, it seems like this is happening. When looking at the details, one will find that most if not all of these take-overs failed or ended in a 'voluntary' merger. Hence, while the large firm model has been changing and seems slowly to be adapting to increased global competition, the embeddedness of the model explains that its deep-rooted features are preserved and remain visible through the changes.

> It is perhaps illustrative that the bid of Krupp-Hoesch (Krupp) for Thyssen AG in 1997 provoked an outbreak of public opposition from politicians, union representatives, the media and employees, as well as the management of the target company. The leader of the IG Metall union, Klaus Zwickel, accused Krupp management of using 'wild west' methods, and Chancellor Helmut Kohl urged both parties to find a 'prudent solution' based on careful consideration of their 'social responsibility'.

The Japanese model of corporate governance
Capital markets and regulation

Rather like the Rhineland model, the Japanese model is characterized by corporate *reliance on bank lending or on retained earnings*. In contrast to the German banks, Japanese banks were not universal banks; until the Financial System Reform Act was introduced in 1993, there was a clear separation between commercial banks (specializing in deposits and loans) and securities firms (in charge of securities underwriting and dealing).

Table 6.3   The Anglo-Saxon and Rhineland models compared

	Anglo-Saxon model	Rhineland model
Focus	shareholder value	stakeholder value
Finance	liquid capital markets	bank/debt finance
Structure of ownership	widely dispersed	concentrated
Relationship between stakeholders and management	arm's length	long-term relationship built on trust
Corporate control	market	supervisory board
Corporate restructuring	take-over mechanism	under assistance of banks
Company law	unitary board	dual board

From the late 1980s onwards, large Japanese firms have shown high levels of self-finance and increased use of securities markets (at home and abroad). From that time onwards, the large city banks, which used to concentrate on providing loans to large firms, were forced to actively seek new borrowers and started to channel funds into the smaller firms. Until 1985, Japan's small and medium-sized firms had to rely on their local banks, which did not have sufficient resources. From the late 1980s onwards, the small and medium-sized firms have, thus, found borrowing restrictions easing. From the 1990s onwards, the crisis in the financial sector under the recession forced banks to become more selective in their lending habits. Smaller firms in particular have been hit hardest by these changes. Unable to go to the bond markets and restricted in their bank borrowing, these firms face hard times.

Also rather like the German situation, in Japan the corporate governance and finance models seem to be moving towards a hybrid model. That is, the traditional bank model continues to be used in the small and medium-sized firm model, while the large firm model incorporates some elements of the Anglo-Saxon model. As with the Rhineland model, however, we cannot speak of convergence towards the Anglo-Saxon model as this would imply more fundamental change.

The structure of ownership

The majority of shares of major corporations in Japan are held by *stable shareholders*, which include other corporations in the same business group, major creditors and major customers/suppliers. These shareholders hold shares primarily to maintain their relationships rather than for financial gain. Often, shareholding is reciprocal and forms a dense network of cross-shareholding.

For example, in 1990, Mitsubishi Corporation owned 1.6 per cent of Mitsubishi Heavy Industries, which, in turn, owned 3.2 per cent of Mitsubishi Corporation.

Although these cross-holdings are usually small on a bilateral basis, between 10 per cent and 25 per cent of all the outstanding shares of group members are generally held within the *keiretsu* (corporate group) itself.

Banks and insurance companies often number among the major shareholders of their main large clients. While, until recently, Japanese banks were prohibited by law from holding more than 5 per cent of the outstanding stock of any other firm, the main bank could mobilize shareholdings by the group-affiliated trust bank, insurance company, trading company and other firms for reasons of concerted voting or to protect a customer firm from hostile take-over. Banks thus also allow large firms to have a long-term strategy.

The bank crisis and the need for Japanese banks to boost their capital-to-asset ratios at the end of the 1990s forced banks to sell some of their shareholdings. The banks did not, however, sell shares of companies in which they held a larger amount of the companies' stocks than any other bank, and thus for which they represented the 'main bank'. Hence, like German firms, Japanese companies can invest while not having to worry about short-term profits for reasons of stock market performance.

Similar to the German *Mittelstand*, Japanese SMEs are also usually family owned and, if listed on the stock market, are tied to larger companies, thus providing them with stable shareholdership. Until now, and despite some changes, the deep-rooted and typical features of the Japanese system continue to survive. Indeed, even after the stock market bubble had burst, a survey of 2426 companies in 1999 showed that 42 per cent of outstanding shares were deemed stable, and 16 per cent were believed to be cross-held.

The relationship between stakeholders and management

Rather like the German situation, relationships between stakeholders and management in large, small and medium-sized Japanese companies are close. Relationships are especially close between a company and its 'main bank'. The relationship between a main bank and its customer can be viewed as a particularly intense manifestation of relationship banking. The main bank not only positions one of its employees as a board member, when requested it also seconds bank officers to customer clients as full-time employees. The main bank also plays the leading role in monitoring and, if essential, in intervention.

Indeed, the most powerful safeguard in the Japanese corporate governance system is the ability of one or more equity-owning stakeholders to intervene directly and explicitly in the affairs of another company when this is required in order to correct a problem. This is by no means a frequent occurrence, but it is common – indeed, expected – in certain circumstances. Such assistance can be as modest as helping a troubled company generate new sales, or as dramatic as injecting new capital, restructuring assets and replacing top management. As indicated, and like the German situation, such intervention is typically led by a company's main bank, usually to remedy non-performance in the face of impending financial distress. Unlike in Germany, however, intervention in Japan is by no means limited to banks. Although less common, major industrial stakeholders will sometimes take quick, decisive steps to supplant an important supplier's or customer's autonomy with temporary de facto administrative control when non-performance becomes imminent (Kester, 1996).

The stability of cross-shareholding patterns in Japan could be seen as an indication of the fact that, as in Germany, Japanese capital markets will tend to remain relatively illiquid and will continue to be prevented from playing an active role in corporate control in the foreseeable future. Unlike in Germany, however, as a result of the morally hazardous behaviour[7] of banks during the stock market boom, the Japanese banks' monitoring abilities have been called into questioned. Moreover, the banks' diminished control over the supply of capital to the large firm segment and the practice of *zaiteku* [8] has greatly reduced both the ability of the banks to undertake corrective action as well as to perform their corporate control function effectively. As a consequence, and given the continuing importance of major aspects of the traditional model, one option could be the strengthening of the role of the board of directors and the introduction of a legislative requirement for outside directors to occupy a certain number of seats on the board (Koen, 2001).

Company law and the structure of top management institutions

Like the Anglo-Saxon model, Japanese corporate law is based on the *unitary board* system. Though outwardly similar in some respects, Japanese boards differ from those of most Anglo-Saxon companies in numerous ways. The Japanese Commercial Code stipulates that a shareholders' meeting elects directors and makes decisions about 'fundamental changes' to the company, such as a merger, a sale of all the firm's assets and amendments to the firm's charter. There must be at least three directors. Directors constitute the board of directors. The board elects representative directors, the Japanese counterparts of US and UK executives. There must be at least one representative director. Representative directors are managers, and they run the company.

In reality, the board of directors in a typical large Japanese company consists of about 20 to 25 directors, most of whom are at least 50 years old. However, unlike normal practice in Anglo-Saxon economies, it is rare to find independent, outside directors on Japanese boards. Japanese company law does not require outside directors. Instead, virtually all Japanese directors are *inside* managing directors chosen from the ranks of top management itself. Although, formally, shareholders are supposed to elect (usually unanimously) directors at annual meetings, the majority are nominated by management itself. Indeed, most members of the board are appointed as a reward, near the end of their careers, and regard the position as an honour rather than an opportunity to contribute (Williams, 2000). Major share-owning stakeholders in a Japanese company often obtain indirect representation through former executives that assume positions on the boards of companies with which their former employers do business. Typically, an executive from a share-owning corporation, bank or other financial institution who is well into his career (most often in his mid-fifties) will be 'retired' from his first job and start a 'second career' as a director of the associated company in question. In some instances, mid-career executive transfers become permanent when the transferred executive rises relatively quickly to the position of managing director (Lightfood, 1992).

Any control over the president in the past came from the banks; however, now these are much weakened by their own severe problems, any controls largely come from the

---

[7] Japanese banks were not selective in lending money and lent to dubious companies. Morally hazardous behaviour is behaviour without an appropriate level of care.

[8] *Zaiteku* means profit-seeking financial activity by the corporate treasury departments of large Japanese companies, which has resulted in an uncoupling of financial policies and financial executive decisions from overall corporate strategy.

president's predecessors: they are normally appointed, frequently for life, as advisers (*soudan-yaku*) or senior advisers (*meiyo-yaku*), who generally have to be consulted on all major decisions (Williams, 2000). Moreover, instead of outside directors, Japanese company law requires *kansayaku*, often (somewhat misleadingly) translated as 'statutory auditors'. These are elected at the shareholders' meeting and do not have to be accountants or other professionals. *A statutory auditor* is responsible for overseeing the activities of management. This is understood to include the legality of management's activities. The statute requires collaboration between accounting auditors and statutory auditors.

Consensus and the institutions of employee representation

Japanese company law operates on a one-tier board system. Employee participation, or codetermination, has not been adopted in Japan. Employees are, however, important constituencies in Japan. A traditional, and frequently uttered, statement is that Japanese companies are run in the best interests of employees and not in the interests of shareholders. Thus a common phenomenon is that when a Japanese company is facing financial distress, management will cut dividends before it starts firing employees. In fact, lifetime employment, compensation tied to seniority and company-by-company labour unions (as discussed in detail in Chapter 5) are often singled out as the distinctive characteristics of Japanese companies, and have functioned to keep employee supremacy alive in the past decade (Hideki Kanda, 1998).

Corporate restructuring

Rather like the German situation, as a consequence of stable shareholding patterns, a hostile take-over is very difficult to implement and in fact rarely happens in Japan. Also rather like the German situation, mergers and rescue operations to aid financially troubled firms are generally set up by the main bank. In addition, past research suggests that the Japanese government has also been closely involved in the corporate governance process by initiating mergers and persuading banks to set up rescue operations. Hence, despite the fact that the government is not a shareholder, it has intervened substantially in corporate governance issues.

> For example, the Ministry of International Trade and Industry (MITI) played an active role in the merger between two large automobile companies, Nissan and Prince, in 1965, and in the merger of two major steel companies, Fuji and Yawata, in 1970. MITI is also argued to have played a key role in persuading Sumitomo bank to rescue Mazda.

Case: Corporate Governance in Russia

After the break-up of the Soviet Union in 1991 and the election of Boris Yeltsin as president, corporate managers soon became de facto owners as a result of the Russian government's privatization programme. One objective of privatization, launched in 1993, was to place shares of formerly state-owned enterprises into the hands of managers, other employees and all Russian citizens. By the time the privatization process ended in 1994, many enterprise managers had become majority or large shareholders in their firms, accumulating shares at nominal cost from other employees and the public. Many managers utilized their powerful positions to engage in self-enriching practices such as asset stripping and setting up false subsidiaries through which they channelled cash and valuable assets. Owner-managers, in addition, often crushed the rights of other shareholders by not holding shareholder meetings, deleting names from stock registers and other crude practices (McCarthy and Puffer, 2002).

Banks were able to keep some control over the financial accounts of enterprises through legislation that required all enterprises to hold their accounts in a single bank, and allowed banks to intervene in decisions on how to divide up enterprise profits between consumption and investment funds. The enforcement of such measures was, however, haphazard (Litwack, 1995). Moreover, the vast majority of Russian banks did not participate actively in the privatization process. Minor participation in enterprise privatization was followed by the banks' minor involvement in corporate governance. In addition, inflation led to the popularity of short-term lending, making unnecessary and cost-ineffective any monitoring of the borrower's performance (Belyanova and Rozinsky, 1995). Industrial management control thus remained unchallenged by the banks.

Major exceptions to this general picture of the Russian bank sector are the so-called 'hard-currency islands' – banks specializing in hard-currency operations (including hard-currency-denominated loans), with Russian exporters as their main customers. This small group of 'export-sector banks' (ESBs) has tended to overcome the Russian banks' general inability to interfere in corporate governance. The specialization of these banks in hard-currency operations, supported by their larger-than-average size and lending capacity, has determined their capacity to exercise control over the industrial enterprises.

In general, it could be argued that ineffective and conflicting laws, lack of enforcement and a limited infrastructure for protecting shareholders' rights help to explain Russia's dysfunctional corporate governance system in the aftermath of the privatization process. A major example is Russian company law. This law, though defining a two-tier structure for corporate governance boards, promoted a governance structure that was strongly dominated by major shareholders. The law did not allow outsiders who did not represent the interests of the major shareholders on to the board of directors. Neither did it automatically allow representatives of insiders, such as managers or workers, on to the board unless they were also significant shareholders or their legal representatives. A shareholders' meeting directly appoints a president and a management board head from the members of a board of directors. The auditing committee, as a supervisory board, is also appointed directly by shareholders.

One damaging result of the enormous power of the owner-managers and the consequent malpractice was that the prospect of attracting investment to Russian enterprises had all but vanished. Indeed, the implications of the privatization process in Russia virtually blocked equity market development. On the one hand, managers and employees are expected to be very conservative shareholders, reluctant to sell their shares; on the other hand, industrial shares are not as attractive as some others to potential buyers because of the low dividends they offer and the virtual impossibility of obtaining large blocks of shares. The equity market, therefore, tends to be thin and incapable of providing adequate control mechanisms (Belyanova and Rozinsky, 1995).

The 1998 economic crisis, which had a very adverse effect on Russian corporate life, made large Soviet companies aware of the fact that effective corporate governance is a crucial underpinning to business success. With the election of Vladimir Putin at the turn of the decade, and Putin's law-and-order platform, which included steps to stabilize the economy and crack down on crime (including destructive business activities), Russia chose to move forward with reform of the corporate governance system. The subsequent development of institutions to support effective corporate governance was a joint effort of Putin's team and private business groups, who shared this objective. This business–government collaboration resulted in new legislation and keener enforcement, as well as a developing culture of more openness and responsibility. The combined result of these developments, together with the need to attract investment capital, as well as the prospect of benefiting more from public listing than from private plundering, motivated enterprises, among other things to:

- operate in a way that benefits all shareholders

- maintain a focus on long-term financial returns

- disclose to shareholders, and the appropriate regulatory and international bodies, accurate, consolidated and timely information

- use internationally accepted standards and accounting principles verified by an independent, qualified audit

- disclose their ultimate ownership structure, including beneficial share ownership by executive officers, board members and any group holding more than 5 per cent

- to have a board of directors that is elected by and accountable to the shareholders, and that includes qualified non-executive directors.

While there is still a long way to go to improve corporate governance practices in Russian business, compared with the situation in the past, it could be argued that substantial progress has been made. This is especially so since Russia started with a blank slate, with no institutional, knowledge or cultural basis on which to base a market economy.

Questions

1. Explain the definition of corporate governance that is used in this case. Use evidence from the case to support your argument.

2. What corporate governance aspects are mentioned in the case that help to explain that some companies in some countries are better at attracting investment capital than others?

3. What corporate governance system would, do you think, be most appropriate in the Russian context – the Japanese or German bank-based system of corporate governance, or the Anglo-Saxon system, and why?

4. Is corporate social responsibility (CSR) important in the Russian corporate governance system? How is this expressed?

Corporate governance systems in western Europe

As indicated above, continental European models of corporate governance are situated between the Rhineland and Anglo-Saxon models. As a consequence of the implementation of European directives, and as a result of the need to adapt to the requirements of the financial markets (the role of which has become more significant), changes have been introduced in the corporate governance systems of continental European countries.

The *central part of internal company life and structure* has been left outside this harmonization, mainly as a consequence of member states' reluctance to modify the internal company structure, which is often based on delicate balances of influence and power. These matters deal with core rules in the governance debate, such as:

- the structure of the board
- the corporate control market, especially the regulation of take-overs and protection against them
- the rules on groups of companies, and
- the protection of minority shareholders (Wymeersch, 1998).

Hence, while change and harmonization efforts have taken place in European corporate governance, differences in policy practice and philosophy have frustrated efforts to agree on a number of measures, hampering the development of a common system of European corporate governance.

The complexity of the comparative analysis of many countries makes it essential to use more descriptive statistics than in the first section of this chapter. Comparative statistics help to provide a clear picture of the diversity in corporate governance and finance practices that exists in Europe. This section closes with a case study of the Chinese corporate governance situation. The Chinese case is interesting in that it provides us with another example of a major post-communist country in transition.

Capital markets and regulation

All European states have their own stock exchanges – usually one per country, although some states have maintained several, albeit increasingly integrated, exchanges. In order to measure the significance of the stock exchange phenomenon in the different economies of Europe several yardsticks are being used. The traditional yardstick is the relationship between market capitalization[9] and GDP (Table 6.4). Market capitalization is assumed to be related to GDP because a larger economy would normally produce larger firms and hence a higher capitalization.

Table 6.4 rates the EU member states according to their relative involvement in the securities (bonds and shares) business in the 1990s. In the hypothesis that there should be a linear relationship between market capitalization and GDP it is apparent that five states show a higher than average intensity in the use of the securities markets. The UK, with 11.2 per cent of EU GDP, holds a concentration of 35.49 per cent of the capitalization of the entire Union. Similar disparities are shown for Switzerland, Sweden, the Netherlands and Luxembourg. All of these are states in which the securities business has experienced the strongest development. These states are also most concerned with market organization, regulation of the securities business and financing in general. This evidence partly suggests that the Netherlands, Sweden, Luxembourg and Switzerland are exhibiting a tendency to shift from the insider model of corporate control to the outsider model, in which corporate control is left to the markets.

At the opposite end of the spectrum, Spain, Austria, Italy, France and Germany are the states in which capital markets play a less important role in comparison to their relative economic weight. The figures are particularly striking for Germany and Italy, two states that stand for 40 per cent of EU GDP and for 36 per cent of EU population, but only for 18.95 per cent of capitalization. This also means that the industry in the aforementioned five states – or 67 per cent of the European economy – is mainly supported by financing means other than securities financing, and that securities financing has not been widely practised in two-thirds of Europe. The latter figures are the more striking as these states contain some of the larger European firms (Wymeersch, 1998).

In between are the smaller European economies – that is, Belgium, Portugal, Greece, Ireland, Finland, Denmark and Norway, where securities capitalization is more or less in balance with their economic weight. The findings from this comparison confirm the divide between the Anglo-Saxon and the Rhineland models, as well as the fact that the vast majority of European states are *not* market-orientated. Almost inevitably, since the degree of market capitalization could be seen as the most clear expression of the choice of a certain type of corporate governance model, the dividing line that appears in this data shows up in many other fields of corporate organization and regulation.

The number of shares available on a market also illustrates its importance. In this respect, Table 6.5 once again confirms that, in the 1990s, the Rhineland model was still less market orientated than the Anglo-Saxon model. The US and the UK markets show the highest capitalization ratio. The higher ratio of Japan in comparison with Germany and France indicates that large Japanese firms are turning more to the securities markets for financing than are large German and French firms.

---

[9] Market capitalization, also called market value, is the number of shares in existence multiplied by the share price.

Table 6.4 Markets classified by % of GDP (1996)

Market	Market capitalization ecu mn*	GDP ecu bn	Market capitalization in % of GDP
Austria (Vienna)	28,719	233.3	12.31
Italy (Milan)	206,997	1,087.2	19.04
Portugal (Lisbon)	19,706	99.8	19.75
Germany	**531,533**	**2,412.5**	**22.03**
Greece (Athens)	18,988	77.8	24.41
France (Paris)	471,426	1,537.6	30.66
Denmark (Copenhagen)	57,281	173.3	33.05
Spain (Madrid)	194,681	559.6	34.79
Belgium (Brussels)	95,751	269.2	35.57
Finland (Helsinki)	49,444	125.0	39.56
Ireland	27,658	64.3	43.01
Norway (Oslo)	45,792	103.4	44.29
Netherlands (Amsterdam)	223,452	395.5	56.50
Sweden (Stockholm)	194,045	230.6	84.15
Switzerland	322,354	306.1	105.31
UK (London)	**1,382,809**	**1,010.8**	**136.80**
Luxembourg	25,909	10.6	244.42

*ecu mn = US$1.2 million

Source: Wymeersch (1998).

Table 6.5 Selected European markets compared with the world markets (1996)

Countries	Cap. ecu mn	GDP ecu bn	Cap. GDP %	Number of securities	Domestic turnover ecu mn
France	471,426	1,538	30.66	686	220,608
Germany	531,553	2,413	22.03	681	621,454
UK	1,382,809	1,011	136.80	2,339	452,019
US	6,702,115	5,967	112.32	7,740	5,525,408
Japan	2,398,523	3,626	66.15	1,766	703,127

Source: Wymeersch (1998: 1061).

The structure of ownership

An analysis of the patterns of share ownership can be carried out in several ways. One method of research relies on macro figures and yields information on the amount of capital shares held by the different classes of securities holder, such as physical persons, institutional investors, and so on (Table 6.2) or on the amount of voting rights (Table 6.6).

Looking at Table 6.6, it appears that there are clear differences between nations, giving the impression of strong national effects. For example, as already indicated, dispersed ownership is common in the UK and (to a lesser extent) in the Netherlands, but rare or non-existent in the rest of Europe. Foreign ownership is predominant in Belgium and Spain, but is uncommon, or much less frequent, in the rest of Europe. Government ownership is common in Italy, Austria and, until recently, in France, but not in the Netherlands, the UK or Belgium. These differences in ownership structure can largely be explained by historical facts. Moreover, the evolution of ownership structures is path dependent.

Ownership structures in French corporations to some extent depart from the path-dependent evolution. French corporations used to be characterized by a large share of government ownership. This was partly a consequence of nationalization after the Second World War and by the Mitterand government in the early 1980s. It also, however, reflected the French tradition of government intervention. Large-scale privatization, in recent times, explains why the large share of government ownership in France has been reversed. Another interesting feature of French ownership structure is the role played by holding companies originally established by industrial companies to overcome financing constraints, which also helps to explain the frequency of cross-holdings and dominant minority ownership.

The high degree of government ownership in Austria dates back to nationalization after the Second World War. Finland was a late industrializer, which may help to explain why the government was given a role in the catch-up process (especially in forest products). Italy is notable for the extent of state ownership, which dates back to industrial reconstruction after the Second World War. State ownership of some large Norwegian energy companies (Norsk, Hydro, Statoil) may be explained by a combination of nationalism and inadequate domestic finance.

In Belgium, the strategy of attracting foreign direct investment from the USA in particular became a national economic strategy after the Second World War, which helps to explain the high frequency of foreign ownership. Spain has a large number of multinational companies, which in part reflects a conscious policy to attract foreign direct investment initiated by the Franco government. A high frequency of family and cooperative ownership in Denmark is partly attributable to the small size of the average company and a relative factor advantage in agricultural products. Sweden's large share of dominant minority ownership is partly a consequence of the German-style industrialization in which banks and large entrepreneurs played a major role. As indicated, in Germany banks played an active role in the industrialization process and financial institutions continue to exercise dominant minority control over many large companies, although founding families have often continued to exercise some control (by large shareholdings) even in limited companies. The UK was the first nation to industrialize, and funds for large

Table 6.6 Ownership of the 100 largest companies in 12 European nations (1990) (share of total turnover in parentheses)

	Dispersed ownership	Dominant ownership	Family owned	Foreign owned	Cooperative	Government owned
Austria	0	7 (4.7)	25 (17.9)	38 (33.5)	10 (9.9)	20 (33.9)
Belgium	4 (7.7)	20 (28.5)	6 (7.8)	61 (46.7)	3 (1.0)	6 (8.2)
Denmark	10 (11.5)	9 (6.5)	30 (30.1)	23 (18.1)	17 (19.9)	11 (13.2)
Finland	12 (9.9)	25 (35.3)	23 (11.1)	11 (4.6)	10 (11.5)	19 (27.6)
France	16 (17.7)	28 (25.4)	15 (9.4)	16 (9.7)	3 (1.3)	22 (36.4)
Germany	9 (15.7)	30 (40.5)	26 (17.3)	22 (16.1)	3 (1.6)	10 (8.8)
UK	61 (59.6)	11 (13.8)	6 (4.8)	18 (18.9)	1 (0.5)	3 (2.4)
Italy	0	22 (32.0)	20 (16.7)	29 (13.5)	0	29 (37.9)
Netherlands	23 (47.4)	16 (12.3)	7 (5.4)	34 (27.1)	13 (4.4)	7 (3.4)
Norway	6 (8.3)	14 (12.7)	29 (15.2)	19 (15.9)	19 (8.8)	13 (39.1)
Spain	6 (6.2)	22 (23.0)	8 (7.4)	45 (34.2)	5 (1.9)	14 (27.2)
Sweden	4 (7.7)	31 (40.3)	18 (18.6)	14 (7.7)	12 (10.7)	21 (14.9)

Source: Pedersen and Thomsen (1997: 795).

Notes:

Dispersed ownership	No single owner owns more than 20 per cent of the company's shares.
Dominant ownership	One owner (person, family, company) owns a sizeable (voting) share (20% < share < 50%) of the company.
Personal/family ownership	One person or a family owns a (voting) majority of the company. Foundation (trust) ownership is included in this category because it reflects the will of a personal founder and often gives the family (heirs) some degree of control.
Government ownership	The (local or national) government owns a (voting) majority of the company.
Foreign ownership	A foreign multinational (MNE) owns a (voting) majority of the company.
Cooperative	The company is registered as a cooperative or (in a few cases) is majority owned by a group of cooperatives.

enterprises had to be attracted from a number of individual investors. The Netherlands is said to have been influenced by its proximity to the UK, which may have increased the frequency of dispersed ownership (Pedersen and Thomsen, 1997).

The relationship between stakeholders and management

In general, relationships between companies and stakeholders tend to be closer in continental Europe than in the UK and the USA. In continental Europe shareholder value, and thus the shareholders, are not exclusively given priority as in the Anglo-Saxon model. While there is increasing attention to shareholder value, the stakeholder model, with its attention to wider social concerns, is still prevalent.

In most continental European countries, relationships between banks and companies have not been as close as in Germany and Japan. Banks did, and do, provide finance to companies but generally do not perform the same role as in the Rhineland model. Moreover, the relatively close relationships, based on trust, between banks and companies have become harder to maintain. EU legislation has limited bank holdings in all EU countries. International capital adequacy rules agreed under the auspices of the Bank for International Settlements (BIS) and largely incorporated into the EU through the EU's Capital Adequacy Directive, have increased the costs of bank equity holdings. Deregulation has resulted in increased competition among banks as well as between banks and other financial institutions. This has tended to undermine relationship banking.

Company law and the structure of top management institutions[10]

The unitary-board system

In most EU member states, listed companies are obliged by statute to organize a board of directors, which is usually composed of three directors. Most European company laws have adopted the unitary board structure. Unitary boards are the exclusive board structure in the UK, Belgium (except for banks), Denmark, Greece, Ireland, Luxembourg, Spain, Italy, Sweden and Switzerland.

In most systems with unitary boards, the UK excepted, members are formally elected by a general meeting of shareholders, which also determines the number of seats on the board. In all systems, research results show that the main sources of influence on the appointment of directors come from the chairman of the board, or CEO, often supported by the full board. Only in Germany, France and Belgium, do shareholders have a stronger (in Germany because of the *Aufsichtsrat*) or weaker (in France and Belgium) influence on appointments. For France and Belgium, institutional investors are also mentioned as having a significant influence on board nomination: one can probably identify these 'institutional investors' as 'holding companies', in which case the finding would be comparable to that made in Germany. In each case, the larger or largest shareholder has a significant influence on the nomination of board members (Wymeersch, 1998: 1090).

In the systems where shareholders have an overwhelming influence, independent directors are seen as instrumental in balancing shareholder influence in favour of other

---

[10] I am grateful to Wymeersch (1998) for most of the information in this section.

shareholders (mainly small investors). Independent directors can only exercise 'balancing' power, keeping in check the overwhelming influence of the dominant shareholder without being able to actively direct the firm's policy. The dominant shareholder will not easily surrender this influence – except on a de facto basis – particularly as this would reduce the value of his shares. Therefore, it has been more difficult to impose independent directors on continental European schemes than in a system with wide share ownership, such as that of the USA and the UK. In Germany, where the boards are composed of representatives of either capital or labour, the issue of independent directors seems to be pointless. The debate about the designation of independent directors is still in its infancy in many European states; codes of conduct are increasingly recommending their appointment. Some larger companies seem to be following the recommendation and have publicly announced the appointment of independent directors. Their role in decision-making, their internal position and their actual practices, however, are still undefined or poorly documented (Wymeersch, 1998: 1100).

Case: Parmalat–The Failure of Italy's Corporate and Market Regulation

Next up, million of dollars worth of Parmalat bonds were sold to an estimated 100,000 unwitting mom-and-pop investors before that company's Dec. 24 bankruptcy.

'Italians feel betrayed,' says Rosarios Trefiletti, president of Federconsumatori, a Rome-based consumers' group that's filing suits and staging noisy demonstrations.

'We Italian investors get no help at all from the government,' laments Vincenzo Nieri, a retired manager of a Bristol-Myers Squibb unit in Milan. 'Nobody has ever taken the initiative to protect investors.'

Meanwhile, Berlusconi & Co. have wilfully overlooked the need for stiff penalties for accounting irregularities. ... Berlusconi's government, by contrast, essentially decriminalized most kinds of fraudulent accounting in 2001 by making it a mere misdemeanor instead of a felony. The law should be revised – but only some factions of Berlusconi's coalition agree. That hardly sends the right signal to Italy Inc. Moreover, little of the government debate on financial market reform has focused on key issues like the need for more independent board members and an autonomous audit committee. Crony boards are flourishing in Italy. Parmalat had one – stacked with family and friends of boss Calisto Tanzi. Italy urgently needs to extend the law giving minority shareholders the right to choose independent board members. It now covers only privatized former state-owned companies.[11]

---

[11] Extracts from 'Italy Needs a Renaissance in Corporate and Market Regulation, *Business Week*, 2 February 2004.

The dual-board system

In some jurisdictions, companies are headed by a two-tier board: mostly called a 'supervisory' board or a 'managing' board. In some jurisdictions this two-tier system is optional; in others it is compulsory. Membership of employees, here called 'codetermination', is usually placed at the level of the supervisory board, although in some legal systems it has been introduced in the managing board.

Systems with an *optional* two-tier board system that is not necessarily linked to co-determination can be found in Finland, in France and in smaller firms in the Netherlands. Two-tier boards without obligatory worker representation are *compulsory* for Portuguese companies. This structure is also found in Italy, where the managing board is headed by a *collegio sindacale*, whose powers and influence, however, are considerably less than those of the traditional supervisory board. Belgium is often wrongly classified among those systems with a two-tier board. This is a consequence of banking law, which recognizes the use of two-tier boards in credit institutions. No other companies may, technically, introduce a two-tiered board. Aside from Germany's large companies, the two-tier board with compulsory worker representation is also found in large Dutch and Austrian firms.

Finland has introduced an optional regime: companies opting for a one-tier board should provide for the designation of a board of three members to be elected by the general meeting of shareholders. However, the charter can stipulate for a minority of board members to be appointed by a different method (i.e. by the employees). Larger companies must appoint a 'managing director' to act within the limits of his assignment by the board of directors. Larger companies may provide for a two-tier system: the supervisory board must be composed of at least five members, elected by the general meeting or in a different way, allowing for employee representation. Although there is no compulsory system of employee representation, there is a widespread practice of organizing voluntary representation: 300 companies are reported to have voluntarily introduced this type of industrial democracy.

In **France**, too, a two-tier system may be introduced by charter provision in a public company limited by shares (*Société Anonyme,* SA). However, this is found in only about 12 per cent of French companies (Williams, 2000). The members of the management board, called *directoire*, are appointed by the supervisory board. The number of its members varies from one to five, or seven if the company is listed. The president is also appointed by the supervisory board. Members of the supervisory board cannot be members of the *directoire*. The supervisory board is appointed by the shareholders. It is composed of three to twelve members, to be increased to twenty-four in the case of a merger. In general, however, French companies are argued to be ruled by the *Président Directeur Général* (PDG), who is both chairman of the board and CEO. The possibility of challenges to the PDG is limited by the culture of the French corporate establishment, in which a very large number are graduates of a very small number of *écoles normales supérieurs* (elite universities), and there are numerous interlocking directorships and shareholdings: it is not hard for the PDG to handpick those he or she believes will support him or her (Williams, 2000).

Since 1971, **Dutch** company law has prescribed the 'structure regime' to be adopted by large corporations. The regime applies to firms that meet the following three conditions during a three-year period:

1. outstanding capital (issued capital and reserves) of at least 12 million euros according to the balance sheet
2. a works council[12]
3. at least 100 employees of the company and its dependent companies employed in the Netherlands.

When these criteria are met, the 'large' company is legally obliged to establish a supervisory board. Each of the members of this board is appointed by the board itself (called co-optation). The general meeting of shareholders and the works council is allowed to object to candidates if they believe they are not qualified, or if they judge the composition of the board to be inappropriate. Moreover, the general meeting of shareholders, the works council and the managing board is allowed to recommend candidates for appointment to the supervisory board. These recommendations are binding.

The supervisory board of the structure corporations is legally endowed with a number of compulsory powers that, under the normal regime, are allotted to the general meeting of shareholders. Thus the structure regime transfers some major competencies from the shareholders to the supervisory board. These competencies include the right to appoint and dismiss members of the managing board and to adopt the annual accounts. Furthermore, a number of major managerial decisions are compulsory, subject to approval by the supervisory board. These include the issue of shares, investment plans and company restructuring.

Companies that do not meet the aforementioned criteria for large companies are legally allowed to voluntarily opt for the structure regime by including this in their articles of association. This is only possible if they have a works council in the company. Certain types of 'large' company may request exemption from the application of the structure regime. This is granted to international concerns that have their principal headquarters in the Netherlands, function merely as management companies, and employ the majority of their employees outside the Netherlands. The Dutch subsidiaries that meet the criteria for 'large' company are then subject to a milder regime, which implies that they must have a supervisory board. However, this milder regime means that the supervisory board is not given the right to appoint and dismiss members of the managing board or to adopt the annual accounts. If a parent company, which has its principal seat in the Netherlands, is fully or partly subject to the structure regime, its subsidiary is exempt from the regime.

Under the normal regime, the establishment of a supervisory board is optional. In such a case, the members of the supervisory board are appointed by the general meeting of shareholders. The latter is endowed with considerably more power than it would be under the structure regime since it retains a number of important decision rights.

Austria has maintained the former German approach, dating back to the 1937 German law. A two-tier board is compulsory, with at least one person at management level (*Vorstand*) acting on his own responsibility. At the supervisory level, there should be at least three members. Members are elected by the general meeting, but one-third may be appointed – or revoked – by specific shareholders, such as the holders of a class of shares. The number varies according to the size of the capital.

Belgian law recognized the two-tier board, but only in the field of credit institutions. In Belgium, banks may (in practice, they are urged to) introduce a two-tier board. In

---

[12] The Dutch law on works councils requires firms with 35 employees or more to install a works council.

major Belgian banks, the board of directors acts as a supervisory board; it deals with general policy issues and is in charge of overseeing the management board's actual banking. Initially, the rules governing the composition of the board served to isolate the bank's actual management from the influence of the controlling shareholders, with the aim of ensuring that the bank was run in its own interests, rather than the interests of its controlling or referee shareholders. In the early 1990s, shareholders took over the reins of power. The objective is no longer to reduce the influence of the dominant shareholder, nor to avoid the bank functioning in the exclusive interests of its shareholders. Instead, the rule aims to exclude undesirable shareholders.

Technically, the **Italian** *società per azione* is also characterized by the presence of two levels of 'boards'. The larger companies are managed by a board of directors – the *consiglio di amministrazione* – composed of inside and outside directors. This board often elects an internal managing board, the *comitato esecutivo*. In addition, Italian law provides for a surveillance body, the *collegio sindacale*, composed of members elected by the general meeting and in charge of supervising the activities of all company organs, including the general meeting. Italian legal writers do not consider this board to be comparable to the German supervisory board, however. Instead, they classify the Italian system as belonging to the unitary board system.

Consensus and the institutions of employee representation

In some of these jurisdictions, the presence of labour representatives or other stakeholders at board level has been introduced. Boards with employee representation are, first and foremost, a German–Dutch phenomenon. However, in the 1970s, employee representation was introduced in several other European states, either as part of the unitary board's functioning or, more usually, in the two-tier structure. Apart from mandated codetermination, most states have voluntary systems of co-decision-making at board level, based either on employer-organized co-decision-making or on collective labour agreements. These evolutions are not very well documented and have not been investigated in detail (Wymeersch, 1998: 1141).

In addition to representation at board level, employees may be able to influence decision-making through their participation in other bodies, most frequently the 'enterprise council'. These are parallel bodies that are mandatory for all larger organizations whether they are engaged in business or not. These bodies are mostly not involved in corporate decision-making, but are restricted to employment conditions, including layoffs and plant closures. At the European level, a 'European Works Council' has become compulsory for all larger undertakings or groups of undertakings with at least 1000 employees within the EU, of which there are at least 150 employees in two or more member states. In the UK, however, this system continues to be opposed by the industry. The fear is that the introduction of the Works Council would be a step towards employee representation at board level.

The institution of employee representation
One-tier board systems and employee representation

Employee representation is obligatory in the one-board system in Denmark, Sweden, Luxembourg and France, and, as just explained, optional in Finland.

In **Denmark**, the Companies Act provides that half the number of the members of the boards elected by the shareholders, or by the other parties entitled to appoint directors, will be elected by employees, with a minimum of two. Companies and groups (parents and subsidiaries) located in Denmark and with at least 35 employees are subject to this regime, which is applicable to the parent companies.

In the 1977 Codetermination Act, **Sweden** introduced a system of compulsory co-determination with respect to all companies – of SA or cooperative type – that employ more than 25 people: two labour representatives must be appointed to the board. If there are more than 1000 employees, three members of the board must be designated. However, since representatives are reportedly reluctant to intervene in the board's decision-making, participation is essentially regarded as serving informational purposes only.

In **Luxembourg**, labour representation was introduced by law in 1974 with respect to public limited companies established in Luxembourg with more than 1000 employees. These companies must have a board composed of at least nine members: one-third should be elected by employees. Election is indirect: members are elected by the representatives of the employees.

In **France**, there is a threefold system of voluntary codetermination within the unitary board. Codetermination had long been opposed both by employers and employees, the unions refusing to be involved with running the firm. Gradually the idea began to gain momentum, though, and in 1982 a form of compulsory representation was introduced to public-sector firms, followed in 1986 by an optional minority codetermination system in the private sector. A 1994 law rendered the system compulsory for privatized state enterprises. The system of codetermination was introduced in all firms with an enterprise council: two representatives of this council take part on the board, as observers and without votes. Their influence is actually very limited: the decisions are made by the directors in a preliminary meeting. This type of codetermination decision-making has been referred to as 'a mockery'.

Another system of codetermination in France is based on a voluntary scheme; this can be introduced by the general meeting by way of a charter amendment. Representatives of employees of the firm – numbering between two and four, and occupying a maximum of one-third of the board seats – are elected by their peers, not by the general meeting. They take part in the meetings of the board in the same position as the other directors. In practice, however, board meetings are often split into two parts, with the representatives invited to the formal part. Hence the system is reportedly not very effective, especially as a result of the fear that the representatives might divulge information. Also, the directors fear that co-decision-making will increase the union's power. The number of companies that have opted to adopt this regime is unknown, but is probably rather small.

France has introduced a more elaborate system of codetermination for its privatized public-sector enterprises, including firms that are majority owned by the French state. Apart from representatives of the state and expert members (both one-third), one-third of members of the supervisory board or of the management board are representatives of the employees. In general, employee representatives on French boards are relatively rare: in only 14 of the CAC (French stock index) 40 companies were there employee representatives. These represented only 7 per cent of the overall number of employees.

In **Switzerland**, although the law does not call for employee participation at board level, some companies have voluntarily introduced codetermination. Examples are Nestlé and the retail distributors Migros and Co-op.

In **Ireland**, the Worker Participation (State Enterprises) Act 1977 introduced board-level employee participation at a selected number of state-owned enterprises employing 43,700 employees. Members are appointed by the minister competent for the state firm in question, and are nominated either by the union or by a percentage of the employees (a minimum of 15 per cent). In addition, only employees of the firm may be appointed. The system has not been extended to the private sector, although proposals have been made to that purpose.

In **Italian** business firms, employees are not represented at the board level. The Italian union tradition is based on confrontation not on *co-gestoine*. In **Belgium** there is no labour representation at board level. In some state-owned firms there may be limited representation of labour (e.g. in the national railway company, where three members are nominated by the unions and elected by the employees). Belgian (unitary) boards usually comprise internal managers, representatives of large shareholders, and independent outsiders. In **Spain**, there is no legally imposed system of codetermination. Spain abolished its system, which was introduced in 1962–65, but it can be continued on a voluntary basis. The latter is the case in state-owned enterprises.

Two-tier board systems and employee representation

The **Dutch** system of labour representation is based on the consensus between the two traditional production factors: capital and labour. Labour representation at the level of the supervisory board is indirect and based on co-optation of members of the board who, without being labour representatives, enjoy the confidence of the employees. Therefore, members of the supervisory board are in a specific position of independence: they do not represent labour interests, but have to take care of 'the interests of the company and its related enterprises' as a whole.

Austria has introduced employee representation more or less along the lines of the original German patterns: at the level of the supervisory board in large companies, one-third of the members should be employee representatives. These are appointed for an indefinite time period by the works council or, in larger firms, by the central works council, and chosen from among their members. Union influence is reported to be strong.

As indicated, there is no legally imposed system of codetermination in the two-tier system in **Portugal**.

Corporate restructuring

As with issues concerning the structure of boards, the corporate control market (especially in terms of the regulation of take-overs and protection against them) has escaped European harmonization and is still determined nationally. Diverging features of share ownership and related regulations explain, to a large extent, the relatively wide diversity in the way the corporate control market is organized and functions. While, as indicated, public take-overs and comparable transactions are common in the UK, they occur less frequently in continental European countries. Between 1988 and 1996, about 8 to 10 per cent of the listed companies in the UK were involved as targets of a take-over that were effected successfully. If one adds the number of transactions that were taken into consideration, even those that have not materialized or were not publicized, one arrives at a figure between 15 and 20 per cent. In comparison, in France, for example, with regard to the number of listed companies, about 2 to 3 per cent of all listed companies have been involved in a take-over situation over the same period.

Akin to the practices of the Rhineland model, company restructuring in most continental European countries takes place by voluntary measures rather than on the markets. The frequency and importance of mergers and acquisitions in Europe illustrate this. In all states there is an active 'private' market for corporate assets and corporate control. In terms of the number of transactions, about half those taking place worldwide involve European companies, whether on the buying or the selling side. This 'private' market for corporate assets and control runs through the communication channels of the large accounting firms and investment banks that operate across Europe. The transactions mostly, if not exclusively, relate to privately owned firms, including subsidiaries and divisions of listed companies. Both in terms of the number of transactions and turnover, the mergers and acquisitions market largely exceeds the more visible markets for public take-over bids (Wymeersch, 1998: 1189). In this respect, Tables 6.7 and 6.8 show that, while the Anglo-Saxon countries stand out both in terms of value and of numbers of merger and acquisition transactions, most continental European countries, and especially France and Germany, also experience relatively high numbers of mergers and acquisitions. The high number of acquisitions in Japan in the 1990s is related to the bursting of the stock market bubble and the fact that many companies experienced problems as a consequence.

Table 6.7 Mergers and acquisitions in value of transactions ($bn)

Country	1990	1991	1992	1993	1994	1995
France	18.9	26.8	21.7	29.8	21.2	20.9
Germany	15.1	20.3	21.4	11.4	10.1	16.5
Italy	20.0	7.5	23.3	16.5	9.0	9.2
UK	**77.4**	**56.6**	**45.5**	**42.3**	**36.4**	**124.2**
Belgium	5.9	3.1	1.0	4.9	1.4	1.6
Netherlands	13.9	5.9	15.5	8.3	5.2	8.5
Spain	8.5	15.5	10.6	9.0	7.3	4.1
Sweden	6.9	11.5	6.9	12.5	7.7	8.8
Switzerland	5.8	0.7	2.2	3.4	2.7	8.2
Rest of Europe	13.3	12.1	12.0	12.2	10.0	24.3
Europe	185.7	160.0	160.1	150.3	111.0	226.3
USA	108.2	71.2	96.7	176.4	226.7	356.0

Source: Wymeersch (1998: 1189).

Table 6.8 Mergers and acquisitions in number of transactions

	Acquisitions		Selling transactions	
	1995	1996	1995	1996
Belgium	49	55	55	89
France	*378*	*343*	*350*	*332*
Germany	*444*	*450*	*362*	*322*
Italy	109	130	170	162
Netherlands	273	319	145	136
Spain	32	46	160	107
UK	**664**	**664**	**449**	**468**
Sweden	93	152	72	120
Switzerland	186	192	76	74
Rest of Europe	365	463	645	745
Europe	2593	2814	2484	2564
Canada	298	323	180	250
USA	1228	1553	699	849
Japan	351	445	89	69
Rest of World	842	817	1890	2220
Total	2719	3138	2858	3388

Source: Wymeersch (1998: 1190).

Case: Corporate Governance in China[13]

From 1978 onwards, the Chinese government embarked on an ambitious programme of economic reform. One of the most important creations was that of the firm as an independent business entity. Under the central planning regime, China's industrial and commercial enterprises were not autonomous but were workshops and production units with no independent decision-making power. The central plan replaced the function of the market, and the conditions for the existence of a firm (as understood in market economies) were absent. All means of production were nominally owned by the state; contracts and market transactions were not needed for organizing production activities.

The workshop and production units within the central input–output planning matrix have been replaced by business enterprises with independent legal status (regardless of ownership composition). These have now become the primary form of productive organization. The emergence of the company as a basic economic entity was accompanied by a process of financial reform that has turned the newly created or reorganized state-owned banks into the primary providers of finance for Chinese enterprises, replacing the old system of state budgetary grants. Most working capital needs of state-owned enterprises (SOEs) are met through bank lending. The banks were encouraged to use economic criteria for evaluating loan applications on the basis of market demand for the enterprises' output, the availability of raw materials and the profitability of investments. The transformation of the Chinese banking system into a truly commercial one, however, is proving an extremely slow process. Some party officials have been reluctant to increase the independence of the central bank and of other banks because officials have been exploiting the banks to finance their own needs. The Chinese government also continues to use the banks to siphon surplus funds from private enterprises to subsidize the losses of state enterprises. Moreover, the political upheaval and mass unemployment involved in making the banks themselves efficient further contribute to slowing the pace of progress. Hence, while banks are technically more independent, in practice they are to a large extent still acting as cashiers for the state and can hardly play a useful role in corporate governance.

From the mid-1980s onwards, when grass-roots efforts to develop China's capital markets began spontaneously, shareholding companies were formed. To raise funds, state and collective enterprises issued various forms of shares and bonds, and informal securities trading could be found in most major Chinese cities. China's first securities and brokerage company was established in Shenzhen in 1987. In the following year, securities companies were set up in every province under the auspices of the local branches of China's central bank. By 1991, China's two official stock exchanges in Shanghai and Shenzhen were ready for full operation. Approval for a company to obtain listing on these markets, however, is determined by the government on the basis of an annual quota broken

[13] The majority of the information in this case is based on On Kit Tam (2002), Eu (1996) and Lin (2001).

down to each province and ministry. The latter then select companies to fill the allocated quotas. The listing of a company is thus usually decided not on its commercial merit but for political and sectional reasons. Just like the state banking system, which supports SOEs through the debt market, the securities market in China is essentially a state securities market, conceived and operated primarily to support corporatized SOEs.

Chinese-listed companies are in the main partially privatized SOEs. That is, their major shareholder is the state in its various forms, including other state-owned enterprises. Shares owned by the state and by state-owned enterprises are not permitted to be traded. The high degree of concentrated state ownership has restricted the capacity of China's equity market to perform a financial disciplinary role in the corporate governance of listed firms. Movements in stock price are generated mainly by the trading of shares among individual shareholders. Because of the high rate of saving and the very limited range of investment instruments available in China, individual investors in the stock market have from the beginning exhibited a highly speculative tendency with a very short investment horizon.

Despite its majority ownership, the state does not exercise *effective control* over its companies. Control of China's companies rests primarily with the insider management and their party–ministerial associates. The Chinese government, together with the party organization, exercise *influence* through, for example, recruitment policy. For listed companies with the state as a majority shareholder, the pool for appointment to the positions of chief executive, most senior managers and a high proportion of the directors on the company board is restricted and subject to government influence or direct intervention. Moreover, many company executives may still have an affiliation to their previous state organization.

In the Chinese system, companies operating under the country's company law have a two-tier board. The board of directors is essentially made up of executive directors. There are few independent directors in Chinese companies. In addition to the board of directors, Chinese companies also have a supervisory board. This board is small in size and usually has labour union and major shareholder representatives. However, it only has a loosely defined monitoring role over the board of directors and managers, and has not so far played any effective governance role. The interests of employees are safeguarded primarily by party representatives in consultation with the controlling shareholder, which is usually the state.

While there has been progress in developing accounting standards, professional organizations and media reports on company activities in China, it is still a long way from achieving the degree of effectiveness and independence that is required for the Anglo-Saxon model to work. It is widely believed that false accounting and financial misreporting are pervasive among Chinese SOEs and companies. However, as in other emerging markets, particularly those in transitional economies, a company's reputation for integrity and performance is often not required in order to raise capital in the stock exchange. Indeed, the unpredictable movements generated by market manipulation may, in fact, at times be applauded by some investors, who hope to profit from such speculative waves and are eager to follow the 'winners'.

Many of the shortcomings in the actual practice of corporate governance in China derive from weaknesses in the policy and institutional environment, as well as from peculiar cultural and political governance traditions. For example, collusion among insiders, and lack of transparency and disclosure to outsiders on the actual performance and workings of the firms have been explained as a consequence of the tradition of insiders versus outsiders with a built-in convention of secrecy among insiders. Family or clan members, as 'insiders', are expected to bear collective responsibility for promoting and safeguarding the interests of the unit. The interests of outsiders are either secondary or irrelevant. Safeguarding the interests of the unit involves maintaining confidentiality on internal affairs, and disclosures are regarded as a betrayal of the unit's interests. Also important is the impact of political governance on corporate governance. Since the Chinese system of political governance itself lacks accountability and transparency, it is difficult, and perhaps incongruous, for corporate governance to be effective and institutionalized. Moreover, the market-orientated legal system, and the corporate and securities law framework in China has only been developed over the past two decades and is still relatively rudimentary and untested in many aspects.

Questions

1. In an attempt to foster enterprise performance, China increased enterprise autonomy, decentralizing investment and production decisions. From this case it is clear, however, that increasing enterprise autonomy might be a necessary but not sufficient condition to optimize allocative efficiency. What in your opinion must be developed to achieve this aim?

2. Explain in what direction the Chinese corporate governance and finance system seems to have evolved – towards a more Anglo-Saxon type of system or towards the Rhineland system? Use the institutional–cultural framework to support your explanation.

3. In your opinion, which corporate governance and finance system would be most beneficial under the current conditions in China?

4. What can you learn from this case with respect to shareholder and other stakeholder rights?

6.3 Conclusions

The comparative analysis of corporate governance systems and of their institutional–cultural roots is not only useful in its own right but also for building an understanding of the impact these systems might have on competitive advantage of national industries. It also enables us to make a sensible judgement on the type of system that could best be developed in less advanced and transitional countries. A comparative analysis of the type that is conducted in this chapter shows that – aside from economics – history, politics and societal traditions are important forces in shaping the development of financial and corporate governance institutions. Corporate governance systems do not exist in an institutional or historical vacuum. The lesson to be learned is that financial and corporate governance reforms must adapt to the unique history and social–political structure of a country. Less advanced and transitional countries cannot blindly follow the financial and corporate governance reforms of other countries.

A striking example in this respect is the advice of the Japanese to top Chinese economic officials not to hasten the development of securities markets. In their view, ordinary Chinese people do not yet understand the risks of stocks and bonds. Moreover, strong securities markets undermine a tool of economic control that Japan found useful during its own development. The Japanese think China should keep its firms dependent on bank loans rather than securities, so making it easier for the government to control who gets capital and when (Eu, 1996).

This chapter also shows that both the Anglo-Saxon and the Rhineland models of corporate governance have their strengths and weaknesses, which help to explain their divergent impact on industrial competitiveness (see Table 6.9). Major strengths of the Anglo-Saxon system of corporate governance include efficiency, flexibility, responsiveness and high rates of corporate profit. More explicitly, the Anglo-Saxon system is good at re-allocating capital among sectors, funding emerging fields, shifting resources out of 'unprofitable' industries, and achieving high private returns each period, as measured by higher corporate returns (Porter, 1997). Major weaknesses of the system stem essentially from two of its features: the unitary board system and its short-term character. The unitary board system, while allowing for efficient decision-making by management, impedes effective monitoring of management performance. Managerial failures in the UK during the 1980s and a number of cases of blatant malpractice in the USA and the UK are an expression of the flaws in this system of corporate control. The election of outside directors (which happens on a voluntary basis in the UK), the use of proxy voting mechanisms, and, as in recent times, the development of shareholder advisory committees have emerged in the Anglo-Saxon system as preferred techniques for solving many of these control problems. When these governance techniques fail, corporate control becomes entirely dependent on the market.

Theoretically, the threat of a hostile take-over should ensure that assets are controlled by those best able to manage them, and in the USA and UK, with their well-developed markets for corporate control, a hostile take-over is the ultimate check on management. When shareholders fail to take an interest in the governance of a company, or when their governance proves ineffective, low-quality managers are able to remain in power or management's allegiance to the shareholder may falter. In either of these cases, a company's share price should drift lower so as to form a gap between the stock's actual price and its potential value. If the gap between a company's market value and its perceived potential value were to grow large enough, a take-over would ensure that control over the company's assets eventually goes to those who can earn a higher return on those assets (Lightfood, 1992).

Moreover, the unitary board system, combined with the threat of take-over, helps to explain the difficulty of the Anglo-Saxon system with aligning the interests of private investors and corporations with those of society as a whole, including employees, suppliers and local communities. Indeed, the market for corporate control often disregards its effects on both human and social capital. Short-term capital is also argued to contribute to impeding the creation of the organizational competencies necessary for firms competing in sectors characterized by incremental innovation processes (Streeck, 1992). In other words, the system fails to encourage sufficient investment to secure competitive positions in existing business. It also induces investments in the wrong forms. It heavily favours acquisitions, which involve assets that can easily be valued, over internal development projects that are more difficult to value and that constitute a drag on current earnings (Porter, 1997).

Major strengths of the Rhineland model are that it encourages investment to upgrade capabilities and productivity in existing fields; it also encourages internal diversification into related fields – the kind of diversification that builds on and extends corporate strengths. The Rhineland model comes closer to optimizing long-term private and social returns. The focus on long-term corporate position – encouraged by an ownership structure and governance process that, together, incorporate the interests of employees, suppliers, customers and the local community – allows the German economy to utilize more successfully the social benefits of private investment (Porter, 1997: 12–13). Downsides of the Rhineland model, however, are the tendency to over-invest in capacity, to produce too many products, and to maintain unprofitable businesses. Moreover, the stable, long-term relationships between banks and firms are increasingly seen as inhibiting the formation and growth of firms in new sectors. As indicated above, the long-term stable shareholder relationships typical of the Rhineland model impede the development of a large, liquid capital market. A large capital market is critical for risk capital or venture capital providers, as it creates a viable 'exit option' via initial public offering (IPO) and mergers or acquisitions (Casper, 1999). Without this exit option, it is difficult for venture capitalists to diversify risks across several investments and to create a viable refinancing mechanism.

The comparative approach of this chapter helps reveal the fact that there is no such a thing as a 'perfect' or the 'best' system. While, at present, the majority view is that the shareholder model will prevail due to the increasing dominance of institutional investors on international capital markets (Lazonick and O'Sullivan, 2000), the intense and ongoing competition between the Anglo-Saxon and the Rhineland models in Europe provides evidence to counter this argument. The impact of this competition provides few signs of change in the UK and only small step-changes, incorporating some elements of the Anglo-Saxon model into the 'large firm' Rhineland model in Germany. Since national forms of corporate governance are embedded in established 'practices' and 'regulatory policies', change in one area does not involve a change in the entire system.

In fact, as the example of Germany shows, modifications of the existing approach to corporate governance that accommodate the new circumstances are more likely. Real change would require root-and-branch change, and as there is not even a consensus on the need for change, let alone a consensus on what that change should be, root-and-branch change in both the UK and Germany – the European representatives of the two strongest models of corporate governance – has not yet occured, and is unlikely to. Hence,

Table 6.9 The Anglo-Saxon and Rhineland models of corporate governance: major weaknesses and strengths		
	Anglo-Saxon model	**Rhineland model**
Major strengths	good reallocation of capital between sectors	encourages investment to upgrade capabilities and internal diversification in related fields
	funding of emerging fields	
	shifting resources out of 'unprofitable' industries	utilizes the social benefits of private investments more successfully
	high rates of profit	
		effective monitoring
	efficient decision-making by management	
Major weaknesses	*Stemming from board system* ineffective monitoring	*Stemming from stable bank ties* tendency to over-invest in capacity
	Plus threat of take-over no incentives to invest in organizational capabilities	tendency to produce too many products
	favours acquisitions instead of internal development projects	tendency to maintain unprofitable business
		tendency to impede the development of liquid capital markets and, as a result,
		tendency to inhibit the development and growth of firms in new sectors

for the foreseeable future, companies within different countries will continue to be characterized by different forms of governance. Evidence shows that there is, and will continue to be, a spectrum of approaches, ranging from the Anglo-Saxon to the Rhineland model.

Study Questions

1. Explain the main differences between the 'shareholder' and the 'stakeholder' models of corporate governance.

2. What is the broad definition of corporate governance?

3. What do you understand by 'effective corporate governance'?

4. The text gives examples of Ford Motor Company adopting extensive cross-ownership relationships through equity holdings and German firms adopting US financial disclosure practices. Explain why this happens?

5. Explain how the German accounting system differs from the US one.

6. Explain the main differences between the Anglo-Saxon and the Rhineland model of corporate governance.

7. What are the main strong and weak points of these two main systems of corporate governance?

8. What is meant by the term 'private' capital markets?

9. What is meant by the terms 'exit' and 'voice' in the governance area?

10. What are the main strong and weak points of the Japanese system of corporate governance?

11. Explain why the take-over option of the Anglo-Saxon model of corporate governance has militated against enterprise growth from small to medium size.

12. Is the German model converging towards the Anglo-Saxon model of corporate governance? Give reasons for your argument.

13. Would it be economically beneficial for the German model to converge towards the Anglo-Saxon model?

14. Which material preconditions are essential for a shareholder value economy?

15. What would you take into account when thinking of a 'best fit' model of corporate governance for developing countries, and why?

16. What is the link between corporate social responsibility and corporate governance?

17. Explain the effects of globalization forces on corporate governance systems.

Further Reading

Aoki, M. and Kim, Hyung-Ki (1995) Corporate governance in transitional economies. Washington, DC: World Bank.

Interesting book paying special attention to insider control, the possible role of banks in corporate governance, and the desirability of taking a comparative analytic approach to finding solutions.

Hopt, K.J., Kanda, H., Roe, M.J., Wymeersch, E. and Prigge, S. (1998) *Comparative Corporate Governance: the State of the Art and Emerging Research.* Oxford: Oxford University Press.

Extremely interesting book. It explains a wide range of corporate governance topics in different countries.

Jürgens, U., Naumann, K. and Rupp, J. (2000) Shareholder value in an adverse environment: the German case. *Economy and Society* 29(1), 54–79.

This article provides an interesting analysis of the ability of the German corporate governance system to change in the direction of shareholder value.

Sheard, P. (1998) Japanese corporate governance in comparative perspective. *Journal of Japanese Trade and Industry* 1, 7–11.

This article offers a brief but critical comparative analysis of the Japanese and Anglo-Saxon systems of corporate governance.

Zhuang, J., Edwards, D. and Capulong, V.A. (2001) *Corporate Governance and Finance in East Asia: a Study of Indonesia, Republic of Korea, Malaysia, Philippines, and Thailand.* Manila, Philippines: Asian Development Bank.

One of the few and excellent books that treats the topic extensively in these East Asian countries.

Case: Barings – a Case of Corporate Social Responsibility[14]

At the time of its collapse, Baring Brothers & Co., Ltd (BB&Co) was the longest-established merchant banking business in the City of London. Since the foundation of the business as a partnership in 1762 it had been privately controlled and had remained independent. BB&Co was founded in 1890 to carry on the business of the bank in succession to the original partnership. In November 1985, Barings plc acquired the share capital of BB&Co and became the parent company of the Barings Group.

In addition to BB&Co, the two other principal operating companies of Barings plc were Barings Asset Management Limited (BAM), which provided a wide range of fund and asset management services, and Barings Securities Limited (BSL), itself a subsidiary of BB&Co, which generally operated through subsidiaries as a broker dealer in the Asia Pacific region, Japan, Latin America, London and New York.

The business of what became BSL was acquired from Henderson Crosthwaite by BB&Co in 1984. BSL was incorporated in the Cayman Islands, although its head office, management and accounting records were all based in London. BSL had a large number of overseas operating subsidiaries, including two that are of particular relevance to this case study, namely Baring Futures (Singapore) (BFS) and Baring Securities (Japan) Limited (BSJ).

BFS, a Singaporean-registered company, was an indirect subsidiary of BSL. BFS was originally formed to allow Barings to trade on the Singapore International Monetary Exchange. At the time of the collapse, BFS employed 23 staff. BSL's other significant Singaporean subsidiary was Baring Securities (Singapore)

---

[14] This case is based on information from the website risk.ifci.ch.

Pte Limited (BSS), which employed some 115 staff. BSS's principal activity was securities trading.

From late 1992 to the time of the collapse, BFS's general manager and head trader was Nick Leeson. Leeson started work for Barings in London in 1989 in a back office capacity (the settlements department). In 1992, he transferred to Barings Futures Singapore. He would occupy the same position and in addition he would also become floor manager of SIMEX (the Securities and Futures Authority of Singapore). As time went by, Leeson was also put in charge of both the dealing desk and the back office, settling his own trades.

The back office records, confirms and settles trades transacted by the front office, reconciles them with details sent by the bank's counter-parties and assesses the accuracy of prices used for its internal valuations. It also accepts and releases securities and payments for trades. Some back offices also provide the regulatory reports and management accounting. In a nutshell, the back office provides the checks necessary to prevent unauthorized trading and minimize the potential for fraud and embezzlement. Since Leeson was in charge of the back office, he had the final say on payments, ingoing and outgoing confirmations and contracts, reconciliation statements, accounting entries and position reports. He was perfectly placed to relay false information back to London.

Leeson engaged in unauthorized activities almost as soon as he started trading in Singapore in 1992. He took proprietary (that is, trading for own or, in this case, for Barings' account) positions on SIMEX on both futures and options contracts. His mandate from London allowed him to take positions only if they were part of 'switching' (a form of arbitrage trading) and to execute client orders. He was never allowed to sell options. Leeson lost money from his unauthorized trades almost from day one. Yet he was perceived in London as a wonderboy and turbo-arbitrageur, who single-handedly contributed to half of Barings Singapore's 1993 profits and half of the entire firm's 1994 profits. However, in 1994 alone, Leeson lost US$296 million; his bosses thought he made a profit of US$46 million, so they proposed paying him a bonus of US$720,000. However, the unauthorized trading activities within BFS, which intensified in January and February 1995, built up such massive losses that, when discovered on 23 February 1995, they led to the collapse of Barings.

Leeson was able to deceive everyone around him by using the vehicle of cross-trade. A cross trade is a transaction executed on the floor of an exchange by just one member, who is both buyer and seller. If a member has matching buy and sell orders from two different customer accounts for the same contract and at the same price, he is allowed to cross the transaction (execute the deal) by matching both his clients' accounts. Leeson entered into a significant volume of cross-transactions between account '88888', an account which he set up, and account '92000' (Barings Securities Japan – Nikkei and JGB Arbitrage), account '98007' (Barings London – JGB Arbitrage) and account '98008' (Barings London – Euroyen Arbitrage). The bottom line of all the cross-trades, which Leeson executed, was that Barings was counter-party to many of its own trades. Leeson bought from one hand and sold to the other, and in doing so did not lay off any of the firm's market risk. Barings was thus not arbitraging between SIMEX and the Japanese exchanges but taking open and very substantial positions, which were buried in account '88888'.

Leeson set up account '88888' in July 1992 – it was designated an error account in the Barings Futures Singapore system, but as a Barings London client account in SIMEX's system. Abusing his position as head of the back office, Leeson suppressed information on account '88888'. Barings London did not know of its existence since Leeson had asked a systems consultant, Dr Edmund Wong, to remove error account '88888' from the daily reports BFS sent electronically to London. This state of affairs existed from on or around 8 July 1992 until the collapse of Barings on 26 February 1995. Information on account '88888' was, however, still contained in the margin file sent to London. Error accounts are set up to accommodate trades that cannot be reconciled immediately. A compliance officer investigates the trades, records them on the firm's books and analyses how they affect the firm's market risk and profit and loss. Reports of error accounts are normally sent to senior officers of the firm.

Barings' management compounded their initial mistake of not segregating Leeson's duties by ignoring warnings that prolonging the status quo would be dangerous. An internal auditor's report in August 1994 concluded that his dual responsibility for both the front and back offices was 'an excessive concentration of powers'. The report warned that there was a significant risk that the general manager (Nick Leeson) could override the controls. The audit team recommended that Leeson be relieved of four duties: supervision of the back office team, cheque signing and signing off SIMEX reconciliations and bank reconciliations. These recommendations were never implemented. At the local operational level Simon Jones, who had responsibility for Barings' operations in Singapore and was a director of BFS, seems to have taken no significant steps to put the recommended segregetion of duties into effect; even though, in his management response to the report, he had stated that, with immediate effect, Leeson would cease to perform certain functions and that he [Jones] would ensure the adequate supervision of all settlement and recording processes. Moreover, the director of BFS and regional manager of the South Asian region failed to concern himself with, or even to check, the implementation of the internal audit report.

Senior management at Barings were happy to enjoy the fruits of the 'success' of the Singapore branch, but were not keen on providing adequate resources to ensure a sound risk-management system for a unit that, alone, ostensibly accounted for one-fifth of its 1993 profits and almost half of its 1994 profits. The CEO's response to the internal auditor's report, which called for a suitably experienced person to run Singapore's back office, was that there was not enough work for a full-time treasury and risk manager even if the role incorporated some compliance duties. No senior manager in London checked whether key internal audit recommendations on the Singapore back office had been followed up.

The crux of the Barings collapse, then, lay in senior management's careless attitude to its derivative operations in Singapore. Every major report on managing derivative risks has stressed the need for senior management to understand the risks of the business, to help articulate the firm's risk appetite and to draft the strategies and control procedures needed to achieve these objectives. Barings' senior managers had a very superficial knowledge of derivatives and did not want to probe too deeply into an area that was 'bringing in the profits'. However, arbitraging the price differences between two futures contracts is a low-risk strategy. How could it then generate such high profits if the central axiom of modern finance theory is low risk–low return? And if such a risk, along with relatively simple arbitrage, could yield so much profit, why were Barings' better-capitalized rivals (all with much larger proprietary trading teams) not pursuing the same strategy? Two of Barings' most senior derivatives staff, and Leeson's bosses, were not familiar with the operations of the SIMEX floor. They thought that the significant and large profits were possible due to the competitive advantage that BFS had, arising from its good inter-office communications and its large client order flow. As the exchanges were open and competitive markets, this suggests a lack of understanding of the nature of the business and the risks inherent in combining agency and proprietary trading.

Questions

1. Identify and discuss the role of the UK's system of management education in the Barings' story.

2. Would corporate governance institutions play a role in an explanation of the case?

3. Is there a role for the human resource system of Barings in helping to understand Leeson's motivation?

Case: The Ahold Scandal

As the post-Enron wave of corporate scandals washed over America last year, a common response in Europe was: it couldn't happen here. Far from having the world's best-policed markets, the United States, many European politicians claimed, suffered uniquely from a lethal combination of greedy and overpaid bosses, conflicted auditors and investment bankers, reliance on accounting rules not principles, and an obsession with quarterly profit numbers. In America, as many as 1,200 companies have been forced to restate their accounts in the past five years; in Europe the number is barely in double digits. So it is outrageous, many Europeans now argue, that America is seeking to impose the unwieldy Sarbanes-Oxley act, passed in the wake of Enron and WorldCom, on European companies listed in New York.

As more sensible European regulators recognise, this smugness was never justified: it is only necessary to recall scandals such as Vivendi, ABB, Elan and EM.TV. But Europe's claim of immunity from corporate sleaze has now been blown out of the water by this week's revelations that Royal Ahold of the Netherlands, the world's third-biggest food retailer, overstated its profits for 2001–02 by as much as $500m. Its chief executive and chief financial officer have both quit.

It is true that Ahold's accounting deficiencies mainly involved American subsidiaries that it bought in a decade-long acquisition binge though they also stretched to Argentina and Scandinavia. But the company's Amsterdam-based auditors, Deloitte & Touche, failed to pick the problems up in 2001, even though worries about Ahold's accounts were widely expressed in the markets for most of last year. Ahold's board, far from questioning the chief executive closely, tamely extended his term for up to seven years as recently as last spring. The Dutch market regulator admitted this week that it had no powers of discipline over faulty auditing.

What about the relative numbers of restatements? Because America's GAAP accounting system relies on thousands of pages of rules, it is more vulnerable to manipulation than Europe's more principles-based approach. Wall Street's excesses of the 1990s were also more egregious than Europe's. But given the largely non-existent regulation of auditors and the poor corporate governance prevalent in much of Europe, a more plausible conclusion is that Europe has had fewer accounting scandals than America mainly because nobody has seriously looked for them, not because they are not there.

This is not to say that Europe should adopt Sarbanes-Oxley *in toto*. That hastily drafted law was designed for America's very different system; it precludes the two-tier boards that are common in Europe, for example. Many of the law's rules on managers and boards seem unduly intrusive even for America. But statutory, independent regulation of auditors, as prescribed by Sarbanes-Oxley, makes sense everywhere. So do rules to stop accounting firms doing consulting work for audit clients; and it is also worth considering mandatory rotation of auditors (Deloitte had audited Ahold for 15 years).

The case for independent regulation is the stronger because European Union companies are due to adopt international accounting standards by 2005. It is little use taking this welcome step towards tougher standards, which the Europeans are urging on America in the interests of global harmonisation, if there is nobody to oversee the rules. Yet the European Federation of Accountants admits that, in six EU countries, there is in effect no enforcement at all.

Bad apples and oranges

After Enron and WorldCom were followed by the bankruptcy and criminal conviction of Andersen, which had audited both companies, the remaining Big Four hinted that Andersen had been an exceptional case: a rotten apple amid a barrel of good ones. Andersen does seem to have been peculiarly culpable. Yet most of the other firms have now also been tarnished by scandal in the past year or so: KPMG over Xerox, PricewaterhouseCoopers over Tyco, Deloitte over Adelphia, for example. This litany means that statutory regulation of auditors is now essential if investors are to regain their shattered confidence in the financial markets.

It is, in any event, pointless for politicians to crow about the merits of their respective systems. As companies such as Ahold go global, they run into countless national regulators and supervisors – and it is the weakest link that is always most likely to prove their (and their investors') undoing. The right response is to adopt the strongest, not the laxest, regimes possible. And that means both enforcement of international accounting standards and tough regulation of auditors.[15]

Questions

1. What explains the occurrence of the Ahold scandal?

2. Should the Ahold case be seen as a failure of the (Dutch) two-tier board system? Please explain your opinion of this issue.

3. The US$500 million overstatement was due primarily to Ahold's US subsidiaries. Would you, therefore, argue that Ahold is less a European problem than yet another US accounting failure?

4. Would the Ahold scandal occur typically in 'global' corporations or could a similar situation arise in companies operating in only one nation?

References

Aoki, M. (1999) *Convergence and Diversity in Corporate Governance Regimes and Capital Markets.* Law and Economics Conference, Evoluon Conference Center, Eindhoven.

Baums, T. (1994) The German banking system and its impact on corporate finance and governance, in Aoki, M. and Patrick, H. (eds) *The Japanese Main Bank System.* Oxford: Clarendon Press.

Belyanova, E. and Rozinsky, I. (1995) Evolution of commercial banking in Russia and the implications for corporate governance, in Aoki, M. and Hyung-Ki Kim (eds) *Corporate Governance in Transitional Economies.* Washington, DC: World Bank, 185–214.

Casper, S. (1999) *High Technology Governance and Institutional Approaches.* WZB discussion paper FS I 99-307. Berlin: Wissenschaftszentrum für Sozialforschung Berlin.

Casper, S. (2000) Institutional adaptiveness, technology policy, and the diffusion of new business models: the case of German biotechnology. *Organization Studies* 21(5), 887–914.

---

[15] Extracts from 'Ahold Out' © *The Economist Newspaper Limited*, London (1 March 2003).

Clarkson, M.B.E. (1995) A stakeholder framework for analyzing and evaluating corporate social performance. *Academy of Management Review* 20(1), 92–117.

Deeg, R. (1997) Banks and industrial finance in the 1990s. *Industry and Innovation* 4(1), 53–73.

Eu, D. (1996) Financial reforms and corporate governance in China. *Columbia Journal of Transnational Law* 34(2), 469–502.

Friedman, M. (1962) *Capitalism and Freedom.* Chicago, IL: University of Chicago Press.

Gelb, D.S. and Strawser, J.A. (2001) Corporate social responsibility and financial disclosures: an alternative explanation for increased disclosure. *Journal of Business Ethics* 33, 1–13.

Hideki Kanda (1998) Notes on corporate governance in Japan, in Hopt, K.J., Kanda, H., Roe, M.J., Wymeersch, E. and Prigge, S. (eds) *Comparative Corporate Governance.* Oxford: Oxford University Press.

Hughes, A. (1990) *Industrial Concentration and the Small Business Sector in the UK: the 1980s in Historical Perspective.* Working Paper No. 5, Small Business Research Center, University of Cambridge (August).

Kester, W.C. (1996) American and Japanese corporate governance: convergence to best practice?, in Berger, S. and Dore, R. (eds) *National Diversity and Global Capitalism.* London: Cornell University Press.

Koen, C. (2001) *The Japanese Main Bank Model: Convergence or Hybridisation?* Mimeo. Tilburg: Tilburg University.

Lane, C. (1994) European business systems: Britain and Germany compared, in Whitley, R. (ed.) *European Business Systems.* London: Sage.

Lazonick, W. and O'Sullivan, M. (2000) Maximizing shareholder value: a new ideology for corporate governance. *Economy and Society* 29 (February), 13–35.

Lightfood, R.W. (1992) *Note on Corporate Governance Systems: the United States, Japan, and Germany.* Harvard Business School Note 9-292-012. Harvard: Harvard Business School Publications.

Lin, C. (2001) Corporatisation and corporate governance in China's economic transition. *Economics of Planning* 34, 5–35.

Litwack, J.M. (1995) Corporate governance, banks, and fiscal reform in Russia, in Aoki, M. and Hyung-Ki Kim (eds) *Corporate Governance in Transitional Economies.* Washington, DC: World Bank, 99–120.

McCarthy, D.J. and Puffer, S.M. (2002) Russia's corporate governance scorecard in the Enron era. *Organizational Dynamics* 31(1), 19–34.

Nowak, E. (2001) Recent developments in German capital markets and corporate governance. *Journal of Applied Corporate Governance* 14(3), 35–48.

OECD (1998) *Tendances des Marches de capiteaux* no. 69 (February). Paris: OECD.

On Kit Tam (2002) Ethical issues in the evolution of corporate governance in China. *Journal of Business Ethics* 37, 303–320.

Pedersen, T. and Thomsen, S. (1997) European patterns of corporate ownership: a twelve-country study. *Journal of International Business Studies* 4, 759–78.

Porter, M. (1990) *The Competitive Advantage of Nations.* New York: Free Press.

Porter, M.E. (1997) Capital choices: changing the way America invests in industry, in Chew, D.H. (ed.) *Studies in International Corporate Finance and Governance Systems.* Oxford: Oxford University Press, 5–17.

Reich, R.B. (1998) The new meaning of corporate social responsibility. *California Management Review* 40(2), 8–17.

Roe, M.J. (1994) Some differences in corporate governance in Germany, Japan, and America, in Baums, T., Buxman, T. and Hopt, K.J. (eds) *Institutional Investors and Corporate Governance*. Berlin: Walter de Gruyter.

Rubach, M.J. and Sebora, T.C. (1998) Comparative corporate governance: competitive implications of an emerging convergence. *Journal of World Business* 33(2), 167–84.

Sabel, C., Herrigel, G., Deeg, R. and Kazis, R. (1987) *Regional Prosperities Compared: Massachusetts and Baden-Württemberg in the 1980s*. Discussion Paper of the Research Unit Labour Market and Employment, Wissenschaftszentrum für Sozialforschung Berlin.

Schaede, U. (2000) *The German Financial System in 2000*. Harvard Business School Case Study 9-700-135. Boston: Harvard Business School Publishing.

Schlie, E.H. and Warner, M. (2000) The 'Americanization' of German management. *Journal of General Management* 25(3), 33–49.

Seibert, U. (1997) Kontrolle und Transparenz im Unternehmensbereich (KonTraG): der Referenten-Entwurf zur Aktienrechtsnovelle. *Zeitschrift für Wirtschafts- und Bankrecht* 51 (January), 1–48.

Streeck, W. (1992) On the institutional conditions of diversified quality production, in Streek, W. (ed.) *Social Institutions and Economic Performance*. London: Sage, 21–61.

Vitols, S. (2001) Varieties of corporate governance: comparing Germany and the UK, in Hall. P.A. and Soskice, D. (eds) *Varieties of Capitalism*. Oxford: Oxford University Press.

Vitols, S. and Woolcock, S. (1997) *Developments in the German and British Corporate Governance Systems*. Discussion Paper, Workshop on Corporate Governance in Britain and Germany, Berlin, WZB.

Williams, A. (2000) Developments in corporate governance around the world. *Benefits & Compensation International* June, 3–9.

Wood, D.J. (1991) Corporate social performance revisited. *Academy of Management Review* 16(4), 691–718.

Woolcock, S. (1996) Competition among forms of corporate governance in the European community: the case of Britain, in Berger, S. and Dore, R. (eds) *National Diversity and Global Capitalism*. London: Cornell University Press.

Wymeersch, E. (1998) A status report on corporate governance rules and practices in some continental European states, in Hopt, K.J., Kanda, H., Roe, M.J., Wymeersch, E. and Prigge, S. (eds) *Comparative Corporate Governance*. Oxford: Oxford University Press.

7

Managing Resources: Production Management

Learning Objectives

By the end of this chapter you will be able to:

- understand the origin of the main production models

- explain the main differences between different production systems

- critically assess the advantages and disadvantages of these models

- reflect on the societal effect of production systems and production management

- link human resource management and corporate governance to modes of production

- understand the concept of fit in the context of production models and production management

- assess the possibilities of applying different production models within divergent societal contexts

- evaluate whether convergence is feasible in the domain of production systems and management.

Chapter Outline

7.1   Introduction

7.2   Characteristics and Types of Production System
Taylorism, or scientific management (1890–1911)
Fordism, or mass production
Flexible production
Lean production
Case: Japanese Production Practices in China
Swedish Uddevallaism

7.3   Production Systems and the Societal Environment
Mass standardized societal systems of production
Societal systems of flexible production
The societal system of lean production
The German societal system of diversified quality production
The Swedish societal system and Uddevallaism
Short-termism and institutional inertia: the difficult transition in the USA

7.4   Conclusions
Study Questions
Further Reading
Case: Manufacturing Machine Tools in Germany and France
References

7.1 Introduction

Many of you may wonder what a topic such as production management is doing in a textbook on comparative international management. Indeed, in most, if not all, textbooks on international business and management, production management is conspicuous by its absence. However, most of you will also have noticed that there are substantial differences in production systems and methods of production management between countries. This suggests that it may be interesting to explore how and why such variations in patterns of work organization and control across societies develop and are reproduced over substantial periods.

While, previously, the superior efficiency of some production models was emphasized, it is now increasingly acknowledged that in order to be effective, there has to be some degree of fit between the production system and the societal environment (see e.g. Streeck, 1991). Hence there is, for instance, a large and successful population of medium-sized investment goods engineering firms in Germany; more competitive in the UK and France are either large batch producers or defence, electronics and specialized 'high-tech' manufacturers (Sorge and Maurice, 1990). In this respect, it has also been argued that while Taylorism, or scientific-management, principles were once thought to represent the only efficient way of structuring work activities, they are now seen as historically and societally contingent patterns of work organization that depended on a number of circumstancial factors to become established in the USA, and that by no means dominated industrial organization in Europe. It is also apparent that Fordist production systems have had many variants and have not always proved as effective as some adherents claimed (Whitley, 1999: 88). Similarly, more recent modes of production, such as Japanese Toyotism, Swedish Uddevallaism and German diversified quality production – which are explained below – developed in specific societal contexts and, when applied elsewhere, had to be, and have been, adapted to the different societal circumstances.

Different production systems are characterized by contrasting ways of work organization, organization structure, skill and knowledge requirements in jobs, methods of educating and training employees of all kinds, working careers, remuneration systems and industrial relations. The societal context in which production systems develop is able to explain why some production systems are characterized by quite different patterns in the fields just mentioned and contribute to maintaining them. It can be seen that such patterns are specific to a certain society, prevailing without regard for different industrial goals and contexts (nature of products, production technology, size of units, dependence, regional location) (Sorge and Maurice, 1990: 142). Differences between US and German skills and practices, and managerial identities, for instance, reflect variations in labour-market institutions, and educational and industrial relations systems, as well as general conceptions of professional expertise and status.

Drawing on societal differences, this chapter compares and contrasts the key differences in major production systems and management across four capitalist societies, and suggests how we might explain the prevalence – or relative absence – of particular kinds of production system, such as the ideal type of Toyotism and flexible production.[1] The

---

[1] Obviously, there are many variants on each type of production system. For theoretical and explanatory purposes, however, we focus here on ideal types against which diversity can be gauged.

emphasis is on how particular societal constellations tend to encourage the development and reproduction of distinctive kinds of work organization, and control and discourage antithetical ones. This chapter discusses the USA, Japan, Germany and Sweden because the societal contexts of these nations have contributed to the development of major production systems. Specifically, Taylorism and Fordism developed within the US societal context from where they spread to Europe. Toyotism, which developed within the Japanese societal context, Uddevallaism, which developed in Sweden, and diversified quality production, which developed within the German context, were all inspired by the flexible production of high-quality products. With the dissolution of the Taylorist–Fordist production control systems in the 1980s and 1990s, these three flexible models were seen as the future production models.

The next section explains the key characteristics of these production systems. This discussion is targeted especially at readers who do not have a background in production or operations management. Inevitably, the information in this section might not be new to all readers. Readers who already have some knowledge of production systems and their features can turn immediately to the subsequent section, which can be read entirely separately from the first section. It provides an explanation of the connections between the features of the production systems that are described in the first section and the societal contexts in which these systems developed.

7.2　Characteristics and Types of Production System

Taylorism, or scientific management[2] (1890–1911)

At the turn of the century, a US engineer (and former worker) called Frederick Taylor undertook the first systematic steps in the area of production management. As Taylor's ideas (referred to as scientific management, or Taylorism) have remained highly influential up to the present day – albeit often in a vulgarized or adapted form – they merit closer examination (Lane, 1989: 140).

Based on his long experience as a worker, first-line supervisor and manager, Taylor held a somewhat low opinion of workers, although he was not anti-worker. He made a distinction between what he termed the '*first-class* man' and the '*average* man'. In Taylor's view, a first-class man is highly motivated and pushes forward with his work rather than wasting time or restricting output. Ideally such men should be selected for the appropriate task and supported by management through financial incentives. In Taylor's experience, restriction of output was the norm in the many workshops he had encountered and he described the phenomenon as 'soldiering' (Sheldrake, 1996: 15). He further classified soldiering as either *natural* – or the tendency of the average man to take it easy and to work slowly through lack of incentive and through peer pressure – or *systematic* – the tendency to reduce output with the deliberate objective of keeping employers ignorant of how fast the work could be done.

Taylor's response to these problems was the application of what he termed a 'systematic and scientific time study', breaking each job down into simple, basic elements and

---

[2]　This section is based mainly on Sheldrake (1996), chapter 2 and Lane (1989), chapter 6.

working out precisely what kinds of body movement were required by able workers to execute *individual tasks* in the shortest possible time without increasing the intensity of labour. Timings of the basic elements were then placed on file and, with appropriate weightings built in, used as the means to construct standard times for various jobs (ibid.). Task management also stimulated management's ability to take greater control of all aspects of production, including tooling, machines, materials, methods and job design, thus enhancing the continued replacement of skill with the standardized approach favoured by US production techniques (Sheldrake, 1996: 16). 'Central to Taylor's system was the desire to rationalize and standardize production techniques in the interests of the economy, efficiency and mutual prosperity' (Sheldrake, 1996: 23). As Lane explains, 'Taylor's advocacy (though not invention) of the principle of maximum decomposition of work tasks implied the minimization of skill requirements – deskilling – in the resulting manual tasks and introduced two new kinds of division of labour. The first, and most insidious, is the separation of mental labour (or conception, planning of labour) from manual labour (or execution, doing); the second is the divorce of direct from indirect labour, i.e. the production tasks from those of setting up, preparation and maintenance' (Lane, 1989: 141).*

Taylor summed all of this up in three central principles:

1. 'the substitution of a science for the individual judgement of the workers;
2. the scientific selection and development of the worker, after each has been studied, taught and trained – instead of allowing the workers to select themselves in a haphazard way, and
3. the intimate cooperation of the management with the workers, so that they do the work together in accordance with the scientific laws that have been developed, instead of leaving the solution of each problem in the hands of the individual worker' (Sheldrake, 1996: 18).

Taylorism demonstrated that expert knowledge of the technical means of production, coupled with time study and financial incentives, could substantially improve efficiency levels. Tayloristic forms of production management have gained huge increases in productivity, achieved both directly and indirectly through enhanced control over the labour process. Taylor was aware that the greater the level of technical complexity, the greater the need for managerial control and the less autonomy required for the individual worker. Ironically, the greatest publicity has been given not to Taylor's management of the interface between complex technology and the worker but to the situation where the level of technical complexity is negligible and the attributes of the worker limited to brute strength and stamina (Sheldrake, 1996: 19).

Taylor's insight into the general logic of industrial work was combined with particular assumptions about human psychology and a particular approach to the problem of incentives (Sheldrake, 1996: 22). He argued that the goals of the worker had to be brought into line with the goals of the enterprise. This problem was to be solved by gearing the worker's wage to his production output through a system of incentive wages. 'He suggested that this problem could be solved if management used the following two

---

* Reproduced with permission of C. Lane.

'motivators'. First, the workman has to be given precise standards as to what amount of labour is expected of him in a given timespan so that he can judge his progress and achieve satisfaction in the attainment of his target. But Taylor believed in the natural laziness of workers and, therefore, recommended close supervision throughout the work. Control of work is, of course, made easier by the fact that tasks are simple and contain no indeterminate 'mental labour' requirements. Secondly, Taylor postulated that individuals would be willing to work in this way if their pay was made to rise with the amount of effort they invested. Taylor thus propagated a view of human nature which, with its exclusive emphasis on extrinsic rewards and its implied a high degree of toleration of monotonous and meaningless activity' (Lane, 1989: 141).*

Criticism and opposition notwithstanding, because of the tremendous advantages this approach brought to management, the insights and techniques of Taylor's work steadily became popular. Taylorism spread from the USA all over the industrialized and industrializing world, and was widely accepted by European management from the 1930s onwards. 'The subsequent world-wide diffusion of Taylorism has not always entailed the adoption of all its elements and frequently involved a merging with elements of other management philosophies and/or techniques of work organization to suit specific national traditions or economic conditions' (Lane, 1989: 142).* A legitimate definition of Taylorism, therefore, should be precise and should include its main features in order to avoid confusion and dispute about the true nature of the system. The following criteria are widely accepted as constituting such a working definition of Taylorism:

- a high degree of division of labour
- a low degree of worker discretion
- close task control
- a minimum-interaction employment relationship, based only on the cash nexus.

'Diffusion of Taylorism was aided by the internationalization of technology – which was usually accompanied by American management techniques, and by the spread of multinational companies' (Lane, 1989: 144–5).* Important to the widespread acceptance of Taylorism was the emergence of vast mass markets for industrial goods, in the more advanced industrial countries, from the 1930s onwards. 'The principles of Taylorism are, of course, particularly adapted to the production of large quantities of standardized and relatively cheap goods by special-purpose machinery' (Lane, 1989: 145).* 'This was first spectacularly demonstrated by Henry Ford in the first decades of this century with his mass production of Model-T cars, based on assembly-line technology and the labour of semi-skilled operatives. A few decades later, European industrialists such as the Michelin brothers strove to emulate him, and gradually Taylorism, or at least Taylorist techniques became accepted in all three societies. But Scientific Management has never penetrated the three European societies to the same extent and today still shows a correspondingly different hold on their production organization. It had to interact with, and adapt to, pre-existing national economic strategies, managerial culture, industrial relations systems and, above all, with the extant qualification structure of the labour force and expectations of both managers and workers resulting from it' (Lane, 1989: 145).*

* Reproduced with permission of C. Lane.

Fordism, or mass production[3]

Around 1914, Henry Ford's adaptation of Taylor's ideas to the operation of specialized machinery further intensified both the division of labour and its intensity, which became dictated by the machine. Ford developed a system, that he called mass production. *Mass production* can be defined as the manufacture of standardized products in high volumes using special-purpose machinery and predominantly unskilled labour.

Mass production seeks to profit from economies of scale. Higher levels of production make possible a greater degree of task differentiation with commensurately lower training requirements and qualifications for workers. Higher levels of production also make it more attractive to produce parts in-house instead of depending on external suppliers. There is, however, a downside to this approach. Lower levels of training of workers also invite greater opportunities for human error. The complexity of the production process increases as more items are manufactured in-house. To prevent errors from paralysing the entire operation, extra reserves are stockpiled that function as buffers between various departments. Similarly, parts from outside suppliers are stored to ensure a consistently available inventory of suitable quality (Dankbaar, 1995).

Ford was able to dominate what soon became the world's largest industry by becoming the first to master the principles of mass production, which made productivity increase immensely. 'Rather, it was the complete and consistent interchangeability of parts and the simplicity of attaching them to each other. These were the manufacturing innovations that made the assembly line possible' (Womack *et al.*, 1990: 27).*

'The key to interchangeable parts, as we saw, lay in designing new tools that could cut hardened metal and stamp sheet steel with absolute precision. But the key to inexpensive interchangeable parts would be found in tools that could do this job at high volume

---

Box 7.1: ❧ **The Main Characteristics of Craft Production**

> ❧ *A workforce that is highly skilled in design, machine operation and fitting.* Most workers progressed through an apprenticeship to a full set of craft skills. Many could hope to run their own machine shops, becoming self-employed contractors to assembler firms.
>
> ❧ *Organizations that are extremely decentralized, although concentrated within a single city.* Most parts and much of the vehicle's design came from small machine shops. The system is coordinated by an owner/entrepreneur in direct contact with everyone involved: customers, employers and suppliers.
>
> ❧ *The use of general-purpose machine tools* to perform drilling, grinding and other operations on metal and wood.
>
> ❧ *A very low production volume* – 1000 or fewer automobiles a year, only a small number of which (50 or fewer) were built to the same design. Even among those 50, no two were exactly alike since craft techniques inherently produced variations.

---

[3] Unless indicated otherwise, this section is based on Womack *et al.* (1990), chapter 2.

* Extracts on this page are reprinted with the permission of Rawson Associates/Scribner, an imprint of Simon and Schuster Adult Publishing Group, from *The Machine That Changed The World* by James P. Womack, Daniel T. Jones and Daniel Roos. ©1990 by James P. Womack, Daniel T. Jones, Daniel Roos, and Donna Sammons Carpenter.

with low or no set-up costs between pieces. That is, for a machine to do something to a piece of metal, someone must put the metal in the machine, then someone may need to adjust the machine. In the craft-production system – where a single machine could do many tasks but required lots of adjustment – this was the skilled machinist's job' (Womack *et al.*, 1990: 35 –6).*

'Ford dramatically reduced set-up time by making machines that could do only one task a time. Then his engineers perfected simple jigs and fixtures for holding the work piece in this dedicated machine. The unskilled worker could simply snap the piece in place and push a button or pull a lever for the machine to perform the required task. This meant the machine could be loaded and unloaded by an employee with five minutes' training.

In addition, because Ford made only one product, he could place his machines in a sequence so that each manufacturing step led immediately to the next. . . . Because set-up times were reduced from minutes – or even hours – to seconds, Ford could get much higher volume from the same number of machines. Even more important, the engineers also found a way to machine many parts at once. The only penalty with this system was inflexibility. Changing these dedicated machines to do a new task was time-consuming and expensive' (Womack *et al.*, 1990: 36).*

As indicated, these dedicated machines allowed Ford to eliminate the skilled fitters who had always formed the bulk of every assembler's labour force. In fact, what had been a handicraft form of production was transformed into a series of divided, repetitive tasks marked by extremely restricted autonomy and great physical burden. Indeed, Ford not only perfected the interchangeable part, he perfected the interchangeable worker. Ford took Taylor's division of labour to its ultimate extreme. 'The skilled fitter in Ford's craft production plant of 1908 had gathered all the necessary parts, obtained tools from the tool room, repaired them if necessary, performed the complex fitting and assembly job for the entire vehicle, then checked over his work before sending the completed vehicle to the shipping department.

'In stark contrast, the assembler on Ford's mass-production line had only one task – to put two nuts on two bolts or perhaps to attach one wheel to each car. He didn't order parts, procure his tools, repair his equipment, inspect for quality, or even understand what the workers on either side of him were doing' (Womack *et al.*, 1990: 31).*

'Someone, of course, did have to think about how all the parts came together and just what each assembler should do. This was the task for a newly created professional, the industrial engineer. Similarly, someone had to arrange for the delivery of parts to the line, usually a production engineer who designed conveyor belts or chutes to do the job. Housecleaning workers were sent around periodically to clean up work areas, and skilled repairmen circulated to refurbish the assemblers' tools. Yet another specialist checked quality. Work that was not done properly was not discovered until the end of the assembly line, where another group of workers was called into play – the rework men, who retained many of the fitters' skills' (Womack and *et al.*, 1990: 30).*

'With this separation of labor, the assembler required only a few minutes of training. Moreover, he was relentlessly disciplined by the pace of the line, which speeded up the

* Extracts on this page are reprinted with the permission of Rawson Associates/Scribner, an imprint of Simon and Schuster Adult Publishing Group, from *The Machine That Changed The World* by James P. Womack, Daniel T. Jones and Daniel Roos. ©1990 by James P. Womack, Daniel T. Jones, Daniel Roos, and Donna Sammons Carpenter.

slow and slowed down the speedy. The foreman – formerly the head of a whole area of the factory with wide-ranging duties and responsibilities, but now reduced to a semiskilled checker – could spot immediately any slacking off or failure to perform the assigned task. As a result, the workers on the line were as replaceable as the parts on the car' (Womack *et al.*, 1990: 31–2).*

'In this atmosphere, Ford took it as a given that his workers wouldn't volunteer any information on operating conditions – for example, that a tool was malfunctioning – much less suggest ways to improve the process. These functions fell respectively to the foreman and the industrial engineer, who reported their findings and suggestions to higher levels of management for action. So were born the battalions of narrowly skilled indirect workers – the repairman, the quality inspector, the housekeeper, and the rework specialist, in addition to the foreman and the industrial engineer. These workers hardly existed in craft production. . . . However, indirect workers became ever more prominent in Fordist, mass-production factories as the introduction of automation over the years gradually reduced the need for assemblers' (Womack *et al.*, 1990: 32).*

'Ford was dividing labor not only in the factory, but also in the engineering shop. Industrial engineers took their places next to the manufacturing engineers who designed the critical production machinery. They were joined by product engineers, who designed and engineered the car itself. But these specialists were only the beginning.

'Some industrial engineers specialized in assembly operations, others in the operation of the dedicated machines making individual parts. Some manufacturing engineers specialized in the design of assembly hardware, others designed the specific machines for each special part. Some product engineers specialized in engines, others in bodies, and still others in suspensions or electrical systems' (Womack *et al.*, 1990: 32).*

'These original "knowledge workers" – individuals who manipulated ideas and information but rarely touched an actual car or even entered a factory – replaced the skilled machine-shop owners and the old-fashioned factory foremen of the earlier craft era. Those worker-managers had done it all – contracted with assembler, designed the part, developed a machine to make it, and, in many cases, supervised the operation of the machine in the workshop. The fundamental mission of these new specialists, by contrast, was to design tasks, parts, and tools that could be handled by the unskilled workers who made up the bulk of the new motor-vehicle industry work force' (Womack *et al.*, 1990: 32–33).*

'In this new system, the shop-floor worker had no career path, except perhaps to foreman. But the newly emerging professional engineers had a direct climb up the career ladder. Unlike the skilled craftsman, however, their career paths didn't lead toward ownership of a business. Nor did they lie within a single company, as Ford probably hoped. Rather, they would advance within their profession – from young engineer-trainee to senior engineer, who, by now possessing the entire body of knowledge of the profession, was in charge of coordinating engineers at lower levels. Reaching the pinnacle of the engineering profession often meant hopping from company to company over the course of one's working life' (Womack *et al.*, 1990: 32–3).*

Flexible production[4]

During the 1970s, the western industrial world was characterized by a revolt against Taylorism and degrading work in mass production. However, it wasn't until the first half of the 1980s that the debate on new forms of production and work organization took a more dramatic turn in most advanced economies. The new developments in the organization of production in advanced societies not only called into question Taylorist practices of work organization but also presented a more comprehensive *new industrial strategy* in which a new approach to product markets had coalesced with the emergence of *more sophisticated production technology* and *new forms of utilizing labour power* (Piore and Sabel, 1984 as in Lane, 1989: 67). This new model of industrial production organization was called *flexible specialization* or *flexible production*. The new model seemed to be able to attain superior competitiveness in world markets through the sophisticated application of information technology, a diversified product range, and non-price-competitive marketing strategies, combining all these with high wages, skilled labour and a flexible, non-Taylorist organization of work.

The new strategy was regarded as a reaction to worldwide economic changes, which rendered problematic the old form of industrial development – mass production of standardized goods with the use of special-purpose machines and semi-skilled labour. As indicated, such production requires large and stable markets and, during the 1970s, various economic developments combined to undermine this stability. The most important of these was a shift in the international division of labour and world trade. The emergence of industrial economies in low-wage East and South-east Asian and Latin American countries, which produced standardized goods cheaper than the advanced industrial countries, has forced the latter to reconsider their role in the international division of labour and to look for alternative markets. The production of specialized/customized and/or high-quality goods, particularly producer goods, suggested itself as a new strategy. This also applied to home markets, where the demand for standardized goods was often saturated and where the development of more sophisticated tastes required more individualized goods as well as more frequent changes in product.

This changeover to a new market strategy was facilitated – and sometimes stimulated – by the emergence of new technology (Lane, 1989: 164). Micro-electronics was one of the technical innovations to gain momentum in the 1970s, and the use of upgraded micro-electronic applications has become particularly widespread since the late 1970s. Since then, micro-electronic circuits have become increasingly integrated, information-processing time has been reduced, and the price of switching functions has fallen proportionally. Improved computer performance has led to the incorporation of computers in equipment, installations and machinery in order to expand, improve and accelerate processing capacity (Sorge, 1995: 270). Computerized equipment made production more flexible as it made possible the frequent conversion of machinery and its adaptation to the production of small batches and/or individual customized products at relatively low costs. It also made possible instant adjustments of machinery to changing

---

* Extracts on this page are reprinted with the permission of Rawson Associates/Scribner, an imprint of Simon and Schuster Adult Publishing Group, from *The Machine That Changed The World* by James P. Womack, Daniel T. Jones and Daniel Roos. ©1990 by James P. Womack, Daniel T. Jones, Daniel Roos, and Donna Sammons Carpenter.

[4] Unless indicated otherwise, I am indebted to Lane (1989) and Streeck (1991) for the information in this section.

market demands – hence the term 'flexible specialization' or 'flexible production' to characterize the new form of production. The computer-controlled machinery not only facilitated the production of specialized goods at greater speed but also at a higher degree of precision and thus to higher quality standards. In fact, products of a craft type could be produced at a similar speed and price as were standardized mass goods. Further advantages flowing from the new technology are that the shorter production runs commit less capital, and that its flexible nature, making the enterprise less dependent on large and stable markets, renders investment in machinery a less precarious matter.

In order to be able to analyse the alternative manufacturing policies that were enabled by the new technology three variables are important: the degree to which products are standardized, the type of competition they try to meet, and the volume of output. The first two factors appear to be closely related in that standardized products are generally sold in price-competitive markets, whereas customized products tend to be quality-competitive. This suggests a distinction between *standardized price-competitive* and *customized quality-competitive* production, on the one hand, and *low-* and *high-volume* production on the other. Crossing the two dimensions generates four alternative product or manufacturing strategies (as depicted in Figure 7.1), two of which – the *low-volume production of customized quality-competitive* goods ('craft' production) and the *high-volume production of standardized price-competitive* goods ('Fordist' production) – were quite conventional. Indeed, with some simplification one could say that before the advent of micro-electronic technology, these would have been the only production patterns possible.

This simple picture, however, became considerably more complicated as a result of technical change. Among other things, new technology seemed to have lowered the break-even point of mass production, both enabling traditional mass producers to survive with shorter production runs and, perhaps, making it easier for artisanal low-volume producers to achieve economies of scale and enter mass-type markets. At the same time, the capacity of the new technology for fast and inexpensive retooling seemed to have made it

Figure 7.1 Categorization of work systems

Volume of output	**Differentiation of output:** Small Standardized Competitive prices	**Differentiation of output:** Large Customized Competitive quality
Small	Specialized component parts	Craft production
Large	Mass production ('Fordism')	Diversified quality production

Source: adapted from Sorge (1995).

attractive for small component producers dependent on large assemblers to differentiate their product range and move into an advanced form of craft production, so as to reduce their exposure to price fluctuations and monopsonistic demand (one buyer and many sellers).

The most important impact of the new technology on manufacturing strategy, however, seemed to be that it had created a new option for firms in the form of *high-volume production of customized quality-competitive* goods. In many manufacturing sectors, micro-electronic circuitry had eroded the traditional distinction between mass and specialist production. The high flexibility of micro-electronic equipment, and the ease and speed with which it can be reprogrammed enabled firms to introduce a hitherto unknown degree of product variety, as well as product quality. The result was a restructuring of mass production in the mould of customized quality production, with central features of the latter being blended into the former and with small-batch production of highly specific goods becoming enveloped in large-batch production of basic components or models. This pattern was what came to be called *diversified quality production*. It can be approached by firms through two different paths of industrial restructuring: by craft producers extending their production volume without sacrificing their high-quality standards and customized product design, or by mass producers moving upmarket by upgrading their products' design and quality, and by increasing their product variety, in an attempt to escape from the pressures of price competition or from shrinking mass markets.

As suggested, flexible specialization or production also implied a new way of deploying labour power. The operation of the more complex technology, and the frequent changes required, were more satisfactorily accomplished by the utilization of skilled labour and the organization of work along the old 'craft' lines. The Taylorist strategy of designing high-specialization/low-discretion jobs or work roles was replaced by one seeking a high degree of overlap between specialisms and flexibility of deployment, as well as the exercise of 'craft' judgement and skill. Thus, polyvalency of skill was given particular emphasis in the new form of worker deployment. Workers were assigned more holistic work tasks, had enriched jobs, and enjoyed greater autonomy and responsibility.

During the 1980s, when flexible specialization was in its developmental phase, scholars were already debating the feasibility of adopting these new technologies, and the new form of work organization they implied in all advanced societies. Some argued that only societies with a surviving craft tradition (i.e. a tradition relying on skilled, all-round workers, operating in a high-trust environment, free from detailed or continuous management control) would be able to successfully adopt the new form of work organization. They identified such remnants of a craft tradition in Germany, Italy and Japan, and saw the new production concept emerging mainly in these societies. In the USA and France, in contrast, they suggested, the extinction of this tradition, and the extant forms of union and state control, respectively, militate against the adoption of the strategy of flexible specialization (Piore and Sabel, 1984). The next section elaborates on this argument and explains the difficulties of US manufacturers in shifting from mass to flexible production.

Lean production[5]

The widespread popularity of, as well as the many misconceptions regarding, lean production explain the amount of attention that is paid to the concept in this chapter. Forced by societal circumstances, Japanese producers were experimenting with flexible production techniques from the 1950s onwards. It all began when Eiji Toyoda, a young Japanese engineer from the Toyoda family, and Taiichi Ohno, his production genius, after a visit to a US Ford plant, realized that mass production could never work in Japan. The problems facing the Toyota company were as follows.

1. 'The domestic market was tiny and demanded a wide range of vehicles – luxury cars for government officials, large trucks to carry goods to market, small trucks for Japan's small farmers, and small cars suitable for Japan's crowded cities and high energy prices.

2. The native Japanese work force, as Toyota and other firms soon learned, was no longer willing to be treated as a variable cost or as interchangeable parts. What was more, the new labor laws introduced by the American occupation greatly strengthened the position of workers in negotiating more favorable conditions of employment. Management's right to lay off employees was severely restricted, and the bargaining position of company unions representing all employees was greatly reinforced. The company unions used their strength to represent everyone, eliminating the distinction between blue- and white-collar workers, and secured a share of company profits in the form of bonus payments in addition to basic pay.

   Furthermore, in Japan there were no "guest workers" – that is, temporary immigrants willing to put up with sub-standard working conditions in return for high pay – or minorities with limited occupational choice. In the West, by contrast, these individuals had formed the core of the work force in most mass-production companies.

3. The war-ravaged Japanese economy was starved of capital and for foreign exchange, meaning that massive purchases of the latest Western production technology were quite impossible.

4. The outside world was full of huge motor-vehicle producers who were anxious to establish operations in Japan and ready to defend their established markets against Japanese exports' (Womack *et al.*, 1990: 49–50).*

In order to become a full-range car producer with a variety of new models, Taiichi Ohno realized that neither Ford's tools and methods nor its craft production methods were suitable. He needed a new approach. From this tentative beginning was born what Toyota came to call the Toyota Production System and, ultimately, lean production.

An important example, which demonstrates some lean production techniques, concerns the production of the different metal parts of a car from sheet steel. Mass producers of cars start with a large roll of sheet steel. They run this sheet through an automated 'blanking' press to produce a stack of blanks slightly larger than the final part they want.

---

[5] Unless indicated otherwise, this section draws on Womack *et al.* (1990).

* Extracts on this page are reprinted with the permission of Rawson Associates/Scribner, an imprint of Simon and Schuster Adult Publishing Group, from *The Machine That Changed The World* by James P. Womack, Daniel T. Jones and Daniel Roos. ©1990 by James P. Womack, Daniel T. Jones, Daniel Roos, and Donna Sammons Carpenter.

'They then insert the blanks in massive stamping presses containing matched upper and lower dies. When these dies are pushed together under thousands of pounds of pressure, the two-dimensional blank takes the three-dimensional shape of a car fender or a truck door as it moves through a series of presses.

'The problem with this second method, from Ohno's perspective, was the minimum scale required for economical operation. The massive and expensive Western press lines were designed to operate at about twelve strokes per minute, three shifts a day, to make a million or more of a given part in a year. Yet, in the early days, Toyota's entire production was a few thousand vehicles a year' (Womack et al., 1990:52).*

'The dies could be changed so that same press line could make many parts, but doing so presented major difficulties. The dies weighed many tons each, and workers had to align them in the press with absolute precision. A slight misalignment produced wrinkled parts. A more serious misalignment could produce a nightmare in which the sheet metal melted in the die, necessitating extremely expensive and time-consuming repairs' (Womack et al., 1990: 52).* In order to avoid these problems, die changes were assigned to specialists. Die changes were undertaken methodically, and typically required a full day to go from the last part with the old dies to the first acceptable part from the new ones. Western manufacturers, selling a large enough volume, found that they could often 'dedicate' a set of presses to a specific part and stamp these parts for months, or even years, without changing dies.

Toyota's budget, however, was unable to finance the hundreds of stamping presses needed to make all the parts needed for the car and truck bodies. Its capital budget dictated that practically the entire car be stamped from a few press lines. This gave rise to the idea of developing simple die-change techniques and to change dies frequently – every two to three hours versus two to three months – using rollers to move dies in and out of position, and simple adjustment mechanisms. 'Because the new techniques were easy to master and production workers were idle during the die changes, Ohno hit upon the idea of letting production workers perform the die changes as well' (Womack et al., 1990: 52).* After endless experiments, from the late 1940s onwards, Ohno eventually perfected his technique for quick changes. 'By the late 1950s, he had reduced the time required to change dies from a day to an astonishing three minutes and eliminated the need for die-change specialists. In the process he made an unexpected discovery – it actually cost less per part to make small batches of stampings than to run off enormous lots.

'There were two reasons for this phenomenon. Making small batches eliminated the carrying cost of the huge inventories of finished parts that mass-production systems required. Even more important, making only a few parts before assembling them into a car caused stamping mistakes to show up almost instantly.

'The consequences of this latter discovery were enormous. It made those in the stamping shop much more concerned about quality, and it eliminated the waste of large numbers of defective parts – which had to be repaired at great expense, or even discarded – that were discovered only long after manufacture' (Womack et al., 1990: 53).*

* Extracts on this page are reprinted with the permission of Rawson Associates/Scribner, an imprint of Simon and Schuster Adult Publishing Group, from *The Machine That Changed The World* by James P. Womack, Daniel T. Jones and Daniel Roos. ©1990 by James P. Womack, Daniel T. Jones, Daniel Roos, and Donna Sammons Carpenter.

However, while Toyota made having small or zero inventories a priority and thus chose to concentrate on small-batch manufacturing, the objective was still similar to that of mass production: to produce the highest possible cumulative volume of each product. Long total runs were (and are) decisive for the careful preparation of the manufacture of each part; standardizing tools, methods and operations; streamlining suppliers; and developing the just-in-time (JIT) flow. It cannot be said, then, that the Toyota system is the antithesis of mass production; it is rather the antithesis of large-batch manufacturing. Flexibility is a matter of switching quickly between a number of standardized models – of retooling from model A to model B, for instance. The high frequency of such switching in the Toyota system has also meant that 'resetting work' could itself be standardized and intensified. It has become part of the highly rationalized system of mass production. The Toyota system's flexibility of mass production has therefore been argued to represent an extension of the sphere of influence of scientific management (Berggren, 1992: 28–9).

In contrast to large-batch mass production, however, in order to make the small-batch system work – a system that ideally produced two hours or less of inventory – an extremely skilled and highly motivated workforce was needed. (See Table 7.1 for a contrast between mass and lean production.) If workers failed to anticipate problems before they occurred, and didn't take the initiative to devise solutions, the work of the whole factory could easily grind to a halt. Holding back knowledge and effort – repeatedly noted by industrial sociologists as a salient feature of all mass-production systems – would swiftly lead to disaster in Toyota. As indicated, labour conditions had changed in Japan after the Second World War; strong unions combined with severe restrictions on the ability of company owners to fire workers led to protracted negotiations between unions and owners at many plants, including Toyota. These negotiations resulted in the development of a compromise that, to a large extent, remains the formula for labour relations in the Japanese auto industry today. Specifically, employees were granted lifetime employment and seniority pay, and often received access to company facilities such as housing, recreation, and so forth (see Chapter 5 for a full explanation). In return, the company expected that most employees would remain with the company for their entire working lives. The employees also agreed to be flexible in work assignments and active in promoting the interests of the company by initiating improvements rather than merely responding to problems.

This new approach to human capital allowed Toyota to eliminate other types of waste (*muda*) that characterized mass production – that is, wasted effort, materials and time. At Toyota it was thought that assembly workers – instead of performing one or two simple tasks, repetitively as in mass production – could probably do most of the functions of the Fordist specialists and do them much better because of their direct acquaintance with conditions on the line. Toyota started to group workers in teams with a team leader rather than a foreman. 'The teams were given a set of assembly steps, their piece of the line, and told to work together on how best to perform the necessary operations. The team leader would do assembly tasks as well as coordinate the team, and, in particular, would fill in for any absent worker – concepts unheard of in mass-production plants' (Womack *et al.*, 1990: 56).* The team was also given the job of

* Extracts on this page are reprinted with the permission of Rawson Associates/Scribner, an imprint of Simon and Schuster Adult Publishing Group, from *The Machine That Changed The World* by James P. Womack, Daniel T. Jones and Daniel Roos. ©1990 by James P. Womack, Daniel T. Jones, Daniel Roos, and Donna Sammons Carpenter.

Table 7.1   Lean and mass production systems compared

	Lean system	Mass system
Type of production	Small-batch flexible mass production	Large-batch mass production
Complexity	*Low* • elimination of waste in structure • fewer functional hierarchical levels	*High* • allows complex and redundant structure • more hierarchical levels and more differentiated divisions
Formalization	*Low* • emphasis on teamwork • flexible job responsibilities • encourages multiple job skills and expertise	*High* • high division of individual labour • strict rules for individual job responsibilities • discourages multiple job skills
Centralization	*Low* • lateral communication is encouraged and decisions are made collectively on a team basis • encourages participation from lower-level employees and lateral-level co-workers	*High* • communication and decision-making is based on strict vertical individual command chain • discourages participation from lower-level employees or lateral-level co-workers
Problem-solving attitude	*Proactive* • workers actively search for problems • workers are trained to tackle problems	*Reactive* • workers wait passively for problems to happen • workers are trained to pass rather than to tackle problems

Source: adapted from Zhiang Lin and Chun Hui (1999).

housekeeping, minor tool repair and quality checking. Finally, once the teams were running smoothly, time was set aside periodically for them to suggest ways of improving the process. This continuous, incremental improvement process (*kaizen*) took place in collaboration with the industrial engineers, who were still present but in much smaller numbers than in the mass-production plants (ibid.).

In striking contrast to the mass-production plant (where stopping the line was the responsibility of the senior line manager), to eliminate the passing on of errors until the end of the line, in the Toyota plant a cord was placed above every workstation and workers were instructed to stop the whole assembly line immediately if a problem emerged that they couldn't fix. Then, the whole team would come over to work on the problem. It was reasoned that the mass-production practice of simply passing on errors in order to keep the line running caused errors to multiply endlessly. Because problems would not be discovered until the very end of the line, a large number of similarly defective vehicles would have been built before the problem was discovered.

Moreover, in mass-production plants, problems tended to be treated as random events. The idea was simply to repair each error and hope that it didn't recur. Toyota instituted a system of problem-solving, which taught production workers to systematically trace every error back to its ultimate cause, then to devise a fix, so that it would never occur again. After a while the result was that the line practically never stopped, the amount of rework needed before shipment fell continually and the quality of the shipped cars improved steadily. This was for the simple reason that quality inspection, no matter how diligent, simply cannot detect all the defects that can be assembled into today's complex vehicles.

A major strength of the lean production system is the *lean supply chain*. The task of a final assembly plant, which assembles the major components into a complete vehicle, accounts for only 15 per cent of the total manufacturing process. 'The bulk of the process involves engineering and fabricating more than 10,000 discrete parts and assembling these into perhaps 100 major components – engines, transmissions, steering gears, suspensions, and so forth.

Coordinating this process so that everything comes together at the right time with high quality and low cost has been a continuing challenge to the final assembler firms in the auto industry' (Womack *et al.*, 1990: 58).*

While Ford's initial answer to this problem was complete or 100 per cent vertical integration, after the Second World War, the company disintegrated to 50 per cent. The world's mass-production assemblers ended up adopting widely varying degrees of formal integration, ranging from about 25 per cent in-house production at smaller specialist firms (i.e. Porsche and Saab) to 70 per cent at General Motors. The central engineering staffs of mass-production assemblers such as Ford and GM designed most of the parts needed in a vehicle and the component systems they comprised. A number of suppliers – whether formally part of the assembler firm or independent businesses – were given the drawings and were asked for bids on a given number of parts. Among all the outside firms and internal divisions that were asked to bid, the lowest bidder got the business. In general, success depended on price, quality and delivery reliability, and the car makers often switched business between firms at relatively short notice.

At Toyota, it was found that the real question was not the make-or-buy decisions that occasioned so much debate in mass-production firms, but rather how the assembler and the suppliers could work together smoothly to reduce costs and improve quality, whatever formal, legal relationship they might have. The solution to this problem was found in taking a new, lean production approach to components supply. The first step was to organize suppliers into functional tiers. First-tier suppliers were responsible for working as an integral part of the product-development team in developing a new product – for instance, a steering, braking or electrical system that would work in harmony with the other systems. Toyota stimulated cooperation among its first-tier suppliers in order to improve the design process. 'Because each supplier, for the most part, specialized in one type of component and did not compete in that respect with other suppliers in the group, sharing information was comfortable and mutually beneficial. Then, each first-tier supplier formed a second tier of suppliers under itself. Companies in the second tier were assigned the job of fabricating individual parts. These suppliers were manufacturing specialists, usually without much expertise in product engineering but with strong backgrounds in process engineering and plant operations' (Womack *et al.*, 1990: 60–1).* Second-tier suppliers were also grouped into supplier associations to exchange information on advances in manufacturing techniques.

Such a high degree of cooperation and information sharing cannot be obtained through marketplace relationships, and Toyota did not wish to vertically integrate its suppliers into a single, large bureaucracy. 'Instead, Toyota spun its in-house supply operations off into quasi-independent first-tier supplier companies in which Toyota retained a fraction of the equity and developed similar relationships with other suppliers who had been completely independent. As the process proceeded, Toyota's first-tier suppliers acquired

Case: Japanese Production Practices in China[6]

China has become an increasingly important destination for Japanese foreign direct investment. China is second only to the USA as a location for Japanese overseas investment. Moreover, Japan is the second largest inward investor to China, behind the quasi-overseas Hong Kong and Taiwan. The question to be answered in this context is to what extent Japanese production management techniques have been transferred to Japanese plants in China. The societal arguments of similarities in the social relationships of work tend to indicate that the 'process of Japanization' should be much easier in Asia than in western countries.

In order to evaluate this question, 20 Japanese manufacturing plants based in China were investigated. Of the 20 plants, 12 were located in Guangdong Province and four each in Nantong and Tianjin. Categorized by industry, there were eight chemical-related plants, seven consumer-electrical, four apparel and one machining (auto parts) factory. Japanese investors held majority share ownership in over half the plants. The average age of the plants was a little over five years, with the oldest 14 years old and the youngest only 1 year old. The primary objective for 13 of the Japanese firms setting up manufacturing operations in China was to take advantage of cheap land, labour and raw material costs. This was especially evident in Guangdong Province. In five cases, proximity to Hong Kong was a major objective and, in four, it was access to China's growing market.

* Extracts on this page are reprinted with the permission of Rawson Associates/Scribner, an imprint of Simon and Schuster Adult Publishing Group, from *The Machine That Changed The World* by James P. Womack, Daniel T. Jones and Daniel Roos. ©1990 by James P. Womack, Daniel T. Jones, Daniel Roos, and Donna Sammons Carpenter.
[6] This case is based on Taylor (1999).

In half of the cases, the Chinese partner was a government agency and/or a state-owned enterprise. For the Chinese partners the transfer of hard technology and modern 'capitalist' management systems was of primary importance. In three cases, the Chinese managers also considered employment opportunities and stimulation of international competitiveness as being important in cooperating with the Japanese.

The plants had generally only a few (three to six) Japanese personnel members on site. There were two exceptions to this: one where a plant had 150 Japanese and over 3000 local staff making precision electronic goods and CD drives, and another employing over 8000 locals and about 70–80 Hong Kong and Japanese staff, which made earphones, speakers and similar audio products. Both these product lines required a reasonably high degree of technical support in order to ensure such processes as quality management and machine maintenance. At least one more firm also required such high-level quality assurance, but this was achieved by other means.

With respect to production technology, it was found that, in half the cases, most of the machinery was imported from Japan. In general, the plants in China had more or less the same physical sort of factories as would be found in Japan, though sometimes on a smaller scale.

With respect to production and inventory management, however, there were significant differences between plants in China and those in Japan. In Japan, production varies according to consumer demand. At its most sophisticated, JIT production allows output to correspond to final demand through a system of pulling production through the factory, significantly reducing the need for inventories. In addition, the ultimate in lean arrangements allows multiskilled workers to work on a range of products in short runs so as to rapidly match market demands, leading to mixed production, which has been regarded as a key feature of JIT.

In eight Chinese plants, there was no variation at all in production output over a year. These firms included five chemical and three electronics plants, the latter being two component suppliers to Japan and one electronics multinational producing facsimile machines for export. Among these plants, only two held very low levels of stock of finished goods on-site. This reflects highly predictable production output rather than the achievement of JIT production.

The other 12 firms coped with fluctuations in product demand primarily through traditional techniques of either producing for stock or varying working time. Five plants, mainly labour-intensive apparel, leather products and electronics manufacturers coped with variations in product demand using overtime work. The other seven firms, including leather goods producers, three chemical firms and two electronics plants (making laser pitches and stereos), employed temporary workers at peak times. Other plants tried to maintain steady production, sometimes despite seasonal variations in demand. Thus, stocks were accumulated either to maximize machine utilization or in order to preserve regularity in plant operations, large variations in activity being seen as disruptive to work routines.

Another aspect of Japanese production techniques – that is, frequent and fast changes in production runs, requiring workers to have knowledge of various types of product – was also applied only marginally. While all 20 firms had some kind of variation in their product lines over time, this was usually limited to workers having no more than one product change a day or three a week. Moreover, these changes in products usually had minimal impact on line workers' jobs. In chemical production, change-overs took much longer than in, say, electronics, resulting in production-line stoppages of hours at a time. Consequently, the notions of flexible and mixed production were not really applied, the costs of 'retooling' far outweighing any benefits from lower stockholding.

Chinese employees pointed to Japanese workers' excessive attention to detail. Such detail included ascertaining and reducing rejection rates from individuals and machines, regulating 'wasted time' from toilet breaks and machine set-ups, as well as frequent management meetings to review and plan. Japanese management, on the other hand, was frustrated by the lack of urgency or seriousness that the Chinese workers applied to this 'attention to detail'; a reflection of the apparent Chinese lack of interest in Japanese efforts towards continuous improvement.

Japanese firms are also well known for the quality of their products, brought about in large part by the efforts of shop-floor workers, whether this involvement is voluntary or coerced, or a combination of the two. What is seen as distinctive about Japanese quality management is the organization of shop-floor employees so that they are involved in continuous quality control and quality improvement. In China, all 20 firms were submitted to the strict quality management measures being introduced by the Japanese. However, quality control was in the hands of Japanese experts, and involved multiple checking, goods inward and outward checks, and checks at various stages of production. Moreover, the Japanese concern with quality was backed with incentive pay schemes that took account of rejects attributed to individual workers. Thus, strong pressure from material incentives was placed on workers to conform to quality standards, with hardly any inculcation of quality consciousness among Chinese workers. In two firms, the work group rather than the individual was held accountable for quality targets, so that the group's bonus was dependent on each individual's performance. Thus, on the whole, there was little evidence that sufficient concern was given to incorporating workers' intrinsic motivation towards developing a consciousness of quality.

Questions

1. What does the case tell you about the transferability of Japanese production techniques to China?

2. Explain how, if at all, the Japanese firms adapted their techniques to the Chinese environment?

3. Assess whether the production techniques explained in the case could be transferred to the US and German production environment.

much of the rest of the equity in each other' (Womack *et al.*, 1990: 61).* Toyota also encouraged its suppliers to perform work for other assemblers, and for firms in other industries, because outside business almost always generated higher profit margins. Toyota also shared personnel with its supplier-group firms in two ways. 'It would lend them personnel to deal with workload surges, and it would transfer senior managers not in line for top positions at Toyota to senior positions in supplier firms' (Womack *et al.*, 1990: 61).*

Finally, to coordinate the flow of parts within the supply system on a day-to-day basis, the famous just-in-time (JIT) system, known as *kanban* at Toyota, was developed. The idea behind it was to simply convert a vast group of suppliers and parts plants into one large 'machine', like Ford's plant, by dictating that parts would only be produced at each step to supply the immediate demand of the next step; the mechanism was the containers carrying parts to the next step. As each container was used up, it was sent back to the previous step, and this became the automatic signal to make more parts. This simple idea was enormously difficult to implement as it eliminated practically all inventories and meant that when one small part of the vast production system failed, the whole system came to a standstill (Womack *et al.*, 1990: 62).

While lean production represents a major advance in productivity, working conditions and the character of work didn't seem to have changed much from the classical Fordist system. If anything, the rhythm and pace of the work on the assembly line is more inexorable under the Japanese management system than it ever was before. Off-line jobs, such as those in subassembly (the senior workers' favourite positions, in which a personal work pace was possible) have been outsourced or are geared strictly to the main line by means of JIT control. Idle time is squeezed out of each workstation through the application of *kaizen* techniques, while work pressure has been intensified and staffing drastically reduced in the name of eliminating all 'waste' (*muda*) (Berggren, 1992: 5–6). The combined JIT and quality pressure (zero defects) of the modern 'Japanized' lines demand a high degree of mental concentration on work that is still very standardized. Acquiescent unions and highly dependent workers who submit to the relentless demands explain that, until the late 1980s, Japanese auto makers had never had to confront and change the character of the work itself (Berggren, 1992: 6).

From the early 1990s onwards, as the Japanese labour market pool has reduced in size, criticisms of the industrial conditions, the long working hours and the trying physical environment have become widespread. Manufacturing firms have been encountering mounting recruitment difficulties, and there has been a soaring turnover among new hirees. It seemed, then, that the prescription of some (i.e. Womack *et al.*, 1990) that the West must adopt the Japanese production system was out of sync with the debate in Japan in the 1990s. In fact, many of the demands raised in the Japanese debate were strikingly similar to the goals of the Swedish work reforms, which were applied from the mid-1980s onwards (see below) and, more generally, to the European human-centred concept of work. Indeed, while the emphasis used to be one-sidedly, on productive efficiency at the cost of workers' needs for fulfilment, the Swedish concept widened the perspective and stressed the humanitarian concern that work should also provide worker satisfaction. It was recognized that the effectiveness of work is greatly influenced by the degree of satisfaction workers derive from it.

Swedish Uddevallaism[7]

From the late 1960s, some countries and some companies began to develop programmes to humanize work. The clear goal of this project was to seek ways of organizing production so that it would be more suited to the requirements of a younger generation with little desire to enter the manufacturing industry. Hence, initial efforts at robotization were designed to eliminate the most tedious and dangerous tasks. Modifications were made to the principles of the assembly line – for instance, through experiments with semi-autonomous groups. Without doubt, it was in Sweden that this work was developed most resolutely and systematically (Boyer and Durand, 1997).

From the 1970s onwards, rather like what happened in most advanced industrial countries (including Sweden), the movement against Taylorist work practices fostered widespread interest in organizational reform and socio-technical engineering. In Sweden this interest became permanent and gathered new momentum in the second half of the 1980s, with the development of a distinctive assembly design and work organization in the Swedish auto industry. Swedish car manufacturer Volvo was searching for an approach that differed from the international mainstream in that it intended to create a 'human' workplace. By the late 1980s, new solutions had materialized in a number of new facilities, with Volvo's Uddevalla plant being the prototype of the Swedish 'experiment in humanistic manufacturing' (Berggren, 1992: vii).

The Uddevalla project began in 1985, the year in which Volvo was the world's most profitable car manufacturer. 'Sweden was in a period of intensive economic expansion, during which labour shortages were acute. At the same time, an extensive debate was taking place about repetitive strain injuries (RSIs) in industrial jobs. More broadly, there was renewed general interest in the reform of working life' (Berggren, 1992: 12). While different sections of the auto industry launched projects for change, Uddevalla had the most comprehensive and consistent ambitions. At Volvo's Uddevalla plant, small, autonomous teams build complete cars (in ergonomically correct positions) in work cycles lasting several hours (a traditional assembly line has short work cycles, often lasting only minutes). The plant attracted wide public interest as an example of the most fundamental attempt so far to solve the problems of the auto industry: the inexorable rhythm of the line (with no opportunity to vary the pace), the overwhelming monotony and repetitiveness of the work, the heavy physical strain, the lack of free movement, and the difficulty of gaining a sense of purpose and meaning in the fragmented work process (ibid.)

The novelty of 'Uddevallaism' was that it combined small-scale assembly with a largely automated materials-handling process, a computer-integrated information system, a comprehensive development of new assembly tools, and significant new forms of vocational training (Berggren, 1992: 13). The plant's practices embodied a radical shift away from line assembly. Volvo decided to mass-produce cars at Uddevalla without using assembly lines. In fact, at Uddevalla, the anthropocentric strategy within the Volvo Group

---

[7] Unless indicated otherwise, the explanation of Uddevallaism in this section draws on Berggren (1992).

culminated in what was called a 'transcendent' production system: assembly work was transcending the confinements of Taylorized fragmentation, thereby attaining a new intellectual quality. 'Workers could arrive at an intimate understanding of the production process and its individual functions, as well as a sense of meaningful participation in a large productive organization' (ibid.). Moreover, there was an appreciable reduction in physical strain thanks to the production design and efforts in the area of ergonomics. The assemblers were able to control the pace of their work; they were freed from detailed administrative or technical control. The plant was not only a bold step in creating a humane workplace, however, but was also a success in a wide range of performance measures. Rapidly improving productivity (the Uddevalla plant reached the productivity levels of Volvo's 'mass production' plant in Gothenburg in 1991, two years into operation) and quality was combined with superior flexibility (in the sense that minimal effort was needed to build new models), low-cost tooling, unparalleled customer orientation, and a unique responsiveness to market demands (short lead times – the time span between customer order and delivery; dealers could offer customers individually specified and equipped cars within four weeks).

Box 7.2: Uddevallaism

Uddevallaism combines the most radical reorganization of the division of labour (elimination of the assembly line, fixed station assembly and greatly extended cycle times) with a capital–labour compromise situated at the national level (centralized negotiations over wages, training and work time).

In general, the Swedish model differs in four important respects from the Japanese one. First, the organizational changes are strongly linked to changes in the production arrangement, which aims to create conditions whereby functional groups have some technical autonomy (Berggren, 1992: 7). Instead of using the assembly line, assembly was completely stationary and teams were responsible for an entire car. Hence, subdivided and monotonous mass-production work was integrated to produce more dignified and holistic tasks. The Swedish assembly trajectory demonstrated that alternatives to repetitive and confined work structures are technically feasible, compatible with varied market demands and socially highly desirable in that they result in qualitative improvements in the working conditions, reducing physical workloads as well as mental stress. The design of the building at Uddevalla was an important part of this new concept. Space was created for six separate assembly shops, which underlined the commitment to small-scale final assembly. Moreover, the integrated assembly line, signifying a low horizontal division of labour, had its counterpart in a decentralized organization: plant manager, shop manager and work teams (low vertical division of labour). The Japanese work teams, by contrast, were organized directly on the line. In fact, the new organization flattened the hierarchy and brought management and labour close together, although it did not eliminate the white-collar/blue-collar distinction.

Second, Swedish teamwork differed from the Japanese approach in that it involved considerable autonomous decision-making and, thus, a substantial reduction in the vertical division of labour (Table 7.2 provides an overview of the differences between the Swedish and the Japanese forms of teamwork). The teams often selected their own leaders

Table 7.2 The Japanese and Swedish models of teamwork

Characteristic	Japanese	Swedish
Production arrangement	Trimmed lines with JIT control	Socio-technical adaptation and increased work content, most radically in complete assembly
Relationship between groups	Elimination of all buffers and variation in individual work pace	Reduction of group interdependencies by increasing worker autonomy and allowing variations in individual work pace
Supervision and coordination	Dense structure and strengthened role vis-à-vis both staff and subordinates; foremen decide matters concerning training, promotion and wages	Reduced control (how much is a contested issue); tasks shifted towards planning, and daily responsibility is delegated to the teams
Administrative control	Team leader is selected by first-line management; suggestions by the workers encouraged but decisions are taken hierarchically to ensure standardization	Group leader/representative chosen by the team; the post is often rotated, but this is a controversial question
Work intensity and performance demands	Intense managerial and peer pressure for maximum performance; no upper performance limits	Performance limits are specified in contract between company and union; actual work intensity varies, depending on wage system and peer pressure
Union role	Work organization, production pace and job design defined exclusively by company	Job content, wage system and prerogatives regulated by contract; unions engaged in questions of plant management's structure and staffing
	Clear structure of interests Team closely tied to plant management	*Autonomy – a social compromise* Work organization expresses partly opposed interests

Source: Berggren (1992: 9).

or group representatives, and performed tasks that had previously been done by foremen and industrial engineers. The Swedish model was, however, less uniform and fixed. It represented a *social compromise* between different interests: between management's interest in delegating tasks and responsibility without yielding control and the trade union's aspirations to achieve a genuine shift in the balance of power. The degree of the work teams' autonomy and decision-making power varied according to the state of production, the managerial policy, the labour situation and other factors affecting the local balance of forces.

Third, the role of first-line management was changed from that of having direct control to coordinating, planning and supporting. At those Japanese 'transplants' investigated, in contrast, teamwork usually went hand in hand with a strengthening of the managerial structure. In many cases – for example, Nissan in the UK or Toyota in Kentucky, USA – the team was organized directly around the foreman. These forms of teamwork entailed a reduction of worker autonomy and an increase in managerial control. In Japan, teams were organized around a team leader rather than a foreman, and the team leader would carry out assembly tasks as well as coordinate the team, and, in particular, would fill in for any absent worker. Similar to the situation in the transplants, however, the team leader decided on matters regarding wages, promotion, and so on, and control led the team members.

Fourth, in Sweden, the Metal Workers' Union strongly committed itself, both centrally and locally, to the development of this new organizational form. It was especially interested in strengthening the teams' decision-making prerogatives, as well as their prospects for developing collective competence.

The Uddevalla factory closed in 1993, hit by a decline in Volvo sales and a consequent contraction of production capacity. This does not imply, however, that the production principles it sought to develop were inferior. Moreover, the factory's reopening in 1996, following its conversion to produce sport and luxury models, suggests that this technological trajectory has not yet fulfilled its true potential. It has been suggested that the Uddevalla experiment may not only provide an alternative to Toyotism but may also surpass it, with its total abandonment of the assembly line, maximization of multiple skills among the workforce as a function of cognitive abilities to memorize a set of complex tasks, moderate level of automation, and close attention to the motivations and expectations of operators (Boyer and Durand, 1997: 53–4). It is not surprising, then, that by the end of the 1980s certain Japanese companies were envisaging the introduction of programmes combining elements of the Scandinavian model with the traditional Toyotist model.

7.3 ❖ Production Systems and the Societal Environment[8]

From the 1980s onwards, there has been wide acceptance of the argument that production systems cannot operate in isolation from the rest of the society and, hence, cannot be understood in isolation from their societal context. The emergence and stability of production systems are seen as dependent on their compatibility with society-wide social relations, such as industrial relations and skills formation, along with some forms of state intervention. Clearly, the skills of workers have to be acquired either within schools and training institutes or on the job within the firm. The pay system and the nature of the hierarchy within the firm are influenced by the style of industrial relations and the stratification of competencies at a society-wide level. Societal conceptions about fairness necessarily interfere with the internal management and influence income differentials across skill levels, firms or regions. Even the organization of capital markets must be considered. Some mass-production industries require such a vast amount of capital that the very characteristics of financial intermediation play an important role in the viability of

[8] Unless indicated otherwise, this section is based on Hollingsworth (1997).

any production system. Finally, the state delivers – or does not – some general precondi-tions for productive efficiency to prosper: clear rules of the game concerning property rights, but also labour law, international trade, access to knowledge, and so on. We could call this complementarity between private management tools and their embeddedness into more general, society-wide relationships a *societal system of production.*

A societal system of production is, then, a configuration of complex institutions which include the internal structure of the firm along with the society's industrial relations, the training system, the relationships with competing firms, their suppliers and distributors, the structure of capital markets, the nature of state intervention and the conceptions of social justice (Boyer and Hollingsworth, 1997: 2). Given these comple-mentarities at each period and for a given society, there exist a limited number of such societal systems of production, since a coalescence of various institutional arrangements assumes a mutual adjustment among a number of different institutions. And even if a society may have more than one societal system of production, one generally imposes its flavour, constraints and opportunities on other production systems. One may label such a societal system of production, the *dominant societal system of production.* This is the one that is tuned to the core societal institutions concerning labour, finance and state inter-vention, and is more involved with an international regime. While there is considerable variability in the way production is organized within a particular society, that variability generally exists within the broad parameters of a single societal system of production (Boyer and Hollingsworth, 1997).

The following discussion includes the institutional configurations of the societal systems of mass and flexible production. Japanese lean production, German diversified quality production and Swedish Uddevallaism are included as examples or variants of flexible production. As indicated, the discussion also includes the institutional configura-tion of the US societal system of production as an example of a powerful economy that has, historically, been embedded in a societal system of mass standardized production, and largely for that reason its economic actors find it very difficult to mimic the practices and performance of their Japanese and German competitors. The latter analysis demon-strates how a society's societal system of production limits its capacity to compete in certain industrial sectors, but enhances its competitiveness in others.

Mass standardized societal systems of production

As indicated, not just any country could have a mass standardized production system as its dominant form of production. For such a social system to be dominant, firms have to be embedded in a particular environment, one with a particular type of industrial relations system, education system and financial markets, one in which the market mentality is very pervasive, civil society is weakly developed, and the dominant institutional arrangements for coordinating a society's economy tend to be markets, corporate hierarchies and a weakly structured regulatory state. As already suggested, firms that successfully employ a mass-production strategy have to use specific types of machinery – that is, specific-purpose machines – and relate in particular ways to other firms in the manufacturing process. Firms engaged in mass standardized production require large, stable and relatively well-defined markets for products that are essentially slow in their technological complexity and relatively low in their rate of technological change (see Table 7.3).

Table 7.3 A typology of societal systems of production

Variables	Mass standardized production	Flexible production
Work skills	Narrowly defined and very specific in nature	Well-trained, highly flexible and broadly skilled workforce
Institutional training facilities	Public education emphasizing low level of skills	Greater likelihood of strong apprenticeship programmes linking vocational training and firms
Investment in work skills by firm	Low	High
Labour–management relations	Low trust between labour and management; poor communication and hierarchical in nature	Relatively high degree of trust
Industrial relations	Conflictual labour–management relations	High social peace between labour and management
Internal labour market	Rigid	Flexible
Work security	Relatively poor security	Long-term employment, relatively high job security
Relationship with other firms	Highly conflictual, rather impoverished institutional environment	Highly cooperative relationships with suppliers, customers and competitors in a very rich institutional environment
Collective action	Trade associations poorly developed and where in existence are lacking in power to discipline members	Trade associations highly developed with capacity to govern industry and to discipline members
Modes of capital formation	Capital markets well developed; equities are highly liquid	Capital markets are less well developed, strong bank–firm links, extensive cross-firm ownership, long-term ownership of equity
Anti-trust legislation	Designed to weaken cartels and various forms of collective action	More tolerance of various forms of collective action
Type of civil society in which firms are embedded	Weakly developed	Highly developed
Degree of pervasiveness of market mentality of society	High	Low

Source: adapted from Hollingsworth (1997: 274–5).

'Because specific purpose machines operate in relatively stable markets, firms either engaged in backward integration or were in a strategic position to force their suppliers to invest in complementary supplies and equipment. Once firms announced their need for specific types of parts, suppliers had to produce at very low costs or lose their business. Over time, those firms that excelled in mass production tended to develop a hierarchical system of management, to adopt strategies of deskilling their employees, to install single-purpose, highly specialized machinery, and to engage in arm's-length dealings with suppliers and distributors based primarily on price. In the long run, the more a firm produced some standardized output, the more rigid the production process became – e.g. the more difficult it was for the firm to produce anything that deviated from the programmed capacity of its special purpose machines. On the other hand, such firms were extraordinarily flexible in dealing with the external labor market. As employees in firms engaged in standardized production had relatively low levels of skill, one worker could easily be exchanged for another. Management had little incentive to engage in long-term contracts with their workers or to invest in the skills of their employees' (Hollingsworth, 1997: 269).*

As mass production has been developed in the USA, it should come as no surprise that historians found that US schools were historically integrated into a societal system of mass standardized production and that the education system was vocationalized. 'In such a system, schools for most of the labor force tended to emphasize the qualities and personality traits essential for performing semi-skilled tasks: punctuality, obedience, regular and orderly work habits' (Hollingsworth, 1997: 270).* 'Hogan argues that schools in a social system of mass production provide skills that are less technical than social and are less concerned with developing cognitive skills and judgments than attitudes and behavior appropriate to mass production organizations and their labor process' (Hollingsworth, 1997: 271).* 'Because labor markets in such a system were segmented, however, educational systems also tended to be segmented, but intricately linked with one another. Thus, such a system also had some schools for well-to-do children that emphasized student participation and less direct supervision by teachers and administrators' (Hollingsworth, 1997: 270).*

Where societal systems of mass standardized production have been highly institutionalized, such as in the USA, the financial markets have also been highly developed. 'Large firms in such a system – in comparison with those in other societies – have tended to expand from retained earnings or to raise capital from the bond or equity markets, but less frequently from bank loans.

'Once financial markets become highly institutionalized, securities become increasingly liquid. And the owners of such securities tend to sell their assets when they believe their investments are not properly managed. Since management embedded in such a system tends to be evaluated very much by the current price and earnings of the stocks and bonds of their companies, it has a high incentive to maximize short-term considerations at the expense of long-term strategy' (Hollingsworth, 1997: 271).* (See Chapter 6 for an extended explanation of this topic.)

'This kind of emphasis on a short-term horizon limits the developments of long-term stable relations between employers and employees – a prerequisite for a highly skilled and broadly trained workforce. Instead, the short-term maximization of profits means that firms in a societal system of mass standardized production tend to be quick to lay off workers during an economic downturn, thus, being heavily dependent on a lowly and narrowly skilled workforce' (Hollingsworth, 1997: 271).*

* Hollingsworth, R. (1997) Continuities and changes in social systems of production: the cases of Japan, Germany, and the United States. In *Contemporary Capitalism: the Embeddedness of Institutions*, edited by J. Rogers Hollingsworth and Robert Boyer, Cambridge: Cambridge University Press © J. Rogers Hollingsworth and Robert Boyer 1997, reproduced with permission of the author and publisher.

Societal systems of flexible production

Flexible production is the production of goods by means of general-purpose resources, a system of production that can flexibly adapt to different market demands. 'In systems in which flexible production is dominant, there is an ever-changing range of goods with customized designs to appeal to specialized tastes' (Hollingsworth, 1997: 272).* Similar to what has just been argued for mass production, not all countries can have flexible production as their dominant societal form of production. Moreover, because the institutional arrangements of each social system of flexible production are system-specific, they are not easily transferable from one society to another.[9] Societies with societal systems of flexible production tend to have most, if not all, of the following characteristics, all of which are mutually reinforcing (see also Table 7.3):

- 'An industrial relations system that promotes continuous learning, broad skills, workforce participation in production decision-making, and is perceived by employees to be fair and just.
- Less hierarchical and less compartmentalized arrangements within firms, thus enhancing communication and flexibility.
- A rigorous education and training system for labor and management, both within and outside firms.
- Well-developed institutional arrangements, which facilitate cooperation among competitors.
- Long-term stable relationships with high levels of communication and trust among suppliers and customers.
- A system of financing that permits firms to engage in long-term strategic planning' (Hollingsworth, 1997: 277).*

In contrast to mass standardized production, flexible production requires workers who have high levels of skills and who can make changes on their own. 'This means that there is much less work supervision than in firms engaged in mass production. Because of the need to shift production strategies quickly, management in firms engaged in flexible production must be able to depend on employees to assume initiative, to integrate conceptions of tasks with execution, and to make specific deductions from general directives. . . .

'A key indicator to the development of a social system of flexible production in a society is its industrial relations system. Highly institutionalized social systems of flexible production require workers with broad levels of skills and some form of assurance that they will not be dismissed from their jobs. Indeed, job security tends to be necessary for employers to have sufficient incentives to make long-term investments in developing the skills of their workers' (Hollingsworth, 1997: 272–3).*

---

* Hollingsworth, R. (1997) Continuities and changes in social systems of production: the cases of Japan, Germany, and the United States. In *Contemporary Capitalism: the Embeddedness of Institutions*, edited by J. Rogers Hollingsworth and Robert Boyer, Cambridge: Cambridge University Press © J. Rogers Hollingsworth and Robert Boyer 1997, reproduced with permission of the author and publisher.

[9] Historically, however, there were always examples of flexible production in societies where a social system of mass standardized production was dominant, and examples of standardized production occurred in societies in which flexible production was most common.

Moreover, firms engaged in flexible production methods tend to become somewhat more specialized and less vertically integrated than those firms engaged in mass production. As a result, such firms must be in close technical contact with other firms. 'To be most effective in employing technologies of flexible production, management must have a willingness to cooperate and have trusting relationships with their competitors, suppliers, customers, and workers. But the degree to which these trust relationships can exist depends on the institutional environment in which firms are embedded. ... But firms in social systems of flexible production are embedded in environments with highly developed institutional forms of a collective nature which promote long-term cooperation between labor and capital as well as between firms and suppliers. And the market mentality of the society is less pervasive. The collective nature of the environment also facilitates cooperation among competitors' (Hollingsworth, 1997: 273).*

'The economic importance of institutional arrangements for rich and long-term relationships between labor and capital and among suppliers, customers, competitors, governments, universities, and/or banks is that such arrangements link together economic actors having relatively high levels of trust with each other, and having different knowledge bases – a form of coordination that is increasingly important as technology and knowledge become very complex and change rapidly' (Hollingsworth, 1997: 273).* For a societal system of flexible production to thrive, firms must be embedded in a *community, region* or *country* in which many other firms share the same and/or complementary forms of production. Firms that adhere to the principles of a societal system of production over long periods of time tend to do so either because of communitarian obligations or because of some form of external coercion.

'Moreover, for a social system of flexible production to sustain itself, firms must invest in a variety of redundant capacities. Such redundancies are likely to result only if firms are embedded in an environment in which associative organizations and/or the state require such investments. Firms acting voluntarily and primarily from a sense of a highly rational calculation of their investment needs are unlikely to develop such redundant capacities over the longer run. Manufacturing firms engaged in flexible forms of production require a workforce that is broadly and highly skilled, and capable of shifting from one task to another and of constantly learning new skills. But firms that are excessively rational in assessing their needs for skills are likely to proceed very cautiously in their skill investments; in such firms, accountants and cost benefit analysts are likely to insist that only those investments be made that will yield predictable rates of return. In a world of rapidly changing technologies and product markets, firms that invest *only* in those skills for which there is a demonstrated need are likely over time to have a less skilled workforce than they need. ... With knowledge and technology becoming more complex and changing very rapidly, excessive rational economic thinking along the principles inherent in a social system of mass production may well result in poor economic performance. Thus, firms engaged in flexible production require excess or redundant investments in work skills, and can sustain this over time only if they are embedded in a social system of flexible production – which by definition has highly developed collective forms of behavior

* Hollingsworth, R. (1997) Continuities and changes in social systems of production: the cases of Japan, Germany, and the United States. In *Contemporary Capitalism: the Embeddedness of Institutions*, edited by J. Rogers Hollingsworth and Robert Boyer, Cambridge: Cambridge University Press © J. Rogers Hollingsworth and Robert Boyer 1997, reproduced with permission of the author and publisher.

with the capacity to impose communitarian obligations among actors' (Hollingsworth, 1997: 273–6)*

'Another redundant investment – one that is somewhat complementary – involves efforts to generate social peace. High quality and flexible production can persist only if there is social peace between labor and management. The maintenance of peace is costly, and it is impossible for cost analysts to demonstrate how much investment is needed in order to maintain a high level of social peace. Thus, just as highly rational managers are tempted to invest less in skills than will be needed over the longer term, so also they tend to underinvest in those things that lead to social peace. But for a firm to have a sufficient supply of social peace when needed, it must be willing to incur high investments in social peace when it does not appear to need it. In this sense, investment in and cultivation of social peace create a redundant resource which is exposed to the typical hazards of excessive rationality and short-term opportunism' (Hollingsworth, 1997: 276).*

'Investment in the redundant capacities of general skills and social peace tend to require long-term employment relationships. And while firms may occasionally develop such capacities based on *voluntarily* imposed decisions, such decisions tend to be less stable and less effective for the development of broad and high level skills and social peace than socially imposed or legally compulsory arrangements which originate from institutionalized obligations. Social systems of mass standardized production represent a social order based on contractual exchanges between utility-maximizing individuals, and most firms in such systems underinvest in the skills of their workers and in social peace. Social systems of flexible production require cooperative relations and communitarian obligations among firms, as well as collective inputs that firms would not experience based purely on a rational calculation of a firm's short-term economic interests' (Hollingsworth, 1997: 277).*

The societal system of lean production

As explained in the first section of this chapter, Japanese lean production involves a small-batch flexible mass-production system and, hence, is based on flexible production techniques. As a consequence, most of the societal features that support the development of flexible production as the dominant societal system (mentioned in Table 7.3) also support the development of lean production systems. One of the most important features of the Japanese societal system of production, from which many have been derived and which contributes to the development of flexible production systems, is the distinctiveness of Japan's capital markets (Hollingsworth, 1997: 279). As discussed at length in Chapter 6, Japanese firms have long been dependent on outside financiers for capital, such as the main banks and the large firms and banks of the major financial groups. These relationships are strengthened by cross-ownership and interlocking directorships. This kind of mutual stockholding obviously diversifies risk and buffers firms from the uncertainties of labour and product markets (ibid.). 'The extensive cross-company pattern of stock ownership in Japan is an important reason why Japanese firms can forsake short-term profit

* Hollingsworth, R. (1997) Continuities and changes in social systems of production: the cases of Japan, Germany, and the United States. In *Contemporary Capitalism: the Embeddedness of Institutions*, edited by J. Rogers Hollingsworth and Robert Boyer, Cambridge: Cambridge University Press © J. Rogers Hollingsworth and Robert Boyer 1997, reproduced with permission of the author and publisher.

maximization in favor of a strategy of long-term goals – a process very much in contrast with the pressures on American managers to maximize short-term gains. Moreover, the patterns of intercorporate stockholding also encourages many long-term business relationships in Japan, which in turn reinforce ties of interdependence, exchange relations, and reciprocal trust among firms' (Hollingsworth, 1997: 280).* These kinds of relationship have also led to low transaction costs among firms, high reliability of goods supplied from one firm to another and close coordination of delivery schedule. 'Because Japanese trade associations are highly developed and span a variety of suppliers, buyers, and related industries, they too have played an important role in developing cooperation among competing and complementary firms, as well as in facilitating the clustering of industries' (Hollingsworth, 1997: 283).*

'Having the option to develop long-term strategies, large Japanese firms have had the ability to develop the kind of long-term relations with their employees, on which invest-ment in worker training and flexible specialization are built' (Hollingsworth, 1997: 280).* Inter-corporate ties explain that many large firms – particularly in steel, ship-building and other heavy industries – have been able to shift employees to other companies within their industrial group during economic downturns rather than dis-missing the workers altogether. Moreover, firms with long-term job security have the capacity to implement a seniority-based wage and promotion system, which in turn, pro-motes employee motivation and identification with the company. Long-term job security also enables the implementation of a system of job rotation (in work teams) and flexible job assignments, and intensive in-firm instruction and on-the-job training. In addition, however, lifetime employment combined with seniority pay, involves a high degree of employee dependence on the firm. Indeed, since all large firms recruit externally only for positions at the bottom of the job hierarchy and train their specialists for better jobs through on-the-job training and job rotation, there is no further possibility of advance-ment outside that firm (Dohse et al., 1989). The unitary school system in Japan (see Chapter 5 for an explanation), with its poorly developed system for providing practical or vocational training, explains that Japanese firms offer this type of training. And, because of the existence of long-term job security, employees and unions accept that training is highly firm-specific and not very generalizable to other organizations. This, of course, further increases inflexibility in the external labour market.

Moreover, as indicated, the Japanese industrial relations system is characterized by company unions. Company unions constitute a much more advantageous arena of nego-tiations for management than more comprehensive unions. The ties of company unions to the individual company make them much more strongly dependent on market success, and hence the productivity and cost structure of their firm. As a consequence, the scope of labour union demands is restricted; conflictual goals with respect to the utilization of labour (i.e. working conditions) are avoided in favour of positions that can be of benefit to both sides. This pacification function, which is inherent in the structure of the company union, was stabilized in the 1950s through destruction of the militant unions. The inten-sive labour struggles of the 1950s were a decisive phase in the constitution of the current

*Hollingsworth, R. (1997) Continuities and changes in social systems of production: the cases of Japan, Germany, and the United States. In Contemporary Capitalism: the Embeddedness of Institutions, edited by J. Rogers Hollingsworth and Robert Boyer, Cambridge: Cambridge University Press © J. Rogers Hollingsworth and Robert Boyer 1997, reproduced with permission of the author and publisher.

Japanese system of labour relations. In the course of this conflict, Japanese firms succeeded, in particular in the automobile industry, in destroying the militant postwar unions, which had an industry-wide orientation, and firing union representatives. In this way, Japanese automobile industry firms were able to prevent from the outset the development of a strong labour union movement, to particularize the interest representation of employees into plant or company unions, and to considerably limit the scope of labour union demands.

Any discussion of the Japanese institutional configuration would be incomplete without mention of the Japanese state. The Japanese state has been closely involved in industrial development – though its role is somewhat less pronounced today. The Japanese state has developed many forms of protection to keep out foreign competition, it has fostered an environment for cooperation among fierce competitors, it has channelled subsidies into targeted areas of research and development, and has encouraged and helped firms to mobilize internal resources. Moreover, for many years, it adopted a set of macro-economic policies designed to fuel economic growth with a yen that was under-valued compared to the dollar (Hollingsworth, 1997: 282–3).

The German societal system of diversified quality production

While the Japanese case is an example of a societal system that emphasizes diversified quality *mass* production, the German societal system promotes another variant of flexible production: diversified quality production in which the emphasis is less on large- and more on small-scale production. While there are other forms of societal systems of flexible production (e.g. the societal systems of flexible production in parts of northern Italy or western Denmark), the Japanese and German systems stand out because they have been conducive to high and continued investment in human resources in large firms. 'Streeck and others have suggested that there is some similarity in the social systems of flexible production of West Germany and Japan, including a high degree of social peace, a workforce that is highly and broadly trained, a flexible labor market within firms, a relatively high level of worker autonomy, a financial system with close ties between large firms and banks, a high degree of stable and long-term relationships between assemblers and their suppliers: overall, a social system of production, which results in very high quality products. Despite similarity in these characteristics, there are major differences in the social systems of production in the two countries' (Hollingsworth, 1997: 288).*

'In Germany, industrial unions are highly developed, whereas in Japan the emphasis has been on company unions. In Germany, both labor and business are politically well-entrenched in most levels of politics, whereas this is not at all the case with labor in Japan. And in Germany, there is nothing resembling the *keiretsu* structure which is so prevalent among large Japanese firms. Moreover, the Germans tend to focus on the upscale, high-cost segments of many markets, whereas the Japanese – with their emphasis on large market share of various products – tend to be more concerned with low-priced, but high-quality products. In Germany, the institutional arrangements underlying the rich

*Hollingsworth, R. (1997) Continuities and changes in social systems of production: the cases of Japan, Germany, and the United States. In *Contemporary Capitalism: the Embeddedness of Institutions*, edited by J. Rogers Hollingsworth and Robert Boyer, Cambridge: Cambridge University Press © J. Rogers Hollingsworth and Robert Boyer 1997, reproduced with permission of the author and publisher.

development of skills have some continuity with corporate associations, which histori-cally have strongly supported and sponsored vocational training. Vocational education has long been important as a precondition for access to certain sectors of the labor market in Germany, whereas historically Japan has had a much more limited public vocational training program' (Hollingsworth, 1997: 288).*

'This type of long-term relationship between firms and banks has encouraged firms to be much more immune to the short-run fluctuations of the price of equities than their competitors in the US and to take a long-term perspective concerning their industry needs. This capacity on the part of management has meant that German firms have had more incentive to engage in the long-term development of products and have been less likely to lay off workers during a modest economic downturn, as has so often been the case with their American competitors who have been more constrained by short-term fluctuations in the financial markets' (Hollingsworth, 1997: 285).* However, unlike Japan, in Germany there is no *keiretsu* structure, which means that during economic downturns, temporarily redundant workers cannot be placed within friendly companies.

'Unlike Japan, another set of institutional arrangements, which contribute to long-term strategic thinking within German companies, is the country's industrial relations system.'* The key to the German industrial relations system is that it is shaped by the highly developed centralized employer and business associations as well as the trade unions. 'Peak association bargaining, mediated by the state, not only has played an important role in shaping distributional issues but also has played a role of great importance in influencing the quality and international competitiveness of German products' (Hollingsworth, 1997: 286).* As indicated, in contrast to Japan, German trade unions have relatively encompassing and centralized organizational structures (see Chapter 5 for a more com-plete explanation of this topic). 'Unions are responsible for collective bargaining and participation – through policies of codetermination – in corporate boardrooms, while elected work councils participate in organizing working conditions inside firms and ensuring that protection laws are obeyed by management. . . . Collectively, these arrange-ments have been instrumental in reducing conflict between labor and management, and in enhancing flexible production inside firms' (Hollingsworth, 1997: 286).*

'The job security enjoyed by labor, under codetermination policies, has encouraged firms to invest in the long-term training of their labor force. When management has real-ized that it cannot easily dismiss workers in the event of economic adversity, it has had an incentive to engage in the investment of employees with skills high and broad enough to adjust to complex and rapidly changing technologies and unstable markets. And in Germany, the rigidity imposed by strongly organized industrial unionism and works coun-cils has encouraged firms to invest in more skills and social peace than management would otherwise have invested under flexible external market conditions, a process which has directly contributed to a diversified quality, flexible social system of production – the key to Germany's high level of competitiveness in the world economy' (Hollingsworth, 1997: 286–7).* Moreover, the lack of employer freedom in hiring and firing has largely been counteracted by the fact that unions and works councils support a flexible

*Hollingsworth, R. (1997) Continuities and changes in social systems of production: the cases of Japan, Germany, and the United States. In *Contemporary Capitalism: the Embeddedness of Institutions*, edited by J. Rogers Hollingsworth and Robert Boyer, Cambridge: Cambridge University Press © J. Rogers Hollingsworth and Robert Boyer 1997, reproduced with permission of the author and publisher.

deployment in qualitative terms. The move to greater functional flexibility in labour deployment is not regarded as a threat to union power as unions are neither organized along craft lines nor do they support demarcation between crafts.

The new technology involved in flexible production also requires that management possess the necessary technical skill to assess the feasibility of investing in this technology, as well as the ability to understand the implications for the organization of work, for manpower requirements and for training needs. The engineering and technical educational background of most German managers (see Chapter 5) explains their high level of managerial technical competence.

'Managers of many German firms found the system quite distasteful. They would like to have followed the practices of their American colleagues in the face of stiff international competitiveness by cutting wages and reducing the size of the workforce. Yet, because they were constrained by the system of codetermination (regulated at the plant level by the Works Constitution Act of 1972 and at the enterprise level by the Works Constitutions Act of 1952, superseded in 1976) which resulted in a high wage system, German firms were forced – with little choice – to become engineering and highly skill intensive, with diversified and high quality producers. With the rigidities that firms faced in dealing with job protection and high wages for their workers, it was highly rational for management to

Table 7.4 Models of flexible production organization

Swedish model	German model	Japanese model
Semi-skilled workers with high initial training (quasi-apprenticeship)	Skilled workers deployed on direct production jobs after full apprenticeship	Semi-skilled workers with generally high starting qualification
Work totally uncoupled from the production cycle	Work (partially) uncoupled from the production cycle	Work tied to the production cycle
Holistic tasks with long work cycles (> one hour)	Job enlargement with work cycles below one hour	Highly repetitive work; cycle times around one minute on the assembly lines, around five minutes in the machining areas where multimachine work is the norm
Homogenous groups	Mixed teams of 'specialists'	Homogenous groups
High partial autonomy for teams through process layout	Little partial autonomy for team through automation and module production	No partial autonomy for the teams through JIT design
De-hierarchization with elected speaker and self-regulation of group affairs	Controversial role of group speaker/leader and of degree of self-regulation	Strong hierarchical structures, group leader appointed by management, no group self-regulation

Source: Jürgens (1995: 204).

*Hollingsworth, R. (1997) Continuities and changes in social systems of production: the cases of Japan, Germany, and the United States. In *Contemporary Capitalism: the Embeddedness of Institutions*, edited by J. Rogers Hollingsworth and Robert Boyer, Cambridge: Cambridge University Press © J. Rogers Hollingsworth and Robert Boyer 1997, reproduced with permission of the author and publisher.

invest more in the training of their workforce than they would have been inclined to do were they simply following market signals. Almost unintentionally, German firms were pushed to develop one of the world's most skilled labor forces' (Hollingsworth, 1997: 287).*

The Swedish societal system and Uddevallaism

Rather like the situations in Japan and Germany, the case of Sweden confirms that there are various configurations of production that come under the umbrella of flexible production (see Table 7.4 for a comparison of the main traits of these three flexible production models). In many respects the societal data on Scandinavian economies are closely related to those on Germany: the role and importance of strong unions, the range of issues covered by collective bargaining, inclusion of the need for competitiveness in employment negotiations, widespread acceptance of technical change as a means of promoting better standards of living and maintaining employment levels, and the significance accorded to quality and product differentiation.

Yet the German and the Swedish production models are not identical, as is demonstrated by the way skill development and work is organized (Table 7.4). Whereas in Germany, the nature of training is theoretical and practical, in Sweden it is theoretical and *technical* (see Chapter 5). Whereas in Germany, training takes place within the educational system, but also in the company through full apprenticeships, in Sweden, the state and regional institutions offer training. Moreover, issues that in Germany are handled by negotiations between employers' associations and trade unions are organized in Sweden by regional or national bodies that adopt an integrated approach to the management of restructuring, unemployment benefits, training and retraining, and even the placement of workers in new jobs. In both instances, the societal context encourages flexibility aimed at the continuous improvement of skills, yet they are far from identical (Boyer and Durand, 1997).

By fully decoupling work from the production cycle and the rhythm of the machines Sweden has evolved at a level beyond Germany and far beyond Japan in enriching and enlarging work content. Uncoupling work from the flow of production is the prerequisite for a type of labour that holds increased possibilities for self-regulation and offers increased levels of responsibility. Hence, Swedish teams have more autonomy than their German and Japanese counterparts, and have the freedom to elect a speaker and self-regulate their own affairs. The latter appears more controversial in Germany between those social partners who can offer different solutions at the various local sites. In stark contrast to the Swedish model, the Japanese teams have little autonomy in organizing the work process due to the JIT principle of production control, and there is no democratic system of regulating teams' internal affairs or of electing a team speaker (Jürgens, 1995).

The simultaneous pressure from product and labour markets in Sweden helps to explain the creation of a production system adapted to human demands. Unlike most of the

*Hollingsworth, R. (1997) Continuities and changes in social systems of production: the cases of Japan, Germany, and the United States. In *Contemporary Capitalism: the Embeddedness of Institutions*, edited by J. Rogers Hollingsworth and Robert Boyer, Cambridge: Cambridge University Press © J. Rogers Hollingsworth and Robert Boyer 1997, reproduced with permission of the author and publisher.

rest of the world, from the 1970s onwards in Sweden there has been constant pressure from the labour market. At the close of the 1980s, more than 85 per cent of the population between 16 and 64 years of age was in the labour force. 'At the same time, the wage differentials between different sectors and companies were small. This made it very hard for companies to compensate for a bad working environment and arduous work with high wages and good benefits. It also increased the engagement and interest of the trade unions in the work environment and organization. The greatly increased product variation in the auto industry during the 1980s was yet another motive for developing more flexible and integrated production systems. The heightened demand for flexibility and quality increased companies' dependence on a stable and committed workforce. Concurrently, the high employment level made it difficult to recruit and keep workers in Taylorized industrial jobs'. Creating new production systems adapted to human needs – such as in Uddevalla – came to be seen as a strategic necessity for coping with personnel problems. Under these conditions, of course, the influence of the unions in the companies' planning and investment decisions also increased (Berggren, 1992: 11). Once more we arrive at the important idea that, to be viable, a production system must cohere with the societal context and organizational forms governing the rest of the economy. The next section offers a further example of this.

Short-termism and institutional inertia: the difficult transition in the USA

While Taylorism and Fordism have been developed within the US societal system of production, US manufacturers have had a hard time shifting to flexible production. The ability of the USA to move towards a societal system of flexible production is argued to be limited by its prevailing practices of industrial relations, its education system and its financial markets – or, in short, by the *constraints of its past societal system of production* (Hollingsworth, 1997: 292). 'And while these types of incentive and skill systems have become quite widespread in the core of the Japanese and German economies, in the United States manufacturing employment has tended to be much more job-specific, workers have been less broadly trained, internal labor markets have been much more rigid, and employers have had much less incentive to invest in their workers' skill development. Because the US has one of the world's most flexible external job markets, it has been much easier for American workers to leave jobs for other firms than is the case in countries where workers have long-term job security' (Hollingsworth, 1997: 292).* Unsurprisingly, this has provided a disincentive for US employers to invest in worker training.

A reorganization of the productive apparatus from mass to flexible production requires a management committed to technological innovation, confident to forge ahead, and competent both to acquire the right type of equipment, and to put it into operation and maintain it without too much disruption of the production process. Such an approach, however, requires a high level of technical expertise among management and

---

* Hollingsworth, R. (1997) Continuities and changes in social systems of production: the cases of Japan, Germany, and the United States. In *Contemporary Capitalism: the Embeddedness of Institutions*, edited by J. Rogers Hollingsworth and Robert Boyer, Cambridge: Cambridge University Press © J. Rogers Hollingsworth and Robert Boyer 1997, reproduced with permission of the author and publisher.

support staff at all levels, which is not sufficiently present in US manufacturing companies.

'The American industrial relations system is shaped in large part by the weakly developed business associations and trade unions. The large size and complexity of the American economy, combined with the racial, ethnic, and religious diversity of the working class have created substantial heterogeneity of interests among both labor and capital, making it difficult for each to engage in collective action. And the weak capacity of both capital and labor to organize collectively has placed severe limits on the ability of the United States to move more rapidly in developing a social system of flexible production' (Hollingsworth, 1997: 292).*

'Countries with firms tightly integrated into highly institutionalized systems of business associations (e.g. Japan and Germany) have rather rigid external labor markets but flexible internal labor markets. The United States, with weak associative structures, tends to have more flexible external labor markets but more rigid internal labor markets' (Hollingsworth, 1997: 292–3).*

'The capital markets in the United States have also placed constraints on the development of broad employee skills by encouraging firms to engage in short-term maximization of profits. In the United States, the equity markets were highly institutionalized by the end of World War I, and managers of large firms have subsequently had low dependence on commercial banks for financing. . . . However, the Clayton Antitrust Act of 1914 made interlocking directorships among large banks and trusts illegal. Moreover, it also forbade a corporation to acquire the stock of another if the acquisition reduced competition in the industry. In the longer term, the Clayton Act tended to reduce the ability of investment banks and firms to carry out a long-term strategy of promoting a community of interests among firms either in the same or in complementary industries. In addition, the American government in 1933 forced a sharp separation between commercial and investment banking. From that point on, investment banks lost much of their access to capital. As a consequence, American nonfinancial corporations became dependent for raising capital on liquid financial markets rather than on banks. Increasingly, corporate managers became dependent on the whims and strategies of stockholders and bond owners. This resulted in an emphasis on a short-term horizon for large firms which has limited the capacity of American management to develop long-term stable relations between employers and their employees – a prerequisite for a highly skilled and broadly trained work force and a flexible or diversified quality social system of production' (Hollingsworth, 1997: 293).*

7.4 🧩 Conclusions

Different societal conditions may give rise to different *production patterns* that may represent *functionally alternative*, and sometimes *functionally equivalent*, responses to common economic challenges. It seems that markets and hierarchies work well when firms are

*Hollingsworth, R. (1997) Continuities and changes in social systems of production: the cases of Japan, Germany, and the United States. In *Contemporary Capitalism: the Embeddedness of Institutions*, edited by J. Rogers Hollingsworth and Robert Boyer, Cambridge: Cambridge University Press © J. Rogers Hollingsworth and Robert Boyer 1997, reproduced with permission of the author and publisher.

embedded in a societal environment impoverished by collective forms of economic coordination. However, *institutionally impoverished economies* that rely solely on markets and hierarchies for the governance of economic activities (such as the USA and the UK) do not necessarily perform better than societies where economic behaviour is more socially regulated (Streeck, 1991). 'But the Japanese and German cases demonstrate that diversified quality forms of production work best when they are embedded in an environment with institutional arrangements which promote cooperation between producers and suppliers, and among competitors, especially an environment which facilitates the exchange of information among competitors. It requires firms to engage in collective behavior far in excess to what is needed for markets and hierarchies to function effectively and in excess of what single firms are likely to develop for themselves. Flexible and diversified quality production systems function best when they are embedded in an institutional environment with rich multilateral or collective dimensions: cooperative action on the part of competitors, rich training centers for workers and managers, and financial institutions willing to provide capital on a long-term basis' (Hollingsworth, 1997: 295).* Hence, it could be argued that a *repertory of social institutions* that *exceeds the neoclassical minimum* may in specific conditions make a *positive contribution* to competitive market performance (Streeck, 1991).

'Because of the low levels of skill of American labor in most manufacturing sectors and because American management has tended to be recruited from marketing, financial, and legal rather than engineering and production backgrounds, American manufacturing firms have been less successful in improving upon products once developed than their Japanese and German competitors. And because American consumers are less demanding of product quality than the Japanese and Germans, American firms – particularly in the consumer goods industries – have been more competitive in the production of low-cost standardized products which can be mass marketed and easily discarded. Also, in contrast to the German and Japanese, the Americans – particularly in many manufacturing industries – have been more willing to compromise on design, quality, and service and to compete in terms of price' (Hollingsworth, 1997: 296).*

'Relationships among producers and suppliers in the United States have been more opportunistic and based more on hard-nosed bargaining over prices than in Japan and Germany. This kind of intense bargaining over price has also had an adverse effect on the Americans' ability to sustain product quality and to achieve a high level of competitiveness in global markets. There are industries in which the technology is not very complex and does not change, and, given the large size of the American market, mass standardized production is still effective in such industrial sectors. For example, paper products, breakfast cereals, soft drinks, bug sprays, floor wax, deodorants, soaps, shaving cream, and hundreds of other products remain symbolic of the familiar hierarchical form of corporate America' (Hollingsworth, 1997: 296).*

However, Germany and Japan, like all other countries, have firms that compete and perform well in some industrialized sectors, but not very well in others. 'By focusing attention on Japan, Germany, and the United States, it becomes quite obvious that why

---

* Hollingsworth, R. (1997) Continuities and changes in social systems of production: the cases of Japan, Germany, and the United States. In *Contemporary Capitalism: the Embeddedness of Institutions*, edited by J. Rogers Hollingsworth and Robert Boyer, Cambridge: Cambridge University Press © J. Rogers Hollingsworth and Robert Boyer 1997, reproduced with permission of the author and publisher.

countries succeed in certain sectors depends less on such classic factor endowments as climate, natural resources, and land than on their national traditions, values, institutional arrangements, quality of labor and management, and the nature of capital markets' (Hollingsworth, 1997: 283).*

The crowded living conditions and tight space constraints throughout Japan have stimulated the Japanese to produce compact, portable, quiet and multifunctional products. 'They have excelled in producing compact cars and trucks, small consumer electronic equipment (TV sets, copiers, radios, and video sets), motorcycles, machine tools, watches and clocks, and a number of business related products such as small computers, fans, pumps, and tools' (Hollingsworth, 1997: 283).* 'Even though the Japanese have been enormously successful in improving upon existing products, they have been less successful in developing new products – primarily because of their particular institutional configuration. Their educational system emphasizes rote learning rather than creative synthesis or critical analysis. Their universities are structured to facilitate consensus decision-making and group conformity' (Hollingsworth, 1997: 284).* The overall weakness of Japanese universities as research institutions is an important reason why the Japanese have lagged behind in industries involving chemistry and biotechnology, and other fields heavily dependent on basic science (see Chapter 8 for a discussion of this issue).

The structure of the German institutional landscape also helps to explain why Germany has excelled in competing in the production of machine tools, automobiles and chemical products, as well as in many traditional nineteenth-century industrial products.

'They have been especially successful in applying the latest microelectronic technology to the production of traditional products and to new production processes. On the other hand, the Germans have been less competitive in many newer industries, e.g. computers, semiconductors, and consumer electronics. In other words, the Germans have placed less emphasis on developing entirely new technologies and industries than in applying the latest technologies to the production of more traditional products. And it is the specific type of German industrial relations system (high job security, the high levels of qualification, and continuous training of German workers) which is conducive to the rapid diffusion of the latest technology to the production of more traditional but high quality products. In addition the strong engineering and technical background of senior management, the high levels of skill of the workforce, and a strong consumer demand for high-precision manufacturing processes have contributed to the development of various manufacturing sectors with very high quality products' (Hollingsworth, 1997: 289–90).*

As explained extensively in Chapter 5, Sweden is different from Germany and Japan in that it has both a large traditional Taylorist industry as well as modern flexible production in some sectors (such as the car industry). The fact that the Swedish societal environment is relatively similar to that of Germany explains that some Swedish sectors (such as the car and truck industries, and the machinery industry) could easily shift to flexible production. Traditional production methods and low-skilled workers are used in the traditional industries, which successfully exploit Sweden's main raw material resources: wood and iron ore.

*Hollingsworth, R. (1997) Continuities and changes in social systems of production: the cases of Japan, Germany, and the United States. In *Contemporary Capitalism: the Embeddedness of Institutions*, edited by J. Rogers Hollingsworth and Robert Boyer, Cambridge: Cambridge University Press © J. Rogers Hollingsworth and Robert Boyer 1997, reproduced with permission of the author and publisher.

Study Questions

1. Which societal features could help to explain why Taylorism and Fordism developed in the USA?

2. Why do you think Toyotism, or lean production, developed in Japan long before flexible production was recognized in the West?

3. Explain how lean supply chain management fits the societal features of Japan and Germany.

4. Explain the links between human resource management systems and corporate governance modes to mass production, and to the lean and flexible modes of production.

5. Explain why lean production is more difficult to implement in the USA.

6. Explain the main differences between mass and flexible production systems, and link these differences in features to the differences in the societal institutions that are needed to develop these models.

7. Explain the concept of Uddevallaism and explain how it is linked to the Swedish societal system and the specific socio-economic circumstances at the time of its development.

8. Explain whether the German diversified quality production model was able to function in Sweden. If so, why? If not, why not?

9. Explain whether Swedish Uddevallaism could be implemented in Germany. If so, why? If not, why not?

10. Explain whether, in your opinion, convergence can occur in the areas of production systems and production management.

Further Reading

Delbridge, R. (1998) *Life on the Line in Contemporary Manufacturing: the Workplace Experience of Lean Production and the 'Japanese' Model*. Oxford: Oxford University Press.

The book provides us with a sophisticated story of the actual work process on the assembly lines in two UK factories: a Japanese-owned television assembly plant and a European-owned automotive parts supplier. Through detailed ethnographic accounts, it convincingly dispels many myths about the humanization of factory life and the innovatory potential of Japanese investment in the West.

Sorge, A. (1991) Strategic fit and the societal effect: interpreting cross-national comparisons of technology, organization and human resources. *Organization Studies* 12(2), 161–90.

Case: Manufacturing Machine Tools in Germany and France[10]

Now, machine-tool producers in all countries are distinctive, compared to other industrial sectors, for an absence of very large firms, an often rather artisanal mode of production, strong continuity from workers' to technicians' and engineers' jobs, training backgrounds and contents, and required skills and knowledge (Sorge and Maurice, 144).* Since these sectoral patterns correspond to societal patterns in Germany, it is an industry in which Germany has held a very strong position since the turn of the century. It has also held this position reasonably well under the Japanese onslaught from the mid-1970s.

Surprisingly, contrary to the characteristics that apply in the French societal context, and in general far removed from the prevailing industrial norm, which is associated with continuous process production regimes and a hierarchical culture, the French machine tool industry had even more customized development and production, smaller production runs, much smaller average plant and enterprise sizes, more skilled craft workers and fewer semi-skilled workers, and fewer engineers than the German one. The German machine tool firms had many more unskilled workers and fewer craft workers because they concentrate on larger batch sizes. The much larger share of engineers in the German industry can be explained by the greater effort that goes into product development and design, as well as by larger batch size production. Despite the more artisanal approach to machine tool production, however, the French industry experienced a more severe sectoral crisis after the mid-1970s than the German one whether ... functional equivalence or its obverse affinity between societal and sectoral regimes applies in this particular industry... (Sorge and Maurice, 145).*

Qualitatively, the differences between the two sectors can be summarized as follows.

- The industry in France was less export-oriented and its exports were concentrated on specific markets: Eastern Europe and Africa. The German industry exported more and exports were more evenly spread.

- Producers in Germany specialized more systematically with regard to specific metalworking processes and machine types, such as lathes, milling, drilling, grinding, honing/lapping, stamping, presses, forging etc. French manufacturers had a larger product range, combining on average more machining processes in their product spectrum.

- French firms more frequently made machines to order, customizing according to the requirements of individual clients. This is related to the fact that they also made special-purpose machines more frequently, which are customized almost by definition. The German firms made more universal

[10] This case draws essentially on Sorge and Maurice (1990) and Sorge (1991).

machines, with modular modifications and additions, selling more frequently by catalogue and producing for stocks.

- Production batches were larger in the German firms, and production planning and systematization efforts more pronounced.

- Plant and enterprise sizes were much higher in Germany, on average twice as large as in France (Sorge and Maurice, 146).*

By all accounts, the professional careers of workers and works management and supervision, on the one hand, and design and development, on the other, are generally more separated in France, and the geographical distance between head office/development functions and production is sometimes greater in France (Sorge and Maurice, 147).* This finding is in accordance with the general institutional and cultural or societal patterns in France. Here, we have a finding which is in greater accord with previously conducted general Franco-German comparisons; these had shown greater continuity of working careers in Germany, starting from basic education and training processes, from production into higher technical functions (ibid.).*

There are also important differences in the way the two machine tool industries are embedded in their respective economies and societal settings. In Germany, it enjoys numerous and close relationships with technical universities. The production engineering and machine-tool departments enjoy high standing, draw good students, are quite generously staffed, and maintain close collaboration with firms in development projects (Sorge and Maurice, 147).*

In France, the opposite applies on many counts. Departments of production engineering and machine-tools have low prestige in the leading engineering schools (*grandes écoles*). There is less contract research and development for the machine-tool industry, and overall research and teaching staff in production engineering departments is much smaller. The industry is not backed up by an academic establishment as large and reputed as in Germany, and the cross-fertilization between the two is much less in evidence (Sorge and Maurice, 148).*

In France, mechanical engineering plays a quite inferior role and occupies a vulnerable competitive position. It is easy to understand, then, that other industrial sectors are more important clients for the French machine tool industry than mechanical engineering. Domestically, French machine-tool makers have been confronted with a clientele that is prone to segment workflow hierarchically and laterally to a greater extent, and which goes for single-purpose automation and, therefore, tailor-made installations. This favours concepts of machines which are not strong on the professional autonomy and responsibility of machine-tool setter-operators (Sorge and Maurice, 149).* Hence, the French machine tool industry has come to specialize in customer-specific single-purpose machines, the production of which necessitates craft-dominated artisanal work processes. At the same time, however, the societal environment imposed segmented career and organization structure patterns on the industry.

The contrary applies in Germany; this country's machine-tool makers confront more firms which emphasize less organizational differentiation of work-flow, requiring flexible but standard machine tools and favouring the socialization and use of professionally autonomous setter-operators (ibid.).* Consequently, German machine tool enterprises and plants are much larger than French ones; work processes are characterized by less artisanal principles in production but, as a result of societal influences, also by less overall lateral and hierarchical segmentation of work careers and functions.

It seems, then, that machine tool making firms are almost the inverse of the norm structures that apply in their clientele. A manufacturing industry dominated by large batch or mass production firms and large concerns will be congenial to manufacturers of customized machine-tools, which have a market strategy and personnel structure that is opposed to that of their clients. A manufacturing industry in which small-batch production of investment goods for more differentiated markets is more typical will go together with a machine-tool industry that makes more flexible but standard machines, and hence has a market orientation, production systems and personnel structure of a more industrial kind, i.e. closer to that of its clients (Sorge and Maurice, 149–50).*

During the immediate postwar period and until the early 1970s, the French machine tool industry outpaced its German counterpart. During this period there was no evidence of a technological gap between the two countries. If anything, the French industry had benefited from its close relations with the aerospace client industry which is strong in France, for an earlier adoption of NC (numerical control) systems which had largely been pioneered by the aerospace and armaments industries, first in the United States and then in Britain and France. This innovation, the bases for which were laid during the 1950s, at first led to piece-meal changes of machine-tool technology and a slow progression of NC machine sales and utilization (Sorge and Maurice, 153).*[11] The then new technique required substantial development of organizational, personnel and planning capacities for programming machines largely away from the shop floor, and for de-bugging and running in job and batch specific machining programmes. It was therefore a technique more fitting for manufacturers with the capacity and will to install substantial planning groups, i.e. larger enterprises and firms in "elite" industries (Sorge and Maurice, 153).* The requirements of this NC technology were one of the reasons why French machine tool producers outpaced their German counterparts at that time. When automated machines for larger batches are in demand in the domestic market, alongside the development of a slowly increasing number of advanced NC machines for industries such as aerospace, it seems that a 'French' type of societal environment is favourable.

This situation changed significantly after the mid-1970s. A worldwide crisis in

[11] NC systems are the earliest forms of machine, using computerized machine tools. They became current in the early 1950s and were dominant until the mid-1970s. The operations of machine tools were determined and controlled first by an electronic plug-board and later by a simple computer. In this early form the sequence of operations that the machine was meant to perform was contained on a paper or magnetic tape. The computer was separate from the machine tool and usually not on the shop floor at all. To change the operations of the machine tool – previously a complex and costly task – one now simply had to change the tape.

machine tools started to develop just at that time, for slower growth of disposable income and of goods markets reduced the need for additions to single-purpose automation and investment goods on the whole (Sorge and Maurice, 153).* While both Germany and France were hit by this crisis, it came at a different time for each, and was dealt with differently in the two countries. But it is significant that from roughly 1977 onwards, CNC machines which improved on the earlier NC generations and became attractive for a wider clientele beyond the original core of NC users, started to be sold more widely (Sorge and Maurice, 155).*

CNC was more quickly, more early and more widely seen in Germany as offering the potential for an original improvement on previous NC techniques, and was more in tune with the work organization and human resource patterns (see Chapter 5) of large parts of the clientele of German machine tool producers. It would appear that German machine-tool users jumped on CNC machines more quickly since they saw them as breaking with the previous cumbersome division of labour between planning, programming and machine operation (Sorge and Maurice, 155).*

The distinctive factor is, as was shown in previous comparisons, the professional continuity and propinquity between worker, technician and engineering occupations in Germany, and the professional discontinuity and distance in France, regarding status, education, remuneration and careers (Sorge and Maurice, 158).*

The perpetuation of professional and organizational structures therefore does not simply happen in response to the evolution of techniques or markets; it also predisposes enterprises to go for particular variants of new techniques and explore particular markets which have an affinity with these structures (Sorge and Maurice, 158).*

German machine-tool producers were already previously more prepared to manufacture universal, non-dedicated machines which can be operated flexibly, and they continued along this way by entering more systematically the market for universal CNC machines with operating flexibility, made in batches. Domestic user concepts stressing flexibility in universal machines thus went hand in hand with a more industrialized machine-tool industry which produced catalogue machines on a larger scale (Sorge and Maurice, 163–4).*

It can be seen that the German industry explored new markets more quickly because its own structure and user expectations prepared it better for entering the new markets for CNC machines (Sorge and Maurice, 163–4).*

The German industry could apparently better afford backward integration into CNC system design and manufacture, since it had much larger firm and plant

---

[12] Computer numerically controlled machines operate along much the same lines as NC machines but with a more advanced form of computer. The new *micro*-computer was built into the machine tool itself and had a 'dialogue' video display unit and keyboard. Thus, the process can be monitored and machines can be adjusted while production is under way. Alternations or refinements dictated by production conditions at a given time can be taken into consideration. The need for human intervention directly with the machine is still further reduced. The more sophisticated computer allows the production of more complex and sophisticated parts with ever greater precision.

sizes, which provided for better opportunities to spread overhead and development costs on the basis of greater economies of scale and larger development departments (Sorge and Maurice, 164).*

Another important element in the explanation is that despite individually greater backward integration into CNC system design and manufacture, there was also greater co-operation between makers of machines, and between them and electronics firms, software houses, non-industrial research and development institutes and users of machines. Intensive collaboration alleviated problems with which individually operating firms are confronted. However, not only the extent of co-operation is important. Also, the better status of production engineering within German industry and academia *vis-à-vis* other specialisms, and the higher status of machine-tool firms *vis-à-vis* other reputed industrial manufacturers must be considered (Sorge and Maurice, 164).*

Throughout the discussion of the German machine-tool industry, it became clear that it has been closer in its profile to user industries, intertwined craft and higher engineering functions, brought artisanal and research and development work closer to each other, put manufacturers into more intimate collaboration with reputed and technologically advanced institutions outside the industry, bridged the gap between mechanical and electronic and software engineering more comfortably (Sorge and Maurice, 168).*

The German machine-tool industry was favoured by the fact that institutionalized social structures and relations are conducive to bridging gaps between artisanal and industrial systems of production, between practices in small and large firms, between craft and technological professions, between noble and less noble branches of engineering (Sorge and Maurice, 168).*

It conforms with the more general argument: In this specific industrial case, the German firms do better, because their existing markets and their less artisanal profile in internal operations prepared them better for achieving a fit with the requirements existing for the industrialized development and manufacture of CNC machines to capture new markets for an innovation (Sorge and Maurice, 166–7).*

The opposite story emerges as we summarize the findings for French machine-tool makers. These opened up new markets through CNC less quickly and to a lesser extent. They were already previously less presented in these markets but more successful in dedicated customized machines requiring less flexibility of operation, installed with users in "high-tech" industries, larger companies or plants with longer production runs.

The French industry entered the crisis later, and its reaction was negatively prejudiced through this later start but also through its orientation towards market segments and user interests different from those that provided latent new demand for CNC machines. Furthermore, collaboration between makers to share professionally novel (electronic and software) development efforts was much more difficult to get off the ground, which was all the more serious in an industry characterized much more than the German one by small firm and plant sizes, enjoying less status *vis-à-vis* other industries and being more cut off from non-industrial research and development institutes and prestigious higher engineering schools (Sorge and Maurice, 164–5).*

Because of these interconnected disadvantages, the backward integration of machine tool makers into CNC systems and software development got stuck in the beginning. However, the industry was not only less prepared to explore new export markets, this being a disadvantage inherited from its industrial history, but was also less able to tap the new domestic markets that became more profitable in the drive towards differentiated quality production. Hence, the emerging markets were more captured by the foreign, notably Japanese, competitor. But it is again also true that demand for CNC machines was, in France, slower to take off and assert itself in a wider scale as it did in Germany (Sorge and Maurice, 165).* As already suggested, this has something to do with the structure of the industry in France, which has previously been weaker in investment goods manufacturing in mechanical engineering but stronger in precisely those sectors where flexible universal machines were much less required than dedicated purpose-specific machinery.

* Source: Sorge, A. and Maurice, M. (1990) 'The societal effect in strategies and competitiveness of machine tool manufacturers in France and West Germany', *International Journal of Human Resource Management* 1, Taylor & Francis Ltd, http://www.tandf.co.uk/journals.

One of the few – if not the only – article to study manufacturing systems and management within the societal effect approach. It provides three excellent cases.

Takahiro Fujimoto (1999) *The Evolution of a Manufacturing System at Toyota*. Oxford: Oxford University Press.

Excellent book describing how, in the early 1990s, Toyota had to change its assembly lines to make them more worker-friendly.

Taylor, B. (1999) Japanese management style in China? Production practices in Japanese manufacturing plants. *New Technology, Work and Employment* 14(2), 20 129–42.

Through an examination of 20 Japanese-owned manufacturing plants in China, this article questions the usefulness of identifying Japanese competitive success as being associated with specific Japanese production management techniques.

References

Berggren, C. (1992) *Alternatives to Lean Production*. New York: ILR Press.
Boyer, R. and Durand, J.P. (1997) *After Fordism*. London: Macmillan.
Boyer, R. and Hollingsworth, R. (1997) The variety of institutional arrangements and their complementarity in modern economies, in Hollingsworth, J.R. and Boyer, R.

(eds) *Contemporary Capitalism*. Cambridge: Cambridge University Press.

Dankbaar, B. (1995) The crisis of Fordism: restructuring in the automobile industry, in Van Ruysseveldt, J., Huiskamp, R. and Van Hoof, J. (eds) *Comparative Industrial and Employment Relations*. London: Sage, 293–314.

Dohse, K., Jürgens, U. and Malsch, T. (1989) From 'Fordism' to 'Toyotism'? The social organization of the labor process in the Japanese automobile industry. *East Asia* 5.

Hollingsworth, R. (1997) Continuities and changes in social systems of production: the cases of Japan, Germany, and the United States, in Hollingsworth, J. R. and Boyer, R. (eds) *Contemporary Capitalism: the Embeddedness of Institutions*. Cambridge: Cambridge University Press, 265–310.

Jürgens, U. (1995) Group work and the reception of Uddevalla in the German car industry, in Sandberg, A. (ed.) *Enriching Production*. Aldershot: Avebury, 199–213.

Lane, C. (1989) *Management and Labour in Europe*. Aldershot: Edward Elgar.

Piore, M.J. and Sabel, C. (1984) *The Second Industrial Divide*. New York: Basic Books.

Sheldrake, J. (1996) *Management Theory*. London: International Thomson Business Press.

Sorge, A. (1995) New technologies, organizational change and employment practices, in Van Ruysseveldt, J., Huiskamp, R. and Van Hoof, J. (eds) *Comparative Industrial and Employment Relations*. London: Sage, 266–314.

Sorge, A. and Maurice, M. (1990) The societal effect in strategies and competitiveness of machine tool manufacturers in France and West Germany. *International Journal of Human Resource Management* 1, 141–72.

Streeck, W. (1984) Guaranteed employment, flexible manpower use, and cooperative manpower management: a trend towards convergence, in Tokunaga Shigeyoshi (ed.) *Industrial Relations in Transition*. Tokyo: University of Tokyo Press.

Streeck, W. (1991) On the institutional conditions of diversified quality production, in Streeck, W. (ed.) *Beyond Keynesianism: the Socio-Economics of Production and Full Employment*, edited by E. Matzner and W, Streeck Aldershot: Edward Elgar, 21–61.

Taylor, B. (1999) Japanese management style in China? Production practices in Japanese manufacturing plants. *New Technology, Work and Employment* 14, 2.

Whitley, R. (1999) *Divergent Capitalisms: the Social Structuring and Change of Business Systems*. New York: Oxford University Press.

Womack, J.P., Jones, D.T. and Roos, D. (1991) *The Machine that Changed the World*. New York: HarperCollins.

Zhiang Lin and Chun Hui (1999) Should lean replace mass organizations systems? A comparative examination from a management coordination perspective. *Journal of Business Studies* 30(1), 45–80.

Questions

1. Explain the relationships between organizational patterns and societal features in the German and French machine tool industries.

2. Identify the link between the human resource practices and inter-organizational relationships in the French and German machine tool industries and the rest of the domestic industry.

3. Explain comparative advantage in the French and German machine tool sectors on the basis of human resources, organization patterns and the embeddedness of firms in the societal structure.

4. Explain the concept of 'fit' in the context of the French and German machine tool industry. In what sense can 'fit' help to explain the competitiveness described in this case?

8

Managing Resources: National Innovation Systems

Learning Objectives

By the end of this chapter you will be able to:

- appreciate the difference between incremental and more radical types of innovation

- explore the link between the 'techno-economic paradigm' shift and dramatic change in national institutions

- identify the major institutions involved in innovation processes

- assess the role of these different institutions in innovative systems

- compare and explain the differences in the main features of the innovation systems of the USA, Japan, Germany and France

- explain how these divergencies help to understand differences in national innovation trajectories.

Chapter Outline

8.1 Introduction

8.2 Technological Advancement: a Taxonomy
Incremental innovations
Radical innovations
Changes of 'technology system'
Changes in 'techno-economic' paradigm

8.3 Innovation: Overview of the Major Institutions Involved
Institutional features affecting the stock of knowledge in research institutes
Institutional features affecting the flow of knowledge between research
Institutions and industry
Organizational practices affecting the stock of knowledge in industry

8.4 The American Innovation System

8.5 The Japanese Innovation System

8.6 The German Innovation System

8.7 The French Innovation System

8.8 Conclusions
Study Questions
Further Reading
Case: The German and Japanese Pharmaceutical Industries
References

8.1 ❖ Introduction

The slowdown of growth in the 1970s and again from the late 1990s onwards in the advanced industrial nations, the rise and fall of Japan as a major economic and technological power, the relative decline of the USA, and the widespread concerns in Europe about lagging behind have induced research and policy concerned with supporting the technical innovative competence of national firms. At the same time, the enhanced technical sophistication of firms from Korea, Taiwan and other newly industrializing countries (NICs) has broadened the range of nations whose firms are competitive players in fields that used to be the preserve of only a few, and has led other nations, who today have a weak manufacturing sector, to wonder how they might emulate the performance of the successful NICs (Nelson and Rosenberg, 1993: 3).

Against this background, a recent body of scholarship has underscored the importance of the national institutional context as an explanation for differences in national patterns of innovation (e.g. Dosi *et al.*, 1990; Lundvall, 1992; Kogut, 1993; Nelson, 1993). From this perspective, technological development is rooted in the skills, capabilities and knowledge that accumulate over time in the *national innovation system*. Country-specific technological paths are argued to be shaped by the structural components of society (such as political and educational systems) that influence the accumulation and diffusion of knowledge required for industrial innovation.

Institutional perspectives highlight two ways in which the national institutional context shapes specific country patterns of innovation. First, they show how the societal institutions that support industrial innovation vary cross-nationally. For example, the policies and practices of a nation's universities and government research institutes are shaped to a large extent by that nation's singular historical development. Universities and research institutes provide knowledge and human capital to firms in technology-driven industries. As a consequence, the features of these institutions influence the technological performance of a country's firms (Ergas, 1987; Porter, 1990; Nelson, 1993).

Second, the national context influences the institutional arrangements and behavioural patterns of firms themselves. For example, the organization of work and patterns of communication within and between firms, or between firms and universities, reflects broader societal characteristics that have been imprinted on firms and institutionalized over time (Kogut, 1991; Powell and DiMaggio, 1991). Such institutionalized arrangements are particularly important in emerging science-based technologies, such as biotechnology, in which the relative success of different countries will depend on the successful coordination of scientific infrastructure and industrial capabilities (Dosi *et al.*, 1990).

This chapter draws on these institutional arguments to explain how the national institutional environments of different countries shape nationally specific innovation patterns. Before that, it first provides some background information on the existing types of innovation, in Section 8.2. In Section 8.3, it offers a brief discussion of the major institutions that can be involved in innovation processes. Sections 8.4 to 8.7 discuss the dominant features of the innovation systems of the USA, Japan, Germany and France. This discussion should enable the reader to understand the link between the nationally specific institutional features and technological trajectories of these countries. At the same time, and as a result of this discussion, you will become aware of the importance of 'location' to successful innovation (Porter and Stern, 2002). Innovation-centred organizations should not be driven only by input costs, tax incentives, subsidies or even wage rates for scientists and engineers; they should also take into consideration locational advantages – rooted in, for example, special relationships with local universities and companies, preferential access to local institutions, and so on.

Finally, the case study at the end of the chapter, on the pharmaceutical industries in Germany and Japan, is intended to help you understand the application of the innovation system approach at sector level.

8.2 ⁘ Technological Advancement: a Taxonomy[1]

In order to be able to understand the innovation process and national innovation systems, one has to have some notion of the types of technological development that occur in the modern world. This section provides a brief overview of existing types of technical change.

The taxonomy of innovations, which is discussed below, is based on empirical work. It distinguishes between:

⁘ incremental innovation

⁘ radical innovation

⁘ new technology systems, and

⁘ changes of techno-economic paradigms.

We will now look at each of these in turn.

Incremental innovations

These are small-step innovations that occur more or less continuously in any industry or service activity, although at differing rates in different industries and different countries, depending on a combination of demand pressures, socio-cultural factors, technological opportunities and trajectories.

They may often occur not so much as the result of any deliberate research and development activity, but as the outcome of inventions and improvements suggested by engineers and others directly engaged in the production process, or as a result of initiatives and proposals by users.

They are frequently associated with the scaling-up of plant and equipment, and quality improvements to products and services for a variety of specific applications. Although their combined effect is extremely important in the growth of productivity, no single incremental innovation has dramatic effects, and they may sometimes pass unnoticed and unrecorded.

[1] This section is based on Freeman and Perez (1988: 45–7).

Radical innovations

These are discontinuous events and in recent times are usually the result of a deliberate research and development activity in enterprises and/or universities and government laboratories. There is, for example, no way in which nylon could have emerged from improving the production process in rayon plants or the woollen industry.

Radical innovations are unevenly distributed over sectors and over time, and whenever they occur, they are important as a potential springboard for new markets, and for the surges of new investment associated with economic booms.

They may often involve a combined product, process and organizational innovation. Over a period of decades, radical innovations, such as nylon or the contraceptive pill, may have fairly dramatic effects (i.e. they do bring about structural change but, in terms of their aggregate economic impact, they are relatively small and localized, unless a whole cluster of radical innovations are linked together in the rise of new industries and services, such as the synthetic materials industry or the semiconductor industry).

Changes of 'technology system'

These are far-reaching changes in technology, affecting several branches of the economy, as well as giving rise to entirely new sectors. They are based on a combination of radical and incremental innovations, together with organizational and managerial innovations affecting more than a few companies. An example is the cluster of synthetic materials innovations, petro-chemical innovations, and machinery innovations in injection moulding and extrusion.

Changes in 'techno-economic' paradigm

Also known as 'technological revolutions', these are far-reaching changes in the technology system that are such that in their effects they have a major impact on the behaviour of the entire economy.

A change of this kind carries with it many clusters of radical and incremental innovations, and may eventually embody a number of new technology systems.

A vital characteristic of this fourth type of technical change is that it has pervasive effects throughout the economy – that is, it not only leads to the emergence of a new range of products, services, systems and industries in its own right, it also affects, directly or indirectly, almost every other branch of the economy.

The expression 'technological paradigm' is used because the changes involved go beyond engineering trajectories for specific product or process technologies, and affect the input cost structure and conditions of production and distribution throughout the system. Moreover, once this new technological paradigm is established as the dominant influence on engineers, designers and managers, it becomes a 'technological regime' for several decades. From this perspective, cycles of economic development can be linked to a succession of 'techno-economic paradigms' associated with a characteristic institutional framework, which, however, only emerges after a painful process of structural change.

8.3 Innovation: Overview of the Major Institutions Involved

The rise of science-based technology has led to a dramatic change in the nature of the people and institutions involved in technological advance. Through much of the nineteenth century, strong formal education in a science provided an inventor – such as, for example, Thomas Alva Edison – with little or no advantage in problem-solving. By 1900, formal training in chemistry was virtually becoming a requirement for successful inventive effort in the chemical products industries. Indeed, the days when unschooled geniuses such as Edison could make major advances in the electrical technologies were coming to an end, and the major electrical companies were busy staffing their laboratories with university-trained scientists and engineers (Nelson and Rosenberg, 1993).

In general, industrial innovation depends on 'the complex interweaving of basic research', which is concentrated primarily in research institutes and universities, 'and market-induced applied R&D' (Tapon, 1989: 199). However, the integration of basic research with market opportunity does not happen automatically. 'Investments in basic research, while important in seeding possibilities for commercial innovation, will not lead to competitive advantage unless transmitted to and further developed by industry' (Porter, 1990: 80–1). Below, we explain the mechanisms that shape the interplay between basic and industry-specific research. We do so on the basis of a discussion of the major features of the national institutional context that affect national innovation patterns. These are:

- tradition of scientific education
- patterns of basic research funding
- linkages with foreign research institutions
- degree of commercial orientation of academia
- labour mobility
- venture capital system, and
- national technology policy.

Most of these features will crop up again in the sections on the specific country explanations. While the first three features affect the stock of knowledge in research institutes, the others affect the flow of knowledge between research institutes and industry. In addition, in the following, we also explain two types of organizational practice that affect the stock of knowledge in industries: inter-firm collaboration and exploitation of foreign technology.

Institutional features affecting the stock of knowledge in research institutes

National tradition of scientific education

A nation's pool of specialized human resources – such as molecular biologists, for example – is created through investments made by individuals seeking to develop their skills. The particular choices of skill development made by individuals are reinforced by social institutions or governments that hope to benefit society or the economy (Porter, 1990). A strong tradition of scientific education endows a country with a base of well-developed institutions devoted to scientific research, which signals to that society's members that scientific research is a worthwhile calling (Locke, 1985). Countries in which it is socially desirable and financially rewarding to pursue a scientific career will tend to produce a greater number of scientists per capita.

National funding of basic research

Advances in basic scientific research are not driven by a motive of return on investment, but rather by 'the logic of scientific advance as perceived by academic scientists' (Tapon, 1989: 199). Because of the very long research cycles in sciences like molecular biology, for example, and the enormous costs of laboratory equipment and materials, long-term government support of most fundamental research is a critical factor affecting a country's stock of scientific knowledge (Mowery and Rosenberg, 1993). The manner in which research funding is allocated is also important, as it influences which types of institution (e.g. universities, government laboratories) become the central performers of scientific research.

Linkages with foreign research institutions

The openness of a nation's research institutions to scientific development in other parts of the world can be important for the stock of knowledge. Strategically tapping into the knowledge bases of other countries can help a country's research institutions to develop expertise in areas in which the country lags, thus complementing its existing knowledge base (Porter, 1990; Shan and Hamilton, 1991).

Nations vary in the degree to which their research institutions seek to learn from foreign research (Yuan, 1987, cited in Bartholomew, 1997), reflecting differences in historical development of the country's educational institutions. While countries that have been 'early industrializers' (e.g. the UK) have a tendency to focus on domestic invention, 'late industrializers' (e.g. Japan) have a stronger pattern of borrowing and adapting knowledge from other countries (Hampden-Turner and Trompenaars, 1993; Westney, 1993).

Institutional features affecting the flow of knowledge between research institutions and industry
Degree of commercial orientation of research institutions

In most societies, research institutions and firms have profoundly different missions. While the central goal of universities and research institutes is to create and disseminate knowledge, the principal mandate of firms is to maximize the wealth of shareholders (Swann, 1988; Nelsen, 1991). The *degree* of cultural distance between academia and industry, however, is rooted in the historical foundations of the educational system unique to each country (see e.g. Mowery and Rosenberg, 1993). A greater commercial orientation in a nation's research institutions translates into a smaller cultural distance between the worlds of academia and industry, which in turn facilitates the flow of knowledge between the two communities. National differences in the commercial orientation of academia, and/or differences in government programmes for technology diffusion have an impact on the extent to which firms collaborate with research institutions (Kenney, 1986; Ergas, 1987).

Labour mobility

Greater movement of individuals between university and industry promotes greater accessibility of firms to the stock of human and technological capital (Ergas, 1987: 201), and greater awareness among academics of commercial markets, thus enhancing the flow of knowledge between research institutions and firms (Swann, 1988). The norms and practices of a nation's research institutions affect the degree to which scientists move between academia and industry. For example, evaluation and promotion systems in universities that allow scientists to pursue contracts in industry can provide an incentive to academics to blend academic and industrial research in their careers, including engaging in industrial consulting (Bartholomew, 1997). Labour mobility between research institutions and firms also reflects the relative 'opportunity cost' of leaving academia for industry (i.e. the potential loss of social prestige or academic standing) as well as the opportunity cost of staying in academia (i.e. the forfeiting of significant financial reward) (Sharp, 1989). How a society confers status on its members – whether according to social position, academic achievement or financial status – thus influences the mobility of scientists between academia and industry.

Availability of venture capital

One option open to scientists is to leave their research institution to start up their own firm. In the field of biotechnology, in particular, start-up companies funded by venture capital serve a particularly important role in diffusing scientific knowledge from research institutions to industry: not only does vital scientific knowledge 'walk out the door' with the academic scientist who establishes the new firm; the new firm also gains an immediate social network of scientists in academia to facilitate ongoing knowledge diffusion (Bartholomew, 1997). The availability of venture capital markets to fund start-up firms varies substantially cross-nationally (Ergas, 1987; Porter, 1990) and is an institutional reflection of a society's degree of individualism and its related view of speculative finance (Lodge, 1990; Hampden-Turner and Trompenaars, 1993).

National technology policy

Nations vary substantially in the underlying orientation of the state towards industry (Lenway and Murtha, 1994). In nations with an individualistic orientation, government assumes a limited role in industrial development, allowing the marketplace to regulate competition among firms. By contrast, in nations with a more collectivist orientation, government takes a more direct role in defining the needs of the community and setting the direction of industrial development to help meet these needs (Lodge, 1990).

Differences in the fundamental orientation of the state also have direct implications for the manner in which technology is diffused from research institutions to industry. Collectivist-orientated states often follow 'diffusion-orientated' innovation policies, in which technology diffusion is considered to be an explicit part of the government's mandate; accordingly, programmes, institutions and structural linkages are established by government expressly for this purpose of facilitating industry's appropriation of new scientific developments (Ergas, 1987; Ostry, 1990). By contrast, individualistic-orientated states leave the flow of knowledge between research institutions and firms to be carried out by market forces.

Organizational practices affecting the stock of knowledge in industry

Inter-firm collaboration

Inter-firm collaboration can be advantageous as a research and development (R&D) strategy because it allows partnering firms 'to realize economies of synergies as a result of pooling resources, production rationalization, risk reduction, and utilization of assets to the efficient scale and scope' (Shan and Hamilton, 1991: 420).

Countries vary in the extent to which inter-firm collaboration is a favoured practice, reflecting historically based societal differences in the underlying view of the nature of cooperation and competition (e.g. Hamel *et al.*, 1989; Hampden-Turner and Trompenaars, 1993). The practice of inter-firm cooperation may be further reinforced by a strong government role in coordinating pre-competitive cooperative R&D (Saxonhouse, 1986; Brock, 1989; Westney, 1993). An example of the latter is the organization by the Japanese Ministry of International Trade and Industry (MITI) of research consortia (see Section 8.5 for an extended explanation).

Exploitation of foreign technology

Cross-border R&D alliances, whether among firms, or between firms and research institutions, contain an additional benefit for firms beyond those gained from domestic collaboration. Although a firm may form one or more international cooperative relationships for economic, strategic and other reasons similar to those that drive it to domestic partnerships, an international cooperative venture may provide the firm with access to country-specific advantages embedded in its partners (Shan and Hamilton, 1991: 419). For example, cross-border collaboration can offer biotechnology firms access to the stock of knowledge created by other national systems of biotechnology innovation.

Firms from different countries vary in how much they strategically source external technology and engage in international R&D activity, reflecting differences in the historical context of economic development (Mansfield, 1988). For example, reliance on foreign technology can be instrumental in late-industrializing economies trying to 'catch up' with economies that industrialized at an earlier date (Hikino and Amsden, 1994). However, in the process of borrowing technology developed by firms from more advanced countries, the late-industrializing country also acquires distinct capabilities in importing and adapting foreign knowledge. This strategy of 'learner' may thus be retained by firms long after the economic 'catch-up' has occurred (Westney, 1993).

The following explanation of the main features of the national innovation systems of the USA, Japan, Germany and France illustrates the importance of each of the aforementioned institutional and organizational features for the specific innovation trajectories in these different countries.

8.4 The American Innovation System[2]

The period between 1900 and 1940 witnessed the formation of the structure of the private sector component of the US national innovation system. The turn of the century ushered in the rise of the giant multi-product corporation; this development was supported by industrial research, which ensured the survival of such initiatives. Since federal funding for non-agricultural research was sparse until about 1940, state government support, particularly to universities, provided the primary impetus. Universities rose to the occasion to accommodate and recognize the requirements of industry, agriculture and mining. Although by later standards their research budgets could be seen as minute, to say the least, university research thrived and eventually included collaborations of all sorts with flourishing research departments within private firms.

What distinguishes the US innovation system from its counterparts in other countries? The most obvious trait is its **scale**: US **R&D investment** – for most of the post world war era – exceeded the combined investment of all other OECD countries. Another key difference in the innovation system in the US can be seen in the triad structure of industry, universities and the federal government in the performance and funding of research. Unique to the US innovation system is the extent to which **new firms** have been behind the commercialization of new technologies in the economy. Development and diffusion of microelectronics, computer hardware and software, biotechnology and robotics: these have all been developed and diffused in the last 40 years by rather small startup firms – to a much greater extent in the US than in any other country (with the possible exceptions of only Denmark and Taiwan).

What lies behind the contrasts in structure between the US national innovation system and that of other countries? **Antitrust statutes** in the US importantly affected the structure and performance of the national innovation system. In the late 19th century, the increasingly stringent judicial interpretation of the Sherman Antitrust Act escalated the civil prosecution of agreements among firms regarding price and output controls. In the period 1895–1904 (and particularly after 1898), firms seeking to control prices and protect markets reacted to this new legal environment through mergers, particularly horizontal mergers. As the US Justice Department used further interpretations of the Sherman Antitrust Act to prosecute a wider range of firms, **corporate America was compelled to greater reliance on industrial research and innovation**. Corporate diversification and the use of patents provided firms some maneuvering room, within the law, to attain or retain market power.

Invention and development of new technologies were not the only core tasks of fledgling corporate research laboratories. These in-house labs were also charged with monitoring the environment for technological threats, and with acquiring new technologies through the purchase of patents or firms. Dupont, for example, can attribute much of its success to acquiring many of its major product and process innovations early

---

[2] This section draws essentially on Mowery and Rosenberg (1993: 29–64).

on in its development – often based on the advice of its research lab. Similar monitoring roles were played by research facilities at AT&T, General Electric, and Eastman Kodak (although the latter to a lesser extent).

If Sherman Antitrust legislation spurred on the development of US innovation in the early 20th century, **military R&D and procurement contracts** were the driving force in the latter half of the century. For the past three decades, the federal R&D budget has been dominated by military services, the allotment of which fell below 50 percent of federal R&D obligations in only three years during this time. During the early postwar years, this high level of military R&D investment bolstered high-technology industries. In the semiconductor sector, for example, military procurement may have played an even more important role than direct military R&D outlays. Product development in the electronics industry was determined from the outset by the procurement needs of the military and NASA. Such industries subsequently poured profits and overheads from military procurement contracts into company-funded R&D to generate lucrative spillovers for civilian use.

Another factor setting apart innovation in the US from that of Germany or Great Britain, for example, is the **parallel way that industrial and academic research developed in the US**. Already at the end of the 19th century, the pursuit of research – within both US industry and higher education – was recognized as an important professional activity. German industry and academia had set the example, and competitive pressure from the Germans (felt keenly by industry) provided the impetus. How did the **two kinds of research become so interrelated**? The answer is to be found in the decentralized structure and financial support of the US higher education system, particularly public universities. **Public funding** of US higher education led the system to grow far beyond that of Great Britain, for example. The nature and politics of public support – state rather than federal funding – created unique advantages for the US system. State funding led to curriculum and research at universities becoming more closely tied into commercial opportunities than could be the case in many European systems. State university systems, attuned to the requirements of the local economy, were able to introduce new programs in a timely fashion in emerging sub-fields such as engineering, and, to some extent, mining and metallurgy.

Of vital importance to scientific knowledge and problem-solving techniques are the people trained to use them. The **pool of technically trained personnel** in the US prepared to contend with the rise in scientific know-how, particularly engineers, grew rapidly at the end of the 19th century, in part due to the increased number of engineering schools and programs. Although the training of these engineers was rather rudimentary before World War II, it met the basic needs of the expanding industrial establishment for technicians trained to cope with the larger body of scientific knowledge. Cutting-edge science would come later. At the time, there were far more technicians than 'scientists'. The diffusion and utilization of advanced scientific and engineering knowledge was supported by the broad-based system of training in the US. Higher education during the early 20th century, although basic, proved to be more than sufficient to power scientific and engineering development.

A dramatic shift took place from World War II onwards. Scientific research, both industrial and academic, was then bolstered by dramatically expanded federal government funding. Post-war federal R&D funding has continued to comprise a substantial fraction of an already impressive national R&D budget. The amount of resources dedicated to R&D since the end of World War II is staggering, not only compared with expenditures during other periods in history, but also compared with the investment of other OECD countries. **Federal support for university research** has led to an immense expansion of academic research, tied into contracts and grants for specific research projects. These are issued, for the most part, by a centralized federal authority, although several other federal agencies, each with their own agendas, have contributed to the huge increases in research demand.

Although **federal funds have been especially important to basic research**, only 15 per cent of federally funded basic research is currently performed within the federal research establishment. Universities became more important players in basic research during the postwar period – now accounting for a growing share of total US basic research, which stimulates even more **collaboration between university and industrial research**. This collaboration was well established before 1940, underwent a weakening during the 1950s and '60s, and has now been restored to prominence. Support of industry for university research can be seen in financial support from industry in establishing on-campus facilities for research with potential commercial value. The spectrum of collaborations is too broad to allow generalizations, and each industry has its own peculiarities regarding the industry/university relationship. Biotechnology provides one example of an extremely close connection between university research and commercial technology. The closeness can be attributed perhaps to the radical nature of biotechnology: scientific breakthroughs in recombinant DNA and genetic engineering techniques are quickly transferred to industry and put into practice.

What other roles did the federal government play in the development of university research? On the supply side, federal actions enlarged the pool of scientific personnel and supported high quality research and teaching by funding acquisition of the necessary physical equipment and facilities. The federal government also fostered the universities' commitment to research – which before World War II had a lower priority than teaching. This was done by simultaneously providing funds for education and the support of research within the university community. The US mix of research and teaching in higher education went much further than policies elsewhere in the world. More research is carried out in specialized institutes in Europe and Japan, for example, and in government-run labs.

Despite the shifts in federal government financial support, however, private industry has retained its position as a forerunner in research. In 1985, industry performed 73 percent of total US R&D, and took on more than 50 percent of the total funding. As mentioned earlier, established firms in the US expanded their R&D greatly in response to the war effort and subsequent Cold War hostilities. Yet, interesting to note is **the prominent role played by relatively young industrial firms** in developing the postwar US industrial innovation system. These new firms, which pioneered the commercialization of new product technologies such as semiconductors, computers, and biotechnology, presented a new way forward, compared with the pattern in Japan and Western Europe, where new technology development was the province of established firms in electronics and pharmaceuticals, among others.

What is behind the prominent role taken by new, small firms in the postwar innovation system in the US? One factor is certainly **the labor mobility** in and out of the large basic research 'incubators' in universities, the government and some private firms. Individuals involved in the development of certain technologies were not adverse to taking their innovations with them and founding firms to pursue commercialization. Biotechnology, microelectronics and computer industries were particularly affected by this pattern. Moreover, within regional agglomerations of high-tech firms the above-mentioned labor mobility had other consequences: channeling technology diffusion and attracting other firms in similar or related industries.

Another important factor behind the success of small, new firms in the US has been the **US venture capital market**, which played, for example, a particularly important role in establishing many microelectronics firms in the 1950s and '60s. This sophisticated private financial system also contributed to the growth of the biotechnology and computer industries. Eventually, the supply of venture capital was supplemented by public equity offerings.

A relatively permissive intellectual property regime in certain industries (particularly microelectronics and biotechnology) also supported the commercialization of innovations by new firms, thereby promoting technology diffusion and shielding young firms from litigations over innovations that may have had their roots, in part, in the R&D departments of established firms or other research labs. The 1956 consent decree that settled the federal antitrust suit against AT&T led, among other things, to more liberal licensing and cross-licensing policies for microelectronics. Litigation with regard to biotechnology may have been discouraged by the continuing uncertainty over the nature of intellectual property protection.

Startup firms benefited importantly also from **post-war antitrust policy**. Settlement of the AT&T suit in 1956 had two ramifications for new microelectronics firms: first, liberal patent licensing terms set down by the consent decree, and second, prohibitions constraining AT&T from business activities beyond telecommunications. AT&T, with at the time the greatest technological capabilities in microelectronics, was thus blocked from entering into commercial production of microelectronic devices, which paved the way for startup firms. IBM also lost an antitrust suit in 1956, which mandated liberal licensing of the firm's punch card and reasonable rates for computer patents.. Indirectly, major postwar antitrust suits probably supported startup firms by deterring the established firms from continuing their prewar pursuit of new technology through acquisitions of smaller firms.

A final postwar stimulant for new firms was **US military procurement policy**, which in the 1950s and '60s opened the doors, through low marketing and distribution entry barriers, to startup firms in microelectronics and computers. The possibilities for technological spillovers from military to civilian applications, fueling the already substantial benefits for such firms, were, in fact, often based on military policy. In contrast to its European counterparts, the US military took a chance on awarding major contracts to firms as yet unproved – by the military or any other market. Such contracts attracted startup firms in industries such as microelectronics. Also firms well-established in civilian markets applied for these contracts, eager to extract any commercial applications from their military R&D efforts.

Box 8.1: The Core features of the US innovation system

1. Substantial federal and state level support for university education and research – both basic and commercial.
2. Robust link between research and teaching at universities.
3. Strong research collaboration between universities and industry.
4. Vigorous university–industry labor mobility.
5. Financial support of university research by industry.
6. Substantial civilian spillover resulting from the significant role of military R&D and procurement in a wide variety of sectors, with
7. Prominent role for small startup firms.

8.5 The Japanese Innovation System[3]

In Japan, the *distinctive relationship between government and industry*, and the government's pervasive intervention in the economy and with technology strategy were already present in the nineteenth century. Ever since 1868 – the start of the Meiji era[4] – Japanese central government had worked closely with industry in modernizing the Japanese economy and importing foreign technology. The government built and owned plants and factories in industries such as mining, railroad machinery and textiles, because it was still difficult for the private sector to finance the required investment and to take risks. In 1873, the Meiji government set up the School of Engineering (*Kogakuryo*), which was responsible for education in fields such as civil and mechanical engineering, telecommunications, construction, chemistry, mining, metallurgy and shipbuilding. This college produced graduates who later founded many of the major Japanese manufacturing companies.

Japan's higher education system has been seen as one of the key players in the national innovation system. The education system, which had been expanded by the beginning of the twentieth century to include several public- as well as private-sector universities and other higher-education institutions, started to supply many trained engineers. From the period between the two world wars, Japan has been among the leading countries in the world in terms of educational opportunity, both at the secondary and higher-education levels (especially in science and engineering). Moreover, Japanese universities have not only helped the private sectors by educating engineers and scientists but also by acting as gatekeepers when overseas techniques were imported into industry, making valuable contributions in introducing, assimilating and implementing advanced technology. In recent years, however, in comparing Japan's postgraduate system of education with that of the USA in the fields of science and engineering, it has been argued that curricula formation in Japan is slow in reflecting the changing nature of science and in introducing an interdisciplinary approach, while financial support for graduate and post-doctoral students in Japan is poor. Potentially, these are significant impediments that

---

[3] This section draws on Odagiri and Goto (1993: 76–103), Freeman (1988) and Goto (2000).

[4] The Meiji era (1868–1911) meant the end of the seclusion of Japan, which was imposed on the country by the Tokugawa government (1603–1868), and the inauguration of a non-feudal central government.

may have a long-term detrimental effect on the scientific and technological development of Japanese industry.

Also at the beginning of the twentieth century, several national research institutions were founded. One of the largest and most productive research institutions, established in 1917, was the Institute of Physical and Chemical Research (*Rikagaku Kenkyusho*, known as *Riken*). *Riken* was established with the aim of fostering scientific progress and thereby contributing to industries. Hence, the aim was not purely academic but also practical. Riken was established with roughly half of the funding provided by government and half by the private sector. The Science Council (*Gakujutsu Shinkokai*, known as *Gakushin*) was established in 1933 to promote more basic research and, again, both government and private sector provided the funding. Companies also started their own R&D laboratories. While small, in 1923 there were 162 private R&D laboratories affiliated to companies, cooperatives and other private foundations.

Japanese national technology policies between the 1930s and the end of the Second World War were driven mainly by military imperatives. The government retained plants in military-related industries, such as shipbuilding, aircraft, munitions and steel, and in public utilities including telecommunication. The military-owned plants were also a centre of technological development. They hired a large percentage of, at that time still scarce, engineers and imported advanced machinery from abroad. As in the USA, military technology was subsequently transferred to the private sector as the engineers and skilled workers moved from the military plants to the private sector, especially during the disarmament period following the Russo-Japanese War of 1904–05. Also similar to the situation in the USA, the military not only produced goods within its own shipyards and arsenals, but also procured them from the private sector. Since the military, for obvious defence reasons, preferred to procure goods domestically, procurement gave domestic producers in shipbuilding, steel, machines, electrical equipment, and so on, who were under competitive pressure from larger and technically advanced foreign firms, a chance to increase their production and accumulate knowledge through experience.

In terms of industrial composition, food processing and textiles were the largest industries before the turn of the century. By mid-1910, many companies in the metal, machinery, chemical and other heavy industries had begun to grow quickly. Technological progress was an important source of this growth. This technological progress came from indigenous (traditional and domestic) technology and, especially, from technology imported from advanced countries. Indigenous technology was important in the traditional industries but also in providing the opportunity to choose between the technologies available in developed countries, and in adapting and assimilating them to fit domestic conditions. This fact was most notable in the textile industry, the second largest manufacturing industry at the time (next to food processing) and the largest exporting industry before the Second World War.

The role of indigenous technology was limited, however, in modern industries such as metal and machinery, where *imported technology* played a far greater role. The import of technologies was accompanied by a systematic policy designed to improve these technologies. The method of assimilating and improving on imported technology was mainly some form of 'reverse engineering'. This involved trying to manufacture a product similar to one already available on the world market but without direct foreign investment or transfers of blueprints for product and process design. The widespread use of reverse engineering during the 1950s and 1960s had several major consequences for the Japanese system of innovation. First, Japanese management, engineers and workers grew accustomed to thinking of the entire production process as a system of thinking in an integrated way about product design and process design. This ability to redesign an entire production system has been identified as one of the major sources of Japanese competitive success in industries such as shipbuilding, automobiles and colour television.

Moreover, whereas Japanese firms made few original radical product innovations in these industries, they did introduce many incremental innovations. They also redesigned and reorganized many processes so as to improve productivity and raise quality. In addition, Japanese engineers and managers grew accustomed to the idea of 'using the factory as a laboratory'. The work of the R&D department was very closely related to the work of production engineers and process control, and was often almost indistinguishable. The whole enterprise was involved in a learning and development process, and many ideas for improving the system came from the shop floor. The horizontal linkages between R&D, production and marketing have been pointed to as a most important feature of the Japanese national system of innovation at enterprise level (Freeman, 1988). Hence, rather like the case in Germany, Japanese success in industries such as motor vehicles, steel, semiconductors and machine tools has been based on an *integrative approach within large companies* far more than on small entrepreneurial firms. In the semiconductor industry, for example, the accumulation of experience through high volumes of production made it possible for Japanese firms to slide along the learning curve and to move quickly from one generation of microchips to the next. Each of these developments at the corporate level was supported by the accumulation of knowledge and technological capability. This, in turn, was underpinned by the practice of sharing experiences by means of staff rotation within the company and by the system of 'lifetime employment' (see Chapter 5).

In these various industries, *tacit knowledge* was important in the process of manufacturing and development. Tacit knowledge is derived from experience, cannot be codified and is scattered at the forefront of operations, be this in a manufacturing plant or sales department. For this reason, it was necessary for those people engaged in production, sales and R&D to share their knowledge with one another and to learn about the contexts in which their tacit knowledge was being interpreted. This was the reason why firm-specific skills were regarded as crucial in sectors such as automobiles, steel, machine tools and semiconductors. The Japanese management system and corporate organizational structure promote the efficient use of such tacit knowledge and the accumulation of firm-specific skills.

This Japanese approach to the import of technology may be compared and contrasted with the methods used, on the one hand, in the former Soviet Union and, on the other, in less developed countries. The former Soviet Union, too, was engaged in the large-scale development and import of technology in the twentieth century and also used reverse engineering; but in the Soviet system of that time much of the responsibility for diffusion and development rested with central research institutes or project design bureaus. This meant that much of the 'technological learning process' took place there rather than at the enterprise level, and acute problems were experienced in the transfer of technology from the specialized R&D institutes to factory-level management. This weakness was recognized and the institutional arrangements were changed considerably in the

1970s and 1980s to strengthen R&D at enterprise level and to regroup research activities in close relationship with enterprises.

In many less developed countries, on the other hand, the method of technology transfer was very often either through subsidiaries of multinationals or by the import of 'turnkey' plants, designed and constructed by foreign contractors. Neither of these methods is likely to result in an intense process of technology accumulation in the (relatively passive) recipient enterprise. Dissatisfaction with both of these methods has led, on the one hand, to pressures on multinationals to set up local R&D activities in addition to training. On the other hand, it has led to efforts to 'unpackage' imported technology and to devolve part of the design and development to local enterprises. The Japanese policy of rejecting foreign investment and putting full responsibility for assimilating and improving on imported technology on the enterprise is more likely to lead to 'systems' thinking and to total systems improvement.

Japanese government policies, especially the protection of the domestic market until the early 1970s, played a significant role in Japan's postwar industrial development. Restricting the growing Japanese market, already the second largest in the capitalist economy in the late 1960s, to Japanese firms that were competing intensively among themselves gave a strong incentive to invest in plants, equipment and R&D. In addition, because postwar Japan's Peace Constitution meant that the military was no longer a significant customer to business, industries such as the automobile sector, which had been helped by military procurement before the war but were still in their infancy relative to US and European producers, might have been wiped out were the market made open to foreign competition.

As is the case in most countries, Japan's policies on intellectual property rights were also used to help the indigenous industry. Until the 1970s, the enforcement of the *patent system* was weak and ineffective to allow the development of domestic industry, which, as mentioned, was largely based on copying foreign technologies. Through the 1980s and 1990s, as Japan's technological ability had attained such a level that there was much to be lost by the infringement of intellectual property, patent law was amended several times in order to strengthen patent protection and enforcement. Japan's patent system is still characterized, however, by 'first to file' and 'pre-grant disclosure' practices. This system implies that firms can quickly acquire the research results of their competitors, and explains why the majority of Japanese producers in, among others, the semiconductor industry, employ the same production techniques while their US counterparts, such as Intel, Motorola and National Semiconductor, adopt different technologies in the production process. In other words, other firms' technology is considered an important source of technological information in Japan. It is argued that Japan's patent system is a 'system for diffusion', in contrast to the US 'system of exclusion'. The Japanese companies' learning process, promoted by spillovers, has been responsible for a continuous process of incremental innovation in the industries mentioned above.

However, the system just described may not necessarily be suited to the new industries, such as biotechnology and information technology (IT), which have experienced rapid growth since the late 1980s. Such industries differ from the traditional ones in not lending themselves as easily to achieving advancements in the technology itself. The rapid advances in science and computer technology have been argued to have initiated a shift in the way new technology is developed (Arora and Gambardella, 1994). While in the past, trial and error, the accumulation of experience, and tacit knowledge played a major role in the process of developing innovations, today one has first to identify the underlying principles governing the behaviour of objects or structures. Hypotheses can then be tested using highly sophisticated instruments and powerful and expensive computers.

For such new technologies, accumulated knowledge or skills become less important, because knowledge and skills are codified in an abstract form and belong to those people who have the advanced and specialized knowledge to understand them. The need for sharing the context in which knowledge is interpreted is also reduced, as is the need for involving the production or sales function in R&D. Rather, it is best if functions are left independent so as to enable researchers to concentrate on their own activities. Under the new system, where technological knowledge can be codified to give it a general meaning, the transaction cost of trading knowledge between different organizations is reduced. In addition, various contractual arrangements can be made (and have, for example, been made between large pharmaceutical companies and bio-venture firms) to transmit knowledge successfully. In this world, since the cost of transferring knowledge is reduced, there is no longer any need for a firm to engage in both development of new technologies and in production or sales. Thus, in the fields of biotechnology and IT, instead of the long-lasting, stable relationships typical of the current inter- and intra-firm organization in Japan, a new type of corporate and industry structure seems to be called for.

When discussing the role of the Japanese government in promoting technological change, one can't leave out the Japanese Ministry of International Trade and Industry (MITI). From the early postwar period onwards, MITI saw as one of its key functions the promotion of the most advanced technologies with the widest world market potential in the long term. In this respect, MITI differed from almost all other analogous ministries and departments in western Europe or North America, which mostly did not see themselves as responsible for long-term technology policies until much later (the 1970s and 1980s). The patent policy just discussed and the protection of the domestic market until the industry was sufficiently developed to cope with foreign competition were part of MITI's industrial policy.

MITI's ability to provide a reasonably accurate identification of the key areas in which to concentrate technological effort and new investment explains its success in restructuring the Japanese economy and orientating the leading firms to a desired course of action. In order to be able to provide good forecasts, MITI established a mode of working that depended on a continuing dialogue on questions of technological development, both with industrial R&D people and with university scientists and technologists. The import-ance of this national system of forecasting, however, lay in the diffusion and generalization of these expectations through a large number of companies in a great variety of industries. This helped to create a climate where firms would make investments in new products and processes associated with the new technology on a much larger scale than elsewhere in the OECD area.

MITI also initiated technological development programmes. A number of such schemes have been implemented (e.g. the 'Large Scale Projects' programme, the 'Next Generation Projects' programme and the 'Mining and Engineering Technological Research Association' system). During the period 1961–87, 87 such government-spon-sored 'research consortia' were formed. For MITI, the research consortia were a convenient way to distribute its subsidies in order to promote the technology, which MITI (and the participating firms) believed important, most notably semiconductors and computers. MITI also used these research consortia to avoid favouring particular firms and to minimize the cost of supervising the use of subsidies. The role of these research consortia is argued to have declined as more and more collaborative research activities are now carried out by research institutions funded jointly by companies or under inter-company technology agreements.

Moreover, in former times, when the Japanese industry was going through its 'catch-up' phase, in which the technological target was clear and well defined and the players were relatively few well-established large firms with a long history of working closely with government, MITI was able to obtain sufficient information and expertise about the technological field or the capabilities of the companies involved. Nowadays, however, it has become a near impossible task since, in the fields of biotechnology or IT, rapid changes are continually occurring, and small start-up firms are playing major roles. The efficiency of traditional industrial-technology policy is much more limited in these areas. While it is true that the government played a major role in US successes in these fields, this role was mainly limited to supporting the creation of a pool of knowledge and putting in place the necessary infrastructure on which the private sector could build its business, rather than promoting specific commercial projects or companies.

Finally, rather like the German model, the Japanese model of innovation also permits and encourages a long-term view with respect to research, training and investment. Japanese firms easily amass and allocate resources for long-term objectives via the main banking system. In market situations, there would be strong pressures from the capital markets to improve short-term profitability by sacrificing long-term investments. The downside of the dominance of centralized or bank-centred finance is the underdevelopment of capital markets and, as a corollary, a relative lack of venture capital. Venture capital is essential for the establishment of the small entrepreneurial firms that are characteristic of new sectors such as biotechnology. Hence, as suggested, small biotechnology ventures are largely absent in the Japanese industrial environment.

Box 8.2: The Core Features of the Japanese Innovation System

1. Strong government guidance and protection of the domestic industry until the 1970s.
2. Government-sponsored research consortia.
3. Well-established educational system, especially for engineers and scientists.
4. Universities were helpful with introducing, assimilating and implementing imported technology.
5. Development of national research institutions to foster research.
6. A strong role of military R&D and procurement with spillover to civilian areas.
7. Important role for imported technology and reverse engineering.
8. Integrative approach within large companies.

8.6 The German Innovation System[5]

Among European states, Germany was a latecomer, in both political and economic terms. In the first third of the nineteenth century, Germany turned to foreign countries, mainly to the UK and Belgium, for new machinery and for skilled workers to bring advanced technology to its industries. Technical knowledge was also acquired through German visitors, often with encouragement and financial support from the government, and sometimes by means of industrial espionage. Given the backward state of the polity and the economy, the government played a key role in the country's development.

In the eighteenth century, *academies of science* had been founded in several German states, and scientific research was primarily their task. At that time, many universities were in a poor state and some people called for their abolition. However, some of the states managed to break away from this condition by re-forming their universities or by establishing new ones with a new curriculum. Prominent among these were the universities of Halle and Göttingen. Although the reforms of these universities were important for the further development of the German university system, the origins of the orientation towards research were more widespread.

For example, in the chemical community in Germany there were eleven laboratories in 1780, eight of which were located at medical departments and two at mining schools. Moreover, in the late eighteenth century some apothecaries expanded their pharmacies into private institutes that trained pharmacists, manufactured such drugs and chemicals as were traditionally custom-made by the pharmacies, and also engaged in laboratory research. Some of these institutes reached such a high level that their courses were certified by the government to be equivalent to university courses.

In the early nineteenth century, after several reforms, in general, universities became the institutional focus of scientific research in Germany. By the middle of the nineteenth century, the research orientation was firmly established at German universities. It was supported by an institutional base, comprising institutes with laboratories for the natural sciences, and specialized libraries for the humanities. University research in Germany rose to a high level, and in some fields (such as medicine, chemistry and physics) ascended to world leadership.

Government funds for the universities increased from 1860 to 1910 by a factor of about five in real terms. This expansion fostered specialization, and many universities created separate departments for natural science. The rise of the German universities took place under the close supervision of state officials. State officials not only pursued a strategy of expanding the Prussian universities, but also of raising their standards further.

Whereas, in the area of science, the German university system accomplished a great deal in the nineteenth century, it did nothing for engineering. In the mind of professors and administrators, engineering lacked the dignity of science and, for this reason, it was not admitted to the university. Some engineering schools had been founded in the eighteenth century to train civil servants for government service: as administrators in the

---

[5] This section draws on Porter (1990), Keck (1993), Soskice (1999), Koen (1999) and Casper (2000).

mining industry (which at that time consisted mainly of state enterprises), as civil engineers and architects, or as military engineers and artillery officers.

In the early 1820s, Prussia took the lead in establishing a system of schools to train technicians for private industry. This soon comprised about 20 vocational schools in the provinces providing courses for craftsmen and factory shopmasters. Above the provincial schools, the Technical Institutes (*Gewerbeinstitut*) in Berlin offered courses for technicians with the objective of enabling them to set up and manage factories. Most German states quickly followed by establishing polytechnic schools.

The *vocational schools* expanded by offering one or more years of preparatory courses, and most were gradually transformed into secondary schools for general education that differed from the traditional secondary school in Germany, the *Gymnasium*, only by not teaching Latin and Greek, and by stressing mathematics and natural sciences. In the 1870s, their students were admitted to the university.

In the 1870s, too, the polytechnic schools were elevated to a higher status. They were now called *Technische Hochschulen*, required similar entrance qualifications as the universities, and distinguished their graduates from lesser kinds of engineers by the special designation of *Diplom-Ingenieur*. A further step towards equal status with the universities was achieved in 1899, when the King of Prussia decided in person to give the *Technische Hochschulen* in Prussia the right to grant doctoral degrees. The other states soon followed suit.

As polytechnic schools were upgraded to university level and vocational schools were transformed into secondary schools for general education, a gap opened at the middle level of technical education. Towards the end of the nineteenth century, the states created new technical schools. The basic level of technical training was provided by the traditional apprenticeship. The old craft guilds were abolished in the first half of the nineteenth century but the apprenticeship system lived on with some reforms. Towards the end of the nineteenth century the apprenticeship system was reorganized; chambers of trade were charged with examination.

By the beginning of the twentieth century, Germany had established a sophisticated system of education in scientific, technical and commercial matters, reaching from elementary-school to doctoral level. There was a flow of knowledge between universities and *Technische Hochschulen*, as many areas of science such as chemistry were pursued in both, though usually with a greater emphasis on applied science in the latter. Moreover, there were links between the education system and industrial firms, not only through the supply of trained personnel but also through consultancy by professors in engineering and in areas of applied science.

What set this system apart from that of other countries was not only the relatively high standard of research at universities and *Technische Hochschulen*, but also its large size. For example, during the first decade of the twentieth century about 30,000 engineers graduated from colleges and universities in Germany compared to about 21,000 in the USA. Relative to the size of the population this means twice as many in Germany as in the USA. In 1913, there were about ten times more engineering students in Germany than in England and Wales.

Akin to the case in Japan, in Germany the bank-based system, which evolved during the period of initial industrialization in the second half of the nineteenth century, provided the industry with 'patient capital', allowing a longer-term focus (see Chapter 6 for details). Already in the late nineteenth century, the 'big three' – that is, the Deutsche,

Dresdner and the Commerzbank – and firms became closely intertwined. The special ties between the big banks and the large corporations outlived the early years of industrial growth, and remained intact during the Weimar Republic as well as during the time of National Socialism. The creation of the Federal Republic after the Second World War did not endanger the coalition around the universal banking system; it proved its use once again at a time of massive capital shortages, with industrial sectors facing the costs of rebuilding and gaining competitive strength.

At the beginning of the twentieth century, in addition to the universities, the *Technische Hochschulen*, and the academies of science, central government and the federal states financed some 40 to 50 *research institutes* for specialized research in applied areas such as weather and atmosphere, geography and geology, health, shipbuilding, biology, and so on, some of which had military purposes; most were orientated towards public tasks, such as public health or safety regulation, and some towards supporting technical innovation in the business sector. Some smaller research institutes were financed jointly by the government and the industry. Similarly, the *Kaiser Wilhelm Society* (which, in 1948, became *the Max Planck Society*) was financed jointly by industry and the government. Whereas, the Kaiser-Wilhelm-Society had major activities in applied research, and included institutes such as leather research or textile research, after the Second World War, the Max-Planck-Society moved back towards basic research, which had brought it international recognition in previous decades.

As in all countries that were involved in the war, during wartime the German innovation system redirected its activities towards the war effort. Generally, the two world wars had mixed consequences for the German innovation system. German companies lost export markets and patent protection, as well as their daughter companies in foreign countries.[6] In the period of National Socialism the number of students in higher education was reduced drastically. Moreover, although a large majority of academics tolerated the authoritarian rule of the National Socialists, many scientists and engineers were removed from their posts. Researchers in all fields of scholarship were forced to emigrate, including leaders in their field such as the physicist Albert Einstein and the mathematician John von Neumann. As many émigrés were unwilling, or unable, to return, the National Socialist period had a damaging effect on the quality of German science for more than two decades.

After the Second World War, the basic components of the innovation system were reconstructed: the firms and their laboratories, the schools, the universities and *Technische Hochschulen*, the Max-Planck-Society, government research institutes, and so on. In the western part, the allies introduced a trade union structure that more or less avoided conflicts among specialized trade unions within firms. The western allies also prohibited R&D for military technology as well as for some areas of civilian technology, including nuclear technology, aeronautics, rocket propulsion, marine propulsion, radar, and remote and automatic control. The key injunctions remained in force until the Federal Republic became a sovereign state in 1955. They effectively wiped out the military and aeronautics industries and in some product groups kept German firms away from the technological front for some time. This is one of the reasons for the relatively poor export performance of the German aircraft, electronics and telecommunications industries.

---

[6] Schering, 'Chronik des Unternehmens'. Schering website.

A genuine institutional innovation in Germany was the *Fraunhofer-Society*, which from its establishment in 1949 grew to become a large organization carrying out applied research mainly on contract with clients in industry and government. Six of its institutes work for the Defence Ministry and are totally financed with public funds. The Fraunhofer-Society has close links to universities. Moreover, being dependent on contracts, it has a strong orientation towards serving clients. As such, it provides a link between universities and industry, and thus helped to reduce the gap that opened in the German innovation system as the Max-Planck-Society moved towards basic research.

Since the mid-1970s, the higher-education sector has been neglected in Germany. In particular for the universities, the neglect by government has not only been financial, but also one of governance. Little has been done to install the sort of governance structures that would enable universities to tackle deficiencies in teaching and to adapt with speed and flexibility to new developments in science and technology, in particular such developments that open up new connections between areas that, previously, were distinct and separate from one another.

The creation of better links between industry and the higher-education sector was recognized in the 1980s by federal and state governments as a task for technology policy. Under German law, professors own most intellectual property and generally have long-term relationships with established firms. Universities have thus had little incentive to establish technology transfer labs. Research within the biomedical sciences and other 'pure' research fields has until recently been conducted with minimal attention to possible commercial spin-offs. From the 1980s, state governments have prodded universities to be more sensitive to the needs of regional industry. Most universities and, in some regions, technical and commercial colleges (*Fachhochschulen*) now have a special office for technology transfer.

An *official technology policy* in the sense of a set of government policies designed to support technical change and to guide its direction has existed at the federal level only since the late 1960s, and at the state level only since the 1980s. Since 1983, the federal government has experimented with support for newly created technology-orientated

---

Box 8.3: The core features of the German innovation system

1. Initially imported technology.
2. Establishment by the government of the academies of science.
3. Private laboratories.
4. High standard of research and education at universities and *Technische Hochschulen*.
5. Excellent vocational training.
6. Specialized research institutes funded by the government.
7. Negative influence of war in terms of prohibitions from carrying out research in certain areas.
8. Applied or contract research carried out by the *Fraunhofer-Society*.
9. Federal support for science parks and small start-ups.
10. Strong industry R&D activity.
11. Link between *Technische Hochschulen* and industry.

enterprises. The government provided subsidies that helped to strengthen the infrastructure for risk capital. The government also worked with the financial community to introduce measures designed to stimulate the provision of higher-risk investment capital and allow technology firms to undertake the rapid growth trajectories commonly seen in US technology clusters. Institutional support by the federal government is heavily concentrated on national laboratories and departmental laboratories. Since the 1970s, there have been attempts to improve the links between the national laboratories with industrial technology. Since the 1980s, federal states and some cities have supported *science parks* to attract new high-tech firms to their region or to facilitate the spin-off of new firms from existing organizations. Innovation centres were established, providing space and infrastructure facilities for new science-based firms.

A key factor in the technological strength of any country is the *innovation activities* of business enterprises. R&D is only a part of these innovation activities, but in many industries it is an essential part. In Germany, about 63 per cent of total national R&D is financed by the business sector, a much higher percentage than in the USA, France, the UK or Italy, but a lower percentage than in Japan, where it is 78 per cent. At the aggregate level, government has not been an important source of funds for R&D performed in the business sector. In 1987, for example, it financed about 12 per cent of all R&D performed by the business sector. About 31 per cent of domestic industrial R&D capability (as measured by R&D employees) is accounted for by the six top spenders: Siemens, Daimler-Benz, Bayer, Hoechst, Volkswagen and BASF.

To date, the German industry has shown a strong technical capability in those areas where it has a long tradition of technological strength. Germany has tended to be strong in complex products, involving complex production processes that depend on skilled and experienced employees on whom responsibility can be devolved. Germany is the undisputed leader in improving and upgrading technology in the fields in which its industry is established (e.g. chemicals – BASF, Schering AG, Bayer, Hoechst; machine construction – Bosch; motor vehicles – Daimler-Benz, Volkswagen, Audi, BMW; electrotechnical products – Siemens and AEG).

Where radically new areas of technology emerged in the decades after the Second World War – for example, computers, biotechnology and electronics – or where, because of the post-Second World War policies of the allied countries German industry had to start anew (as in aircraft), industry developed less technological dynamism (with the exception of nuclear power). In industries of large complex systems, where technology is changing rapidly and where government organizations play a key role as customers (such as telecommunications), German industry does not exhibit technological dynamism.

8.7 The French Innovation System[7]

The French system is essentially a creation of the post-Second World War period. The higher-education sector, with its dual component (the universities and the *Grand Ecoles*) dates back to the late eighteenth century and to subsequent developments at given periods of the nineteenth century (the Napoleonic period). But, otherwise, today's institutions

---

[7] This section draws essentially on Chesnais (1993: 192–226).

and mechanisms have all evolved out of those that were built just after the Liberation from 1945 to 1949, and again from 1958 to 1966.

The French national system of innovation consists to a large extent of a set of vertically structured and fairly strongly compartmentalized sectoral subsystems, often working for public markets and involving an alliance between the state and public and/or private business enterprises. The most important subsystems are those that concern electrical power production (conventional and nuclear), telecommunications, space, arms production and electronics. However, the state–enterprise relationship also exists in petroleum, railway equipment and transport systems, civil engineering and marine technology.

Of all sectoral subsystems, the military subsystem of innovation is one of the largest. In fact, a large part of the French high-tech industry (perhaps really all of it outside the medical sector and pharmaceuticals) has been shaped by the pervasive influence of defence markets and military demand (Chesnais and Serfati, 1990, 1992). This influence did not necessarily have positive outcomes. It has, for example, been argued that the disastrous balance of the French electronics industry, despite the attention and financial support it has received, cannot be dissociated from the fact that the military has had priority in setting the industry's R&D and industrial objectives (Serfati, 1991).

Moreover, in instances where new technologies emerge in the defence sector, as in laser technology, the transfer to civilian use has proved a complete failure. The strong vertical organization of innovation in many sectors has been pointed to as a significant obstacle to the horizontal inter-industry and inter-sectoral transfer of technology. Barriers to inter-industry flows of technology have been further accentuated by a strong secrecy stemming from the important military component of technology production.

The pervasive role of the state in the French economy and innovation system has been explained by the historical weakness of French capitalism, along with the need it has to receive state support, and by the important role played by the elite of the *Grandes Ecoles* and the *Grands Corps* in creating particularly strong links between the state apparatus, the public or quasi-public enterprise sector, and the private industrial and financial sector.

By 'corps' is meant a highly trained expert personnel who successfully entered the *polytechnique* and went on to one of the select engineering schools. These people, who come from the same schools, to a large extent run the country's major industrial enterprises, the nationalized industries and the public sector. Thus, at the heart of each of the major innovation subsystems is a group of managers, research directors and private office ministerial advisers belonging to the same 'corps'. These people possess a 'lifelong *passeport*' to the highest and best-paid jobs, within a system in which severe business failure almost invariably goes unpunished (Salomon, 1986).

The strong role of the state in science and industry began in 1676 when Colbert founded the French *Académie Royale des Sciences* with the explicit aim of fostering scientific capacities and fitting them into the machinery of government. Basic science was immediately synonymous with expert science, seeking industrial and military applications. Both the institutional establishment of scientific research and much of manufacturing industry were, from the very beginning, acts of state.

Driven by circumstances, the Napoleonic government tried to root science-based innovation in industry. This led in particular to the birth of the country's chemical industry. However, once the impetus of the Napoleonic state-led and state-supported policies had petered out, French private industry did nothing to pursue the necessary investment and maintain the ties with research. Hence, from the 1840s onwards, science and industry were divorced. This is made manifest most clearly in the almost total absence of the kind of industrial R&D laboratory that developed from the 1890s onwards in the USA and Germany, and so France occupied a weak position in the 'science push' industries.

By contrast, in sectors where technological development took the form of pragmatic, step-by-step innovations, as in aeronautics and automobiles, French inventors and entrepreneurs were very active. Up to the Second World War, the French automobile industry was the second largest world producer. Panhard (today just a military firm, producing tanks) and Peugeot date back to 1890, and Renault to 1899. Michelin produced the first air-tube tyre in 1895. In aviation, too, Frenchmen flying French planes held world records on a par with their US rivals up until the Second World War. Farman and Breguet were major international exporters of planes, and Gnome and Rhone, Hispano and Renault of airplane engines between the two wars.

In general, however, France experienced a slow and uneven development of industrial capacity in the nineteenth century. Industrialization came about in successive bursts on the basis of government-guaranteed and bank consortium-financed demand, notably for railway building (both at home and abroad), ships and arms. The feats of French engineering were principally those of large projects, involving large or very large amounts of capital (e.g. the Suez Canal) and dependent on banks, which were otherwise uninterested in investing. The heart of concentrated French industry was almost from the outset situated in the iron and steel industry, and in products for the railways and the army. In these critical areas, French industrialists went abroad to England and Belgium, and later to Germany, to buy their technology. They even recruited their foremen and skilled operators in these countries.

The legacy of the Napoleonic period, with regard to the organization of teaching and of research in science and technology, proved in time to be an obstacle to the development of science and innovation. When Napoleon undertook the reorganization of French higher education between 1806 and 1811, he largely re-established the centralized structure fashioned in the *Ancien Régime* in keeping with his increasingly conservative policies in many areas. This structure gave primacy to the training of *experts* as distinct from

Box 8.4: The innovation system features that are specific to France

1. A pervasive element of state and military involvement in the production not just of general scientific and technical knowledge, but often of technology per se in the form of patentable and/or immediately usable products or production processes.

2. A dual-education sector producing at least one type of senior technical person little known elsewhere, namely the *Grandes Ecoles* technical experts, elite engineers-cum-industrial managers-cum-high-level political and administrative personnel.

3. The organization and funding of the largest part of fundamental research through a special institution, the National Centre for Scientific Research (CNRS), distinct from the higher-education sector entities, which are funded by the state and governed by scientists in an uneasy relationship with the public authorities.

researchers and *creators*. It was provided in the professional schools, which have come to be known collectively as the *Grandes Ecoles*. The *Ecole Polytechnique*, for example, was founded in 1794 and provided a grounding in engineering and science.

In contrast to the German polytechnic schools (*Technische Hochschulen*), the French engineering schools generally lacked the spirit of modern scientific research. Until well into the twentieth century, most of them suffered from parochialism. Though one had to have an extensive and broad mathematical education to be selected for one of the engineering *Grandes Ecoles*, the training and curriculum at each school were designed to train experts, civil servants and managers for a particular ministry. Students at the *Grandes Ecoles* learned the results of science, not the *methods* of science. They became either abstract mathematicians or production engineers who applied existing knowledge, rather than research engineers, who could make substantial advances in the state of the art. Indeed, while the engineering *Grandes Ecoles* compensate for some of the weaknesses of the university system as far as preserving the level of education is concerned, they do not with respect to the needs of industry (in terms of numbers of trained personnel) and do so less still with respect to long-term basic research. R&D – in particular basic or long-term research – remains weak, and in some instances is still marginal within the engineering schools.

The *Ecole Normale Supérieure* was initially set up to train the teachers required by the newly established system of secondary education. It passed through a precarious existence during much of the first half of the nineteenth century but was able to build up its research potential and develop its ties with the university in Paris. In the latter part of the century, as a result of the reforms of Pasteur, the *Ecole* emerged as the best training ground of French scholars and scientists. However, with its 30 science graduates each year, the *Ecole Normale* represented much too narrow a base on which to build a sound scientific edifice.

The university system, which was abolished by the Revolution and restored in Napoleonic times, was a centrally state-controlled system, which scarcely functioned. Attempts to reform and strengthen the universities took place from the 1880s onwards as part of a wider policy of strengthening through education, the political and social basis of the Third Republic. However, the universities played only a small part in the production of scientific and technical personnel compared with the *Grandes Ecoles*. The provincial universities often found it hard to survive, as Paris attracted both teachers and students, and the competition of the *Grandes Ecoles* attracted a good proportion of students away from the universities. As a result, the universities rarely offered a base for research of any magnitude. Well into the twentieth century, the typical R&D laboratory was of the small personal type that came with the professor's chair. There the professor could pursue his personal inclinations with a few assistants, though the research might not be at the frontiers of scientific advance and the laboratory might be too small, ill equipped and isolated to be efficient.

In some cases, even a scientist of renown might not be lucky enough to have such minimal conditions. Pierre Curie, for instance, had no research funds, no personal laboratory – not even an office. His important work on magnetism was carried out primarily in a corridor. His work with his wife Marie on radium was conducted under extremely adverse conditions.

On being proposed for the *Légion d'honneur*, Pierre Curie wrote to a friend, 'Please be so kind as to thank the Minister, and inform him that I do not feel the slightest need of being decorated, but that I am in the greatest need of a laboratory.' The Paris Radium Institute was established only in 1910, four years after Pierre Curie's death (Chesnais, 1993: 199).

By 1945, France's industrial base was small and often extremely backward technologically. Moreover, the industrial base (also including the coal and iron mines) and the basic economic infrastructure bore the scars of the two earlier decades of chronic underinvestment, the impact of the slump of the 1930s and the destruction of the war. The state of the industry in 1945 also reflected what have been called the *secular Malthusian tendencies* on the part of a large proportion of the owners of capital and landed property. More specifically, France has been described as a 'stalemate society' marked by:

- a preference for stability and protection over growth and competition
- a Malthusian fear of overproduction of material goods and of educated people
- the burden of social, religious and political conflict
- the fragmented structure and conservatism of French industry, and
- the domination of agrarian and colonial interests over domestic industrial concerns (Hoffman, 1963).

Indeed, France has had a number of brilliant scientists, but up to 1939 they had generally been almost completely deprived of adequate resources to carry out their research.

Between 1945 and 1975, however, large investments in R&D and two phases of intensive science and technology (S&T) institution building took place, explaining a process of growth and enormous transformation. The new innovation system that was built was a 'mission-orientated' type of innovation system in which 'big was beautiful'. From 1945 onwards, a premium has constantly been given to large technology-intensive systems (as in the military area, in electrical power, and in rail transport) or to products that are inherently systemic (e.g. aircraft or space products). As a result, markets are almost always conceived by project leaders as being public. At home these are created through *public procurement*.

As suggested, the first phase of institution building took place immediately at the end of the Second World War (1945). In a significant manner it began with the creation of a capacity for R&D and production in nuclear energy, and subsequently for military purposes (lodged in a major agency, the *Commissariat à l'Energie*, CEA). It also included the reorganization and expansion of the National Centre for Scientific Research (CNRS) and the creation under the Ministry of Post, Telegraph and Telephone of the National Centre for the Study of Telecommunications (CNET). Among the numerical technical agencies also established at the time under the Ministry of Defence, the most important was the National Office of Aeronautical Studies and Research (ONERA), which was given a mandate both for military and civil R&D. The major public agencies in the industries that had just been nationalized in energy and basic infrastructure followed suit.

The most portentous step was to move into nuclear research and production. This was subsequently to lead France into one of the largest nuclear energy production programmes in the world. The building of the CEA's central R&D laboratory and pilot plant capacities at Saclay from 1947 onwards symbolized the start of a transformation of French scientific institutions. In place of the small, poorly equipped laboratories of individual professors that had characterized French science, large scientific resources were brought together in a complex of modern laboratories with teams of researchers and supporting technicians. In a country where no large firm had yet set up a major industrial R&D laboratory based on the US and German model, the building of Saclay was France's first real step into twentieth-century fundamental and applied science.

The CNRS, though founded in 1939 as a belated result of the political interest in science, began to play a role only from 1945 onwards. Through the establishment of numerous laboratories and the research facilities that it administers, the CNRS has, since 1945, provided France with an infrastructure of research institutes similar to that created in Germany after 1911 by the Kaiser Wilhelm Society (today the Max Planck Society). In particular the CNRS has been able to establish and administer laboratories in newer fields of research that could not be placed within the French university structure. Moreover, the CNRS has supported the otherwise very weak university research by, among other things, seconding researchers to university laboratories and by providing the numerous services, assistants and equipment required by scientists, which neither the Ministry of Education nor the university budget had supported adequately.

During the period 1945–58, the production and diffusion of technology were driven almost exclusively by the state, and by innovation capacity lodged principally in nationalized or publicly owned firms. In the second phase of institution building, which took place after de Gaulle's return to power and the setting up of the Fifth Republic (1958–66), innovation continued to be driven strongly by the state. However, policies began to be enacted to lodge at least a part of the innovative capacity within the industry's national champions.

Major institutional decisions in science and technology concerned space research, with the creation in 1959 of a Committee for Space Research. In 1962, under the influence of de Gaulle, a national organization for space research was set up: the National Centre for Space Studies (CNES). This time, however, public and private firms were involved in the programme from the outset by contracting out a large part of the R&D to the business sector. The same pattern of state–industry relationship, based on procurement and often involving the same firms, was adopted for the arms industry. Military R&D was moved out of the state sector and reorganized on the basis of R&D procurement to industry. The only exception was the military atomic programme, which did not use firm-based R&D procurement.

After 1965, the problems of the French computer and data-processing industries brought about a further development and yet another pattern of state–industry relationships. Faced with the difficulties of the French computer industry and spurred by a hopeless US embargo decision, the French government launched a new 'Major Programme' in the field of data processing (*le Plan Calcul*) and set up a new private data-processing company, which received massive financial aid from the state. The state also set up an Institute for Research into Data-Processing and Automatism (IRIA) and gave further financial assistance to the French components and peripheral equipment firms.

The 1970s and 1980s brought only shifts in emphasis in the area of overall R&D resource allocation and the location of entrepreneurial capacity, along with a clearer spelling-out of features that were already contained within the system as it had been built in the previous phases. Two developments warrant special attention. The first has been the consolidation, based on institutions built during the earlier periods, of a large military-industrial complex, which encompasses among other things, parts of the space programme, a part of the activity in telecommunications, and the efforts made to maintain a computer and components industry. The industrial elements of the complex now represent France's most powerful and, at least in appearance, most successful high-tech corporations (in particular, Thomson, Aerospatiale and Matra). (The first two are public firms, Matra is private).

The second novel, but totally logical, development concerned the steps taken first to build new links between the research capacity accumulated within the public sector and all firms that are ready to take the innovations to market, and later to authorize and even force public research centres to move downstream towards the market and to become 'technological entrepreneurs' in their own right. These changes are far from a full-scale privatization of public-sector R&D, but they represent a step in that direction. The status of the R&D laboratories was changed in the 1980s from administrative public institutions to a new generic type of status with some attributes of private law. Under this new status, laboratories have been empowered to establish subsidiaries, acquire shares and seek cooperation around specific projects with scientific and industrial partners in public interest groups (GIP) and scientific groups (GS). These possibilities give the major agencies more incentive to involve themselves in exploiting and marketing their innovations.

By the end of the 1980s, however, industrial R&D, or R&D carried out within firms, remained significantly weak. In fact, a group of no more than 150 firms account for the bulk of French R&D. According to a survey, these 150 firms carry out 75 per cent of R&D and receive over 90 per cent of direct government support for R&D. The concentration of R&D by industrial branch is necessarily extremely high. In 1987, eight branches accounted for over 85 per cent of total R&D expenditure: electronics 23.2 per cent; aircraft 17.8 per cent, automobiles 10 per cent; chemicals 10 per cent; pharmaceuticals 7 per cent; energy production 7.2 per cent; data processing 5.2 per cent; and heavy electrical material 4.7 per cent. Industrial branches that account for a significant part of French exports (agriculture and food processing) or still represent fairly important components of French industrial GDP (metallurgy and metal working, textiles, machinery) account for only a very small fraction of industrial R&D. This picture confirms quite logically that, to a large extent, France's innovation system still consists essentially of sectors dominated by public procurement and state funding of technical activities.

8.8　Conclusions

The four-country overview of some of the main institutional features of the national innovation systems shows that there are clear institutional differences between countries, leading to different trajectories of innovation. Aside from the differences, there were a few similarities that seem to be required in order for an innovation to function. In one way or another, in all four countries we found a link between basic research (carried out at universities or research institutes) and applied or commercial research. Military R&D and procurement has played a substantial role in all countries (except Germany, since after the Second World War, as it was not allowed to build up a military complex). The importance of spillover from military to civilian technology can be seen from the relatively poorer performance of the German telecommunications and aircraft industries.

The most striking communal feature, however (albeit to different degrees and in different ways), is government support for research and education. Government support, especially in developing the institutional edifice, seems to be a necessary condition in all countries for firms to innovate. This conclusion underlines the point made by Edquist and Johnson (1997) that innovation activities are so uncertain and conflict-ridden that they need institutional support in order to become an important activity. This is not the traditional view of the relationships between institutions and innovations. It is indeed more common to see institutions as entities that introduce stability, even rigidity, into the economy and act as brakes to innovation rather than accelerators.

But, as we have seen in the case of these countries, the institutional set-up does change over time. Institutional rigidity is, in the long run, a threat to technical change and, as a consequence, would make long-run economic development impossible. We have observed here, however, that institutions may have both supporting and retarding effects on innovation. The balance between them is clearly different between countries and changes drastically over time. The countries discussed have also shown that a specific institutional set-up can neither permanently support nor retard innovation (i.e. France). This picture confirms that an economy's ability to generate growth depends on its ability to generate technical change, and, at the same time, on its ability to adapt and renew its institutions to support growth and innovation.

Study Questions

1. Explain why, despite globalization, the concept of a 'national' innovation system still makes sense.

2. Explain why institutions matter in an analysis of an innovation system.

3. Explain why history matters in systems of innovation analysis.

4. Explain in what way the anti-trust statutes of the USA have had an effect on the structure and performance of the innovation system.

5. Explain the factors that are argued to have contributed to the prominent role of new, small firms in the postwar US innovation system.

6. Explain how government protection in Japan helped the indigenous industry.

7. Explain how the emphasis on tacit knowledge in Japanese industry stimulates as well as hampers innovation.

8. Explain the features of the German system of innovation that contribute to the German industry's strength in chemicals, automobiles and electrotechnical products.

9. Explain the features of the innovation system of France that have contributed to an emphasis on large-scale and systemic innovation.

Further Reading

Amable, B. (2000) Institutional complementarity and diversity of social systems of innovation and production. *Review of International Political Economy* 7(4), 645–87.

This article uses the concepts of complementarity and hierarchy of institutions to analyse social systems of innovation and production. In doing so it explains why no generalized pattern of convergence towards the same economic model should be expected.

Coriat, B. and Weinstein, O. (2002) Organizations, firms and institutions in the generation of innovation. *Research Policy* 31, 273–90.

This paper develops the innovation system analysis by bringing together the 'institutional' and 'organizational' dimensions of the process of innovation at the firm level. In this way it attempts to make progress towards a more exhaustive and better-articulated representation of the innovation process.

Gambardella, A. and Malerba, F. (eds) (1999) *The Organization of Economic Innovation in Europe.* Cambridge: Cambridge University Press.

The collection of papers in this book explains the organization and dynamics of innovative activities in Europe. The book is one of the few attempts within the literature on industrial economics and innovation to build analytical frameworks that are based on the distinctive features and institutional characteristics of Europe, and especially of the EU.

Mowery, D.C. and Nelson, R.R. (eds) (1999) *Sources of Industrial Leadership: Studies of Seven Industries.* Cambridge: Cambridge University Press.

This book analyses how seven major high-tech industries evolved in the USA, Japan and western Europe. The industries covered are machine tools, organic chemical products, pharmaceuticals, medical devices, computers, semiconductors and software. The emphasis here is on the key factors that supported the emergence of national leadership in each industry, and the reasons behind the shifts when they occurred.

Case: Explaining Innovation Strategy: a Case Study of the German and Japanese Pharmaceutical Industries[8]

The international success of the German traditional pharmaceutical industry has been widely documented (i.e. Balance *et al.*, 1992; Taggart, 1993; Sharp *et al.*, 1996). It is also well known that the Japanese pharmaceutical industry has spent most of the postwar period as a laggard, with minimal exports and a negative trade balance. It is less well known, however, that a major proportion of German pharmaceutical products are similar to Japanese ones – that is, of low quality and, as a consequence, lacking the potential to be sold on the world market. This case study explores this paradox and, in particular, considers how the national institutional environment has contributed to this rather dubious difference in levels of achievement in the two countries' pharmaceutical industries.

The case first examines a few sources of competitive success in the global pharmaceutical industry, documenting the relative success of Germany and the failure of Japan. In order to explain the aforementioned paradox, the case discusses two key aspects of product market regulation in the pharmaceutical sector: regulation of product safety and drug prices.

Competitive Performance in Global Pharmaceuticals

Table 8.1 reports various measures of competitive performance for the pharmaceutical sectors of Germany, Japan, the USA and the UK. This data provides an indication of the weak performance of Japan and the better position of German pharmaceutical manufacturers. The comparison with the USA and the UK is made for two reasons: both countries have strong pharmaceutical sectors, and both have been identified as advanced industrial economies with national institutional frameworks (the Anglo-Saxon model) that differ widely from the German and Japanese national institutions (the Rhineland model).

Table 8.1 shows that, in the 1980s and early 1990s, Japan's pharmaceutical trade was weak, while Germany's trade performance was relatively strong. The figures in the table cannot be left unqualified, however. When looking at the world share of sales achieved by firms based in the four countries, it is obvious that the US firms are in the lead, with a 43 per cent market share of the global pharmaceutical industry, and that the Japanese firms are second with a 20 per cent share of world sales. At first glance, these figures suggest that Japan is a strong performer in pharmaceuticals. The reality is that world sales by Japanese firms are almost entirely located in a large home market that is protected by non-tariff

[8] This case study draws on fieldwork research that was carried out as part of my doctoral research during the period 1996–98. For institutional support, I am indebted to the Max-Planck-Institut in Cologne and the Wissenschaftszentrum fuer Sozialforschung Berlin. I also owe a great debt to Canon Foundation Europe, who provided funding for the field research in Germany and Japan.

trade barriers. The market share of 20 per cent represents Japan's protectionism far more than the superior competitive performance of its pharmaceutical firms.

Table 8.1 International comparison of market features

	US	Japan	Germany	UK
World market share 1985	43.3	20.2	10.2	7.4
External share 1985	19.1	0.1	6.2	5.8
Firm market share in the USA 1982	80	n.a.	3.9	5.1
1991	70.2	0.3	4.6	14.6
Percentage discovery global 1965–85	44	9	18	51
Percentage discovery local 1965–85	28	77	49	25
R&D intensity (%)* 1964	7	3	5	5
1974	11	4.5	9	10
1983	10.6	6.7	8.4	11.7
1992	14.3	9.8	9.2	16.3
New chemical entities (NCEs) 1961–70	202	78	112	45
1971–80	154	74	91	29
1981–90	142	129	67	28
Origin of major drugs (%) 1950–66	48.6	0.7	10.9	7.2
1970–83	42	4	10	10
No. of products in top 50 1985	23	5	5	9
1990	27**	2	5	12
No. of products in top 25 1998	16	0	2	5
No. of firms that innovate/R&D 1965–85	3.6	12.2	5.9	4.8

Source: Teso (1980); Grabowski (1989); Thomas (1994); Sharp *et al.* (1996); ABPI (2000), and own calculations.

*R&D intensity is measured as a percentage of sales.
**The three best-selling drugs of SmithKline Beecham are credited to both the USA and the UK, since the company is of joint ownership.

The poor export performance of the Japanese pharmaceutical sector confirms these observations. The Japanese pharmaceutical industry has been one of the least prolific exporters among the pharmaceutical industries of the major producing countries. For most of the postwar period, the Japanese pharmaceutical industry has exported only about 3 per cent of total production (Figure 8.1). In comparison, during the 1980s and 1990s, the USA (the largest drug market) exported approximately 9 per cent of its pharmaceutical production, France 21 per cent, the UK 55 per cent and West Germany 24 per cent. Even in 1993, in Japan, pharmaceutical imports exceeded exports by about two and a half times (Figure 8.2). It must be noted that the relatively low export rate of the USA can be

Figure 8.1 Ratio of exports to production – Japanese pharmaceuticals 1955–93 (percentage)

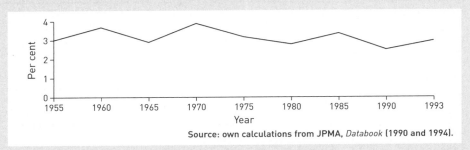

Source: own calculations from JPMA, *Databook* (1990 and 1994).

Figure 8.2 Pharmaceutical trade Japan – 1975–93 (million yen)

Source: JPMA, *Databook* (1994).

explained by the fact that most major US pharmaceutical firms have foreign production facilities (Taggart, 1993: 27). This is not the case for Japanese companies.

The poor performance of Japan's pharmaceutical firms becomes more pronounced when looking at external market share. 'External share' is defined as the sales by firms of a given nation achieved outside that nation's borders as a share of pharmaceutical sales in all external markets (Thomas, 1994: 453). Using this indicator of competitiveness for 1985 we find that Japan is an exceptionally weak performer, with a market share of 0.1 per cent while German performance (6.2 per cent) compares well with that of the UK (5.8 per cent). With an external market share of 19.1 per cent in 1985, the USA is an exceptionally strong competitor.

In addition, Japanese pharmaceutical firms are not competitive in the US market. Firm market share in the USA could be seen as a crude measure of competitiveness because the US market is the most open and competitive in the world (Casper and Matraves, 1998: 4). In 1991, Japan's market share in the USA was negligible (0.3 per cent) in comparison with that of Germany (4.6 per cent) and the UK (14.6 per cent). The German pharmaceutical share of the US market, on the other hand, is low relative to that of the UK. In fact, Table 8.1 shows that Germany's share of the US pharmaceutical market has not increased much from the 1980s onwards and, as a consequence, has dropped far below the UK share. The latter can be clarified partly by looking at the types of innovation in each country's pharmaceutical industry.

In this respect, Table 8.1 shows that strong competitive performers such as the USA and the UK concentrate on developing significant innovations – the so-called global or consensus drugs – that can be marketed effectively in the major pharmaceutical markets (Grabowski, 1989). Between 1965 and 1985, the percentage of innovations discovered in the USA and the UK that were global products was 44 and 51 respectively, while under 30 per cent are less significant local products. Germany and Japan, in contrast, concentrate essentially on the development of local as opposed to global products. During the period 1965–85, German innovation was more local (49 per cent) than global (only 18 per cent). With 77 per cent of its innovations local products and only 9 per cent global, Japan is in the weakest position. While local products do, indeed, represent incremental innovations, they also stand for products that diffuse to only a few countries. This observation, combined with the fact that Germany and Japan are not competitive in the US market (or, in other words, that a large number of the German and Japanese pharmaceuticals are unable to clear the stringent regulatory hurdles of the USA), allows us to argue that Germany and Japan's local products are not always of high quality.

An examination of the number of NCEs, combined with the origin of major NCEs, provides us with confirmation of the dominance of local, lower-quality products among German and Japanese discoveries. The last measure is included to account for the fact that although some NCEs introduced are genuinely original, others may be marginal improvements only, which could make the NCE figures misleading (Sharp et al., 1996: 24).

Looking at R&D intensity, it can be seen that from the 1960s until the late 1980s, the lowest R&D-to-sales ratio was in Japan, although between 1983 and 1992, expenditure did rise substantially. Japan also significantly increased its proportion of NCEs between 1981 and 1990 (from 74 to 129). Evidence shows, however, that if the number of breakthrough NCEs is considered, Japan is in the weakest position (only 4 per cent between 1970 and 1983). The steady rise in UK pharmaceutical performance is expressed in the substantial increase in R&D expenditure from the 1960s onwards. Moreover, while, during the 1971–80 period, only 29 new drugs were developed in the UK, a relatively high percentage of these turned into blockbusters (on average, ten drugs per year turned into blockbusters over the period 1970–83). Germany's position is rather dubious. German pharmaceutical companies developed far more drugs (91 NCEs between 1971 and 1980) and, like the UK, produced a number of blockbusters (an annual average of ten between 1970 and 1983). German companies must therefore have developed a high number of drugs that are marginal improvements at best. The US pharmaceutical industry is the strongest, in terms of the highest introduction of NCEs and the largest number of blockbuster drugs.

A last measure of competitive performance that is discussed here is the distribution of innovative effort among innovating firms. In this respect, Table 8.1 reports the number of innovative pharmaceutical firms for each of the four countries divided by billions of dollars of domestic pharmaceutical R&D. For the strongest competitive performer, the USA, innovative effort is concentrated in a handful of firms. The innovative effort in Germany is slightly more fragmented than in the UK, but less than in Japan. In the weakest competitive performer, Japan, each billion dollars' worth of pharmaceutical R&D expense is fragmented into 12 different firms. Concentration of innovative efforts into a small number of firms in the USA and the UK has led to significant global success (Thomas, 1994). Conversely, the fragmentation of innovative effort into large numbers of minor derivative products discovered by weaker firms in Japan has contributed to competitive failure. Germany's pharmaceutical structure and performance are situated somewhere between those of the UK and Japan.

Summing up this data on country-level performance in pharmaceuticals, it is clear that US and UK pharmaceutical firms are stronger players than German and Japanese ones. Japan shows the weakest performance level. The German pharmaceutical sector, on the other hand, while showing a higher capacity to develop competitive drugs than Japan, nevertheless also adopted strategies that resulted in the development and production of poor-quality drugs. Aside from providing further evidence in this direction, in order to understand the reasons for the strategies pursued by pharmaceutical firms based in Germany and Japan we will turn now to an institutional explanation of firm strategy and performance.

An industrial policy for the pharmaceutical industry – safety regulation

National regulations in the pharmaceutical industry have sought to achieve goals along two broad axes. The first axis, stimulated by the Thalidomide tragedy of the early 1960s, has focused on the safety, quality and efficacy of drugs. The second axis of regulation was stimulated by the rapidly increasing cost of drugs combined with the ageing of the population, and has focused on drug pricing. This case study shows that the way in which governments have approached these two axes of regulation has been a central factor in setting the product market strategies of their domestic pharmaceutical industries.

Turning first to the regulation of drug safety, from the 1960s onwards, most OECD governments, including those of Germany and Japan, enacted an array of nationally distinct regulations to govern the approval of new drugs. With the adoption of the 1967 act, the Japanese government installed a system whose preclinical trials and clinical standards not only differed from those of the West but also required locally generated supporting data. Specifically, this new regulatory regime called for lengthy and costly preclinical and clinical trials to be repeated according to unfamiliar Japanese standards, resulting in delaying the entry of foreign innovators. Moreover, until the mid-1980s, drug approval regulations also prohibited foreign firms from applying for the first step of drug approval, the demonstration of efficacy and safety review. The aggregate impact of all new requirements in Japan was to erect a protectionist edifice, limiting competition in the home market and directing the benefits of the large domestic market primarily to domestic companies (Reich, 1990). As a result Japanese pharmaceutical manufacturers were discouraged to learn to be competitive in the global market.

In addition, the act contained an element that induced the Japanese pharmaceutical industry to take an incremental, low-risk approach to the drug discovery process rather than to pursue high-risk/high-cost pharmaceutical breakthroughs. After 1967, the regulatory system in Japan was predicated on demonstrating merit for a new chemical entity as necessary for approval. However, merit could be shown in a variety of relatively modest ways – for example, improved pharmacokinetics leading to a simplified dosage, higher potency, and the like (Neimeth, 1991: 158–9). The lenient attitude towards innovation, and the neglect of efficacy demands until the late 1980s, explain the local nature of most Japanese drugs.

In Germany, the Thalidomide tragedy intensified debates on drug safety and efficacy. However, until the mid-1970s, no serious government efforts were made to regulate drugs. The medical law of 1961 simply demanded the registration of new and old drugs with the Federal Health Office (Bundesgesundheitsamt, BGA). In fact, the public health administration only occupied itself with industrially produced drugs when it was beneficial for the industry – for example, with the introduction of quality certificates to support the industry's export efforts (Baumheier, 1994). It seems that German policy-makers were concerned more with industrial performance than with drug safety and efficacy.

In the mid-1970s, as a result of a new drug scandal, combined with the fact that drug safety guidelines were being prepared within the European Community, the pressure on the German government to come to a fundamental reform of its drug safety regulations gathered force. At that time, too, the lack of a governmental control system was increasingly hampering exports of German pharmaceuticals. Hence it was, in fact, in the interests of the German pharmaceutical industry that its products could pass official drug safety tests. However, while the 1976 Arzneimittelgesezt (drug safety law) introduced thorough drug safety regulations, its administration was less exacting than its counterparts in the USA and the UK, and mandatory efficacy thresholds were correspondingly lower (Baumheier, 1994). Moreover, companies were given until 1990 to have all of their products registered by the BGA. By 1998, however, there were still products on the market that had not been submitted for BGA approval and that often suffered from poor quality.

The Japanese and German governments' approaches to drug safety regulation had a pronounced effect on the constitution of both countries' pharmaceutical market (which makes the majority of the figures in Table 8.I easy to understand). In Japan, both limited competition in a large domestic market for pharmaceuticals and the approval of small-step innovation resulted in a product market strategy that focused on modest advances by existing agents, whose development was relatively quick, simple, inexpensive and risk free – and whose registration was virtually guaranteed. The late introduction of regulation in Germany, and the lenient administrative controls once regulation was introduced, explain why, rather like Japan, Germany has a substantial amount of local products that are incremental innovations only, not always of high quality, and unsuitable for export to stringent regulatory environments like the USA and the UK.

At the beginning of the 1960s, the UK and the USA introduced stringent safety and efficacy regulations. The stringency of these regulations forced firms that were based in both countries to develop significant innovations of a high quality, as it is difficult, if not impossible, to obtain approval for minor derivative local products in the UK and US markets (Thomas, 1994: 463). It follows that the stringency of regulation in the USA and the UK also helped to explain the significant drop in the amount of new chemical entities discovered in the USA after the adoption of the Kefauver Amendments in 1962, and in the UK after the creation of the Committee on the Safety of Drugs in 1964 (see Table 8.1). The more lenient and protectionist approach to regulation in Germany and Japan respectively explains why the decrease in the development of new chemical entities was markedly less in these countries. It also accounts for the lower degree of research intensity in Germany and Japan than in the UK and the USA (Table 8.I).

The German and Japanese approach to drug regulation also explains why innovative efforts in these countries are more fragmented than in the UK and the USA. The stringency of regulation in the USA and the UK has resulted in a shakeout of innovative firms. At the beginning of the 1960s, after the introduction of safety and efficacy regulations in both nations, a host of smaller and weaker firms were forced from the market, either through acquisition by stronger firms or simple cessation of pharmaceutical innovation (Thomas, 1994: 462). It is essential to note, however, that this was in the early period when biotechnology was not yet popular, and alliances between small and large pharmaceutical firms were of little importance. The belated introduction of official drug-approval processes and the leniency of administrative control in Germany explain why a large number of smaller companies, which concentrate on local products, have been able to survive. Some suggest that the lenient controls over drug approval could be seen as an indication of the forthcoming, almost protectionist, attitude of the German Economics Ministry towards Germany's small- and medium-sized companies. The absence of protectionist elements in regulation, or the existence of an open domestic environment, on the other hand, explains why innovative efforts in Germany are less fragmented than they are in Japan.

The argument that concentrates on the local focus and often poor quality of German and Japanese drugs can be supported further by evidence that shows the degree of access that certain types of drugs have to both countries' pharmaceutical markets. With this in mind, Table 8.2 shows that, with the highest access rate for drugs of all types, Germany is the least restrictive of the major pharmaceutical competitor nations in terms of access to new drugs. Countries with stringent regulatory regimes, such as the USA and the UK, have far lower access rates and thus are less open to new drugs. The protectionist elements in Japanese drug regulations explain that, like the case in the UK and the USA, Japan is far less open to new drugs than Germany. Openness to new drugs does not, of course, in itself explain the focus or quality of these drugs. An indication of quality restrictiveness can be obtained by contrasting the access rate for local products with that of global products. It is noticeable that while Germany is far more open to global than local drugs, it also ranks third in openness to local drugs, the quality of which is often doubtful. Only France and Italy, countries for which the low quality of drugs is well documented, have higher access rates for these types of drugs (see Thomas, 1996). That Japan is slightly less open than Germany to local products is not surprising since it has a protectionist regime, which closes the market to all types of drugs. The leniency of Japanese regulation, on the other hand, explains why its market is more open to local products than the US and UK markets. The in general restrictive character of the Japanese pharmaceutical market is also expressed in its low access rate for global drugs.

Table 8.2	Access rates to nine major competitor nations' markets (1980s)		
	Access all drugs	**Access global**	**Access local**
USA	33.8	72.7	16.9
Switzerland	38.2	78.4	13.1
UK	39.2	90.3	9.6
Germany	**59.4**	**96.3**	**26.5**
France	54.3	86.5	32.3
Italy	54.9	86.2	33.5
Japan	**39.3**	**65.0**	**22.1**
Sweden	19.1	59.6	2.9
Netherlands	25.1	61.0	3.9

Source: Thomas (1996).

An industrial policy for the pharmaceutical industry – drug price regulation

A second foundation of pharmaceutical industrial policy is the regulation of drug prices. Pricing policy is of crucial importance for the pharmaceutical industry. The need to recoup enormous R&D costs during the period that a drug enjoys patent protection means that too-low drug prices would discourage innovation. A too-generous price level, on the other hand, could be seen as a form of promotional policy. In the absence of price intervention, the oligopolistic market structure allows the industry to earn monopoly rents by charging prices above costs that recoup long-term development costs (Koen, 1995: 24–30). Ample reason thus exists to explain why price controls are such a widespread phenomenon in the pharmaceutical industry. This case study argues that absence of government price controls in this sector could, in fact, be seen as an implicit form of industrial policy.

Like safety regulation, pricing policy is handled in different ways in different countries. This case study finds that pricing policy has a pronounced effect on the competitive strategies and performance of firms based in the resulting environment. Also in this case, there are differences between the German and Japanese governments' approach, with similar effects on firm strategy. In Japan, the official reimbursement price for all pharmaceuticals is set by the government with its Drug Tariff. The National Health Insurance (NHI) drug price functions both as the reimbursement rate paid by all health insurers to all medical institutions, and as the official acquisition price recognized by the MHW for budgetary purposes. There is, however, a considerable difference between the official reimbursement price of pharmaceuticals, and the actual price paid by physicians and hospitals (Howells and Neary, 1995). Pharmaceutical companies, as a matter of marketing strategy, offer the drugs to hospitals and private physicians at a discount. Throughout the postwar period, Japanese general practitioners and hospitals had both prescribed and dispensed pharmaceuticals to patients, with the difference between the purchase price from the supplier and the reimbursement price set by the government serving as additional income. By creating economic incentives for private physicians and hospitals to prescribe liberally and to choose products with higher margins, this system has contributed to the expansion of the domestic market (Reich, 1990).

Clearly, since pharmaceutical companies have been able to give substantial discounts on drugs, reimbursement rates must have been generous. Indeed, while international comparisons of pharmaceutical prices are subject to various uncertainties (due to product variation and exchange rates), one study reported Japanese prices as significantly above those in Switzerland, the UK, Italy, Spain and France. This study confirmed that the higher price level in Japan, apart from reflecting the strength of the yen at that time, is also a clear illustration of the fact that Japan has consistently supported its home-based industry (Reich, 1990: 132). In an Office of Health report, Reekie provides further confirmation of Japan's high drug prices. Using different exchange rates and measures for calculating prices, Reekie shows that drugs in Japan are priced consistently higher than their European and US equivalents (Reekie, 1981).

Reimbursement price policy has also played a major role in determining the strategic allocation of corporate R&D funds in Japan. From the mid-1970s onwards, downward price revisions for older drugs, combined with significant price premiums for minor modifications, led to 'excessive innovation for the local market' or, in other words, stimulated companies to concentrate on merely altering existing drugs slightly, rather than on producing new innovative (or global) drugs. Moreover, this policy of rewarding small-step innovation also, inevitably, resulted in an upward price spiral, which led to increasing profits in the pharmaceutical industry. Hence, it could, in fact, be argued that this price system would have, in and of itself, and independently of the safety regulations, encouraged the development of mainly local products.

In recent years, however, while still cutting the prices of older drugs, the Japanese government has only offered premium prices to drugs with a significant therapeutic advantage, thus driving research programmes towards 'breakthrough' drugs. Although this measure is said to be part of the MHW's cost-containment effort, this case argues that this also contains an industrial policy aspect in that it forces firms to develop global drugs and punishes those firms that are unable to do so. Moreover, MHW respondents argued that while pricing policy is used for health policy reasons, it is also the main, if not sole, industrial policy instrument (interviews, Tokyo, 1996–97). Consequently, while this case accepts the argument that, initially, pricing policy could have been used mainly as healthcare policy, it also claims that eventually, when the effect of pricing upon industry behaviour was recognized, the MHW combined the use of pricing policy for healthcare purposes with applying it in order to steer the pharmaceutical industry, thus also using pricing policy as an industrial policy instrument.

In a similar vein, this case argues that, in Germany too, pricing policy – which in Germany means the absence of price controls until the late 1980s – could be seen as part of an industrial policy with considerable influence on product market strategy. Rather like Japan, Germany is also well known to be a high-price country for pharmaceuticals. Table 8.3 shows that Germany is the second highest-price country in Europe.This case argues that a decided non-interventionist stance in an oligopolistic market is tantamount to interventionism. The absence of price controls on pharmaceuticals until the end of the 1980s in Germany, in a market that is known to be oligopolistic, amounts to a policy that promotes the pharmaceutical industry.

At the end of the 1980s, as part of the cost-containment efforts in the healthcare sector, for the first time in history, the German government decided to interfere with drug pricing and introduced a fixed-price scheme. The intention was to stimulate price competition in the pharmaceutical market and to use this to reduce drug spending. However, by fixing reimbursement levels by therapeutic category rather than basing the system on individual drugs, the reference price scheme continues to encourage oligopolistic pricing and discourage radical kinds of drug innovation within the therapeutic categories.

The incremental bias of the German product market strategy received further support in 1995, when the German government changed the original fixed-price scheme. Whereas initially only 'truly innovative' drugs were shielded from the fixed price scheme, from 1995 onwards, on-patent drugs were freed from price controls. Since 'on-patent' drugs do not have to be truly innovative but must include incremental innovations, the government once again sent a clear signal to the industry that it continues to support a product market strategy that is focused on incremental, and thus less costly, innovation.

Table 8.3 International pharmaceutical price indexes in the EU (1993)	
Country index	
Denmark	164
Germany	*152*
Netherlands	152
Austria	129
Ireland	128
Belgium	113
UK	*111*
Luxembourg	110
Finland	108
Sweden	108
EU-15 average	100
Portugal	77
France	76
Italy	72
Spain	63
Greece	51

Source: Senior (1996).

Questions

1. Institutional theory argues that Japan's institutional framework is largely similar to Germany's. It also argues that national institutions largely determine a nation's success in particular sectors. Explain briefly why – given that Germany and Japan have similar institutional environments – the German pharmaceutical sector has been successful internationally, and why Japanese firms have persisted in strategies that have led to failure.

2. Explain why, despite the international success of German pharmaceuticals, German pharmaceutical firms nevertheless also adopted strategies that resulted in the development and production of lower-quality drugs.

3. Explain whether the incremental character of German and Japanese pharmaceutical innovation and those countries' high drug prices support the institutional thesis on innovativeness.

4. Explain whether the local character or low quality of a large number of German and Japanese drugs can also be explained within the institutional framework.

References

Balance, R., Pogany, J. and Forstner, H. (1992) *The World's Pharmaceutical Industries.* Aldershot: Edward Elgar.

Baumheier, U. (1994) *Staat und Pharmaindustry.* Baden-Baden: Nomos Verlag.

Casper, S. and Matraves, C. (1998) *Corporate Governance and Product Market Competition in the Pharmaceutical Industry,* mimeo.

Grabowski, H. (1989) An analysis of US international competitiveness in pharmaceuticals. *Managerial and Decision Economics,* Special Issue.

Howells, J. and Neary, I. (1995) *Intervention and Technological Innovation.* London: Macmillan.

JPMA *Databook* (1990) Tokyo: JPMA.

JPMA *Databook* (1994) Tokyo: JPMA.

Koen, C. (1995) *An Analysis of the Japanese Pharmaceutical Industry and Market.* Unpublished MA thesis. Coventry: University of Warwick.

Neimeth, R. (1991) Japan's pharmaceutical industry, in Gelijns, A. and Halm, E. (eds) *The Changing Economics of Medical Technology.* Washington: National Academy Press.

Reekie, W.D. (1981) *Price Comparisons of Identical Products in Japan, the US, and Europe.* London: Office of Health Economics.

Reich, M. (1990) Why the Japanese don't export more pharmaceuticals: health policy as industrial policy. *California Management Review* 32, 124–50.

Senior, I. (1996) International medicine prices – is a new index needed? *Scrip Magazine* (September).

Sharp, M., Patel, P. and Pavitt, K. (1996) Europe's pharmaceutical industry: an innovation profile. Draft report prepared for DG XIII, European Commission.

Taggart, J. (1993) *The World Pharmaceutical Industry.* London: Routledge.

Thomas, G.L. (1994) Implicit industrial policy: the triumph of Britain and the failure of France in global pharmaceuticals. *Industrial and Corporate Change* 3, 451–89.

Thomas, G.L. (1996) Industrial policy and international competitiveness in the pharmaceutical industry, in Helms, R.B. (ed.) *Competitive Strategies in the Pharmaceutical Industry.* Washington: AEI Press.

References

ABPI (Association of the British Pharmaceutical Industry) (2000) *Pharma Facts and Figures: How the Pharmaceutical Industry Contributes to the Health and Wealth of the Nation.* London: ABPI.

Arora, A. and Gambardella, A. (1994) The changing technology of technological change: general and abstract knowledge and the division of innovative labor. *Research Policy* 23, 523–32.

Bartholomew, S. (1997) National systems of biotechnology innovation: complex interdependence in the global system. *Journal of International Business Studies* 28(1), 24–66.

Brock, M.V. (1989) *Biotechnology in Japan*. London: Routledge.

Casper, S. (2000) Institutional adaptiveness, technology policy, and the diffusion of new business models: the case of German biotechnology. *Organization Studies* 21(5), 887–914.

Chesnais, F. (1993) The French national system of innovation, in Nelson, R. (ed.) *National Innovation Systems*. New York: Oxford University Press, 192–229.

Chesnais, F. and Serfati, C. (1990) L'Industrie d'armement: une locomotive du développement économique français?, in Chesnais, F. (ed.) *Compétitivité internationale et dépenses militaires*. Paris: Economica.

Chesnais, F. and Serfati, C. (1992) *L'Armement en France: genèse, ampleur et coûts d'une industrie*. Paris: Nathan.

Dosi, G., Pavitt, K. and Soete, L. (1990) *The Economics of Technical Change and International Trade*. New York: New York University Press.

Edquist, C. and Johnson, B. (1997) Institutions and organizations in systems of innovation, in Edquist, C. (ed.) *Systems of Innovation. Technologies, Institutions and Organizations*. London: Pinter.

Ergas, H. (1987) Does technology matter?, in Guile, B.R. and Brooks, H. (eds) *Technology and Global Industry: Companies and Nations in the World Economy*. Washington, DC: National Academy Press.

Freeman, C. (1988) Japan: a new national system of innovation?, in Dosi, G., Freeman, C., Nelson, R., Silverberg, G. and Soete, L. (eds) *Technical Change and Economic Theory*. London: Pinter.

Freeman, C. and Perez, C. (1988) Structural crises of adjustment: business cycles and investment behaviour, in Dosi, G. Freeman, C., Nelson, R., Silverberg, G. and Soete, L. (eds) *Technical Change and Economic Theory*. London: Pinter.

Goto, A. (2000) Japan's national innovation system: current status and problems. *Oxford Review of Economic Policy* 16(2), 103–13.

Hamel, G., Doz, Y. and Prahalad, C.K. (1989) Collaborate with your competitors – and win. *Harvard Business Review* 67(1), 133–9.

Hampden-Turner, C. and Trompenaars, F. (1993) *The Seven Cultures of Capitalism*. New York: Doubleday.

Hikino, T. and Amsden, A.H. (1994) Staying behind, stumbling back, sneaking back, soaring ahead: late industrialization in historical perspective, in Baumol, W.-J., Nelson, R.R. and Wolff, E.N. (eds) *Convergence of Productivity: Cross-country Studies and Historical Evidence*, New York: Oxford University Press.

Hoffman, S. (1963) Paradoxes of the French political community, in Hoffman, S. (ed.) *In Search of France*. Cambridge MA: Harvard University Press.

Keck, O. (1993) The national system for technical innovation in Germany, in Nelson, R. (ed.) *National Innovation Systems*. New York: Oxford University Press, 115–57.

Kenney, M. (1986) *Biotechnology: the University–Industry Complex*. New Haven, Conn.: Yale University Press.

Koen, C.I. (1999) Government and the pharmaceutical industry: a comparative study of Germany and Japan. Doctoral dissertation. Unpublished manuscript. University of Warwick, Department of Politics and International Studies.

Kogut, B. (1991) Country capabilities and the permeability of borders. *Strategic Management Journal* 12 (Summer/Special Issue), 33–47.

Kogut, B. (1993) Introduction, in Kogut, B. (ed.) *Country Competitiveness: Technology and the Organizing of Work*. New York: Oxford University Press.

Lenway, S.A. and Murtha, T.P. (1994) The state as strategist in international business research literature. *Journal of International Business Studies* 25(3), 513–36.

Locke, R. (1985) The relationship between educational and managerial cultures in Britain and West Germany: a comparative analysis of higher education from an historical perspective, in Joynt, P. and Warner, M. (eds) *Managing in Different Cultures*. Oslo: Universitetsforlaget AS.

Lodge, G.C. (1990) *Comparative Business–Government Relations*. Englewood Cliffs, NJ: Prentice-Hall.

Lundvall, B.-A. (1992) *National Systems of Innovation: Towards a Theory of Innovation and Interactive Learning*. London: Pinter.

Mansfield, E. (1988) The speed and cost of industrial innovation in Japan and the US: external vs internal technology. *Management Science* 34(10), 1157–68.

Mowery, D.C. and Rosenberg, N. (1993) The US national innovation system, in Nelson, R.R. (ed.) *National Innovation Systems*. Oxford: Oxford University Press.

Nelsen, L.L. (1991) The lifeblood of biotechnology: university–industry technology transfer, in One, R.D. (ed.) *The Business of Biotechnology: From the Bench to the Street*. Boston: Butterworth-Heinemann.

Nelson, R.R. (ed.) (1993) *National Innovation Systems*. Oxford: Oxford University Press.

Nelson, R.R. and Rosenberg, N. (1993) Technical innovation and national systems, in Nelson, R.R. (ed.), *National Innovation Systems*. Oxford: Oxford University Press.

Odagiri, H. and Goto, A. (1993) The Japanese system of innovation: past, present, and future, in Nelson, R.R. (ed.) *National Innovation Systems*. Oxford: Oxford University Press.

Ostry, S. (1990) *Governments and Corporations in a Shrinking World: Trade and Innovation Policies in the United States, Europe and Japan*. London and New York: Council on Foreign Relations Press.

Porter, M. (1990) *The Competitive Advantage of Nations*. New York: Free Press.

Porter, M. and Stern S. (2002) Innovation: location matters. *Sloan Management Review* 42(4), 28–36.

Powell, W.W. and DiMaggio, P.J. (1991) *The New Institutionalism in Organizational Analysis*. Chicago: University of Chicago Press.

Salomon, J.J. (1986) Le Gaulois, le Cowboy et le Samourai: la politique française de la technologie. Paris: Economica.

Saxonhouse, G. (1986) Industrial policy and factor markets: biotechnology in Japan and the United States, in Patrick, H. (ed.) *Japan's High Technology Industries*. Seattle: University of Washington Press.

Serfati, C. (1991) Primauté des technologies militaires, faiblesse des retombées civiles et déclin de compétitivité: le cas the l'industrie électronique française. Paper presented at the conference on the Social Mastery of Technology, Maison Rhone-Alpes des Sciences de l'Homme, Lyon (September).

Shan, W. and Hamilton, W. (1991) Country-specific advantage and international cooperation. *Strategic Management Journal* 12(6), 419–32.

Sharp, M. (1989) European countries in science-based competition: the case of biotechnology. DCR Discussion Paper 72. Science Policy Research Unit, University of Sussex.

Soskice, D. (1999) Divergent production regimes: coordinated and uncoordinated market economies in the 1980s and 1990s, in Kitschelt, H., Lange, P., Marks, G. and Stephens, J.D. (eds) *Continuity and Change in Contemporary Capitalism.* Cambridge, US: Cambridge University Press, 101–34.

Swann, J.P. (1988) *Academic Scientists and the Pharmaceutical Industry: Cooperative Research in Twentieth-century America.* Baltimore, MD: Johns Hopkins University Press.

Tapon, F. (1989) A transaction cost analysis of innovations in the organization of pharmaceutical R&D. *Journal of Economic Behavior and Organization* 12, 197–213.

Teso, B. (1980) *Technical Change and Economic Policy: the Pharmaceutical Industry.* Paris: OECD.

Westney, D.E. (1993) Country patterns in R&D organization: the US and Japan, in Kogut, B. (ed.) *Country Competitiveness: Technology and the Organizing of Work,* New York: Oxford University Press.

Yuan, R.T. (1987) Biotechnology in western Europe. Discussion Paper. International Trade Administration, US Department of Commerce (April).

Chapter 9

Multinational Corporations: Structural Issues

NIELS NOORDERHAVEN

Learning Objectives

By the end of this chapter you will be able to:

- understand the factors leading to the existence of multinational corporations (MNCs)

- reflect on the stages of development and foreign market entry modes of MNCs

- appreciate the influence on MNCs of pressures to adapt to local circumstances and to integrate activities worldwide

- critically assess the 'transnational form' as a response to these conflicting pressures, and be able to reflect critically on the concept of the 'transnational'

- identify the mechanisms of coordination and control that are used in MNCs

- explore the management of headquarters–subsidiary relationships in the MNC

- distinguish between different roles of subsidiaries within the MNC, and relate these roles to the learning capabilities of the MNC

- evaluate the impact of cultural and institutional differences on the management of MNCs

- understand the country-of-origin effect as it produces itself within MNCs.

Chapter Outline

9.1   **Introduction**

9.2   **The Internationalization Processes of MNCs**
Why do MNCs exist?
Internationalization as a learning process
Foreign market entry modes
Stages of development of MNC organization structures
Transnational management
Complex realities

9.3   **Coordination and Control within MNCs**
Coordination and control mechanisms
Headquarters–subsidiary relationships

9.4   **Knowledge Management in the MNC**
Exploitative and explorative learning in the MNC
The costs of transnational management

9.5   **The MNC and Cultural and Institutional Differences**
How do MNCs respond to cultural and institutional diversity?
The country-of-origin effect on MNCs
Study Questions
Further Reading
Case: Heineken
Case: Integration of the Operations of the London Branch of a German Bank
References

9.1 Introduction

In this chapter we will concentrate on the type of organization that, arguably, deals most intensively with international differences in management and organization: the multinational corporation (MNC). While almost all firms have to deal with international diversity issues more or less frequently, the MNC has to internalize this diversity within its organization in the course of its daily operations. MNCs are not only important as the place where international comparative management is practised; these organizations are also growing in economic importance. According to the World Investment Report (WIR) (2000) international production by MNCs is growing fast, and now spans virtually all countries and industries. The gross product of all MNCs together (about 63,000 parent firms with 690,000 affiliates) comprises one-quarter of the total gross production in the world. Between one-third and one-half of world trade takes place between within MNCs (Kumar, 1999; WIR, 2000). Hence, the MNC is a factor of immense importance in the world economy.

What is a multinational corporation? This question is not so easy to answer. Of course, in order to be called 'multinational' a firm should engage in business activities in more than one country. The United Nations defines multinational enterprises as 'enterprises that own or control production or service facilities outside the country in which they are based' (United Nations, 1988: 16). The phrase 'own or control' is of importance. It implies that MNCs are actively engaged in international activities. The control mentioned may be based on (partial) ownership, but this is no necessity: foreign expansions may also take the form of contractual arrangements with local firms. On the other hand, foreign investments are not always made with the purpose or effect of gaining control. Some foreign investments are part of a portfolio of non-controlling interests, and are made with the motive of spreading risk. In contrast, foreign direct investments (FDIs) are made with the motive of exerting control over the activities financed. Although not all FDI is performed by MNCs, most of it is, and we may say that FDI is an important hallmark of the MNC.

There is no consensus whether the international business activities should be above a minimum level (e.g. 10 per cent of turnover) or of a specific kind (e.g. production and sales as opposed to sales only) before a firm should be called a multinational. The most sensible approach is to assume that MNCs form no homogenous group, but that these firms can be ranked according to their level of 'multinationality' or 'transnationality'. In the World Investment Reports, published by the United Nations, the transnationality index for the world's largest MNCs is published yearly. This index is the average of three ratios:

1. foreign to total assets
2. foreign to total sales, and
3. foreign to total employment (WIR, 2000: 83).

When this criterion is applied, the most 'transnational' among the large MNCs are typically those from small home countries and/or producing consumer products like food and beverages, like Nestlé (Switzerland) or ABB (Switzerland and Sweden) (WIR, 2003). This stands to reason, for consumer goods like foods and beverages are more sensitive to cultural and institutional differences than, say, capital goods like machinery. Hence companies active in these sectors need more of a presence in foreign countries if they want to sell there, and for companies from smaller home countries the international market becomes important very quickly, if they want to continue to grow.

In our discussion of MNCs in this chapter we will first, in the following section, discuss the internationalization processes of MNCs. Subsequently, we will focus on coordination and control within the MNC. In the final section of the chapter we will focus in on the ways in which MNCs deal with international diversity.

9.2 ✦ The Internationalization Processes of MNCs

Practically all MNCs have started off as companies operating in their home country and have, later, gradually added activities in foreign countries. Exceptions are MNCs that acquired bi-national status at a very early stage of their development (e.g. British-Dutch Shell), and MNCs that are the result of an international merger and have since developed into a new entity (e.g. Swedish-Swiss ABB). Most other MNCs first developed at home, and then started adding international activities. Before discussing the modalities of international expansion and the typical growth paths of MNCs, a preliminary question must be answered: 'Why do MNCs exist at all?' At first sight, this question may seem absurd, so much have MNCs become a fact of life. But from a theoretical point of view that MNCs should exist is not so obvious at all. After all, the previous chapters of this book have been emphasizing the differences between the business environments in different countries. This means that a firm that has experience in one particular country must have a significant disadvantage, vis-à-vis local firms, once it begins operating in another country. There must, then, be advantages that more than offset the disadvantage of not being familiar with the local business environment or the 'liability of foreignness'.

Why do MNCs exist?

Various theories have been developed to explain the existence and continuing growth of MNCs. John Dunning put the most important explanations together in what he called 'the eclectic paradigm' of international investment and production (Dunning, 1993). Dunning focuses on three sets of explanatory factors: ownership factors, location factors and internalization factors.

Starting with the ownership factors, given the 'liability of foreignness' a firm must have certain advantages over local companies if it is to compete successfully in foreign markets. These advantages can be of various kinds. A firm may, for instance, possess specialized technology that cannot easily be bought or developed by local firms. This is true, for instance, of chip-maker Intel. While its chip-making technology is not unique, it is confined to a quite small group of companies, operating worldwide. Another possibility is that a firm may have built up a valuable brand name, which allows it to compete successfully even without superior or hard-to-imitate technology or products. McDonald's is an example of a company that possesses this type of ownership advantage. The company-specific advantage may also be that the firm has certain technological or management skills. Finally, a company may have privileged access to certain raw materials, like bauxite or petroleum. This type of ownership-specific advantage is often of a political nature – that is, it has been granted to the company by the government of the country from which the raw materials originate. All these firm-specific advantages should be difficult and/or costly to create or acquire (otherwise they would not constitute a sustainable advantage), but at the same time they must be relatively easy to transfer to other locations at low cost.

The possession of company-specific advantages is no sufficient explanation for the existence of MNCs. Why would the company that has these advantages not simply put them to use within its home country, and then export its products to foreign markets? For a firm to invest abroad, some location-specific factors must also exist. Location-specific advantages, like firm-specific advantages, can be of many kinds. Historically, an important reason for firms to invest in production facilities abroad was the existence of high import tariffs for finished goods, making it more economical to perform at least part of the production process in the end market. This is an important explanation behind the many local assembly plants set up by manufacturing firms before the Second World War. Somewhat comparable is production in foreign countries to minimize transportation costs. Beer brewer Heineken, for example, has production facilities in many countries, to avoid the high transportation costs of a product consisting of 95 per cent water. Other location-specific advantages may stem from production factors, in particular cheap labour. This is an important reason for overseas investment in labour-intensive industries, like in the apparel industry in Madagascar. Finally, some locations offer a particularly attractive environment for specific types of activity, like the City of London for the financial sector and Silicon Valley in the USA for information technology. These types of location advantage are of a more dynamic nature, since they originate in a historic process of cumulative causation, which gradually makes a particular location attractive for particular activities, mainly because of a concentration of specialized producers and service providers.

However, even the combination of firm-specific advantages and location-specific advantages is insufficient to explain the FDI that makes a company into an MNC. Why would the firm not sell or contract out its specific advantages to a local firm in the country it wishes to enter? The local firm could in that way combine the firm-specific advantages with the location-specific advantages, without being hindered by the liability of 'foreignness'. The explanation put forward in the eclectic paradigm is that markets for firm-specific advantages often fail. Trading technology over a market interface is not impossible, but can be difficult and risky, especially when the technology is very innovative. The buying partner will want to have a deep insight into the technology before deciding about the deal but, in disclosing too much, the selling firm may in fact be giving away the very thing it wants to sell. Protection of intellectual property rights is never very easy, and even less so in the international arena. This is why R&D-intensive firms that expand abroad tend to internalize their international activities. In the case of advertising-intensive firms, the motive is predominantly to avoid the damage to their reputation that would be the result of poor-quality services offered by local representatives, which would decrease the quality of their product or service as perceived by consumers (Hennart, 1991).

Internationalization as a learning process

The reasons MNCs exist have been discussed above. Even if there are excellent rationales, however, MNCs do not come about overnight. The main reason for this is the 'liability of foreignness' problem, which can only be overcome by learning. On the basis of a study of the internationalization process of four Swedish firms, Johanson and Wiedersheim-Paul (1975) were the first to stress that internationalization is often a gradual and incremental process. From a purely domestic function with production and sales only in Sweden, these companies first moved into export through independent representatives, then at a certain point in time they decided to set up their own sales subsidiaries in foreign countries, and only after that they moved on to setting up production facilities overseas. This 'establishment chain' shows a gradual increase in the commitment to foreign markets; as the firm learns about these markets, the perceived uncertainty decreases and it commits more resources to them (Johanson and Vahlne, 1977). Not only do companies gradually increase their commitment to foreign markets, they also enter new foreign markets in an incremental way. They start with countries that are similar to their home country in terms of culture, language, institutions, political system, and so on, and only after having successfully established in these countries move on to more dissimilar countries. In this way, they minimize the 'psychic distance' that has to be bridged in their initial steps on the internationalization path, and thus keep the uncertainty they have to deal with within manageable bounds. The initial theory developed by Johanson and Wiedersheim-Paul was based on only a very small number of observations, but later studies have, at least in part, confirmed the gradual stepwise internationalization process (Erramilli, 1991; Hadjikani, 1997). Of course, this general description is not applicable to all firms in all cases. By acquiring existing local firms, MNCs can accelerate their learning process. MNCs can also transfer what is learned from experiences within in a particular country to other units operating in the same country, or even to other units operating in other countries. MNCs can sometimes also use their business contacts (buyers and suppliers) as sources of information to expedite learning (Forsgren, 2002). Nevertheless, the internationalization process model helps to understand the learning process necessary for the formation and development of an MNC.

Foreign market entry modes

The internationalization process view suggests that the MNC with production subsidiaries in different countries is the end point of a development process. However, it is also the case that fully-fledged MNCs may continue to use foreign market entry modes other than wholly owned subsidiaries. Adapting their mode of entry to local circumstances and regulations MNCs may enter different markets in different ways, or they may be at different stages of the internationalization learning process in different regions or product areas. Hence, in order to understand the MNC and the way in which this type of organization deals with international diversity we need to look in more detail at the modalities of foreign market entry.

In classifying modes of foreign market entry, two dimensions can usefully be distinguished: the degree of control the MNC can exert over the activities abroad and the extent of resource commitment. The various modalities of foreign market entry that we will discuss can be seen as a series of alternatives implying increasing degrees of both control and resource commitment. The mode that implies the lowest extent of commitment of resources, and also the lowest level of control, is production in the home country with export to foreign countries. International control is low in this mode since although the firm has total control over the production of its goods, it has little or no control over their distribution in foreign markets. Exports can be indirect via export agents or confirming houses. This does not necessitate the firm having to conduct any special international activities. If the firm is to engage in the organization of its exports itself, this means that the necessary knowledge needs to be present. If exports as a proportion of total sales become more important, a special export department is often formed within the company, in which all expertise regarding foreign sales is bundled. Eventually the firm may decide to set up its own marketing and sales subsidiary in foreign markets that are particularly important.

Depending on the type of product (e.g. costs of transportation, labour intensity of the production process) and the country (e.g. regulations concerning 'local content' such as the proportion of the end value of a product that has to be added within the country in question), the firm can decide that it is better to produce abroad. If this is the case, there are two options: it can either sell or rent its advantages to a local firm (through licensing or franchising) or exploit them itself, and launch foreign manufacturing (Hennart 1991). Licensing implies the lowest level of commitment to foreign production. A licensing agreement gives a firm in the host country (the 'licensee') the right to use the intangible resources of the firm (e.g. patents, registered designs, trademarks, know-how). In return, the licensee pays royalties, either in the form of a one-time fee or as a percentage of, say, sales revenue, or a combination of the two.

Licensing is often the foreign entry mode of choice when the focal firm's advantage consists mainly of process technology. But not all forms of proprietary technology are fit for this mode of entry. The technology in question should be relatively explicit and easy to codify. As codified knowledge can be transferred from one firm to the other relatively easy, this is the type of knowledge that lends itself most readily to licensing agreements. Codified knowledge is often associated with older technologies. This is confirmed by research into the use of licensing, which shows that the probability that a firm uses this entry mode, instead of engaging in own production abroad, is greater the older the technology, the more peripheral it is to the licensing firm's business, the smaller the investment in R&D necessary to develop it has been, and the greater the firm's experience in international licensing (Davidson and McFetridge, 1984). However, some types of knowledge are *tacit* – that is, non-verbalizable, intuitive and/or not well articulated (Polanyi, 1962). This may, for instance, be know-how with regard to arrangements for the organization of the production process within which the technology to be transferred is to be applied.

Like exporting, licensing is a low-commitment, low-control mode of foreign country entry. However, both the level of control and the level of resources that need to be committed will in most cases be substantially higher than in the case of exporting. The level of control is higher because various kinds of restriction may be written in the licence agreement. However, the licensing firm also needs to commit more resources, first of all because licensing agreements are complicated contracts and, second, because in many cases a combination of codified and tacit knowledge are needed in order to make the technology transfer work (WIR, 1999). This may mean that the firm has to send some of its own employees to the licensee, at least initially.

The main advantages of licensing are that there is no need for heavy investment, and the risk incurred is limited. However, there are also some notable disadvantages. The company becomes to a certain extent dependent on the local licensee, who may not exert the marketing efforts needed to realize the full market potential of the product, or may reduce the consistency of product or service quality. Also, the licensee may use the licence to learn about and eventually 'engineer around' the production technology, and in this way the firm that grants the licence may be opening itself up to a future competitor.

A contractual form of market entry that offers more control is franchising. Franchising is a form of licensing of intangible property in combination with assistance over an extended period. Franchising is most often used to transfer the right to use a brand name or trademark, and is primarily used in services and retailing (e.g. McDonald's). In comparison with a licensing contract, franchising offers greater control, while at the same time allowing for rapid international expansion. It is often used in retailing and services, like the fast-food sector, because the firm granting the licence can make use of the local knowledge of the franchisee, which can be an important advantage in consumer markets. A disadvantage is that the control cost can be hefty. As in the case of licensing, the interests of the licensor and licensee can easily diverge. For the firm granting the licence its brand name is often its most important asset, hence it will want to prevent its licensees from performing any activities that will erode the value of its brand name. However, for the licensees any damage to the brand name caused by their actions is, to a large extent, an 'externality' (i.e. they do not bear much of the cost). Thus, if a licensee of an international fast-food chain decides to compromise quality, it bears only a fraction of the costs in terms of the reduced value of the licence, while pocketing all the advantages in terms of lower costs. The only way the licensing firm can avoid this danger is through intensive control.

One step further in the commitment chain is when the MNC decides to enter into a more strategic cooperation with a local company. This can take two general forms: purely contractual or involving equity. In the case of an equity-based cooperation, for our purposes, we will speak of a joint venture, which is an example of a purely contractual arrangement of a strategic alliance. Both strategic alliances and joint ventures can have various activities as their purpose. Hence, this mode of foreign market entry does not necessarily imply local production, but may also remain confined to marketing and sales arrangements. The difference with the entry modes discussed so far, however, is the degree of commitment from the side of the entering firm. In the forms of market entry discussed so far this commitment remains restricted, and most of the business risk can be said to fall upon the local firm. In strategic alliances and joint ventures, in contrast, the risk is shared between the partners. This risk sharing can be in divergent proportions (in the case of a joint venture, normally as a function of the proportion of equity invested). The fact remains, however, that moving from export, licensing or franchising to an international strategic alliance constitutes a quantum leap on the path of internationalization.

Strategic alliances and joint ventures can have different functions in the overall flow of activities of the MNC. The most common forms are forward integration, backward integration and buy-back arrangements (Buckley and Casson, 1988). In the case of forward integration, the MNC cooperates with a local company in setting up or using a distribution system. Backward integration is used, for example, in raw material sourcing. Backward integration through joint ventures is frequently used in the petroleum industry, where full ownership by foreign multinationals is often ruled out by local government regulations. These kinds of restriction often play a decisive role when MNCs enter into alliances or joint ventures with local government agencies, rather than with private companies. Buy-back joint ventures or strategic alliances are used when companies cooperate in a particular phase or process in the production process. An example is the production of engines in the automobile industry, where the minimum efficient scale is much larger than in most other activities in the production process. This is the rationale for, for instance, BMW and Chrysler's Tritec Motors Ltd, a joint venture for the production of engines in Brazil.

The advantages of both strategic alliances and joint ventures are that, compared with wholly owned subsidiaries (as discussed below), the investments and the risks are reduced. Furthermore, they allow the cooperating companies to combine their strengths, and to learn from each other. An additional advantage for the MNC may be that, compared with some of the other entry modes, they help to create a more 'local' image. The disadvantages are that the MNC has no full control. Related to this, the cooperation may lead to conflicts between the partners. In particular, 50/50 joint ventures are renowned for being conflict-ridden. Furthermore the learning potential mentioned as an advantage of the collaborative entry modes may turn into a disadvantage if the local partner 'out-learns' the MNC to the point that it no longer needs the collaboration and becomes a full-blown competitor. Strategic alliances and joint ventures tend to be unstable; many of these collaborative ventures are discontinued after a relatively short time (Yan and Zeng, 1999). In a sense, in using these entry modes, MNCs can be seen as 'buying options': if the entry succeeds and the local market is attractive enough, the MNC can choose to 'strike' the option by acquiring the joint venture or turning the alliance into a wholly-owned subsidiary (Bowman and Hurry, 1993).

Finally, the entry mode requiring the largest commitment and also surrendering full control is setting up a wholly owned local subsidiary. With this entry mode, MNCs have two possibilities: either they start up a new facility from scratch, or they buy an existing local firm. In the first case we speak of 'greenfield' investment, in the second of an acquisition. Acquired companies are sometimes restructured extensively in order to fit into the MNC (e.g. in terms of quality management). If this is the case, the term 'brownfield' is sometimes used, indicating that this is a hybrid mode of entry, with characteristics of both a greenfield investment and an acquisition (Meyer and Estrin, 2001). The advantage of an acquisition, or brownfield investment, is that local resources – for example, in the form of management – can be incorporated in the MNC. The disadvantage may be that the acquired company often also brings with it numerous local practices and/or inefficiencies that are difficult to reconcile with the MNC's overall policies. A greenfield start-up can be moulded to the MNC's liking to an extent often impossible with acquired companies, because of the sometimes strong resistance to change in existing organizations. The general advantages of wholly owned subsidiaries as modes of foreign market entry are that they offer complete control and that the activities in the target country can be integrated within the global strategy of the MNC to a larger extent than with the other entry modes. The disadvantages are that the resources required are more extensive (since there is no other investor) and hence there is higher risk exposure.

If the MNC decides to set up a wholly owned subsidiary it has to decide about its legal structure. Two options exist: the subsidiary can have the legal status of a branch (i.e. no independent legal status) or of a subsidiary in the legal sense (Daniels and Radebaugh, 2001: 541). The choice between these options will depend, among other things, on the disclosure requirements in the host country and regulations regarding the limited liability of owners of joint stock companies.

Stages of development of MNC organization structures

Building on our discussion of modes of foreign market entry in the previous section, we will now look at the question of how MNCs organize for the management of the increasing diversity they will meet in the internationalization process.

Stopford and Wells (1972) studied the development of the organizational macro structures of US MNCs, focusing on two factors influencing these structures: foreign sales as a percentage of total sales, and foreign product diversity (see Figure 9.1). The macro structure of an MNC reveals the criterion on which the basic grouping of activities within the MNC is based. The first dimension of Stopford and Wells measures the importance of foreign activities, relative to those in the home country. The second dimension can be seen as a proxy for the degree of complexity the MNC meets in managing its international activities. Stopford and Wells describe two distinct paths of development. Most MNCs started with an international unit (a department or a division) taking care of all overseas activities. This is possible only if foreign sales are relatively low and if foreign product diversity is limited. Otherwise it becomes impossible for a single international division or department to manage all foreign activities effectively.

The direction in which MNCs developed depended on what became the most pressing issue first: the sheer volume of foreign sales or the product diversity of international sales

Figure 9.1 Evolution or organizational macro structures of MNCs

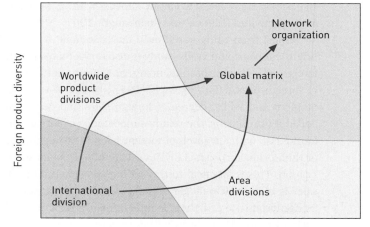

Source: Stopford and Wells (1972).

and production. In the first case, the solution was typically to base the organization on geographical divisions. In the second case, the organization would be structured into product divisions, each of which has a worldwide mandate. Each of the two solutions has its advantages and disadvantages. Geographically based divisions have the advantage that all local market know-how is concentrated within a single organizational unit. This allows for flexible adaptation to local circumstances. However, if the MNC produces and sells divergent products, it will be difficult for the area-based units to build and maintain all the necessary product and technological expertise. In contrast, worldwide operating product divisions have the advantage of bundling all the expertise concerning a particular class of product and the associated production technologies. However, they will have more difficulty in dealing with country-specific issues.

If both foreign sales and foreign product diversity continue to increase, MNCs need an organizational structure that strikes a balance between the advantages and disadvantages of product-based and area-based divisions. Such a structure can be a matrix structure, in which all major activities are coordinated by both product and area-related managers. This means that a basic classical principle of organization – the unity of command – is abolished. A number of managers in a matrix organization have two bosses. In a well-balanced matrix these bosses are equally powerful, meaning that in case of disagreement the parties concerned must discuss and negotiate until agreement is reached. As a result, matrix organizations tend to be cumbersome, in that they entail high coordination costs and may slow down decision-making. We will return to this point later.

Research by Franko (1976) has shown that the typical growth paths of European MNCs are different from those identified by Stopford and Wells in their study of US MNCs. Because of the smaller size of their home-country economies, these MNCs were forced to respond to the international dimension of their activities at an earlier stage than was the case for their counterparts in the USA. Also, the cultural and linguistic diversity within Europe prompted the European MNCs to grant their local foreign operations more decision-making power. The result was that, for European MNCs, the geographical division structure was a more important organizational form than for US MNCs. This structure is more likely when, in contrast with US MNCs, no single region dominates the MNC's activities (Daniels and Radebaugh, 2001: 524).

Apart from being based on a biased sample (in that all MNCs studied were of US origin) Stopford and Wells' study is also not completely satisfactory in that they focus on foreign sales as a factor influencing the organizational form of MNCs, but neglect the role of foreign production. Egelhoff (1988) looked at the two dimensions distinguished by Stopford and Wells (degree of foreign sales and degree of product diversification), but added a third factor: the relative importance of foreign production (see Figure 9.2). He found that, with low levels of foreign sales, MNCs opt for either the international division or the worldwide product division structure, depending on the degree of product diversification. This is identical to the findings of Stopford and Wells. If the degree of foreign sales is high, however, the organizational form depends on the relative importance of foreign production. If there is little foreign production, MNCs can continue to function with a worldwide product division structure. If there is much foreign production, MNCs rather opt for divisions based on geographical regions (if the product diversification is low) or for a matrix form (if product diversification is high).

Figure 9.2 Organizational macro structure of MNCs and the relative importance of foreign production

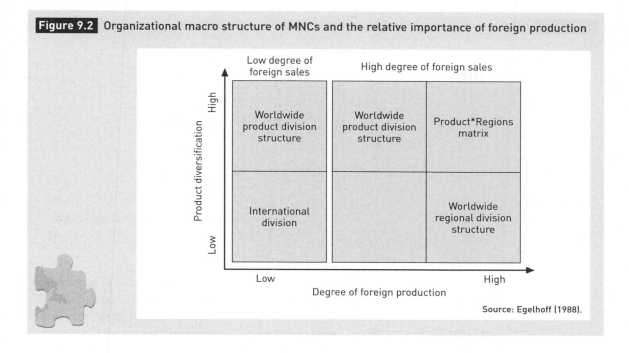

Source: Egelhoff (1988).

Transnational management

Building on the literature discussed above, and their own research into the structures and strategies of MNCs, Christopher Bartlett and Sumantra Ghoshal (2000) elaborate further on the management of this type of firm. Their approach centres on the local-versus-global dilemma that all MNCs have to face when deciding where in the organization to vest what sort of decision-making authority. MNCs in their operations have to be adaptive to local circumstances, to the extent that consumer preferences, market structures and government regulations differ between countries. But they also have to integrate activities at a global level if they want to realize economies of scale to the fullest extent possible. Moreover, if the MNC wants to avoid costly duplication of efforts in, say, research and development, it must coordinate and integrate these activities across borders. If the pressures to adapt to local circumstances and to integrate globally are, for the sake of simplicity, assumed to be either high or low, a two-by-two matrix can be drawn in which the four possible MNC strategies proposed by Bartlett and Ghoshal can be positioned (Figure 9.3).

If both the pressures for localizing and for globalizing are weak, the most likely MNC strategy is the *international* strategy. This is the traditional form of MNCs based in large domestic markets such as the USA. The international activities receive little special attention. Products are typically developed for the domestic market and sold overseas with little or no adaptation. In as far as production abroad takes place, this is largely in response to transportation costs or to host-country government policies regarding local content requirements. This form is most adequate for MNCs in certain business-to-business markets, like machinery and equipment manufacturing. If there are strong pressures for localizing, and weak forces towards global integration, the organizational form predicted

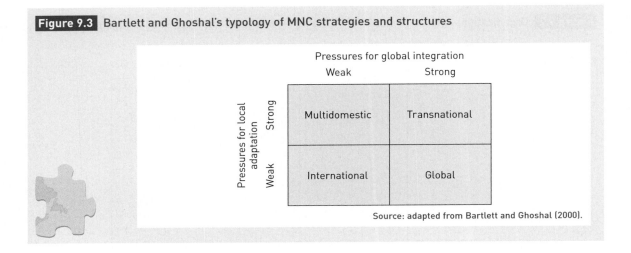

Figure 9.3 Bartlett and Ghoshal's typology of MNC strategies and structures

Source: adapted from Bartlett and Ghoshal (2000).

is that of the *multidomestic firm*. This is most fitting in consumer markets, in particular for products that need to be adapted to local tastes, like food and beverages. Local subsidiaries of the MNC act as quasi-independent firms, focusing on their own geographical market, and typically having almost complete freedom in determining their local strategies. The heydays of this type of MNC were in the first half of the twentieth century (Martinez and Jarillo, 1989). In that period, tariff and non-tariff barriers between many countries were still a major factor. The opposite situation to that of the multidomestic type is that of strong forces for globalization and weak forces for local adaptation. The associated type of MNC is the *global firm*. Here global integration of R&D, design and production dominates at the cost of local adaptation. This form is most likely where economies of scale are intensely important, as in the production of industrial chemicals. According to Martinez and Jarillo (1989), this type of MNC was most prevalent in the period 1950–80.

So far, Bartlett and Ghoshal's description is a variation on the earlier research findings described above. The most interesting contribution made by Bartlett and Ghoshal, however, pertains to the situation in which both those forces driving towards local adaptation and those pressing for global integration are strong. In earlier publications, the matrix form was associated with this situation; but Bartlett and Ghoshal go beyond this structural solution to discuss the mentality that companies need to develop in order to thrive under such demanding conditions. Companies that have the mentality that enables them to simultaneously adapt to local circumstances and to integrate activities across borders are called *transnationals*. It is important to note that 'transnational' is not just another word for 'matrix structure'. Transnationals will often have matrix-like structures, but that is not the essence of their nature. This lies in the combination of a strategy, a structure *and* the mentality of the top management of the companies. In the view of Bartlett and Ghoshal, the organizational structure is a dependent rather than an independent variable: if an MNC wants to be a transnational, it first has to change its mentality from the one-size-fits-all thinking characteristic of global management, or from the idea that differences between countries are so fundamental that coordination across national subsidiaries is unfeasible or even undesirable. Some transnationals adopt a formal matrix structure, while others maintain a macro structure centred on either regions or products but dramatically change the way it operates (Westney, 1999). People-orientated coordination mechanisms, such as horizontal communication and the building of a strong corporate culture are seen as more important than the hierarchy or formal rules. Ghoshal and Nohria (1993: 28) refer to 'normative integration' through the 'socialization of managers into a set of shared goals, values, and beliefs that then shape their perspectives and behavior'. However, as Welch and Welch (1997) rightly remark, corporate cultures are difficult to change or to 'manage', and the loss of central control may have negative consequences for the MNC, like increased duplication of effort and dysfunctional inter-unit rivalry.

The transnational adapts to local circumstances where necessary, but at the same time achieves a far greater degree of coordination across countries than is the case with the multidomestic company. On top of that, the transnational MNC manages its subsidiaries in such a way that the whole integrated system acquires the flexibility necessary to adapt to changing circumstances, and to allow learning to take place not only between local subsidiaries and headquarters, and vice versa, but also among subsidiaries. We will return to this issue in Section 9.4, on knowledge management in the MNC.

Bartlett and Ghoshal's ideas about the transnational form are not entirely new. In earlier work, 'network organizations' or 'heterarchies' (Hedlund, 1986) have been proposed as organizational forms capable of squaring the circle of local adaptation and global integration. In addition, the importance of the mentality of MNC top management has also been recognized by Perlmutter (1969) in his seminal essay on 'the tortuous evolution' of the multinational company. All in all, there seems to be reason enough to expect something like the transnational form to make headway within the population of MNCs, but what is the empirical evidence?

While we have no historical data that would enable us to gauge the penetration of transnational-like organizational forms, there have been some empirical studies suggesting that the Bartlett and Ghoshal typology rings true. Harzing (2000) gives an extensive overview of typologies of MNCs, together with an indication of the empirical support for each of them. She also tests the Bartlett and Ghoshal typology on data from 166 subsidiaries of 37 MNCs. Overall, she found considerable support for the existence of MNCs with characteristics of the multidomestic, global and transnational type. (The international type of MNC was not included in her study, since it was not as clearly defined as the other types, and had not received much empirical support in earlier studies.) The overall conclusion was that Bartlett and Ghoshal's typology does indeed help to categorize MNCs in groups that share important characteristics.

Below, we will look at the mechanisms MNCs use for achieving internal coordination and control, and then focus on the relationship between headquarters and subsidiaries within the MNC. First, however, a note of caution with regard to the extent of the simplification of our discussion of macro organizational structures of MNCs.

Complex realities

The previous subsection illustrated the complexity of the issue of MNC organizational structures. In reality, this complexity is even far greater than suggested by the discussion above. As a consequence of their historical growth paths, as well as because of growth through foreign acquisitions rather than organic growth, many MNCs display a mixed organizational macro structure (Daniels and Radebaugh, 2001: 525). Recently acquired subsidiaries often do not fit very well into the existing organizational structure – for instance, because they perform a combination of activities that is uncommon within the MNC. An important issue to keep in mind is that whatever structure the MNC chooses, the international dimension has to be factored in at some point. If the MNC opts for geographical division, then it is very likely that within these divisions there will be departments specializing in the various product categories the MNC carries. Likewise, if the MNC is organized according to product divisions, the responsibility for different geographical areas will be assigned to organizational units within the divisions. A decision-making authority may also be allocated to regional or product-based units depending on the type of decision. For instance, all contacts with local authorities and institutions like labour unions may be delegated to a country or regional manager, while all responsibility for the internal activities of the MNC may be allocated to managers of product-based divisions. An example of such a structural set-up is the Swiss-Swedish producer of power plants and related products, ABB. Finally, for the sake of simplicity, our discussion above neglected the middle-layer structures MNCs often adopt – for example, with some kind of regional headquarters coordinating all product-based divisions within a certain geographic area.

Also the way in which the forces towards local adaptation and towards global integration work out in a particular MNC and its various units is more complicated than suggested above. Bartlett and Ghoshal (1989) illustrate this with the example of Unilever. At the level of the business unit (e.g. Unilever's detergent business), a balance must be struck between local adaptation and global integration. However, if one looks more closely at the various functions performed within the business unit, like marketing, production or product development, the need for local adaptation and/or global integration may well vary. For instance, the sales function is likely to require more adaptation to local markets than the product development function; we could look even more closely at the particular tasks that are performed within each function in the business unit. Also at this level we are likely to find tasks that need more or less local adaptation and/or global integration. Sales promotion activities are, most of the time, geared specifically to a national market, but in determining the product policy, local managers must coordinate carefully with their colleagues in other countries.

Taking into account this complexity of MNC strategies and structures, we will now look in more detail at the mechanisms MNCs use to coordinate and control their activities.

9.3   Coordination and Control within MNCs

In the previous section we discussed the macro structures of MNCs; but the formal macro structure, although important, is but one of the mechanisms MNCs use for organizing their international activities. In this section we will look into the more subtle processes and systems MNCs employ in order to coordinate and control their activities. After that, we will concentrate on the headquarters–subsidiary relationship within MNCs, and discuss the ways in which these relationships are managed.

Coordination and control mechanisms

The terms 'control' and 'coordination' are often used without it being clear whether there is any difference between them. Control can be defined as 'the regulation of activities within an organization so that they are in accord with the expectations established in policies and targets' (Child, 1973: 117). Coordination is 'an enabling process to bring about the appropriate linkages between tasks' (Cray, 1984: 86). Both control and coordination pertain to the direction of efforts towards organizational goals. The concept of 'control' suggests a power difference that is not implicit in that of 'coordination' (Harzing, 1999: 9). However, as the two concepts are strongly related, and as coordination/control mechanisms based on power differentials and on other bases in practice coincide, we will use the terms interchangeably.

Synthesizing the literature on control mechanisms, Harzing (1999: 21) distinguishes between direct and indirect mechanisms on the one hand, and personal and impersonal mechanisms on the other. On this basis, she categorizes control mechanisms into four groups (Figure 9.4).

Figure 9.4 Four categories of coordination and control mechanism

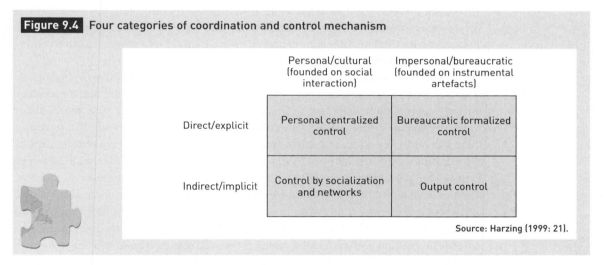

	Personal/cultural (founded on social interaction)	Impersonal/bureaucratic (founded on instrumental artefacts)
Direct/explicit	Personal centralized control	Bureaucratic formalized control
Indirect/implicit	Control by socialization and networks	Output control

Source: Harzing (1999: 21).

Personal centralized control is based on the organizational hierarchy, and works through supervision and intervention by managers. *Bureaucratic formalized control* consists of the formulation of rules, procedures and standards for the work activities to be performed in the organization. *Output control*, in contrast, does not specify work procedures, but plans targets for the organizational units, while these units have a large degree of freedom in deciding how to reach these targets. *Control by socialization and networks*, finally, is a mixed bag of coordination activities that have as a common characteristic that they are neither hierarchical nor bureaucratic. Mechanisms that belong to this category are the socialization of managers and employees, the informal exchange of information (i.e., not as part of formalized control or reporting procedures), and the formalized lateral relationships between organizational units (but not based on hierarchy, unlike in the case of personal centralized control).

The extent to which these various types of control mechanism are used by MNCs depends on many factors. An important factor is size. Large organizations can rely only to a limited extent on personal centralized control, otherwise the number of managers would be too large and there would be too many layers in the hierarchy. Hence, these large MNCs tend to have a relatively strong emphasis on bureaucratic formalized control. Another factor is the organizational macro structure, discussed earlier in this chapter. The macro structure can be seen as a schematic rendering of the most important formal authority relations within the MNC. Hence, the structure shows who reports to whom at the top of the MNC, both in the sense of personal supervision and of bureaucratic control. Furthermore, we can assume that in the multidomestic form, the control mechanism used in the relationship between the corporate headquarters and the division will be predominantly of the output control type. Bureaucratic formalized control or personal centralized control would make little sense, as headquarters does not want to interfere in the day-to-day operations of the local subsidiaries. However, the organizational macro structure as such gives little clues as to the mix of control mechanisms used to realize coordination in the organization as a whole (i.e. below the top management level). An exception is the matrix structure. International matrix-like structures are indicated as the structure of choice in situations of high foreign-product diversity and high foreign sales (Stopford and Wells, 1972, or in situations where there are strong pressures to localize *and* strong forces to integrate across borders (Bartlett and Ghoshal, 2000). In this type of situation, and with this kind of macro structure, a strong emphasis on more informal control mechanisms, in particular socialization and networks, is to be expected.

Just as the organizational structure of the MNC can never be based on a single criterion (e.g. product categories or geographical regions), no MNC can achieve the necessary internal coordination with just a single coordination mechanism. The mechanisms should be seen as complements, rather than substitutes (Harzing, 1999: 23). In reality there will always be a mix of control mechanisms, but the balance between the various mechanisms used differs between MNCs and within MNCs at different hierarchical levels. Even at one particular level, different control mechanisms may dominate in different places. For instance, in the relationship between headquarters and some subsidiaries, output control may dominate, while in other subsidiaries a much more direct supervision of the personal centralized type is exerted. This is likely to depend on the roles of the subsidiaries in question within the MNC, a subject we will discuss later in this chapter.

There are several reasons to expect that it is more difficult for an MNC to exert control and realize coordination of its activities than for a firm operating within a single country. Daniels and Radebaugh (2001: 518) note that four factors cause these greater difficulties, compared to single-country firms:

1. the greater geographical and cultural distance between units of the MNC
2. the greater diversity in the environments (in terms of market conditions, standards, currencies, etc.) in which the MNC works
3. factors that limit the control of MNC headquarters over all the activities of the firm, such as local stockholders, local government regulations, and so on
4. the higher degree of uncertainty (e.g. because of a lack of accurate and timely data).

As a result, in the context of the MNC the various control mechanisms meet with a number of specific difficulties. Personal centralized control is made more difficult because local managers may give little support to headquarters interventions, which may easily be seen as ignoring local circumstances and developments. Likewise, bureaucratic formalized control, because of its standardized nature, will often ignore the heterogeneity of the countries in which the MNC operates. The effectiveness of output control is restricted because the limited information flow from subsidiaries to headquarters gives unscrupulous subsidiary managers opportunities for manipulation. Working with socialization and networks is more difficult in MNCs because, for these mechanisms, frequent face-to-face contacts and interactions are essential. Moving around staff in expatriate positions can be a way to promote socialization and the formation of a common organizational culture (although it can also be part of a strategy of centralized personal supervision). However, because of the high cost, the use of this mechanism between headquarters and subsidiaries, as well as among subsidiaries, can only be limited.

Over time, and in conjunction with changing organizational macro structures, MNCs have started to use a more diverse mix of control mechanisms. Centralized personal control, partly through the use of expatriates, was the dominant coordination mechanism for multidomestic MNCs in the period 1920–50 (this and the following is based on Martinez and Jarillo, 1989). On top of this, output control (mainly financial performance) was used. Global MNCs (most prominent from 1950–80) relied more heavily on bureaucratic formalized control in the form of formal planning and budgeting systems. Martinez and Jarillo (1989) observe that these bureaucratic controls were complemented by output control in US MNCs, but more by cultural control (among other things, through the use of expatriates) in Japanese MNCs. As the pressures towards both local adaptation and global integration increased (from 1980), and MNCs moved towards the transnational form, more and more emphasis has been put on the informal control mechanisms belonging to Harzing's (1999) category of socialization and network control. The use of these mechanisms is, however, cumulative: they are used on top of the three other categories of control mechanism. Hence we can say that from the point of view of organizational control MNCs tending towards Bartlett and Ghoshal's 'transnational' type are very complex organizations.

Headquarters–subsidiary relationships

Christopher Bartlett and Sumantra Ghoshal (1989) make the point that responding simultaneously to pressures of local adaptation and global integration requires more than just a structural solution. More subtle forms of control and organization – like those discussed above under the heading of 'socialization and networks' – are also necessary. Most of all, these authors called for a new *mentality*, which was seen as necessary in order to achieve the flexibility required. This new mentality not only pertains to the macro structure and the mix of coordination mechanisms used, but also more in general to the relationship between headquarters and subsidiaries.

Bartlett and Ghoshal (1986) observe two dysfunctional 'syndromes' in headquarters–subsidiary relationships in MNCs. The 'UN model' syndrome implies that MNC headquarters' relationships with subsidiaries are based on the assumption that these should be treated in a uniform manner. Subsidiary roles and responsibilities are expressed in the same general terms, planning and control systems are applied uniformly and all subsidiaries typically enjoy the same degree of autonomy. The 'headquarters hierarchy' syndrome points at the tendency in many MNC headquarters to keep all key decisions centralized. The two syndromes are related: because headquarters have the tendency to treat all subsidiaries in the same way, all subsidiaries receive the same low degree of autonomy and play the same restricted role within the MNC (Bartlett and Ghoshal, 1986: 88). By treating their subsidiaries in this uniform way, MNCs deny the possibility that subsidiaries develop in different directions and acquire new capabilities that enable them to play a lead role within their area of competence. The existence of multiple subsidiary roles is one of the essential characteristics of the transnational form.

Building on Bartlett and Ghoshal (1986) and a number of empirical studies, Birkinshaw and Morrison (1995) distinguish between three subsidiary roles (see Table 9.1). *Local implementers* typically operate within a single country. The main responsibility of this type of subsidiary is to adapt global products to the needs of the local market. Within that local market the subsidiary operates with a certain level of autonomy. *Specialized contributors* have considerable expertise, but in a narrowly defined area. Their activities are strongly intertwined with those of other units of the MNC; hence their autonomy is limited. Subsidiaries with a *world mandate*, finally, have a worldwide (or at least region-wide) responsibility for a product line or certain types of value-adding activity. Thus there is worldwide integration, but the activities are coordinated not by headquarters, but from the subsidiary.

In Table 9.1, a number of dimensions in which the three types of subsidiary differ are indicated. The world mandate subsidiary has the largest strategic autonomy, the local implementer the smallest (all three types score equally in operational autonomy). The 'product dependence on the parent' dimension reflects the extent to which the products of the subsidiary are also produced by the parent company. The assumption is that, if this is the case, the subsidiary is more dependent on the parent with regard to these production

Table 9.1 Roles of MNC subsidiaries	Local implementer	Specialized contributor	World mandate subsidiary
Strategic autonomy	low	medium	high
Product dependence on the parent	high	high	low
Inter-affiliate purchases	high	high	low
International dispersion of manufacturing	low	high	medium
International dispersion of downstream activities	low	high	medium
Pressures for national responsiveness	high	medium	low

Source: adapted from Birkinshaw and Morrison (1995: 748).

activities. This dependency is lower for world mandate subsidiaries than for the two other types. Inter-affiliate purchases are products or components that the subsidiary buys from other parts of the MNC. Local implementers and specialized contributors are strongly bound to the MNC by such material flows, world mandate subsidiaries more weakly. International dispersion of manufacturing and of downstream activities shows to what extent the activities performed by the subsidiary also take place at other locations within the MNC. The activities of local implementers tend to be specific to their location, and hence are not replicated elsewhere in the MNC. The activities of specialized contributors are more strongly linked to like operations elsewhere in the world; world mandate subsidiaries fall between these two types in this respect.

If we tentatively link the three subsidiary roles with the MNC typology of Bartlett and Ghoshal, a first remark should be that each of the three kinds of subsidiary could be assumed to exist within each of the four types of MNC. However, the description of the subsidiary roles suggests that the local implementer may be assumed to be particularly prominent in international MNCs and multidomestic MNCs. Within the second type of MNC the local implementer will have more autonomy than within the first. The specialized contributor is more likely to be found in the global MNC. The world mandate subsidiary, finally, fits best with the transnational MNC. In this type of MNC the idea that different capabilities may be concentrated in different subsidiaries, and that, consequently, some subsidiaries (rather than headquarters) should have central authority in some fields, is most likely to be accepted.

Birkinshaw and Morrison (1995), in their study, also checked for the need for global integration and the need for local responsiveness, as perceived by the subsidiaries. While there were no significant differences between the three subsidiary types regarding the perceived need for global integration, local implementers expressed a significantly higher need for local adaptation than world mandate subsidiaries. Specialized contributors fall in between. The link between the management of headquarters–subsidiary relationships and the environment was further explored in a study of 618 headquarters–subsidiary relationships by Ghoshal and Nohria (1989). These authors linked parameters describing the degree of centralization, formalization and socialization (comparable with Harzing's personalized supervision, formalized bureaucratic and socialization network control types, respectively) in these relationships to the complexity/stability of the environment and the local resources commanded by the subsidiaries. In their relationships with subsidiaries operating in complex environments and commanding abundant local resources, MNC headquarters rely relatively little on centralization of authority, and relatively much on formal control and socialization. Centralization is lowest when local resources are abundant, but the local environment is stable. These subsidiaries are left to look after themselves, one might say. If the environmental complexity is high but local resources are limited, centralization is intermediate and formalization is low. The picture with regard to subsidiaries with limited local resources and operating in a stable environment was less clear, in that no statistically significant differences between these subsidiaries and any of the other group were found. Although not directly comparable to the study of Birkinshaw and Morrison (1995), these results suggest that important environmental variables influence the headquarters–subsidiary relationship.

In a later study, Ghoshal and Nohria (1993) focused on the differentiation of subsidiary roles within MNCs. They looked at the pressures to localize and those to globally integrate in the environment of the MNC, and at the internal integration and differentiation in headquarters–subsidiary relationships. A high internal integration means that the MNC intensively uses authority hierarchies, formalized bureaucratic systems and/or socialization mechanisms to achieve a high degree of coordination across its different units. The differentiation dimension pertains to the question of whether the mix of coordination mechanisms used and/or their intensity differs between subsidiaries, or that MNC headquarters manages all subsidiaries in a uniform way. Putting these two dimensions together, Ghoshal and Nohria (1993) specify four patterns of the overall structuring of headquarters–subsidiary relationships (see Figure 9.5).

Figure 9.5 Patterns of structuring of headquarters–subsidiary relationships

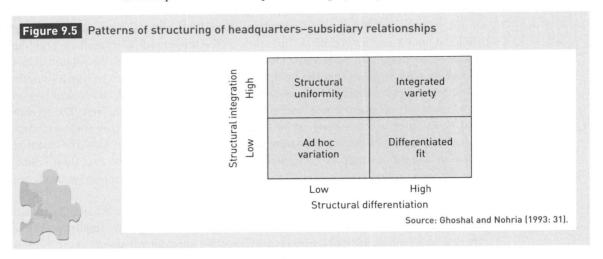

Source: Ghoshal and Nohria (1993: 31).

Structural uniformity is the pattern in which the structural integration (through hierarchy, bureaucratic means and/or socialization) is strong and uniform throughout the MNC. There is one 'company way' of managing subsidiary relationships. In the *differentiated fit* variety, different coordination mechanisms are used for different subsidiaries. This is also true for the pattern of *integrated variety*, but in this case the MNC overlays one dominant integrative mechanism (which may be of a hierarchical, bureaucratic or socializing kind) for all relationships. Hence, there is more integration of coordination mechanisms than in the previous category. In the case of *ad hoc variation*, finally, there is neither a dominant coordination mechanism nor a clear pattern of differentiation of coordination mechanisms used across subsidiaries.

Ghoshal and Nohria (1993) predicted that MNCs that matched their pattern of headquarters–subsidiary relationship to their environment would be most successful. The differentiated fit pattern was expected to do best in an environment characterized by high pressures for localizing and weak pressures for globalizing (i.e. calling for a multidomestic approach). The structural uniformity pattern fits best in an environment with strong pressure to globalize and weak pressure to localize (the global approach), and the integrated variety pattern in environments with both strong pressures to localize and to globalize (transnational management). Based on their limited dataset of 41 MNCs the authors came to the conclusion that MNCs that managed their headquarters–subsidiary relationships in a way that fits their environment did indeed perform better than the other MNCs, in terms of return on net assets, growths of these returns and revenue growth.

The upshot is that effective MNC management does not only mean that the MNC should have the right macro organizational structure and apply the right mix of coordination mechanisms, but should also be able to differentiate its approach to different kinds of subsidiary, as the modern MNC is a differentiated network of units, in which the function of each element to the whole determines the pattern of coordination mechanisms to be used. In the next section we will put this complex picture in a more dynamic light, by focusing on the question of how the internal management of MNCs enables them to learn and develop over time.

9.4   Knowledge Management in the MNC

Increasingly, the competitive advantage of companies is seen as residing in their unique sets of competencies and capabilities. As competencies and capabilities can be acquired or copied by competitors, a firm has to work continuously on their further development if it is to remain competitive (Senge, 1990). The concept of the transnational MNC fits very well in this new perspective, as it emphasizes the importance of MNCs' capacity to learn, combining knowledge inputs from all of its dispersed units in flexible ways. In this section, we will discuss the learning MNC in more detail.

Exploitative and explorative learning in the MNC

Looking at the concept of learning, it is first of all important to distinguish between exploitative and explorative learning (March, 1991). Exploitative learning consists of the MNC trying to become better in what it is already capable of doing; its effect is more efficient operation in known fields. The essence of explorative learning is experimentation with new alternatives. The outcome is more uncertain, but may consist of the MNC starting completely new activities. In order to be effective, the MNC must engage in both exploitative and explorative learning, but the balance may differ between companies, industries and time periods. Traditional theories of the MNC, such as Dunning's eclectic paradigm, discussed at the beginning of this chapter, have concentrated predominantly on exploitative learning: the MNC has a particular capability and looks for new locations to better exploit that capability. Hence the emphasis is on the flow of knowledge from headquarters (or the home-country organization) to subsidiaries abroad. However, if we also focus on explorative learning, the two-way flow of information and knowledge, both between subsidiaries and headquarters and among subsidiaries, becomes more important. Moreover, a more balanced view of the motives for foreign expansion is due. MNCs not only invest abroad to further exploit their existing capabilities, but also to be able to acquire new knowledge. This type of foreign investment can be called 'knowledge-seeking FDI' (Makino and Inkpen, 2003: 239). This means that the MNC invests in certain countries or regions because it seeks critical capabilities that are bound to those locations (e.g. because they reside in local inter-firm networks). An example is the City of London as an attractor of FDI from knowledge-seeking MNCs in the financial services sector (Nachum, 2003).

Organizing for explorative learning puts different demands on the MNC: 'the distance in time and space between the locus of learning and the locus for the realization of returns is generally greater in the case of exploration than in the case of exploitation, as is the uncertainty' (March, 1991: 85). Hence, it becomes unpredictable where in the MNC new knowledge will originate, and where it will be put to use. As a consequence, the MNC also cannot tell which of the many potentially important intra-firm relationships it has to invest in and foster. For the transnational this is a crucial issue, for the capability of the MNC to effectively transfer know-how and capabilities from one unit to another is far from self-evident (Cerny, 1996). Buckley and Carter (1999: 80) observe that 'organizational and cultural barriers internal to the firm become a prime concern when the firm's management is seeking the most effective use of its intangible knowledge assets' ('intangible knowledge assets' referring to know-how and capabilities).

Gupta and Govindarajan (1991) distinguish between four types of subsidiary, in as far as their role in MNC knowledge development is concerned. Some subsidiaries, 'global innovators', serve as the source of knowledge in a particular field for all other parts of the MNC. Other types of subsidiary ('implementers') receive knowledge from headquarters or other subsidiaries and apply it locally, without transferring any knowledge back to other parts of the MNC. 'Integrated players' both give and take, sometimes and in some areas functioning as the source of information, and at other times or in other areas of knowledge as the receptor. 'Local innovators', finally, do develop new knowledge, but this remains specific to their own area of application, and is not shared with other parts of the MNC. Traditionally, MNCs consisted predominantly of foreign subsidiaries acting as implementers and local innovators, the bulk of the innovation coming from the home country organization. This made the demands placed on the MNC organization in terms of communication and coordination relatively easy and predictable. Local innovators and implementers require less communication and coordination than the two other types of subsidiary. Gupta and Govindarajan (1991) predict that global innovators and integrated players will be linked to the rest of the MNC through various integration mechanisms and more intense communication.

In a later empirical study, these authors found that coordination mechanisms allowing for rich information transmission (in terms of the informality, openness and density of the communication) positively and significantly influence both the outflow of knowledge from subsidiaries to other parts of the MNC and the inflow into the subsidiary of information from other parts of the MNC (Gupta and Govindarajan, 2000). They found this effect both for formal integrative mechanisms (liaison personnel, task forces, permanent committees) and for more informal corporate socialization mechanisms (job transfers among subsidiaries, and between subsidiaries and headquarters, participation in multisubsidiary executive programmes, participation in corporate mentoring programmes). These types of coordination mechanism all seem to fall under the rubric of what we have called 'socialization and networks'.

The costs of transnational management

The upshot of the discussion in the previous subsection seems to be that transnational management emphasizing both exploitative and explorative learning not only requires the MNC to invest in intensive, and hence costly, coordination mechanisms, but also impedes a strict a priori selection of the intra-firm links to invest in. With regard to this second issue, headquarters cannot predict where in the MNC network crucial new knowledge can be developed by what combination of subsidiaries, so all possible links should, in principle, be kept open. This strategy, however, obviously entails costs that can easily become prohibitive. The theoretical number of links varies between network structures. In a 'star structure', one central node is connected to all other nodes, which remain unconnected to each other. In this structure, the number of links is equal to the number of nodes. If an MNC with such an internal structure has n subsidiaries, it also has n intra-organizational links to maintain. This would be the archetypical international or multidomestic type of MNC, in which only headquarters–subsidiaries relationships are invested in, and links between subsidiaries remain unimportant. The transnational, however, can better be compared with the theoretical structure of the 'fully connected network', in which each node is directly connected to each other node. Here, if n is the number of nodes, the number of links becomes $(n^2-n)/2$. As an example, take an MNC with 20 local subsidiaries. In a star structure, the number of intra-firm relationships would be 20; but in a fully connected network, the number of links to be maintained would be no less than 190. Clearly the costs of maintaining a network of this size can become a serious competitive disadvantage, at least if the links are to be of the kind that enables the exchange of knowledge that is often difficult to codify.

This brings us to the other point. Transnational MNCs rely relatively much on expensive forms of coordination. Hierarchical coordination and bureaucratic control processes are less important than in the more traditional forms of MNC management. These coordination mechanisms – and the same is true of output control – are not very conducive to the speedy, improvised and high-quality exchange of ideas associated with explorative learning in a differentiated network of MNC units. The knowledge to be exchanged will very often be partly implicit and difficult to codify. As a result the MNC must extensively use coordination mechanisms that allow unstructured information to be exchanged between units in a flexible way. As a result there will be, relatively, much emphasis on coordination through socialization and networks.

This can be clarified with the distinction Thompson (1967) made between various types of interdependence between individuals or units. Thompson distinguished between three types of interdependency (see Figure 9.6). In the case of *pooled interdependence*, two units depend on the inputs from a third unit for their own tasks. However, after having received this input the two units can function independently from each other. If there is *sequential interdependence*, one unit depends on the inputs from a second unit for the fulfilment of its task, and a third unit in turn is dependent on its own output. *Reciprocal interdependence*, finally, is the term Thompson uses for situations in which units depend on each other's outputs in complex and unpredictable ways.

The three kinds of interdependency can be linked to the types of coordination mechanisms discussed earlier in this chapter. Pooled interdependence exists, for instance, between the subsidiaries of a multidomestic MNC. They are all dependent on headquarters' decisions with regard to targets and budgets, but once these have been decided upon, each subsidiary can go its own way. This type of interdependence can be managed through output control. Sequential interdependence is typical of the relationship between functional departments within a firm. Within an MNC the various production units will often be organized internally along these lines (the following discussion is based on Egelhoff, 1993). Sequential interdependence can effectively be managed through bureaucratic formalized control if the issue is of a routine nature, and through hierarchical

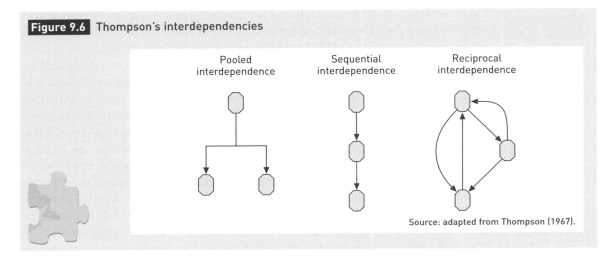

Figure 9.6 Thompson's interdependencies

Pooled interdependence

Sequential interdependence

Reciprocal interdependence

Source: adapted from Thompson (1967).

referral (personal centralized control) if it concerns non-routine issues. Reciprocal interdependence is the kind of interdependence between parties engaged in complex tasks. This is the type of interdependence that at the micro level can be found within departments of units. If this type of interdependency pertains to routine issues, it can be managed through information systems that allow all parties concerned access to a dynamic and interactive database. If the issue is non-routine, however (as in the case of explorative learning within the MNC), the information that needs to be exchanged and discussed will typically not be the type of standard data one can find in the company's computer systems. Hence, coordination forms that allow for rich, face-to-face information exchange are called for. These are the socialization and networking kinds of coordination mechanism, like task forces consisting of members from different units and/or departments, teams, managers with integrating roles, and so on. It is not possible to unambiguously rank the coordination mechanisms according to their cost. For instance, personal centralized control requires little set-up cost, but the ongoing costs of maintaining this type of coordination are relatively high. For bureaucratic formalized control, it is just the other way around. At any rate, control by socialization and networks can be characterized as high cost, meaning that the management of transnationals as envisaged by Bartlett and Ghoshal (1989) may very well be prohibitively expensive.

9.5　The MNC and Cultural and Institutional Differences

In this final section of the chapter we will discuss how cultural and institutional differences impact on the MNC. In a way, the entire chapter has focused on this issue, for it is mainly because of this cultural and institutional diversity that the management and organization of MNCs is different from that of large domestically operating firms. Here, however, we will first reiterate what the influence of cultural and institutional diversity on MNCs can be expected to be, and inspect the (scarce) relevant empirical evidence. After that, we will look at the issue from a different angle, and explore the question of 'country-of-origin' effects on MNCs or, in other words, how the management and organization of the MNC as a whole is influenced by its home country.

How do MNCs respond to cultural and institutional diversity?

The decision of an MNC concerning the macro structure most suited to dealing with the institutional and cultural diversity of the environments in which the company is operating can be compared to the 'order penetration point' decision. In deciding where the order penetration point will be located, a firm determines which of its activities will be influenced by market fluctuations, and which not. In mass production, the production process itself is normally scheduled ahead, but the distribution of the final product is determined by the demand. In case of production to order, all or part of the production processes are influenced by the demand fluctuations while, for instance, purchasing activities may be scheduled ahead. By analogy, we could speak about the 'diversity penetration point' in the MNC. In a multidomestic MNC the main interface between the cultural and institutional diversity in the MNC's various environments and the core of the MNC (i.e. that part of the MNC that does not adapt to the specificities of any of the localities in which it does business – other than that of the home country, see the next subsection) lies between headquarters and the regional divisions. The regional divisions adapt to the specific demands of their environments, as well as the diversity in the subenvironments they are dealing with. Headquarters guards over the common characteristics and capabilities of the MNC. In the global MNC the interface between the diverse environments and the MNC is in the relationships between product-based divisions and their subsidiaries in different countries. This means that this intercultural and inter-institutional interface has to be managed in many more intra-firm relationships than in the multidomestic MNC, which will be possible only if the cultural and institutional diversity is smaller or of less relevance. In the transnational, finally, the situation is more complex. Here there is a diversity interface between the product-based part of the organization and the subsidiaries in different countries. This interface will in many cases be managed in coordination with the region-based part of the MNC (assuming a matrix-like macro organizational structure). On top of this, however, relationships between subsidiaries are also more frequent and important, meaning that cultural and institutional differences will also have to be managed in these relationships. As a consequence, the number of diversity interfaces is multiplied in comparison with the global MNC. This may be problematic, as the transfer of knowledge across cultural boundaries confronts the MNC with increased complexities (Inkpen, 1998).

The task of operating the interface between the different cultures within which the MNC operates is more difficult the greater the cultural distance between the units concerned. Hence we may expect that MNCs adapt their control strategy to this cultural distance. The small number of empirical studies focusing on this issue provides some clues that this is indeed the case. Hennart and Larimo (1998) found that a larger cultural distance between the home country of the MNC and the subsidiary country made it more likely that the MNC would choose shared ownership of the subsidiary (i.e. a joint venture) rather than a wholly owned subsidiary. Although the scope of this study is restricted (only two home countries and one host country, and only ownership of subsidiaries as dependent variable), it does indeed suggest that the cultural diversity an MNC has to deal with has an influence on its internal management. On the basis of this finding one would be inclined to speculate that when the cultural distance that needs to be bridged is larger, MNCs opt for less strict control and more flexibility. This is confirmed by Harzing's (1999) study of 287 subsidiaries of 104 MNCs, in which she found that a larger cultural distance was associated with more use of personal centralized control, and less use of output control and bureaucratic formalized control. However, whereas the findings from these two studies suggest that with a larger cultural distance MNC headquarters leave more room for local adaptation, Rosenzweig and Nohria (1994), in a study of human resource management (HRM) practices in 249 US subsidiaries of MNCs from eight foreign countries, found that a larger cultural distance made it somewhat less likely that the MNC followed local US HRM practices. Furthermore, they found that as MNCs use more expatriates and as there is more frequent communication between the subsidiary and headquarters, it is more likely that home-country (instead of host-country) HRM practices are maintained.

Although the findings pertaining to the adaptation of MNC policies to local culture discussed above are far from conclusive, a study by Newman and Nollen (1996) provides some evidence that this type of adaptation does in fact lead to greater effectiveness. These authors studied 176 work units in 18 foreign subsidiaries of one US corporation, and found that units with practices better fitting the local culture (operationalized along Hofstede's dimensions) performed better than units with less fitting practices. This corresponds to the general trend in the literature that, although the empirical evidence is scarce, consistently points at the importance for MNCs of taking cultural differences into account in their internal management. For instance, Brock *et al.* (2000) theorize that differences in national culture will affect the planning approaches preferred by headquarters and subsidiaries. Welch and Welch (1997) put forward that national cultural differences will make it more difficult for MNCs to impose parent–company values on their diverse foreign affiliates, hence this favoured coordination mechanism may in fact be difficult to implement. Hofstede (2001: 442) opines that, in particular, power distance differences in which MNC headquarters is influenced by a high power–distance culture, and the subsidiary by a low power–distance culture, lead to problems; the opposite situation would be much easier to deal with. On the other hand, Hofstede expects differences in uncertainty avoidance to be equally problematic, whichever way they go. The conclusion can be drawn that, whereas there are many indications that cultural diversity is indeed an important factor in the management of MNCs, as yet it is difficult to offer specific guidance as to the best way to deal with this diversity.

The situation is not significantly different if we look at institutional differences. The general thrust of the literature is that MNCs need to adapt to local institutional idiosyncracies, but there is a paucity of systematic empirical research (Westney, 1999). Furthermore, there is an overlap between the presumed influence of institutional differences and that of cultural differences. For instance, Hofstede (2001: 443) states that cultural values become (partly) institutionalized in, say, legislation, labour union structures and organizations of stakeholders. In addition, some categories of institution, like the normative component of the institutional profile of a country described by Kostova and Roth (2002: 217) as 'the values, beliefs, norms and assumptions about human nature and human behavior held by the individuals in a given country', seem to be identical to culture. However, institutional environments are assumed to influence MNCs in ways that are different from that ascribed to culture. Culture enters into the equation through the beliefs and preferences of individuals, predominantly in their roles as managers, employees and other stakeholders of the MNC.

The adaptation of the MNC to local institutions is assumed to be a more conscious process. Three mechanisms are usually distinguished (Westney, 1993). Institutions may have a 'coercive' influence, meaning that the MNC is forced by a powerful authority, usually the state, to adapt its organization in a certain way. A second possibility is that the institutional influence is 'normative' – that is, organizational patterns that are deemed to be appropriate within a certain environment are championed (but not coercively prescribed) by, say, professional associations. Third, the influence may be of the 'mimetic' kind, in that the MNC copies organizational features from other companies (local companies or other MNCs) that are seen as successful. In all cases, the MNC adapts its organization to acquire or maintain legitimacy in the perspective of powerful stakeholders, and in this way to increase its chances of survival and success. However, this adaptation is restricted to the extent that the MNC also strives for integration across countries and regions (Westney, 1993).

All organizations are subject to institutional influences, but what is typical for the MNC is that it is subject to a variety of different and potentially contradictory influences in the different environments in which it operates (Westney, 1993: 60). At the same time, because of the need for global integration in order to utilize organizational capabilities worldwide, there will be an internal drive in the MNC towards standardization of structures and processes within the company. As a result the MNC faces a unique institutional complexity, and local subsidiaries are faced with 'institutional duality': they have to maintain legitimacy both in their local environment and within the MNC (Kostova and Roth, 2002: 216). The tension between institutional pressure from the environment and from the MNC is felt within the local subsidiaries. Kostova and Roth show how the extent to which subsidiaries adopt practices institutionalized within the MNC (in their research this was a quality management system) depends, among other things, on the degree of fit between the practice and their local institutional environment. Some of the other factors influencing the extent of adaptation pertain to the subsidiary–parent relationship. The expectation would be that stronger subsidiaries (in terms of capabilities, value added and influence within the MNC) will have stronger local links with customers and suppliers, and will adapt relatively more to local institutions and less to MNC practices (Rosenzweig and Singh, 1991). However, Kostova and Roth's (2002) findings point in the opposite direction: subsidiaries that seem to be more dependent on the MNC report *lower* degrees of adaptation to MNC practices. This suggests that much more research is needed in order to unveil the true interplay of institutional influences on the MNC.

The complexity is further increased because the influence of local institutions will vary from situation to situation. For instance, it is likely to depend on the industry in which MNC operates. For MNCs in service industries, acquiring local legitimacy is essential, because of the intangible nature of services. For this reason the ability to engage in local networks and adaptation to local institutions may be particularly important (Campbell and Verbeke, 1994). Second, MNCs may choose to locate in regions within a country where local institutional pressures are weakest. This is, for instance, the case with many Japanese automobile manufacturing subsidiaries in the USA, which were targeted at regions where the influence of the traditional automobile labour union was weak or non-existent (Westney, 1993). The influence of state policies may be assumed to vary with the policy credibility of the government in question. When the government is not perceived to be credible in its commitments (e.g. because of past policy changes, or because of its attitude towards business enterprises in general) attempts to influence MNCs will be likely to have only a marginal effect on MNCs, but will not fundamentally change MNC strategies (Murtha and Lenway, 1994). This is particularly true if the government's institutional pressure is of the normative, rather than coercive, kind (i.e. requirements do not take the form of formal laws, but rather of informal expectations and demands). Finally, local institutions not only influence the MNC, but this also works the other way around: the introduction by an MNC subsidiary of a new organizational practice in a country may challenge the legitimacy of existing practices, and in this way erode or change local institutions (Westney, 1993). This tendency was also documented by Lane (2000) in a study of the strategies of UK and German MNCs. Her study also made clear, however, that the strategies of these companies for the time being remain heavily influenced by their home countries. We will now turn to this 'country-of-origin effect'.

The country-of-origin effect on MNCs

In the globalization literature the MNC is presented as a harbinger of global practices (Dicken 1998). However, far from being 'nationless', even the most global MNCs in many respects still seem to be strongly rooted in their country of origin (this section is based on Noorderhaven and Harzing, 2003). Various studies have pointed at this 'country-of-origin' effect. In particular, human resource management practices (Ngo *et al.*, 1998) and control strategies (Lubatkin *et al.*, 1998; Harzing and Sorge, 2003) reflect specific influences of the home countries of MNCs. Country-of-origin effects can be caused by both the cultural and the institutional specificities of the home country of the MNC. The underlying assumption of the culturalist approach is that individual inhabitants of a country are 'mentally programmed' by the way they were raised by their parents and peers, and by the institutions of the country (Hofstede, 2001). This makes them adopt broad preferences for certain states of affairs that they share with their compatriots. In the institutionalist perspective – for example, the 'business systems' approach (Whitley and Kristensen, 1996), differences in the structures and operations of firms 'clearly stem from variations in dominant social institutions such as the state and the financial system' (Whitley, 1992: 1).

Why, though, would these national factors influence MNCs operating in dozens of countries? A possible explanation is corporate inertia. MNCs may continue to operate in ways attuned to their cultural and institutional home country, but not necessarily to their present multifarious environments. This effect is strengthened by the fact that most MNCs continue to hire country-of-origin nationals for many of their key management positions (Perlmutter, 1969; Lane, 2000). These managers share the cultural background of their home country, and their perceptions are influenced by the institutional environment in which they grew up and were trained. The question could be asked, however, what country can be assumed to be the country of origin of an MNC? This may be another country than that in which the MNC headquarters are located, as this may be relocated (e.g. for tax reasons) at a time when the original 'imprint' of the country of origin has already been made. It makes more sense to assume that the country of origin is determined by the 'historical experience and the institutional and ideological legacies of that experience' (Pauly and Reich, 1997: 4). This means that the country in which the MNC originally 'grew up' is most relevant.

While there is mounting evidence that MNCs are indeed subject to a 'country-of-origin effect' (for an overview, see Noorderhaven and Harzing, 2003), there is less clarity about the specifics. What country specifics cause what types of MNC behaviour, and under which conditions are these effects stronger or weaker? Much work remains to be done. The following sketchy comments mainly serve as a warning that elements of national idiosyncracy can be found even within the actor that is often seen as the herald of globalization: the MNC.

Bartlett and Ghoshal (cited in Birkinshaw and Morrison, 1995: 738) had already recognized the importance of the parent country of origin, and on the basis of their observations noted that socialization was a predominant coordination mechanism in European MNCs, centralization in Japanese MNCs and formalization in US MNCs. Lubatkin *et al.* (1998), comparing the behaviour of UK and French parent firms after an acquisition, noted that the French companies made more use of expatriate management, and relied more on centralized control than the UK parent companies. More generally, reasoning from a culturalist perspective, Hofstede (2001) opines that differences in power distance and uncertainty avoidance are the most important cultural differences for MNCs (see Chapter 2). Hofstede speculates that MNCs originating in countries with a small power distance will be better able to manage subsidiaries in large power distance cultures than the other way around (Hofstede, 2001: 442). Regarding uncertainty avoidance, Hofstede expects the flexibility to use different degrees of and bases for coordination in different businesses and different parts of the world to be more prevalent in MNCs based in weak uncertainty avoidance countries than in MNCs based in strong uncertainty avoidance cultures (Hofstede, 2001: 444). This suggests that the ability to manage the MNC as a differentiated, but at the same time strongly integrated network of subsidiaries, is at least in part determined by the cultural background of the MNC. Hence, the applicability of the 'transnational solution' may not only depend on industry conditions, but also on the administrative heritage of the MNC.

Study Questions

1. Discuss the three conditions leading to the existence of multinational corporations (MNCs). Why is there no need for an MNC to arise if one of the conditions is *not* present?

2. MNCs historically have tended to develop through a number of stages. Describe these stages, and explain the factors influencing an MNC's progress through successive stages.

3. Describe the types of MNC that arise under varying combinations of weak/strong pressures for local adaptation and for global integration.

4. Describe and critically discuss the 'transnational form' of MNCs.

5. Describe the main mechanisms of coordination and control used in MNCs.

6. Discuss possible roles of subsidiaries in MNCs, in relation to the learning capabilities of the MNC.

7. Discuss the 'country-of-origin effect' on MNCs.

Further Reading

Bartlett, C.A. and Ghoshal, S. (2000) *Transnational Management: Text, Cases, and Readings in Cross-Border Management* (3rd edn). Boston, MA: McGraw-Hill.

This book is a rich source on the management of MNCs, paying particular attention to the transnational form.

Harzing, A.-W.K. (1999) *Managing the Multinationals: an International Study of Control Mechanisms*. Cheltenham, UK: Edward Elgar.

An empirical study of the use of control mechanisms within MNCs, with much attention paid to the roles and functions of expatriates.

Case: The Evolving International Structure of Heineken

Case written by N.G. Noorderhaven on the basis of interviews at Heineken corporate headquarters, and the Heineken website.

The history of Heineken beer breweries dates back to 1863. The first international expansion consisted of the opening of a brewery in Indonesia in 1931. At that time, Indonesia was a colony of the Netherlands. In the 1970s Heineken actively used licensing as an instrument of further internationalization, to France, Ireland, Spain and Italy, among other places. At present Heineken is the number two beer brewery in the world. During its history, Heineken has gone through a series of organizational structures to adapt to the growing complexity of its operations and environment. In the 1960s the company was organized into two major groups: Heineken Nederland and Heineken International. The latter was responsible for handling foreign subsidiaries and participations, and international licensing. Heineken Nederland was responsible for the home market as well as for exports (the famous 'green bottles'). Around 1970, as an answer to growing internationalization and diversification, Heineken shifted to a geographical structure, with all domestic operations (beer as well as soft drinks and distilled beverages) remaining in one group, and the international activities coordinated in four regional groupings: Europe, Asia/Australia, Africa and the 'Western Hemisphere'. Around 1983 the company had gradually moved towards a matrix structure with, on the one hand, the operating companies that had increasingly gained independence, and on the other, five regional coordinating directors (the Western Hemisphere had been split into the USA, Canada and the Caribbean and South America). A number of functional central staff departments, like Financial and Economic Affairs and Technical Affairs, provided support to the regions, and also tended to be organized along geographic lines (while all being located in the Netherlands). As the functional staff departments could have a strong influence on the operations of the operating companies, there was in practice almost a three-dimensional matrix (see Figure 9.7).

Figure 9.7 Heineken organizational structure around 1983 (simplified)

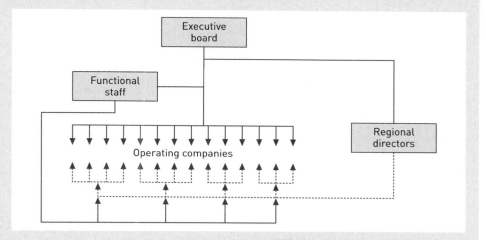

In more recent years Heineken has become an increasingly decentralized company. This was accelerated when Freddy Heineken stepped down as chairman of the executive board in 1995. His successor, Karel Vuursteen, exerted a much less dominating influence on the company. Compared to the situation in 1983, a substantial part of the corporate staff has been decentralized to the level of the regional clusters. The cluster directors are responsible for profit performance in their area, and form a liaison point between the executive board and the breweries and other plants in their region. These plants function as 'quasi-operating companies', meaning that they have a certain degree of autonomy, but not as much as that of the 'real' operating companies (OCs). These OCs report directly to the executive board. The present structure of Heineken is depicted graphically in Figure 9.8.

The policy of Heineken is to form an OC if the activities within a certain country or region exceed above a certain threshold and come to be of strategic importance. OCs work within a set of guidelines concerning financial ratios, brand policies, production standards and HRM. The aim of Heineken is to think and act both globally and locally. The company is very much aware of maintaining a strong positive corporate image, and pursues worldwide policies in the fields of employee healthcare and education, terms of employment, and adherence to environmental regulations, and regulations concerning alcohol consumption.

Figure 9.8 Organizational structure of Heineken around 2004 (simplified)

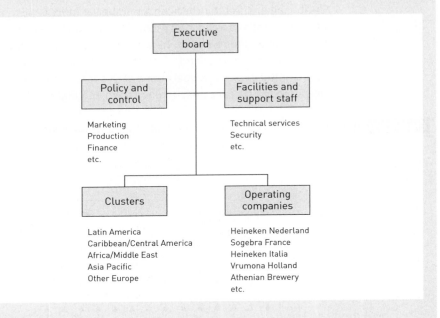

Question

1. Discuss the factors requiring Heineken to operate both in a centralized *and* in a decentralized way.

Case: Integration of the Operations of the London Branch of a German Bank

Case written by N.G. Noorderhaven on the basis of Moore (2003).

The organization described in this case is the London branch of an unidentified major German bank, headquartered in Frankfurt. The London branch was opened in 1981 and, for many years, was managed as a quasi-independent operation. Of the 160 staff members, around a third were German, Swiss or Austrian, one-tenth were non-German-speaking foreigners, the rest were British. In the summer of 1999 the bank began the implementation of a new international matrix structure. Whereas, previously, most of the contacts between the London branch and headquarters in Frankfurt had been maintained by the general manager of the branch, now individual department heads had to report directly to their superiors in Frankfurt. This integrated the activities of the London branch into the overall operations. This shift brought about considerable tensions in the London branch and, in the process, fault lines between various categories of employee became increasingly visible. In the first place there were the German expatriates sent to the London branch by headquarters for a limited period of time; these expatriates saw themselves as a bridge between the London branch and headquarters. However, for many other employees they were seen as unfit to play this role, as the assumption was that their main loyalty was with headquarters. A second group of employees was formed by locally hired Germans: employees who, although of German nationality, had been hired directly by the London branch, and hence were not in expatriate positions. These employees emphasized that their nationality did not colour their view of the relationship between the branch office and headquarters. A third category of employees, the 'Germanophiles', were those that were not German but had some particular connection to Germany or the German culture (e.g. because their spouse was of German origin). Observing the growing tensions between the expatriates and the other groups of employees, they interpreted this as a clash between two parochialisms: that of headquarters, which wanted to impose practices that were supposed to be 'global' but were in reality rooted in Germany, and that of the local staff of the London branch, who resisted any change initiated from abroad. The local UK employees, finally, framed the situation as the imposition of a hostile foreign culture. The overall effect was increased tension and suspicion between employee groups and resistance to the implementation of the matrix structure. Headquarters, while aware of this resistance, did not recognize the differences between the various groups of employees, except for the distinction between expatriates and local employees. The resistance against the matrix structure was interpreted in terms of cultural differences between the British and the German. The assumption that all employees of the London branch but the expatriates would be hostile to greater headquarters' interference alienated those groups (locally hired Germans and 'Germanophiles') who could have functioned as a bridge between headquarters and the branch office. One can speculate to what extent this made the difficulties of implementing the new structure more serious than would have been necessary.

Questions

1. What are plausible reasons for an international bank to switch to an international matrix structure?

2. What could headquarters have done differently in implementing the international matrix structure, in order to minimize resistance from the London branch?

References

Bartlett, C.A., and Ghoshal, S. (1986) Tap your subsidiaries for global reach. *Harvard Business Review* 64, 87–94.

Bartlett, C.A. and Ghoshal, S. (1989) *Transnational Management: Text, Cases, and Readings in Cross-Border Management*. Boston, MA: McGraw-Hill.

Bartlett, C.A. and Ghoshal, S. (2000) *Transnational Management: Text, Cases, and Readings in Cross-Border Management* (3rd edn). Boston, MA: Irwin.

Birkinshaw, J.M. and Morrison, A.J. (1995) Configurations of strategy and structure in subsidiaries of multinational corporations. *Journal of International Business Studies* 26, 729–53.

Bowman, E. and Hurry, D. (1993) Strategy through the option lens: an integrated view of resource investments and the incremental-choice process. *Academy of Management Review* 18, 760–82.

Brock, D.M., Barry, D. and Thomas, D.C. (2000) 'Your forward is our reverse, your right, our wrong': rethinking multinational planning processes in light of national culture. *International Business Review* 9, 687–701.

Buckley, P.J. and Casson, M. (1988) A theory of cooperation in international business, in Contractor, F.J. and Lorange, P. (eds) *Cooperative Strategies in International Business: Joint Ventures and Technology Partnerships Between Firms*. Lexington, MA: Lexington Books, 31–53.

Buckley, P.J. and Carter, M.J. (1999) Managing cross-border complementary knowledge. *International Studies of Management & Organization* 29(1), 80–104.

Campbell, A.J. and Verbeke, A. (1994) The globalization of service multinationals. *Long Range Planning* 27(2), 95–102.

Cerny, K. (1996) Making local knowledge global. *Harvard Business Review* 74 (May/June), 22–38.

Child, J. (1973). Predicting and understanding organization structure. *Administrative Science Quarterly* 17, 168–85.

Cray, D. (1984). Control and coordination in multinational corporations. *Journal of International Business Studies* 15 (Fall), 85–98.

Daniels, J.D. and Radebaugh, L.H. (2001) *International Business: Environments and Operations* (9th edn). Upper Saddle River, NJ: Prentice-Hall.

Davidson, W.H. and McFetridge, D.G. (1984) International technology transactions and the theory of the firm. *Journal of Industrial Economics* 32, 253–64.

Dicken, P. (1998) *Global Shift: Transforming the World Economy*. London: Paul Chapman.

Dunning, J.H. (1993) *Multinational Enterprise and the Global Economy*. Harrow: Addison-Wesley

Egelhoff, W.G. (1988) Strategy and structure in multinational corporations: a revision of the Stopford and Wells model. *Strategic Management Journal* 9, 1–14.

Egelhoff, W.G. (1993) Information-processing theory and the multinational corporation, in Ghoshal, S. and Westney, D.E. (eds) *Organization Theory and the Multinational Corporation*. New York: St Martin's Press, 182–210.

Erramilli, M.K. (1991) The experience factor in foreign market entry behavior of service firms. *Journal of International Business Studies* 22, 479–502.

Forsgren, M. (2002). The concept of learning in the Uppsala internationalization process model: a critical review. *International Business Review* 11, 257–77.

Franko, L.G. (1976) *The European Multinationals: a Renewed Challenge to American and British Big Business*. London: Harper & Row.

Ghoshal, S. and Nohria, N. (1989) Internal differentiation within multinational corporations. *Strategic Management Journal* 10, 323–37.

Ghoshal, S. and Nohria, N. (1993) Horses for courses: organizational forms for multinational corporations. *Sloan Management Review* 34(2), 23–35.

Gupta, A.K. and Govindarajan, V. (1991) Knowledge flows and the structure of control within multinational corporations. *Academy of Management Review* 16, 768–92.

Gupta, A.K. and Govindarajan, V. (2000) Knowledge flows within multinational corporations. *Strategic Management Journal* 21, 473–96.

Hadjikani, A. (1997). A note on the criticism against the internationalization process model. *Management International Review* 37(2), 43–66.

Harzing, A.-W.K. (1999) *Managing the Multinationals: an International Study of Control Mechanisms*. Cheltenham: Edward Elgar.

Harzing, A.-W.K. (2000) An empirical analysis and extension of the Bartlett and Ghoshal typology of multinational companies. *Journal of International Business Studies* 31(1), 101–20.

Harzing, A.-W.K. and Sorge, A. (2003) The relative impact of country-of-origin and universal contingencies on internationalization strategies and corporate control in multinational enterprises: world-wide and European perspectives. *Organization Studies* 24, 187–214.

Hedlund, G. (1986). The hyper-modern MNC – a heterarchy? *Human Resource Management* 25(1), 9–35.

Hennart, J.-F. (1991) The transaction cost theory of the multinational enterprise, in Pitelos, C.N. and Sugden, R. (eds) *The Nature of the Transnational Firm*, London: Routledge.

Hennart, J.-F. and Larimo, J. (1998) The impact of culture on the strategy of multinational enterprises: does national origin affect ownership decisions? *Journal of International Business Studies* 29(3), 515–38.

Hofstede, G. (2001) *Culture's Consequences: Comparing Values, Behaviors, Institutions and Organizations across Nations* (2nd edn). Thousand Oaks: Sage.

Inkpen, A.C. (1998) Learning and knowledge acquisition through international strategic alliances. *Academy of Management Executive* 12(4), 69–80.

Johanson, J. and Vahlne, J.-E. (1977) The internationalization process of the firm: a model of knowledge development and increasing foreign market commitments. *Journal of International Business Studies* 8, 23–32.

Johanson, J., and Wiedersheim-Paul, F. (1975) The internationalization of the firm: four cases. *Journal of Management Studies* 12, 305–22.

Kostova, T. and Roth, K. (2002) Adoption of an organizational practice by subsidiaries of multinational corporations: institutional and relational effects. *Academy of Management Journal* 45, 215–33.

Kumar, N. (1999) Multinational corporations: general principles, issues and concepts, in Tung, R.L. (ed.) *The IEBM Handbook of International Business*. London: Thomson, 424–9.

Lane, C. (2000) Understanding the globalization strategies of German and British companies, in Maurice, M. and Sorge, A. (eds) *Embedding Organizations: Societal Analysis of Actors, Organizations and Socio-economic Context*. Amsterdam: John Benjamins, 189–208.

Lubatkin, M., Calori, R., Very P. and Veiga, J.F. (1998) Managing mergers across borders: a two-nation exploration of a nationally bound administrative heritage. *Organization Science* 9, 670–84.

Makino, S. and Inkpen, A.C. (2003) Knowledge seeking FDI and learning across borders, in Easterby-Smith, M. and Lyles, M.A. (eds) *The Blackwell Handbook of Organizational Learning and Knowledge Management*. Oxford: Blackwell, 233–52.

March, J.G. (1991) Exploration and exploitation in organizational learning. *Organization Science* 2(1), 71–87.

Martinez, J.I. and Jarillo, J.J. (1989) The evolution of research on coordination mechanisms in multinational corporations. *Journal of International Business Studies* 20, 489–514.

Meyer, K.E. and Estrin, S. (2001) Brownfield entry in emerging markets. *Journal of International Business Studies* 32, 575–84.

Moore, F. (2003) Internal diversity and culture's consequences: branch/head office relations in a German financial MNC. *Management International Review* 43 (Special Issue 2003/2), 95–111.

Murtha, T.P. and Lenway, S.A. (1994) Country capabilities and the strategic state: how national political institutions affect multinational corporations' strategies. *Strategic Management Journal* 15, (Special Issue Summer), 113–29.

Nachum, L. (2003) Liability of foreigness in global competition? Financial service affiliates in the city of London. *Strategic Management Journal* 24, 1187–208.

Newman, K.L. and Nollen, S.D. (1996) Culture and congruence: the fit between management practices and national culture. *Journal of International Business Studies* 27, 753–79.

Ngo, H.-Y., Turban, D. Lau, C.-M. and Lui, S.-Y. (1998) Human resource practices and firm performance of multinational corporations: influences of country of origin. *The International Journal of Human Resource Management* 9, 632–52.

Noorderhaven, N.G. and Harzing, A.-W.K. (2003) The 'country-of-origin effect' in multinational corporations: sources, mechanisms and moderating conditions. *Management International Review* 43 (Special Issue 2003/2), 47–66.

Pauly, L.W. and Reich, S. (1997) National structures and multinational corporate behavior: enduring differences in the age of globalization. *International Organization* 51, 1–30.

Perlmutter, H.V. (1969). The tortuous evolution of the multinational company. *Columbia Journal of World Business* (Jan./Feb.), 9–18.

Polanyi, M. (1962) *Personal Knowledge*. London: Routledge.

Rosenzweig, P.M. and Nohria, N. (1994) Influences of human resource management practices in multinational corporations. *Journal of International Business Studies* 25, 229–51.

Rosenzweig, P.M. and Singh, J.V. (1991) Organizational environments and the multinational enterprise. *Academy of Management Review* 16, 340–61.

Senge, P.M. (1990) *The Fifth Discipline: the Art and Practice of the Learning Organization*. London: Century Business.

Stopford, J.M. and Wells, L.T. (1972) *Managing the Multinational Enterprise: Organization of the Firm and Ownership of the Subsidiaries*. London: Longman.

Thompson, J. (1967) *Organizations in Action*. New York: McGraw-Hill.

United Nations (1988), *Multinational Corporations in World Development*. New York: United Nations.

Welch, D. and Welch, L. (1997) Being flexible and accommodating diversity: the challenge for multinational management. *European Management Journal* 15(6), 677–85.

Westney, D.E. (1993) Institutionalization theory and the multinational corporation, in Ghoshal, S. and Westney, D.E. (eds) *Organization Theory and the Multinational Corporation*. New York: St Martin's Press, 53–76.

Westney, D.E. (1999) Organisational evolution of the multinational enterprise: an organisational sociology perspective. *Management International Review* 39 (Special Issue 1), 55–75.

Whitley, R. (1992) Introduction, in Whitley, R. (ed.) *European Business Systems: Firms and Markets in their National Contexts*. London: Sage, 1–3.

Whitley, R. and Kristensen, P.H. (eds) (1996) *The Changing European Firm: Limits to Convergence*. London: Routledge.

WIR (1999) United Nations Conference on Trade and Development, *World Investment Report 1999*.

WIR (2000) United Nations Conference on Trade and Development, *World Investment Report 2000*.

WIR (2003) United Nations Conference on Trade and Development, *World Investment Report 2003*.

Yan, A. and Zeng, M. (1999). International joint venture instability: a critique of previous research, a reconceptualization and directions for future research. *Journal of International Business Studies* 30, 397–414.

Chapter 10

Multinational Corporations: Comparative Corporate Strategy

ASWIN VAN OIJEN AND PATRICK VAN ROOY

Learning Objectives

By the end of this chapter you will be able to:

- understand the concept of corporate strategy
- appreciate the different types of corporate strategy that firms adopt
- understand the different theories that are used to explain corporate strategies
- evaluate the usefulness of these theories for explaining differences and similarities in cross-national corporate strategies
- critically assess the ability of institutional theory to explain comparative corporate strategy
- explain the variables that firms should ensure that they take into account when they choose a corporate strategy
- assess whether corporate strategies converge or diverge across regions.

Chapter Outline

10.1 Introduction

10.2 Corporate Strategy

10.3 Theoretical Approaches to Corporate Strategy
Universalistic Explanations of Corporate Strategy
Particularistic Explanations of Corporate Strategy

10.4 Comparative Empirical Studies
Kogut, Walker and Anand
Mayer and Whittington
The car and steel industry

10.5 Model
Strategic planning
The model
Expectations

10.6 Conclusions
Study Questions
Further Reading
Case: Examples of Five Different Firms
References

10.1 Introduction

Strategy occupies the minds, not only of managers, but also of other important stakeholders of the firm, such as directors, shareholders and unions. The reason is that strategic decisions are both influential and enduring. They have major consequences for many stakeholders. Moreover, they commit a firm for a long period, because revocations are difficult, costly or both.

The importance of strategy is reflected in the academic literature. Following the seminal contributions from Ansoff (1965), Chandler (1962) and Rumelt (1974), strategy has developed into one of the largest fields, if not *the* largest field, within management research. It should come as no surprise, then, that strategy today is a rich field, encompassing a rather wide variety of more specific topics, such as entry modes (Chapter 9), decision-making processes, implementation mechanisms and different types of strategy, like functional strategy, business strategy, global strategy and corporate strategy.

In this chapter, we confine ourselves to corporate strategy. This type of strategy represents the highest level of firm strategy. Developments in corporate strategy are often highly visible, making it to the headlines of newspapers (at least of their financial sections) every day. We examine whether and how corporate strategy is influenced by the environment of the firm, and whether corporate strategy is characterized by convergence or divergence across countries. More precisely, we try to answer whether there are differences or similarities between the corporate strategies adopted by firms in different countries and whether they are becoming smaller or larger.

Before we answer these questions, for readers who do not have a background in strategy, in the next section, we briefly explain the concept as well as the different types of corporate strategy firms can adopt. Readers who are familiar with these topics can go immediately to Section 10.3, which discusses several theories that can be used to explain corporate strategy. Section 10.3 starts by addressing the widely used universalistic explanations of corporate strategy. Next, it explains how the institutional approach can be usefully applied to explaining differences in corporate strategy between countries.

The application of institutional theory to corporate strategy is relatively new and few studies have applied it in their empirical analysis. Nevertheless, there are some interesting studies of which we think students of international comparative management should be aware. Hence, in Section 10.4, we present a summary of two larger-scale empirical studies that compare corporate strategies across countries – the study by Kogut *et al.* (2002) and research by Mayer and Whittington (1999, 2000). We add the results of our own study on the car and the steel industry in the USA, Germany and Japan. The analysis in these three studies is based on institutional theory. This provides us with a blunt illustration of the limits of the approach for explaining cross-national differences and similarities in corporate strategy.

In Section 10.5, we present a model that should help us to arrive at a more complete understanding of cross-national corporate strategies. The model should also enable us to predict the direction of change in corporate strategy across countries – in other words, whether corporate strategies will converge or diverge across countries. The model incorporates factors from both the particularistic and universalistic theories. The last Section, 10.6, presents the conclusions to this chapter.

10.2 Corporate Strategy

Different types of strategy can be distinguished: international strategy, corporate strategy, business strategy and functional strategy. Each type of strategy answers a distinct question. International strategy answers the question 'In what geographic regions does a company compete?' For example, a company could limit its activities to its home country or expand globally. Corporate strategy deals with the question 'In what industries or businesses does a company compete?' A company could be, for example, active in just one industry or in many different industries. The question that is central to business or competitive strategy is 'How does a company compete in a given industry or geographic region?' For example, a company could compete by minimizing its costs, enabling it to charge lower prices for its products or services than competitors do and thus attract many customers. Alternatively, the company could compete by offering a product or service with unique features, enabling it to attract customers who are prepared to pay a premium price (Porter, 1985). Finally, functional strategy revolves around the question 'How does a company improve the competitiveness of functional activities within the company?' Examples of functional activities are production, marketing, finance, and research and development. In production, for example, a company could embrace Taylorism or the Japanese model.

This chapter is about corporate strategy. Other types of strategy that are interesting from a comparative management perspective are treated in different parts of the book. For example, international strategy is explained in Chapter 9. Aspects of finance strategy and production strategy are discussed in Chapters 6 and 7, respectively. Strategy in this chapter deals with the industries in which a company is active, or, in other words, its portfolio of businesses.

Within the broad category of corporate strategy, various more specific options exist. Several schemes to classify these options have been developed (see e.g. Ansoff, 1965; Porter, 1980; Palepu, 1985). Probably the best-known scheme was designed by Rumelt (1974). Rumelt assigns firms to nine different diversification categories, depending on their scores on a number of quantitative and qualitative criteria. For our purpose, a less elaborate classification is sufficient (Figure 10.1). We distinguish two dimensions – level and direction – which, in combination, lead to three types of corporate strategy.

With respect to the level, a distinction can be made between companies that generate their sales in just one industry or business, and companies that generate their sales in more than one industry or business. Consequently, there are single-business companies and diversified companies. In the second case, the businesses can be related or unrelated. This results in, respectively, related-diversified companies and unrelated-diversified companies. Companies that are active in many unrelated businesses can also be referred to as conglomerates.

This classification scheme may seem quite straightforward. The application in practice, however, often proves to be tricky. There is always an element of judgement involved. For example, it is not always clear what constitutes a separate industry or business and, as a result, whether a company is active in one industry or in several industries. Furthermore, there is no clear separation between related and unrelated. Some similarities between a company's activities can always be detected, but the question is whether

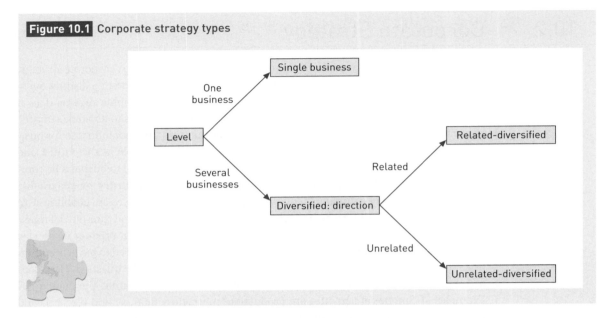

Figure 10.1 Corporate strategy types

these are strong enough to allow the label related-diversified instead of unrelated-diversified. Since unrelated diversification has been in bad odour with the financial media, top managers often maintain that their companies' activities are related, whereas, in reality, the relationships are often superficial. A final caveat is that companies might actually belong to more than one category. Hanson Trust, for example, consisted of four clusters of businesses that were clearly unrelated. Nevertheless, within each cluster the similarities were very strong.

10.3 ☙ Theoretical Approaches to Corporate Strategy

Various theories have been used to explain corporate strategy. Following the suggestions presented in the introductory chapter, these theories can be divided into universalistic and particularistic. This section starts off by explaining several universalistic theories that are commonly used to explain corporate strategy. Subsequently, we discuss industrial organization, transaction cost economics, agency theory, dominant logic, the resource-based view of the firm, the organizational learning perspective and strategic contingency theory.

After that, we focus on institutional theory as the sole example of a particularistic theory, which has been applied to explaining corporate strategy. The application of other particularistic theories, like the cultural approach, to corporate strategy has yet to take off in the literature.

Universalistic explanations of corporate strategy
Industrial organization

According to the structure–conduct–performance paradigm from industrial economics, the structure of an industry determines the behaviour of the firms active in that industry, which, in turn, drives their performance. For example, if the concentration in the industry is low (i.e. there are many competitors with small market shares), firms are expected to engage in fierce competition, which reduces their profitability. In this view, firms diversify because this gives access to market power, which reduces competition and, consequently, boosts their performance (Montgomery, 1994).

Diversified firms can use several instruments to reduce competition (Williamson, 1975; Palepu, 1985; Montgomery, 1994). Cross-subsidization involves the use of profits gained in one industry to support activities in another. Specifically, a diversified firm can afford 'predatory pricing', charging low prices that attract many customers, but do not cover all the costs. A single-business competitor, which presumably lacks the 'deep pockets' required to sustain low price levels, may eventually be forced to exit the industry. Reciprocal buying and selling can be applied if a firm's potential customer is, at the same time, the firm's potential supplier. The firms can then come to an agreement like 'I buy from you if you buy from me' (Williamson, 1975: 163). The chances that a firm can be supplier and buyer simultaneously are higher when it is diversified into several businesses. The result is that markets are closed to undiversified competitors. A final instrument is mutual forbearance. Diversified firms meeting each other in multiple industries sooner or later recognize their mutual dependence. For example, if a firm competes too fiercely in one industry, a diversified competitor can retaliate in this particular industry, but also in all the other industries they share. Therefore, the decision could be made to compete less vigorously.

Product diversification to wield market power can thus be very beneficial to the financial health of the firm. The verdict from a policy-maker's perspective is the reverse, though. Any strategy that has anti-competitive effects is seen as potentially harmful to society as a whole.

Transaction cost economics

Transaction cost economics can be seen as a response to neoclassical economics. Departing from the neoclassical economist's strong belief in the infallibility of markets, firms are, at best, irrelevant. However, Williamson (1975) identified a number of factors that lead to high transaction costs and, as a result, cause market failure. Activities should then be coordinated within firms, instead of across markets.

Product diversification can also be regarded as a response to market failure. In theory, activities in two different industries could be assigned to two independent firms. Any necessary coordination between the two firms could take place via the market. For example, if one firm produces jet engines and the other produces aircraft, the two could write a contract for the supply of jet engines. Nevertheless, markets can fail, necessitating the coordination of the activities in the different industries within one firm, which then becomes diversified. Two types of market have been emphasized: the capital market and the market for excess resources.

A company may need to attract outside capital to fund an investment proposal. However, it is likely to be reluctant to disseminate all relevant information to potential outside investors, since they could use the information opportunistically and copy the investment proposal to start their own activities or pass the information on to competitors. This danger would be greatly reduced if the company were not independent, but part of a multibusiness corporation. All businesses would present their investment proposals to corporate headquarters, which has no incentive to use the information opportunistically. Subsequently, corporate headquarters would reallocate the cash flows it has withdrawn from the businesses to the most attractive investment proposals. This creates, in effect, an internal capital market, in which the allocation of funds is more efficient than in the external capital market. Besides, corporate headquarters has at its disposal a wide range of subtle mechanisms to motivate business managers. The external capital market only has crude mechanisms to discipline managers (Williamson, 1975).

A single-business company could possess excess resources (Teece, 1982). It may have physical equipment or know-how that is not needed for its current activities, but that could be put to use in a new industry. Because the costs of developing the resources have already been incurred, economies of scope would be the result. Economies of scope arise when the cost of combined production of several products or services are lower than the cost of producing each product or service separately (Panzar and Willig, 1975). Economies of scope do not provide a sufficient reason for a single-business company to diversify, since the excess resources could also be traded across a market to another company active in a different industry. However, markets for excess resources may also fail. For example, know-how often cannot be described in the form of a blueprint or formula because it has a tacit and learning-by-doing character. Therefore, the transfer of the know-how to the buying company necessitates continuing support by a team of people from the selling company. This may be costly to organize across markets. To economize on these transaction costs, the managers of the single-business company may decide to use the excess resources to start activities in the other industry on their own, or, in other words, to *diversify*.

Because the same resources can only be used when the activities in the different industries are similar, economies of scope can only be achieved in the case of related diversification. In contrast, the internal capital market can be realized both by unrelated-diversified and by related-diversified firms. Since economies of scope and the internal capital market require different and conflicting implementation mechanisms, related-diversified firms have to focus on either economies of scope or the internal capital market (Hill and Hoskisson, 1987).

Agency theory

Agency theory revolves around the conflict of interest between principal and agent. The agent is hired to perform some activity on behalf of the principal, but the agent also has his or her personal interests, which may urge him or her not to act in the best interests of the principal. Traditionally, and also in the context of corporate diversification, the principals are the owners or shareholders of a firm, while the agents are the firm's top managers (Berle and Means, 1932). Firms, in particular those that are active in mature industries, often have what Jensen (1986) calls 'free cash flow'. Free cash flow is cash flow in excess of that needed to fund all projects with a positive net present value (when discounted at the relevant cost of capital). Free cash flow should be returned to the shareholders, since reinvestment in the firm would harm its value. Nevertheless, the top managers are reluctant to surrender the free cash flow, as this would reduce the resources they control and the power they wield. Instead, they prefer to spend the free cash flow on wasteful projects, such as diversification.

Apart from the pleasures of empire building, top managers have various motives for choosing diversification (Hoskisson and Hitt, 1990; Montgomery, 1994). Diversification and firm size are strongly correlated. The same goes for firm size and the level of compensation of its top managers. As a result, top managers can use diversification to boost their compensation. The second motive is managerial entrenchment. Top managers may choose particular diversification strategies to increase demand for their own particular skills. A final motive is reduction of employment risk. Shareholders can 'diversify away' risks by holding a portfolio of stock of several firms. One firm's bad financial performance, or even bankruptcy, is then compensated by the good results of another firm. In contrast, for a top manager, diversification of employment risk by being in charge of a number of independent firms is not an option. However, diversification of his or her firm into several businesses can serve as a substitute.

In conclusion, agency theory does not represent a very positive view of diversification. Diversification is used to promote the interests of top managers, at the expense of the firm's shareholders. On the other hand, in practice, various mechanisms are available that serve to align the interests of shareholders and top managers. For example, top manager compensation can be tied to firm profitability by awarding bonuses or stock options. Furthermore, if there is an effective market for corporate control, firms that are performing poorly as a result of the wrong diversification moves are taken over by competing management teams, which then immediately replace opportunistic top managers.

Dominant logic

A dominant general management logic is defined as 'the way in which managers conceptualise the business and make critical resource allocation decisions' (Prahalad and Bettis, 1986: 490). Grant (1988) and Goold and Campbell (1987) have made this concept more tangible by translating it into administrative mechanisms like formulating and coordinating business strategies, allocating resources to businesses, and setting and monitoring performance targets for businesses. The dominant logic has to match the strategic characteristics of the businesses, otherwise hidden costs ensue. Hidden costs encompass inappropriate and tardy responses as a result of a lack of understanding of the businesses.

For corporate strategy, the implication is that the dominant logic of a firm's top management team drives the portfolio of businesses that can be managed successfully. If the top management team has a single dominant logic, the firm should either stick to one business or diversify into businesses with similar strategic characteristics. Diversification into businesses with different strategic characteristics can only be successful if the top management team adopts multiple dominant logics, which, in turn, at least requires altering the composition of the top management team. In essence, this represents a break with the more traditional notions of relatedness, which have emphasized similarities in end products or services, or the resources that are used to produce them. Instead, dominant logic involves a focus on similarities in strategic characteristics, such as the maturity and high-tech nature of the businesses. This could then explain the success of some conglomerates with small head offices with limited management capacity. Their businesses may appear unrelated, but could, in fact, be strategically very similar. Moreover, dominant logic may explain the failure of take-overs that, beforehand, seem to offer a large potential for synergies. After the take-over, the businesses turn out to require different dominant logics, which the top management team cannot provide.

Resource-based view

The ideas underlying the resource-based view originate from 1959, when Edith Penrose's 'The theory of the growth of the firm' was published. Only after its rediscovery by Wernerfelt (1984) did the resource-based view really start to take off in strategic management. The resource-based view of the firm can be seen as a response to the dominant influence on firm behaviour and performance that industrial economics assigns to the industry. Instead, the resource-based view emphasizes a firm's resources. Resources include assets – such as plants, patents and cash flow – and competencies, which represent the know-how to create a new asset or expand existing assets (Markides and Williamson, 1996). If the resources possess certain characteristics, such as non-tradability, non-substitutability and non-imitability, they can serve as the source of competitive advantage for a firm.

Mahoney and Pandian (1992) discuss a number of applications of the resource-based view to diversification strategy. For example, the resource-based view can explain the motivation for diversification, the direction of diversification and the performance of diversification. A firm can use its excess capacity in resources in a different industry, leading to diversification (Penrose, 1959), as already explained under transaction cost economics, above. In general, tangible resources (e.g. machines) and intangible resources (e.g. brand names) can only be used for a relatively narrow range of products or services. Therefore, a firm with excess capacity in these areas chooses related diversification. More flexible resources – in particular, financial resources – can also be used for unrelated diversification (Chatterjee and Wernerfelt, 1991). Finally, only if the resources that are used for diversification have the characteristics required for competitive advantage, will diversification increase firm performance. Excess financial resources, for example, could easily be returned to the capital market and then be made available to other companies. In contrast, excess tangible and intangible resources may be difficult to trade across markets and thus provide a more solid foundation for profitable diversification. This might help explain the general pattern that has been found, in which related diversified firms outperform single-business and unrelated-diversified firms (Rumelt, 1974; Palich et al., 2000). Nevertheless, each firm has a unique bundle of resources. Therefore, the decision to diversify, the direction of diversification and its performance are highly firm specific, according to the resource-based view.

Organizational learning perspective

The underlying premise of the organizational learning perspective is that organizations can learn from experience, which translates into future actions and their success. The quality of learning improves as the degree of environmental diversity to which an organization is exposed and the frequency of actions that are undertaken increase, but is also subject to organizational constraints (Barkema and Vermeulen, 1998).

The organizational learning perspective has not been established as an important explanation of corporate strategy, but it does provide an interesting direction for future research. For example, it could help explain why single-business firms are less profitable than related-diversified firms. Learning by single-business firms is limited, since they have only a narrow pool of experiences to draw on. Moreover, the organizational learning perspective would predict that, for firms that have already diversified, further diversification would be more feasible and successful than for firms that have no experience with diversification at all. As a final example, it could help to understand why related acquisitions are more successful than unrelated acquisitions (Bergh, 2001). Whereas the resource-based view of the firm would relate this to the resources that can be transferred, the organization learning perspective would point to the limited usefulness of a firm's experiences for unrelated activities. What is important to note, though, is that, according to both the resource-based view and the organizational learning perspective, corporate strategy and its success are highly firm specific, since they depend on, respectively, accumulated resources and experiences, which are unique to every firm.

Strategic contingency theory

The final explanation of corporate strategy is provided by strategic contingency theory (Venkatraman, 1989). The underlying notion is that a fit between a firm's strategy, on the one hand, and external and internal conditions or contingencies, on the other, increases performance. Consequently, corporate strategy can be seen as a response to various external and internal contingencies (Hoskisson and Hitt, 1990). Relevant external contingencies are government policy and market failure. An important aspect of government policy is anti-trust law. Through anti-trust law, policy-makers try to prevent large concentrations of power in an industry. If anti-trust policy is stringent and firms still want to grow, they are forced to expand in a different industry and thus diversify. Market failure as an incentive for diversification has already been discussed under transaction cost economics, above. If markets fail, coordination of activities in different industries within a firm is more efficient. The firm then becomes diversified.

Examples of internal contingencies are low performance, uncertainty and risk reduction. If a firm performs weakly in an industry, it may flee to a different industry, in an attempt to improve results. Similarly, uncertainty surrounding future cash flows that can be earned in the current industry may drive a firm to a new industry. Finally, firms may diversify into several industries in order to spread risks. As already explained under agency theory, above, risk reduction is a suspicious reason for diversification in the eyes of the shareholders. However, for other stakeholders, such as the managers, it may be a valid incentive to diversify.

The previous examples of contingencies suggest that the distinction between external and internal contingencies is not always clear-cut. For instance, the internal contingency uncertainty may actually be induced by external demand conditions. Also, the ability to exploit market failure depends on internal implementation mechanisms. Furthermore, some of the contingencies have already appeared as part of other theories.

In sum, strategic contingency theory does not seem to be a very precise theory, but more of a repository for various factors that have or have not appeared elsewhere. Therefore, in contrast with most of the other theories discussed in this chapter, it has never become widespread in studies of corporate diversification.

In this section, we have discussed a number of universalistic theories that have been used to explain corporate strategy. What makes these theories universalistic is that they do not take differences between countries explicitly into account. However, they do not necessarily imply convergence of corporate strategies among various countries. They may contain factors that are, and remain, different between countries. As an example, take transaction cost economics. According to this theory, the rationale behind the diversified firm is its ability to overcome market failure. Consequently, the corporate strategies that are adopted by the firms in a country become dependent on the functioning of the markets in that country. If the strength of the markets differs from country to country, as has been claimed for the capital market, for instance, one should expect to observe different corporate strategies.

Particularistic explanations of corporate strategy
Institutionalism

Institutional theory, which is discussed in the introductory chapter and, more extensively, in Chapter 4, is built on the idea that organizations are deeply embedded in wider institutional environments. This means that organizational practices are often reflections of or responses to rules and structures in their environments (Powell, 1998). It is a matter of debate how strongly national institutions influence the behaviour of firms. Whitley (1992, 1994, 1997) believes this influence is strong, and that firm behaviour has to be in agreement with the rules and structures of the stable institutional environment. Sorge (1995) leaves room for behaviour that is not similar to the rules and structures of institutions, because, in his approach, institutions are continuously modified by the behaviour of firms in a process called non-identical reproduction (see Chapter 4). Clark and Mueller (1996) suggest that large firms, in particular, are relatively autonomous to the national institutions, because they function simultaneously in both a national institutional environment and an international institutional environment. Since they function in both environments, large firms can arbitrage between them.

As discussed in Chapter 4, Whitley (1992) identifies several key institutions that govern economic activities. The institutional environment constructed by these institutions is or is not the same as a country. Some institutions, such as government policy, can vary within a country. For example, the state of Delaware has corporate laws that differ from those of most other states in the USA. Therefore, firms in Delaware face an institutional environment that differs from the ones in other US states. 'However many of the key institutions that structure economic relationships vary significantly between nation states' (Whitley, 1994: 176). Among these key institutions, a difference can be discerned between institutions that structure general patterns of trust, cooperation, identity and subordination in a society, and those that are more directly involved in the economic system and constitute the more direct business environment.

Because our aim is to focus on institutions that are able to explain differences in corporate strategies, we will focus on the latter institutions, which Whitley calls 'proximate social institutions'. The three major categories these institutions can be divided into are the political system, the financial system and the labour system (Whitley, 1997). In order to explain differences in corporate strategies between various countries, several scholars (Mayer and Whittington, 1999; Kogut *et al.*, 2002) have identified various institutional factors. These can all, except for one, be placed in one of the three categories mentioned above, which have an impact on the decision of a firm to diversify.

Political system

Government policy can have a strong impact on corporate strategies. For example, anti-trust laws can influence corporate strategy. Also, the willingness of a government to share economic risks with private firms is important. If government is willing to share economic risks, firms do not have to cope with those risks on their own and a strategy of unrelated diversification as a way of hedging against economic risks becomes less likely (Whitley, 1997). Therefore, this might affect the direction of diversification strategy that is favoured in a country. In addition, tax laws can have an influence on corporate strategy, especially on the level of diversification. High taxes on dividends, in combination with lower taxes on capital gains, can induce shareholders to stimulate firms to retain funds, in order to invest these in other high-profit industries. If the stock value increases, shareholders may receive a better return than through dividends, because capital gains would be taxed more lightly than dividends (Hoskisson and Hitt, 1990).

Financial system

The way the financial system in a country functions can also have an impact on corporate strategies, especially on the level of diversification in a country. In Chapter 6, financial systems are discussed in detail. This chapter distinguishes between two types of systems: a capital-market-based system and a credit-based system. In a capital-market-based system, firms raise capital in a variety of ways, depending on costs and terms. So their relationships with banks tend to be impersonal, short-term and specific to certain transactions (Whitley, 1992). Banks and other financial institutions concentrate on allocating funds on a portfolio basis to a range of borrowers. Therefore, they are less concerned with building a long-term relationship with a single customer than with the relative attractiveness of competing investment projects. In this system, it is less likely that banks and other financial institutions are willing to share long-term economic risks with client firms. Consequently, firms will be more likely to try to spread their economic risks by diversifying into other businesses. In a credit-based system, the situation is quite the opposite. Because the capital market is not highly developed in this system, banks and financial institutions cannot trade financial assets easily. This causes banks and financial institutions to invest in personal relationships with their client firms, since they depend on their success. Firms are also motivated to invest in a personal relationship with particular banks and other financial institutions because they are dependent on their willingness to support investment plans as there is no highly developed financial market, and banks and other financial institutions will only invest in firms they know and have confidence in. This all leads to a situation in which risk sharing between financial institutions and firms is much more common than in a capital-market-based system. Consequently, firms will be less likely to try to spread their economic risks by diversifying into other businesses.

Another aspect of the financial system that can have an impact on corporate strategies is the market for corporate control. When there is a highly developed market for corporate control, it is easier for firms to undertake hostile take-overs and, thus, easier to get access to other industries. Therefore, a highly developed market for corporate control can lead to more diversification. Nevertheless, it is important to note that a highly developed market for corporate control also makes it easier to break up conglomerates through a hostile take-over and, by doing so, to end diversification.

Ownership and boards are also mentioned as institutional factors that have an influence on corporate strategies (Kogut et al., 2002). Ownership and boards have an influence because important decisions, like corporate strategy, have to be approved by the owners and the board members. When ownership is dispersed and weak boards have little influence and power, it is easier for managers to act in their own interests at the expense of the owners and give in to their personal motives to choose a diversification strategy. These motives, like managerial entrenchment, higher wages and reduction of their employment risks, are discussed in Section 10.6.

Labour system

The labour system also influences corporate strategy. The way management development is organized can influence the way managers rate different directions of diversification (Mayer and Whittington, 1999). This can be illustrated by an example given by Lane (1995: 35–8), in which she points out the implications for corporate strategy of the traditional lack of technical and engineering skills of UK top managers. UK managers are more financially orientated and therefore supposed to prefer unrelated diversification, while the more technologically orientated German managers are assumed to favour related diversification. Therefore, the labour system might affect the direction of diversification strategy that is most common in a country.

Others

One institutional factor named by Kogut et al. (2002) cannot be placed in the categories listed above. The existence of inter-firm networks has an impact on the ability of firms to conduct a diversification strategy. When a firm decides to enter a new industry, this may threaten the position of incumbent firms. These incumbents may try to prevent the firm from gaining access to the resources needed to enter the industry by calling in the help of their network. If the ties between firms are strong, incumbents can successfully block the entrance of new firms and make diversification difficult.

In sum, anti-trust laws, tax laws, the functioning of the financial system and the existence of inter-firm networks influence the level of diversification in a country, while the willingness of governments to share economic risks and the way managers are trained have more impact on the direction of diversification that is favoured in a country. Research in this field is still limited, so more institutional factors influencing the level of diversification, the direction of diversification, or both, might be discovered in the future. In addition, it should be noted that some institutional factors in a country may favour diversification, while others do not. Hence, it is important to take account of institutional complementarities (see Chapter 4), and their effect on the level and direction of diversification in a specific country.

10.4 ❧ Comparative Empirical Studies

So far, there have been only a limited number of studies of differences or similarities in corporate strategies between countries that try to explain these differences or similarities via national institutions. Three of those studies are discussed in this section. We start with the study of Kogut *et al.* (2002), who look at national divergences in diversification behaviour in France, Germany, Japan, the UK and the USA. Then we discuss the study of Mayer and Whittington (1999, 2000) of corporate strategies and structures in France, Germany and the UK. We end this section with a discussion of our own research about corporate strategy in the car and steel industry in Japan, Germany and the USA.

Kogut, Walker and Anand

The study of Kogut, *et al.* (2002) consists of two parts. In the first part, they examine inter-industry diversification patterns in France, Germany, Japan, the UK and the USA. The study is limited to the 75 largest, domestically owned firms. The data are taken from previous studies, conducted primarily in the 1970s, like the study of Dyas and Thanheiser (1976) for Germany and France. These 75 largest firms are categorized by industry. Firms are categorized according to their industries, because, according to Teece *et al.* (1994), linkages in technological and market characteristics cause firms to diversify in a common pattern across industries. Teece *et al.* seem to implicitly assume that these linkages are constant in countries at an advanced state of market capitalism and, therefore, should be robust to institutional influences. This leads to the first hypothesis that is tested:

H1: patterns of inter-industry diversification are similar across countries.

Kogut *et al.* pose a second, opposite, hypothesis:

H2: country-specific institutions cause different patterns of inter-industry diversification.

The country-specific institutions they mention are ownership, boards, inter-firm networks and government policy. We discussed the influence of these institutions on strategy in Section 10.3. Kogut *et al.* conclude that large institutional differences exist between the countries. For example, state ownership of key enterprises has been an important influence in France, somewhat less in the UK, and even less so in Germany and Japan, though different German regional governments have substantial interests in large enterprises like automobile manufacturer Volkswagen and steel mill Salzgitter. In the USA, state ownership of enterprises is almost non-existent. The empirical findings suggest that there are no similarities in patterns of inter-industry diversification across France, Germany, Japan, the UK and the USA, and thus support the second hypothesis. Differences in country-specific institutions cause different patterns of inter-industry diversification.

In the second part of the study, Kogut *et al.* (2002) present two case studies that show institutional influences on diversification efforts. In 1967, Leasco, a US leasing company, tried to acquire Chemical Bank through a hostile take-over. The take-over failed due to the fact that Chemical Bank was part of an influential inter-firm network that included the banks that were supposed to finance the take-over bid. The network also included members of the state assembly, which promptly banned conglomerate take-overs. So the attempted diversification by Leasco failed because the inter-firm network enabled Chemical Bank to prevent the hostile take-over.

The second case study is situated in France. In 1969, the newly formed packaging and bottling firm, BSN, undertook a hostile takeover bid for the 300-year-old chemical and glass company St Gobain. On the board of one of the banks supporting the take-over bid was a member of St Gobain, who managed to slow down the attack, until a white knight was found in Pont-à-Mousson. Pont-à-Mousson was an old firm that had ties with important families in the region, and which had already mediated in a fight between the families owning St Gobain. So the attempted take-over by BSN failed and St Gobain merged with Pont-à-Mousson. Soon after, BSN expanded into food products instead of glass making and eventually became Danone.

Kogut *et al.* (2002) conclude that institutions shape the possibilities that individual firms have to realize the economic advantages of diversification.

Conclusions to this section

Differences in country-specific institutions cause different patterns of inter-industry diversification. Institutions shape the possibilities that individual firms have to realize the economic advantages of diversification.

Mayer and Whittington

Mayer and Whittington (1999, 2000) come to a different conclusion in their study of the strategy and structure development of the top 100 domestically owned industrial firms in France, Germany and the UK in the period 1950–93. Strategy is measured using the diversification categories developed by Rumelt (1974), which were mentioned in Section 10.2. The firms are classified in a diversification category every ten years over the period 1950–93. Mayer and Whittington also investigate three different institutions that are assumed to influence strategy and structure development: ownership, management control and management development. These institutional factors are indices of the broader institutional frameworks of finance and management. The influence of these institutions on strategy corresponds to the influence of institutions mentioned in Section 10.3. Exceptions are the influences of the institutions described under the categories political system and inter-firm networks, which are not explicitly taken into account; the same goes for the influence of boards. The way the institutions develop in the period 1950–93 is measured by the way the firms develop in terms of ownership, management control and management development.

The institutional environment was found to remain quite different in the three countries over the period of time under investigation. Hence, following the institutional approach, differences in strategy and structure development between French, German and UK firms could be expected. However, the predictions according to the institutional approach prove to be inaccurate. For example, it is not the professionally managed, capital-market-driven, finance-dominated firm of the UK that appears to be more like a conglomerate, but the technically orientated, bank-backed German firm (Mayer and Whittington, 1999: 951). The conclusion is that small differences in strategy and structure in France, Germany and the UK remain, but that these differences cannot be explained by existing institutional theories.

Conclusions to this section

Over the period 1950–93, there are only small differences in strategy and structure between firms in France, Germany and the UK, which cannot be explained by existing institutional theories.

The car and steel industry

The third study concerns our own research in the US, German and Japanese steel and car industries.[1] This study investigates the influence of national institutions on corporate strategy development in those industries. It should be noted beforehand that these industries have a rather global character, which might influence the results; the results in other, more multidomestic, industries could be different. The study takes almost all the institutional factors, mentioned in Section 10.3, into account for the USA, Germany and Japan. The political, financial, educational and inter-firm cooperation systems differ considerably between the three countries, although there are quite a few similarities between Germany and Japan.

The **political system** differs in the three countries. For example, in the USA, the government is, in most cases, not willing to share economic risks with firms, while this is much more common in Germany and Japan. Germany also has a history of (partially) state-owned firms, like the aforementioned Volkswagen and Salzgitter. In Japan, the influence of the government on business is also more direct, especially through the role played by the Ministry of International Trade and Industry (MITI). This ministry tries to coordinate economic activity in Japan, and issues plans that state how the Japanese economy should develop in subsequent years. Firms are encouraged to follow these plans through a system of administrative guidance (Bernstein, 1997). This means that civil servants use their power to favour firms that follow the plans and punish firms that do not. For example, the Ministry of Finance uses its power to allocate financial resources to firms that follow MITI's plans, and makes it hard for firms that do not follow the plans to get access to financial resources.

There are also differences in the **anti-trust laws** between the three countries. The USA is known for its severe anti-trust laws and policy.[2] Until the end of the 1990s, the Bundeskartelamt, which supervises observance of the German anti-trust laws, was not very active. Subsequently, the European Union coordinated the anti-trust policies in its member states, so a more active attitude was expected of the Bundeskartelamt. Japanese anti-trust policy is not severe because the Japanese government does not favour strong

---

[1] The research is described in more detail in a working paper by the two authors of this chapter, on which the synopsis presented here is based.

[2] Remember the Microsoft case? This company was almost forced to split up because of alleged misuse of market power.

competition among Japanese firms, in order to give them a stronger position on the world market, although, during the economic crisis of the 1990s, efforts were made to increase competition in Japan.

The **financial system** also differs between the USA, Germany and Japan (see Chapter 6 for a more detailed discussion). Germany and Japan are characterized as bank-centred, credit-based systems, while the USA has a more capital-market-based system. Ownership is dispersed in the USA (Lorsch and Graff, 1996), while ownership is concentrated in Germany (Dietl, 1998). In Japan, ownership is concentrated in inter-firm networks, like the *keiretsu*. The boards are relatively weak in the USA and Japan. In the USA the CEO, who in most cases also acts as chairman of the board, dominates the board and is able to control meetings. Many other board members are high-ranking managers of friendly firms (Lorsch and Graff, 1996). Japanese boards are dominated by present or former 'inside' senior managers and have relatively low influence on the corporate decision-making process. In most cases, former high-ranking civil servants or the retired company president are asked to become chairman of the board. This practice strengthens the influence of the government on business strategy. German boards have the strongest influence, in part due to their two-tier boards and the fact that the supervisory board is totally made up of directors who cannot be members of the management board. So these directors in the supervisory board, half of whom are elected by the owners and the other half by the employees, are all outsiders and can, therefore, limit the power of the management board.

The last aspect of the financial system that is discussed is the market for corporate control. This market is highly developed in the USA. Hostile take-overs are common practice and seen as an efficient way to deal with agency conflicts (see Section 10.3). The situation is quite different in Germany. Not so long ago, hostile take-overs were unthinkable. It was not until 1989 that the first German hostile take-over took place. Hostile take-overs are also very rare in Japan, and are almost seen as a crime (Tachibanaki and Taki, 2000). However, the Japanese economic crisis in the 1990s made hostile take-overs more common.

In addition, the way **management development** is organized differs between the three countries (see Chapter 5). Most US top managers have a financial background and have attended a business school. They do not have a real commitment to a specific product or industry (Fligstein, 1990). German managers, on the other hand, mostly have a technical background, although young German managers increasingly attend business schools (Lane, 1992). Japanese top managers mostly come from a couple of top Japanese universities. Companies recruit students from these universities and develop them into managers through an extensive job-rotation programme that may take three years. The aim of that programme is not to make specialists of those future managers in one field, but to turn them into generalists (Deller and Flunkert, 1996). Due to the extensive job-rotation programme, Japanese managers are aware of the know-how and specific skills that are available in their company. Because of their awareness of these specific skills and know-how, Japanese managers are expected to pay close attention to finding new opportunities to make use of them. Another interesting aspect is that Japanese companies frequently exchange managers between companies inside a *keiretsu*. This strengthens the influence of inter-firm networks.

Accordingly, the final institutional factor in the USA, Germany and Japan is the role of **inter-firm networks**. The USA is notable for the weakness of its inter-firm ties (Kogut *et al.*,

2002). These ties are much stronger in Germany. It is common practice that firms have large stock interests in other firms and that their officials have positions on each other's supervisory boards. Ties are especially tight between firms in the same industry. These ties are maintained with the support of trade and employer organizations (Grant, 1986). In Japan, inter-firm ties are also tight; there are several kinds of network between firms, of which the *keiretsu* is the best known.

It is quite clear that the institutional environment differs between these three countries. Based on the influence on corporate strategy of the various institutional factors we discussed in Section 10.3, and the way these institutional factors function in each country (as discussed above) we formulate different expectations about the level and direction of diversification in the three countries. The distinction in level and direction was made in Section 10.2. In Table 10.1 we have summed up the factors that influence the level of diversification in a country, and labelled each factor for the USA, Germany and Japan with a plus (+) if a factor indicates a higher level and a minus (−) if a factor indicates a lower level of diversification.

Table 10.1 indicates that:

- the highest level of diversification is expected in the USA

- Germany and Japan seem to have a similar environment, but due to the weaker Japanese boards a slightly higher level of diversification is expected in Japan than in Germany.

In Table 10.2, the institutional factors that influence the direction of diversification are summed up for each country and labelled in the same manner as in Table 10.1. However, this time a plus (+) indicates a preference for unrelated diversification and a minus (−) a preference for related diversification.

According to Table 10.2:

- US firms are expected to favour unrelated diversification

- German and Japanese firms are expected to favour related diversification.

Table 10.1 The expected influence of institutional factors on the level of diversification			
	USA	**Germany**	**Japan**
Anti-trust laws	Strict anti-trust policy (+)	Lenient anti-trust policy (−)	Lenient anti-trust policy (−)
Financial system	Capital-market-based (+)	Credit-based (−)	Credit-based (−)
Ownership	Dispersed (+)	Concentrated (−)	Concentrated (−)
Boards	Dominated by executive management (+)	Influential, independent supervisory board (−)	Dominated by insiders (+)
Inter-firm networks	Weak (+)	Strong (−)	Strong (−)

Table 10.2　The expected influence of institutional factors on the direction of diversification

	USA	Germany	Japan
Government's willingness to share business risks	Low (+)	Moderate (−)	High (−)
Management development	Generalist (+)	Technical (−)	Generalist within one company (−)

The expectations regarding level and direction of diversification in the USA, Germany and Japan are tested for firms in the automobile and steel industry. The three biggest US, German and Japanese companies in the two industries are selected on the basis of production data (number of cars and tons of steel in the year 2001 for both industries). Their strategy development is measured for the period 1985–2000. The firms selected in the automobile industry are General Motors, Ford, DaimlerChrysler, Volkswagen, BMW, Toyota, Nissan and Honda.

Some remarks have first to be made about DaimlerChrysler and Nissan. DaimlerChrysler is the outcome of a merger between German-based DaimlerBenz and US-based Chrysler in 1998 (see the case in Chapter 3). Therefore, the strategy development before 1998 is measured for the two separate companies. Since 1999, Nissan has been under the control of the French company Renault, so the strategy of Nissan is measured until 1999. Our aim is to investigate the national, institutional effects on corporate strategy. This aim makes it important that strategy is developed in the country, the institutions of which are taken into account. Therefore, in Nissan's case, this would be Japan and not France.

The firms selected in the steel industry are US Steel, Bethlehem Steel, Nucor, ThyssenKrupp, Nippon Steel, NKK and Kawasaki Steel. ThyssenKrupp is the outcome of a merger between Thyssen and Krupp in 1999. Krupp had taken control of another German steel manufacturer, Hoesch, in 1992. The strategies of the different companies are measured separately until the last year of their independence. This means that the strategies of Thyssen and Krupp are measured until 1999 and the strategy of Hoesch is measured until 1992.

Strategy development is measured using the scheme developed by Rumelt (1974). According to this scheme, firms are assigned to nine different diversification categories, depending on their scores on a number of quantitative and qualitative criteria. Each company is assigned to a category, first in 1985 and then every five years until 2000. In addition, for each company and each industry in a country a pattern is established that indicates whether the level of diversification is higher or lower than in the period before. The level of diversification is measured with the help of the diversification categories of Rumelt (1974), where single business is the lowest possible level of diversification and unrelated business the highest.

The results for the two industries are mixed. In the automobile industry, all companies, except for one, stay in the same diversification category for the whole of the period 1985–2000 and they all end in this category in 2000. This category is dominant-vertical. This means that the automobile companies earn 70–95 per cent of their total revenues from the sale of cars, trucks and semi-finished products like spare parts. The remaining part of the total revenues is earned with other activities; one of these activities, which all automobile companies have in common, proves to be automotive financing. Other activities, further, include, for example, the sale of motorcycles in the case of BMW and Honda, and the car-rental business, Europcar, of Volkswagen.

The only exception in this pattern appears to be DaimlerBenz. Until 1995, this company seemed to be developing into an industrial conglomerate, with interests in the aircraft industry, the market for domestic appliances and even the market for mobile communications. After 1995, however, the company refocused on the automobile industry and sold most of its interests in other industries. As already mentioned, in 1998 DaimlerBenz merged with Chrysler to form DaimlerChrysler.

These results illustrate that our expectations regarding the level and direction of diversification did not come through in the automobile industry. All companies seemed to have developed similar strategies. These results suggest that national institutional environments have a very limited influence on corporate strategy in global industries like the automobile industry. Forces of international competition may compel companies in the automobile industry to adopt similar strategies.

Other theories, especially industrial organization, could be used to explain the results found in the automobile industry. As indicated in Section 10.3, the paradigm used in industrial organization states that the market structure determines the conduct of firms. According to this line of reasoning, the results can be explained as follows. Due to the global structure of the automobile industry, firms cannot afford to adopt a radically different strategy from those of other firms because this can give them a competitive disadvantage. The large multinational firms making up the automobile industry have to deal with different national institutional environments, of which the national environment of the country of origin is only one. The global structure of this industry enables it to arbitrate between the different institutional environments.

Also, results in the steel industry do not confirm our expectations based on the different national institutional environments in the USA, Germany and Japan. It is not the US but the German companies that have reached the highest level of diversification. The German steel companies seem to favour unrelated diversification instead of related diversification, a result completely opposite to our expectations. Differences remain in strategies between companies in the three countries, but in the period 1995–2000, the overall level of diversification drops in all three countries. This suggests some convergence to less diversification, although the convergence is not as strong as in the automobile industry. The results seem to indicate that the steel industry is less of a global industry than the automobile industry, which leaves more room for divergence of strategies between countries. A further interesting note is that most companies defend their diversification efforts by pointing out their poor results and perspectives in the steel market.

Conclusions to this section

The results suggest that national institutional environments have a very limited influence on corporate strategy in global industries like the automobile industry. Forces of international competition may compel companies in the automobile industry to adopt similar strategies.

Although our expectations regarding diversification strategies based on the national institutional environments in the USA, Germany and Japan did not come through, we did find some striking results that seem to indicate that there might still be country-specific influences on corporate strategy. In both the automobile and the steel industry, we found some typical diversification moves within a country. For example, in one period, all the Japanese steel companies are active in the market for semiconductors, while the US and German steel companies are not. German steel companies all diversify in machine construction and automotive parts, while US and Japanese steel companies do not. In the automobile industry, Toyota and Nissan are both producers of lift trucks, while other companies in other countries are not. The US automobile companies General Motors and Ford both start to develop satellites at a certain moment, while other automobile companies in other countries do not. These examples seem to indicate that, despite the general tendency to converge, there are still some country-specific factors influencing firms to diversify in a specific direction.

To sum up, the studies in this section have produced different results.

✦ Based on earlier research, primarily from the 1970s, Kogut *et al.* (2002) found a strong influence of national institutions on strategy.

✦ Mayer and Whittington (1999, 2000) found small differences in strategy between firms in different European countries, but these differences could not be explained by reference to national institutions.

✦ The research in the car and steel industry in the USA, Germany and Japan indicates an influence of industry characteristics on strategy development. Firms in more global industries, like the automobile industry, seem to be less influenced by national institutional environments than firms in less global industries like the steel industry.

10.5 ✦ Model

The previous section shows that institutional theory is not always able to help us explain cross-national differences and similarities in corporate strategy. Obviously, then, if we want to come to more precise explanations of cross-national corporate strategies, we have to move beyond institutional analysis and consider variables other than institutions. In Section 10.3, we have presented universalistic explanations. These explanations point to variables such as corporate resources, industry-specific variables, and so on, that can help us to explain corporate strategy. In this section, we develop a model that can be used to order these factors and, as such, can be helpful in generating new insights regarding the convergence or divergence question. The section is divided into three subsections: strategic planning, the model and expectations.

Strategic planning

The model is based on the well-known strategic planning process.[3] The process is used by many firms to develop their strategy. The starting point of the process is the definition of a firm's mission and goals. The mission indicates why the firm exists and what it should be

---

[3] The strategic planning process is described in almost any handbook on strategy. A detailed description can be found in, for example, Hill and Jones (2001).

doing. As such, the mission expresses if, how and also in what order the firm tries to look after the interests of its stakeholders, such as shareholders, customers, employees and society in general.

The mission of Tyco (see the case at the end of this chapter), for example, is 'We will increase the value of our company and our global portfolio of diversified brands by exceeding customers' expectations and achieving market leadership and operating excellence in every segment of our company'. Therefore, Tyco seems to give priority to increasing its value and thus the interests of its shareholders, while the satisfaction of customer needs only seems instrumental in this purpose.

The goals indicate what the firm wants to achieve in the long term. For example, one of Tyco's goals was to attract and retain, at every level of the company, people who represent the highest standards of excellence and integrity.

After the definition of the mission and goals, the next steps of the strategic planning process are the internal analysis and external analysis. The internal analysis refers to an analysis of the firm itself in order to identify its strengths and weaknesses. The external analysis entails an analysis of the firm's environment to discover the opportunities and threats it presents to the firm. Next, in the SWOT analysis, the **S**trengths, **W**eaknesses, **O**pportunities and **T**hreats are brought together to support the identification of alternative strategies that build on the strengths, eliminate the weaknesses, take advantage of the opportunities and avoid the threats. Subsequently, a strategy is chosen that matches the firm's mission and contributes to the achievement of its goals. Finally, the chosen strategy can be implemented.

The strategic planning process has been criticized for a number of reasons. For example, it assumes the predictability of the future, whereas, in reality, even the most thoroughly prepared strategic plans are often thwarted by unexpected developments.[4] A criticism that is perhaps more relevant in the context of this book is that the approach may be culturally biased. Its main contributions originate from the USA. Elsewhere, the strategic planning process may not be a very relevant approach to strategy development. Nevertheless, it can still be used to order the factors that underlie corporate strategy, according to the previous sections.

The model

Figure 10.2 shows the underlying factors, together with the main elements of the strategic planning process.

Mission and goals

Both **agency theory** and **institutional theory** can explain the mission and goals a firm adopts. According to agency theory, top managers have personal motives to diversify, such as increase in compensation, managerial entrenchment and risk reduction (Jensen, 1986; Hoskisson and Hitt, 1990; Montgomery, 1994). In the absence of powerful countervailing mechanisms or institutions, like strong boards and concentrated ownership (Kogut *et al.*,

---

[4] For a thorough discussion of the various approaches to strategy formation and their weaknesses see, for instance, Mintzberg *et al.* (1998).

2002), the personal motives of the top managers become the firm's explicit or implicit mission and goals, and this is expected to result in diversification.

This line of reasoning assumes that shareholders are the firm's chief stakeholders and that diversification is not in their interests, since it destroys value. However, diversification can also be attractive for shareholders. Diversification, in particular if it is of the related kind, could lead to synergies and thus increase firm value. Also, shareholders may not always be in a position to 'diversify away' their risks by holding an efficient stock portfolio, which makes firm diversification to reduce risks an appealing alternative. This could, for instance, be the case in regions where the capital market does not offer a large number of good investment opportunities or in situations in which the main shareholder is a family that wants to remain in control of the firm. Furthermore, besides shareholders, the firm has other stakeholders, like employees, suppliers, customers, debt providers and government agencies. These stakeholders might also benefit from a firm that diversifies to reduce risks, since it is usually difficult for them to diversify away their risks.

To sum up, if shareholders are the principal stakeholders, and if they do not have a special stake in the firm but plenty of investment alternatives in the capital market, then conglomerate diversification to reduce risks is not a good strategy and will only emerge if moves to rein in management are weak. In contrast, when the interests of other stakeholders are taken into account, or when shareholders do not have sufficient investment alternatives in the capital market at their disposal, risk reduction as mission or goal of the firm, and the accompanying strategy of unrelated diversification, would be attractive for the firm. The influence of stakeholders, institutions and the capital market (as part of the factor markets) is shown in Figure 10.2.

Figure 10.2 Model of corporate strategy development

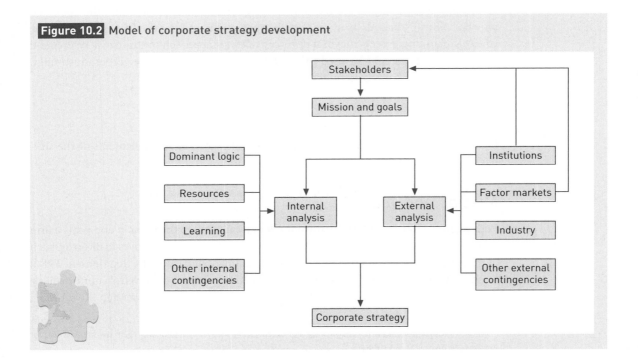

Internal firm-specific factors

Figure 10.2 also shows the influence of several internal, firm-specific factors, which are suggested by dominant logic, the resource-based view, organizational learning and strategic contingency theory.

According to the first perspective, the **dominant logic**(s) of the top managers, instead of their personal motives, drive(s) a firm's corporate strategy (Prahalad and Bettis, 1986). If the top management team possesses a single dominant logic, then the firm should stick to one business or a number of related businesses that require a similar dominant logic. Diversification into strategically dissimilar businesses only makes sense if the top management team has multiple dominant logics.

The **resource-based view** argues that each firm constitutes a unique bundle of resources. Excess resources that meet certain characteristics can be used to diversify into new industries. The type of resources determines the direction of diversification (Mahoney and Pandian, 1992).

According to the **organizational learning** perspective, learning by firms from previous diversification experiences facilitates further diversification (Bergh, 2001). Similar to the resources, this factor is unique to every firm.

The final internal factor is a reservoir of various internal **contingencies** that shape a firm's corporate strategy (Venkatraman, 1989). For example, diversification could be the response of a firm to low performance in the current activities.

External factors

The external factors that influence corporate strategy are derived from institutional theory, transaction cost economics, industrial organization and, again, strategic contingency theory.

Institutional theory offers a number of institutions that contain a rather wide range of more specific factors. A political system that includes flexible anti-trust laws, no willingness to share economic risks with the private sector, and tax laws that encourage firms to retain and reinvest cash flows encourages firms to diversify (Hoskisson and Hitt, 1990; Whitley, 1997). Diversification is also stimulated in a financial system that is capital market based (as opposed to credit based) (Whitley, 1992).[5] Another aspect of the financial system that promotes diversification is the absence of strong boards and concentrated ownership (Kogut *et al.*, 2002). This has already been mentioned in the mission and goals part of the model, because it facilitates the adoption of the personal motives of the top managers as the firm's explicit or implicit mission and goals. A final factor that is part of the financial system is the presence of a highly developed market for corporate control. Such a market offers an opportunity for firms that want to diversify through acquisition.

---

[5] In combination with the remarks we made in the mission and goals part of our model, an interesting situation emerges. In a capital-market-based system, the inability to share risks with financial institutions poses a threat to the firm, which can be countered through diversification. However, in a highly developed capital market, the then presumably dominant shareholders have no need for diversification to spread risks and will oppose attempts to make this part of the firm's mission and goals. In a credit-based system, there is no need for a firm to diversify to reduce risks, since firms can share risks with financial institutions. However, managers face less opposition from shareholders when they set the firm on a diversification course for other, personal, motives.

At the same time, it poses a serious threat to firms that have followed a value-destroying diversification strategy. The third institution is the labour system. The type of management development enables or disables specific directions of diversification (Mayer and Whittington, 1999).[6] The final institution that encourages diversification is the absence of strong networks that help incumbent firms to retaliate against diversifying newcomers in an industry.

The latter institution is strongly related to **industrial organization**, the next theory that provides external incentives for a firm's corporate strategy. In general, industrial organization stresses the importance of the industry for the strategies firms adopt. More specifically, it has been worked out as a number of opportunities to reduce competition that firms can take advantage of through diversification.

The third theory is **transaction cost economics**. Firms diversify in response to inefficient markets. The conventional markets that have been used as examples are the capital market and the markets for unused resources, like physical equipment and know-how. However, other factor markets, like the labour market, could also be included.

Strategic contingency theory is the final perspective we mention here. Again, it is a reservoir of various contingencies that influence corporate strategy. However, here it includes contingencies that are external to the firm, like government policy and market failure. These aspects have been dealt with already.

Expectations

The model shown in Figure 10.2 indicates that the corporate strategy a firm adopts is unique. The internal factors, like dominant logic, resources and learning, in particular, tend to be firm specific. The other factors apply to more firms, but it is still unlikely that the same constellation of factors will be relevant to multiple firms. The upshot is that any strategy can be found among the firms in a country. So perhaps the institutional environment in the USA has become less beneficial to conglomerates, although there are still flourishing conglomerates.

One example is Illinois Tool Works, which successfully ran 600 different business units. According to *Forbes*, somebody forgot to tell CEO W. James Farrell that the conglomerate went out with the trilobite.[7] The firm owed its success mainly to a unique dominant logic, or capability, involving the instilment of the '80/20 process' at each acquired unit. This process implied focusing exclusively on the 20 per cent of customers or products that provide 80 per cent of sales, and methodically getting rid of smaller buyers and lesser product lines. Although the concept seems straightforward, the implementation in practice is very hard. Apparently, it took the firm ten years to work it out, making imitation by competitors difficult.

Nevertheless, despite this 'anything goes' principle, the factors firms face might be more similar *within* countries than *across* countries. Consequently, in general, the corporate strategies adopted within a specific country might display more similarities than those adopted in different countries. This would support the expectation of divergence of

---

[6] This institution actually seems to be translated into a firm's strategy through its dominant logic.

[7] www.forbes.com, 15 April 2002. A trilobite is a hard-shelled, segmented creature that existed over 300 million years ago in the earth's ancient seas. More information on Illinois Tool Works' dominant logic can be found in *Business Week*, 24 September 2001.

corporate strategies across countries. So, for example, in one country a larger percentage of firms might adopt a single business strategy than in another.

To decide whether this kind of divergence can be anticipated we have to look again at the factors of the model presented in Figure 10.2. For the sake of convenience, we divide these factors into three, sometimes overlapping, categories:

1. factors that pertain to countries (including the institutions, like the political system, the financial system, the labour system and networks)
2. factors that pertain to collections of firms (like factor markets and industry)
3. firm-specific factors (like stakeholders, dominant logic, resources and learning).

Factors that pertain to countries

Many elements of the institutional environment differ from country to country (Kostova and Roth, 2002). For example, the market for corporate control is highly developed in the USA, while in many other countries, such as the Netherlands, firms are protected by take-over barriers, making hostile take-overs an exception. The institutional differences enable divergence of corporate strategies across countries. However, there are many trends that reduce the differences between countries. For instance, the demise of communism and its centrally planned economies, the rise of free-trade zones like NAFTA, and even more extensive integration in other regions like the European Community, together with the large political, military and economic influence of the USA have led to more harmonization among the national institutions. Anti-trust law, for example, had, in comparison with the USA, always been very relaxed in most European countries. Under the influence of European Community regulations, anti-trust law and its enforcement have become much stricter across the board. The European Committee even successfully blocked a merger between General Electric and Honeywell, two US-based companies. This provides a uniform incentive for unrelated diversification to firms that seek external growth, both in Europe and elsewhere.

Factors that pertain to collections of firms

The factors of the second category, involving industries and factor markets, are less obviously tied to countries. Levitt (1983) even foresaw the emergence of huge global markets for standardized consumer products, due to the convergence of customer preferences across countries. As examples, he mentioned the worldwide acceptance of standardized products from Levi's, McDonald's and Coca-Cola. However, all these firms have been forced to adapt their products to different local circumstances. Coca-Cola, for example, traditionally had not performed many activities outside the USA, besides bottling. After lower financial results and an erroneous response to a crisis in consumer confidence in

---

[8] See *Business Week*, 3 July 2000. Similarly, Unilever had to adapt the washing powder it offers in various countries for a number of reasons. For example, US consumers prefer liquid detergents, while Europeans prefer powder and, increasingly, tablets and sachets. Washing powder in India has to be able to cope with curry stains, while it has to clean tomato and barbecue stains in South America. Phosphates are forbidden in Scandinavia, while they

Belgium, however, it switched to locally adapted advertising campaigns, packaging, products, organization, Internet sites and press relations.[8]

In general, a multinational corporation may face pressures for responsiveness to local or national circumstances, such as differences in customer needs, in distribution channels, in the presence of local competitors and in a host government demands. On the other hand, the corporation may face pressures for more global integration or coordination of activities, such as universal customer needs, the demands of multinational customers, the presence of multinational competitors and cost reductions (Prahalad and Doz, 1987). Taken together, these pressures lead to the distinction between global industries, in which the pressures for global integration prevail, versus multidomestic industries, in which the pressures for local responsiveness prevail (Hout *et al.*, 1982).

Of course, the distinction between global and multidomestic industries is somewhat simplified. For example, in some industries, both responsiveness and integration are highly important (Bartlett and Ghoshal, 1989). An important implication for our purposes, however, is that more global industries possess few country-specific features that firms have to take into account when they develop their corporate strategy. If they still follow deviant strategies, they run the risk of punishment by global competitors, which are able to realize large cost savings through their more integrated strategies. On the other hand, the strategies of firms active in more multidomestic industries have to be more responsive to country-specific conditions, otherwise more adaptive competitors corner them. To sum up, more convergence of corporate strategies can be expected in global industries, whereas more divergence should be the outcome in multidomestic industries. Given the huge number of different industries, it is very difficult to tell whether the number of global industries exceeds the number of multidomestic industries. As suggested earlier, Levitt's (1983) claim of the emergence of global markets seems to be hyperbole. Nevertheless, it also seems to be increasingly difficult to find examples of industries that are purely multidomestic. Retail, for example, used to be a rather multidomestic industry, due to different customer preferences. However, retailers are increasingly active on a global scale. Carrefour (from France), Wal-Mart (from the USA) and Tesco (from the UK) have even entered Japan, which had always been difficult to access for foreign competitors.[9] Obviously, they need to adapt their activities to local differences. Wal-Mart found out the hard way, when its 'cookie cutter' approach did not go down well in Germany.[10] At the same time, the worldwide players give the industry a more global character – for example, through their global sourcing policies and worldwide application of best practices.

Similar observations can be added for factor markets. Some markets are already very global, stimulating convergence of corporate strategies across countries. An example is

are still allowed in the UK. With respect to washing machines, US consumers prefer top loaders, whereas front loaders are preferred in Europe. Also, in India, washing machines have to be closed at the bottom to prevent rats and cockroaches from creeping in. In rural China, the machines are also used to wash vegetables. US consumers prefer short programs and cold water, while in Europe longer programs and warm water are generally used. Finally, advertising campaigns for washing powder in India can emphasize a superior's appreciation for an office worker's stainless white shirt, whereas they can emphasize erotic aspects in Europe. See *NRC-Handelsblad*, 8 April 2002.

[9] See *NRC-Handelsblad*, 11 June 2003.

[10] See *Business Week*, 3 September 2001. German customers did not like all the products and the pricing policy. Suppliers had problems delivering their products to Wal-Mart's central warehouses. Government regulations concerning permission to open new stores were very time-consuming, compared with the USA.

the capital market, in which investors who do not like the investment opportunities in one country can move their money to a different country in a flash. This reduces the scope for firms to follow strategies that are very country-specific. Other markets, like the labour market, still have a more multidomestic character, which encourages divergence of corporate strategies across countries. For example, in the USA, the labour market facilitates the rapid movement of employees from one company to another, while this is discouraged in Japan. Therefore, for newly formed US companies it is much easier to attract experienced personnel than it is for new Japanese companies. As a consequence, the start-up of new activities by existing firms makes more sense in Japan than it does in the USA. Accordingly, Japanese companies could be expected to diversify to a larger extent than their counterparts from the USA do, at least from this perspective. Nevertheless, here also the trend seems to be towards more similarity among countries. A very convincing example is presented by the European Community, in which successful attempts have been made to create common markets, enabling the free flow of capital, goods and people.

Firm-specific factors

Finally, we will look at the category of firm-specific factors. At a first glance, it seems difficult to link factors like stakeholders, dominant logic, resources and learning to convergence or divergence across countries, since they can differ from firm to firm, rather than from country to country. However, Porter's (1990) 'diamond of national competitive advantage' suggests that the competitive advantage of companies is influenced by their national environment. In particular, excellent factor endowments (such as raw materials, land, labour, capital, technological know-how and infrastructure), sophisticated and demanding local customers, internationally competitive related and supporting industries, and tough local competition all increase the competitive strength of firms. So, for example, BMW's capability in the development of sophisticated, upmarket automobiles is partly based on the availability of highly skilled employees, the lack of speed limits, the presence of very critical customers, the availability of world-class suppliers, and strong competition from Mercedes-Benz, Porsche and Audi in Germany. It is difficult for car manufacturers located in countries with less favourable conditions to equal BMW's competitive strength in this respect. As a consequence, firm-specific factors may be linked with country-specific factors. We believe enough has been said already about differences between countries, trends that may reduce these differences, and their consequences for the divergence or convergence of corporate strategies. We would only like to add here that the mobility of resources has increased through technological developments. For example, container shipping, jet aircraft and the Internet have drastically reduced the costs of moving goods, people and ideas, respectively. Hence, it has become easier to transfer resources that were once peculiar to a specific company located in a specific country to a company located in another country. This creates an additional pressure for convergence of corporate strategies across countries.

Conclusions to this section

To sum up, each firm is faced with a unique constellation of factors that underlie corporate strategy. Therefore, the corporate strategy a firm adopts is also unique. None the less, many firm-specific factors, factors that are related to collections of firms, and factors that are related to countries, are more similar within countries than they are across countries. Consequently, we expect that there is plenty of room for divergence of corporate strategies among countries (and some convergence within countries). However, in all three categories of factors, there are strong trends towards greater similarity across countries. As a result, we expect to observe divergence of corporate strategies across countries, but the divergence could very well be diminishing.

10.6 Conclusions

In this chapter we have investigated the relationship between corporate strategy and institutional variables such as the political system, the financial system and the labour system. Differences in these factors across countries might result in divergence in corporate strategy. The relationship has been investigated in a number of larger-scale empirical studies. The variety in the samples, data and methods that were employed in these studies implies that only tentative inferences can be drawn. Still, we might conclude that convergence of corporate strategy has increased over time. A study that was based on older data found no similarities across countries, while studies that included more recent data found strong similarities across countries.

This allows us to conclude that institutional theory offers, at best, a partial explanation of corporate strategy. While there are still some differences between the corporate strategies adopted by firms in different countries, these are becoming smaller.

This is not entirely good news for the explanatory power of institutional theory in the area of corporate strategy. Generally speaking, institutional theory implies sustained diverg-ence of corporate strategy, given that institutions vary across countries and are assumed to be fairly stable over time. Furthermore, the differences in corporate strategy across countries that were observed could not always be explained by institutional factors. We also found that the degree of convergence might differ among industries. This suggests the existence of at least one additional factor that is relevant for the convergence or divergence of corporate strategy.

In our case, the explanation offered by institutional theory is, at best, incomplete. In order to offer a more complete picture, we developed a model that, aside from institutions, also incorporates additional theories and variables that explain corporate strategy. The variables could be assigned to three categories:

1. factors that are specific to firms
2. factors that pertain to collections of firms, and
3. factors that pertain to countries.

Companies that possess firm-specific factors that are subject to country influences, that are active in multidomestic industries and factor markets, and that originate from countries with unique institutions have ample scope for country-specific strategies. In contrast, companies with firm-specific factors that are not peculiar to a given country, that are active in global industries and factor markets, and that originate from countries with more common institutions, have little room for the adoption of country-specific strategies. Therefore, in some circumstances, corporate strategies could be very different across countries, whereas, in other circumstances, corporate strategies could be very similar across countries. However, since the mobility of resources, the global character of industries and factor markets, and the homogeneity among institutions (at least those that are relevant for corporate strategy) are all increasing, we believe that the trend is towards more convergence of corporate strategy.

Our final conclusion, based on existing and our own larger-scale empirical research, and the inferences drawn from our model, is that, under the right circumstances, divergence of corporate strategies across countries can still be observed, but convergence is gaining the upper hand.

An interesting question is what the convergence will entail. A meta-analysis performed by Palich *et al.* (2000) indicated that related diversification, in general, outperformed both single-business and unrelated-diversification strategies. So if we assume that financial performance determines sustainability in the long term, we assume that the most widely adopted corporate strategy worldwide will be related diversification.

Study Questions

1. Explain what you understand by corporate strategy.

2. Describe the different types of corporate strategy that a firm can adopt.

3. Provide a critical assessment of the usefulness of institutional theory for explaining cross-national differences and similarities in corporate strategy.

4. Explain how the political, financial and labour market systems have an impact on the corporate strategies of firms.

5. Evaluate how industrial organization theory, transaction cost economics and agency theory can help to explain corporate strategy.

6. Evaluate the explanatory power of dominant logic, the resource-based view, organizational learning and strategic contingency theory in the area of comparative corporate strategy.

7. Legitimize your own theoretical choice for understanding corporate strategy.

8. Assess whether and why corporate strategies will converge or diverge across countries.

Further Reading

Davis, G.F., Diekmann, K.A. and Tinsley, C.H. (1994) The decline and fall of the conglomerate firm in the 1980s: the deinstitutionalization of an organizational form. *American Sociological Review* 59, 547–70.

This article is highly interesting because of its institutional analysis of the extinction of the highly and unrelated diversified firms in the USA.

Mayer, M.C.J. and Whittington, R. (2000) The European corporation: strategy, structure, and social science. Oxford: Oxford University Press.

Provides an excellent historical study of the evolution of strategy and structure of European corporations.

Mintzberg, H., Ahlstrand, B. and Lampel, J. (1998) *Strategy Safari: a Guided Tour Through the Wilds of Strategic Management*. New York: Free Press.

This book offers an overview of various perspectives of strategic management.

Montgomery, C.A. (1994) Corporate diversification. *Journal of Economic Perspectives* 3, 163–78.

Case: Examples of Five Different Firms

This case treats a number of examples of firms from various countries. Each firm has followed a unique strategy. At the same time, the cases discussed illustrate the developments in the firms' home countries. Successively, we will look at Tyco International, Buhrmann, Vivendi Universal, Siemens and Tata. After that, there is a brief conclusion.

Tyco International[11]

Tyco International Ltd was founded in 1960 as a US research laboratory. In 1964, the company went public. Management had soon recognized the commercial potential of its research and began to look for acquisitions to develop complementary capabilities in production and marketing. In 1965, Tyco acquired its first company, Mule Battery Products. This was followed by a long list of other acquisitions. However, financial performance was not consistent. For example, Tyco was hit by recessions in the late 1970s, early 1980s and early 1990s. In 1992, L. Dennis Kozlowski became the company's CEO.

When Kozlowski took over, Tyco had four, mostly unrelated, divisions. Despite this apparent diversity, the vast majority of the revenues depended on just one industry – commercial construction – which was highly volatile. Therefore, Kozlowski set out to reduce the cyclicality. An important first step was the successful acquisition of Kendall International, a producer of disposable medical supplies. Kendall became the core of a new division, the Tyco Healthcare Group. Many acquisitions were to follow, totalling US$60 billion, creating a huge

---

[11] Besides the references mentioned in the text, this case is mainly based on Tyco International's corporate website (www.tyco.com) and several articles from *Business Week* (e.g. 'The rise and fall of Dennis Kozlowski', 23 December 2002). The description of Tyco's organization is derived primarily from Collis and Montgomery (1998) and Montgomery *et al.* (2001). Information on General Electric Company is obtained from its corporate website (www.ge.com) and the description in the *International Directory of Company Histories*, Detroit (MI): St James Press.

conglomerate, offering, for example, fire protection and security products and services, valves, pipes and other flow-control products, packaging materials, electrical and electronics components, and medical supplies and devices.

The divisions were allowed to operate in a very autonomous way. The corporate staff was tiny, ensuring little interference from corporate headquarters. At the same time, financial control was tight. Division presidents were held strictly accountable for the financial performance of their individual divisions. High-powered incentives to maximize performance were offered. Fixed salaries were low, but bonuses, which were mainly paid in stock, could be large. Together with the acquisition policy, this management style was regarded as the reason for Tyco's success. Under Kozlowski, market capitalization increased seventyfold. From 1997 to 2001, revenues rose by almost 50 per cent a year, while pretax margins improved to more than 22 per cent. Kozlowski and others began to view Tyco as the second coming of General Electric, whose excellent financial results it even outperformed.

Perhaps in an effort to copy General Electric's successful financial service activities, Kozlowski made a very costly strategic mistake. In 2001, Tyco acquired the CIT Group, a commercial and consumer finance company, for the huge sum of US$9.2 billion. The deal turned out to be a disaster. Tyco would eventually divest the company, incurring a loss of approximately US$7 billion. Kozlowski made a second strategic mistake. To boost the already falling stock price, in January 2002 a plan was announced to separate Tyco into four independent, publicly traded companies. Shareholders, who were already nervous because of the recent Enron debacle, were taken by surprise and began to suspect accounting problems. They became even more confused when the plan was withdrawn a few months later.

By then, Kozlowski had run into more serious trouble. He was accused of dodging US$1 million sales tax due on fine art. Even worse, together with two other corporate officers, Kozlowski was accused of, first, obtaining US$430 million from Tyco through improper sales of stock and, second, stealing US$170 million directly from the company. A few examples of the second category were:

- the use of company funds to throw a lavish birthday party for Kozlowski's wife on Sardinia (costing more than US$1 million)

- the reimbursement of US$1 million for items such as jewellery, clothing and wine

- the inappropriate use of a relocation plan to rent a lavish apartment in New York at an annual rent of US$264,000, paid for by Tyco

- the use of an interest-free loan to buy, at a low price, a company-owned apartment, which was later decreed to Kozlowski's ex-wife

- the sale of a home to Tyco for significantly more than its market value the purchase by Tyco of another apartment for Kozlowski for US$16.8 million, plus US$3 million in improvements and US$11 million in furnishings

- the use of an employee loan programme for a wide variety of personal needs, including yachts, antiques and furniture

- the commitment of donations and pledges to charitable organizations with Tyco money amounting to more than US$106 million, of which at least US$43 million was represented as personal donations.

Consequently, the media started to publish stories about 'The Great Tyco Robbery' and began to liken Kozlowski to Al Capone. Kozlowski had to resign at the beginning of June 2002. After his departure, the future of Tyco was uncertain. Tyco was left with a huge debt. Market capitalization fell by approximately US$90 billion in 2002.

In general, after the 1980s, only few conglomerates seemed to be able to thrive in the USA. Together with General Electric, Tyco belonged to one of the very few exceptions. Some of the fundamental causes of the fall of the conglomerate were the complexities of the management of very diverse businesses. In the end, this type of risk led to the punishment of conglomerates with a 'conglomerate discount' instead of a favourable valuation in the stock market (Porter, 1987: 50). In the second place, during the 1980s, under the Reagan administration, regulatory policy changed considerably (Davis *et al.*, 1994). Anti-trust policy that had made diversification the only viable mode of external growth had disappeared. Moreover, legal impediments that had protected conglomerates against hostile take-overs were removed. This created an effective market for corporate control, in which raiders such as Carl Icahn and T. Boone Pickens realized huge profits by acquiring conglomerates, breaking them up, and selling the separate parts to finance the deal. To prevent this, many conglomerates opted for voluntary restructuring of their portfolio of businesses.

Hence, Porter (1987) argued that it is no longer a valid model for corporate strategy in advanced economies. Only in developing countries, with few large firms, undeveloped capital markets and scarce professional management expertise, might the conglomerate model still work.

Buhrmann[12]

Buhrmann NV is a public corporation that was created in 1993, as a result of the merger between three Dutch companies: KNP, BT and VRG. All three were long-established companies, with roots in the nineteenth or early twentieth centuries. KNP, or, in full, NV Koninklijke Nederlandsche Papierfabriek (Royal Dutch Paper Mill), was mainly a producer of paper, cardboard and packaging. BT or, in full,

[12] The description of Buhrmann is mainly based on the annual reports of the various companies involved, press clippings, in particular from *NRC Handelsblad* and *Het Financieele Dagblad* (two Dutch newspapers), and Buhrmann's corporate website (www.buhrmann.com). We are also indebted to Mario Schijven for his research assistance.

Bührmann-Tetterode NV, was also active in the packaging industry, as a producer and distributor. In addition, BT supplied office products, was a merchant in paper, and distributed and serviced graphic and office systems. Finally, VRG or, in full, Van Reekum-Gepacy NV, was, like BT, a paper merchant,and a distributor of graphic and office systems. Consequently, there were overlaps between the activities of the three companies before the merger. Also, formal ties between the companies were present, in particular in the form of two joint ventures between KNP and BT, and a share of more than 50 per cent of VRG held by KNP.

In the year preceding the merger, all three companies had experienced a sharp drop in their profitability, mainly because of adverse economic conditions. Thus some sort of strategic response seemed appropriate. A merger could, because of the overlaps between the activities, lead to synergies. For example, the combination of activities might reduce direct competition and increase bargaining power over suppliers and customers in certain markets. Moreover, expertise could be exchanged, for instance between the business units that were involved in paper production and those involved in paper trade. Another advantage of the merger could be a more efficient use of working capital. A central treasury department could reallocate funds from business units with a surplus, to business units with a shortage of working capital, thus cutting out banks as an expensive intermediary. However, the primary motive behind the merger may have been risk reduction.

Paper production is highly cyclical. On the one hand, demand for paper is not very stable – for instance, because the number of job advertisements that are printed in newspapers and magazines depends on the state of the economy. On the other hand, supply cannot be adjusted smoothly to demand fluctuations, since production involves huge investments in paper mills, which are slow to build up and slow to break down. The ensuing imbalances between supply and demand give rise to large price fluctuations. The other activities of the merging companies were also vulnerable to economic trends, although to a lesser extent than paper production. For each company, the merger represented entry into new industries, or diversification, and, as a consequence, an opportunity to reduce risks. If some parts of the merged company were to be faced with adverse conditions, this could, at least in theory, be compensated by the better performance of other parts.

Nevertheless, despite these possible advantages, the merger was criticized after its announcement. For example, sceptics claimed that the merger partly involved companies that were active in different parts of the same business chain (like paper production and the subsequent distribution). Therefore, the diversification was, at the same time, vertical integration. Vertical integration can actually make a firm more vulnerable to economic cycles. For instance, if end demand for paper drops by 50 per cent, a distributor of paper could halve the amount of paper that is obtained from a paper producer. However, if the paper producer is part of the same corporation, costs will not be halved, since a large proportion of the costs is not variable, but tied to the investments in the paper mill. Therefore, vertical integration raises the proportion of fixed costs for a distributor, which, in turn, increases the chance that the company incurs losses in the case of a drop in demand. Different criticism came from the European Commission, which feared that market power in certain areas would become too large. Eventually, the merger was approved. The merger created a corporation with sales of approximately €5 billion, about 30,000 employees and over 150 subsidiaries in 30 countries. The subsidiaries could be divided into three main sectors: paper production, packaging production and distribution activities.

There was no smooth sailing for NV Koninklijke KNP BT, as the corporation was somewhat awkwardly named after the merger. More than the traditional Dutch public corporation, KNP BT stressed the importance of creating shareholder value. However, it was precisely in this area that the corporation failed to perform. Over 1993, the year of the merger, a net loss of more than €10 million was incurred, but this could still be blamed on unfavourable economic circumstances instead of the merger. In the following two years, net income rose considerably, but eventually not as much as the shareholders had expected. In 1996, net income fell below the level of 1994. The share price lagged increasingly far behind the general index of the Amsterdam Stock Exchange.

A number of causes of the disappointing performance can be identified. The potential synergies resulting from the merger had probably been overestimated. The realization of synergies among subsidiaries requires more central coordination. At the same time, this impairs the ability of subsidiaries to respond in an appropriate way to new local circumstances. In particular in the area of distribution and trade, the resulting loss of responsiveness often outweighs the synergies realized. Furthermore, the cycles in the paper industry, which seemed to become shorter and fiercer, continued to have a destabilizing effect on the financial results of the merged corporation. Also, the firm was accused of not informing the shareholders adequately about important developments. Specifically, according to the Vereniging van Effectenbezitters, an influential Dutch association of owners of securities, a profit warning was issued too late. Finally, shareholder confidence was wrecked by disagreement among the senior officers about the most suitable course for the firm. For example, at one point the chairman of the executive board wanted to sell the distribution division to Hagemeyer, a large competitor, but the board of directors refused to go along with this.

This conflict led to the resignation of the chairman of the executive board. An important measure that had already been taken was the sale of most of the paper production to Sappi Ltd, a South African paper producer. However, even after these two measures, the market value of the corporation was calculated to be substantially lower than the break-up value. Therefore, splitting up the company into separate parts was an alternative that warranted serious consideration.

In 1998, the packaging activities were divested. Also, a new name for the corporation was adopted: Buhrmann. After the failed diversification of the past, the corporation was to focus exclusively on growth in distribution and service. A major step in this respect was the friendly acquisition of US-based Corporate Express, Inc. Corporate Express was a large, international distributor of office and computer products. A more hostile move was the bid on Samas-Groep NV and

Koninklijke Ahrend NV, two Dutch competitors in the office industry. Perhaps in an attempt to ward off a hostile take-over, the two companies had announced their intention to merge. Ironically, this may have triggered the bid by Buhrmann. Both Samas and Ahrend resisted the bid and further increased the take-over barriers that had already been in place. At the end of 2000, though, a compromise was reached, according to which Buhrmann would take over part of the activities of Samas. The bid for Ahrend was subsequently withdrawn.

The take-overs established Buhrmann as a leading international player in the office and graphic markets. For example, Buhrmann had become the world's largest distributor of office products. However, the take-overs also involved two disadvantages. First of all, about half of the total net sales were now generated in the USA, making the corporation very dependent on cycles in the US economy. This became very clear in 2001, when many firms in the USA started to lay off office workers, and other firms began to economize on their office supplies, forcing Buhrmann to issue a series of profit warnings. The second disadvantage was that Buhrmann incurred a great deal of debt in financing the acquisitions. This gave the lending banks power over Buhrmann and further increased its vulnerability to economic downturns, because of the large fixed-interest payments.

Debt could be reduced through use of the money generated by the divestment of activities. In 2003, Buhrmann announced the sale of its paper merchanting business to Paperlinx, an Australian company. After the divestment, Buhrmann would be almost a single-business firm. By far the largest division was Office Products, which sold, distributed and serviced office and computer products for the business market. The only other division was Graphic Systems, which supplied graphic machines, materials and related services to the graphic industry. Naturally, this undiversified character, in combination with an increased dependence on the USA, meant that the opportunity to spread risks was very limited. Still, shareholders responded very positively to the announcement of the divestment, leading to an increase in the stock price of 40 per cent.

In conclusion, Buhrmann stems from the need of three companies to diversify. The reasons for diversification were altogether not very convincing and the subsequent financial performance was disappointing. Therefore, under increasing pressure from shareholders the diversification strategy was largely dismantled and replaced by a strategy of international expansion. Many other Dutch corporations – like Aegon, KPN, VendexKBB, VNU and Vopak – have also opted for international expansion, often through acquisitions, in a reduced number of core activities.

Vivendi Universal[13]

Vivendi was founded in 1852 in France as the Compagnie Générale des Eaux. It started as a private water company. Soon after its foundation, it won important

---

[13] This case is based on the description of Vivendi Universal in the *International Directory of Company Histories*, Detroit, MI: St James Press, an article in the Dutch magazine *FEM Business* (10 May, 2003), an article in the Dutch newspaper *NRC Handelsblad* (8 November 2002) and an article in *Business Week* (21 April 2003).

contracts in Lyon and Nantes and, in 1860, it won a contract in Paris. In 1940, Générale des Eaux supplied water to 50 per cent of all French town dwellers.

Générale des Eaux remained a water company until Guy Dejouany became president and director general of the company. He first advocated a thermal energy programme in the 1960s and 1970s. He also moved the company into urban cleaning and maintenance, waste management, electrical contracting, house building and construction. These diversification efforts proved to be very successful and profits grew to FFr331 million. This success attracted the attention of other companies. In 1983, Saint-Gobain announced it had a 33 per cent interest in Générale des Eaux. Dejouany managed to convince the government to stop the nationalized Saint-Gobain from taking over Générale des Eaux. Eventually, Saint-Gobain lowered its interest in Générale des Eaux.

With the threat of a hostile take-over gone, the company started to expand both nationally and internationally. It acquired water distribution activities in Spain, Portugal, Italy, the UK and the USA, collected waste in Prague and Bogotá, cleaned the streets of Madrid, and supplied cable television in the UK and Montreal. The company also acquired private hospitals in the UK.

In France, the company expanded in communication, construction and waste management. By 1991, Générale des Eaux had become a leading operator of cable networks in France. Its interests included CANAL+ and a mobile phone network. Furthermore, the company acquired several construction companies and became active in the prestigious La Defense project. Générale des Eaux also won contracts to clean the Louvre and the Museé d'Orsay, and collected waste for Peugeot, Air France and Nestlé.

In 1996, Dejouany retired and Jean-Marie Messier took over. By that time, the media were referring to Générale des Eaux as a 'corporate octopus', with interests in the property, construction, energy, mobile phones, health, amusement parks, cable television and railway industries. Messier developed an ambitious strategy to turn Générale des Eaux into a world-leading company in the environmental service industry as well as in the media and communication industry. Messier, known in the French press as 'Jean Marie Messier Moi-Même Maître du Monde', spent US$77 billion to achieve his goals in a period of six years. He changed the name from Générale des Eaux to Vivendi and split off the water company under the name Vivendi Environment. With the pledge of Vivendi Environment and its steady cash flows, Messier could convince banks to finance his strategy. First, Messier created Cegetel, a subsidiary that operated in the fixed and mobile phones business in France. Vivendi merged with Havas, a publishing company, in 1998 and acquired Cendant Software, an electronic publishing firm. At the peak of the Internet hype Vivendi took over Seagram, owner of Universal Studios and the Universal Music Group, for US$34 billion. Then Messier changed the name of the company again, this time to Vivendi Universal.

However, after the burst of the Internet bubble, there were difficult times for Vivendi. In 2001, the company announced a loss of no less than €13.6 billion, and by 2002 the loss has grown to €23.3 billion. Furthermore, the company had a huge debt. The international finance industry lost faith in Vivendi and attracting new loans became very difficult. Then the board took action and sent Messier home. Rumour has it that it was French president Jacques Chirac personally, who asked Jean-René Fourtou to save Vivendi Universal. Fourtou started a reorganization programme and sold off large parts of the company. Vivendi Environment was the first part to be sold. After that, the publishing subsidiaries were sold. Fourtou was also planning to sell Universal Studios, Universal Music Group, and the US cable network USA Networks. The new strategy of Vivendi Universal is to concentrate on its telecoms business, Cegetel, and the French part of the cable network CANAL+.

To sum up, Vivendi had been a real conglomerate for a long time. However, after the burst of the Internet bubble, the company was forced to limit its activities and concentrate on the telecoms business.

Siemens[14]

In 1847, in Germany, Werner von Siemens and Johann Georg Halske founded the company that later developed into Siemens AG. The German company grew into a huge enterprise, with 426,000 employees, representation in 190 countries all over the world, and net sales exceeding €84 billion (fiscal year 2002). Siemens was not only big, but also very diverse. It divided its activities into eight broad business segments: automation and control, information and communications, power, transportation, medical, lighting, financing and real estate, and affiliates. In turn, each segment consisted of a number of separate business groups. Together, they supplied a large number of different products and services to various business and consumer markets. Some examples of its products and services are process automation, automotive parts, telephone and communications systems, power plants, locomotives, imaging systems for medical diagnosis, lamps, insurance products, mobile phones, computers and washing machines. This made Siemens into an archetypal conglomerate.

Siemens' corporate strategy was heavily criticized, particularly by stock analysts and investment bankers. They argued that the corporation lacked focus, that it was slow and overly cautious, and that it was squandering opportunities for growth. ABB, the result of a merger between Asea from Sweden and Brown-Broveri from Switzerland, was set as an example to Siemens. Under the leadership of its renowned CEO Percy Barnevik, ABB had concentrated on high-growth businesses and sold the rest. For example, it had divested its traditional activities in power-generation equipment, while making 160 acquisitions in other areas.

Nevertheless, Siemens stuck to its corporate strategy. It refused to sell boring activities such as power-generation equipment and 'be drawn into the excesses of the New Economy', according to President and CEO Dr Heinrich von Pierer in his letter to the shareholders (annual report 2002). Siemens' businesses were subject to different cycles. Many businesses – like power generation,

---

[14] This case is based mainly on several articles from *Business Week* and *NRC-Handelsblad*, and the corporate website of Siemens (www.siemens.com) and its annual reports.

medical equipment and rail systems – were subject to long-term market cycles. Others – like automation and lighting – were faced with regular short-term market cycles. Then there were businesses, like information and communication, that had to cope with sudden drops in demand. In sum, the diverse portfolio of businesses stabilized overall financial results. This did not imply cross-subsidization. Each group was responsible for its own profitability. If necessary, measures like reorganization, alliances with other firms or divestment were taken. Apart from risk reduction, several additional advantages of being a conglomerate were pointed out by corporate officers. For example, the shared reputation and brand name allowed the recruitment of talented employees all over the world. Also, Siemens was able to offer customers integrated solutions for most of their needs. A hospital, for instance, could go to Siemens for its needs in transportation, lighting, communication, power and medical systems. Finally, Siemens' worldwide presence facilitated entry into new markets. If a subsidiary wanted to start activities in China, for instance, it could depend on the support of the dozens of joint ventures that other parts of Siemens had already established over there.

The corporate strategy seemed to work. Siemens was less affected than other companies by the unfavourable macro-economic environment and high-tech bust at the beginning of the twenty-first century. Despite a sharp decrease in demand from telecoms operators, for example, the conglomerate still produced satisfactory results, because it could rely on profits from the more traditional activities. In contrast, ABB was struggling to survive. It had acquired huge debts to finance the acquisitions, making it vulnerable to economic downturns. Furthermore, one of the companies ABB had acquired was Combustion Engineering, which was later to face asbestos-related claims that threatened the very existence of the company.

In conclusion, Siemens is an example of a firm that withstood the perhaps short-sighted interests of shareholders and stuck successfully to its corporate strategy of extensive, unrelated diversification. Naturally, critics are never at a loss for an argument. They claimed that Siemens' returns on shares still lagged behind those of General Electric, the well-known US-based conglomerate.

Tata[15]

In 2003, the Tata Group comprised 80 companies, which were active in seven broad sectors: materials, engineering, energy, chemicals, consumer products, communications and information systems, and services. Some examples of the activities of the 80 companies were steel manufacturing, advanced composites manufacturing, commercial and passenger vehicle manufacturing, industrial engineering and construction services provision, power generation, chemicals and fertilizer production, tea and coffee manufacturing and marketing, chinaware

[15] The information used in this case is primarily derived from the description of Tata Iron & Steel Co. Ltd in the *International Directory of Company Histories*, Detroit, MI: St James Press, and the website of the Tata Group (www.tata.com). The authors would also like to thank, in alphabetical order, Rejie George and Rekha Krishnan for their help. Any remaining errors are the sole responsibility of the authors.

production, publishing, basic telephony, cellular and Internet services provision, information technology consultancy, management consultancy, hotel chain operation, real estate development, life insurance coverage and asset management. Given the number and scope of these activities, Tata clearly qualifies for the label 'conglomerate'. However, the origination of Tata differs from that of a traditional western conglomerate.

The foundations for Tata were laid in 1868, when Jamsetji Nusserwanji Tata started a trading firm in India. In 1874, the first manufacturing activities began, through the establishment of the first indigenous Indian textile mill. At the time, since India was still under UK rule, its economy was dominated by UK economic interests, which dictated that India should serve as supplier of the required raw materials and buyer of its manufactured products. The advancement of an independent India was an important motive behind Jamsetji Tata's further plans. Based on his international travels, he had identified three activities that he saw as essential to a modern industrial economy: steel manufacturing, hydroelectric power generation and technical education. Although he died before his plans for any of these three activities bore fruit, he did lay the foundations on which later generations of his family were able to realize his vision.

A few important milestones in this respect were: the birth of the Tata Iron and Steel Company in 1907, the creation of the Tata Hydro-Electric Power Supply Company in 1910, and the establishment of the Indian Institute of Science in 1991. Other significant diversification moves were the entries into consumer goods such as soaps, detergents and cooking oils (1917), commercial aviation (1932), chemicals (1939), commercial vehicles (1945), cosmetics (1952), tea (1962), consultancy (1968), publishing (1970), computer hardware (1977), passenger cars (1985), telecoms hardware (1988), fertilizers (1989), insurance (1995) and telecoms services (1996). Several of these entries took the form of a joint venture with a foreign partner. For example, the insurance activities were started together with the American International Group from the USA. For a long time, a joint venture was the only legal option for a foreign firm that wanted to enter India. Tata's own international expansion started modestly, with the establishment of a London office in 1907, and increased gradually, culminating in the take-over in 2000 of the Tetley Group, a tea company, from the UK. This represented the first major acquisition of an international brand by a firm from India.

Meanwhile, in particular during the late 1960s and 1970s, Tata had been faced with developments that posed a serious threat to its survival. The Indian government appeared to prefer a Soviet-style centrally planned economy to one with large private enterprises. Therefore, legislation became increasingly unfavourable or even hostile towards enterprises like Tata. For example, dividends were restricted, expansion into certain industries was constrained, and attempts were made to nationalize certain parts. As a result, Tata had to assume a low profile. Until 1970, central control was achieved through the managing agency system. According to this system, investments in India were managed by firms of agents who, in return, received commission. After the abolishment of the system, formal control was preserved through shares in the Tata companies owned by Tata

Industries Ltd. whose chairman was a distant relative of the founder, Jamsetji Tata. However, because of the unfavourable political environment, the group was compelled to emphasize the independent character of all Tata companies. Also, it was stressed that trusts set up to promote non-commercial goals held the majority of the companies' shares. In reality, however, the family managed to hold the group together through informal consultation, the appearance of identical names among the directors, and a shared office in Bombay.

Starting in the 1980s, government policy became less negative for private enterprises. As a result, the 'coming out' of Tata could slowly commence. A number of changes became apparent. In 1999, a new corporate mark and logo were launched, which were to be centrally promoted and protected. Furthermore, in 2001, a group executive office was set up. This office had to design and implement change in the group and guide the group's future strategy. Finally, financial performance was emphasized to a greater extent than it had been in the past. Tata had often been accused of keeping all companies alive, irrespective of their profitability. However, at the start of the new millennium the need to critically review companies that were consistently underperforming was recognized. According to Ratan N. Tata, the group chairman, the companies were faced with ever increasing competitive pressures, both in domestic and foreign markets, due to the growing integration of the Indian economy into the world economy.

To sum up, a number of differences between Tata and a typical western conglomerate, such as General Electric or Tyco, can be pointed out. First of all, Tata's mission was not single-minded profit or shareholder value maximization. It was founded with the idealistic, anti-colonial motive of self-sufficiency for India. The second, and related, difference is the path to growth. Tata did not rely on external growth through the acquisition of existing companies; instead, most of its diversification originated from its own internal start-ups and subsequent expansions of new activities and, in addition, from domestic joint ventures with companies from abroad. In fact, this seems to be the main reason for Tata's survival and success as a conglomerate. In countries with substantial market imperfections, in particular in the capital and managerial labour markets, a conglomerate that is capable of allocating capital and expertise to promising new ventures can perform a very valuable role. Also, as probably the best-known and most respected Indian company, Tata represented an attractive joint venture partner for foreign firms that were not allowed to have wholly owned subsidiaries in the country. Another difference is the structure, which does not entail a clearly defined corporate office with hierarchical authority over a number of divisions that are fully owned, but is much less explicit. For example, there are multiple central coordinating companies. In addition, companies do not have to be fully owned by a central holding company, but can also have their own public listing. A final related difference is the influence of the family. While a western conglomerate is controlled by independent, professional managers, Tata is still controlled by the family that gave the group its name. Nevertheless, as became clear in the previous paragraph, a more mainstream government policy in India, in combination with increasing international competition, has caused Tata to adopt a number of characteristics, which mean that it is starting to resemble a western conglomerate.

Based on the firms discussed in this case, two general observations can be made. First, their backgrounds show that the organization or governance of corporate strategy differs between countries. In the firms from the USA and Europe, diversification is mainly organized through formal control of subsidiaries active in different industries by a central holding company, which is based on full, or at least majority, ownership of the subsidiaries. In the examples from Asia, governance of diversification seems to be more informal, meaning that companies active in different industries are grouped together via a number of mechanisms like cross-shareholdings, officials with positions in several companies, and companies that perform coordinating roles.

Next, in the USA, the successful conglomerate had become almost extinct by the late 1980s. After that, ill-advised diversification moves were rapidly and severely punished in a demanding capital market. The examples from the other countries indicate that extensive diversification was sustainable for a much longer period of time. However, in all those cases, conglomerates were under mounting pressure to critically evaluate, and possibly restructure, the existing portfolio of businesses.

Questions

1. Trace the differences and similarities in the corporate strategies of the five companies studied in this case.

2. Explain whether you find more evidence of divergence or of convergence.

3. Provide, where possible, an institutional explanation for the corporate strategies of the companies discussed in this case.

4. Evaluate whether and how the theories discussed in this chapter could be used to explain the corporate strategies of the companies examined in this case.

This article is especially interesting for its overview of several universalistic theories of product diversification.

References

Ansoff, H.I. (1965) *Corporate Strategy: an Analytical Approach to Business Policy for Growth and Expansion*. New York: McGraw-Hill.

Barkema, H.G. and Vermeulen, F. (1998) International expansion through start-up or acquisition: a learning perspective. *Academy of Management Journal* 41, 7–26.

Bartlett, C.A. and Ghoshal, S. (1989) *Managing Across Borders: the Transnational Solution*. Boston, MA: Harvard Business School Press.

Bergh, D.D. (2001) Diversification strategy research at a crossroads: established, emerging and anticipated paths, in Hitt, M.A., Freeman, R.E. and Harrison, J.S. (eds) *The Blackwell Handbook of Strategic Management*. Malden, MA: Blackwell, 362–83.

Berle, A.A. and Means, G.C. (1932) *The Modern Corporation and Private Property*. New York: Macmillan.

Bernstein, J.R. (1997) Japanese capitalism, in McCraw, T.K. (ed.) *Creating Modern Capitalism: how Entrepreneurs, Companies, and Countries Triumphed in Three Industrial Revolutions*. Cambridge, MA: Harvard University Press, 441–89.

Chandler, A.D. (1962) *Strategy and Structure: Chapters in the History of the Industrial Enterprise*. Cambridge, MA: MIT Press.

Chatterjee, S. and Wernerfelt, B. (1991) The link between resources and type of diversification: theory and evidence. *Strategic Management Journal* 12, 33–48.

Clark, P. and Mueller, F. (1996) Organizations and nations: from universalism to institutionalism. *British Journal of Management* 7, 125–40.

Deller J.F. and Flunkert, U. (1996) Recruitment and development of up-and-coming managers in Germany and Japan: an exemplary comparison. *Career Development International* 2, 5–9.

Dietl, H.M. (1998) *Capital Markets and Corporate Governance in Japan, Germany and the United States: Organizational Response to Market Inefficiencies*. London: Routledge.

Dyas, G.P. and Thanheiser H.T. (1976) *The Emerging European Enterprise: Strategy and Structure in French and German Industry*. London: Macmillan.

Fligstein, N. (1990) *The Transformation of Corporate Control*. Cambridge, MA: Harvard University Press.

Goold, M. and Campbell, A. (1987) *Strategies and Styles: The Role of the Centre in Managing Diversified Corporations*. Oxford/New York: Basil Blackwell.

Grant, R.M. (1988) On 'dominant logic', relatedness and the link between diversity and performance. *Strategic Management Journal* 9, 639–42.

Grant, W. (1986) *Why Employer Organization Matters*. University of Warwick, Working Paper No. 46.

Hill, C.W.L. and Hoskisson, R.E. (1987) Strategy and structure in the multiproduct firm. *Academy of Management Review* 12, 331–41.

Hill, C.W.L. and Jones, G.R. (2001) *Strategic Management: an Integrated Approach* (annual update (5th ed). Boston, MA: Houghton Mifflin.

Hoskisson, R.E. and Hitt, M.A. (1990) Antecedents and performance outcomes of diversification: a review and critique of theoretical perspectives. *Journal of Management*, 16, 461–509.

Hout, T., Porter, M.E. and Rudden, E. (1982) How global companies win out. *Harvard Business Review*, 60 (September/October), 98–108.

Jensen, M.C. (1986) Agency costs of free cash flow, corporate finance, and takeovers. *American Economic Review* 76, 323–9.

Kogut, B., Walker, G. and Anand J. (2002) Agency and institutions: national divergences in diversification behavior. *Organization Science* 13, 162–78.

Kostova, T. and Roth, K. (2002) Adoption of an organizational practice by subsidiaries of multinational corporations: institutional and relational effects. *Academy of Management Journal* 45, 215–33.

Lane, C. (1992) European business systems: Britain and Germany compared, in Whitley, R. (ed.) *European Business Systems: Firms and Markets in their National Contexts.* London: Sage Publications, 64–97.

Lane, C. (1995) *Industry and Society in Europe: Stability and Change in Britain, Germany and France.* Aldershot: Edward Elgar.

Levitt, T. (1983) The globalization of markets. *Harvard Business Review* 61 (May/June), 92–102.

Lorsch, J.W. and Graff, S.K. (1996) Corporate governance, in Warner, M. (ed.) *International Encyclopedia of Business and Management.* London: Routledge, 772–82.

Mahoney, J.T. and Pandian, J.R. (1992) The resource-based view within the conversation of strategic management. *Strategic Management Journal* 13: 363–80.

Markides, C.C. and Williamson, P.J. (1996) Corporate diversification and organizational structure: a resource-based view. *Academy of Management Journal* 39, 340–67.

Mayer, M.C.J. and Whittington, R. (1999) Strategy, structure and 'systemness': national institutions and corporate change in France, Germany and the UK, 1950–1993. *Organization Studies* 20, 933–59.

Mayer, M.C.J. and Whittington, R. (2000) *The European Corporation: Strategy, Structure, and Social Science.* Oxford: Oxford University Press.

Mintzberg, H., Ahlstrand, B. and Lampel, J. (1998) *Strategy Safari: a Guided Tour Through the Wilds of Strategic Management.* New York: Free Press.

Montgomery, C.A. (1994) Corporate diversification. *Journal of Economic Perspectives* 3, 163–78.

Palepu, K. (1985) Diversification strategy, profit performance, and the entropy measure. *Strategic Management Journal* 6, 239–55.

Palich, L.E., Cardinal, L.B. and Miller, C.C. (2000) Curvilinearity in the diversification-performance linkage: an examination of over three decades of research. *Strategic Management Journal* 21, 155–74.

Panzar, J. and Willig, R. (1975) Economies of scale and economies of scope in multi-output production. Unpublished working paper. Murray Hill, NJ: Bell Laboratories.

Penrose, E.T. (1959) *The Theory of the Growth of the Firm.* Oxford: Blackwell.

Porter, M.E. (1980) *Competitive Strategy: Techniques for Analyzing Industries and Competitors.* New York: Free Press.

Porter, M.E. (1985) *Competitive Advantage: Creating and Sustaining Superior Performance.* New York: Free Press.

Porter, M.E. (1987) From competitive advantage to corporate strategy. *Harvard Business Review* 65 (May/June), 43–59.

Porter, M.E. (1990) The Competitive Advantage of Nations. New York: Free Press.

Powell, W.W. (1998) Institutional theory, in Cooper, C.L. and Argyris, C. (eds) *The Concise Blackwell Encyclopedia of Management.* Malden, MA: Blackwell, 301–3.

Prahalad, C.K. and Bettis, R.A. (1986) The dominant logic: a new linkage between diversity and performance. *Strategic Management Journal* 7, 485–501.

Prahalad, C.K. and Doz, Y.L. (1987) *The Multinational Mission: Balancing Local Demands and Global Vision*. New York: Free Press.

Rumelt, R.P. (1974) *Strategy, Structure, and Economic Performance*. Boston, MA: Harvard Business School Press.

Sorge, A. (1995) Personnel and organization from a comparative perspective, in Harzing, A.W. and van Ruysseveldt, J. (eds) *International Human Resource Management*. London: Sage, 199–223.

Tachibanaki, T. and Taki, A. (2000) *Capital and Labour in Japan: the Functions of Two Factor Markets*. London: Routledge.

Teece, D.J. (1982) Towards an economic theory of the multiproduct firm. *Journal of Economic Behavior and Organization* 3, 39–63.

Teece, D.J., Rumult, R., Dosi, G. and Winter, S. (1994) Understanding corporate coherence: theory and evidence. *Journal of Economic Behavior and Organization* 23, 1–30.

Venkatraman, N. (1989) The concept of fit in strategy research: towards verbal and statistical correspondence. *Academy of Management Review* 14, 423–44.

Wernerfelt, B. (1984) A resource-based view of the firm. *Strategic Management Journal* 4, 171–80.

Whitley, R. (1992) *European Business Systems: Firms and Markets in their National Contexts*. London/Newbury Park/New Delhi: Sage Publications.

Whitley, R. (1994) Dominant forms of economic organization in market economies. *Organization Studies* 15, 153–82.

Whitley, R. (1997) Business systems, in Sorge, A. and Warner, M. (eds) *International Encyclopedia of Business and Management: The Handbook of Organizational Behaviour*. London: International Thomson Business Press, 173–86.

Williamson, O.E. (1975) *Markets and Hierarchies: Analysis and Antitrust Implications*. New York: Free Press.

Chapter 11

Networks and Clusters of Economic Activity

SJOERD BEUGELSDIJK AND GERT-JAN HOSPERS

Learning Objectives

By the end of this chapter you will be able to:

- understand why networks and clusters are important for business life
- analyse the positive and negative aspects of the network relationships of firms
- explore how geographical clustering can enhance a firm's competitive position
- critically assess the insights of several theoretical frameworks for understanding the concepts of networks and clusters
- assess the argument that institutions are important in industrial districts
- appreciate the difference between the sectoral approach and the cluster approach.

Chapter Outline

11.1 **Introduction**

11.2 **Balancing Competition and Cooperation**

11.3 **Networks from a Theoretical Perspective**
Transaction cost theory and networks
Network theory: structural hole theory
Network theory: the Swedish network approach

11.4 **From Networks to Clusters**
Industrial districts
Porter's concept of clusters

11.5 **Innovative Milieux**

11.6 **Conclusions**
Study Questions
Further Reading
Case: Networks in China or Guanxi
References

11.1　Introduction

Over the past ten years the concepts of networks and clusters have gained popularity in international business in the advanced countries. These concepts refer to a certain kind of strategic cooperation between various organizations, mostly firms. At present, pleas can be heard for the logic of cooperative ventures in doing international business. Generally speaking, cooperation is increasingly seen as a necessary organizational survival strategy in today's intensely competitive business environment. Some authors even suggest that cooperation strategies are part of a new industrial order ('alliance capitalism'), in which international competitiveness depends on the continuous collabouration of firms with external sources of knowledge (Best, 1990; Dunning, 1997; Dicken, 1998; Porter, 1998). In spite of its current popularity, the idea of inter-organizational cooperation is, of course, not new. For example, it is well known that the UK cotton industry of the late nineteenth century derived much of its competitiveness from the well-developed cooperation of producers with suppliers of machines and transport facilities (Lazonick, 1992).

What *is* new, however, is both the aim and the complexity of modern cooperative efforts. Often, they are aimed at the collaborative research and development (R&D) needed for the realization of innovations, that is, new products, services and processes. In many cases, the technology-based aim of these cooperative strategies involves a complex interplay of different parties (e.g. firms, universities and private research institutes), providing each other with complementary knowledge. This type of cooperation has led to the emergence of different types of network and geographically concentrated clusters of economic activity.

While it is hard to give a definition of networks and clusters that encompasses all variants of economic cooperation, in general, networks can be seen as chains of competitors, suppliers, customers and/or knowledge institutes with the aim of creating value added. Clusters could then be seen as constituting a subgroup of networks, in that they have a clear geographical dimension. There are, for example, many cross-border networks of firms operating in the field of semiconductors (e.g. cooperation between Toshiba, Hitachi and AT&T). Simultaneously, however, there are some geographically concentrated clusters in this branch of activity. Well-known examples of such regional clusters in semiconductors are Silicon Valley in California and Cambridge in the UK.

The increasing popularity of networks and clusters in international business explains its inclusion in this text. Both management and policy-makers are interested in the power of network- and cluster-type relationships for increasing the international competitiveness of companies and entire sectors. In order to provide you with a good grasp of the fundamentals of networks and clusters, this chapter discusses network theory and, subsequently, the concept of clusters. As a result, the text is essentially theoretical and probably demanding, but it offers most that there is to know about the topic in a nutshell. The case at the end of the chapter will help you to test your knowledge of networks and clusters in a comparative setting. It requires you to take a comparative view and combine the insights generated in this chapter with the insights discussed in previous chapters.

The chapter starts with a brief examination of the drivers of networking and clustering – that is, the increasing need for innovation and specialization. Next, the fundamentals of transaction cost theory are discussed, as networking can be perceived as a hybrid form of governance. After that, networks are discussed from two complementary theoretical perspectives: structural hole theory and the embeddedness perspective.

Subsequently, the chapter stresses the geographical dimension of inter-firm cooperation. In this context, concepts such as industrial districts, Porter's cluster approach and the innovative milieux are introduced. The chapter ends with an overview of the different dimensions of networking and clustering that can be identified in practice. The chapter shows that networks and clusters are not only important carriers of business life, but are also complex inter-organizational structures with many different faces, because they are rooted in different societal structures.

11.2 Balancing Competition and Cooperation

The emergence of networks and clusters as important vehicles in business life can be related to trends that have been going on in the world economy for some time. These developments include, in particular, globalization, technological developments and changes in market demand (Dicken, 1998). Through the combined effect of these trends, market rivalry has not only intensified, but has also changed character. As explained in the introduction, globalization refers to the phenomenon of an increasing number of economic relations in today's world economy. Due to the liberalization of world trade, the opening of previously sheltered economies (e.g. eastern Europe and China) and the resulting increase in foreign direct investments (FDIs), more and more and different types of relationship between parties in the market place are emerging. The phenomenon of globalization seems to induce integration of activities that are geographically dispersed with no company or country being able to operate in a totally independent manner. This new global context forces companies to change their competition strategies in the market.

Besides globalization, there is a tendency for an accelerating pace of technological development. In particular developments in the information and communication technologies (ICTs) have caused a reduction in transportation costs for people, goods, services and information (Dicken, 1998). Although these 'space-shrinking technologies' have resulted in cost reductions, simultaneously the R&D needed to develop new technologies has become more expensive. The latter is caused by the fact that, nowadays, most innovations are realized by combining separate complex technologies ('crossroads technologies'); modern examples are mechatronics and biochemistry.

Another important market development is the change of preferences at the demand side of the economy. Contractors and consumers both place heavier demands on the quality of the products and services they buy. As a result, products and services have to be tailored to the individual customers' requirements. This process of 'customization', which started in the capital goods industry, has also penetrated the market for consumer goods. An example of the changing pattern of demand can be found in the automobile industry. Because the demand for automobiles has matured, producers have to supply a far greater variety of vehicle types than they did previously. In this way, they hope to create new markets and attract new customers.

These trends in the world economy have resulted in the paradoxical situation that *firms have to cooperate in order to remain competitive*. Success stories of clusters, in which competition and cooperation co-exist with an innovating economy, show that firms are able to resolve the paradox. An illustration of this can be found in the Italian region of Emilia Romagna, where firms producing ceramic tiles are cooperating in the field of purchasing and research on materials, while, at the same time, competing aggressively with each other in the marketplace (Pyke, 1995).

The idea that competition and cooperation should go hand in hand can be found in several recent contributions in the literature too. According to Enright (1996), for instance, firms should not ask themselves whether to compete or to cooperate, but rather on *what dimensions* to compete and cooperate. This question involves a trade-off between access to more resources versus potential loss of firm-specific knowledge to competitors.

Related to such arguments is Audretsch and Thurik's point (1997) that, currently, a fundamental shift is taking place from a 'managed economy' with homogeneous mass production as the central issue towards a so-called 'entrepreneurial economy'. In this kind of economy, the competitiveness of companies is primarily based on entrepreneurship, heterogeneity and innovativeness. Here, competition and cooperation are not substitutes any more, but rather complements.

It must be noted, however, that not all firms in all countries are equally good at cooperating and that, partly based on cultural and institutional features, in some countries entrepreneurship and innovativeness are more prevalent than in others. Indeed, the type and intensity of cooperation, as well as the ways in which cooperation and innovation are successfully achieved, differ between countries. In Germany, for example, entrepreneurship and innovation in the biotechnology sector only developed after significant government involvement and adaptation of the institutions at the sector level. The Japanese *keiretsu*, on the other hand, are a different type of inter-organizational cooperation that developed in response to the lack of efficiently functioning institutions after the Second World War, combined with market-distorting government policies. The case at the end of this chapter is a further illustration of these arguments.

11.3 Networks from a Theoretical Perspective

To explore the issue of networking and clustering from a theoretical point of view, both the insights derived from transaction cost economics and network theories are discussed here. Transaction costs theory offers an economic perspective on networking, whereas network theories perceive the network type of cooperation more as a societal activity than a sole economic decision based on costs and benefits.

Transaction cost theory and networks
The choice of market, hierarchy or hybrid forms

Coase (1937) and, particularly, Williamson (1975, 1985) have developed transaction cost economics. The focus of these authors is on the organization of economic transactions between parties. They do not take the neoclassical notion of a representative firm as their unit of analysis. Instead, they take transactions between economic actors as the analytical starting point. According to Williamson (1985), 'a transaction occurs when a good or service is transferred across a technologically separable interface. One stage of activity terminates and another begins.' When economic parties execute transactions, they meet transaction costs – that is, the costs of information and communication needed to find, negotiate, agree upon and monitor contracts. As an example, just think of the marketing costs a producer has to incur in order to attract new customers.

In general, these costs may be divided into three categories: contact costs, contract costs and control costs (Nooteboom, 1999). Costs of contact and contract may appear in the phase before doing business (ex ante), while control costs may arise when parties have carried out transactions and one of the parties is, say, cheating (ex post). The main argument of transaction cost economics is that parties will look for the most efficient governance structure to coordinate their transactions. Ultimately, they will choose that mode of governance in which the sum of both transaction costs and production costs is minimized.

In his first book, Williamson (1975) follows Coase (1937) and only sees market and hierarchy (merger) as alternative governance structures. In his later work (1985), however, he replaces this dichotomy by a continuum on which 'hybrid forms' (cooperative forms such as networks and clusters) are positioned between the poles of market and hierarchy. The efficiency of each of these governance structures depends on the properties of human behaviour as well as on the characteristics (dimensions) of transactions.

The assumptions of transaction cost theory regarding human behaviour are 'bounded rationality' and 'opportunism'. Bounded rationality means that individuals have restricted cognitive capabilities so that their behaviour can be seen as 'intendedly rational but only limited so' (Simon, 1961). Opportunism is a form of strategic behaviour and reflects the incentive of individuals to cheat if this will improve their position. In consequence, Williamson (1975) defines opportunism as 'self-interest seeking with guile'. Both the bounded rationality and the opportunism of individuals cause costs in executing transactions. The height of these transaction costs is determined by three dimensions of transactions – that is, their asset specificity, uncertainty and frequency.

The first dimension of a transaction is its asset specificity, or the degree to which the transaction has to be supported by investments in special assets, which have no or little use outside the transaction. These investments create a relationship of dependency between the transaction partners. A classic example of a transaction-specific investment is a mould a supplier develops for a customer to use to press the coachwork of a special model of car (Nooteboom, 1999). The second dimension is the frequency of a transaction, referring to the question of how often it takes place. The last dimension, the uncertainty surrounding transactions, is inherent in economic activities, since human behaviour is assumed to be bounded rational.

Why markets and hierarchies are not always efficient

When both the degree of asset specificity, the frequency and the uncertainty of a transaction are relatively low, transaction cost theory predicts that the market is the most efficient governance structure to coordinate transactions. In this case, the transaction costs for parties are low because the price mechanism can coordinate their transactions. However, when transactions are characterized by high asset specificity, frequency and uncertainty, the market is no longer efficient. At that moment, internalization of the transaction in a hierarchy (i.e. an organization governed by authority), involves reduced transaction costs for the partners. For the less extreme, intermediate cases, hybrid forms between market and hierarchy are suitable alternatives (Williamson, 1991).

As suggested, in countries such as Japan (the *keiretsu*) and Korea (the *Chaebol*), these hybrid forms of transactions, such as networks, emerged as a reaction to the business environment in which the firms operate. Supplier networks, like the one around Japanese firm Toyota, developed in reaction to the domestic environment after the Second World War and a specific combination of government policies. By forming its own supplier network, Toyota gained an advantage over competitors in the USA because it was relieved of two major transaction costs: those linked to internalization and decomposed subcontracting. In addition, successful networks like Toyota's develop intra-group understandings that lead to significant reductions in both inter-firm coordination costs and direct production costs per unit of output (Edwards and Samimi, 1997).

In general, it has been suggested that 'hybrid vertical inter-firm relations' might be more efficient than market and hierarchy (Noorderhaven, 1994). In this light, seven in-depth case studies among Dutch companies indicate that, since the 1980s, the number of inter-firm relationships has grown compared with the strategic options of market and hierarchy, and that the competitive positioning of the cooperating firms has been strengthened (Commandeur, 1994). On the basis of an analysis of surveys among about 700 firms in the Dutch province of Brabant in the period 1987–92, a significant positive correlation was found between the results of innovating and the joint R&D efforts of suppliers and users (Oerlemans, 1996). The conclusion from this finding is that cooperating firms can use knowledge from their environment more efficiently than firms innovating in isolation. The problem with this conclusion, however, is that not all national institutional environments allow for cooperation and, further, that not all national cultures are equally prone to adopt cooperative business practices.

The latter indicates clearly that transaction cost economics offers a more economic view of cooperation. This view has been criticized, however, for being too rigid, mechanical and pessimistic, reducing cooperation to only a cost–benefit problem. In reality, as suggested, cooperation is also a societal phenomenon through which different parties complement each other and can develop trust relationships. Below we address two theoretical approaches that build on the notion that firms are influenced by their societal context and that a firm's competitive advantage is influenced by its position in a network.

First, we introduce Burt's theory on the societal structure of competition. This weak-tie approach argues that a large network of arm's-length or weak ties is most advantageous. The second approach is the embeddedness perspective, which is also referred to as the 'Swedish school'. This strong-tie approach assumes that a closed, tightly knit network of embedded or close ties is most advantageous. In reality, firms have a portfolio of embedded and atomistic neoclassical arm's-length ties. These two theoretical approaches, however, are also important for understanding inter-firm relationships and the creation of competitive advantage.

Network theory: structural hole theory

Burt (1992) argues that the structure of the player's network, and the location of the player in the social structure, build competitive advantage. His theory is based on the idea that an actor is in a better position to profit from interactions and transactions with others if these other actors are connected to actors who are not connected with the actor himself. These connections provide additional opportunities and the lack of connections are defined as *structural holes*. By occupying the structural location between otherwise unconnected nodes (a structural hole), the so-called *tertius gaudens*, or the third that profits, realizes greater returns on the social capital extant within his network. The social network becomes a social resource. The central argument made by Burt is that an optimal position is characterized by two qualities:

1. the connections of an actor are surrounded by structural holes, and
2. the actor him/herself is not surrounded by these structural holes.

In essence, Burt's argument is that some network positions are better than others, namely those that provide for least constraint and take least effort to maintain while still providing the most access to (flows of) information or other goods.

A fundamental idea that inspired Burt's structural hole theory is Granovetter's description of the 'strength of weak ties' (Granovetter, 1973). Granovetter argued that access to new information is obtained through an ego's weak ties to nodes at a distance from his own local network. The reasoning is that information within the local network is widely shared locally. Hence, most of the local contacts are redundant. New information comes from non-redundant ties. Although weak ties and structural holes seem to describe the same phenomenon, the new element of Burt's theory, contra Granovetter (1973), is that the crucial element is not the strength or the weakness of the ties, but their redundancy or non-redundancy in relation to the ties that you have already established.

Moreover, Burt constructs a conceptualization of power relationships (i.e. the so-called *tertius gaudens* controls the flows of resources between the other two nodes, placing him in a position of greater power). According to Burt, networks are especially important when competition is imperfect. This is in line with Uzzi's argument (1997), which stated that, especially if the transactions between actors are non-reciprocal and are deals in which costs are everything, the competitive market mechanism may work; but as conditions change under which the transactions take place – that is, more tacit elements like quality and service (instead of quantities and prices) are present and important (the weaker the ability of prices to distil information) – the more organizations will form embedded ties. Relations go beyond the level of the neoclassical concept of buyer–seller relationships, and include trust, altruism, and so on. Repeated interactions and the resulting social networks facilitate informal collective economic and social punishments for deviant behaviour.

A critical perspective on the structural hole approach

There are several problems with Burt's theory of structural holes and his concept of networks. First, just like transaction costs economics, the individual (atomistic), static and rational actor approach makes it hard to link Burt's network theory with other literature on networks. By taking the individual actor perspective, Burt does not take into account the collective nature of organizational action and the role of networks in maintaining stable collective structures (Salancik, 1995). In Burt's theory societal factors cannot be incorporated, because Burt does not discuss the nature of the ties. He 'assumes away' the problems of trust and reciprocity when it comes to forging and sustaining network ties. The making and breaking of ties is based solely on the actor's competitive access to resources within the network. But would systems like the Japanese *keiretsu* exist if the actors selected network contacts out of purely individualistic motives?

A second related problem concerns the closure of social networks. Closure of the social structure is important for the existence of effective norms and the trustworthiness of social structures. In Burt's theory the structural hole is the most efficient position one could take in a network. As is illustrated in Figure 11.1, in the diagram on the left-hand side, Burt's theory of structural holes is more or less fulfilled by actor A. By having contact with B and C, A is also able to reach D and E. However, in this situation of an open structure, actor A can carry out actions that impose negative externalities on B or C, or both. Since they have no relationships with one another, but with others instead (D and E), they cannot sanction A in order to constrain the actions. A's actions with negative externalities can continue until B or C alone is sufficiently harmed and has the power to sanction A.

Figure 11.1 Network closure versus openness

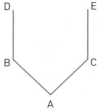

Burt's structural hole Coleman's closure of networks

In the second diagram on the right-hand side of Figure 11.1, all actors are related to each other. In terms of Burt's theory this would be an inefficient structure for A. However, in a closed structure like this one, B and C can team up to provide a collective sanction, or either can reward the other for sanctioning A. Reputation cannot arise in an open structure, and collective sanctions that would ensure trustworthiness cannot be applied. Bearing in mind the fact that closure creates trustworthiness in a social structure and Burt's theory assumes open structures, it can be argued that Burt's theory cannot effectively handle norms and trustworthiness in relationships.

A third problem relates to the information flow in networks. Who guarantees that an actor is receiving the correct information? The *tertius gaudens* is completely dependent on the first and only tie he has to a certain network. The problem of opportunistic behaviour is left out in Burt's perception of the ideal network position. A fourth problem arises when Burt simply assumes away the issue of the 'who'. Burt argues that 'who' accesses resources is less important and secondary to 'how' one accesses those resources over the network structure (Burt, 1992: 61). However, if people develop relationships with people like themselves, and the issue of 'who' is therefore unimportant, the influence of culture and values is paradoxically left out. After all, if culture and values are different between persons, the *tertius gaudens* will not come into being, because he or she will only consider relationships between people like him/herself. As Burt assumes away the issue of 'who' by stating that strong relations will only originate between similar people, his theory of structural holes cannot be used when one is studying the influence of culture on economic relationships, and the dynamics of these relationships; or it can only be used to explain why such relationships do *not* come into being between actors with different cultural backgrounds.

Finally, in analysing business networks, one could argue that the most interesting and profitable relationships from an economic point of view are the ties between different firms (cf. Granovetter, 1973). Similar firms are in competition with each other, and ties between these firms are, in general, not the norm. Ties between firms are made to have direct access to particular resources that the firm itself does not have. The question of 'who' seems to be crucial in this situation. Summarizing, one could say that Burt's theory of structural holes can be used as a powerful and insightful theory when it is plausible to assume that actors are motivated by pure self-interest. But when cultural and normative elements like trust and reciprocity are introduced, when studying the creation and destruction of ties within networks, Burt's theory of structural holes does not suffice. The strength of Burt's model lies in its generalizability. Its weakness lies in Burt's reluctance to admit environmental causal factors that influence the dynamic, processual aspects of the network's structuration. An approach that takes these environmental elements into account explicitly is the Swedish network approach.

Network theory: the Swedish network approach

The Swedish network approach is closely related to the social embeddedness approach 'developed' by Granovetter (1985). It is often seen as a reaction to the neoclassical mainstream, like the aforementioned transaction cost economics approach. The core of the arguments in this stream of research is that firms develop ties with other firms in which trust plays a crucial role.

The concept of embeddedness was 'introduced' by Karl Polanyi in his classic book *The Great Transformation* (1944). He describes the anarchy in nineteenth-century England when the social foundations of the economy for a short period crumbled. Polanyi finds it unrealistic to assume that economic actors act separate from society. Economic action without the societal element would be only the 'bare bones'.

As suggested, a famous and more recent contribution in this respect is Granovetter's 1985 paper. In this paper, the author explores to what extent economic action is embedded in the structures of social relations in modern industrial society. He discusses two strands of literature that are related to the issue of social structure and economic action. First the Benthamian approach, which assumes rational, utility-maximizing individuals that are not, or are only slightly, affected by social relations. Second, the new institutional economics, personified by Williamson, argues that behaviour and institutions can best be understood as resulting from the pursuit of self-interest by rational, more or less atomized individuals.

Granovetter presents his own view, which diverges from these schools of thought. He argues that social relationships, rather than generalized morality (over-socialized conception) or institutional arrangements like contract or authority structures (under-socialized conception), are mainly responsible for the production of trust in economic life.

Granovetter notes (1985: 485) that both under- and over-socialized views share the same conception of human action regarding atomized actors. He notes that, in the under-socialized account, atomization results from the narrow utilitarian pursuit of self-interest and, in the over-socialized account, from the fact that behavioural patterns have been internalized and ongoing social relations have thus only peripheral effects on behaviour. In other words, the fact that the internalized rules of behaviour are social in origin does not differentiate this argument decisively from a utilitarian one.

Furthermore, he states that modern attempts by economists to incorporate social influences are often done in the over-socialized way and these conceptions are rather mechanical. Once the individual's social class is known, everything else in a person's behaviour is automatic. He opposes the view that individuals are not seen in their social network, but as atomistic. A fruitful analysis of human action requires us to avoid the atomization implicit in the theoretical extremes of under- and over-socialized conceptions. Actors do not behave or decide as atoms outside a social context, nor do they adhere slavishly to a script written for them by the particular intersection of social categories that they happen to occupy. Their attempts at purposive action are instead embedded in concrete, ongoing systems of societal relations (Granovetter, 1985).

Zukin and DiMaggio (1990) distinguish four different kinds of embeddedness.

1. *Cognitive embeddedness* refers to the ways in which rational economic action is limited by uncertainty, complexity and the costs of information.

2. *Political embeddedness* observes that economic action is always carried out in a greater political context.

3. *Structural embeddedness* refers to the fact that economic exchange always takes place in a larger social structure of ongoing interpersonal relations. It focuses on the social embeddedness of economic action.

4. Finally, *cultural embeddedness* observes that economic assumptions, rules and rationality are limited and shaped by culture. Collective understandings and norms shape economic strategies and goals.

It is obvious that all these four forms of embeddedness are interrelated. The structural embeddedness perspective is closely related to the Swedish network theory. Uzzi is explicit about the embeddedness perspective:

> Whereas neo-classical accounts focus predominantly on asocial and price-determined allocative mechanisms, the structural embeddedness approach emphasizes how social networks achieve outcomes that may equal or even surpass market alternatives. (Uzzi, 1996: 682)

The cultural embeddedness perspective focuses more on elements of social capital and trust (see Chapter 1). It should be clear that these perspectives are very much intertwined. The Swedish network approach takes these two embeddedness perspectives as points of reference.

Håkansson (1987, 1989; Håkansson and Johanson, 1993) and his colleagues in Uppsala have developed an alternative view to the neoclassically orientated concept of networks as seen from a transaction cost perspective. In their so-called industrial network theory, which is also referred to as the 'Swedish network approach', the basic assumption is that, over time, the partners in a network involve themselves in a process of social exchange that gradually builds mutual trust. Instead of the neoclassical point of departure of transaction cost economics, the Swedish Network Approach takes a more sociological perspective. Actors are embedded in a societal context of relationships. A basic assumption in this view is that economic behaviour is path dependent and dynamic. Relations are viewed as a set of more or less implicit rules, which imply a mutual orientation of the actors to one another (Håkansson and Johanson, 1993). In other words, in a (industrial) network there is a web of interdependent activities performed on the basis of the use of a certain constellation of resources. Industrial networks can therefore be defined as sets of connected exchange relationships among actors performing industrial activities (Håkansson and Johanson, 1993).

As the dynamic aspect is a core assumption of this approach, the Swedish network approach is often used to analyse innovation and cooperation (Lundvall, 1992; Håkansson et al., 1999), in which learning fulfils an important role. The extent to which learning takes place is highly related to the existence of connections between the relationships. The more a single relationship is part of a larger network, the more a company, on average, seems to learn from it. Hence, networking increases learning.

A critical perspective of the Swedish network approach

The Swedish network approach, in which embeddedness plays a prominent role, not only creates the advantages discussed earlier. There are negative elements as well. Maintaining social ties generates costs, but the social relations of an actor in a network also create obligations towards the other network members (implicit contract). The necessary condition for a dense social network is trust. A crucial element of trust is reciprocity, and reciprocity creates obligations. Therefore, the positive side of being embedded in a network is the advantages of transacting with less transaction cost. The negative side of being a member – the other side of the trust coin – is the obligational side. These obligations expose an actor to 'free riding' by other members of his network on his own resources. Hence, cosy inter-group relationships can give rise to the problem of free riding (Portes and Sensenbrenner, 1993).

The second negative aspect of social capital is the fact that a dense network and the accompanying community norms can place constraints on individual behaviour. Membership of a tightly knit or dense social network can subject one to restrictive social regulations and sanctions, and limit individual action. All kinds of levelling pressures keep members in the same situation as their peers, and strong collective norms and very 'solid' communities may restrict the scope of individuals (Portes and Sensenbrenner, 1993; Meyerson, 1994; Brown, 1998); or, as Woolcock puts it

> high levels of social capital can be 'positive' in that it gives group members access to privileged 'flexible' resources and psychological support while lowering the risks of malfeasance and transactions costs, but may be 'negative' in that it also places

high particularistic demands on group members, thereby restricting individual expression and advancement, permits free riding on community resources; and negates, in those groups with a long history of marginalization through coercive non-market mechanisms the belief in the possibility of advancement through individual effort. (Woolcock, 1998)

Embeddedness may therefore reduce adaptive capacity. This may imply the danger of lock-in effects and path dependency. These lock-in effects may be strengthened by processes of cognitive dissonance in tight groups (Meyerson, 1994; Rabin, 1998). Individuals that make up a dense network tend to develop a commitment to one another and to their group. Information that disturbs the consensus of the group's perception of reality is likely to be rejected. Woolcock (1998) uses the term *amoral familism* to describe the presence of social integration within a group but no linkages outside this group. In his view, amoral familism undermines the efficiency of all forms of economic exchange by increasing transaction costs. On the other hand, there is *amoral individualism*. In this case, there is no familial or generalized trust at all and only narrow self-interested individuals exist. Individuals are not embedded in a cohesive social network. A theoretical approach like transaction cost economics fits very well in this view. In this theory there is no room for social networks and trust relationships that are based on reciprocity.

In a study of the apparel industry in New York it has been shown that there is a U-shaped pattern between the likelihood of failure of a firm and the degree of embeddedness, which implies that there is an optimal degree of embeddedness. In a study of the banking sector, similar results were found (Uzzi, 1996, 1999). Firms are more likely to secure loans and receive lower interest rates on loans if their network of bank ties has a mix of embedded ties and arm's-length ties. Embeddedness seems to yield positive results up to a certain threshold (see Figure 11.2). Hence, the positive effects of being a member of a network are the same mechanisms that cause negative effects.

Figure 11.2 Economic success and degree of network closure

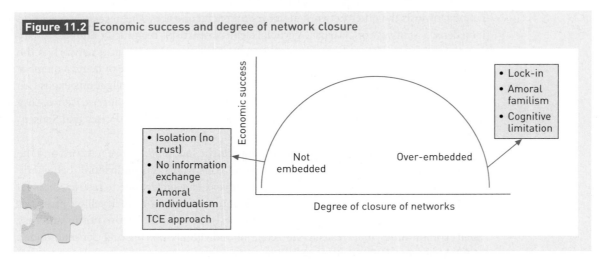

11.4 From Networks to Clusters

Until now, we have considered networks of economic activity as sets of relationships, without paying attention to the spatial dimension. Many networks are, indeed, not bound to a certain location. Just think of the network of shoe manufacturer Nike. At Nike's headquarters in Oregon, USA, there are only 900 employees. The rest of this company's activities are performed by a close network of suppliers that supply parts of the production process (e.g. laces, plastic, heels) from all over the world. Besides such aspatial, international networks, however, many networks are stuck to a certain place; they are geographically concentrated and may contribute to a large extent to regional economic development. Despite all tendencies that point to the decay of distance, in the end, all economic actions have to be located somewhere. As is the case with networks, several concepts are used to denote these spatially concentrated networks.

In the next section, some of the most important notions in this respect are discussed. Subsequently, attention is paid to industrial districts, Porter's conceptualization of clusters and the innovative milieux. The main message of all these approaches is that networks of firms that are geographically concentrated may enhance a firm's competitive position.

Industrial districts
How firms benefit from geographical clustering

The historical roots of the cluster concept can be found in the literature on 'industrial districts'. The notion of industrial districts goes back to Alfred Marshall, who presented an economic analysis of the location of industries. In his handbook *Principles of Economics* (1890), Marshall explains the development of geographically concentrated clusters, which he calls 'industrial districts', by three factors: specialized labour, dedicated intermediate inputs and knowledge spillovers. Firms are attracted to a particular location by a labour market with highly skilled workers. These workers not only possess specialized technical skills, but also knowledge about people and their activities in the industrial district. Next, location near a pool of specialized intermediate inputs provides advantages to a firm. In this way, the firm can obtain equipment, tools, technologies and services from supporting industries. Moreover, firms can absorb knowledge spillovers in an industrial district, because it is easier to realize information exchange within the same location than over great distances. The various benefits of regional concentration are external to the particular firms ('external economies'), but internal to the industrial district as a whole. Marshall argues that the achievement of these benefits depends on the existence of close social relationships between firms, creating an 'industrial atmosphere' within the district. It is clear that such an atmosphere favours the learning and innovation process of the firms in the region:

> Good work is rightly appreciated, inventions and improvements in machinery, in processes and the general organization of the business have their merits promptly discussed: if one man starts a new idea, it is taken up by others and combined with suggestions of their own; and thus becomes the source of further new ideas. (Marshall, 1890 (1947 edn): 225)

The importance of institutions in industrial districts

Marshall left most of his ideas on industrial districts undeveloped. However, over the last 15 to 20 years, his analysis has played an important role in explaining the economic success of clusters of small firms in the north of Italy (Pyke, 1995). In the region of Emilia Romagna, for example, clusters producing machine tools, ceramic tiles, knitting and footwear can be found. Although around three quarters of the manufacturing workers are employed in firms with 100 employees, the region has developed from one of the poorest in Italy to one of the richest in Europe. The success of the clusters in northern Italy attracted the interest of policy-makers and researchers (see Box 11.1).

Clusters of small firms in other countries were also identified and studied. Well-known examples of such so-called 'Marshallian industrial districts' are Jutland (Denmark), the Basque country (Spain), Baden-Württemberg (Germany), Toyota City (Japan), Sinos Valley (Brazil), Daegu (Korea), Silicon Glen (Scotland), Flanders Language Valley (Belgium) and Silicon Valley (California). In the analysis of these success stories, however, the researchers place more emphasis on the role of institutions than did Marshall (You and Wilkinson, 1994). In addition to inter-firm linkages, linkages with institutions, such as trade associations, research institutes and government agencies, can also be important factors in explaining the success of industrial districts.

Further research on industrial districts was stimulated by Piore and Sabel. In their book *The Second Industrial Divide* (1984), these authors identify fundamental shifts in the social organization of production and exchange in industrial economies. They argue that, since the 1970s, the system of mass production has been in crisis. An indication of the possible end of this period of 'Fordism' is the emergence of networks of small firms. The firms in a network can acquire competitive advantage by using their flexibility to specialize in niche markets. By cooperating with firms and institutions they can benefit from cost advantages ('collaboration economies'). Because cooperation is facilitated by face-to-face contact and local institutions, the emerging cluster will often be situated in one region.

Industrial districts: exhibiting a mix of competition and cooperation

In the 1990s the concept of 'industrial districts' benefited from renewed interest thanks to Krugman's work (1991). In his contribution, the original ideas of Marshall (1890) are formalized and brought up to date. Krugman stresses the importance of large-scale firms, with increasing returns to scale for the emergence of a cluster at a particular location. These firms will attract supplier firms in order to lower transportation costs and they will stimulate the development of a local pool of skilled labour around these firms. Through the exchange of specialized inputs, services and labour, the firms within the cluster learn from each other continuously. In this way, they can profit through 'agglomeration economies'. The author thus views geographic clustering of production as a means for firms to create sustainable competitive advantage, even in a world economy that is becoming more and more closely integrated.

Other authors (Best, 1990; You and Wilkinson, 1994) in the 1990s see the key to understanding the success of an industrial district in the particular mix of competition and cooperation among its firms. The firms in an industrial district are specialized, but complement each other through cooperation in the field of product design or manufacturing. At the same time, the firms have to compete in the product market with other firms supplying similar products and services in the district. The cooperative aspects of inter-firm relationships help the firms to overcome their disadvantage of small size, while the competitive aspects provide them with the flexibility that large, integrated firms often do not possess. A balance between competition and cooperation thus seems crucial for the functioning of industrial districts. Reviewing the various contributions in the literature, Rabellotti (1998) concludes that *an industrial district can be identified by four stylized facts*:

1. *proximity* – a group of geographically concentrated and specialized small- and medium-sized enterprises (SMEs)

2. *common behaviour* – a common behavioural code as the various actors are linked by the same cultural and social background

3. *linkages* – a set of linkages between firms based on the exchange of goods, services, labour and information;

4. *institutions* – a network of public and private local institutions supporting the various actors in the cluster.

Box 11.1: Industrial Districts in Northern Italy

Generally, northern Italy is seen as a set of industrial districts par excellence. In contrast to the poor south, the Mezzogiorno, the northern part of Italy, has shown high growth rates based on network structures in such artisan sectors as textiles, clothing, leather, shoes and ceramics. Santa Croce, for example, a town between Florence and Pisa, is a breeding place for production and innovation in high-quality leather manufacturing (Amin and Thrift, 1994). At the beginning of the 1990s, 300 small- and medium-sized firms specializing in tanning cooperated with 200 suppliers of raw leather. Unlike the worldwide leather market, which was gradually approaching maturity, this network proved to be very stable and less vulnerable to cyclical movements. As reasons for this stability, Amin and Thrift (1994) point to four factors related to the embeddedness of the leather producers in Santa Croce.

To start with, the agglomeration in the field of leather encouraged the growth of complementary firms in paint, chemicals and marketing. Next, by cooperating, the firms were able to yield scale and scope economies, leading to efficiency gains and process innovations. Furthermore, semi-public organizations, such as local chambers of commerce, municipal bodies and local training centres, played a supporting role in Santa Croce. Finally, the close ties between the firms were not only maintained for economic reasons. The entrepreneurs also met each other in civic associations and at social occasions throughout the town. Interestingly, it was the Communist Party that helped to create this atmosphere of collectivity among the local entrepreneurs, thus also facilitating cooperation in the economic field.

To sum up, regional economic development is not only about economics; local institutional and cultural factors also play a role.

Porter's concept of clusters

How firms derive their competitive advantage from their embeddedness in clusters

Undoubtedly, Porter's book, *The Competitive Advantage of Nations* (1990), has made the most influential contribution in the field of clustering. He is interested in why only certain countries generate many firms, which become successful international competitors in one or more industries. For his research on the competitive advantage of nations Porter has carried out case studies in ten different countries (including Germany, Japan and the USA). In his analysis, Porter focuses on the individual firm and its position in the structure of a particular cluster of firms. He suggests that domestic competition continuously creates pressures on firms to innovate. In his view, firms and their linkages of competition and cooperation with other organizations are the key to the competitive advantage of these firms, but also to that of the whole nation. Porter argues, then, that these innovative firms derive competitive advantage from their place within a group of four sets of factors (determinants), which he calls the 'diamond'. These factors are as follows.

1. *Factor conditions.* This determinant refers to a nation's position with regard to factors of production. Competitive advantage is not so much created by basic factors (cheap unskilled labour, natural resources, etc.), but rather by advanced factors, which have to be upgraded constantly (e.g. highly skilled labour and a modern infrastructure).

2. *Demand conditions.* The nature of home market demand for a product or service influences the success of a firm in international markets. This depends on the relative size and growth of the home market, the quality of demand and the presence of mechanisms transmitting domestic preferences to foreign markets.

3. *Related and supporting industries.* These play an important role in the ability of firms to compete internationally. The existence of industries that provide firms with inputs for the innovation process stimulates competition and cooperation. Often, the exchange of these inputs is facilitated by geographical proximity.

4. *Firm strategy, structure and rivalry.* Differences in national economic structure, organizational culture, institutions (e.g. the capital market) and history contribute to national competitive success. These conditions determine how firms are created, organized and managed, as well as how intense the domestic rivalry is.

The determinants of the diamond reinforce each other and together create the national environment in which firms operate. If this context is dynamic and challenging, nations will ultimately succeed in one or more industries, since firms are stimulated to upgrade their advantages over time.

Porter also mentions two additional factors that play a role in national competitive advantage.

5. *Chance events.* Chance factors can cause shifts in a nation's competitive position and include elements such as major technological changes, shifts in exchange rates or input prices, and important political developments.

6. *The government.* Governments play an important role in influencing the dynamics between the four determinants of the diamond through regulations related to business, policies towards the physical and educational infrastructure, and so on.

If all the factors in the diamond are functioning well, the result is a cluster of successful firms, both between and within given industries. Originally, Porter defined such a cluster as follows:

> a group of rival firms, suppliers and customers, specialized research centers and skilled labor pools that are able to draw on common skills, ideas and innovations generated by the cluster as a whole, which would not be present if the firm operated in isolation. (Porter, 1990)

Eight years later, Porter seems to have been influenced by ideas originating from the industrial district approach, when he describes a cluster as:

> a geographically proximate group of interconnected companies and associated institutions in a particular field, linked by commonalities and complementarities. (Porter, 1998)

The value chain approach to clustering

Porter's view on clusters is based on his earlier publication, *Competitive Advantage* (Porter, 1985), in which he uses the concept of 'value' to analyse the competitive position of a firm. Porter argues that a firm can be seen as a value chain – that is, the collection of activities that are performed to design, produce, market, deliver and support a product that creates value for the buyers. Each of these activities can contribute to lower costs for the firm, and creates a basis for product differentiation. The firm's value chain is embedded in a larger stream of activities, which is called the 'value system'. The value system includes suppliers, delivering products and services to the firm, and various channels. On its way to the buyer the product passes through the value chains of these channels, which perform additional activities for the firm (such as distribution activities).

Thus creating and sustaining competitive advantage not only depends on the firm's value chain, but also on the question of how the firm fits into the overall value system. As a result, clusters of competitive industries emerge, providing primary goods (end products), machinery for production, specialized inputs and associated services. According to Porter, these clusters of related and supporting industries are crucial for competitive success. An important element of Porter's value chain approach to clustering is its emphasis on the end use of products. Consequently, Porter distinguishes 16 possible clusters in terms of the final products that result from them, divided up as follows.

1. *Upstream clusters*: materials/metals, semiconductors/computers, forest products, and petroleum/chemicals.
2. *Supportive clusters*: transportation, energy, office, telecommunications, defence, and other multiple business services.
3. *Downstream clusters*: food/beverages, housing/household, leisure, healthcare, textile/clothing, and personal affairs.

Porter considers the performance of products made in a cluster on the world market as a main indicator of its competitiveness. By including only the more competitive half of all clusters in a country, one can draft a 'cluster chart', which can be used to make a comparison of the relative specialization patterns between countries. This relatively simple idea of clusters has had considerable influence on researchers and policy-makers over the years. In various countries (the USA, the Netherlands, Italy, Denmark, Sweden and Finland) the diamond and value chain analysis have been used as a framework to analyse the competitiveness of (parts of) the national economy.

How both horizontal and vertical linkages play a role in clusters

In his recent works Porter (1997, 1998) emphasizes that the cluster approach offers an alternative to the traditional sectoral approach. The latter approach takes sectors (industries) as the units of analysis and deals only with horizontal relationships and competitive interdependence (i.e. relationships between direct competitors in the same product market). The cluster approach focuses on horizontal relationships too, but also on vertical relationships and synergetic interdependence between suppliers, main producers and users.

Thus the cluster approach cuts through the classical division in sectors and provides a new way of looking at the economy (see Table 11.1). In addition to his earlier thoughts on clustering Porter (1998) pays extensive attention to the link between clusters and competitive advantage in his book, *On Competition*. He argues that clusters stimulate the competitiveness of firms and nations in three different manners. First, participating in a cluster allows firms to operate more productively. They have a better access to the means needed for carrying out their activities – such as technology, information, inputs, customers and channels – than they would have when operating in isolation. Second, this easier access will not only enhance the participants' productivity, but also their ability to innovate. Third, an existing cluster may provide a sound base for new business formation, as the relationships and institutions within the cluster will confront entrepreneurs with lower barriers of entry than elsewhere.

In summary, with the help of different concepts (the diamond, the value chain, the value system), Porter stresses the importance of clusters in creating and sustaining competitive advantage, not only for individual firms, but also for a nation as a whole.

11.5 Innovative Milieux

Similar to the industrial district approach and Porter's theory on clustering, the notion of innovative milieux studies the firm and its partners in their broader environment (Camagni, 1991; Maillat *et al.*, 1995). As the term *innovative milieux* suggests, this idea was identified by authors in France and French-speaking Switzerland. Proponents of this approach have grouped themselves in GREMI (Groupe de Recherche Europeen sur les Milieux Innovateurs). The concept of an innovative milieu may, in fact, be seen as the French variant of the Italian notion of industrial districts. The literature on innovative milieux has its roots in Perroux's *growth pole* approach. Perroux, a French economist, stressed the asymmetric and cumulative effects innovations may have in space.

Table 11.1 The sectoral approach versus the cluster approach

Sectors	Clusters
Focus on one or a few end-product industries	Comprise customers, suppliers, service providers and specialized institutions
Participants are direct or indirect competitors	Include related industries sharing technology, information, inputs, customers and channels
Hesitancy to cooperate with competitors	Most participants are not direct competitors, but share common needs and constraints
Dialogue with governments often aimed at subsidies, protection and limiting competition	Wide scope for improvements on areas of common concern, improving productivity and raising competition
Less pay-off to investments	Induce investments by both the private and the public sectors
Risk of dulling local competition	Forums for a more constructive and a more efficient business–government dialogue

Source: Porter (1997).

Box 11.2: The Engineering Cluster in Baden-Württemberg

A traditional case of clustering can be found in the German region of Baden-Württemberg. This region is widely seen as one of the biggest industrial success stories within Europe over the past 30 years, though it is currently having some problems in remaining competitive. Still, however, the region is contributing a great deal to maintaining Germany's image as a renowned car- and machinery-producing nation. The region's success is based on the presence of an engineering cluster that is deeply embedded in the economy. Leading firms, including Daimler-Benz, Bosch, Audi and IBM, cooperate fruitfully with small supplier firms (*Mittelstand*) in the field of automotive, electronics and machine tool engineering. A number of knowledge institutes (universities, polytechnics, basic and applied research institutes, as well as technology transfer centres) provide these firms with the latest research findings.

The literature has put forward several factors to explain Baden-Württemberg's success. First of all, the importance of history has been emphasized. The tradition of clustering within Baden-Württemberg can be traced back to the existence of pre-industrial crafts (Cooke *et al.*, 1995; Hassink, 1997). Thus, there has been a fruitful base on which to build. Interestingly, this industrial tradition has proved to be advantageous even in modern times. The region's recent specialization in multimedia has its roots in the engineering cluster, and Baden-Württemberg has had an active cluster policy for years. The regional state, often in the form of the former minister-president Lothar Späth himself, has been proactive in promoting cooperation between 'state, industry and science' for a long time. Many state-sponsored programmes have been designed to help market parties in the process of clustering. Examples are the formation of a technology transfer system ('Steinbeis Stiftung') and financial aid to firms wishing to cooperate. As this 'best practice' makes clear, the cluster perspective may be an interesting way of thinking, both for firms and for governments.

The GREMI group mainly points to institutional and societal factors in explaining an innovative milieu's and its firm's successful development. According to authors such as Maillat *et al.* (1995), organizations operating in innovative milieux differ in three respects. First, they are relatively autonomous in terms of decision-making and strategy formulation. The interaction between organizations contains an element of both cooperation and rivalry (cf. the industrial district approach).

Second, the local milieu is characterized by a specific set of material elements (e.g. physical and telecommunications infrastructure), immaterial factors (knowledge) and institutional arrangements (e.g. the relevant legal framework). All of these elements make up a complex of relationships within the innovative milieu. Finally, the interaction leads to collective learning processes and improves the ability of organizations to cope with the dynamics of their environment. In sum, in the GREMI literature the innovative milieu is seen as a local production organization in which firms cooperate collectively in the field of innovation. Innovation is the result of a joint learning process in which local actors learn how to transfer material and immaterial assets into products and services with new characteristics.

Box 11.3: Innovation in the Swiss Watch Industry

A well-known and often cited example of an innovative milieu is the Swiss watch industry (Camagni, 1991; Weder and Grubel, 1993). In the 1970s this industry met with severe problems due to increasing competition from cheap Japanese watches. Based on artisan production dating back to the seventeenth century, the Swiss Jura d'Arc had developed an international reputation for watch making, machine tools and micro-electronics ('Swiss made' still stands for high quality). Looking back at the economic history of the Swiss watch history in the 1970s, one may say that the local parties working in the watch industry more or less became victims of the so-called 'Icarus paradox': due to their centuries-long success, they lost the connection to the worldwide trend of micro-electronics that had also invaded the world of watch manufacturing. The result was a delayed reaction to the Japanese threat: most Swiss watch makers reacted only when the market for traditional watches had already collapsed. The region more or less fell into the trap of 'institutional lock-in' due to over-embedded relationships between local firms and institutions. Consequently, the number of workers in the Swiss watch industry decreased from 90,000 in 1970 to 33,000 in 1985.

Interestingly, thanks to the relationships between the local parties in the Jura d'Arc, the region was able to recover from this crisis. The close ties between local firms and institutions now proved to be an advantage: they facilitated collective learning and innovative action. Here, the notion of an innovative milieu really came to the fore. With the help of local government, business associations and research centres, plans were developed on how to turn the tide, while building on unique local factors. The result of this collective search for regional renewal was twofold. On the one hand, in combating the Japanese competitors the focus still remained partly on producing expensive quality watches. On the other hand, the region's industry associations also decided to develop cheap but trendy watches under the brand name Swatch (Swiss watch). In terms of price these new devices aimed to rival the watches made in Japan. In particular this last strategy turned out to be a fruitful approach. Swatch as a 'new combination' of traditional Swiss quality and trendy marketing was soon a popular concept that contributed to the revival of the local watch industry. Nowadays, the Swiss watch-making firms can still profit from being part of a close network of formal and informal institutions in the Jura d'Arc. In short, they are part of an innovative milieu.

11.6 Conclusions

In this chapter we have identified globalization, technological developments and changes in market demand as trends in the world economy that have not only intensified competition, but have also changed its character. The competitiveness of firms has become increasingly dependent on their ability to innovate and cooperate with other parties in innovative clusters. As a result, firms have to find a balance between competition, on the one hand, and cooperation on the other. The notion of networking and clustering has been studied by several authors over time.

Transaction cost considers networks as alternatives to markets and hierarchies. Additionally, network theory conceptualizes networks as separate forms of economic co-ordination in which social and institutional factors play an important role. The spatial dimension of cooperation is emphasized in literature on industrial districts, as well as Porter's work on clustering.

The approaches of networking and clustering essentially try to combine several dimensions of clusters. In fact, the ideas discussed in this literature only differ to the extent that they stress one or more dimensions of (spatial) cooperation in particular. By combining the several views, a multidimensional cluster approach arises that can take into account the pluriformity of networks and clusters in business life. Moreover, by combining the insights of authors working in transaction cost economics, the network theory, the industrial district tradition, the ideas of Porter and the innovative milieux literature, the following dimensions for defining clusters can be derived.

1. A *horizontal dimension*: linkages between firms that perform similar activities and that are direct competitors outside the cluster on the product market.

2. A *vertical dimension*: (innovative) cooperation between synergetic interdependent firms (suppliers, main producers and users) in a value chain.

3. A *geographical dimension*: a concentration of economic activities in a region with the presence of a skilled labour pool and firms providing specialized inputs to other firms.

4. An *institutional dimension*: a cluster as a cooperative in which, apart from firms, several institutions (e.g. knowledge institutes) are involved.

These cluster dimensions can be illustrated with many examples of existing clusters. To conclude, three Dutch examples will be discussed (see Boxes 11.4–11.6): the Océ-cluster, the TIMP-cluster and the Mass Individualization Network (Klein Woolthuis *et al.*, 1996; Ministry of Economic Affairs (EZ), 1997).

Box 11.4: The Océ-cluster

Situated in the southern part of the Netherlands, this is an example of a geographically concentrated cluster in which networks of small supplying firms cooperate with a large company (Océ) in the development of innovations. Océ makes use of up-to-date digital technologies to develop new colour printers and colour copiers. In order to remain competitive in the industry this company cooperates with about 45 supplier networks in the south-east of the Netherlands. Each network of suppliers has the task of developing a module for a new product, such as the control panel of a copier. Thus, Océ wants its suppliers to combine both the R&D and the production of the module. This type of cooperation has enabled Océ to shorten product development times and, ultimately, to produce better printers and copiers (Klein Woolthuis *et al.*, 1996).

Box 11.5: The Twente Initiative for the Development of Medical Products (TIMP)

TIMP is another interesting example. The network illustrates all the dimensions mentioned above. The cluster is situated in the Dutch region of Twente and is composed of parties maintaining both horizontal and vertical technological relationships. In the cluster, two main producers, six small suppliers, two regional economic development agencies and the University of Twente contribute to the development of new medical technologies for homecare and rehabilitation. The cluster appears to be successful because the cooperation reduces the lead times and the costs of new technologies. Klein Woolthuis *et al.* (1996) argue that this success can be explained by both economic and regional factors. The economic factors include the joint interest of the parties in exploiting market opportunities, and the availability of subsidies for cooperation. In addition, the regional aspect is important for the cluster's success. Because the parties involved have the same cultural, educational and professional background, they feel strongly connected with each other and behave cooperatively within the cluster.

Box 11.6: The Mass Individualization Network

This is a national cluster in which the Dutch Ministry of Economic Affairs and about 50 large and small competitors (e.g. retailers) participate (Ministry of Economic Affairs (EZ), 1997). The cluster is based on the observation that the preferences of consumers are becoming more and more individualized and unstable. This trend of 'customization' clearly creates economic opportunities for the market parties. However, responding to different customer needs requires a more flexible organization of firms and a good network for the provision of information. Therefore, with the assistance of the Ministry, the firms cooperate in projects to find solutions to handle the trend of customization. The example of the Mass Individualization Network illustrates two important points regarding clustering. First, though clusters are often regionally embedded, this is not always the case. Second, the innovations resulting from clusters are not restricted to new technologies or products; the clustering can also be directed to the development of innovative services that are important in fields like retailing.

These examples make it clear that networks and clusters are composed of several parties (e.g. large firms, small firms, public institutions) and can be understood as a combination of different dimensions. It is important to realize that each of these cluster dimensions requires 'tailor-made' firm strategies related to clustering (Jacobs and de Man, 1996). In consequence, a multidimensional approach is needed to understand the variety of networks and clusters in practice.

Study Questions

1. Explain why networks and clusters are important for business life.

2. Discuss how geographical clustering can enhance a firm's competitive position.

3. Explain how Burt's structural hole theory can help us understand the increased competitiveness of firms located in networks.

4. Assess the explanatory power of the concept of 'cultural embeddedness'.

5. Discuss how industrial districts exhibit a mix of cooperation and competition.

6. In recent years, firms that are part of the Japanese *keiretsu* and the Korean *Chaebol* are argued to experience deteriorating performance precisely because they are part of a network. Use network theory to explain these negative side-effects.

7. Silicon Valley is a successful example of an innovative cluster of firms. Use the knowledge introduced in this chapter to explain why and under what conditions, or why not, governments should try to emulate the Sillicon Valley story.

Further Reading

Ebers, M. (1997) *The Formation of Inter-Organizational Networks*. Oxford: Oxford University Press.

This book includes excellent papers that all focus on the recent trend among organizations to form networks with competing organizations. Most of the theory presented also applies to networks among non-competing organizations.

Faust, K. and Wasserman, S. (1999) *Social Network Analysis: Methods and Applications*. Cambridge: Cambridge University Press.

For the diehards among you; this book is highly recommended for those wishing to carry out quantitative analysis on networks.

Murphy, J.T. (2002) Networks, trust, and innovation in Tanzania's manufacturing sector. *World Development* 30(4), 591–619.

Excellent article, which explores the societal dimension of innovation for a group of manufacturers in Mwanza and Tanzania.

Parrilli, M.D. (2001) The social roots of successful economic policies: the cases of the third Italy and Nicaragua. *L'institute Discussion Paper 18*, Institute for Industrial Development Policy: Ferrara, Italy, www.linstitute.org/papers/.

On the basis of an analysis of the districts of the third Italy and of Nicaragua's clusters, this paper shows that the difficulty that policy-makers have in replicating successful stories in developing contexts stems from a neglect of the 'real society that exists behind the market' that surrounds the local production system.

Case: Networks in China or Guanxi

Case written by Carla Koen on the basis of Davies *et al.* (1995); Xin and Pearce (1996); Tsang (1998); Park and Luo (2001).

The People's Republic of China (PRC) is becoming a major economic power, with a population making up approximately one-fifth of the world's consumer market. For a number of reasons, the situation in the PRC changed significantly in the course of 1992 and 1993. First, leader Deng Xiaoping made a highly publicized tour of rapidly growing areas in South China, giving his explicit support to the pace and direction of change in those areas, and encouraging other parts of the country to emulate their success. Second, the Fourteenth Party Congress, held in October 1992, confirmed that the commitment to market-based reform would be maintained, thereby increasing confidence that rapid growth rates could be continued. Third, it became clear that the reported figures for national income, and, hence, the size of the Chinese market, are almost certainly quite substantial underestimates. Finally, there have been strong signs of the existence of a large consumer market. McKinsey estimated that the number of relatively affluent Chinese consumers is around 200 million; the Beijing branch of McDonald's is reported to be one of the largest and most profitable in the world; and Avon has 15,000 salesladies in Guangdong Province alone.

At the same time, the Chinese government has made further moves to reduce controls over the economy and to open the vast domestic market to foreign competition. Price controls have been relaxed for many kinds of raw materials and commodities, customs duties have been reduced for over 200 types of consumer and industrial goods, and the attempt to accommodate the GAT requirements for membership have led to liberalization of imports and the removal of further structural constraints.

Despite the opportunities now presented by the Chinese market, however, the evidence suggests that doing business in China can be cumbersome and strenuous. Generally, the daunting outcomes experienced by western business-people arise from the need for investment in network building, after which the transacting process may be quite efficient. The establishment of personalized trust through networks is particularly crucial to the conduct of business in China. Networks, translated as *guanxi*, have been the dominant form of transactional governance in China long before the concept was taken up by western scholars. The concept refers to the drawing on a web of connections to secure favours in personal and organizational relations. It has been pervasive for centuries in every aspect of Chinese social and organizational activities; and modern Chinese society still operates within the realm of these countless social and business *guanxi* networks.

A good illustration of the latter is provided by an experienced US general manager of a joint venture packaging company in Nanjing who observes that, 'The most common contrast between western and Chinese management practices lies in the emphasis placed on written contracts and procedures in the former, compared with personal relationships in the latter.'

Guanxi, or Chinese networks, are characterized by continuous relationships, which require that activities undertaken by the parties in a relationship cannot be completed without the active and reciprocal involvement of both parties (or continuing reciprocal obligation). A person is viewed as untrustworthy when he or she fails to return a favour, and he or she does not follow the rules of reciprocity. The rules of reciprocity establish a structural constraint that curtails self-seeking opportunism. Therefore, in China, transactions often follow successful *guanxi*, while in the West a relationship follows successful transactions.

As suggested, trust and credibility are two other important ingredients of *guanxi*. In fact, trust and credibility sometimes play a more salient role than legal contracts.

An illustration of the importance of these two concepts is provided in the following example.

> A Chinese deputy general manager of a Sino-foreign joint venture urgently needed certain components in her factory. The components were in short supply, but through her *guanxi*, she managed to obtain them from a friend in a factory in another city. Based on mutual trust, a cash-on-delivery price was agreed verbally and the components were sent to her factory. However, her factory was experiencing a cash-flow problem when the components arrived. In order to uphold trustworthiness, she paid the bill out of her own savings – an amount roughly equal to her annual salary. She says that if she had not done so, the *guanxi* with her friend would have been blemished (Tsang, 1998: 66).

Clearly, the long-term viability of *guanxi* depends on the members' commitment to *guanxi* and to one another. *Guanxi* does not specify the range or frequency of exchanging favours. *Guanxi* members are tied together through an invisible and unwritten code of reciprocity and equity. Failure to respect the commitment damages one's reputation, leading to a humiliating loss of prestige, or face.

Face is a key element in the development and maintenance of *guanxi*. As suggested, face is an individual's public image, gained by performing one or more specific social roles that are recognized by others. Though highly abstract, the concept of face is treated by the Chinese as something that can be quantified and measured. How much face an individual has depends partly on his or her *guanxi* or network. The larger one's *guanxi* – and the more powerful the people connected with it – the more face one has. In addition, one needs to have a certain amount of face in order to cultivate a viable *guanxi*.

Guanxi is utilitarian rather than emotional. It is based entirely on the exchange of favours, not on emotional attachment. Accordingly, *guanxi* does not necessarily involve friendship, although friendship is preferred.

The practice of *guanxi* stems from Confucianism, which fostered the broad cultural aspects of collectivism manifested in the importance of networks of interpersonal relations. It is deeply embedded in China's culture with a history of over 5000 years. Chinese society has been functioning as a clan-like network since Confucius codified societal rules, values and hierarchical structures of authority during the sixth century BC. *Guanxi* operates in concentric circles, with close family members at the core and with distant relatives, classmates, friends and acquaintances arranged on the periphery, according to the 'distance' of the relationship and the degree of trust involved. When a situation arises that is beyond an individual's capacity, the *guanxi* network is mobilized to accomplish the desired results.

In the present-day Chinese environment, *guanxi* has become even more entrenched, with strong and direct implications for social attitudes and business practices. China's recent economic transition has produced a high degree of institutional uncertainty. Despite ongoing attempts to facilitate market transactions, China's economic reform remains incomplete, with a mix of both plan and market systems operating in the economy. China's transitional economy is characterized by weak capital structures, poorly specified property rights, and institutional instability, of which a lack of coherent business law is an example. These characteristics make market exchanges uncertain and costly. Hence, transaction costs remain high for firms to secure necessary inputs and legitimize their existence. As institutional uncertainty increases, firms more eagerly turn to *guanxi* to lower external dependence for key resources. Thus *guanxi* helps firms to overcome the lack of resources to accommodate growth while alleviating substantial bureaucratic costs that would result from internalizing operations. As a loosely structured network, *guanxi* is an efficient mechanism to facilitate economic exchanges and to overcome administrative interventions by the Chinese government.

Moreover, the ambiguity regarding property rights, and the fact that production factor markets are inoperative, explains why the survival of firms also depends largely on their networking with local governments. Private firms have grown quickly, while the control of financing and key scarce resources remains largely with the state. In a country with uncertain property rights, the potential for threatening interference and expropriation from party and governmental officials is great. Given such institutional uncertainty, private firms nurture a long-term reciprocal relationship with local government through various formal and informal ties (i.e. *guanxi*). Facing ineffective factor markets and ambiguous property rights, *guanxi* substitutes for government-instituted, formal channels of resource allocation and dispersal.

Moreover, as market information is greatly distorted in a transition economy, *guanxi* becomes a reliable source of necessary information for the making of strategic decisions. *Guanxi* is thus a valuable entrepreneurial tool for bridging gaps in information and resource flows between unlinked firms, and between firms and important outside stakeholders.

Additionally, given the uncertainty and confusion in China's transition economy, firms develop *guanxi* to broker structural holes and alter the existing network structure. Firms use *guanxi* to mobilize complementary benefits by arbitraging different networks and even potentially negotiating between competing networks. There are substantial rewards, such as commissions, bonuses and promotions, for managers' personal *guanxi* utilized for organizational purposes to source key inputs and marketing products.

Furthermore, small or newer organizations can overcome legitimacy barriers through involvement in *guanxi*, thus gaining wider opportunities to influence the local, political and/or regulatory environments. The following testimony from the general manager of a small private computer company is illustrative.

> My company had bad luck. We were audited for income tax fraud. The Auditing Bureau has red eye disease [jealousy]. Whenever they see a private company doing well, they come and find problems.
>
> The tax auditor just showed up one day and wanted to see company books. There are no standardized rules on how to keep books in China, especially for small private companies like ours. If they want to find errors in your income tax, they will always find something wrong. If we had been found guilty of tax fraud we could have faced thousands of yuan in fines and the possible suspension of our business licence.
>
> Our accountant was very worried. I called my administrative assistant, X, into my office and told him the situation. He smiled and said: 'Give me a 2500 yuan allowance [equivalent to a middle managers' six-month salary] and I will take care of everything.' I had no choice. So I said, 'I will give you 2500 yuan but you will lose your job if you cannot handle this crisis.'
>
> By noon, my phone rang. X asked me to go to lunch with the auditors, at the best restaurant in the city. We hired a Mercedes Benz and went to lunch. The auditors kept saying that they only needed a working lunch. After expensive drinks and Peking duck, the head auditor started to praise our accounting system, saying how good and efficient it looked. After lunch the head auditor left me a notice requesting a 2500 yuan income tax supplement. The reason he had to force us to pay the supplement was that he had to report to his boss on what he had accomplished that day. Later on I found out that X's father is a good friend of the head auditor. (Xin and Pearce, 1996: 1652–3).

Indeed, organizations in China receive different treatment and resource allocations from the government depending on their institutional and organizational orientations – such as ownership, size, experience and skills. Therefore, there is a great deal of variation across Chinese firms in terms of their institutional advantages and disadvantages and, hence, in terms of the use of *guanxi*.

Questions

1. Assess and discuss whether transaction cost theory can help you explain the current use of guanxi *fully*, or whether other explanations are needed and, if so, which ones.

2. In accordance with Hofstede's national cultural dimensions, China is a collectivist country. Discuss what type of inter-organizational relationships one should expect in collectivist countries, and explain whether the case confirms this picture.

3. Explain, on the basis of this case, the influence of the institutional environment on the type of network that has developed in China.

4. Would you assume that, if the institutional setting became more stable and reliable, the current type of network:

    (a) would change (and, if so, in what direction?)

    (b) become disfunctional, or

    (c) disappear all together?

    Explain your answer.

References

Amin, A. and Thrift, N. (1994) (eds) *Globalization, Institutions and Regional Development in Europe*. Oxford: Oxford University Press.

Audretsch, D.B. and Thurik, A.R. (1997) *Sources of Growth: the Entrepreneurial versus the Managed Economy*. Discussion paper. Rotterdam: Tinbergen Institute.

Best, M. (1990) *The New Competition: Institutions of Industrial Restructuring*. Cambridge, MA: Harvard University Press.

Brown, T.F. (1998) *Theoretical Perspectives on Social Capital*. Working paper. Program for Comparative and International Development. Baltimore: Johns Hopkins University.

Burt, R. (1992) The social structure of competition, in Nohria, N. and Eccles, R. (eds) *Networks and Organizations, Structure, Form and Action*. Boston, MA: Harvard Business School Press.

Camagni, R. (1991) *Innovation Networks: Spatial Perspectives*. London: Belhaven.

Coase, R.H. (1937) The nature of the firm. *Economica* 4, 386–405.

Coleman, J. (1988) Social capital in the creation of human capital. *American Journal of Sociology* 94, S95–S120.

Commandeur, H.R. (1994) *Strategische samenwerking in netwerkperspectief: een theoretisch netwerk voor industriële ondernemingen* (Dutch). Alblasserdam: Haveka.

Cooke, P., Morgan, K. and Price, A. (1995) The future of the *Mittelstand*: collaboration versus competition, in O'Doherty, D.P. (ed.) *Globalization, Networking and Small Firm Innovation*. London: Graham & Trotman.

Davies, H., Leung, T.K.P., Luk, S.T.K. and Wong, Y.-h. (1995) The benefits of guanxi: the value of relationships in developing the Chinese market. *Industrial Marketing Management* 24, 207–14.

Dicken, P. (1998) *Global Shift: Transforming the World Economy* (3rd edn). London: Chapman Publishing.

Dunning, J.H. (1997) *Alliance Capitalism and Global Business*. London: Routledge.

Edwards, C.T. and Samimi, R. (1997) Japanese interfirm networks: exploring the seminal sources of their success. *Journal of Management Studies* 34(4), 489–510.

Enright, M.J. (1996) Regional clusters and economic development: a research agenda, in Staber, U.H., Schaefer, N.V. and Sharma, B. (eds) *Business Networks: Prospects for Regional Development*. Berlin: Walter De Gruyter.

Granovetter, M. (1973) The strength of weak ties. *American Journal of Sociology* 78, 1360–80.

Granovetter, M. (1985) Economic action and social structure: the problem of embeddedness. *American Journal of Sociology* 91, 481–510.

Håkansson, H. (ed.) (1987) *Industrial Technological Development: a Network Approach*. London: Croom Helm.

Håkansson, H. (1989) *Corporate Technological Behaviour, Cooperation and Networks*. London: Routledge.

Håkansson, H. and Johanson, J. (1993) The network as a governance structure, in Grabher, G. (ed.) *The Embedded Firm, on the Socioeconomics of Industrial Networks*. London: Routledge.

Håkansson, H., Havila, V. and Pedersen, A.-C. (1999) Learning in networks. *Industrial Marketing Management* 28(5), 443–52.

Hassink, R. (1997) What distinguishes 'good' from 'bad' industrial agglomerations?, *Erdkunde* 51, 2–11.

Jacobs, D. and de Man, A.P. (1996) Clusters, industrial policy and firm strategy: a menu approach. *Technology Analysis and Strategic Management* 8, 425–37.

Klein Woolthuis, R., Schipper, D. and Stor, M. (1996) *How Entrepreneurial Networks can Succeed: Cases from the Region of Twente*. Paper presented at the High Technology Small Firms Conference, Enschede, September.

Krugman, P.R. (1991) *Geography and Trade*. Cambridge, MA: MIT Press.

Lazonick, W. (1992) *Organization and Technology in Capitalist Development*. Aldershot: Edward Elgar.

Lundvall, B.A. (1992) *National Systems of Innovation*. London: Pinter.

Maillat, D., Lecoq, B., Nerneti, F. and Pfister, M. (1995) Technology district and innovation: the case of the Swiss Jura Arc. *Regional Studies* 29(3).

Marshall, A. (1890, 1947 edn) *Principles of Economics*. London: Macmillan.

Metcalfe, J. (1995) Technology systems and technology policy in an evolutionary framework. *Cambridge Journal of Economics* 19, 25–46.

Meyerson, E.M. (1994) Human capital, social capital and compensation: the relative contribution of social contacts to managers' incomes. *Acta Sociologica* 37, 383–99.

Ministry of Economic Affairs (EZ) (1997) *Opportunities through Synergy: Government and the Emergence of Innovative Clusters in the Private Sector*. Letter from the Minister of Economic Affairs to the Second Chamber, Second Chamber document 25518, no. 1.

Noorderhaven, N.G. (1994) Transaction cost analysis and the explanation of hybrid vertical interfirm relations. *Review of Political Economy* 6, 19–36.

Nooteboom, B. (1999) *Inter-firm Alliances: Analysis and Design*. London: Routledge.

Oerlemans, L.A.G. (1996) *De ingebedde onderneming: Innoveren in industriële netwerken* (Dutch). Tilburg: Tilburg University Press.

Park, S.H. and Luo, Y. (2001) *Guanxi* and organizational dynamics: organizational networking in Chinese firms. *Strategic Management Journal* 22, 455–77.

Piore, M.J. and Sabel, C.F. (1984) *The Second Industrial Divide: Possibilities for Prosperity*. New York: Basic Books.

Polanyi, K. (1944) *The Great Transformation*. New York: Rinehart.

Porter, M.E. (1985) *Competitive Advantage: Creating and Sustaining Superior Performance*. New York: Free Press.

Porter, M.E. (1990) *The Competitive Advantage of Nations*. New York: Free Press.

Porter, M.E. (1997) *Knowledge-based Clusters and National Competitive Advantage*. Presentation to Technopolis, Ottawa, 12 September.

Porter, M.E. (1998) *On Competition*. Cambridge, MA: Harvard University Press.

Portes, A., and Sensenbrenner, J. (1993) Embeddedness and immigration: notes on the social determinants of economic action. *American Journal of Sociology* 98(6), 1320–50.

Pyke, F. (1995) Endogenous development in a global context: the scope for industrial districts, in O'Doherty, D.P. (ed.) *Globalisation, Networking and Small Firm Innovation*. London: Graham & Trotman.

Rabellotti, R. (1998) Collective effects in Italian and Mexican footwear industrial clusters. *Small Business Economics* 10, 243–62.

Rabin, M. (1998) Psychology and economics. *Journal of Economic Literature* 36, 11–46.

Salancik, G.R. (1995) WANTED: a good network theory of organization. *Administrative Science Quarterly* 40, 345–49.

Simon, H.A. (1961) *Administrative Behavior*. New York: Macmillan Press.

Tsang, E.W.K. (1998) Can *guanxi* be a source of sustained competitive advantage for doing business in China? *Academy of Management Executive* 12(2), 64–73.

Uzzi, B. (1996) The sources and consequences of embeddedness for the economic performance of organizations: the network effect. *American Sociological Review* 61, 674–98.

Uzzi, B. (1997) Social structure and competition in interfirm networks: the paradox of embeddedness. *Administrative Science Quarterly* 42, 35–67.

Uzzi, B. (1999) Embeddedness in the making of financial capital: how social relations and networks benefit firms seeking financing. *American Sociological Review* 64, 481–505.

Weder, R. and Grubel, H.G. (1993) The new growth theory and Coasean economics: institutions to capture externalities. *Weltwirtschaftliches Archiv*, 488–513.

Williamson, O.E. (1975) *Markets and Hierarchies: Analysis and Antitrust Implications*. New York: Free Press.

Williamson, O.E. (1985) *The Economic Institutions of Capitalism*. New York: Free Press.

Williamson, O.E. (1991) Comparative economic organization: the analysis of discrete structural alternatives. *Administrative Science Quarterly* 36, 269–96.

Woolcock, M. (1998) Social capital and economic development: toward a theoretical synthesis and policy framework. *Theory and Society* 27, 151–208.

Xin, K.R. and Pearce, J.L. (1996) *Guanxi*: connections as substitutes for formal institutional support. *Academy of Management Journal* 39(6), 1641–58.

You, J. and Wilkinson, F. (1994) Competition and cooperation: towards understanding industrial districts. *Review of Political Economy* 6, 259–78.

Zukin, S. and DiMaggio, P. (eds) (1990) *Structures of Capital: the Social Organization of the Economy*. Cambridge: Cambridge University Press.

Chapter 12

Globalization, Convergence and Societal Specificity

Learning Objectives

By the end of this chapter you will be able to:

- explain the complementarity of three core societal institutions – that is, the systems of corporate governance, personnel and industrial relations

- understand the need to distinguish between different levels of analysis when tracing the impact of globalization forces

- analyse the effect of the so-called globalization forces upon the three aforementioned societal frameworks

- reflect critically on the plausibility of path-deviant change in organization and management

- appraise whether institutional theory is sufficiently powerful to analyse the impact of globalization pressures

- evaluate the role of cultural characteristics in explaining change at the societal, organization and management levels

- reflect on the link between globlization and MNCs.

Chapter Outline

12.1   **Introduction**

12.2   **Corporate Governance**

12.3   **The Personnel and Industrial Relations Systems**
Germany
Japan

12.4   **Conclusions**
Study Questions
Further Reading
Case: Global Outsourcing: Divergence or Convergence?
References

12.1 Introduction

As mentioned in the introduction to this book, the different opinions on the consequences of global forces form the starting point of this chapter. As also explained in the introduction, the globalization literature exhibits divergent opinions on the consequences of globalization, which can be summarized in four possible scenarios.

1. Convergence towards the Anglo-American neoliberal market system (i.e. Dore, 1996; Streeten, 1996; Streeck, 1997).

2. Greater specialization of national models in accordance with domestic institutional and cultural characteristics (Vitols, 2001; Sorge, 2003).

3. Incremental adaptation of the domestic institutional context in a largely path-dependent manner (i.e. Whitley, 1994; Casper, 2000)

4. Hybridization with change in a path-deviant manner (i.e. Whitley, 1999; Lane, 2000).

In Chapter 4, we developed some theoretical concepts, which can help us understand institutional change as a result of global pressures. Among other things, these concepts stress that when we consider only single social institutions in trying to understand the effects of globalization, this may be misleading because it denies the genuine nature of the social institutional architecture, which is combinative. We argued that, in order to understand the impact of globalization on the domestic context and as a corollary on management and organization, we need to study how social institutions are complementary to one another, in the sense that one institution functions better because some other particular institutions or forms of organization are present (Amable, 2000). Hence, when analysing the effects of global pressures, we have to take account of the possible (destabilizing) effect of change and resilience in one element of the social system on other elements.

This chapter uses the dynamic concepts, explained in Chapter 4, to analyse further the directions of change in the relevant managerial fields that have been studied in this book. It tries to identify the impact on management and organization of diverging and/or converging tendencies in major societal institutions in Germany and Japan in comparison with the USA and the UK. The chapter is restricted to these four countries as they are the prototype countries of the two major societal models: the Rhineland model and the Anglo-Saxon model, respectively. Most, if not all, other industrialized countries are situated somewhere on the continuum between the two. It could be argued that if globalization were to have an impact, we should be able to identify changes in the societal context of the core representatives of the two major capitalist models.

While we have identified societal change in the relevant chapters of this book, we have postponed to this chapter the drawing of conclusions. In view of the complementary character of institutions, and because the different chapters concentrate on only one set of societal institutions, we were unable to make legitimate claims for one or other direction of change. We did reflect somewhat on the predictions of many scholars, which suggest convergence of the Rhineland model towards the Anglo-Saxon model. This claim should be seen against the background of the recession, in Japan and Germany, from the late 1990s onwards, and the establishment of regulatory changes by the German and Japanese governments in answer to this recession.

This chapter, in contrast, while recognizing that these reforms are path deviant and seem to point towards convergence, explains how they, nevertheless, induced path-dependent adaptation of organization and management practices as well as further specialization of the industrial profile. This observation leads to the warning that it is important to make a clear distinction between the levels at which one analyses the impact of globalization. Analysis at the societal level, while having an impact on organization and management, is not sufficient to legitimize claims for all types of change. True, it could be argued that the effect of societal change on management and organization might be slower than the effect of globalization on the societal level. In Chapter 4, we argued, however, that path-deviant change at the societal level does not necessarily lead to path-deviant change in organization and management, as there are other dynamics at work at that level of analysis.

We will concentrate in this chapter on assessing the direction and type of change in three main societal frames – that is, the corporate governance system and the personnel and industrial relations systems. From Chapter 7, on production management, and Chapter 8, on national innovation systems, it should be clear that these three societal settings are complementary and that change in one of them would necessarily trigger change in another in order to preserve the coherence, efficiency and stability of the entire societal system. In these chapters, it was shown that the combination of these three societal frames allows us to explain the differences in production models and innovation systems between countries.

Briefly, in Chapter 7 we saw that the combination of capital market finance, absence of substantial training for workers, short-term contracts and arm's-length industrial relations helped us to explain the competitive position of the USA and the UK in mass-production sectors. Conversely, long-term patient capital, high-quality training, long-term employment, and close industrial relations helped us to understand the competitive position of the German and Japanese flexible production models. Chapter 8 showed that the combination of venture capital, which allows high risk taking, an active labour market of the scientists and financial experts needed to form start-up companies, and strong financial incentives based on share options, helps us to explain the competitive position of US and UK firms in radical forms of innovation. Conversely, constraints on the provision of venture capital created by the broadly bank-centred orientation of German and Japanese capital markets, rigidities in the labour market for scientists and managers, and inadequate performance incentives within German and Japanese firms, help us to explain the competitive position of German and Japanese firms in incremental types of innovation.

So, in the following, we will first discuss recent changes in the societal systems of corporate governance, personnel and industrial relations. Next, we briefly elaborate on the conclusions that are drawn from these changes and, finally, we look at the significance of our conclusions for managing multinational operations.

12.2 Corporate Governance

To simplify the discussion of a complex topic, it is useful to distinguish between the two main models of corporate governance, which are discussed at length in Chapter 6, on corporate governance: the 'outsider', or the Anglo-Saxon system, and the 'insider' model, like the German and Japanese systems. The distinction between the two systems is often made in terms of whether the banks play a dominant role or whether the stock market is the main locus of monitoring and control. The take-over mechanism is at the heart of the Anglo-Saxon open market model of corporate governance. Any party can bid for the control rights of a listed company by accumulating a large enough ownership stake. The building blocks of the insider-based system of corporate governance in Germany and Japan are the important role played by the banks as large creditors and large parent firms, and the high degree of interlocking shareholdings. In contrast to UK and US views of the firm as a property of owners, who are the sole 'residual claimants', German and Japanese corporate governance has drawn lesser distinctions between the private rights of owners and social or political obligations in the context of social groups or society.

In the context of the globalization debate, neoclassical orthodoxy claims that one or the other corporte governance model is economically superior and that, over time, we should see convergence towards this model of 'best practice'. The shareholder or outsider model was heavily criticized in the early 1990s for its tendencies to under-invest and to focus on short-term results (Porter, 1990). At present, however, the majority view is that the shareholder model will prevail due to the globalization of capital markets and the growing power of institutional investors. The argument is that, since international capital markets are increasingly dominated by diversified portfolio investors (such as mutual funds and pension funds) seeking higher returns, companies must adopt the shareholder model or be starved of the external capital needed to invest and survive (Lazonick and O'Sullivan, 2000, cited in Vitols, 2001).

The main question is: '*Is the stakeholder model of corporate governance changing towards the shareholder model as a result of globalization pressures?*' In order to investigate this claim – that is, in order to be able to judge the plausibility of a shift of the insider-orientated model towards the outsider or shareholder model – it is useful to look at the developments of four major interrelated and complementary categories of the German and Japanese corporate governance systems:

1. formal legal and regulatory changes

2. changes in the structure of corporate ownership

3. growth of the stock market, and

4. emergence of a market for corporate control (Coffee, 2001).

Taken in isolation, one aspect of a system, such as stable shareholding arrangements in Germany and Japan, may appear arbitrary or even reprehensible when wanting to judge the direction of change. Especially since – despite the lack of agreement on the direction of causality – there is widespread agreement in the literature that changes in one of these categories would affect the others (Nowak, 2001). One school of thought holds that law affects the economic system (La Porta *et al.*, 1997; Roe, 1997), while another argues that law and regulation are likely to be a result of the economic system (Easterbrook, 1997). In any case, the assumptions of dialectical relationships between systemic elements and the tendency for institutional coherence imply that, when change in one of the aforementioned categories occurs, we should expect change in another.

The most important regulatory changes in Germany and Japan in the past few years in the area of corporate governance have been in the area of company law and financial regulation. In the 1990s, to increase the attractiveness of German capital markets, German legislators initiated the Second and Third Laws for the Promotion of Financial Markets. The Second Law (established in 1994) set up an Anglo-Saxon-style Federal Securities Supervisory Office (*Bundesaufsichtsamt für Wertpapierhandel*) and imposed the first formal German prohibition of insider trading. The Third Law (passed in 1997) liberalizes restrictions on mutual funds and venture capital companies, and allows more liberal listing requirements, to try to encourage more German and foreign companies to list on the German stock exchanges, and also to expand the access to capital of small and medium-sized enterprises (Schaede, 1999; Nowak, 2001; Vitols, 2001).

A significant reform of German company law was effected through the Law for Corporate Control and Transparency in Large Companies (*KonTraG*), which modifies the Joint Stock Company Law 1965 (*Aktiengesetz*). The law was an initiative of the Kohl government as a political response to a number of major failures of supervisory board administration. The primary goals of the *KonTraG*, which became effective in May 1998, were to improve the monitoring effectiveness of German supervisory boards and corporate disclosure to the investment community. In addition, the legal liability of the management board in case of dishonest or fraudulent behaviour was also tightened. In order to provide the management with proper performance-based incentives, the *KonTraG* also simplifies the use of stock option programmes through share buybacks and capital increases, allowing German companies to adopt 'typical' Anglo-Saxon practices (Nowak, 2001).

Although these reforms have led to a somewhat more liquid and transparent stock exchange for the largest German companies (particularly the largest 30 companies contained in the Deutscher Aktienindex, or DAX), most significant are the elements of continuity that remain. The vast majority of German companies are not listed on the stock exchange, remain embedded in 'relational networks', including their local banks, and continue to receive their external finance mainly in the form of bank loans. The most important banking group – especially for the vast *Mittelstand* (small and medium-sized companies) – remains the publicly owned municipal savings bank sector (*Sparkassen*), which continues to account for more than half of all banking system assets in Germany (Vitols, 2001: 348).

Small- and medium-sized enterprise (SME) owners have been criticized for avoiding listing in order to prevent any dilution of their control and for their unwillingness to reveal profitability (*Herr im Hause Mentalität*). Such SMEs have not made much use of share capital as a means of fulfilling their growing financing needs, despite reforms aimed at making it easier for them to do so (the 1986 introduction of a Second Market, or *geregelter Markt* and the 1994 Law on Small Public Companies, or *Gesetz über Kleine Aktiengesellschaften*). The SMEs, on the other hand, argue that there remain barriers to listing. For example, continuing credit institutions – in effect, banks – must be involved in the first segment of trading (i.e. issuing shares). As the banks are concerned about their reputation, they are thought to be careful about dealing with new entrepreneurs (Vitols and Woolcock, 1997).

Against this background, Table 12.1 shows that, despite regulatory changes, the majority of German firms (but also other European firms operating within the Rhineland model) do not show a preference for market-based transactions. From the table it is clear that, by the end of the 1990s, the number of German and other European (with the exception of the UK) corporations that issued tradable shares remains small. In the EU, on average 64.3 per cent of trading volume is accounted for by 13 firms; for Germany, this is 85.5 per cent by 35 companies; for the UK, in contrast, this is 59.9 per cent by 102 firms and 51.4 per cent by 113 firms on the NYSE. In general, the concentration of stock trading in a few companies remains higher in Rhineland-model countries than in Anglo-Saxon countries. Table 12.2 confirms this picture by showing the differences in the degree of liquidity and depth of financial markets between the two models. There are still substantial differences in the ratio of capitalization to GNP between the USA, the UK and Germany. Even in 2000, German stock markets remained minor players in comparison to the US and UK markets.

Deregulation of the financial markets in Japan started from the late 1970s. Important measures were the easing of restrictions in 1979 and 1981 on the issuing of unsecured straight and convertible bonds and approval in the mid-1980s for banks to issue convertible bonds (Koen, 2000). After the bad loans crisis of 1996, the Japanese government implemented further deregulatory measures to foster the restructuring of the financial sector and to revitalize financial markets.[1] From 1997 onwards, Japan embarked on a stepwise reform of its general accounting rules, including, among others things, the adoption of market value reporting, as opposed to the current book value reporting, for all securities holdings in March 2001, and the adoption of market value estimation of cross-held shares in March 2002. In 1998, the Foreign Exchange Law was revised, which resulted in a complete liberalization of cross-border transactions. Foreign investments into Japan became legally unrestricted, although many informal restrictions on corporate take-over remain. In 1998, too, a new Financial Holding Company Law allowed bank holding companies, and, in 1999, brokerage commissions were deregulated. Moreover, rather like the situation in Germany, Japan reformed corporate law in 1997, and introduced stock options, share buybacks and holding companies.

At first glance, it seems that regulatory change in Japan did succeed in creating a deeper capital market with a high number of listings. Table 12.1 shows that the volume of share trading in the Japanese capital markets is not concentrated in only a few firms – as in the other Rhineland-model countries – but instead is spread over a more or less similar number of firms, as in the USA and the UK. From the late 1970s onwards, large Japanese corporations started to make greater use of the bond and securities markets, issuing convertible bonds and other equity-linked debt instruments. The change in the pattern of corporate financing was accelerated in the mid-1980s, when the Japanese economy experienced a huge and steady rise in stock prices following the Plaza Accord of October 1985. Prices on the Tokyo Stock Exchange increased by two and a half times between 1985 and 1989. Bond issuance in the domestic market, which was mainly composed of convertible bonds, grew sharply from 1986 onwards (Hideaki Miyajima, 1998).

Table 12.2, on the other hand, shows that market capitalization as a percentage of GDP, while somewhat higher than in Germany, still points to a relatively illiquid and thin market in comparison with that of the USA and the UK. Related to this conclusion is a Bank of Japan study, which argues that, to date, the redesigning of Japan's financial system in the 1990s has not produced a striking increase in financial transactions via

[1] A complete schedule of financial system reform is available at the Ministry of Finance (MOF) website at www.mof.go.jp.

capital markets. According to Japanese flow of funds accounts, the percentage of bank loans in the financial liabilities of non-financial businesses remains virtually unchanged from 38.9 per cent at the end of 1990 to 38.8 per cent at the end of 1999. During the same period, the percentage of shares, equities and securities increased from 38.9 per cent to 43.1 per cent (Baba and Hisada, 2002).

Moreover, like Germany, Japan has a large SME sector, which is not listed and is embedded in 'relational networks' including local banks. The SME sector accounts for 99.7 per cent of all Japanese firms and contributes to about 80 per cent of employment.[2] In terms of shipment value, the SME manufacturing subsector accounts for about 51 per cent of the total and nearly 50 per cent of the productivity of its industry as a whole (Sunday I. Owualah, 1999). In the 1970s, as the large firms tapped alternative sources of funds in the capital markets, commercial banks began to provide funding to SME companies. Commercial banks, in conjunction with regional, long-term credit and trust banks, are now the dominant source of finance for SMEs in Japan. At the end of the 1990s, 77 per cent of financing for plant, equipment and long-term operating funds for SMEs was provided by commercial, regional and trust banks (Sunday I. Owualah, 1999). It is even argued that if the relationships between banks and these borrowers were to weaken, a large number of businesses might be forced into bankruptcy; their performance will deteriorate if they cannot secure financial assistance (Baba and Hisada, 2002).

Moreover, despite regulatory changes to revitalize the market mechanism, Table 12.3 shows that owner–company relations in the Rhineland model are still most often characterized by one or more large shareholders with a strategic (rather than pure share value maximization) motivation for ownership. A total of 90 per cent of listed companies in

Table 12.1 Concentration in stock exchange trading in international comparison (in % of trading volume accounted for by largest 5% of corporations)

	1988	1993	1998	Number of firms representing top 5%
Germany	**61**	**85.9**	**85.5**	**35**
France	48.8	61.3	63.4	37
Italy	55.6	62.5	60	12
Sweden	28	58.8	72.7	12
Greece	n.a.	n.a.	50.1	11
Euro countries average	48.4	54.7	64.3	13
UK	**n.a.**	**34.5**	**59.8**	**102**
Japan				
Tokyo	55.4	42.9	62	90
Osaka	47.4	62.7	79.7	63
USA				
NYSE	n.a.	38.6	51.4	113
Nasdaq	n.a.	64.5	78.8	275
Amex	46.1	n.a.	n.a.	32

Source: Deutsches Aktieninstitut, DAI Factbook (1999: 6-4-2).

[2] Ministry of Public Management, Home Affairs, Posts and Telecommunications, *Establishment and Enterprise Census* (1999).

Table 12.2	National capitalization (market value as a percentage of GDP)			
	UK	**USA**	**Germany**	**Japan**
1997	161	132	40	53
1998	155	141	48	53
1999	216	191	72	87
2000	187	152	66	66
2001	166	152	61	50

Source: Rebérioux (2002: 113); *Tokyo Stock Exchange Fact Book 2003*; Bank of Japan (www.boj.jp).

Germany have a shareholder with at least a 10 per cent stake in the company. The types of investor likely to have strategic interests – enterprises and banks – together hold 52 per cent of shares (or 42 per cent and 10 per cent, respectively). Enterprises generally pursue strategic business interests. Large German banks have tended to view their shareholdings as a mechanism for protecting their loans and strengthening their business relationships with companies, rather than as a direct source of income. The ownership types having smaller shareholdings – investment funds, pension funds/insurance companies and households – account for only 35 per cent of total shareholdings of the large German companies (or 8 per cent, 12 per cent and 15 per cent respectively). The Rhineland system is thus characterized by concentrated ownership by actors pursuing a mix of financial and strategic goals (Vitols, 2001: 343). Hence, despite the tendency for the German financial model to adopt features of the Anglo-Saxon model of finance, a critical distinction remains: the majority of the German firms continue to have stable, long-term shareholdership, protecting firms from the short-termism of Anglo-Saxon capitalism.

Box 12.1: Resisting the Force of the Anglo-Saxon Model

While there have been moves in the direction of Anglo-Saxon corporate governance by some German executives, there are still powerful opposing forces. Evidence of these is the forcing out by his supervisory board of Ulrich Schumacher, the showy, American-style boss of Infineon, a semiconductor firm, at the beginning of April 2004. Mr Schumacher was famous for launching his firm's initial public offering in 2000 dressed as a racing driver. He later irritated trade unionists and worker representatives with his repeated threats to relocate the Munich-based firm to Switzerland.

By contrast, some top German managers, who in the USA or in the UK might have been dismissed for poor performance, are still in power because they play the consensus game. A well-known example is Juergen Schrempp, head of loss-making DaimlerChrysler, who remains in charge, despite DaimlerBenz's unfortunate merger with Chrysler. (*Economist*, 3 April 2004, Kultur clash, 63)

Despite the changes, many fundamental aspects of German company law have been preserved. Neither the dual-board system nor the principle of employee board representation were ever seriously questioned. The basic principle of the Joint Stock Company Law 1965 – that neither shareholders, top managers, nor employees should exert unilateral

Table 12.3 Structure of ownership (% of outstanding corporate equity held by sectors, 1998)				
	USA	**UK**	**Germany**	**Japan**
Households	49	21	15	24
Non-financial firms	–	1	42	24.1
Banks	6	1	10	22
Insurance enterprises and pension funds	28	50	12	11
Investment funds and other financial institutions	13	17	8	2.2
Non residents	5	9	9	9.8

Source: Rebérioux (2002: 114); *Tokyo Stock Exchange Fact Book 1999*, for Japan.

control in the company – remains intact (Vitols, 2001: 347). The fact that employee representation is safeguarded also means that the concentration of ownership rights, which is a core feature of the Rhineland model, will also persist. This conclusion is supported by a study from Pedersen and Thomsen (1999), in which the impact of employee board representation on ownership structure is tested. The study found that employee representation stimulates the creation of countervailing power (i.e. a concentration of ownership rights) to ensure that owner interests are represented on the board.

As in Germany, and despite signs of change, share ownership is still essentially institutionalized in Japan. In this respect, Table 12.3 shows that, at the end of the 1990s, the major shareholders were financial institutions and industrial corporations, which serve as stable shareholders. Moreover, while the accounting change is said to have induced the sale of cross-shareholdings among affiliated firms it is hard to find strong evidence for this claim. In order to mitigate the impact of stock price movement on their profits, many Japanese firms and banks would have started to reduce their stockholdings in other firms (Yoshikawa and Phan, 2001). A survey of 2426 companies in 1999, however, showed that 42 per cent of outstanding shares were still considered stable, and 16 per cent were believed to be cross-held (Schaede, 1999). In the late 1990s, the large horizontal *keiretsu* still held, on average, some 18 per cent of all outstanding shares within their group. It seems, then, that, as in Germany, there is continuity in the Japanese system in the midst of change. Indeed, the importance of the pattern in the rise of foreign ownership and the decline in cross-shareholding is that it is not evenly distributed. The impact of the change in ownership pattern is greater in some firms than in others.

This argument is further supported by data, from the end of the 1990s, on the ownership structure of Japanese firms in the automobile and electronics industries (Table 12.4). These industries are most exposed to the competitive global product and capital markets, and hence, have to respond more quickly to changes than firms in other industries. Looking at Table 12.4, it is clear that the majority of the shares of companies with group affiliations, but also of independent companies (Sony and Honda Motor), is stable. The diverse impact of foreign ownership on ownership structure in Japan is also clear from Table 12.4. Only Sony's ownership structure is notable for the large proportion of shares held by foreign investors. In 1998, foreign investors held 43.6 per cent of Sony's shares as compared to 13.8 per cent on average of the shares of the other corporations.

Table 12.4 Foreign ownership and stable shareholding positions of major group affiliated* and independent Japanese electronics and automotive companies (1998)

Company group	Foreign ownership (%)	Stable shareholding positions (%)	Corporate affiliation
Mitsubishi Electric	11.0	61.0	Mitsubishi
Hitachi	27.5	49.3	Fuyo, Sanwa, DKB**
Toshiba	9.4	59.1	Mitsui
Matsushita	20.3	60.9	Matsushita
Sony	43.6	43.4	Independent
Sharp	11.8	72.4	Sanwa
Fujitsu	14.5	68.0	DKB
NEC	13.7	67.2	Sumitomo
Honda Motor	17.8	74.3	Independent
Toyota Motor	8.1	85.4	Mitsui
Nissan Motor	10.6	79.4	Fuyo
Mitsubishi Motors	7.3	84.0	Mitsibishi

*Groups: Mitsui, Mitsubishi, Sumitomo, Fuyo, Sanwa, DKB.
**DKB: Dai-Ichi Kangyo Bank Group.

Source: Yoshikawa and Phan (2001: 193, 195).

In the literature, it has been argued that the biggest step that could be taken to radically change the distribution of ownership of financial assets, or the distribution of assets between categories, is to promote US- and UK-style pension funds and mutual funds by creating tax incentives for employers and employees to defer compensation (Vitols, 2001: 348).[3] Such a proposal was made by the nascent mutual fund industry in Germany but, due to opposition from the insurance industry, this was dropped (Vitols, 2001: 348). Thus, although the financial markets have been somewhat liberalized, the increase in the relative importance of the type of institutional investor dominant in the UK and the USA (i.e. pension funds and mutual funds) is limited. Table 12.5 confirms this picture; it shows that despite the gradual increase in financial assets (as a percentage of GDP) of institutional investors in different countries, Germany and Japan, as well as other Rhineland-model countries, are lagging far behind the USA and the UK. In addition, the composition of the portfolios of institutional investors in Germany and Japan, the prototype countries of the Rhineland model, still shows a preference for bonds and loans, as opposed to a preference for shares in the Anglo-Saxon countries (Table 12.6).

Pension reform in Japan includes the introduction of an Anglo-Saxon style (that is, a 401(k)-type) pension scheme, from 1 October, 2001. This reform, it is hoped, will bring about the engagement of households in the capital markets in Japan. Participation in this defined-contribution scheme is compulsory and includes the allocation of the assets into

---

[3] A large proportion of US shares is held in 401(k) pension plans. These are financed from employee – and frequently also employer – contributions. The contributions are paid from income before tax, and the accumulated assets only become liable to tax when the capital is disbursed. The name is taken from section 401(k) of the 1978 US Internal Revenue Code.

Table 12.5 Financial assets of institutional investors* (as % of GDP)

	1992	1993	1994	1995	1996	1997	1998	1999	2000
Germany	34.0	38.9	41.3	45.3	50.6	58.7	66.1	76.8	79.7
Denmark	55.7	63.9	62.2	65.1	70.6	77.5	84.8	98.0	n.a.
Norway	36.4	42.0	41.4	42.4	43.5	46.6	47.7	53.9	n.a.
Sweden	88.8	105.7	97.9	102.9	118.5	136.8	123.2	137.8	n.a.
Japan	78.0	83.4	81.6	89.3	89.3	87.6	91.7	100.5	n.a.
UK	131.3	163.0	143.8	164.0	173.4	195.5	203.6	226.7	n.a.
USA	127.2	136.3	135.9	151.9	162.9	178.4	192.0	207.3	195.2

*Insurance companies, investment companies, pension funds and other forms of institutional saving.   Source: OECD (2001).

bonds and investment trusts, for example. Members have to select the type of investment themselves. The Japanese government is faced with a very serious pension fund shortfall in coming decades. In the hope of reducing the severity of this situation, the government is expanding the investment opportunities available to the population. It is hoped that this scheme will gradually encourage private investors to include shares in their long-term financial planning, thus increasing the volume of capital flowing in to the stock market. Up to now, Japanese households' operations in the stock markets have been on a relatively small scale. Japanese private investors are known to be risk averse, and to attach greater importance to the safety and liquidity of their capital than to its profitability. At the end of 2000, for example, Japanese households held more than half of their financial assets in cash and deposits with credit institutions (Deutsche Bank Research, 29 October 2001). The extended downturn in the Japanese stock markets, combined with the risk averseness of the population, makes it highly likely that most households will go for bonds instead of shares to set up their pension schemes.

A law reform that is thought to enable and stimulate the unwinding of the complex 'web' of cross-shareholdings in Germany is the tax reform enacted in 2000, especially the amended paragraph 8b of corporate tax law, which states that public companies' capital gains on the sale of shareholdings will generally be tax-free as of 1 January 2002 (Deutsche Bank Research, 7 February 2002). It has been argued that the 'web' of cross-shareholdings and *Konzerne* had partly been maintained by a stiff tax of over 40 per cent on the sale of shares by corporations (Schaede, 2000). However, the small number of large listed public companies, combined with the fact that in some of the sectors in which German companies are among the most competitive in the world, the prevailing owner-ship structures are highly concentrated (automotives, telecoms, post and insurance), suggest that the number of large-scale transactions as a corollary of the tax law reform is unlikely to be high. Moreover, while companies from sectors such as utilities, steel-making and electrical engineering are looking to divest business and subsidiaries that no longer form part of their core activities, these divestments are sometimes part of reciprocal activities. In addition, these companies are looking to use the proceeds from these divest-ments to acquire shareholdings and companies in their core business, thus preserving the pattern of concentrated ownership (Deutsche Bank Research, 7 February 2002).

Table 12.6 Portfolio composition of institutional investors (as % of total financial assets)										
	1990	**1991**	**1992**	**1993**	**1994**	**1995**	**1996**	**1997**	**1998**	**1999**
Germany										
Bonds	39	41	42	43	42	43	43	42	43	40
Loans	47	45	43	40	40	40	38	34	30	28
Shares	*9*	*10*	*10*	*12*	*12*	*12*	*14*	*19*	*22*	*28*
Other	5	5	4	5	6	5	5	5	5	5
Japan										
Bonds	31	36	37	38	41	44	47	48	49	49
Loans	26	29	29	28	29	26	26	26	23	21
Shares	*32*	*24*	*22*	*22*	*18*	*19*	*17*	*15*	*16*	*19*
Other	10	11	12	13	12	11	10	11	12	11
UK										
Bonds	14	13	14	15	16	16	16	16	17	14
Loans	2	1	1	1	1	1	1	1	1	1
Shares	*66*	*70*	*68*	*70*	*69*	*68*	*67*	*68*	*65*	*68*
Other	18	16	16	15	15	15	16	16	17	17
USA										
Bonds	45	44	45	45	44	40	38	35	34	32
Loans	16	14	13	11	11	10	9	9	8	8
Shares	*25*	*29*	*30*	*33*	*33*	*38*	*42*	*46*	*48*	*51*
Other	14	13	12	11	11	11	11	10	10	10

Source: OECD (2001).

Similarly, the recent corporate tax reform in Japan is argued to enable companies to reorganize around their holding companies by way of either 'spinning off' or 'spinning in'. Holding companies are said increasingly to be used to spin off and separate unprofitable business units (i.e. divisions, departments and subsidiaries) from profitable ones so that not only tax advantages are gained, but also the non-competitive units can be disposed of in the M&As market (Ozawa, 2003). At the same time, however, there seems to be a 'Japanized', or culturally specific way, in which the new holding structure has begun to be used, a way in which some parent companies are merely avoiding their announced layoff plans for corporate restructuring by creating new, unlisted subsidiaries and hiving workers off the parent's books.[4]

Finally, while take-overs are increasingly becoming part of economic normality in Germany and Japan,[5] Anglo-Saxon style 'hostile' take-overs following public bids remain rare (Deutsche Bank Research, 7 February 2002).[6] In fact, the history of German industry reveals only very few cases of hostile take-overs, some of which either led to a consensus in the final stages of the dispute or failed outright.[7]

---

[4] *Economist*, 'The way Enron hid debts' (2002).

[5] Following the Financial Holding Companies Law of 1998, in order to improve the long-term health of the bank system, a move towards mega-mergers among the largest banks took place.

[6] 'Hostile' here means directed against the interests of the target company's management.

[7] Until the UK company Vodafone acquired Mannesmann AG in 2000, a German company had never been acquired in a hostile take-over.

Box 12.2:	'Corporate Greed on Trial'

In April 2004, the *Economist* reported on the most spectacular trial in German corporate history. The trial concerned extra bonuses paid to senior managers of Mannesmann after the take-over of Mannesmann by Vodafone in February 2000. Six former Mannesmann officials, including Josef Ackermann, the chief executive of Deutsche Bank, were accused of committing a breach of trust in being awarded bonuses worth 57 million euros. Questions were raised with respect to the level of the bonuses, the sloppy way in which the paperwork was done, the instigator(s) of, and the reasons for, the bonuses. The German public is said to have seen this as corporate greed on trial. The prosecutors tried to suggest that the bonuses were bribes to secure the biggest hostile take-over in history. (*Economist*, 3 April 2004, Kultur clash, 63)

In general, in Japan, there has been reluctance on the part of the Japanese business community, and society as a whole, to engage in take-overs even between Japanese companies. The Japanese business community still attaches great value to the traditional Japanese management style of long-term perspective, stable employment and protection against corporate raids.[8] The major institutional reason for the absence of hostile take-overs in the form of public bids in both countries is the complex ownership structures of many large companies, which put up barriers to transfers of control, thus providing incentives for the management of the target company and bidder, as well as controlling and influencing shareholders on both sides to seek a consensus.

To sum up, while there have been formal legal and regulatory changes in Germany and Japan, these only had a minor impact on:

- the structure of ownership
- growth of the stock market, and
- patterns of corporate control.

12.3 The Personnel and Industrial Relations Systems

The previous section underlines that corporate governance is part of nationally specific institutional configurations that help condition the coalitions between capital, labour and management in the governance of the firm. The structure of top management institutions (i.e. unitary or two-tier boards), for example, affects the management–labour nexus. 'Patient capital' in Germany and Japan enables a different set of coalitions between capital and labour than is feasible in the UK and US systems. Insulation from shareholder pressure to maximize returns, even at the expense of cutting labour costs and employment, exhibits a strong 'institutional interlock' with the system of lifetime and stable employment, in-company training, seniority-based wages and promotion (in Japan),

[8] *Nikkei Weekly*, 20 September 1999: 3.

a relatively low stratification of rewards, and the social perception of the firm as a community (Dore, 1994). As such, the system of corporate governance is embedded in the systems of industrial relations and human resources. The complementarity of these institutions requires us to move beyond the analysis of change in a single institutional domain. Since each institutional complex depends for its viability on the others, serious erosion tendencies in one complex will, in the longer run, produce erosion tendencies in the other two. This section, therefore, analyses the dialectics of change in the systems of industrial relations and human resources.

Germany

The German system of industrial relations has been seen as a vital part of the German system of diversified quality production (see Chapter 7, on production management, for an explanation of this system), both in its capacity for securing social peace and through its impact on the quality and stability of labour (Streeck, 1991). The most important features of the system in these respects are the relatively centralized and coordinated form of collective bargaining, and the integration of labour at the enterprise level through codetermination mechanisms, together with the clear separation of functions between unions and works councils. At the enterprise level, relatively high levels of employment security, secured through codetermination mechanisms, combined with patient capital, which allows for long-term strategies, have provided management with the incentive to invest in high levels of skill training and internal promotion.

Bargaining within industries has been credited with considerable advantages for both labour and management: a high coverage rate and a relatively egalitarian wage distribution, promoting solidarity and union strength; social peace and the predictability of wage demand have enabled employers to combine the payment of relatively high wages with constant rises in labour productivity (Lane, 2000: 212).

Box 12.3: ⬛ **Vital Features of the German Personnel and Industrial Relations System**

- ⬛ A relatively centralized and coordinated form of collective bargaining
- ⬛ Codetermination mechanisms
- ⬛ Clear separation of functions between unions and works councils
- ⬛ High levels of employment security

Despite the challenges in recent years, from external political and economic changes, the most important pillars of the industrial relations system have proved their resilience. While there has been some decentralization of bargaining, with works councils assuming more influence over negotiations so as to better match bargaining outcomes to the economic performance of firms, centralized negotiations are still prevalent (Begin, 1997: 181). Moreover, hardship clauses, permitting an employer to avoid an industry agreement, still have to be authorized centrally (Hassel and Schulten, 1998). In general, social partnership is still valued by most employers because the social peace it creates affords the stability, predictability and cooperation needed for the German production model. This is particularly true in the many firms where export activity remains more important than foreign production (Lane, 2000), but also in the globalizing firms.

While it has been argued that the internationalization of German firms would facilitate the erosion of organizational regulation and interest representation (Streeck, 1997), until now, there has been only minor evidence in support of this fear. Admittedly, in some sectors, such as the car and electrical engineering industries, the development of transnational production chains has forced works councils into concession bargaining. However, concessions remain more the exception than the rule in industry-wide bargaining (Jackson, 1997) and have involved mainly working time flexibility (Lane, 2000). Internationalization did result in weakened competencies of plant-level codetermination by bringing centralization of strategic decision-making at the *Konzerne* level. Plant management within large internationalized German firms, which are the traditional negotiating partners of the works councils, is losing its competencies in terms of strategic decisions (Streeck, 1995). However, works councils can use a variety of options to coordinate across enterprises and bypass negotiations with partners who lack 'sovereignty'.[9]

In addition, as already indicated, labour's representation on supervisory boards remains unquestioned, thus supporting the stakeholder 'mentality' and impeding the adoption of Anglo-Saxon style hire-and-fire policies. Share options are used in some German firms as a management incentive, but because one-sided decision-making is limited, they tend to be targeted at groups rather than individuals (Casper, 2000), or are available to all employees, not just managerial ones, as at VW (Lane, 2000: 220). In general, German workers continue to be among the highest paid, as well as the socially most secure in the developed world. The realization that the viability of the German production policy continues to depend on its core workforce is argued to still have a hold on most German management (Lane, 2000).

Japan

Rather like Germany, Japan's system of industrial relations plays an important role in its production strategy. Unlike in Germany, however, and with very few exceptions (e.g. the Seamen's Union), Japanese unions are enterprise unions, each representing the employees of a different firm and organizing both blue- and white-collar employees; also dissimilar to the situation in Germany, Japanese corporate law is based on the unitary board system. Hence, employee participation, or codetermination, is not adopted in Japan. Despite the structural dependence on the firm, however, Japanese unions have had a considerable stake in, and have fought hard to defend, two core institutions of the Japanese human resource system: lifetime employment and seniority-based pay and promotion[10] (Lincoln, 1993). These institutions have been credited by both management and labour with major advantages. Management views them as a way to secure labour peace and retain skilled workers. For the unions they were ways to stave off management's tendency to lay workers off in order to adjust labour costs and to beat the threat of an inflated cost of living in the early postwar period (Ornatowski, 1998).

---

[9] See Jackson (1997) for an extended discussion of these options.

[10] Seniority-based pay and promotion is a system or practice that emphasizes the number of years of service, or age and educational background, in determining pay and promotion.

Box 12.4:	Vital Features of the Japanese Personnel and Industrial Relations System

Seniority-based wages
Lifetime employment

More than in Germany, lifetime employment is an important part of Japanese management practice as a whole because it reduces the significant commitment problems associated with firm-based private-sector training. In the unitary education system of Japan, the state focuses on the provision of general education, leaving firms to organize and invest in their own firm-specific technical training (Nishida and Redding, 1992). Lifetime employment provides incentives for workers to stay with the company that trains them, which, in turn, makes it safe for the firm to invest heavily in skills without fear of workers absconding with these skills to other firms (Thelen and Kume, 1999). As in Germany, this practice is linked to the nature of corporate governance in Japan, which is less subject to short-term financial disciplines and tends to put off radical restructuring of industrial activities and to avoid taking drastic measures if at all possible (Nohara, 1999).

Unlike in Germany, however, lifetime employment is not protected by codetermination rights in Japan, but is firmly grounded in legal precedents set by the Japanese court, which has made it almost impossible for employers to terminate or lay off their regular-status employees without the employees' or their unions' consent (Morishima, 1995). Also dissimilar to the situation in Germany, lifetime employment has always applied to the core full-time workers or the 'insiders' only in the biggest companies,[11] representing probably no more than one-third of the entire workforce.[12] Moreover, while the Japanese lifetime employment rule means long-term stable employment, it has never excluded massive dismissal.[13] The system has also always been seen as a flexible one in which only about 20 per cent of all employees serve continuously at the same company from youth until the age of 60. Intra-group transfers, temporary and permanent – in a sense a sub-system of the lifetime employment system – help corporate groups shift the workforce, yet avoid laying off their core employees and are responsible for much of the system's inherent flexibility.[14] Similarly, the current growth of part-time employment as a response to the downturn and the need for firms to cut costs, is at the same time, a means of maintaining the security and benefits accorded to core workers. It is seen as a flexible strategy aimed at sustaining a relatively rigid and costly commitment to lifetime employment of the core (Osawa and Kingston, 1996).

Rather like the case in Germany, and despite the challenges to the system in recent years, patterns of change and resilience are closely interwoven. As a result of the ongoing recession, there have been pressures for change in life-time employment and in the seniority

[11] The group of so-called more 'peripheral' workers, or 'outsiders', usually includes women, youths and older workers.

[12] Japan Institute of Labor, 'The labor situation in Japan, 2002/2003', 22; *Economist*, 18 November 1999, 'The worm turns'; 23 August 2001, 'An alternative to cocker spaniels'.

[13] *Japan Labor Bulletin*, Mid- and long-term prospects for Japanese-style employment practices, 33(8), 1 August 1994.

[14] *Japan Labor Bulletin*, 'The labor situation in Japan 2002/2003', 22.

system in particular. In order to cut labour costs large Japanese companies have shed an increasing amount of their labour force. Well-known examples are Nissan, which has closed five car plants and shed 21,000 jobs to stave off bankruptcy; Nippon Steel, which shed 40 per cent of its 10,000 white-collar workers between 1993 and 1997; Sony, which got rid of 17,000 jobs; and NEC which disposed of 15,000.[15] Such dramatic cuts explain the plethora of articles in the popular business press that predict the demise of lifetime employment.

However, the fact that the Japanese lifetime employment system has always been limited to a small proportion of the workforce, combined with the diversity of practices that have always been used by Japanese corporations to cut labour costs in times of distress, demands caution when examining, and making bold statements about so-called dramatic changes to the system. In general, a lot of Japanese firms still tend to rely on traditional responses to negative situations (Tanisaka and Ohtake, 2003). These include a reduction in working hours and overtime payment for currently employed full-time core workers; an increase in 'service overtime' (overtime without pay); less employment for new graduates; and an increase in *shukko* (temporary transfers between firms) and *tenseki* (transfers to another company, or change of long-term employment), both of which effectively reallocate workers within the internal labour market (Mroczkowski and Hanaoka, 1997; Sato, 1999; Fujiki *et al.*, 2001; Genda, 2003). Moreover, many of the current job cuts are argued to have been designed to minimize job losses in Japan and to maximize those elsewhere; some of them are said to be part of early-retirement programmes;[16] and others affect the peripheral rather than the core workforce.[17]

Moreover, labour shedding via dismissals and calls for voluntary retirement, which happens increasingly during the ongoing recession, is still considered the very last resort for Japanese firms in streamlining their structures, and to be a measure that only these firms in critical condition would resort to (Tanisaka and Ohtake, 2003). Indeed, while most Japanese firms have adopted a mandatory retirement system with the age of 60 as the common retirement age, the system at the same time functions to secure employment for full-time regular workers until the mandatory retirement age (Sato, 1999). It seems more appropriate, then, to see the new conditions of employment as modifications of the lifetime employment system, not a contradiction of it (Kono and Clegg, 2001). Until now, the basic structure of the Japanese employment system has remained intact. Lifetime employment of the core is retained – not only because it is a protected right, but also because of the heightened dependence on stable and predictable relationships with labour at the plant level, in the context of tightly coupled production networks and the demands of producing at high quality on a just-in-time basis.

Similarly, while a few major Japanese employers have made the choice to modify the rules regarding seniority-based pay and promotion,[18] this is far from being a modal practice. In the early 1990s, the recession and the emphasis on the creation of new

---

[15] *Economist*, 9 October 1997, 'On a roll'; 18 November 1999, 'The worm turns'; 23 August 2001, 'An alternative to cocker spaniels'.

[16] *Japan Labor Bulletin*, September 2003, 4.

[17] *Economist*, 9 October 1997, 'On a roll'; 23 August 2001, 'An alternative to cocker spaniels'.

[18] In 1999, Matsushita changed its seniority-based wage system for its 11,000 managers. This behaviour was followed by some other big companies; i.e. by Fujitsu, Fuji Xerox, Asahi Glass, Asahi Breweries, Kansai Electric and Itochu Corporation (*Economist*, 20 May 1999, 'Putting the bounce back into Matsushita').

technological resources in Japan induced large Japanese companies to renew their incentive mechanisms, particularly their wage systems. Some firms have introduced a lump-sum salary that is renegotiated annually and depends to a large extent on individual performance and on the performance of the employing organization. By linking employee compensation to both kinds of performance, employers expect that wage levels will be more flexible in response to changes in individual performance and the economic prosperity of the firm (Morishima, 1995). The new system is also intended to provide incentives for employees to increase their productivity and commitment to the goals of their employing organization, as well as to encourage autonomy and individual creativity, particularly among white-collar workers, whose productivity is considered rather mediocre, even if this development means sacrificing some of the benefits of cooperation (Nohara, 1999). Most importantly, the reforms are seen as essential to maintaining the stability of long-term employment.

The combined review of both employment and seniority systems could probably best be understood in terms of the need to recover the 'lost' balance between jobs, ability and wages. Technological developments in the past decade have outstripped the skills of experienced workers, and the need to fill the gap has unleashed fierce competition among firms for promising young workers because of their adaptability to new technology. Younger employees, however, are increasingly less tolerant of the principle of equality of results and patiently waiting for the promotion implied by the traditional seniority system (Ornatowski, 1998). Older workers, on the other hand, are highly paid as a result of seniority-based wage components but do not possess the skills necessary to do the new sophisticated jobs (Sato, 1999). Reforms of the wage system have thus been motivated by attempts to achieve advantage in competition with other firms over the most desirable young workers, as well as by a desire to make it less costly for firms to retain older workers. However, partly as a result of the system's enterprise-orientated incentives, the new human resource practices are diffusing only slowly in Japan (Jacoby, 1995).

12.4 Conclusions

This chapter has shown that the internationalization of national economies is reshaping the characteristics of the systems of corporate governance, industrial relations and human resources in Germany and Japan – the prototype countries of the Rhineland model. To some extent, this reshaping involves the adoption of practices that conform more closely to Anglo-Saxon standards (i.e. the adoption of new accounting practices in Germany and Japan). As a consequence, the propagation of the globalization myth with path-deviant changes in the Rhineland model has been possible and credible. In general, the effects of the new practices on German and Japanese organization and management, however, are less proof of path deviance or convergence towards the Anglo-Saxon model than they are of resilience and small-step adaptation within the existing model. This chapter has assessed the impact of globalization tendencies on organization and management by assessing changes in three core components of the German and Japanese production and innovation systems.

The systems of corporate governance, industrial relations and human resources have all been affected by these tendencies, albeit to a different degree. The corporate governance system has been most affected. However, in this case, it could also be argued that the most radical changes at the institutional level, while showing tendencies to convergence towards the Anglo-Saxon model, revitalize the existing model far more than producing path-deviant change. Changes in financial regulations and corporate law in Germany and Japan have not produced any clear movement towards equity-centred systems of corporate finance and an 'outsider' model of corporate governance. Ownership still tends to be concentrated and stable, and there is not much of a market in corporate control. Instead, control over companies is held by a majority of stakeholders. The traditional stakeholder 'mentality' and reality (especially since there are still codetermination and comparatively strong labour organizations in Germany and enterprise unions in Japan) still prevail in both countries.

The stakeholder mentality of the insider model – which requires broad consensus – helps to explain why the industrial relations and human resource systems of both countries, while experiencing reform, still rest on the pillars of enduring social partnership and employment security. Moreover, the correlation between culture and labour market institutions, which is identified in the research of Nickel and Layard (1997) and Inglehart and Baker (2000), underlines that these pillars are not likely to change in the near future.[19] In addition, it seems unlikely that major stakeholders, such as the unions, will accept the dilution of established rights. In both countries, the unions are strengthened in their positions by the fact that the current features of the systems of corporate governance, industrial relations and human resources jointly support the production model of internationally competitive domestic industries. The preservation of these production models depends on the combined availability of long-term, patient capital; social peace and partnership between capital, management and labour; highly skilled labour; and a network of long-term and cooperative relationships. These requirements are irreconcilable with Anglo-Saxon-style capitalism, which emphasizes short-termism in managerial strategy and relationships, and instant hire-and-fire practices. Hence, we would argue that far more than leading to the demise of the existing German and Japanese systems, by injecting a healthy dose of competition at all levels, reforms, even though they are path deviant, will help to remodel and improve them.

Contrary to Lane (2000), and consistent with Whitley (1999), we would also argue against hybridization. As indicated, hybridization implies change in a path-deviant manner. It is argued to result from the process of integration into the global system of individual companies. Subsidiaries, which enjoy a high level of resources and a relatively high degree of autonomy, also become embedded in their host countries. This will lead to learning processes and to the adoption of new organizational structures, practices and competencies. Organizational learning from host country experience by affiliates will, in integrated TNCs, initiate organizational learning and hybridization at company level. Such hybrid companies, it is argued, if they belong to the core companies of a country, may eventually affect the domestic business system (Lane, 2000). In support of Whitley (1999), we would regard hybridization as an unlikely development for corporations from cohesive and highly integrated home economies such as Germany and Japan.[20] We consider that

[19] Inglehart and Baker (2000) and Nickell and Layard (1997) found major differences in labour market institutions between 20 countries, which changed only very slowly over time. This research identifies the correlation between culture and labour market institutions as the underlying reason for this.

[20] Moreover, evidence on France, Italy and Spain also argues against hybridization. See Deeg and Perez (1998) for further information.

while there is evidence of path-deviant change at the institutional level (i.e. regulatory change) in both countries, it has not led to hybridization or path-deviant change at the organization level.

While it is true that some of the large Germany companies, such as Hoechst, Bayer and BASF, have restructured their organizations, this was less an expression of organizational hybridization, as Lane claims (2000), than of 'greater specialization in national industrial profiles' (Vitols, 2001: 360; Sorge, 2003). Unable to enter new growth fields (i.e. biotechnology),[21] which require more radical innovation, these three companies disposed of their pharmaceuticals subsidiaries. Initially, all three companies relocated their innovative activities in pharmaceuticals to the USA, either through the establishment of new research facilities there or through the acquisition of existing firms (particularly in the biotechnology area). More recently, however, it seems that German companies are simply disappearing from the pharmaceutical industry. Hoechst disappeared as a German pharma company by merging with the French Rhône-Poulenc, with the new company's headquarters (Aventis) in France. BASF has sold all of its pharmaceutical operations to a US company, and Bayer is also argued to have increased its focus on core competencies, and the current preference is towards maintaining chemicals activities and selling off pharmaceuticals (Vitols, 2001). It seems, then, that far more than hybridization, what is happening in this industry points to further specialization.

Further specialization does not occur at the level of societal institutions, however, as was also predicted by the second assumption. Rather, as indicated, we have discussed some evidence of path-deviant change at that level. In fact, it seems that path-deviant reforms in Germany and Japan, which allow for Anglo-Saxon-style management practices, contribute to intensified specialization at the industrial level. For example, the tax reform in Germany, which was expected to lead to the unwinding of cross-holdings, rather than doing so, in general stimulated the divestment of non-core activities. Similarly, in Japan, in order to attract young employees, some companies bypassed the institutionalized seniority-based wage system and implemented Anglo-Saxon-style remuneration packages that are performance-based. However, rather than diluting the entire system, these measures, at the same time, enabled these companies to preserve lifetime employment, which is one of the cornerstones of the Japanese production model. This model has a comparative advantage in the so-called medium-tech sectors characterized by incremental innovation and large firm-specific human capital investments.

In general, it would not be wrong to argue that there is more evidence of path dependency and resilience than of hybridization or path-deviant change at the organization and management level. This finding can perhaps best be explained by the dynamics of bargaining processes within the insider or stakeholder model, which strive to obtain an equilibrium situation between diverging interests and acquired rights, including those of labour. While it is true that regulatory reform shows tendencies that could be perceived as path-deviant in both Germany and Japan, its effects point to the wish to preserve and revitalize the current model. These findings lead to the conclusion that the choice of a particular level of analysis, to a large extent, determines the type of evidence one obtains and, thus, the argument that one is able to defend. When the research focus is on societal

---

[21] See Casper (2000) for an extended explanation of incremental adaptation in a largely path-dependent way in German biotechnology companies.

institutions such as regulations and laws, one can find evidence that point to path-deviant change and hybridization. When looking at the level of the firm, though, there is evidence of incremental adaptation and path dependency as well as further specialization of the industrial profile. There is no evidence, however, in support of the convergence argument within institutional or societal frameworks.

Similarly, within the cultural framework, there is no evidence in support of the convergence argument. Research that focuses exclusively on cultural analysis – whether from the etic or emic viewpoints – finds considerable differences between cultures and these differences seem to be path dependent. Perhaps an important proof of this argument is that the country scores on Hofstede's national cultural dimensions, which were calculated on the basis of a dataset from the 1980s, are still valid and used widely in today's research.

Additional evidence in this direction comes from a study by Inglehart and Baker (2000). These authors tested the thesis that economic development is linked with systematic changes in basic values. Their research was informed by modernization theorists from Karl Marx (1867) to Daniel Bell (1973, 1976), who argued that economic development brings pervasive cultural changes. It was also based on research by scholars such as Max Weber ([1904] 1958) and Samuel Huntington (1993, 1996), who have claimed that cultural values are an enduring and autonomous influence on society. Using data from the three waves of the World Values Surveys, which include 65 societies and 75 per cent of the world's population, Inglehart and Baker found evidence both of massive cultural change and the persistence of distinctive cultural traditions. Economic development was found to be associated with shifts away from absolute norms and values, towards values that are increasingly rational, tolerant, trusting and participatory. Cultural change, however, was found to be path dependent. The broad cultural heritage of a society – Protestant, Roman Catholic, Orthodox, Confucian or communist – was found to leave an imprint on values that endure despite modernization. Moreover, the differences between the values held by members of different religions within given societies were found to be much smaller than are cross-national differences. Once established, such cross-cultural differences are argued to become part of a national culture transmitted by educational institutions and mass media. Hence, while there is some talk of global communications and worldwide cultural standardization, as in McDonaldization and Coca-Colonization, the basic systems of national values endure in the midst of change.

This argument provides us with further confirmation for our claim that societal institutions, while surely experiencing change, are not converging and will not converge in the future. Since national culture is embedded in the societal institutions, full convergence at the institutional level would imply convergence of cultural traditions. Following Inglehart and Baker's study, we can argue here that since the latter is not happening, full institutional convergence will not take place.

A final important question to answer in this last chapter is 'What does all of this imply for the management of multinational companies (MNCs)?' If the world political economy becomes globalized, as some argue, then multinationals should gradually be losing their national characters, and converging in their fundamental strategies and operations. This assumption fits with Theodore Levitt's 1983 paper, which is in favour of the global company. He argues that the global company will outperform the multinational company by concentrating 'on what everyone wants rather than worrying about the details of what everyone thinks they might like' (1983: 2). Nowadays, however, an increasing amount of research talks about the 'myth of globalization' and the fact that most of the largest companies operate in only one of the three dominant clusters – the EU, Japan and North America (Rugman, 2001) – and not on a global scale. It is argued that globalization is misunderstood – it does not and has never, existed in terms of a single world market with free trade (Rugman, 2001: 11).

Moreover, in a study on retail companies, Rugman and Girod (2003) argue that the likelihood that a (retail) firm will act globally is determined to a great extent by the size of its primary market. A total of 83 per cent of their study's domestic-only firms come from the USA, a fact that the authors attribute to the size of the US market. They explain that most US firms do not have to go abroad to generate sufficient growth. The bi-regional MNCs, by contrast, come mainly from small European nations and have larger sales in North America than in Europe. Rugman and Girod argue that this was a strategic choice carried out through acquisitions since the 1960s. They write that these companies acted as locals as much as possible, not using European names in North America. The conclusion drawn from this study is that, while the retail industry is becoming more international and there is an overall need for firms to expand abroad in order to generate new growth, this is not global activity. Most of the international activity is within the local home region of the retail MNC. Hence, Rugman advises managers not to buy in to the globalization myth but rather to concentrate on building strategies that create advantage in their major regional markets (Rugman, 2001).

Additional confirmation of the absence of global companies, and the absence of global pressures leading to convergence, can be found in a study of German, Japanese and US multinationals (Pauly and Reich, 1997). This study shows that German, Japanese and US MNCs continue to diverge fairly systematically in their internal governance and long-term financing structures, in their approaches to research and development (R&D), as well as in the location of core R&D facilities, and in their overseas investment and intra-firm trading strategies. Consistent with the line of thinking in this book and, especially, with Chapter 10, on MNCs, the study shows that durable national institutions and distinctive ideological traditions still seem to shape and channel crucial corporate decisions. Indeed, the evidence of this study suggests 'a logical chain that begins deep in the idiosyncratic national histories that lie behind durable domestic institutions and ideologies and extends directly to the structures of corporate governance and long-term corporate financing' (Pauly and Reich, 1997: 23). Those structures, it is argued, in turn appear plausibly linked to continuing diversity in the corporate foundations of national innovation systems. The latter is precisely what we concluded from Chapter 9, on national innovation systems, and what we have repeated at the beginning of this chapter.

It would not be wrong to argue, then, that sufficient evidence exists to legitimize the ending of this chapter and, at the same time, of this book, by disagreeing with those who, despite all evidence to the contrary, maintain expectations regarding the emergence of a truly global political economy with truly global corporations acting as the sinews of convergence in the world economy. It is clear that the globalization template upon which much current theoretical and policy debate rests remains weak. Convergence may be apparent at the level of popular culture, and perhaps not coincidentally in the sales report and marketing campaigns of MNCs; but below the surface, where the roots of leading MNCs remain lodged, this book suggests durable sources of resistance.

Study Questions

1. Explain the complementarity of three core societal institutions – that is, the systems of corporate governance, personnel and industrial relations.

2. Why is it essential to distinguish between different levels of analysis when analysing the impact of globalization forces?

3. Analyse the effect of the so-called globalization forces on the following societal systems in Germany and Japan: the systems of corporate governance, personnel and industrial relations.

4. Would path-deviant change in organization and management generally be feasible in German and Japanese corporations?

5. Evaluate whether institutional theory is sufficiently powerful to analyse the impact of globalization pressures and to arrive at credible conclusions.

6. Evaluate the role of cultural characteristics in explaining change at the societal, organization and management levels.

7. Explain whether the MNC drives globalization and whether it needs to be prepared for globalization.

Further Reading

Govindarajan, V. and Gupta, A. (2000) Analysis of the emerging global arena. *European Management Journal* 18(3), 274–84.

In contrast to mainstream opinion nowadays, and despite all evidence to the contrary, both authors maintain the claim that globalization is one of the main issues facing companies today. They claim that twin forces – that is, ideological change and technology revolution – underline the existence of globalization.

Pauly, L.W. and Reich, S. (1997) National structures and multinational corporate behavior: enduring differences in the age of globalization. *International Organization* 51(1), 1–30.

This article focuses on German, Japanese and American MNCs, and examines whether they are losing their national characters, and are converging in their fundamental strategies and operations as a result of globalization. The article shows that MNCs continue to diverge fairly systematically and that durable national institutions and distinctive ideological traditions still seem to shape and channel crucial corporate decisions.

Ruigrok, W. and Van Tulder, R. (1995) *The Logic of International Restructuring.* London: Routledge.

This book offers an integrated and interdisciplinary framework to analyse the dynamics of the international economy. The authors explain in a very clear way that the nationality of companies continues to be a decisive factor in today's supposedly 'borderless' economy.

Global Outsourcing: Divergence or Convergence?

They also resent an insinuation underlying the debate over 'outsourcing': that all countries such as India have to offer is cheap labour and a telecommunications link. Just look, they say, at the extent of the high-end research and development (R & D) work being undertaken in India.

Yet by the crude measure of patents earned by the Indian subsidiaries of multinational firms, a significant amount of innovation now stems from India. Last year, Intel's Indian subsidiary filed 63 patents. Its president, Ketan Sampat, says that the 1,500 IT professionals employed by the firm in R & D in Bangalore are engaged in 'engineering challenges as complex as any other project on the planet.' They use the fastest supercomputer in India (ranked as the 109th most powerful computer in the world) and are divided into four product-design divisions covering ultra-wideband radio, enterprise processors, mobile and wireless chip-sets, and communications.

For Intel, which has a similar-sized R & D operation in Israel, and smaller facilities in Russia and China, the attractions of Bangalore are simple: the best climate in India and 'very smart people', who are technically well-educated and speak good English. D. B. Inamdar, the senior civil servant in the provincial government's IT Department, says that some 140,000 IT professionals now work in Bangalore – about 20,000 more than in Silicon Valley. Some 50 colleges produce 40,000 more each year. Intel's approach is to hire and train college graduates, supplementing them with about 100 senior engineers, mostly (like Mr Sampat) returning expatriates.

Intel and others also point to the congenial 'ecosystem' developed as technology companies have clustered in Bangalore.

For SAP, a German software firm, the appeal of the Bangalore ecosystem includes the presence of its customers, its global partners and, crucially, some 3,000 engineers trained in SAP software on the books of Indian IT services such as Wipor, Infosys and Tata Consultancy Services. SAP has 850 staff in Bangalore, a number likely to grow by 500 this year, but can, with a local phone call, quickly add qualified engineers for particular projects.

Wipro's boss, Vivek Paul, says that R & D is becoming 'like the movies'. Firms, like film studios, are increasingly unwilling to keep expensive teams together between projects. For Wipro, providing firms with an alternative to doing R & D with permanent in-house teams has become a big business, accounting for one third of its $1 billion in annual revenues, and employing 6,500 people. It is probably the world's biggest R & D services firm.

Its customers include all the big telecoms-equipment vendors (except

Germany's Siemens). Its smallest commitment to any of these clients is 300 people. Elaborate procedures protect the customer's intellectual property, including mandatory 'cooling-off' periods for engineers between clients, and sometimes a right of veto on their redeployment. The corollary is that the breadth of industry knowledge is part of the sales pitch.

The approach, says Mr Paul, varies from micro-management by the customer, who takes on Wipro engineers virtually as members of his own staff, to 'total product ownership' – the handing over to Wipro of a mature product and all its global development and maintenance requirements, such as adaptation for a particular market. This allows customers to redeploy their own engineers to the next big thing.

Sarnoff's Mr Cherukuri calls this the 'globalisation of innovation' – continuing the erosion in the past 20 years of the old model of corporate R & D, dominated by the big firms with big budgets able to erect big barriers to entry to their markets.

This is part of a broader trend, prompted partly by a rising number of entrepreneurial innovators and growing amounts of venture capital to finance them, towards a more 'dispersed" model of R & D. Now, the internet has removed geographic barriers to using far-flung talent, and the popping of the dot-com bubble 'has spread innovation off-shore". The dispersal is becoming global.[22]

Question

1. Explain why 'outsourcing' in the area of innovation demands divergence combined with some degree of convergence.

References

Amable, B. (2000) Institutional complementarity and diversity of social systems of innovation and production. *Review of Political Economy* 7(4), 645–87.

Baba, Naohiko and Hisada, Takamasa (2002) *Japan's Financial System: its Perspective and the Authorities' Role in Redesigning and Administrating the System.* Tokyo: Bank of Japan, Institute for Monetary and Economic Studies. Discussion Paper No. 02-E-1.

Begin, J.P. (1997) *Dynamic Human Resource Systems: Cross-National Comparisons.* Berlin: Walter de Gruyter.

Bell, D. (1973) *The Coming of Post-industrial Society.* New York: Basic Books.

Bell, D. (1976) *The Cultural Contradictions of Capitalism.* New York: Basic Books.

Casper, S. (2000) Institutional adaptiveness, technology policy, and the diffusion of

---

[22] Extracts from 'Innovative India' © *The Economist Newspaper Limited*, London (3 April 2004).

new business models: the case of German biotechnology. *Organization Studies* 21(5), 887–914.

Coffee, J.C. (2001) The rise of dispersed ownership. Columbia Law School Working Paper, No. 182.

Deeg, R. and Perez, S. (1998) International capital mobility and domestic institutions: corporate finance and governance in four European cases. Paper presented at the 1998 Annual Meeting of the American Political Science Association, Boston, 3–6 September.

Deutsche Bank Research (2001) Japan's investors becoming less risk-averse? *Frankfurter Voice*, 29 October.

Deutsche Bank Research (2002) Corporate takeovers in Germany and their regulation. *Frankfurt Voice*, 7 February.

Dore, R. (1994) Financial Structures, Motivation and Efficiency. Unpublished manuscript. London: London School of Economics.

Dore, R. (1996) Convergence in whose interest?, in Berger, S. and Dore, R. (eds) *National Diversity and Global Capitalism* New York: Cornell University Press.

Easterbrook, F. (1997) International corporate differences: markets or law? *Journal of Applied Corporate Finance* 9(4).

Fujiki, H., Kuroda Nakada, S. and Tachibanaki, T. (2001) Structural issues in the Japanese labour market: an era of variety, equity, and efficiency or an era of bipolarization? *Monetary and Economic Studies* (Special Edition), February.

Genda, Y. (2003) Dangers facing businessmen in their 20s and 30s who work for large companies. *Japan Labour Bulletin*, February, 7.

Hassel, A. and Schulten, T. (1998) Globalization and the future of central collective bargaining: the example of the German metal industry. *Economy and Society* 27(4), 486–522.

Hideaki Miyajima (1998) The impact of deregulation on corporate governance and finance, in Carlile, L.E. and Tilton, M.C. (eds) *Is Japan Really Changing its Ways?* Washington, DC: Brookings Institution Press.

Huntington, S.P. (1993) The clash of civilization? *Foreign Affairs* 72(3), 22–49.

Huntington, S.P. (1996) *The Clash of Civilizations and the Remaking of World Order.* New York: Simon & Schuster.

Inglehart, R. and Baker, W.E. (2000) Modernization, cultural change, and the persistence of traditional values. *American Sociological Review* 65, 19–51.

Jackson, G. (1997) Corporate governance in Germany and Japan: developments within national and international contexts. Draft paper. Cologne: Max-Planck-Institut für Gesellschaftsforschung.

Jacoby, S.M. (1995) Recent organizational developments in Japan. *British Journal of Industrial Relations* 23(4), 645–50.

Koen, C. (2000) The Japanese main ban model: evidence of the pressures for change. Unpublished paper. Tilburg: Tilburg University.

Kono, T. and S. Clegg (2001) *Trends in Japanese Management.* Houndsmills, Basingstoke: Palgrave.

Lane, C. (2000) Globalization and the German model of capitalism – erosion or survival? *British Journal of Sociology* 51(2), 207–34.

La Porta, R., Lopez-de-Silanes, F., Shleifer, A. and Vishny, R. (1997) Legal determinants of external finance. *Journal of Finance* 52, 1131–50.

Lazonick, W. and O'Sullivan, M. (2000) Maximizing shareholder value: a new ideology for corporate governance. *Economy and Society* 29 (February), 13–35.

Levitt, T. (1983) The globalization of markets. *Harvard Business Review* 61 (May/June), 92–102.

Lincoln, J.R. (1993) *Work Organization in Japan and the United States.* Oxford: Oxford University Press, 54–74.

Marx, K. (1867) *Das Kapital: Kritik der politischen Ökonomie.* Vol. 1. Hamburg: O. Meissner.

Morishima, M. (1995) Embedding HRM in a social context. *British Journal of Industrial Relations* 33(4), 617–37.

Mroczkowski, T. and Hanaoka, M. (1997) Effective rightsizing strategies in Japan and America: is there a convergence of employment practices? *Academy of Management Executive* 11(2), 57–67.

Nickel, S. and Layard, R. (1997) Labour market institutions and economic performance. Discussion paper series 23. Oxford: Centre for Economic Performance.

Nishida, J.M. and Redding, S.G. (1992) Firm development and diversification strategies as products of economic cultures: the Japanese and Hong Kong textile industries, in Whitley, R. (ed.) *European Business Systems, Firms and Markets in their National Contexts*, 241–67.

Nohara, H. (1999) Human resource management in Japanese firms undergoing transition, in Dirks, D., Huchet, J.-F. and Ribault, T. (eds) *Japanese Management in the Low Growth Era*, Berlin: Springer, 243–62.

Nowak, E. (2001) Recent developments in German capital markets and corporate governance. *Journal of Applied Corporate Finance* 14(3), 35–48.

OECD (2001) *Recent Trends: Institutional Investors Statistical Yearbook.* OECD.

Ornatowski, G.K. (1998) The end of Japanese-style human resource management? *Sloan Management Review, Cambridge* 39(3), 73–84.

Osawa, M. and Kingston, J. (1996) Flexibility and inspiration: restructuring and the Japanese labour market. *Japan Labour Bulletin* 35(1).

Ozawa, T. (2003) Japan in an institutional quagmire: international business to the rescue? *Journal of International Management* 9, 219–35.

Pauly, L.W. and Reich, S. (1997) National structures and multinational corporate behavior: enduring differences in the age of globalization. *International Organization* 51(1), 1–30.

Pedersen, T. and Thomson, S. (1999) Business systems and corporate governance. *International Studies of Management and Organization* 29(2), 43–59.

Porter, M. (1990) *The Competitive Advantage of Nations.* New York: Free Press.

Rebérioux, A. (2002) European style of corporate governance at the crossroads: the role of worker involvement. *Journal of Common Market Studies* 40(1), 111–34.

Roe, M. (1997) The political roots of American corporate finance. *Journal of Applied Corporate Finance* 9(4).

Rugman, A. (2001) *The Myth of Global Strategy.* AIB Newsletter, second quarter, 11–14.

Rugman, A. and Girod, S. (2003) Retail multinationals and globalizations: the evidence is regional. *European Management Journal* 21(1), 24–37.

Sato, A. (1999) Employment and treatment of middle-aged and older white-collar employees after the bubble. *Japan Labour Bulletin* 38(6), June.

Schaede, U. (1999) *The Japanese Financial System: from Postwar to the New Millenium.* Harvard Business School Case Study 9-700-049. Boston: Harvard Business School Publishing.

Schaede, U. (2000) *The German Financial System in 2000.* Harvard Business School Case Study 9-700-135. Boston: Harvard Business School Publishing.

Sorge, A. (2003) Cross-national differences in human resources and organization, in Harzing, A.-W. and Van Ruisseveldt, J. (eds) *Human Resource Management* (2nd edn). London: Sage.

Streeck, W. (1991) On the institutional conditions of diversified quality production, in Matzner, E. and Streeck, W. (eds) *Beyond Keynesianism* Aldershot: Edward Elgar, 21–61.

Streeck, W. (1995) Industrial democracy beyond co-determination? Paper presented at the Conference on Worker's Participation in Europe: Institutions, Industrial Relations and Technology, Centro di Studio Economici Sociali e Sindacali (CESOS), Rome, 9–10 November.

Streeck, W. (1997) German capitalism: does it exist? Can it survive?, in Crouch, C. and Streeck, W. (eds) *Political Economy of Modern Capitalism.* London: Sage.

Streeten, P. (1996) Free and managed trade, in Berger, S. and Dore, R. (eds) *National Diversity and Global Capitalism.* New York: Cornell University Press.

Sunday I. Owualah (1999) Banking crisis, reforms, and the availability of credit to Japanese small and medium enterprises. *Asian Survey* XXXIX(4), July/August.

Tanisaka, N. and Ohtake, F. (2003) Impact of labour shedding on stock prices. *Japan Labour Bulletin*, January, 6.

Thelen, K. and Kume, I. (1999) The effects of globalization on labour revisited: lessons from Germany and Japan. *Politics and Society* 27(4), 477–505.

Vitols, S. (2001) Varieties of corporate governance: comparing Germany and the UK, in Hall, P.A. and Soskice, D. (eds) *Varieties of Capitalism: The Institutional Foundations of Comparative Advantage.* Oxford: Oxford University Press.

Vitols, S. and Woolcock, S. (1997) *Developments in the German and British Corporate Governance Systems.* Discussion paper. Workshop on Corporate Governance in Britain and Germany, Berlin, WZB.

Weber, M. [1904] (1958) *The Protestant Ethic and the Spirit of Capitalism.* Translated by T. Parsons. Reprint, New York: Charles Scribner's Sons.

Whitley, R. (1994) Dominant forms of organization in market economies. *Organization Studies* 15(2), 153–82.

Whitley, R. (1999) How and why are international firms different? The consequences of cross-border managerial coordination for firm characteristics and behavior. University of Manchester. Paper presented at the 15th EGOS colloquium, University of Warwick, 4–6 July.

Yoshikawa, T. and Phan, P.H. (2001) Alternative corporate governance systems in Japanese firms: implications for a shift to stockholder-centered corporate governance. *Asia Pacific Journal of Management* 18, 183–205.

Index

acculturation, mergers 114, 116–17
achieved status vs. ascribed status, cultural
    dilemmas 73
acquisitions see mergers
actor-structure relationship, societal effect (SE)
    approach 180–2, 187
adaptation, globalization 18–19
agency theory, corporate strategy 450–1, 465–6
Ahold scandal
    case study 302–4
    corporate governance 302–4
Alvesson, M., culture as diagnostic instrument
    125–7
America see USA
analysis levels
    dimensions 60–2
    ecological indexes 59
    national cultures 59–60
    reverse ecological fallacy 59–60
    typologies 60–2
Anglo-Saxon model, corporate governance 256,
    260–4
    capital markets/regulation 260
    company law 262–3
    consensus 263–4
    corporate restructuring 264
    employee representation 263–4
    management 262–3
    ownership structure 260–1
    resisting 530
    cf. Rhineland model 272, 294–7
    stakeholders 261–2
anti-trust laws
    corporate strategy 459–60
    national innovation systems 367, 370
approaches, comparative international
    management 4–24
ascribed status vs. achieved status, cultural
    dilemmas 73
assimilation, mergers 114–15
assumptions, cultural approach 9–10

Atos Origin
    case study 136–45
    mergers 136–45
Austria
    dual-board system 286
    employee representation 289
automotive industry see car industry
autonomy vs. embeddedness, motivational values
    70–1

background institutions 161–3
BAe, decision rights 85–6
banks/banking
    Barings 299–302
    case study 299–302, 438–9
    corporate governance 299–302
    keiretsu 191–5
    MNCs 438–9
    Nigeria 38–9
    organizational culture 129–31
    RaboBank 129–31
    World Bank 30
    zaibatsu 191–5
Barings bank
    case study 299–302
    corporate governance 299–302
Belgium
    dual-board system 286–7
    employee representation 289
    one-tier board systems 289
boundaries, national cultures 57–9
Buhrmann, corporate strategy 476–9
business systems
    characteristics 157–9
    collaborative 160–2, 165–6
    compartmentalized 160, 162, 165
    coordinated industrial district 160, 162, 165
    dominant institutions 163–6
    features 157–9
    fragmented 160, 162, 164
    highly coordinated 161, 162–6

institutional features 164
state-organized 160, 162, 165, 176–9
types 159–61, 162
business systems approach, national diversity
    155–67
business systems research 155–67
Korea 167–73
national diversity 167–9
non-ownership coordination 158–9
ownership co-ordination 157–8
Taiwan 173–9

capital markets/regulation
Anglo-Saxon model, corporate governance 260
Japanese model, corporate governance 271–2
Rhineland model, corporate governance 264–7
western Europe, corporate governance 279–80
car industry
corporate strategy 459–64
cross-cultural negotiations 85–6
Daimler-Chrysler 118–19
decision rights 85–6
Germany 459–64
Japan 85–6, 205–6, 320–9, 459–64, 531–5
mergers 118–19
Uddevallaism 329–32, 342, 343–4
USA 459–64
case study
Ahold scandal 302–4
Atos Origin 136–45
banks/banking 299–302, 438–9
Barings bank 299–302
Buhrmann 476–9
China 239–42, 265, 292–4, 514–18
corporate governance 265, 266, 275–8, 284,
    292–4, 299–304
corporate strategy 474–85
corruption 38–9
Daimler-Chrysler 118–19
decision rights 85–6
educational systems 38–9
glass ceiling 129–31
Grohe AG 266
Heineken 436–8
human resource management 239–42, 244–9
ICT 136–45

Japan 191–5
Japanese production systems 325–7
keiretsu 191–5
Korea 244–9
KPN WerkplekDiensten 136–45
machine tools manufacture 349–54
mergers 136–45
MNCs 436–8, 438–9
national innovation systems 390–401
Netherlands 244–9
networks 514–18
Nigeria 38–9
organizational culture 136–45
outsourcing 546–7
Parmalat 284
pharmaceutical industries 390–401
phosphate mining 89–90
RaboBank 129–31
Russia 275–8
Siemens 481–2
sticky floor 129–31
Tata Group 482–5
telecoms 88–9
Tyco International 474–6
Vivendi 479–81
Wipro 546–7
Chaebol, Korea 167–9
change
cultural 134–5
environment 131–5
everyday reframing 132
grand technocratic project 132–3
Inglehart's thesis 46–7
institutional 185–9
material 134–5
organic social movement 133
organizational culture 131–5
structural 134–5
types 132–4
China
case study 239–42, 265, 292–4, 514–18
corporate governance 265, 292–4
guanxi 514–18
Haier company 265
human resource management 239–42
networks 514–18

production systems 325–7
Christensen, E.W., organizational culture 102–4
closed vs. open system, organizational culture 142–3
clusters
    Germany 509
    horizontal linkages 508
    innovative milieux 508–11
    Mass Individualization Network 512–13
    Océ cluster 512
    Porter's concept 506–8
    vs. sectors 509
    Swiss watch industry 510–11
    TIMP 512
    value chain approach 507–8
    vertical linkages 508
    see also networks
collaboration
    business systems 160–2, 165–6
    national innovation systems 366
    research 369
Collectieve Arbeidsovereenkomsten (CAOs), Netherlands 208
communitarianism vs. individualism, cultural dilemmas 73
company law
    Anglo-Saxon model, corporate governance 262–3
    Japanese model, corporate governance 274–5
    Rhineland model, corporate governance 269
    western Europe, corporate governance 283–7
comparative corporate strategy, MNCs 444–88
compartmentalized business systems 160, 162, 165
competition
    clusters 493–4
    networks 493–4, 504–5
complementarity, institutional change 187–9
consensus
    Anglo-Saxon model, corporate governance 263–4
    Japanese model, corporate governance 275
    logic 81–2
    Rhineland model, corporate governance 270
    western Europe, corporate governance 287–9
constraint, culture 124–5

contingency perspective
    comparative international management 5–8
    organizational structure 5–8
contract, logic 81–2
control, MNCs 420–7
convergence, globalization 16–18, 522–50
cooperation
    clusters 493–4
    networks 493–4, 504–5
coordinated industrial district business systems 160, 162, 165
coordination, MNCs 420–7
corporate governance 254–306
    Ahold scandal 302–4
    Anglo-Saxon model 256, 260–4, 270, 530
    banks/banking 299–302
    Barings bank 299–302
    case study 265, 266, 275–8, 284, 292–4, 299–304
    China 265, 292–4
    Germany see Rhineland model, corporate governance
    globalization 525–35
    Japanese model 271–5, 525–35
    models 256–9
    Parmalat 284
    Rhineland model 256, 264–71, 525–35
    Russia 275–8
    shareholders 256–9, 526–7
    societal explanation 259–304
    stakeholders 256–9, 526–7
    western Europe 278–91
    see also corruption
corporate restructuring
    Anglo-Saxon model, corporate governance 264
    Japanese model, corporate governance 275
    Rhineland model, corporate governance 270–1
    western Europe, corporate governance 289–90
corporate strategy
    agency theory 450–1, 465–6
    anti-trust laws 459–60
    Buhrmann 476–9
    car industry 459–64
    case study 474–85
    comparative empirical studies 457–64
    comparative international 444–88
    country factors 469

dominant logic 451–2
   examples 474–85
   expectations 468–72
   external factors 467–8
   financial systems 455–6, 460
   firm-specific factors 467, 471
   industrial organization 449
   institutional theory 465–6, 467–8
   institutionalism 454–5
   inter-firm networks 460–4
   Kogut, Walker and Anand 457–8
   labour system 456
   management development 460
   Mayer and Whittington 458–9
   model 464–72
   organizational learning perspective 452–3
   particularistic explanations 454–7
   political system 455, 459
   resource-based view 452
   Siemens 481–2
   steel industry 459–64
   strategic contingency theory 453–4
   strategic planning 464–8
   Tata Group 482–5
   theoretical approaches 448–57
   transaction cost economics 449–50
   Tyco International 474–6
   types 447–8
   universalistic explanations 449
   Vivendi 479–81
corruption
   Nigeria 38–9
   trust relationship 37–41
   World Bank 37–43
   see also corporate governance
country location, Inglehart's thesis 48
country-of-origin effect, MNCs 434–5
craft production, characteristics 314
cross-cultural negotiations
   car industry 85–6
   national cultures 82–6
   phosphate mining 89–90
   telecoms 88–9
cross-cultural research
   methodological dilemmas 60–2
   work-related values 63–9

cultural approach
   assumptions 9–10
   comparative international management 8–11
   emic approach 8–11
   etic approach 8–11
   globalization 30–1
   Inglehart's thesis 44–9
   Weber thesis 31–2
   see also national cultures; societal environment
cultural change see change
cultural clusters
   IDV 74–8
   LTO 74–8
   MAS 74–8
   national cultures 74–8
   PDI 74–8
   UAI 74–8
cultural differences 28–9
   MNCs 430–5
cultural dilemmas 72–4
   achieved status vs. ascribed status 73
   individualism vs. communitarianism 73
   inner-directed orientation vs. outer-directed
      orientation 73
   sequential vs. synchronous time 74
   specificity vs. diffuseness 73
   universalism vs. particularism 73
cultural dimensions, Inglehart's thesis 47–9
cultural fit
   Japan 112–13
   mergers 112–13
cultural logic 81–2
cultural values, organizational culture 109–10
culture
   building block 123–4
   constraint 124–5
   diagnostic instrument 125–7
   societal environment 36–43
   sociologist's stance 43–9
   tool 124–5
culture clash, organizational culture 118–19

Daimler-Chrysler
   car industry 118–19
   case study 118–19
   mergers 118–19

organizational culture 118–19
decision rights, cross-cultural negotiations 85–6
deculturation, mergers 115
Denmark
  employee representation 288
  one-tier board systems 288
diagnostic instrument, culture 125–7
diffuseness vs. specificity, cultural dilemmas 73
d'Iribarne, Philippe, emic approach 78–82
dismissal procedures, employment relationships
  223–7
diversified quality production, Germany 349–54
diversity, national see national diversity
dominant institutions, business systems 163–6
dual-board system, western Europe, corporate
  governance 285–7
dynamism, work-related values 65–6

ecological fallacy, analysis levels 59–60
ecological indexes, analysis levels 59
economic development
  economist's point of view 29–43
  societal environment 26–51
economic performance, organizational culture
  123–7
economist's point of view
  LDCs 30
  societal environment 29–43
educational systems
  France 383–5
  Germany 377–9
  Japan 371
  Nigeria 38–9
egalitarianism vs. hierarchy, motivational values
  71
electronics industries, Japan 531–5
embeddedness, networks 499–502
embeddedness vs. autonomy, motivational values
  70–1
emic approach
  cultural approach 8–11
  d'Iribarne, Philippe 78–82
  vs. etic approach 55–6, 104
  national cultures 78–82
  organizational culture 97–100, 104
empirical studies, corporate strategy 457–64

employee-orientated vs. job-orientated
  organizational culture 142
employee representation
  Anglo-Saxon model, corporate governance
    263–4
  Japanese model, corporate governance 275
  one-tier board systems 288–9
  Rhineland model, corporate governance 270
  two-tier board systems 289–90
  western Europe, corporate governance 287–9
  see also personnel systems; unionism
employment policies
  Korea 169–70
  Taiwan 175–6
employment relationships
  dismissal procedures 223–7
  external recruitment 220–2
  human resource management 217–27
  promotion 220–2
  recruitment and selection 218–23
environment
  change 131–5
  see also societal environment
etic approach
  cultural approach 8–11
  vs. emic approach 55–6, 104
  limitations 79–81
  national cultures 62–74
  organizational culture 100–4
  work-related values 63–9
everyday reframing, organizational culture 133
expectations, corporate strategy 468–72
exploitative learning, MNCs 427–8
explorative learning, MNCs 427–8
exporting, MNCs 411–12
external recruitment, employment relationships
  220–2

factor analysis 39–40
financial assets, institutional investors 532–3
financial systems
  corporate strategy 455–6, 460
  Germany 460
  Japan 460
  Nigeria 38–9
  USA 460

Finland, dual-board system 285
flexible production
  organization 342
  production systems 317–19, 334
  societal systems 336–8
Fordism, production systems 314–16
foreign technology, national innovation systems
    366–7
fragmented business systems 160, 162, 164
France
  dual-board system 285
  employee representation 288–9
  higher education 383–5
  machine tools manufacture 349–54
  national innovation systems 381–7
  one-tier board systems 288–9
franchising, MNCs 413
functional pressures, institutional change 185
functional specialization
  Germany 209, 211
  Japan 209, 210–11
  Netherlands 211–12
  Sweden 209, 210
  UK 209–10
  US 208–9
  work relationships 208–12
funding
  national innovation systems 364, 368–71
  research 368–71

GDP
  societal environment 43
  trust 35–6
geographic clustering, networks 503–5
Germany
  car industry 459–64
  clusters 509
  corporate governance see Rhineland model,
    corporate governance
  dismissal procedures 226–7
  diversified quality production 349–54
  financial systems 460
  functional specialization 209, 211
  higher education 377–9
  industrial relations 536–7
  inter-firm networks 460–4

  machine tools manufacture 349–54
  management development 460
  national innovation systems 377–81, 390–401
  performance-related pay 236–7, 238
  personnel systems 536–7
  pharmaceutical industries 390–401
  Rahmenbedingungen 207
  recruitment and selection 219, 222
  reward structure 238
  steel industry 459–64
  wage systems 233–4, 238
  work relationships 206–7, 209, 211
  see also Rhineland model, corporate
    governance
glass ceiling
  case study 129–31
  organizational culture 129–31
  RaboBank 129–31
globalization 15–19
  adaptation 18–19
  convergence 16–18, 522–50
  corporate governance 525–35
  cultural approach 30–1
  hybridization 18–19
  incremental path-dependent adaptation 18
  industrial relations 535–40
  outsourcing 546–7
  path-dependent adaptation 18
  personnel systems 535–40
  societal specificity 522–50
  specialization 18–19
Gordon, G.G., organizational culture 102–4
grand technocratic project, organizational culture
    132–3
Grohe AG, case study 266
group-coordinated market economies,
    institutional approach 13–15
growth, societal context 43
guanxi, China 514–18

Haier company, China 265
harmony vs. mastery, motivational values 71–2
headquarters-subsidiary relationships 423–7
Heineken
  case study 436–8
  MNCs 436–8

hierarchies, networks 494–6
hierarchy vs. egalitarianism, motivational values 71
higher education
    France 383–5
    Germany 377–9
    Japan 371
highly coordinated business systems 161, 162–6
Hofstede, Geert
    organizational culture 100–4
    work-related values 63–9
Honda, decision rights 85–6
honour, logic 81–2
horizontal linkages, clusters 508
human resource management 198–253
    China 239–42
    employment relationships 217–27
    Korea 244–9
    Netherlands 244–9
    reward structure 227–38
    work relationships 202–17
    see also personnel systems
hybridization, globalization 18–19

IBM survey, work-related values 63–9
ICT see information and communication technology
IDV see individualism vs. collectivism
incremental path-dependent adaptation, globalization 18
independence, institutional 184–5
individualism vs. collectivism (IDV)
    cultural clusters 74–8
    work-related values 65, 67
individualism vs. communitarianism, cultural dilemmas 73
individuation, societal environment 46
industrial districts
    Italy 505
    networks 503–5
industrial organization, corporate strategy 449
industrial relations
    Germany 536–7
    globalization 535–40
    Japan 537–40
industry-coordinated market economies,

institutional approach 13–15
industry culture, organizational culture 119–21
information and communication technology (ICT)
    Atos Origin 136–45
    KPN WerkplekDiensten 136–45
    mergers 136–45
    organizational culture 136–45
    see also telecoms
Inglehart's thesis
    country location 48
    cultural change 46–7
    cultural dimensions 47–9
    modernization theory 44–5
    societal environment 44–9
    survival/self-expression dimension 47–9
    traditional/rational dimension 47–9
inner-directed orientation vs. outer-directed orientation, cultural dilemmas 73
innovation
    incremental 361, 373
    organizational culture 143–4
    outsourcing 546–7
    radical 362
    techno-economic paradigm 362
    technology system 362
    see also national innovation systems
innovative milieux
    clusters 508–11
    networks 508–11
institutional analysis, national diversity 154–5
institutional approach
    comparative international management 11–15
    group-coordinated market economies 13–15
    industry-coordinated market economies 13–15
institutional change
    causes 185
    complementarity 187–9
    functional pressures 185
    national diversity 185–9
    political pressures 185–6
    social pressures 186
    theorizing 186–9
institutional differences, MNCs 430–5
institutional features, business systems 162
institutional independence 184–5
institutional inertia, USA 344–5

institutional influences
    Korea 170–3
    Taiwan 176–9
institutional investors
    financial assets 532–3
    portfolio composition 533–5
institutional theory, corporate strategy 465–6,
        467–8
institutional typology 159–61
institutionalism, corporate strategy 454–5
institutions
    background 161–3
    process 182–4
    proximate 161–3
    societal environment 36–43
    structure 182–4
integration, mergers 115–16
Intel, outsourcing 546
intellectual property, national innovation systems
        370
inter-firm networks
    corporate strategy 460–4
    Germany 460–4
    Japan 460–4
    USA 460–4
internationalization processes, MNCs 409–20
Ireland
    employee representation 289
    one-tier board systems 289
d'Iribarne, Philippe, emic approach 78–82
Italy
    dual-board system 287
    employee representation 289
    industrial districts 505
    one-tier board systems 289

Japan
    car industry 85–6, 205–6, 320–9, 459–64, 531–5
    cultural fit 112–13
    dismissal procedures 225–6
    electronics industries 531–5
    financial systems 460
    functional specialization 209, 210–11
    growth 29–30
    higher education 371
    Honda 85–6

industrial relations 537–40
inter-firm networks 460–4
keiretsu 191–5
lean production 320–9, 338–40
management development 460
MITI 375–6
national innovation systems 371–6, 390–401
organizational culture 112–13
performance-related pay 236, 238
personnel systems 537–40
pharmaceutical industries 390–401
production systems 325–7
recruitment and selection 218–19, 221–2, 223
reward structure 238
steel industry 459–64
teamwork 330–2
Toyota 320–9
wage systems 231–3, 238
work relationships 205–6, 209, 210–11
zaibatsu 191–5
Japanese model, corporate governance 271–5,
        525–35
    capital markets/regulation 271–2
    company law 274–5
    consensus 275
    corporate restructuring 275
    employee representation 275
    management 273–4
    ownership structure 272–3
    stakeholders 273–4
Japanese production systems, case study 325–7
job-orientated vs. employee-orientated
        organizational culture 142
joint ventures, MNCs 413–14

keiretsu, Japan 191–5
Kilman, R.H., organizational culture 102–4
knowledge management, MNCs 427–30
Korea
    business systems research 167–73
    case study 244–9
    Chaebol 167–9
    employment policies 169–70
    human resource management 244–9
    institutional influences 170–3
    labour management 169–70

non-ownership coordination 169
ownership relations 167–9
postwar business systems 169–71
KPN WerkplekDiensten
   case study 136–45
   mergers 136–45
   organizational culture 136–45

labour management
   Korea 169–70
   Taiwan 175–6
labour mobility, national innovation systems 365
law, anti-trust 367, 459–60
law, company see company law
LDCs see less-developed countries
lean production
   Japan 338–40
   cf. mass production 323
   production systems 320–9
   societal system 338–40
less-developed countries (LDCs)
   economist's point of view 30
   trust 37
licensing, MNCs 412–13
logic, cultural 81–2
long-term vs. short-term orientation (LTO)
   cultural clusters 74–8
   work-related values 65–6, 68
Luxembourg
   employee representation 288
   one-tier board systems 288

machine tools manufacture
   case study 349–54
   France/Germany 349–54
management
   Anglo-Saxon model, corporate governance
      262–3
   Japanese model, corporate governance 273–4
   national cultures 52–93
   Rhineland model, corporate governance 269
   western Europe, corporate governance 283–7
management development
   corporate strategy 460
   Germany 460
   Japan 460

   USA 460
management styles, mergers 117–19
Mannesmann/Vodafone merger 535
market economies, types 157–9, 160–1
market entry modes, MNCs 411–15
markets, networks 494–6
masculinity vs. femininity (MAS)
   cultural clusters 74–8
   work-related values 65, 67
Mass Individualization Network, clusters 512–13
mass production
   cf. lean production 323
   production systems 314–16
mass standardized societal production systems
   333–5
mastery vs. harmony, motivational values 71–2
material change 134–5
mergers
   acculturation 114, 116–17
   assimilation 114–15
   Atos Origin 136–45
   boundaries 113–14
   car industry 118–19
   case study 136–45
   cultural fit 112–13
   culture issues 110–18
   Daimler-Chrysler 117–18
   deculturation 115
   ICT 136–45
   integration 115–16
   KPN WerkplekDiensten 136–45
   management styles 117–19
   organizational culture 110–18, 136–45
   separation 116–17
   strategic fit 111–12
   symbols 113–14
   values 291
   Vodafone/Mannesmann 535
methodological dilemmas, national cultures
   55–62
military contracts, national innovation systems
   368, 370
mining phosphate, national cultures 89–90
Ministry of International Trade and Industry (MITI),
   Japan 375–6
MNCs see multinational corporations

modernization theory, Inglehart's thesis 44–5
motivational values 69–72
    embeddedness vs. autonomy 70–1
    hierarchy vs. egalitarianism 71
    mastery vs. harmony 71–2
multi-level shaping, organizational culture 104–10
    macro perspective 106–8
    micro perspective 105–6
    societal culture vs. organizational context
        108–10
multinational corporations (MNCs)
    banks/banking 438–9
    case study 436–8, 438–9
    comparative corporate strategy 444–88
    complex realities 419–20
    control 420–7
    coordination 420–7
    country-of-origin effect 434–5
    cultural differences 430–5
    defining 408–9
    development stages 415–17
    evolution 415–17
    exploitative learning 427–8
    explorative learning 427–8
    exporting 411–12
    franchising 413
    Heineken 436–8
    institutional differences 430–5
    interdependencies 428–30
    internationalization processes 409–20
    joint ventures 413–14
    knowledge management 427–30
    licensing 412–13
    market entry modes 411–15
    national diversity 431–4
    organizational structure 415–17
    reasons for 409–11
    strategic alliances 413–14
    strategies/structures 417–19
    structural issues 406–43
    subsidiaries 414–15, 423–7
    transnational management 417–19, 428–30

national cultures
    analysis levels 59–60
    boundaries 57–9

cross-cultural negotiations 82–6
cultural clusters 74–8
emic approach 78–82
etic approach 62–74
management 52–93
methodological dilemmas 55–62
research methods 56–62
Unisource 88–9
see also cultural approach
national diversity 152–97
    business systems approach 155–67
    business systems research 167–9
    institutional analysis 154–5
    institutional change 185–9
    MNCs 431–4
    societal effect (SE) approach 179–85
national innovation systems 358–404
    anti-trust laws 370
    case study 390–401
    collaboration 366
    commercial orientation 364–5
    foreign technology 366–7
    France 381–7
    funding 364, 368–71
    Germany 377–81
    incremental 361, 373
    institutions 363–7
    intellectual property 370
    Japan 371–6
    labour mobility 365
    military contracts 368, 370
    pharmaceutical industries 390–401
    policy 365–6, 374–5
    technological advancement 361–2
    USA 367–71
    venture capital 365
    see also innovation
negotiations, cross-cultural see cross-cultural
    negotiations
Netherlands
    case study 244–9
    Collectieve Arbeidsovereenkomsten (CAOs) 208
    dismissal procedures 227
    dual-board system 285–6
    employee representation 289
    functional specialization 211–12

human resource management 244–9
performance-related pay 237–8
recruitment and selection 219, 222, 223
reward structure 238
wage systems 234, 238
work relationships 207–8, 211–12, 212–17
networks 490–521
  case study 514–18
  China 514–18
  to clusters 503–5
  competition 493–4, 504–5
  cooperation 493–4, 504–5
  embeddedness 499–502
  geographic clustering 503–5
  guanxi 514–18
  hierarchies 494–6
  industrial districts 503–5
  innovative milieux 508–11
  markets 494–6
  structural hole theory 496–9
  Sweden 499–502
  theoretical perspective 494–502
  theory 496–502
  transaction cost theory 494–6
Nigeria
  banks/banking 38–9
  corruption 38–9
  educational systems 38–9
  financial systems 38–9
normative vs. pragmatic organizational culture
  143

Océ cluster 512
one-tier board systems, employee representation
  288–9
open vs. closed system, organizational culture
  142–3
O'Reilly et al., organizational culture 102–4
organic social movement, organizational culture
  133
organizational culture 94–149
  analysis 140–4
  banks/banking 129–31
  case study 136–45
  change 131–5
  consolidation 128–9

creation 127–8
cultural values 109–10
culture clash 118–19
Daimler-Chrysler 118–19
dimensions 102–3
economic performance 123–7
emic approach 97–100, 104
employee-orientated vs. job-orientated 142
etic approach 100–4
everyday reframing 133
glass ceiling 129–31
grand technocratic project 132–3
ICT 136–45
industry culture 119–21
innovation 143–4
Japan 112–13
KPN WerkplekDiensten 136–45
mergers 110–18, 136–45
multi-level shaping 104–10
normative vs. pragmatic 143
open vs. closed system 142–3
organic social movement 133
process-orientated vs. results-orientated 142
qualitative research 99–100
RaboBank 129–31
research 94–149
research streams 97–104
stability 144
sticky floor 129–31
strategy 121–3
team orientation 144
organizational hierarchy, work relationships
  212–17
organizational structure
  contingency perspective 5–8
  MNCs 415–17
outer-directed vs. inner-directed orientation,
  cultural dilemmas 73
outsourcing
  case study 546–7
  globalization 546–7
  innovation 546–7
  Intel 546
ownership co-ordination, business systems
  research 157–8
ownership relations, Korea 167–9

ownership structure
  Anglo-Saxon model, corporate governance 260–1
  Japanese model, corporate governance 272–3
  Rhineland model, corporate governance 267–8
  western Europe, corporate governance 281–3

Parmalat
  case study 284
  corporate governance 284
particularism vs. universalism, cultural dilemmas 73
particularistic theories
  comparative international management 8–15
  cultural approach 8–11
  institutional approach 13–15
path-dependent adaptation, globalization 18
PDI see power distance
performance see economic performance
performance-related pay 234–8
personnel systems
  Germany 536–7
  globalization 535–40
  Japan 537–40
  see also employee representation; human resource management; unionism; work relationships
pharmaceutical industries
  case study 390–401
  comparisons, international 391
  Germany 390–401
  Japan 390–401
  national innovation systems 390–401
  price regulation 397–400
  safety regulation 394–7
phosphate mining, national cultures 89–90
policy, national innovation systems 365–6
political pressures, institutional change 185–6
political system, corporate strategy 455, 459
portfolio composition, institutional investors 533–5
postwar business systems
  Korea 169–71
  Taiwan 176–9
power distance (PDI)
  cultural clusters 74–8

work-related values 64
pragmatic vs. normative organizational culture 143
price regulation, pharmaceutical industries 397–400
principal-agent framework 33, 35
principal components analysis 39–40
process-orientated vs. results-orientated organizational culture 142
production management 308–56
  production systems 311–32
production systems
  characteristics 311–32
  China 325–7
  flexible production 317–19, 334, 336–8
  Fordism 314–16
  Japan 325–7
  lean production 320–9
  mass production 314–16
  mass standardized societal 333–5
  scientific management 311–13
  societal environment 332–45
  societal systems 332–44
  Swedish Uddevallaism 329–32, 342, 343–4
  Taylorism 311–13
  types 311–32
  work systems 318
promotion, employment relationships 220–2
Protestantism, Weber thesis 31–2

qualitative research, organizational culture 99–100

RaboBank
  case study 129–31
  glass ceiling 129–31
  organizational culture 129–31
  sticky floor 129–31
Rahmenbedingungen, Germany 207
recruitment and selection
  employment relationships 218–23
  Germany 219, 222
  Japan 218–19, 221–2, 223
  Netherlands 219, 222, 223
  Sweden 218, 221, 223
  UK 218, 220–1, 223

US 218, 220, 223
regression analysis 43
research
  collaboration 369
  commercial orientation 364–5
  funding 364, 368–71
  see also national innovation systems
research methods, national cultures 56–62
resources management see national innovation
    systems; production management
results-orientated vs. process-orientated
    organizational culture 142
reverse ecological fallacy, analysis levels 59–60
reward structure
  human resource management 227–38
  performance-related pay 234–8
  . wage systems 228–34
Rhineland model, corporate governance 256,
    264–71, 525–35
  cf. Anglo-Saxon model 272, 294–7
  capital markets/regulation 264–7
  company law 269
  consensus 270
  corporate restructuring 270–1
  employee representation 270
  management 269
  ownership structure 267–8
  stakeholders 268–9
Rover, decision rights 85–6
Russia
  case study 275–8
  corporate governance 275–8

Saffold, G.S., culture as diagnostic instrument
    126–7
Saxton, M., organizational culture 102–4
Schein, Edgar, organizational culture 97–100
Schwartz, Shalom, motivational values 69–72
scientific management, production systems
    311–13
sectors, vs. clusters 509
secularization, societal environment 46
Senegal, phosphate mining 89–90
separation, mergers 116–17
sequential vs. synchronous time, cultural
    dilemmas 74

shareholders, corporate governance 256–9, 526–7
short-termism, USA 344–5
Siemens, corporate strategy 481–2
social capital
  societal environment 32–6
  trust 32–6
social networks, trust 34–5
social pressures, institutional change 186
societal context, growth 43
societal culture vs. organizational context 108–10
societal effect (SE) approach
  actor-structure relationship 180–2, 187
  national diversity 179–85
  process 182–4
  structure 182–4
societal environment
  components 41
  country scores 41–2
  culture 36–43
  economic development 26–51
  economist's point of view 29–43
  GDP 43
  individuation 46
  Inglehart's thesis 44–9
  institutions 36–43
  production systems 332–45
  secularization 46
  social capital 32–6
  sociologist's stance 43–9
  survival/self-expression dimension 47–9
  traditional/rational dimension 47–9
  trust 32–6
  see also cultural approach
societal explanation, corporate governance
    259–304
societal institutions 162
societal production systems 332–44
societal specificity, globalization 522–50
sociologist's stance
  Inglehart's thesis 44–9
  societal environment 43–9
South Korea see Korea
Spain
  employee representation 289
  one-tier board systems 289
spans of control, work relationships 212–17

specialization, globalization 18–19
specificity vs. diffuseness, cultural dilemmas 73
stability, organizational culture 144
stakeholders
    Anglo-Saxon model, corporate governance
        261–2
    corporate governance 256–9, 526–7
    Japanese model, corporate governance 273–4
    Rhineland model, corporate governance 268–9
    western Europe, corporate governance 283
state-organized business systems 160, 162, 165
    Taiwan 176–9
steel industry
    corporate strategy 459–64
    Germany 459–64
    Japan 459–64
    USA 459–64
sticky floor
    case study 129–31
    organizational culture 129–31
    RaboBank 129–31
strategic alliances, MNCs 413–14
strategic fit, mergers 111–12
strategic planning, corporate strategy 464–8
strategy
    comparative corporate strategy 444–88
    organizational culture 121–3
    theorists 119–21
    see also corporate strategy
structural change 134–5
structural hole theory, networks 496–9
structure, organizational see organizational
    structure
subsidiaries, MNCs 414–15, 423–7
    headquarters-subsidiary relationships 423–7
    roles 424–5
    structure 425–7
survival/self-expression dimension, societal
    environment 47–9
Sweden
    car industry 329–32
    dismissal procedures 224–5
    employee representation 288
    functional specialization 209, 210
    networks 499–502
    one-tier board systems 288

performance-related pay 235, 238
recruitment and selection 218, 221, 223
reward structure 238
teamwork 330–2
Uddevallaism 329–32, 342, 343–4
wage systems 229–30, 238
work relationships 204–5, 209, 210
Swiss watch industry, clusters 510–11
Switzerland
    employee representation 289
    one-tier board systems 289
synchronous vs. sequential time, cultural
    dilemmas 74

Taiwan
    business systems research 173–9
    employment policies 175–6
    institutional influences 176–9
    labour management 175–6
    non-ownership coordination 174–5
    ownership relations 173–4
    postwar business systems 176–9
    state-organized business systems 176–9
Tata Group, corporate strategy 482–5
Taylorism, production systems 311–13
team orientation, organizational culture 144
teamwork
    Japan 330–2
    Sweden 330–2
techno-economic paradigm, innovation 362
technological advancement, national innovation
    systems 361–2
technology system, innovation 362
telecoms
    cross-cultural negotiations 88–9
    see also information and communication
        technology
theoretical debate, comparative international
    management 4–5
theorizing institutional change 186–9
TIMP see Twente Initiative for the Development of
    Medical Products
Toyota 320–9
trades unions see unionism
traditional/rational dimension, societal
    environment 47–9

transaction cost economics, corporate strategy 449–50

transaction cost theory, networks 494–6

Trompenaars, Fons 72–4

trust
  corruption relationship 37–41
  functions 35–6
  GDP 35–6
  LDCs 37
  levels 33–5
  social capital 32–6
  social networks 34–5
  World Bank 37–43

Twente Initiative for the Development of Medical Products (TIMP), clusters 512

Tyco International, corporate strategy 474–6

UAI see uncertainty avoidance

Uddevallaism, car industry 329–32, 342, 343–4

UK
  dismissal procedures 224
  functional specialization 209–10
  performance-related pay 238
  recruitment and selection 218, 220–1, 223
  reward structure 238
  wage systems 228–9, 238
  work relationships 203–4, 209–10

uncertainty avoidance (UAI)
  cultural clusters 74–8
  work-related values 65

unionism
  UK 203–4
  US 202–3
  see also employee representation; personnel systems

Unisource, national cultures 88–9

unitary-board system, western Europe, corporate governance 283–4

universalism vs. particularism, cultural dilemmas 73

universalistic theories, comparative international management 5–8

USA
  car industry 459–64
  dismissal procedures 223–4
  financial systems 460

functional specialization 208–9
institutional inertia 344–5
inter-firm networks 460–4
management development 460
national innovation systems 367–71
performance-related pay 235, 238
recruitment and selection 218, 220, 223
reward structure 238
short-termism 344–5
steel industry 459–64
wage systems 228–9, 238
work relationships 202–3, 208–9

value chain approach, clusters 507–8

values see cultural values; motivational values; work-related values

venture capital, national innovation systems 365

vertical linkages, clusters 508

Vivendi, corporate strategy 479–81

Vodafone/Mannesmann merger 535

Volvo, Uddevallaism 329–32

wage systems 228–34

Washington Consensus 30–1

Weber thesis, cultural approach 31–2

western Europe, corporate governance 278–91
  capital markets/regulation 279–80
  company law 283–7
  consensus 287–9
  corporate restructuring 289–90
  dual-board system 285–7
  employee representation 287–9
  management 283–7
  ownership structure 281–3
  stakeholders 283
  unitary-board system 283–4

Whitley, R., business systems research 155–67

Wipro, case study 546–7

women, glass ceiling 129–31

work classification, work relationships 202–8

work coordination, work relationships 202–8

work design, work relationships 202–8

work-related values
  criticism 66–9
  cross-cultural research 63–9
  dynamism 65–6

etic approach 63–9
IBM survey 63–9
IDV 65, 67
LTO 65–6, 68
MAS 65, 67
PDI 64
UAI 65
work relationships 202–17
functional specialization 208–12
Germany 206–7, 209, 211, 212–17
human resource management 202–17
Japan 205–6, 209, 210–11, 212–17
Netherlands 207–8, 211–12, 212–17
organizational hierarchy 212–17

spans of control 212–17
Sweden 204–5, 209, 210, 212–17
UK 203–4, 209–10, 212–17
US 202–3, 208–9, 212–17
work classification 202–8
work coordination 202–8
work design 202–8
see also employee representation; personnel
systems
World Bank 30
corruption 37–43
trust 37–43

zaibatsu, Japan 191–5